DELTA'S
Key to the
TOEFL®
TEST

by
Nancy Gallagher

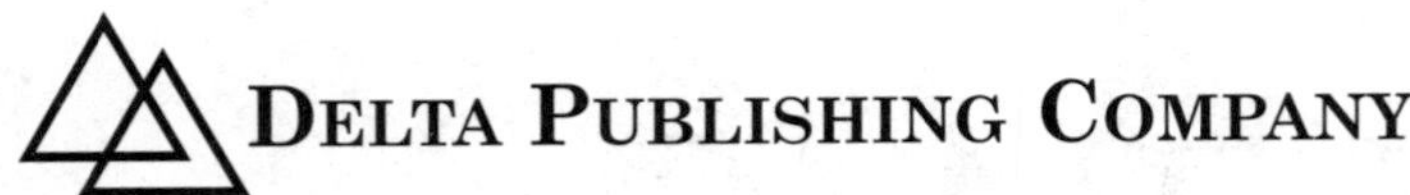

Requests for permission to make copies of any part of the work should be sent to:
Delta Publishing Company
A Divison of Delta Systems Co., Inc.
1400 Miller Parkway
McHenry, IL 60050 USA
(800) 323-8270 or (815) 363-3582
www.delta-systems.com

Copy Editor: Patricia Brenner
Page Layout & Design: Linda Bruell
Artwork Provided By: Kathy Combs and Damon Taylor

Printed in the United States of America

10 9 8 7

1-887744-60-6 Textbook only

1-887744-52-5 Textbook with CD–ROM

Acknowledgments

I would like to thank the following people for their contributions:

Patricia Brenner, for her editorial expertise, understanding of the student perspective, and generosity with yellow stickies.

Jay Kenney, for his direction, narration, and editing of the audiotapes and for allowing the cameos.

Linda Bruell, for her superhuman patience in managing the ten thousand details of page design.

Bob Longman, for his uncanny ability to untangle any computer problem.

Chris Hall, for her input on what TOEFL teachers really want.

All of the teachers and program directors who responded to our surveys, for their practical suggestions.

Delight Willing, for her confidence in me.

Kelly Stapleton, for her friendship at the times it mattered.

CONTENTS

INTRODUCTION

INTRO

Our Purpose

When we set out to create this book, there were certain things we wanted to do and certain things we did not want to do. We also needed to determine what teachers of TOEFL (Test of English as a Foreign Language) preparation courses really wanted. We wanted to incorporate the latest research in language acquisition and cognitive science; we wanted to create a "brain–friendly" environment for the students and a "teacher–friendly" format for the instructor. We wanted to continually demonstrate to the teachers and students how far they had come and how far they had to go.

Teacher Survey

We learned from surveys that teachers required many practice tests and exercises with explanations—clear ones. They wanted to be able to track students' progress. They also wanted the book to be a good value.

It was essential to have a course that treated the new computer–based test. Since the paper–based test will still be given abroad, and recognizing that the "Institutional" version will still be used for years, they also wanted a course that would include the paper–based test.

Teachers wanted the units to comprise the various categories of questions contained in the TOEFL. We have analyzed these questions, categorized them, clearly described each type, and noted in what proportion each appears on the test. We have suggested strategies for the test in general and for each type of question in particular. We have also included discussion of "trick" questions.

Teachers indicated they wanted to teach the English skills *and* the test, so we built on the philosophy that skill building and assessment are interrelated. Our course addresses the specific language skills necessary for success in university studies and on the TOEFL.

Course Design

Cognitive research, language acquisition research, and even quality control processes led us to design the course following an effective framework:

1. Reveal and present the concept/question.
2. Identify models and examples that connect new information to existing knowledge.
3. Support the students as they select examples and link information.
4. Move from directed tasks to independent activities applied to the real world.
5. Evaluate progress and engage the students as analysts and critics.

The study of language fascinates so many of us because it exposes the secrets of how the mind works. For the last twenty years, computer scientists and educators have been trying to program computers to learn as well as to teach. It is not surprising that artificial intelligence is a field that now relies on linguists and instructional designers. *Input*, *analysis*, *output*, and *feedback* are common jargon in human learning, computer systems, and even manufacturing standards.

Researchers believe we learn in "chunks." We learn when we can create these chunks easily, and we associate them with other chunks as we build a structure of knowledge or skills. All adult second–language learners are familiar with the "plateau" learning experience: depressingly long plateaus of no apparent progress, interspersed with the occasional inspiration of making an instant jump to a higher level of facility. Here the jargon of cognitive theorists begins to complement that of applied linguists: *scaffolding learning*, *comprehensible input*, *sequencing*, *facilitative language teaching*.

What works seems like common sense: repetition is essential in language teaching. "Tell them what you're going to teach them, teach them, tell them what you taught them." The feeling of progress is essential to language learning. So, too, is testing.

The objective of an effective learning environment is to minimize anxiety—the enemy of learning—especially since we are preparing students for a test that is usually associated with fear and loathing. While our course can be used in a variety of ways, it is designed to establish a familiar routine. However, predictability does not mean this course must be boring—if the environment is challenging and filled with varied examples.

In a TOEFL prep book, we have the opportunity to maximize students' strong motivation to pass the TOEFL exam as well as their overall goal of learning the language. A lot of practice and a feeling of making progress contribute to this motivation.

If the course accurately simulates the test environment, students will be motivated to study and less anxious during the real test. Teachers agree; they generally want the course focused on the TOEFL, with as many questions and "TOEFL–realistic" exercises as possible.

Delta's Key to the TOEFL Test is designed to be a course—not just a book. It is flexible—adaptable to the particular objectives and time constraints of the instructor, while also accommodating a variety of learning styles. It is a rich, robust course, guaranteed to provide the teacher and student with lots of material and complementary activities that help illustrate and practice the points being covered.

How to Use This Book

This book can be used in a number of ways: as the sole text in a TOEFL preparation course; as a supplementary text in a listening/speaking, grammar, reading, or writing course; or as a general review course in English for the independent–study student.

The book's units of study allow ample opportunities for review and practice of essential English skills. We encourage teachers and students to build their own program of study by choosing the most appropriate of the many components of **Delta's Key to the TOEFL Test**.

Progress Charts and Conversion Tables

Beginning on page 8 are five *Progress Charts* where students can keep a visual record of their performance on all quizzes and tests in the book. The *TOEFL Score Conversion Tables* allow students to determine their approximate TOEFL score for each section of each test. The charts and tables can help students set individual goals and monitor their progress.

Quick Diagnostic Test

Our *Quick Diagnostic Test* is shorter than the actual TOEFL exam, designed to be administered in a 50–minute time slot. Its purpose is to diagnose skill areas where students need to focus, especially if time for test preparation is limited. (For those who prefer a full–length diagnostic test, one of the four *Practice Tests* can be used for this purpose.)

Focus

In *Section 1 – Listening* through *Section 4 – Writing*, each unit opens with an exercise to focus attention, activate prior knowledge, and help students anticipate the content. *Focus* takes an English text—a sentence, conversation, reading passage, or essay paragraph—and challenges the learner to identify the relevant principle. These exercises can be done in class or as homework.

Do You Know...?

This component of each unit provides a thorough description of a specific language skill—such as identifying topic and main ideas, checking subject–verb agreement, or making inferences—along with numerous sample TOEFL items assessing this skill. Included are relevant definitions, explanations of correct and incorrect answers, and discussion of common TOEFL tricks. *Do You Know...?* can be the basis of classroom lectures and discussions or can be studied as homework.

Practice

Practice consists of sets of TOEFL questions for students to apply the fifty–four skills described in the book. The *Practice* exercises in each unit can be done in class or as homework.

Extension

People acquire language through social interaction, so we suggest numerous ideas to foster cooperation, stimulate discussion, extend skill practice, guide peer review, and link the classroom with the real world. *Extension* activities are student–centered, and many engage students in creating their own "TOEFL exams."

Assessing Progress

Regular assessment is an integral part of skill building. *Assessing Progress* consists of thirty–two timed quizzes to simulate parts of the TOEFL. Each quiz covers the content of one to four units of study. Quiz material builds cumulatively, and some of the longer quizzes review several units. Quiz scores can be graphed on the *Progress Charts*.

Review Tests

The three section review tests—Listening, Structure, and Reading—are similar in form and content to the corresponding sections of the actual TOEFL exam. These tests can be taken as midterm or final examinations. Scores can be graphed on the *Progress Charts*.

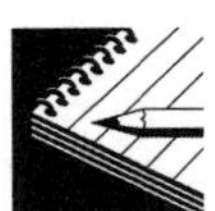

Writing Topics

In the computer–based TOEFL, the essay constitutes one–half of the score for Structure/Writing. Therefore, in *Section 4 – Writing* we provide a list of writing topics used on the actual test, along with the actual criteria used for scoring essays.

Practice Tests

This section consists of four full–length tests which are similar to the actual TOEFL. *Test 1* and *Test 3* are similar to the computer–based test, and *Test 2* and *Test 4* are similar to the paper–based test. Any of the *Practice Tests* can be taken as midterm or final examinations. They can also be used for diagnostic or placement purposes. Scores can be graphed on the *Progress Charts*.

Answer Sheets

Answer sheets accompany the *Quick Diagnostic Test* and the four full–length tests. Although the actual computer–based TOEFL does not have an answer sheet (test–takers use the computer mouse to click on answers), we provide answer sheets for the two practice tests resembling the computer test for students and teachers who want them. All answer sheets are reproducible.

Answer Key

This section consists of answer keys for all tests, quizzes, and practice exercises. The answer keys provide explanations and refer students to appropriate units of study for further review.

Tapescript

This section includes complete tapescripts for all listening material in the practice exercises, quizzes, and tests. In addition to their role in building listening comprehension, the scripts can be used in several ways. The conversations can be used for learning vocabulary and idioms and as models for students to write and perform their own skits. The talks can be used as reading passages for students to write their own "TOEFL questions" about, for example, referents or vocabulary in context.

Cassettes

The set of cassette tapes accompanying this book includes over six hours of listening material. In addition to being used for TOEFL preparation, the cassettes can be used for pronunciation practice, dictation exercises, and vocabulary study, as well as for learning English through academic content.

Sample Course Plans

Objectives will vary from program to program, and from student to student, regarding what content the TOEFL course should cover. However, a good general rule is to allow approximately the same amount of time for Structure/Writing as for Listening/Reading.

The book can be adapted to fit several time frames:

- **Limited Time** (5 to 9 weeks). If time is limited, the program should concentrate on the tests and quizzes. Use the *Quick Diagnostic Test*, answer keys, and progress charts to identify skill areas that require more review and practice. Work systematically through the units in these problem areas.
- **Moderate Time** (10 to 15 weeks). Students should work through as much of the text as possible. See the following sample plan for a *15–week TOEFL Preparation Course*. This course can be shortened to ten or twelve weeks by skipping some material.
- **More Time** (16 to 20 weeks). See the following sample plans for two separate courses, *Listening and Reading Comprehension Course* and *Grammar and Writing Course*. Each course can be shortened by skipping some material.

15–WEEK TOEFL PREPARATION COURSE
(75 hours of instruction)

WEEK	UNITS AND QUIZZES	TOPICS
1	Quick Diagnostic Test 1.1 – 1.6 Listening Quiz 1 and 2	Diagnostic assessment *Short conversations*: Key words; idioms; conditionals, causatives, and modals; negative expressions; time, quantity, and comparisons; intonation
2	1.7 – 1.11 Listening Quiz 3, 4, and 5	*Short conversations*: Implications; inferences *Longer conversations and talks*: Topic and main ideas; details
3	1.12 – 1.15 Listening Quiz 6 and 7	*Longer conversations and talks*: Categories; processes; reasons; inferences
4	Listening Quiz 8 Listening Review Test Test 1	Progress assessment
5	2.1 – 2.6 Structure Quiz 1 and 2	Subjects and objects; appositives; plurals; articles; verbs and auxiliaries; passives
6	2.7 – 2.10 Structure Quiz 3, 4, and 5	Infinitives and gerunds; main and subordinate clauses; noun clauses; adjective clauses
7	2.11 – 2.15 Structure Quiz 6, 7, and 8	Adverb clauses; conditionals; inverted subjects and verbs; subject–verb agreement; pronoun agreement
8	2.16 – 2.21 Structure Quiz 9, 10, and 11	Adjective word order; participial adjectives; negative modifiers; equatives, comparatives, and superlatives; conjunctions; prepositions
9	2.22 – 2.25 Structure Quiz 12 and 13	Word form; word choice; redundancy; parallel structure
10	Structure Quiz 14 Structure Review Test Test 2	Progress assessment
11	3.1 – 3.3 Reading Quiz 1, 2, and 3	Topic and main ideas; details and supporting ideas; referents
12	3.4 – 3.6 Reading Quiz 4, 5, 6, and 7	Vocabulary in context; inferences; organization and purpose
13	3.7 Reading Quiz 8, 9, and 10 Reading Review Test	Coherence Progress assessment
14	4.1 – 4.4	Prewriting and organizing ideas; supporting main idea; introduction, body, and conclusion
15	4.5 – 4.7 Test 3	Paragraph and sentence structure; word choice; scoring essays Progress assessment

10–WEEK LISTENING AND READING COMPREHENSION COURSE
(50 hours of instruction)

WEEK	UNITS	TOPICS	QUIZZES
1	1.1 1.10 3.1	Key words Topic and main ideas (listening) Topic and main ideas (reading)	Reading Quiz 1
2	1.2 3.4	Idioms Vocabulary in context	Listening Quiz 1 Reading Quiz 4
3	1.11 3.2	Details Supporting ideas	Listening Quiz 5 Reading Quiz 2
4	1.3 1.4 1.5 1.6	Conditionals, causatives, modals Negative expressions Time, quantity, comparisons Intonation	Listening Quiz 2
5	3.3	Referents	Reading Quiz 3 Reading Quiz 5 (review) (*Full–length Test)
6	1.7 1.8 1.9 1.14	Implications Inferences Inferences Reasons	Listening Quiz 3 Listening Quiz 4 (review)
7	1.15 3.5	Inferences (listening) Inferences (reading)	Listening Quiz 7 Reading Quiz 6
8	1.12 1.13 3.6	Words and categories Events in a process Organization and purpose	Listening Quiz 6 Reading Quiz 7
9	3.7	Coherence	Listening Quiz 8 (review) Reading Quiz 8 (review) Reading Quiz 9
10			Reading Quiz 10 (review) Listening Review Test Reading Review Test (*Full–length Test)

*Schedule time at midterm and at term's end for a full–length test (from Tests 1 through 4).

10–WEEK GRAMMAR AND WRITING COURSE
(50 hours of instruction)

WEEK	UNITS	TOPICS	QUIZZES
1	2.1 2.2 2.3 2.4	Subjects and objects Appositives Plurals Articles	Structure Quiz 1
2	2.5 2.6 4.1	Verbs and auxiliaries Passives *Essay*: Prewriting	Structure Quiz 2
3	2.7 2.8 4.2	Infinitives and gerunds Main and subordinate clauses *Essay*: Main idea	Structure Quiz 3 Structure Quiz 4 (review)
4	2.9 2.10 4.3	Noun clauses Adjective clauses and phrases *Essay*: Introduction	Structure Quiz 5
5	2.11 2.12 2.13 4.4	Adverb clauses and phrases Conditionals Inverted subjects and verbs *Essay*: Body and conclusion	Structure Quiz 6
6	2.14 2.15	Subject–verb agreement Pronoun agreement	Structure Quiz 7 Structure Quiz 8 (review) (*Full–length Test)
7	2.16 2.17 2.18 2.19 4.5	Adjective word order Participial adjectives Negative modifiers Equatives, comparatives, superlatives *Essay*: Paragraph and sentence structure	Structure Quiz 9
8	2.20 2.21	Conjunctions Prepositions	Structure Quiz 10 Structure Quiz 11 (review)
9	2.22 2.23 2.24 2.25 4.6	Word form Word choice Redundancy Parallel structure *Essay*: Word choice	Structure Quiz 12 Structure Quiz 13
10	4.7	*Essay*: scoring essays	Structure Quiz 14 (review) Structure Review Test (*Full–length Test)

*Schedule time at midterm and at term's end for a full–length test (from Tests 1 through 4).

Progress Charts and Conversion Tables

PROGRESS CHARTS

The Progress Charts enable students to record and monitor their progress on all quizzes and tests in the book.

On Charts 1 through 4, students can graph their scores and refer to relevant units of study. On Chart 5, students can record their test scores and then use the conversion tables to determine their approximate TOEFL scores.

These charts may be reproduced.

- **Chart 1 – *Listening Quizzes and Review Test***
- **Chart 2 – *Structure Quizzes and Review Test***
- **Chart 3 – *Reading Quizzes and Review Test***
- **Chart 4 – *Practice Tests***
- **Chart 5 – *TOEFL Scores for Review Tests and Practice Tests***

Listening Chart Example

% CORRECT	QUIZ 1	QUIZ 2	QUIZ 3	QUIZ 4	QUIZ 5	QUIZ 6	QUIZ 7	QUIZ 8	REVIEW TEST*
				25				25	42
									41
80%	12	12	12	24	12	12	12	24	40
									39
				23				23	38
	11	11	11	22	11	11	11	22	37
									36
70%				21				21	35
									34
	10	10	10	20	10	10	10	20	33
									32
				19				19	31
60%	9	9	9	18	9	9	9	18	30
									29

Practice Test Chart Example

% CORRECT	TEST 1 *			TEST 2 *			TEST 3 *			TEST 4 *		
	Listen	Struct	Read	Listen	Struct	Read	Listen	Struct	Read	Listen	Struct	Read
	37		41	41	33	41	37		41	41	33	41
80%	36	20	40	40	32	40	36	20	40	40	32	40
	35		39	39	31	39	35		39	39	31	39
	34	19	38	38		38	34	19	38	38		38
	33		37	37	30	37	33		37	37	30	37
	32	18	36	36	29	36	32	18	36	36	29	36
70%			35	35	28	35			35	35	28	35
	31	17	34	34	27	34	31	17	34	34	27	34
	30		33	33		33	30		33	33		33
	29	16	32	32	26	32	29	16	32	32	26	32
	28		31	31	25	31	28		31	31	25	31
60%	27	15	30	30	24	30	27	15	30	30	24	30

PROGRESS CHART 1

LISTENING QUIZZES and REVIEW TEST

Circle the number correct on each quiz or test. Draw a line to connect the circles.

% CORRECT	QUIZ 1	QUIZ 2	QUIZ 3	QUIZ 4	QUIZ 5	QUIZ 6	QUIZ 7	QUIZ 8	REVIEW TEST*
100%	15	15	15	30	15	15	15	30	50
				29				29	49 48
	14	14	14	28	14	14	14	28	47 46
90%				27				27	45
	13	13	13	26	13	13	13	26	44 43
				25				25	42 41
80%	12	12	12	24	12	12	12	24	40
				23				23	39 38
	11	11	11	22	11	11	11	22	37 36
70%				21				21	35
	10	10	10	20	10	10	10	20	34 33
				19				19	32 31
60%	9	9	9	18	9	9	9	18	30
				17				17	29 28
	8	8	8	16	8	8	8	16	27 26
50%				15				15	25
	7	7	7	14	7	7	7	14	24 23
				13				13	22 21
40%	6	6	6	12	6	6	6	12	20
				11				11	19 18
	5	5	5	10	5	5	5	10	17 16
30%				9				9	15
	4	4	4	8	4	4	4	8	14 13
				7				7	12 11
20%	3	3	3	6	3	3	3	6	10
UNITS TO STUDY	1.1 1.2	1.3 1.4 1.5 1.6	1.7 1.8 1.9	1.1 thru 1.9	1.10 1.11	1.10 1.11 1.12 1.13	1.14 1.15	1.10 thru 1.15	1.1 thru 1.15

*To convert your Listening Review Test score to a TOEFL score, use the TOEFL Score Conversion Table for Listening on page 15. Record your Review Test score in the appropriate box on Progress Chart 5.

PROGRESS CHART 2

STRUCTURE QUIZZES and REVIEW TEST

Circle the number correct on each quiz or test. Draw a line to connect the circles.

% CORRECT	QUIZ 1	QUIZ 2	QUIZ 3	QUIZ 4	QUIZ 5	QUIZ 6	QUIZ 7	QUIZ 8	QUIZ 9	QUIZ 10	QUIZ 11	QUIZ 12	QUIZ 13	QUIZ 14	REVIEW TEST*
100%	15	15	15	25	15	15	15	25	15	15	25	15	15	25	40
															39
				24				24			24			24	38
	14	14	14	23	14	14	14	23	14	14	23	14	14	23	37
90%															36
	13	13	13	22	13	13	13	22	13	13	22	13	13	22	35
				21				21			21			21	34
															33
80%	12	12	12	20	12	12	12	20	12	12	20	12	12	20	32
															31
				19				19			19			19	30
	11	11	11	18	11	11	11	18	11	11	18	11	11	18	29
70%															28
	10	10	10	17	10	10	10	17	10	10	17	10	10	17	27
				16				16			16			16	26
															25
60%	9	9	9	15	9	9	9	15	9	9	15	9	9	15	24
															23
				14				14			14			14	22
	8	8	8	13	8	8	8	13	8	8	13	8	8	13	21
50%															20
	7	7	7	12	7	7	7	12	7	7	12	7	7	12	19
				11				11			11			11	18
															17
40%	6	6	6	10	6	6	6	10	6	6	10	6	6	10	16
															15
				9				9			9			9	14
	5	5	5	8	5	5	5	8	5	5	8	5	5	8	13
30%															12
	4	4	4	7	4	4	4	7	4	4	7	4	4	7	11
				6				6			6			6	10
															9
20%	3	3	3	5	3	3	3	5	3	3	5	3	3	5	8
UNITS TO STUDY	2.1 2.2 2.3 2.4	2.5 2.6	2.7 2.8	2.1 thru 2.8	2.9 2.10	2.11 2.12 2.13	2.14 2.15	2.1 thru 2.15	2.16 2.17 2.18 2.19	2.20 2.21	2.16 thru 2.21	2.22 2.23 2.24	2.22 2.23 2.24 2.25	2.16 thru 2.25	2.1 thru 2.25

*To convert your Structure Review Test score to a TOEFL score, use the TOEFL Score Conversion Table for Structure on page 15. Record your Review Test score in the appropriate box on Progress Chart 5.

PROGRESS CHART 3

READING QUIZZES and REVIEW TEST

Circle the number correct on each quiz or test. Draw a line to connect the circles.

% CORRECT	QUIZ 1	QUIZ 2	QUIZ 3	QUIZ 4	QUIZ 5	QUIZ 6	QUIZ 7	QUIZ 8	QUIZ 9	QUIZ 10	REVIEW TEST*
100%	10	10	20	10	20	10	10	20	10	20	50 49
			19		19			19		19	48 47 46
90%	9	9	18	9	18	9	9	18	9	18	45 44
			17		17			17		17	43 42 41
80%	8	8	16	8	16	8	8	16	8	16	40 39
			15		15			15		15	38 37 36
70%	7	7	14	7	14	7	7	14	7	14	35 34
			13		13			13		13	33 32 31
60%	6	6	12	6	12	6	6	12	6	12	30 29
			11		11			11		11	28 27 26
50%	5	5	10	5	10	5	5	10	5	10	25 24
			9		9			9		9	23 22 21
40%	4	4	8	4	8	4	4	8	4	8	20 19
			7		7			7		7	18 17 16
30%	3	3	6	3	6	3	3	6	3	6	15 14
			5		5			5		5	13 12 11
20%	2	2	4	2	4	2	2	4	2	4	10
UNITS TO STUDY	3.1	3.1 3.2	3.1 thru 3.3	3.4	3.1 thru 3.4	3.5	3.5 3.6	3.1 thru 3.6	3.7	3.1 thru 3.7	3.1 thru 3.7

*To convert your Reading Review Test score to a TOEFL score, use the TOEFL Score Conversion Table for Reading on page 15. Record your Review Test score in the appropriate box on Progress Chart 5.

PROGRESS CHART 4

PRACTICE TESTS

Circle the number correct on each test section. Draw lines to connect the circles for Listening, Structure, and Reading.

%	TEST 1 *			TEST 2 *			TEST 3 *			TEST 4 *		
CORRECT	Listen	Struct	Read	Listen	Struct	Read	Listen	Struct	Read	Listen	Struct	Read
100%	45	25	50	50	40	50	45	25	50	50	40	50
	44		49	49	39	49	44		49	49	39	49
	43	24	48	48	38	48	43	24	48	48	38	48
	42		47	47		47	42		47	47		47
	41	23	46	46	37	46	41	23	46	46	37	46
90%			45	45	36	45			45	45	36	45
	40	22	44	44	35	44	40	22	44	44	35	44
	39		43	43	34	43	39		43	43	34	43
	38	21	42	42		42	38	21	42	42		42
	37		41	41	33	41	37		41	41	33	41
80%	36	20	40	40	32	40	36	20	40	40	32	40
	35		39	39	31	39	35		39	39	31	39
	34	19	38	38	30	38	34	19	38	38	30	38
	33		37	37		37	33		37	37		37
	32	18	36	36	29	36	32	18	36	36	29	36
70%			35	35	28	35			35	35	28	35
	31	17	34	34	27	34	31	17	34	34	27	34
	30		33	33	26	33	30		33	33	26	33
	29	16	32	32		32	29	16	32	32		32
	28		31	31	25	31	28		31	31	25	31
60%	27	15	30	30	24	30	27	15	30	30	24	30
	26		29	29	23	29	26		29	29	23	29
	25	14	28	28	22	28	25	14	28	28	22	28
	24		27	27		27	24		27	27		27
	23	13	26	26	21	26	23	13	26	26	21	26
50%			25	25	20	25			25	25	20	25
	22	12	24	24	19	24	22	12	24	24	19	24
	21		23	23	18	23	21		23	23	18	23
	20	11	22	22		22	20	11	22	22		22
	19		21	21	17	21	19		21	21	17	21
40%	18	10	20	20	16	20	18	10	20	20	16	20
	17		19	19	15	19	17		19	19	15	19
	16	9	18	18	14	18	16	9	18	18	14	18
	15		17	17		17	15		17	17		17
	14	8	16	16	13	16	14	8	16	16	13	16
30%			15	15	12	15			15	15	12	15
	13	7	14	14	11	14	13	7	14	14	11	14
	12		13	13	10	13	12		13	13	10	13
	11	6	12	12		12	11	6	12	12		12
	10		11	11	9	11	10		11	11	9	11
20%	9	5	10	10	8	10	9	5	10	10	8	10

*To convert your practice test scores to TOEFL scores, use the TOEFL Score Conversion Tables on page 15. Record your TOEFL scores on Progress Chart 5.

PROGRESS CHART 5

TOEFL SCORES for REVIEW TESTS and PRACTICE TESTS

Test	Section	Number Correct*	Paper–based TOEFL Score		Computer–based TOEFL Score	
			Section	Total Test**	Section	Total Test**
Review	Listening					
	Structure					
	Reading					
Test 1	Listening					
	Structure					
	Reading					
Test 2	Listening					
	Structure					
	Reading					
Test 3	Listening					
	Structure					
	Reading					
Test 4	Listening					
	Structure					
	Reading					

*To convert your number correct on the three section review tests and on each section of the full–length practice tests, use the TOEFL Score Conversion Tables on page 15. The Conversion Tables give TOEFL scores for both the paper–based test and the computer–based test.

**To estimate your TOEFL score for the total test, add the TOEFL scores for the three sections and divide the sum by 3.

Test	Section	Number Correct*	Paper–based TOEFL Score		Computer–based TOEFL Score	
			Section	Total Test**	Section	Total Test**
Review	Listening	37	540	537	200	203
	Structure	31	550		220	
	Reading	35	520		190	
Test 1	Listening	28	490	517	160	187
	Structure	19	540		210	
	Reading	35	520		190	
Test 2	Listening	31	490	523	160	193
	Structure	31	550		220	
	Reading	37	530		200	

Example:

On the paper–based test:
Listening score = 540
Structure score = 550
Reading score = 520

$\frac{540 + 550 + 520}{3} = 537$

On the computer–based test:
Listening score = 200
Structure score = 220
Reading score = 190

$\frac{200 + 220 + 190}{3} = 203$

537 on the paper–based test *is equivalent to* 203 on the computer–based test.

TOEFL SCORE CONVERSION TABLES

The paper–based and computer–based tests use different scoring scales. These conversion tables provide approximate TOEFL scores for both versions of the test.

QUICK DIAGNOSTIC TEST

Look under *Total Number Correct* for the number of questions answered correctly on the Quick Diagnostic Test. Read across the table. On the same line, you will find your approximate *TOEFL Score Range* for both the paper–based and computer–based tests. This is not a precise score. Rather, it gives a general idea of where your score might fall in a range of possible scores.

TOTAL NUMBER CORRECT	TOEFL SCORE RANGE	
	PAPER–BASED TEST	COMPUTER–BASED TEST
50	670-680	300
47-49	630-670	270-290
43-46	580-630	240-270
39-42	540-580	210-240
35-38	510-540	180-210
31-34	480-510	150-180
27-30	460-480	130-150
23-26	430-460	110-130
19-22	390-430	90-110
15-18	350-390	70-90
11-14	310-350	50-70
7-10	270-310	30-50

LISTENING, STRUCTURE, AND READING

Separate conversion tables are used for Listening, Structure, and Reading. Make sure you use the correct table for each test section.

For each test section, look in the correct column under *Number Correct* for the number of questions answered correctly on the test you have taken. Make sure you look in the correct column (*Tests 1 & 3 or Review Test/Tests 2 & 4*). Read across the table. On the same line, you will find your approximate *TOEFL Score* for the paper–based test and an equivalent score for the computer–based test.

LISTENING

Number Correct		TOEFL Score	
Tests 1 & 3	Review Test Tests 2 & 4	Paper-based Test	Computer-based Test
45	50	680	300
44	49	660	290
43	48	640	270
42	47	630	270
41	46	610	250
--	45	610	250
40	44	600	250
39	43	590	240
38	42	580	230
37	41	570	220
36	40	560	220
35	39	550	210
34	38	550	210
33	37	540	200
32	36	530	190
--	35	520	190
31	34	520	180
30	33	510	170
29	32	500	160
28	31	490	160
27	30	490	150
26	29	480	140
25	28	480	140
24	27	470	130
23	26	470	130
--	25	460	120
22	24	460	120
21	23	450	110
20	22	440	100
19	21	440	100
18	20	430	90
17	19	430	90
16	18	420	90
15	17	410	80
14	16	400	70
--	15	400	70
13	14	390	60
12	13	370	50
11	12	360	50
10	11	350	40
9	10	340	40

STRUCTURE

Number Correct		TOEFL Score	
Tests 1 & 3	Review Test Tests 2 & 4	Paper-based Test	Computer-based Test
25	40	680	300
--	39	670	290
24	38	660	280
23	37	640	270
--	36	620	260
22	35	600	250
--	34	590	250
21	33	580	240
20	32	560	230
--	31	550	220
19	30	540	210
18	29	540	210
--	28	520	200
17	27	510	190
16	26	500	180
--	25	490	170
15	24	480	170
--	23	470	160
14	22	460	150
13	21	450	140
--	20	440	140
12	19	430	130
11	18	420	120
--	17	410	110
10	16	400	110
--	15	390	100
9	14	380	90
8	13	370	90
--	12	360	80
7	11	340	70
--	10	340	70
6	9	320	60
5	8	300	50

READING

Number Correct	TOEFL Score	
Review Test Tests 1-4	Paper-based Test	Computer-based Test
50	670	300
49	660	290
48	650	280
47	630	270
46	610	260
45	600	250
44	590	250
43	580	240
42	570	230
41	560	220
40	550	210
39	540	210
38	540	210
37	530	200
36	520	200
35	520	190
34	510	180
33	500	170
32	490	170
31	480	160
30	480	160
29	470	150
28	460	150
27	460	140
26	450	130
25	440	130
24	430	120
23	430	120
22	420	110
21	410	110
20	400	100
19	390	90
18	380	90
17	370	80
16	360	80
15	350	70
14	340	70
13	330	60
12	310	60
11	300	50
10	290	50

Section 1

1. (A) (B) (C) (D)
2. (A) (B) (C) (D)
3. (A) (B) (C) (D)
4. (A) (B) (C) (D)
5. (A) (B) (C) (D)
6. (A) (B) (C) (D)
7. (A) (B) (C) (D)
8. (A) (B) (C) (D)
9. (A) (B) (C) (D)
10. (A) (B) (C) (D)
11.

This term	
Next Term	
Next Year	

12. (A) (B) (C) (D)
13. (A) (B) (C) (D)
14. [A] [B] [C] [D]
15. (A) (B) (C) (D)
16. (A) (B) (C) (D)
17. (A) (B) (C) (D)
18. (A) (B) (C) (D)
19.

Quality of relationships	Large number of subjects	Two groups of subjects

20. (A) (B) (C) (D)

Section 2

1. (A) (B) (C) (D)
2. (A) (B) (C) (D)
3. (A) (B) (C) (D)
4. (A) (B) (C) (D)
5. (A) (B) (C) (D)
6. (A) (B) (C) (D)
7. (A) (B) (C) (D)
8. (A) (B) (C) (D)
9. (A) (B) (C) (D)
10. (A) (B) (C) (D)
11. (A) (B) (C) (D)
12. (A) (B) (C) (D)
13. (A) (B) (C) (D)
14. (A) (B) (C) (D)
15. (A) (B) (C) (D)

Section 3

1. (A) (B) (C) (D)
2. (A) (B) (C) (D)
3. (A) (B) (C) (D)
4. (A) (B) (C) (D)
5. (A) (B) (C) (D)
6. (A) (B) (C) (D)
7. (A) (B) (C) (D)
8. (A) (B) (C) (D)
9. (A) (B) (C) (D)
10. (A) (B) (C) (D)
11. (A) (B) (C) (D)
12. (A) (B) (C) (D)
13. (A) (B) (C) (D)
14. (A) (B) (C) (D)
15. (A) (B) (C) (D)

QUICK DIAGNOSTIC TEST

DIAGNOSTIC

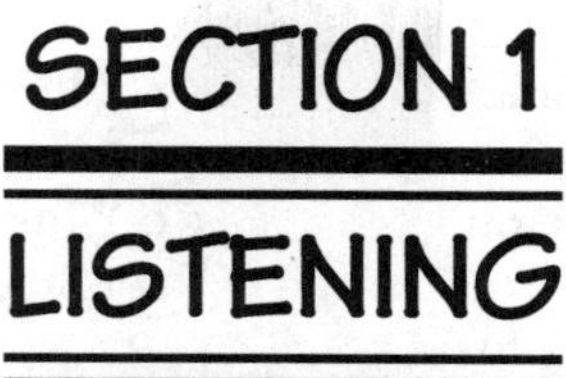

Time—approximately 20 minutes

 *(Start Tape)*

In the Listening section of the test, you will have an opportunity to demonstrate your ability to understand conversations and talks in English. Answer all the questions on the basis of what is stated or implied by the speakers you hear. Do not take notes or write during the test.

PART A

Directions: In Part A you will hear short conversations between two people. After each conversation, you will hear a question about the conversation. The conversations and questions will not be repeated. After you hear a question, read the four possible answers and choose the best answer.

Here is an example.

On the recording, you hear:

In your book, you read:

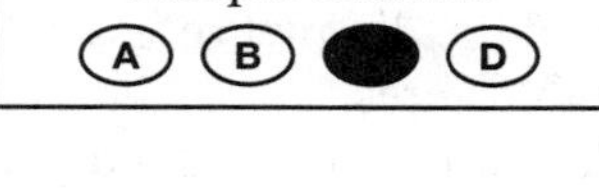

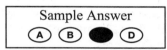

(A) She doesn't want to buy a printer.
(B) She would rather buy something else.
(C) She doesn't want to pay a lot for a printer.
(D) She wants to shop at a better place.

You learn from the conversation that the woman hopes to find a printer at a better price. The best answer to the question, *What does the woman mean?* is (C), *She doesn't want to pay a lot for a printer.* Therefore, the correct choice is (C).

1. (A) At least seventeen managers will come to the training.
   (B) Fewer than seventeen people will be on the train.
   (C) More than seventy people will come to the training.
   (D) She expects to miss the training this year.

2. (A) He prefers reading about real people.
   (B) He would like to borrow the woman's book.
   (C) He should study biology instead.
   (D) He has to lead a geography group.

3. (A) She hasn't seen him in a long time.
   (B) He is never glad to see her.
   (C) He is not as happy as he usually is.
   (D) He seems more cheerful than ever.

4. (A) Firefighter.
   (B) Physician.
   (C) Bus company manager.
   (D) Restaurant manager.

5. (A) He asks if Professor Moore is a picture taker.
   (B) He didn't know Professor Moore was a skater.
   (C) He didn't know Professor Moore was good with figures.
   (D) Professor Moore is a bigger skater now than before.

6. (A) Join a hiking group.
   (B) Go climbing on Mount Adams.
   (C) Take a chemistry examination.
   (D) Study for a chemistry examination.

7. (A) He will wait for Jim on the corner.
   (B) He always turns left at the corner.
   (C) He will work out in the gymnasium.
   (D) He waits there every Saturday.

8. (A) Review the problems.
   (B) Walk to the testing room together.
   (C) Meet later that day.
   (D) Find another time to study.

9. (A) He is not sure what time the field trip starts.
   (B) He never feels lucky on field trips.
   (C) It was hot on the last field trip.
   (D) He does not feel as lazy this time.

This is the end of Part A.

        1

PART B

Directions: In this part of the test, you will hear several conversations and talks. Each conversation or talk is followed by several questions. The conversations, talks, and questions will not be repeated.

For most of the questions, you will read four possible answers and choose the best answer. Some questions will have special directions.

Here is an example.

On the recording, you hear:

Now listen to a sample question.

Sample Answer
(A) (B) ● (D)

In your book, you read:

(A) It helped scientists see the atmosphere more clearly.
(B) It made it easier for scientists to send messages.
(C) It made data collection from weather stations faster.
(D) It helped airplanes fly higher.

The best answer to the question, *How did the telegraph improve the science of meteorology?* is (C), *It made data collection from weather stations faster.* Therefore, the correct choice is (C).

Now listen to another sample question.

In your book, you read:

Choose 2 answers.

[A] Forecast the weather.
[B] Study trends in rocket science.
[C] Solve air pollution problems.
[D] Study costs of building satellites.

The best two answers to the question, *What do meteorologists do today?* are [A], *Forecast the weather*, and [C], *Solve air pollution problems.* Therefore, the correct choices are [A], and [C].

Remember, you should <u>not</u> take notes during the test.

1 1 1 1 1 1 1 1 1

10. (A) He is failing his coursework.
(B) He has trouble breathing.
(C) He thinks his workload is too heavy.
(D) He is bored with being a teaching assistant.

11. Put each letter, A, B, and C, in the correct space below.

(A) Only a few students
(B) A lot of work
(C) More choice in which class to teach

This term	
Next term	
Next year	

12. (A) Do as well as he can in Dr. Chapman's class.
(B) Complain to the department head.
(C) Ask Dr. Chapman for fewer students.
(D) See a different doctor about his problem.

13. (A) How to compete successfully with other companies.
(B) How to succeed as a small business owner.
(C) Business successes and failures.
(D) Training for small business management.

14. Choose 2 answers.

[A] Education in computers and economics.
[B] Education in business and accounting.
[C] Experience in retailing.
[D] Experience in government or law.

15. (A) When it branches out into other fields.
(B) When it can hire professional management.
(C) When it becomes a large corporation.
(D) When it can support itself on its profits.

16. (A) They do not demand hard work from their employees.
(B) They do not expand into large chains.
(C) They have good management but poor products and services.
(D) They do not have enough financial reserves to absorb losses.

17. (A) To define the term *research*.
(B) To describe different types of research.
(C) To compare experimental and qualitative research.
(D) To explain how experiments are conducted.

18. (A) It can determine cause–effect relationships involving treatments.
(B) It obtains information from a large group of people.
(C) It provides an in–depth look at a particular situation.
(D) It can be done by mail, telephone, or on the Internet.

19. Put each letter, A, B, and C, in the correct space below.

(A) Survey
(B) Experimental
(C) Qualitative

Quality of relationships	Large number of subjects	Two groups of subjects

20. (A) What people think about research.
(B) Suitable subjects for research.
(C) A specific research methodology.
(D) Control and treatment groups.

This is the end of Section 1.

 *(Stop Tape)*

SECTION 2

STRUCTURE

DIAGNOSTIC

Time—10 minutes
(including the reading of the directions)
Now set your clock for 10 minutes.

The Structure section of the test measures your ability to recognize language that is appropriate for standard written English. There are two types of questions in this section, with special directions for each type.

Directions: In the first type of question, there are incomplete sentences. Beneath each sentence, there are four words or phrases. Choose the one word or phrase that best completes the sentence.

Example I

Although Chicago is not ------- New York, it has many attractions for visitors.

(A) as large as
(B) larger
(C) larger city
(D) the larger city is

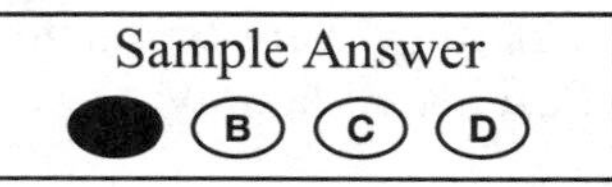

The sentence should read, *Although Chicago is not as large as New York, it has many attractions for visitors.* Therefore, you should choose (A).

The second type of question has four underlined words or phrases. Choose the one underlined word or phrase that must be changed for the sentence to be correct.

Example II

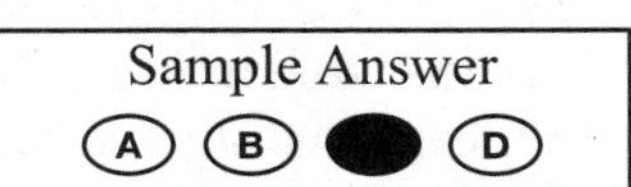

Guglielmo Marconi, the son of (A) a wealthy Italian landowner, made (B) the first successfully (C) transmission using (D) radio waves.

The sentence should read, *Guglielmo Marconi, the son of a wealthy Italian landowner, made the first successful transmission using radio waves.* Therefore, you should choose (C).

Now begin work on the questions.

2 2 2 2 2 2 2 2 2

1. ------- for elementary grade students to sit still for extended periods of time.

   (A) Why it is difficult
   (B) That it is difficult
   (C) It is difficult
   (D) Difficulty

2. Around the core of the earth ------- of heavy crystalline rock.

   (A) is a thick shell
   (B) a thick shell is
   (C) with a thick shell
   (D) a thick shell

3. ------- by the work of Paul Gauguin in Tahiti, artists became interested in a return to much simpler styles.

   (A) They were largely fascinating
   (B) A large fascination
   (C) That they were fascinated largely
   (D) Fascinated largely

4. Haleakala, ------- volcano, forms the eastern bulwark of the island of Maui.

   (A) giant dormant
   (B) a giant dormant
   (C) the giantly dormant
   (D) it is the giant dormant

5. ------- of a tornado is the funnel.

   (A) The distinguishing feature
   (B) The feature distinguishing
   (C) How to distinguish the feature
   (D) The features distinguished

6. European settlers wasted no time (A) in importing many of (B) their technology to North America and applying it (C) to the forests around them (D).

7. In seventeenth century Amsterdam, the house facades were not only (A) harmonious but also distinct (B), unlikely (C) the uniformity (D) of Parisian and English squares.

8. The frost–free period of high summer (A), when (B) mean daily temperatures (C) are above 32 degrees, are short (D).

Go on to the next page

9. The cougar is one of the New World's largest cats, second not only to the jaguar.
A B C D

10. The training manager must estimate the expenses for the program, including costs for its develop, delivery, and evaluation.
A B C D

11. Evaporation is the process that a liquid turns into a vapor at a temperature below its boiling point.
A B C D

12. In paintings of cut flowers, the artist has in most cases devoted just as much care to the vase than to the blooms, and sometimes the vase is the most effective part of the picture.
A B C D

13. Many machines use the centrifugal force generated by a sudden movement to activating catches and ratchets.
A B C D

14. While the bear's vision is poor, their sense of smell is keen, enabling the remarkable bruin to smell food as far away as a mile.
A B C D

15. If a stone thrown into a pond, the ripples will spread out from the point where the stone hits the water.
A B C D

This is the end of Section 2.

SECTION 3

READING

Time—17 minutes (including the reading of the directions) Now set your clock for 17 minutes.

Directions: In the Reading section of the test, you will read several passages. Each one is followed by a number of questions about it. For questions 1–15 below, you are to choose the one best answer, (A), (B), (C), or (D), to each question.

Answer all questions about the information in a passage on the basis of what is stated or implied in that passage.

Read the following passage:

The coffees of Central America profit from the area's steady climate and wealth of mountains. The mountains of the Pacific Cordillera, which stretch in a virtually unbroken line from Guatemala to the middle of Panama, provide the best combination of climate, altitude, and soil.

Guatemala was a relative latecomer to the commercial coffee business, exporting beans only since 1875. This mountainous country is ideally suited for coffee production, and its exports now surpass those of much larger countries. European merchants still take about 50 percent of the Guatemalan beans, with most of the best beans today being exported to England.

Example I

It can be inferred from the passage that coffee grows well

(A) in the northern hemisphere
(B) in mountainous regions
(C) in small countries
(D) near the Pacific Ocean

Sample Answer
(A) ● (C) (D)

The passage implies that the mountainous regions of Central America are ideally suited for coffee production. The other answer choices cannot be inferred from the information given. Therefore, you should choose (B).

Example II

The word "surpass" in line 7 is closest in meaning to

(A) include
(B) surround
(C) exceed
(D) limit

Sample Answer
(A) (B) ● (D)

The word *surpass* in this passage means *exceed*. Therefore, you should choose (C).

Now begin work on the questions.

Go on to the next page

QUESTIONS 1–7

An increasing percentage of newcomers to the U. S. workforce comes from populations that have been underserved in the past because of racial, ethnic, gender, or cultural differences. Social trends indicate that today's minority groups are more likely than those of previous generations to celebrate their own uniqueness and to demand respect and equal treatment from mainstream institutions.

Organizations must manage and train this increasingly diverse workforce. Good management depends on working effectively with other people by understanding and appreciating differences in values and perspectives. Individuals who can function in diverse situations tend to develop cross–cultural communication skills and stronger leadership abilities.

The primary goal of all training and development programs is to provide workers at all levels of an organization with the knowledge, skills, and abilities to perform their jobs and help the organization meet its business goals. Thus, for most organizations, the decision to provide diversity training is a business rather than a moral decision. Effective diversity training targets not only individuals but also the core values, traditions, structure, and culture of an organization. Diversity programs strive to identify and eliminate barriers that prevent individuals and the organization from achieving their goals.

Race, ethnicity, and gender problems in the workplace are increasingly viewed by management as a significant barrier to productivity. Organizations that do not respond to diversity experience lawsuits, high turnover, low morale and productivity, loss of talent to competitors, additional recruitment and training costs, and negative publicity.

1. With what topic is the passage mainly concerned?

(A) Diversity in the U. S. workforce
(B) Responding to diversity in the workplace
(C) Demands of minority groups in the workplace
(D) Techniques of good management

2. The word "those" in line 4 refers to

(A) cultural differences
(B) social trends
(C) minority groups
(D) mainstream institutions

3. What does the author mean by the statement in line 13–14, "…for most organizations, the decision to provide diversity training is a business rather than a moral decision"?

(A) Diversity training is profitable for organizations.
(B) Effective workers are trained in an organization's core values.
(C) The culture of some organizations is immoral.
(D) Diversity training is a growing business.

4. The word "targets" in line 15 is closest in meaning to

(A) alters
(B) aims at
(C) objects to
(D) consists of

5. The word "barrier" in lines 16 and 19 is closest in meaning to

(A) tradition
(B) idea
(C) solution
(D) obstruction

6. Which of the following is NOT mentioned as a consequence of disregarding diversity?

(A) Low productivity
(B) Lawsuits
(C) Violence
(D) Additional costs

7. With which of the following statements would the author most probably agree?

(A) Diversity training does not have to be costly to an organization.
(B) Members of minority groups should be trained in good management.
(C) Communication skills should be the main goal of diversity programs.
(D) Managing diversity benefits both individuals and organizations.

Go on to the next page

QUESTIONS 8–15

Safe within the embrace of the bark is the tree's circulatory system: two cellular pipelines that transport water, mineral nutrients, and other organic substances to all living tissues of the tree. One pipeline, called the phloem—or inner bark—carries the downward flow of foodstuffs from the leaves to the branches, trunk, and roots. The other, called the xylem—or sapwood—carries water and nutrients up from the roots to the leaves. Between these two pipelines is the vascular cambium, a single–cell layer too thin to be seen by the naked eye. This is the tree's major growth organ, responsible for the outward widening of the trunk, branches, twigs, and roots. During each growing season, the vascular cambium produces new phloem cells on its outer surface and new xylem cells on its inner surface.

Within the plump, elongated xylem cells, water molecules adhere to each other and are pulled upward through the trunk and into the branches and leaves by capillary action. Water molecules, drawn into the tree through tiny root tips, bring life–sustaining hydrogen and oxygen into the tree and also carry chemical nutrients from the soil. Exactly how a tree manages to lift gallons of water hundreds of feet into the air against the pull of gravity is a feat of hydraulics that has puzzled naturalists and engineers for centuries and is still not understood completely by today's scientists.

Late in the growing season, xylem cells diminish in size and develop thicker skins, but they retain their capacity to carry water. Over time the innermost xylem cells become clogged with hard or gummy waste products and can no longer transport fluids. A similar situation occurs in the clogging of arteries in an aging human body. When they cease to function as living sapwood, the dead xylem cells become part of the central column of heartwood, the supportive structure of the tree.

8. What is the main purpose of the passage?

(A) To explain how a tree's circulatory system works
(B) To describe the annual growth of a tree's living tissues
(C) To compare the downward and upward flow of water in a tree
(D) To identify the structural components of a tree

9. Which of the following sentences should NOT be included in a summary of the passage?

(A) A tree's inner bark conducts the downward flow of nutrients.
(B) The phloem, xylem, and vascular cambium make up a tree's circulatory system.
(C) The vascular cambium produces xylem and phloem cells.
(D) The outer bark of a tree shows the annual production of phloem.

10. The word "This" in line 7 refers to

(A) xylem
(B) sapwood
(C) vascular cambium
(D) naked eye

11. The phrase "adhere to" in line 10 is closest in meaning to

(A) respond to
(B) cling to
(C) stimulate
(D) control

12. It can be inferred from paragraph 2 that

(A) most of a tree is composed of xylem cells
(B) some properties of trees remain a mystery
(C) a branch of engineering is devoted to studying trees
(D) rainwater enters a tree through its leaves

13. All of the following are functions of the xylem EXCEPT

(A) carrying food from the leaves to the trunk
(B) carrying chemical nutrients from the soil
(C) forming part of the tree's structural support
(D) lifting water upward through the tree

14. Where in the passage does the author compare a tree to another organism?

(A) Lines 1–3
(B) Lines 7–9
(C) Lines 10–11
(D) Lines 19–20

15. The following sentence can be added to paragraph 3.

However, since the vascular cambium manufactures healthy new xylem cells each year, the death of the old cells does not mean the death of the tree.

Where would it best fit in the paragraph? Choose **A**, **B**, **C**, or **D**.

Late in the growing season, xylem cells diminish in size and develop thicker skins, but they retain their capacity to carry water. **A** Over time the innermost xylem cells become clogged with hard or gummy waste products and can no longer transport fluids. **B** A similar situation occurs in the clogging of arteries in an aging human body. **C** When they cease to function as living sapwood, the dead xylem cells become part of the central column of heartwood, the supportive structure of the tree. **D**

This is the end of the Quick Diagnostic Test.

Answers to the Quick Diagnostic Test are on page 627.
TOEFL score conversion tables are on page 14.

SECTION 1 – LISTENING

The Listening Comprehension section of the TOEFL measures your ability to understand conversations and talks in English as it is spoken in North America. You will be tested on your comprehension of vocabulary, idioms, and spoken structures, as well as your overall understanding of the meaning and purpose of the conversations and talks.

Many of the topics covered are informal and conversational. A variety of academic topics are also included. You do not need special knowledge of the topics to answer the questions correctly. All questions are based on what is stated or implied by the speakers.

You will hear each conversation and talk only once. You will not be allowed to take notes during this section.

THE PAPER–BASED TEST

The paper–based TOEFL will continue to be administered in certain parts of the world and by certain educational institutions in North America.

There are 50 questions in the Listening Comprehension section of the paper test.

You have approximately 35 minutes to complete this section. This time includes your reading of the directions for each part.

There are three parts in the Listening section of the paper test:

Part A—Short Conversations (30 questions)

You will hear several short conversations between two speakers. For each conversation, you will answer one question.

Part B—Longer Conversations (7–8 questions)

You will hear two longer conversations between two speakers. For each conversation, you will answer three or four questions.

Part C—Talks (12–13 questions)

You will hear three short talks or lectures, each given by a single speaker. For each talk or lecture, you will answer three to five questions.

THE COMPUTER–BASED TEST

You will use headphones to listen to several conversations and talks. While you are listening, pictures of the speakers or other information will be presented on your computer screen.

The Listening section of the computerized TOEFL is computer–adaptive. This means that the computer will give you test questions that are aimed at your ability level.

How does the computer–adaptive test work? The first question will be of average difficulty.

- If you answer it correctly, the computer will then give you a slightly harder question.
- If you answer it incorrectly, the computer will then give you an easier question.

The second question will match your performance on the first question. In other words, the computer adapts the questions to your ability level.

There are approximately 30 to 50 questions in the Listening section of the computer test. There will be some variation in the length of the test. This means that some test takers will have a slightly longer test than others.

You have approximately 40 to 60 minutes to complete this section. This time does not include the time it takes to listen to the conversations and talks.

There are two parts in the Listening section of the computer test:

Part A – Short Conversations (11–17 questions)

You will hear several short conversations between two speakers. For each conversation, you will answer one question.

Part B – Longer Conversations and Talks (19–33 questions)

You will hear several longer conversations and talks with two or more speakers. For each conversation or talk, you will answer two to six questions.

LISTENING SKILLS ON THE TEST

Fifteen different skills are tested in the Listening Comprehension section of the TOEFL. The approximate distribution of questions by skill is shown below.

LISTENING SKILL	APPROXIMATE NUMBER	
	Paper Test	*Computer Test*
Listening for Key Words	3–4	2–3
Listening for Idioms	7–10	3–5
Listening for Conditionals, Causatives, and Modals	2–3	1–2
Listening for Negative Expressions	1–2	1
Listening for Time, Quantity, and Comparisons	1–2	1
Understanding Intonation	1–2	0–1
Listening for Implications by the Speakers	4–5	2–3
Making Inferences about People	4–5	2–3
Making Inferences about Context	1–2	0
Identifying the Topic and Main Ideas	3	3–5
Comprehending Details	8	8–12
Matching Words and Categories	0	1–2
Sequencing Events in a Process	0	1–2
Determining Reasons	4–5	4–6
Making Inferences and Predictions	4–5	4–6
TOTAL	50	30–50

OVERVIEW OF THIS SECTION

LISTENING

PART A—SHORT CONVERSATIONS

The Listening section of both the paper–based and computer–based test includes several short conversations between two people. Each conversation is followed by one question about it.

QUESTIONS ON THE PAPER TEST

In all of the short conversations on the paper–based test, each person speaks only once. Usually, the questions are about what the second speaker says.

Multiple–Choice Questions

On the paper test, all of the questions in Part A are multiple choice. After each conversation, you will hear a question and choose the one best answer of four possible choices, (A), (B), (C), or (D). Then, on your answer sheet, you will find the number of the question and fill in the space that corresponds to the letter of the answer you have chosen.

The conversations and questions will be presented only once. This means you must answer all questions as you go. You have twelve seconds to read the four answer choices and answer each question.

You will hear a recording of a conversation like this one:

(Woman) Didn't you hear me say your parents were coming over tonight?
(Man) No, I must have been in a fog.
(Narrator) What does the man mean?

In your book, you will read:

(A) He knew his parents were coming over.
(B) He has been outdoors in the fog.
(C) He hadn't noticed what the woman said.
(D) He must have been in another room.

You learn from the conversation that the man *must have been in a fog.* In fog, you cannot see and may feel confused. The man means he was not aware of what the woman had said about his parents coming over. Therefore, the best answer to the question, *What does the man mean?* is (C), *He hadn't noticed what the woman said.*

QUESTIONS ON THE COMPUTER TEST

In most of the conversations on the computer–based test, each person speaks only once, but in some of the conversations, one or both people speak more than once.

Multiple–Choice Questions

On the computer test, all of the questions in Part A are multiple choice. You will use the mouse to click on the one best answer of four possible choices.

The conversations and questions will be presented only once. You must answer all questions as you go.

You can take as much time as you need to answer each question; however, you should work as quickly as possible because the entire Listening section is timed. The amount of time you have left will appear on the computer screen. The time you spend listening to the conversations and questions is not counted in the total time.

You will be able to change your answer as many times as you like—*until you confirm your answer*. When you confirm your answer, the computer will give you the next conversation.

You will not be allowed to return to a previous question. This is because the answer you give helps the computer determine the difficulty level of your next question.

While you are listening to each conversation, a picture of the two speakers will be shown on the computer screen. You will hear a conversation like this one:

(Man) I wonder who just pulled in the driveway.
(Woman) Didn't you hear me say your parents were coming over tonight?
(Man) No, I must have been in a fog.

Then, you will both *see* and *hear* the question before the answer choices appear.

The computer screen with the question and answer choices will look like this:

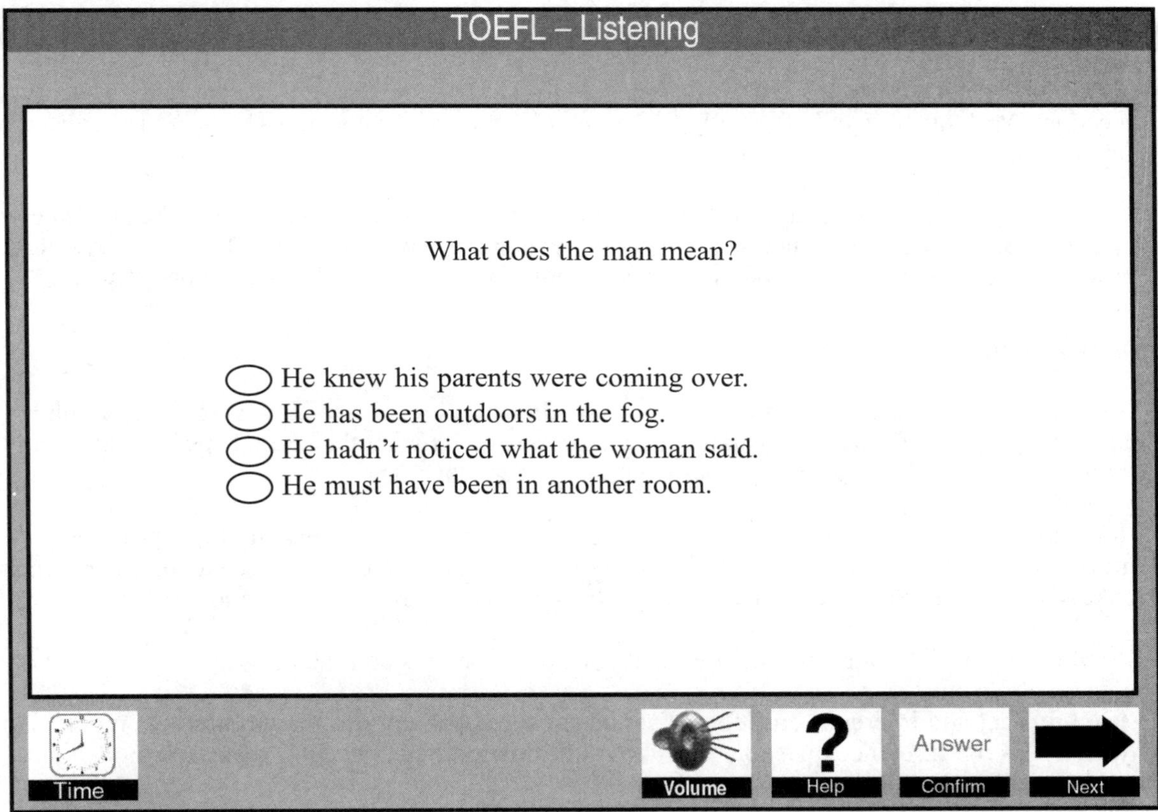

The correct answer is *He hadn't noticed what the woman said.* Therefore, you should click on the third answer choice.

When you click on the oval next to one of the answer choices, the oval will darken. To change your answer, click on a different oval.

When you are satisfied that you have chosen the right answer, click on **Next.** Then click on **Confirm Answer**. When you do this, the computer will give you the next short conversation.

STRATEGIES FOR PART A—SHORT CONVERSATIONS

Prepare before the Test

- Work on building your vocabulary and knowledge of idioms. Use the conversations in this book to become familiar with the informal language in the Listening section.
- Be familiar with the structures that are common in conversational English. This book gives you practice in listening for many of these structures.
- For the computer test, be familiar with the testing tools, such as **Time**, **Next**, and **Confirm Answer**. Practice using the mouse.

Pace Yourself during the Test

- Think only of the question you are currently working on.
- On the paper test, you have only twelve seconds to read the four answer choices and answer each question. Work quickly and efficiently. Do not work on previous questions or try to read ahead to the next question.
- On the computer test, you must answer each question before you can move on to the next one. Confirm your answer only when you are certain you are ready to move on. Once you have moved on to the next question, forget the previous questions. You cannot go back and change them.

Listen for Meaning

- Think about the context of the conversation. The first speaker sets the context, and the second speaker adds key information. Usually, the question is about what the second speaker says. Only occasionally will the question be about what the first speaker says.
- Think about the purpose of the conversation. One speaker may be requesting help, providing information, or making a suggestion. The other speaker may agree or disagree, express an opinion, make a suggestion, or express an emotion such as pleasure, surprise or disappointment.
- Listen for key words, phrases, and idioms that help you understand the message.
- Listen for fact and inference questions. Fact questions ask about information that was mentioned by the speakers. Inference questions ask about information that was not directly mentioned but was implied by the speakers.

Use the Process of Elimination

- If you do not see the correct answer right away, eliminate the answer choices that you know are incorrect. If you can eliminate one or two answer choices, you will improve your chance of answering the question correctly.
- Then, if you are still not sure of the correct answer, guess! On the paper test, your score is based on the number of questions you answer correctly, and wrong answers are not subtracted. On the computer test, if you answer a question incorrectly, the computer will make the next question easier.

Know the Tricks

Be familiar with the various ways the incorrect answer choices try to trick you. The most common tricks are:

- repeating words and phrases from the conversation incorrectly
- having words that sound similar to words in the conversation
- using incorrect meanings of words with multiple meanings
- giving literal meanings of idioms

Try This Exercise

Listen to your teacher read the following conversation. Then read the answer choices and eliminate those that try to trick you.

(Man) Is there anything I can do to help?
(Woman) Would you please cut more meat?
(Narrator) What does the woman want the man to do?

(A) Come meet her.
(B) Cut more wood.
(C) Put the meat away.
(D) Slice some meat.

How many choices were you able to eliminate? How did they try to trick you? (The correct answer is (D).)

1.1 Listening for Key Words

FOCUS

Listen to a conversation. What words in the conversation are keys to understanding the message?

(START TAPE)

(PAUSE TAPE)

For each key word you hear in the conversation, write a ***synonym***, another word with a similar meaning.

Key Words	*Synonyms*

Now, listen to the conversation again. Choose the best answer to the question.

(START TAPE)

- ◯ She is supposed to receive a lizard.
- ◯ There might be a thunderstorm.
- ◯ A snowstorm is predicted.
- ◯ Her friend Liz is coming to visit.

(STOP TAPE)

In the conversation, some key words you may have heard are *forecast* and *blizzard*. These words tell you that the speakers are discussing the weather.

A synonym for *forecast* is *prediction*. A synonym for *blizzard* is *snowstorm*. Therefore, the best answer to the question *What does the woman mean?* is the third choice, *A snowstorm is predicted.*

Why are the other answer choices incorrect? The first choice tries to trick you by using *lizard*, which sounds similar to *blizzard*. The second choice has *thunderstorm*, which is an electrical storm, not a snowstorm. The fourth choice tries to trick you with *Liz is coming*, which sounds similar to *blizzard coming*.

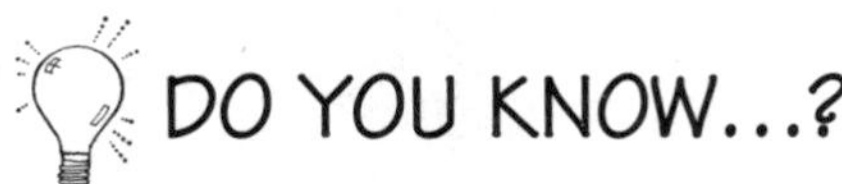

DO YOU KNOW...?

1. Approximately three questions on the TOEFL will test your ability to recognize key words and understand their meaning in the short conversations you hear.

2. Key word questions are about specific information in a conversation. Key word questions sound like this:

   What does the man mean?
   What does the woman say about ____________?
   What does the man want to know?
   What does the woman want the man to do?
   What do you know from the conversation?

LISTENING

3. Some of the answer choices will try to trick you with words that sound similar to the key words in the conversation. Here is an example:

   (Man) Let me help you with that backpack. It looks heavy.
   (Woman) It's not light.
   (Narrator) What does the woman mean?

   ◯ It is not right for the man to help her.
   ◯ The man is mistaken.
   ◯ Her backpack is heavy.
   ◯ Her backpack is dark–colored.

   The first answer choice has *It is not right*, which sounds similar to *It's not light*. The second choice has *mistaken*, which means *not right*. Both of these answers try to trick you by making you think of words that sound similar to the key word *light*.

   The fourth choice tries to trick you with *dark–colored*, which refers to a different meaning of *not light*. In this context, *not light* means *heavy*.

   The best answer is the third choice, *Her backpack is heavy.*

4. Some of the answer choices will try to trick you by using incorrect meanings of key words that have multiple meanings. Here is an example:

   (Woman) I was surprised to see so many rabbits on our hike.
   (Man) So was I. I didn't think they were common around here.
   (Narrator) What does the man mean?

   ◯ The rabbits they saw were a rare type.
   ◯ The rabbits they saw were an inferior species.
   ◯ He didn't know the woman shared his interest in rabbits.
   ◯ He had thought rabbits were not often seen there.

   In this conversation, both speakers express surprise at seeing rabbits, and the man says he didn't think rabbits were *common*. The key word *common* has multiple meanings. Here, it refers to the prevalence of rabbits, that is, how often rabbits are seen. The best answer is the fourth choice, *He had thought rabbits were not often seen there.*

   The first three answer choices refer to other meanings of *common* that are incorrect in this context: *common = not rare*; *common = of inferior quality*; *common = shared.*

PRACTICE

Exercise 1.1.A

Listen carefully to the following conversations. Choose the best answer to each question.

(START TAPE)

1. (A) The mountains are beautiful.
   (B) It is windy in the mountains.
   (C) The air in the mountains is dry.
   (D) The air is thin in the mountains.

2. (A) His neighbors will return to their country.
   (B) His neighbors used to own a restaurant.
   (C) His neighbors refuse to disagree with anyone.
   (D) His neighbors escaped danger in their country.

3. (A) She hoped to pick the new president.
   (B) She wanted to show something to the president.
   (C) She was looking for the president's new office.
   (D) She wanted to see the new president.

4. (A) A spinning cloud is dangerous.
   (B) They can see the cloud better from indoors.
   (C) Clouds make her feel sad.
   (D) It is bad luck to see an early cloud.

5. (A) She was annoyed by the mosquitoes.
   (B) She found the mosquitoes amusing.
   (C) She recommends visiting the lake in August.
   (D) There were too many other tourists there in August.

6. (A) He got lost on the way home.
   (B) He is a dangerous driver.
   (C) He is a kind and gentle person.
   (D) He wouldn't allow anyone else to drive his car.

(STOP TAPE)

Exercise 1.1.B

Listen carefully to the following conversations. Choose the best answer to each question.

(START TAPE)

1. (A) Nadine's home is in bad condition.
   (B) Nadine should not run down the stairs.
   (C) They had to go downstairs to look for Nadine.
   (D) Nadine lives in a basement apartment.

2. (A) He got lost and didn't hear the speech.
   (B) He couldn't see the president from where he was sitting.
   (C) He didn't understand the speech.
   (D) He lost his vision.

3. (A) The woman is pouring drinks.
   (B) The speakers cannot afford a taxi.
   (C) It is raining heavily outside.
   (D) The woman is too tired to walk.

4. (A) Mr. Kendrick fired Jim during the meeting.
   (B) Jim and Mr. Kendrick argued during the meeting.
   (C) Jim and Mr. Kendrick were exciting speakers.
   (D) It was very warm in the room.

5. (A) Her brother means to visit them with a companion.
   (B) Her brother has a lot of dreams about college.
   (C) She doesn't believe her brother has his own company.
   (D) Her brother would like to start a business.

6. (A) His instructor thanked him for the gift.
   (B) His instructor praised his work.
   (C) His instructor criticized his presentation.
   (D) His instructor spoke for a long time.

(STOP TAPE)

Exercise 1.1.C

Listen carefully to the following conversations. Choose the best answer to each question.

 *(START TAPE)*

1. (A) The woman feels up to taking marketing.
   (B) The marketing class will be more interesting than sociology.
   (C) The woman was lucky to be able to take marketing.
   (D) She will be able to fill up with gas at the market.

2. (A) The man must overcome his shyness.
   (B) The man must find the right time to speak to Teresa.
   (C) Teresa may want to stop being friends.
   (D) The man should stop in to ask for Teresa.

3. (A) Her mother is a terrible cook.
   (B) Her mother means to be nice.
   (C) Her mother can still handle her affairs.
   (D) Her mother's hearing is very bad.

4. (A) The man is a building inspector.
   (B) The school is more than two centuries old.
   (C) The woman discovered the school a long time ago.
   (D) The woman found an excellent old school.

5. (A) He expects to decide the next morning.
   (B) He thinks they may find a better apartment.
   (C) They should agree on how much rent they expect to pay.
   (D) They should examine the apartment carefully.

6. (A) She is not impressed with his dog.
   (B) She doesn't know anything about dogs.
   (C) The man should not beat his dog.
   (D) The man will not be able to take his dog on the train.

 *(STOP TAPE)*

Answers to Exercises 1.1.A through 1.1.C are on page 628.

LISTENING

1.1 EXTENSION

1. Working in pairs, students discuss why the three incorrect answer choices in Exercises 1.1.A through 1.1.C are incorrect. How do they try to trick you? Which answer choices have words that sound similar to key words? Which key words have more than one meaning?

2. After listening to the cassette and answering the questions, students read the tapescripts for Exercises 1.1.A through 1.1.C on page 681. Each person takes the part of the woman, man, or narrator. Practice reading the conversations aloud, concentrating on pronunciation.

3. Working in pairs, students choose one of the conversations from Exercises 1.1.A through 1.1.C and rewrite it so that one of the incorrect answer choices is now the correct answer. Use the tapescript on page 681. Each student takes the part of one of the speakers. Practice reading the conversation aloud, concentrating on pronunciation. Present the conversation and question to the class. Classmates take a "live TOEFL exam." Be prepared to explain the new correct answer!

Example:

M: The air feels different here in the mountains.
W: Yes, I can feel how blustery it is.
N: What does the woman mean?

Correct answer: (C) It is windy in the mountains. (Ex. 1.1.A, #1)
Explanation: *Windy* is a synonym for the key word *blustery*.

1.2 Listening for Idioms

FOCUS

Listen to a conversation.

 *(START TAPE)*

 *(PAUSE TAPE)*

What does the man say?

The man uses an idiom, *It's a real load off my mind*. An ***idiom*** is an expression that has a special meaning which is different from the meaning of the individual words. In this conversation, you cannot understand what the man means by knowing only the meanings of the words *load*, *off*, and *mind*.

Now, listen to the conversation again and choose the best answer to the question.

 *(START TAPE)*

- ◯ He feels light–headed from studying.
- ◯ He has a low opinion of his abilities.
- ◯ He is relieved at the news of his acceptance.
- ◯ He does not mind talking about medical school.

 *(STOP TAPE)*

In this context, *It's a real load off my mind* means the man is relieved to learn he was accepted into medical school. Therefore, the best answer to the question *What does the man mean?* is the third choice.

How do the other answer choices try to trick you?

DO YOU KNOW...?

1. At least seven questions on the paper–based TOEFL and three questions on the computer–based TOEFL will test your comprehension of idioms in the short conversations you hear.

2. An ***idiom*** is an expression that has a special meaning. The meaning of an idiom is different from the meaning of the individual words. In other words, the meaning of the whole is different from the sum of the parts. Look at some examples:

COMMON IDIOMS	MEANING
blow it	fail, do poorly
can tell	can comprehend, know instinctively
can't stand	won't or can't tolerate
fed up	disgusted
get out of hand	become uncontrollable
hard to imagine	difficult to accept as being true
keep an eye on	watch, guard
keep in touch	communicate
keep track of	know about; stay informed; keep a record of
kill time	occupy one's time while waiting; waste time
make fun of	joke about (someone or something)
none of one's business	a personal matter that should not be of interest to someone else
out of date	not timely, not fashionable
out of touch	not in contact or communication
pull someone's leg	tease or joke
see eye to eye	agree
take advantage of	use the opportunity for; abuse a kindness
take care of	watch over, be responsible for
up to date	timely, modern, the most recent
worn out	exhausted; in bad condition

A ***phrasal verb*** is another type of idiom that you will hear on the TOEFL. A phrasal verb is a verb + preposition structure and is sometimes called a ***two–word verb*** or ***three–word verb***. A phrasal verb has a special meaning that is different from the meaning of the individual words.

COMMON PHRASAL VERBS	MEANING
back out	withdraw from a promise or agreement
call off	cancel
catch on	begin to understand
catch up (with)	reach the same level or position
check out	investigate
come down with	become ill
deal with	control, manage, or handle (a matter)
drop out	quit school
fall through	fail to happen
get along with	be friendly with, not fight
jump at	accept eagerly
kick out	force (someone) to leave
pass away	die
point out	call attention to
put off	delay, postpone
put up with	tolerate
show up	appear, come
take over	assume responsibility or control of
throw away, throw out	discard, get rid of
turn down	decrease volume or intensity; refuse

Idioms and phrasal verbs are used extensively in spoken English. The best way to acquire them is to listen to and converse with native speakers of English. There are also several excellent books and dictionaries that can help you learn idioms and phrasal verbs.

3. Some of the answer choices will try to trick you by giving literal meanings of the words in an idiomatic expression. A ***literal meaning*** is an exact, dictionary meaning of a word.

Here is an example:

(Man) When are you going to do something about your faucet?
(Woman) Do you have to bring that up again?
(Narrator) What does the woman mean?

- ◯ She wants the man to carry her faucet upstairs.
- ◯ She asks the man to bring her something.
- ◯ She asks the man if he needs anything.
- ◯ She does not want to talk about her faucet.

The woman uses the idiom *bring that up*. In this context, *bring up* means *mention* or *raise the topic of* the faucet. The man mentions her faucet, and the woman communicates that she does not like being reminded of her faucet. Therefore, the best answer is the fourth choice, *She does not want to talk about her faucet.*

The first and second answer choices give literal meanings of *bring up*. The third choice does not fit the context; the woman is not asking the man if he needs anything.

Why do you think the woman does not like being reminded of her faucet?

Here is another example:

(Woman) Well, it's good–bye until I come back to school next year.
(Man) Be sure to drop me a line, OK?
(Narrator) What does the man mean?

- ◯ He wants her to write him a letter.
- ◯ He asks her to visit him any time she likes.
- ◯ He asks her to let a line fall.
- ◯ He wants her to drop out of school.

If you chose the first answer choice, congratulations! You were correct. *Drop a line* is an idiom that means *write a letter*.

The second choice is incorrect because *visit him any time* refers to *drop in* or *drop by* (which are also idioms). The third choice is incorrect because *let a line fall* is a literal meaning for *drop a line*, which does not make sense in this context. The fourth choice is incorrect because the idiom *drop out* means *quit*.

4. Some commonly used exclamations are idiomatic. Here is an example:

(Man) My brother just called to say his wife had twins.
(Woman) You don't say!
(Narrator) What does the woman mean?

- ◯ She thinks the man is lying.
- ◯ She is pleasantly surprised.
- ◯ She thinks the man is teasing her.
- ◯ She doesn't understand what the man said.

In this conversation, the woman uses the idiomatic exclamation *You don't say!* This expression can communicate pleasure, surprise, or both, as in this case, where the woman is responding to the news about the twins.

The best answer is the second choice, *She is pleasantly surprised.*

Why are the other answer choices incorrect?

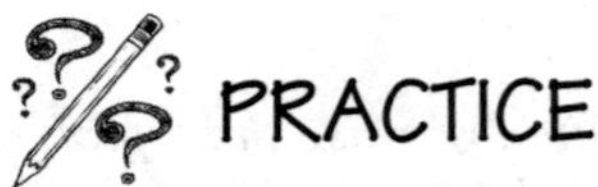

PRACTICE

Exercise 1.2.A

Listen carefully to the following conversations. Choose the best answer to each question.

 *(START TAPE)*

1. (A) He thinks Dr. Williamson robbed him.
   (B) Dr. Williamson gave him incorrect directions.
   (C) He finds Dr. Williamson annoying.
   (D) He likes having Dr. Williamson for a neighbor.

2. (A) She has been crying about her kitten.
   (B) She is overjoyed at having a kitten.
   (C) She got a kitten just like the man's.
   (D) Her house is crowded with nine kittens.

3. (A) She must be careful not to over–exercise.
   (B) She is almost finished with her homework.
   (C) She must do the exercises repeatedly.
   (D) She can't do the exercises correctly.

4. (A) Karen and her sister look alike.
   (B) It is difficult to speak to Karen and her sister.
   (C) You can't tell Karen anything.
   (D) Karen and her sister are always together.

5. (A) She hardly ever sees her boss anymore.
   (B) Her boss never agrees with her.
   (C) Her boss does not see very well.
   (D) She would like to meet with her boss more often.

6. (A) He wants to shake her hand.
   (B) He is giving her advice.
   (C) He will wait for her after the test.
   (D) He is wishing her good luck.

7. (A) Stop worrying.
   (B) Stop hitting her.
   (C) Make his point.
   (D) Come indoors.

8. (A) The speakers called someone about a car.
   (B) Someone in another car shouted at the speakers.
   (C) The speakers almost had an accident.
   (D) The speakers are trying to make a phone call.

 *(STOP TAPE)*

LISTENING

Exercise 1.2.B

Listen carefully to the following conversations. Choose the best answer to each question.

 *(START TAPE)*

1. (A) They should have taken the bus.
   (B) They alternated drivers.
   (C) They turned several times when driving.
   (D) They took a wrong turn.

2. (A) His supervisor gave him too much work to do.
   (B) His boss has been criticizing him.
   (C) His boss sat down on his briefcase.
   (D) His supervisor is not an effective manager.

3. (A) Lend him some money.
   (B) Give him a number.
   (C) Help him with some wood.
   (D) Hand him his laundry.

4. (A) He is an excellent carpenter.
   (B) He said the right thing.
   (C) He is a violent person.
   (D) He prefers to work only with his head.

5. (A) He can't find the letter Aaron sent him.
   (B) He thinks Aaron likes living in Texas.
   (C) He doesn't care how Aaron is doing.
   (D) He never hears from Aaron anymore.

6. (A) Find an easier way to finish the project.
   (B) Talk to his boss about getting help with the project.
   (C) Stop trying to work so hard.
   (D) Make the project easier for his boss to understand.

7. (A) She likes to stay up late.
   (B) She studies the habits of birds.
   (C) She is frequently late for work.
   (D) She prefers working during the day.

8. (A) He never knows what time it is.
   (B) He takes a long time to read the paper.
   (C) He will probably kill someone.
   (D) He wastes a lot of time.

 *(STOP TAPE)*

Exercise 1.2.C

Listen carefully to the following conversations. Choose the best answer to each question.

 *(START TAPE)*

1. (A) He is glad the woman knows that Fred is dishonest.
   (B) He thinks the woman should try to see Fred more often.
   (C) He doesn't think Fred has been lying.
   (D) He is finally going to see Fred again.

2. (A) She can't see in the rain.
   (B) She can't stand the rain.
   (C) She likes to take long walks in the rain.
   (D) The man probably thinks she is crazy.

3. (A) There is a hole in his suit.
   (B) He wants to throw away his suit.
   (C) He wants a new jacket for his suit.
   (D) He would like a red suit.

4. (A) Offer to help her brother paint his house.
   (B) Choose a color for her brother's house.
   (C) Go to the lake with her brother.
   (D) Try to avoid painting her brother's house.

5. (A) Rachel will probably not pass the class.
   (B) Rachel's father passed her on the way home.
   (C) Rachel's father died.
   (D) Rachel dropped the class.

6. (A) They should take a van to the museum.
   (B) They should go to the concert if it is free.
   (C) They should go to a free movie instead of the concert.
   (D) The man should decide what they will do that evening.

7. (A) She is disgusted by having to work on her boat.
   (B) She needs to work less on her boat than she did in the past.
   (C) She would like the man to work on her boat.
   (D) She doesn't eat on her boat anymore.

8. (A) The parents usually bring their children to visit.
   (B) He enjoys introducing his children to people.
   (C) The parents understand their children.
   (D) The parents have raised their children well.

9. (A) His girlfriend promised to show him something.
   (B) He has a job as a waiter in the coffee shop.
   (C) He wants to give his girlfriend a ride home.
   (D) His girlfriend has not arrived yet.

10. (A) The man should stop teasing Shunji.
    (B) Shunji does not have a sense of humor.
    (C) The man should tell funnier jokes.
    (D) Shunji may want to choose his own friends.

(STOP TAPE)

Exercise 1.2.D

Listen carefully to the following conversations. Choose the best answer to each question.

(START TAPE)

1. (A) Think carefully about the job.
   (B) Stay away from Mr. Tung.
   (C) Accept the job.
   (D) Politely refuse the job.

2. (A) Perhaps his grandfather was a captain.
   (B) He would like a boat like his grandfather's.
   (C) He is looking for his grandfather.
   (D) He resembles his grandfather.

3. (A) She needs to discover Stefan's address.
   (B) She wants Stefan to write to his sister.
   (C) She doesn't care where Stefan is.
   (D) She wants Stefan to deliver a letter for her.

4. (A) The woman may have to wait a long time to get an appointment.
   (B) The woman should try calling his dentist.
   (C) The woman must not delay seeing a dentist.
   (D) The woman does not need an appointment to see a dentist.

5. (A) If the man wants to go running before dinner.
   (B) If there is no food at home.
   (C) Which store she should run to.
   (D) Why the man doesn't want to make pizza at home.

6. (A) The man should speak more clearly to Warren.
   (B) The man should avoid Warren.
   (C) The man should buy Warren's term papers.
   (D) The man should be careful not to tear Warren's papers.

7. (A) The man's parents will take a trip to Boston.
   (B) The man's parents anticipate his visit.
   (C) The man's parents will look for him at the airport.
   (D) The man should look for a flight to Boston.

8. (A) They should share their feelings with Masami.
   (B) Masami might like a new chair.
   (C) They should take Masami to see a doctor.
   (D) They should try to make Masami feel happy.

9. (A) Take Nina out more often.
   (B) Cut something outside.
   (C) Stop correcting Nina.
   (D) Put Nina outside.

10. (A) He has bought a motorcycle.
    (B) He borrowed a motorcycle.
    (C) He wrote a check for Greg's motorcycle.
    (D) He has been looking at motorcycles.

(STOP TAPE)

Exercise 1.2.E

Listen carefully to the following conversations. Choose the best answer to each question.

 *(START TAPE)*

1. (A) The woman said something questionable.
   (B) It is not possible for them to move.
   (C) He agrees with the woman.
   (D) The woman must ask a different question.

2. (A) He disagrees with the woman.
   (B) The woman's opinion shocked him.
   (C) The woman said something obvious.
   (D) He could not hear what the woman said.

3. (A) He is surprised by the news.
   (B) He finds the news very sad.
   (C) He doesn't believe the news.
   (D) He contradicts the woman.

4. (A) She is afraid for her life.
   (B) Boxing is her favorite sport.
   (C) She refuses to go to the boxing match.
   (D) She will go to the boxing match with someone else.

5. (A) She doesn't understand the man's request.
   (B) She thanks the man for his kindness.
   (C) She must get the children ready.
   (D) She will not have the man's laundry ready.

 *(STOP TAPE)*

Answers to Exercises 1.2.A through 1.2.E are on page 628.

1.2 EXTENSION

1. With books closed, students listen to the cassette for one of the exercises in Exercise 1.2.A through 1.2.D. Try to identify the idioms in each conversation (usually spoken by the second person). Write down the idioms you hear. In groups of 2 to 4, write a definition for each idiom. Share your results with the class. Then, open your book. Play the cassette again and answer the questions in the exercise. Did you correctly identify and define the idioms?

2. Before listening to the cassette for Exercise 1.2.E, the teacher dictates the idioms listed below. Students write down the idioms. Working in pairs, students discuss possible meanings for each. Choose two expressions and write a short conversation using each. Present the conversations to the class. Then, listen to the cassette and answer the questions.

   Exercise 1.2.E Idioms

   1. You must be kidding!
   2. That goes without saying.
   3. No kidding!
   4. That's out of the question!
   5. Not on your life!

3. Working in groups of 2 to 4, students write a list of idioms and phrasal verbs that use the verbs from the list below. **Example:** *go over, go through with, go away, go crazy, go straight, go jump in the lake.*

call	give	look	run
do	go	make	take
get	keep	put	turn

4. In conversation or reading outside class, students find examples of idioms and phrasal verbs. Bring examples to share in class. In what context did you hear or see the expressions? What do the expressions mean?

5. Students use the lists of idioms and phrasal verbs from activities 1 through 4 (above) to start a dictionary of idioms to help prepare for the TOEFL. Write a definition for each. Include examples showing how the idioms are used in spoken English.

 ASSESSING PROGRESS — 1.1 through 1.2

QUIZ 1 *(Time – approximately 10 minutes)*

(START TAPE)

Directions: In this quiz you will hear short conversations between two people. After each conversation, you will hear a question about the conversation. The conversations and questions will not be repeated. After you hear a question, read the four possible answers and choose the best answer.

Here is an example.

On the recording, you hear:

In your book, you read:

(A) Sarah fell on her trip to Mexico.
(B) Sarah enjoyed her trip to Mexico.
(C) Sarah had a terrible trip to Mexico.
(D) Sarah did not go to Mexico.

You learn from the conversation that Sarah's trip to Mexico fell through. *Fell through* is an idiom that means *failed to happen*. The best answer to the question, *What does the man mean?* is (D), *Sarah did not go to Mexico*. Therefore, the correct choice is (D).

1. (A) He had no salt, so he substituted something else.
   (B) He ran out to buy some miso for the soup.
   (C) He uses a different recipe each time he makes the soup.
   (D) He put in more salt than he usually does.

2. (A) He couldn't hear everything the speaker said.
   (B) He couldn't understand any of the lecture.
   (C) He left the lecture after the opening words.
   (D) He had not heard there would be a lecture.

3. (A) The man does not have much time.
   (B) She wants to leave early.
   (C) They will have to rush if they want to be early.
   (D) The man does not have to hurry.

4. (A) She is a kind of maid.
   (B) She bought them a nice gift.
   (C) She is very considerate.
   (D) She lives by herself.

5. (A) His relationship with his roommate was not satisfactory.
   (B) He never could find a roommate.
   (C) His roommate never wanted to go along with him to the park.
   (D) His roommate was never at home at the same time he was.

6. (A) Watch the woman's dog.
   (B) Tell her when five minutes have passed.
   (C) Watch to see if the number five bus is coming.
   (D) Take care of the woman's handbag.

7. (A) He could have gotten a scholarship if he had worked harder.
   (B) He criticizes himself too harshly.
   (C) He has a very difficult problem.
   (D) The scholarship examination is unusually difficult.

8. (A) He is trying to hurt the woman.
   (B) He is a generous person.
   (C) He is joking with the woman.
   (D) He is going to visit the Algerian ambassador.

9. (A) She wants Taro to keep something for her.
   (B) Taro should hug her to say good–bye.
   (C) Taro should visit her during the summer.
   (D) They should communicate during the summer.

10. (A) His behavior is vulgar.
    (B) He tries to be serious.
    (C) He is in the wrong course.
    (D) He causes problems.

11. (A) Dr. Lim speaks too quickly.
(B) The lectures are too advanced for her.
(C) She has missed most of the lectures.
(D) Dr. Lim's lectures are too long.

12. (A) He agrees with the woman.
(B) He has something else to say.
(C) He is surprised.
(D) He doesn't know what to say.

13. (A) She does not feel like talking.
(B) She agrees to meet the man at her home.
(C) She is recovering from being ill.
(D) She is tired from a long airplane trip.

14. (A) The man is required to take more calculus.
(B) Two of the calculus classes are not very difficult.
(C) Only men must take two years of calculus.
(D) The calculus classes are held in the auditorium.

15. (A) The man's brother lived there for only one month.
(B) The man put his brother's things in a safe place.
(C) The man's brother is difficult to live with.
(D) She never met the man's brother.

(STOP TAPE)

Answers to Listening Quiz 1 are on page 628.

1.3 Listening for Conditionals, Causatives, and Modals

Listen to a conversation and choose the best answer to the question.

(START TAPE)

- ◯ Caleb cares too much about his car.
- ◯ Caleb is probably not annoyed.
- ◯ Caleb does not know about the dent on his car.
- ◯ Caleb never discusses his feelings.

(PAUSE TAPE)

The man wonders if Caleb is still annoyed, and the woman responds, *If he were, he would let you know*. This is a ***conditional statement*** because it expresses a condition and a result (See 2.12).

Condition:	If he were (still annoyed)
Result:	he would let you know

If he were is an unreal condition. The past tense verb, *were*, indicates that Caleb is *not* annoyed. The result, *he would let you know*, means that Caleb usually tells you when he is annoyed, but he has not done so now because he is not annoyed.

The best answer to the question *What does the woman say about Caleb?* is the second choice, *Caleb is probably not annoyed*.

Listen to another conversation and choose the best answer to the question.

(START TAPE)

- ◯ He didn't know anyone in the class.
- ◯ The instructor didn't know what to do.
- ◯ The instructor introduced someone to the class.
- ◯ The students introduced each other.

(STOP TAPE)

The man says, *The instructor had us introduce someone we didn't already know*. The verb phrase *had us introduce* is a ***causative***. It means that the instructor *caused* the students to introduce someone they didn't already know. In other words, *the students*, not the instructor, introduced someone to the class.

The best answer to the question *What does the man say about his class?* is the fourth choice, *The students introduced each other*.

Conditionals and causatives are used frequently in spoken English.

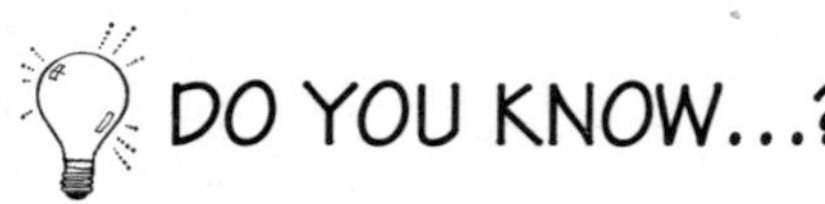

DO YOU KNOW...?

1. Approximately two questions on the TOEFL will test your understanding of conditionals, causatives, and modals in the short conversations you hear.

2. Conditional sentences express a condition that leads to, or does not lead to, a possible result. Look at some examples:

(Man)	If we hurry, we might not miss the bus.
(Narrator)	What does the man mean?
Answer:	They should hurry so that they do not miss the bus.

(Man)	If we had hurried, we might not have missed the bus.
(Narrator)	What does the man mean?
Answer:	Because they did not hurry, they missed the bus.

Wishes are similar to conditional sentences that are unreal or not true. Look at some examples:

(Woman)	I wish this town had a good Italian restaurant.
(Narrator)	What do you know from this statement?
Answer:	There is not a good Italian restaurant in the town.

(Woman)	If this town had a good Italian restaurant, I would eat there often.
(Narrator)	What do you know from this statement?
Answer:	There is not a good Italian restaurant in the town.

(Man)	I wish I knew where to find a reliable used car. If I knew where to find one, I would buy it.
(Narrator)	What does the man mean?
Answer:	He does not know where to find a reliable used car.

Note: You will also review conditionals in 2.12.

3. ***Causatives*** are verbs that cause certain results or cause or allow people to do things. The following verbs can be used as causatives:

make	get	have	let	help

Look at some examples:

(Man)	My instructor makes us type all our papers.
(Narrator)	What does the man mean?
Answer:	He must type all his papers because his instructor requires it.

(Woman)	Bob got his roommate to wash the dishes.
(Narrator)	What happened to the dishes?
Answer:	Bob's roommate washed them.

(Man)	Mona had her assistant prepare the monthly report.
(Narrator)	What does the man say about the monthly report?
Answer:	It was prepared by Mona's assistant.

4. ***Modals*** are auxiliary verbs (See 2.5) that are used to give advice, make suggestions, or indicate preferences. Some modals that occur in TOEFL conversations are:

have to	had better	need to	should	would rather

Look at some examples:

(Woman)	I'd rather stay up late than get up early.
(Narrator)	What does the woman mean?
Answer:	She prefers to stay up late.
(Man)	Ruth had better not fail the next biology test.
(Narrator)	What does the man mean?
Answer:	Ruth must pass the next biology test.
(Man)	I have two books to read and a paper to write, and I haven't slept in days.
(Woman)	I think you need to take it easy.
(Narrator)	What does the woman advise the man to do?
Answer:	He should rest and not work so hard.

5. Some of the answer choices will try to confuse you by repeating words and phrases from the conversation incorrectly. Here is an example:

(Man)	If Tyler can't raise his grade point average, he'll be put on academic probation.
(Woman)	Well, he'd better do something about that.
(Narrator)	What do the speakers say about Tyler?

○ He cannot raise his grade point average.
○ He will have to work harder to stay in school.
○ He has something better to do.
○ He has a better grade point average.

The first answer choice repeats part of the condition stated by the man, *if Tyler can't raise his grade point average*. However, this would be an inaccurate answer because it is only part of what the speakers say about Tyler.

The second choice, *He will have to work harder to stay in school*, is the correct answer because it expresses what both speakers mean. The man states a condition, *If Tyler can't raise his grade point average*, and a probable result, *he'll be put on academic probation*. The woman says that Tyler *had better do something about that*. In other words, Tyler must do something to raise his grade point average to avoid being put on probation.

The third and fourth answer choices incorrectly repeat words from the conversation, such as *something better to do* and *grade point average*.

On the TOEFL, listen for the overall meaning and beware of answer choices that merely repeat some of the words and phrases from the conversation.

PRACTICE

Exercise 1.3.A

Listen carefully to the following conversations. Choose the best answer to each question.

(START TAPE)

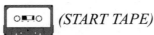

1. (A) Go shopping with him.
   (B) Accompany him to the coffee shop.
   (C) Show him where she buys coffee.
   (D) Buy him a cup of coffee.

2. (A) Dr. Levensky allows students to direct their own learning.
   (B) Dr. Levensky has little experience in teaching sociology.
   (C) Dr. Levensky allows very little flexibility in class.
   (D) Dr. Levensky does not expect students to work very hard.

3. (A) Her brother called her two hours ago.
   (B) Her brother makes long phone calls.
   (C) Her brother does not call her often enough.
   (D) She regrets not having time to talk to her brother.

4. (A) Dr. Grant will not be present in class.
   (B) The students will present their papers in class.
   (C) Dr. Grant requires students to write a lot of papers.
   (D) Dr. Grant will make the introductions.

5. (A) He does not like potlucks.
   (B) He prefers to work on his thesis.
   (C) He does not want to finish his thesis.
   (D) He will go to the potluck late.

6. (A) He agrees to help the woman this weekend.
   (B) He would rather help Troy move this weekend.
   (C) He does not want to help the woman.
   (D) He cannot help her because he has to work.

(STOP TAPE)

Exercise 1.3.B

Listen carefully to the following conversations. Choose the best answer to each question.

(START TAPE)

1. (A) She will ask Dr. Chung for an interview.
   (B) She will ask Dr. Chung for an interview if he is not busy.
   (C) She called Dr. Chung, but his line was busy.
   (D) She does not want to ask Dr. Chung for an interview.

2. (A) She did not go to the beach last weekend.
   (B) She regrets not knowing about the funeral.
   (C) She went to the funeral by herself.
   (D) She did not want to go to the funeral.

3. (A) Her brother borrowed her motorcycle.
   (B) Her brother gave her a ride on his motorcycle.
   (C) She rode her brother's motorcycle to the party.
   (D) She bought her brother a motorcycle.

4. (A) He does not know the grade on his term paper.
   (B) He was disappointed in the grade on his term paper.
   (C) He was absent when his professor gave the papers back.
   (D) He asked his professor for more time to write the term paper.

5. (A) Taking a walk would help the man.
   (B) The man should have walked with her.
   (C) The man should try to finish his paper.
   (D) They could walk as far as the dead end.

6. (A) She will give him the ratchet wrench.
   (B) She does not know what a ratchet wrench is.
   (C) She cannot find the right type of wrench.
   (D) She was not able to catch the wrench.

(STOP TAPE)

Answers to Exercises 1.3.A through 1.3.B are on pages 628 and 629.

1.3 EXTENSION

1. Working in pairs, students identify conditionals, causatives, and modals in the conversations in Exercises 1.3.A and 1.3.B. How do some of the incorrect answer choices try to trick you?
2. Working in pairs, students choose one of the conversations from Exercise 1.3.A or 1.3.B and rewrite it so that one of the incorrect answer choices is now the correct answer. Use the tapescript on page 684. Each student takes the part of one of the speakers. Practice reading the conversation aloud, concentrating on pronunciation. Present the conversation and question to the class. Classmates take a "live TOEFL exam." Be prepared to explain the new correct answer!

Example:

W: Hi, Nick! Do you know where I can get a good cup of coffee?
M: If you'll come with me to my favorite coffee shop, you can treat me.
N: What does the man want the woman to do?

Correct answer: (D) Buy him a cup of coffee. (Ex. 1.3.A, #1)
Explanation: *To treat someone* means to pay for him.

LISTENING

1.4 Listening for Negative Expressions

FOCUS

Listen to a conversation and choose the best answer to the question.

(START TAPE)

- ◯ He does not know who got married.
- ◯ He is very surprised by the marriage.
- ◯ He disagrees with the marriage.
- ◯ He does not believe the marriage took place.

(STOP TAPE)

The man says, *Nothing could surprise me more!* He uses a negative expression to show surprise. The news of the marriage surprises him more than any other news he might hear.

The best answer to the question *What does the man mean?* is the second choice, *He is very surprised by the marriage.*

The incorrect answer choices try to confuse you with other negative expressions. Can you identify them?

Negative expressions and meanings are common in spoken English.

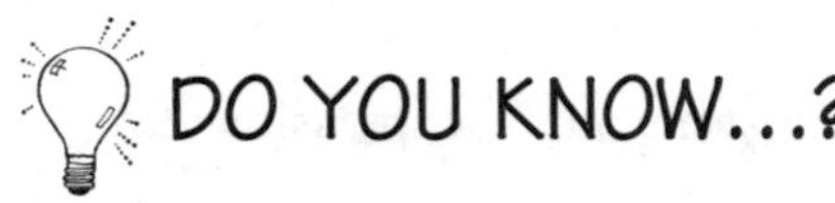

DO YOU KNOW...?

1. At least one question on the TOEFL will test your comprehension of negative expressions in the short conversations you hear.

2. Some negative expressions to listen for are:

neither	never	nobody	no one	nothing
neither...nor	no	none	not	nowhere

(Woman)	Paul isn't going skiing this weekend.
(Man)	Neither am I.
(Narrator)	What does the man mean?
Answer:	He is not going skiing either.

(Man)	Neither Mike nor Kathy is a very good singer.
(Narrator)	What does the man mean?
Answer:	Mike is not a good singer, and Kathy is not a good singer.

(Man)	I'm finished with my paper already.
(Woman)	Not all students are as organized as you are!
(Narrator)	What does the woman mean?
Answer:	The man is one of the most organized students.

3. Negative prefixes can be added to the beginning of some words to give these words an opposite meaning.

   Some negative prefixes to listen for are:

PREFIX	EXAMPLE	MEANING
de-	deactivate	stop, turn off
dis-	disbelief	inability or refusal to believe
il-	illegal	not legal, against the law
im-	impolite	not polite
in-	invisible	not visible, unable to be seen
ir-	irresponsible	not responsible
non-	nonfat	without fat
un-	uninteresting	not interesting

(Woman)	I guess I'm unlucky when it comes to lotteries.
(Narrator)	What does the woman mean?
Answer:	She is not very lucky in lotteries.

(Man)	I hadn't realized it would be informal dress at the party.
(Narrator)	What does the man say about the party?
Answer:	People dressed casually at the party.

Note: A "double negative" (*not* + word with a negative prefix) has an affirmative meaning.

Look at this example:

(Man)	I wonder what the chance of an avalanche is today.
(Woman)	With these warm temperatures, it's not unlikely.
(Narrator)	What does the woman mean?
Answer:	An avalanche is likely to occur today.

4. Some expressions have an "almost negative" meaning. Some "almost negative" expressions to listen for are:

barely	hardly	rarely	scarcely	seldom

(Man) I could barely stay awake during my economics class this morning.
(Narrator) What does the man mean?
Answer: He almost fell asleep in his economics class.

(Woman) I seldom have any free time during the week.
(Narrator) What does the woman mean?
Answer: She is usually busy during the week.

Note: You will also review negative structures in 2.18.

5. Some of the answer choices will try to trick you by using other negative expressions. Here is an example:

(Woman) I was sorry not to see you at the concert last night. The music was wonderful.
(Man) I tried to get in, but they were turning people away.
(Woman) Oh, I know. There were hardly any seats left when I got there.
(Narrator) What does the woman mean?

○ She was unable to find a seat.
○ She got one of the few remaining seats.
○ She did not hear much of the concert.
○ The seats in the concert hall were hard.

The woman says there were *hardly any* seats left when she got to the concert hall. *Hardly any* is an "almost negative" expression, which in this context means there were almost no seats left.

The best answer is the second choice, *She got one of the few remaining seats*.

The first choice tries to trick you with the negative word *unable*. However, you know this is incorrect because the woman heard the concert and enjoyed the music. This means she was able to find a seat. The third choice tries to confuse you with *did not hear much*. You know this is inaccurate because the woman tells the man the music was wonderful.

How does the fourth choice try to trick you?

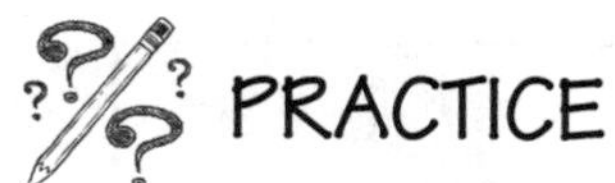

PRACTICE

Exercise 1.4.A

Listen carefully to the following conversations. Choose the best answer to each question.

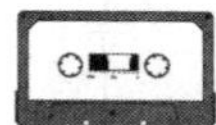
(START TAPE)

LISTENING

1. (A) He wants to take the woman shopping.
   (B) He wants to help the woman practice her driving.
   (C) He is looking for a place to park.
   (D) He can't find the parking lot.

2. (A) He could not decide which classes to take.
   (B) He dropped one of his classes.
   (C) He had to leave school.
   (D) She heard that he missed his old friends.

3. (A) They will have to cancel the picnic.
   (B) Only a few people are coming to the picnic.
   (C) Some people are not able to come to the picnic.
   (D) They do not know how many are coming to the picnic.

4. (A) They are not good dancers.
   (B) They dislike dancing.
   (C) They go to the dance club every Saturday.
   (D) They never go to the dance club.

5. (A) She has not talked to Martin in a long time.
   (B) She does not understand Martin anymore.
   (C) She does not know anyone named Martin.
   (D) She does not want to talk about Martin.

6. (A) The woman may get a good score on the TOEFL.
   (B) It is not possible to do well on the TOEFL the first time.
   (C) The woman should not take the TOEFL.
   (D) The woman has already taken the TOEFL.

7. (A) He did not attend Professor Snow's lecture.
   (B) He was not aware of any difference in Professor Snow.
   (C) He disagrees with the woman.
   (D) He had difficulty understanding Professor Snow.

8. (A) He is always excited about something.
   (B) He is more excited than he has ever been.
   (C) He is nervous about going to Stanford.
   (D) She has not seen Raul recently.

9. (A) She cannot attend the lecture at eight o'clock.
   (B) She doesn't understand the lecture.
   (C) She has never had an eight o'clock lecture.
   (D) She doesn't like having an eight o'clock lecture either.

10. (A) He has not heard of any hotels nearby.
    (B) He does not know how to find their hotel room.
    (C) They might be able to get a room without a reservation.
    (D) She had not heard him make a reservation.

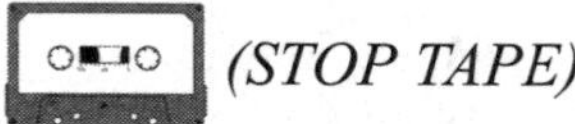
(STOP TAPE)

Answers to Exercise 1.4.A are on page 629.

1.4 EXTENSION

1. The teacher calls out words from the list below, and students must give an ***antonym*** (a word with an opposite meaning). There may be several antonyms for a word. Either the teacher or students may add to the list. Use some of the negative prefixes from the list on page 57.

always	inexpensive	decrease	find
kind	difficult	destroy	satisfied
benefit	exciting	narrow	obey
evil	afraid	sell	pleasant
clean	terrible	catch	import
necessary	wake up	dry	safe
common	borrow	frequently	softer
honest	capable	inside	short

2. Students create "TOEFL conversations" to test their classmates' understanding of negative expressions. Working in pairs, follow this procedure:

(1) Choose an expression from the lists of negative and "almost negative" expressions on pages 57 and 58. Write a short conversation with two speakers.
(2) Pass your conversation to the next pair of students.
(3) With the conversation you now have (written by another pair of students), choose an appropriate "TOEFL question" from the list below. Then, pass the conversation and question to the next pair of students.
(4) With the conversation and question you now have (written by others), write four answer choices. One must be the correct answer!
(5) This conversation is now yours. Show your conversation, question, and answer choices to your teacher. The teacher may make suggestions and return the conversation to you.
(6) Type the answer choices and give copies to the class.
(7) Practice reading your conversation aloud, concentrating on pronunciation.
(8) Present your conversation to the class. The teacher reads the questions, and the class takes a "live TOEFL exam."

TOEFL Questions

What does the _____ mean?
What does the _____ say about _____?
What does the _____ want to know?
What does the _____ want the _____ to do?
What do you know from this conversation?

1.5 Listening for Time, Quantity, and Comparisons

FOCUS

Listen to a conversation and choose the best answer to the question.

(START TAPE)

- ◯ He is looking for a new job.
- ◯ He will ask for a promotion next week.
- ◯ He has two more weeks to find a job.
- ◯ He will begin a new job in two weeks.

(STOP TAPE)

You know the man just got a job because the woman congratulates him. When she asks when the job will start, the man replies, *The week after next.* This means he will begin his new job two weeks from now.

The best answer to the question *What do you know about the man?* is the fourth choice, *He will begin a new job in two weeks.*

This question tests your ability to hear and understand the time expression *the week after next.* It also tests your overall comprehension of the meaning of the conversation, which is given in the first line, *Congratulations on getting the job!* This knowledge allows you to eliminate the first and third answer choices, which imply that the man has not yet found a job.

DO YOU KNOW...?

1. At least one question on the TOEFL will test your comprehension of expressions of time, quantity, and comparison in the short conversations you hear.

2. Some time expressions to listen for are:

after	as long as	earlier	later	until
already	as soon as	first	next	when
as	before	last	once	while

(Man)	I've known Terry for around ten years. How long have you known her?
(Woman)	Oh, at least as long as that.
(Narrator)	What does the woman mean?
Answer:	She has know Terry for more than ten years.

(Woman)	Once my children are in school, I plan to go back to college.
(Narrator)	What does the woman mean?
Answer:	She will go back to college after her children start school.

(Woman)	Did you talk to your adviser?
(Man)	She had already left when I called.
(Narrator)	What does the man mean?
Answer:	He did not talk to his adviser.

Other time expressions:

the day after tomorrow	...means in two days
the week before last	...means two weeks ago
at least three hours	...means three or more hours

3. Some expressions of quantity to listen for are:

almost as many/much	a couple of	half	a lot
as many/much as	double	hardly any/enough	only a few
at least	a few	a little	triple

(Man)	Only a few people showed up at the meeting.
(Narrator)	What does the man mean?
Answer:	There were not many people at the meeting.

(Woman)	There were hardly enough handouts to go around.
(Narrator)	What does the woman mean?
Answer:	They almost ran out of handouts.

(Man)	Membership in the astronomy club has tripled in four years.
(Narrator)	What does the man say about the astronomy club?
Answer:	It has three times as many members as it had four years ago.

4. Some expressions of comparison to listen for are:

as…as	-er…than	more…than	not as…as
better…than	less…than	much more…than	worse…than

(Man) Ruby is not as fussy as her sister.
(Narrator) What does the man mean?
Answer: Ruby is less fussy than her sister.

(Woman) Poor Leo! It seems the more he studies, the worse he does on the tests.
(Narrator) What does the woman mean?
Answer: Leo seems to get lower test scores when he studies a lot.

(Woman) I'm almost finished with breakfast, and then I'll be ready to leave.
(Man) The sooner the better.
(Narrator) What does the man mean?
Answer: He is eager to get going.

Note: You will also review comparative expressions in 2.19.

5. Some of the answer choices will try to trick you by using incorrect expressions of time, quantity, or comparison. Here is an example.

(Man) Tomorrow is Ralf's birthday. Do you know how old he'll be?
(Woman) Well, I know he's older than my brother, who will turn twenty–three next July.
(Narrator) What do you know about Ralf?

- ◯ He will be at least twenty–three tomorrow.
- ◯ He is no more than twenty–three.
- ◯ He is not as old as the woman's brother.
- ◯ He never told them his age.

From the conversation, you know that Ralf has a birthday tomorrow and that he is older than the woman's brother. You also know the woman's brother will be twenty–three next July. You can conclude that tomorrow Ralf will be twenty–three or older.

The correct answer is the first choice, *He will be at least twenty–three tomorrow.*

The second choice tries to confuse you with *no more than*, which means *less than*. The third choice tries to confuse you with *not as old as*, which means *younger than*. You can conclude that the fourth choice is incorrect because the woman has a general idea of Ralf's age: she knows he is older than her brother.

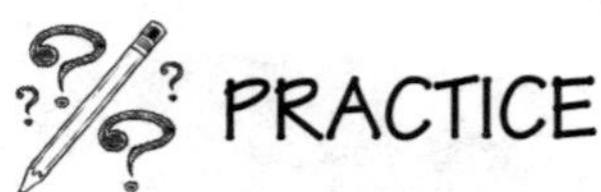

PRACTICE

Exercise 1.5.A

Listen carefully to the following conversations. Choose the best answer to each question.

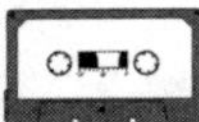

(START TAPE)

1. (A) Her class starts at six o'clock.
   (B) She has to hurry to make her seven o'clock class.
   (C) She needs to leave earlier than the man does.
   (D) The library closes at seven o'clock.

2. (A) He has taught high school for two months.
   (B) He has taught at the same school for several years.
   (C) He moved in next door two years ago.
   (D) He moved in next door after he started teaching.

3. (A) It is the same as the man's.
   (B) It is heavier than the man's.
   (C) It is narrower than the man's.
   (D) It is a darker color than the man's.

4. (A) He met the woman and her cousin around the same time.
   (B) He met the woman after he met her cousin.
   (C) He has not known the woman's cousin very long.
   (D) He has known the woman's cousin for a long time.

5. (A) He is not a good student.
   (B) He should have been able to graduate this year.
   (C) He had to leave school before graduation.
   (D) He has almost enough credits to graduate.

6. (A) They were married more than five years ago.
   (B) They were married last year.
   (C) They have been married longer than he has.
   (D) They have been married too long.

7. (A) He likes having big parties.
   (B) He will probably have several parties.
   (C) His party will be small and intimate.
   (D) He will not invite enough people.

8. (A) Next year tuition will cost twice as much for freshmen.
   (B) Tuition is nearly twice as much as he remembers.
   (C) Freshmen pay lower tuition than other students.
   (D) Tuition doubles every year.

(STOP TAPE)

Answers to Exercise 1.5.A are on page 629.

1.5 EXTENSION

1. Working in pairs, students identify expressions of time, quantity, and comparison in the conversations in Exercise 1.5.A. How do some of the incorrect answer choices try to trick you?

2. Working in pairs, students choose one of the conversations from Exercise 1.5.A and rewrite it so that one of the incorrect answer choices is now the correct answer. Use the tapescript on page 685. Each student takes the part of one of the speakers. Practice reading the conversation aloud, concentrating on pronunciation. Present the conversation and question to the class. Classmates take a "live TOEFL exam." Be prepared to explain the new correct answer!

Example:

M: Tomorrow is Ralf's birthday. Do you know how old he'll be?
W: Well, I know he's younger than my brother.
N: What do you know about Ralf?

Correct answer: He is not as old as the woman's brother. (Example on page 63.)
Explanation: *Not as old as* means *younger than*.

1.6 Understanding Intonation

FOCUS

Listen to a conversation and choose the best answer to the question.

(START TAPE)

- ◯ She has just finished the Acme project.
- ◯ She does not want to be given the Acme project.
- ◯ She thinks the Acme project is wonderful.
- ◯ She wants to hear about the Acme project.

(PAUSE TAPE)

The woman says, *That's just what I wanted to hear*...but is it really? How do you think she feels when she says it?

The woman's falling tone of voice indicates she is not pleased by the news that Mr. Tumpek may be giving her the Acme project. Therefore, you can eliminate the first and third answer choices.

The best answer to the question *What does the woman mean?* is the second choice, *She does not want to be given the Acme project.*

Listen to another conversation and choose the best answer to the question.

(START TAPE)

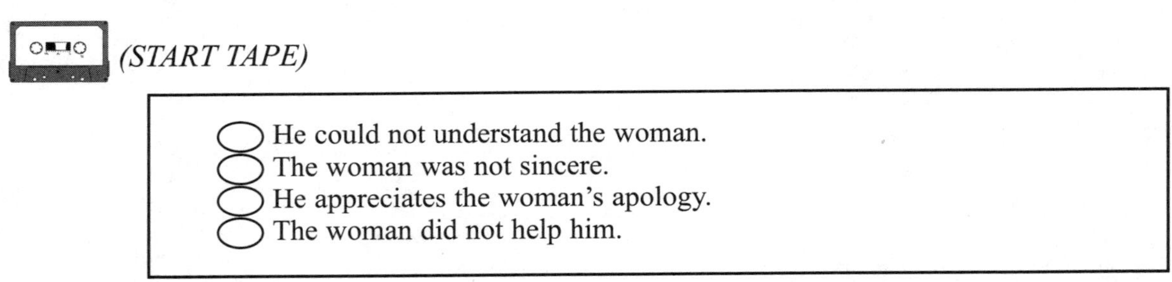

- ◯ He could not understand the woman.
- ◯ The woman was not sincere.
- ◯ He appreciates the woman's apology.
- ◯ The woman did not help him.

(STOP TAPE)

The man says, *That helps me a lot.* How do you think he feels when he says it?

The man's falling tone of voice indicates he is not pleased by the fact that he cannot use his credit card there. His response is sarcastic because his words say the opposite of what he really means. He does not feel that the woman helped him.

The best answer to the question *What does the man mean?* is the fourth choice, *The woman did not help him.*

Both of these conversations show the importance of intonation in conveying meaning in spoken English.

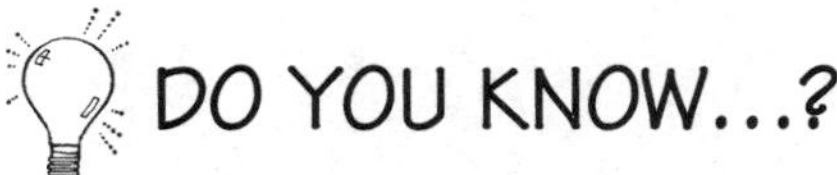

1. At least one question on the TOEFL will test your ability to understand the meaning of intonation in the short conversations you hear.

2. ***Intonation*** is the way people's voices go up and down as they speak. In English, there are different levels of pitch. ***Pitch*** refers to the highness or lowness of the voice.

   Speakers usually use a higher pitch at the beginning and the lowest pitch at the end of sentences. Thus, most sentences have ***falling intonation***, which means the pitch goes from higher to lower. This is especially true of sentences that are statements or commands.

   > ↘
   > There's a video parlor on First Street.

   > ↘
   > Please hand me my umbrella.

   Questions that have a *yes* or *no* answer have ***rising intonation***. This means the pitch of the voice goes from lower to higher.

   > ↗
   > Did you pass the test for your driver's license?

   Questions that begin with *wh–* question words such as *what*, *when*, or *why* have falling intonation.

   > ↗ ↘
   > When will you be finished with your homework?

   Rising intonation can turn a statement into a question.

   > ↗
   > She has the flu and still went to school today?

   > ↗
   > You'll be able to come with us?

   In exclamations, the highest pitch is combined with the strongest stress to show emphasis or to express emotions such as pleasure, enthusiasm, surprise, anger, or disbelief.

   > ↗
   > I couldn't believe my eyes!

   > ↗
   > What a way to go!

3. On the TOEFL, sometimes the meaning of a conversation depends on the intonation of one of the speakers. Listen to the speakers' voices. If a speaker emphasizes certain words with a higher pitch, that may be the key to his or her message.

   Here is an example:

(Woman)	Yusef got the highest grade on our chemistry practicum.
(Man)	Oh, so he *did* stick with chemistry after all!
(Narrator)	What had the man assumed about Yusef?

○ He was not a hard worker.
○ He never studied chemistry.
○ He was a practicing chemist.
○ He had dropped chemistry.

Because the man stresses *did* by giving it a higher pitch, he shows he is surprised that Yusef stuck with, or stayed with, chemistry. This means he had assumed Yusef had *not* stuck with chemistry and had dropped the class. Therefore, the best answer is the fourth choice, *He had dropped chemistry*.

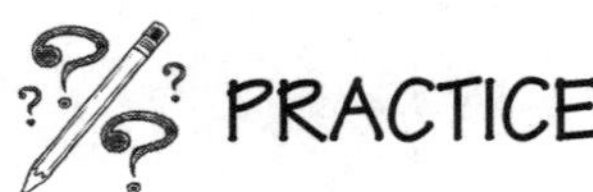

PRACTICE

Exercise 1.6.A

Listen carefully to the following conversations. Choose the best answer to each question.

(START TAPE)

1. (A) The family did not know about the cabin.
   (B) The family could not come this weekend.
   (C) The man did not want to invite his family.
   (D) The man had forgotten to invite his family.

2. (A) He thought Bruce was a poor dancer.
   (B) He did not know Bruce was a dancer.
   (C) He did not know Bruce was a prince.
   (D) He regrets not going to the recital.

3. (A) He has never been to the speedway before.
   (B) The tickets are probably too expensive.
   (C) He would rather do something else on Saturday.
   (D) He would like to go to the speedway with her.

4. (A) Something was wrong with the woman's car.
   (B) The woman had just bought a new car.
   (C) The woman did not want to drive her own car.
   (D) The woman wanted to go running in San Francisco.

5. (A) She loves to babysit her nephews.
   (B) She would rather play with her nephews than write her term paper.
   (C) She is too busy to babysit this weekend.
   (D) She looks forward to seeing her nephews.

6. (A) She is glad the man can help her.
   (B) She looks forward to going to the football game.
   (C) She is frustrated that the man will not help her.
   (D) She appreciates the man's assistance.

7. (A) He was not a lawyer.
   (B) He would not win the case.
   (C) He did not know the man.
   (D) He did not like to celebrate.

8. (A) He didn't know she liked steak.
   (B) He thought she would prefer a hamburger.
   (C) He thought she was a vegetarian.
   (D) He didn't realize she was so hungry.

(STOP TAPE)

Answers to Exercise 1.6.A are on page 629.

1.6 EXTENSION

1. Students practice reading each sentence below in different ways. Read the sentence as a statement, question, command, and exclamation. Change intonation to show different emotions.

   1. I'm driving.
   2. My sister is coming to visit for a week.
   3. You're coming with me.
   4. I need help with this.
   5. You know that.

   On the board, write:

Type of Sentence	**Emotion**
statement	surprise
question	pleasure
command	displeasure
exclamation	disbelief

   Choose one of the sentences to read to the class. Choose one type of sentence and one emotion. **Example:** Read *I'm driving* as a question that shows surprise. Classmates listen and try to determine which type of sentence and which emotion you are expressing.

2. Working in pairs, students choose one of the conversations from Exercise 1.6.A. Change the intonation and rewrite the question and four answer choices. One must be the correct answer! Use the tapescript on page 685. Each student takes the part of one of the speakers. Practice reading the conversation aloud, concentrating on intonation. Write the new answer choices on the board. Present the conversation and question to the class. Classmates take a "live TOEFL exam." Be prepared to explain the correct answer!

   Example:

   M: My sister says we should expect the whole family at the cabin this weekend.
   W: Oh, they're *all* coming…
   N: What does the woman mean?

   (A) She did not know the family could come.
   (B) The family could not come.
   (C) She does not want the whole family to come.
   (D) She wants the whole family to come.

   Correct answer: (C).
   Explanation: The woman's intonation shows displeasure.

ASSESSING PROGRESS — 1.3 through 1.6

QUIZ 2 *(Time—approximately 10 minutes)*

(START TAPE)

Directions: In this quiz you will hear short conversations between two people. After each conversation, you will hear a question about the conversation. The conversations and questions will not be repeated. After you hear a question, read the four possible answers and choose the best answer.

Here is an example.

On the recording, you hear:

In your book, you read:

(A) She must prepare her presentation.
(B) She must help her boss give a presentation.
(C) Her boss is making a presentation tomorrow.
(D) She will miss the presentation tomorrow.

The woman says her boss is making her give a presentation, which means that she, not her boss, will be giving the presentation. The best answer to the question, *What does the woman mean?* is (A), *She must prepare her presentation.* Therefore, the correct choice is (A).

1. (A) She was accepted into graduate school.
   (B) She does not understand the graduate school requirements.
   (C) She does not know if she got into graduate school.
   (D) She does not want to go to graduate school.

2. (A) The man would talk too long on the telephone.
   (B) The man would forget to buy a birthday card.
   (C) The man would be rude to his mother.
   (D) The man might forget his mother's birthday.

3. (A) The roommate will move out at the end of the month.
   (B) The roommate moved out last week.
   (C) The roommate moved out two weeks ago.
   (D) The roommate lived there only a month.

4. (A) She has a class at three o'clock.
   (B) She cannot have coffee with the man.
   (C) She will meet the man for coffee after class.
   (D) She will cancel her appointment with her adviser.

5. (A) He wanted to get there earlier.
   (B) He has to work this weekend.
   (C) He has to leave early to go to work.
   (D) He was allowed to leave work early.

6. (A) It was the same speech that was given last year.
   (B) It was shorter than last year's speech.
   (C) It was longer and less focused than last year's speech.
   (D) It was a big improvement over last year's speech.

7. (A) He had not known about the trip.
   (B) Most people like dangerous activities.
   (C) He does not like dangerous activities.
   (D) No one told him the trip would be so dangerous.

8. (A) He enjoys spending time with her.
   (B) She does not have enough fun.
   (C) She knows how to have a lot of fun.
   (D) He enjoys helping her with homework.

9. (A) She had not known about Eli's party.
(B) She did not attend Eli's party.
(C) Only a few people knew about the party.
(D) Eli's apartment was too small for a party.

10. (A) He can't find the directions.
(B) The chair needs another bolt.
(C) A bolt is missing.
(D) The directions are incomplete.

11. (A) Astrid is not as tall as the woman.
(B) Astrid is taller than the man.
(C) The shirt will be too short for Astrid.
(D) Astrid never wears T–shirts.

12. (A) She thought he did not want a convertible.
(B) She thought he should wait to buy a car.
(C) She did not know he wanted to buy a car.
(D) She wanted to help him decide which car to buy.

13. (A) Her secretary will arrange the details of her trip.
(B) She will arrange to have her secretary accompany her.
(C) She will not go to the conference.
(D) Her secretary will go to the conference.

14. (A) He wishes he received more letters.
(B) His friends do not answer his letters.
(C) He rarely corresponds with anyone.
(D) He does not like to use e–mail.

15. (A) Professor Tran let no one else speak.
(B) Professor Tran did not hear the speech.
(C) Professor Tran probably liked the speech.
(D) Professor Tran is not a good teacher.

(STOP TAPE)

Answers to Listening Quiz 2 are on page 629.

1.7 Listening for Implications by the Speakers

FOCUS

Listen to a conversation and choose the best answer to the question.

(START TAPE)

- ◯ The man should look out the window.
- ◯ The man should not open the window.
- ◯ The man should open the window slowly.
- ◯ The room is close and drab.

(STOP TAPE)

The man wants to open the window. The woman says she just closed it because *it felt drafty in here*. She does not directly tell him she does not want the window opened, yet this is what she *implies*. How do you know this? She says she *just closed* the window because *it felt drafty*.

The best answer to the question *What does the woman imply?* is the second choice, *The man should not open the window.*

People make implications frequently in conversations. One reason is that the speakers understand the context and therefore do not have to mention a lot of details. For example, in the above conversation, it is not necessary for the woman to say, *I do not want you to open the window because it felt drafty in here and I was uncomfortable with the window open, so I closed it.*

Another reason people make implications is because it is sometimes more polite than speaking directly.

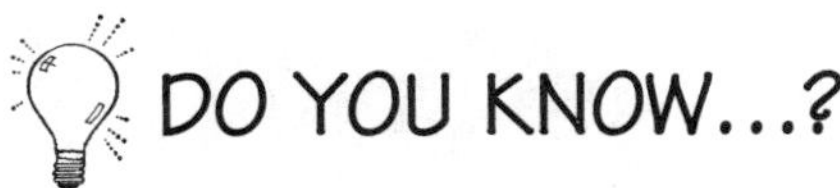

DO YOU KNOW...?

1. At least four questions on the paper–based TOEFL and two questions on the computer–based TOEFL will test your comprehension of implications made by the speakers in the short conversations you hear.

2. An ***implication*** is something that is not stated directly by one of the speakers but is implied or suggested. When a speaker *implies* something, you must *infer* the meaning.

   TOEFL questions about implications sound like this:

   > What does the woman imply?
   > What does the man imply about _____?
   > What does the man suggest the woman do?
   > What does the woman think the man should do?
   > What does the man advise the woman to do?

   Sometimes a speaker will make an implication by asking a negative question. Here are some examples:

(Man)	I'll get the car ready for our trip.
(Woman)	Wouldn't it be more relaxing to take the train?
(Narrator)	What does the woman imply?
Answer:	They should take the train rather than drive.

(Woman)	I need something for my headache.
(Man)	Isn't there a drugstore nearby?
(Narrator)	What does the man imply?
Answer:	The woman can get something for her headache at the drugstore.

3. To understand implications, you must consider:

   - the meaning of key words, phrases, and idioms
   - the meaning of negative questions
   - the context and purpose of the conversation
   - the probable relationship of the speakers to each other

   In questions about implications, some of the answer choices may try to trick you by:

   - repeating words and phrases from the conversation incorrectly
   - having words that sound similar to key words in the conversation
   - being inaccurate: partly incorrect or opposite in meaning
   - being about something not mentioned by the speakers

Here is an example:

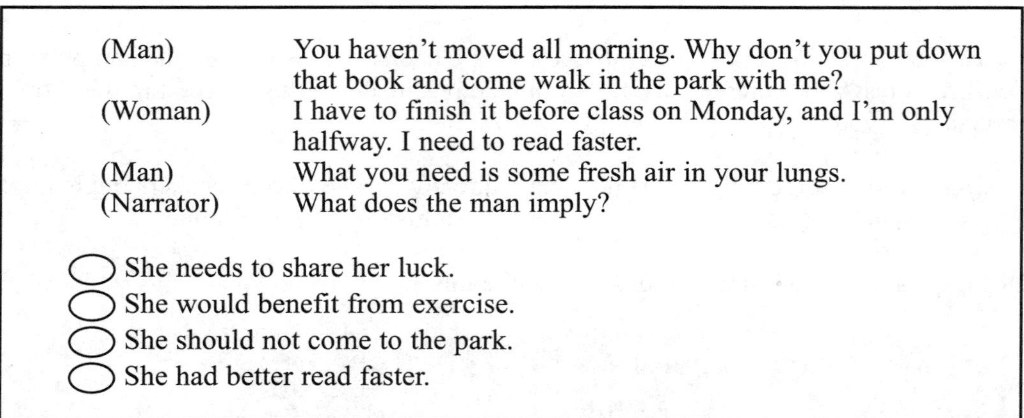

(Man) You haven't moved all morning. Why don't you put down that book and come walk in the park with me?
(Woman) I have to finish it before class on Monday, and I'm only halfway. I need to read faster.
(Man) What you need is some fresh air in your lungs.
(Narrator) What does the man imply?

- She needs to share her luck.
- She would benefit from exercise.
- She should not come to the park.
- She had better read faster.

What is the purpose of the conversation? The man invites the woman to join him for a walk in the park, and she refuses his invitation. The speakers are probably close friends or spouses.

The best answer is the second choice, *She would benefit from exercise*. Some key words that help you understand the man's implication are *need* and *fresh air*.

The first answer choice tries to trick you with words that sound similar to the key words: *needs to share her luck* sounds similar to *need is some fresh air in your lungs*. The third choice is incorrect because it is the opposite of what the man wants. The fourth choice relates more to what the woman says than to what the man implies.

PRACTICE

Exercise 1.7.A

Listen carefully to the following conversations. Choose the best answer to each question.

 *(START TAPE)*

1. (A) She should work full–time.
   (B) She may have planned too much for the summer.
   (C) She should take more than two classes.
   (D) She is not allowed to work full–time.

2. (A) Call the department secretary about his grade.
   (B) Wait patiently for the results of the exam.
   (C) Study for at least two weeks before the exam.
   (D) Complain to the department secretary.

3. (A) The woman should change her attitude about the class.
   (B) The woman should drop the class.
   (C) The woman is used to having more interesting classes.
   (D) The woman needs a different class for graduation.

4. (A) The radio announcer cannot be believed.
   (B) The radio announcer is doing a good job.
   (C) They should follow the radio announcer's advice.
   (D) It makes no difference what the radio announcer says.

5. (A) They should have worked harder on the quarterly report.
   (B) Kimi should be hired full–time for the summer.
   (C) Kimi should work on the next quarterly report.
   (D) The man should hire someone to help Kimi.

6. (A) They should watch the thriller.
   (B) He is thrilled to watch a movie with her.
   (C) Long movies are difficult to understand.
   (D) The historical drama follows the other movie.

7. (A) Look for someone to share his house.
   (B) Introduce her to Yong.
   (C) Become Yong's housemate.
   (D) Look for a new lab partner.

8. (A) He expects a lot of dogs at the party.
   (B) The dog can sleep in a quiet room.
   (C) The dog will enjoy himself at the party.
   (D) She should not bring her dog to the party.

9. (A) He should give up the idea of medical school.
   (B) He should get a less difficult job.
   (C) He should give up one of his jobs.
   (D) He should drop one of his courses.

10. (A) His friend may be able to help her.
    (B) His friend lives nearby.
    (C) His friend's car has a similar problem.
    (D) She should buy a car from his friend.

(STOP TAPE)

Exercise 1.7.B

Listen carefully to the following conversations. Choose the best answer to each question.

 *(START TAPE)*

1. (A) Begin working on her assignment.
   (B) Go to court next week.
   (C) File a weekly report.
   (D) Borrow the book she needs.

2. (A) Maria doesn't like rock climbing.
   (B) He likes the hot climate of Devil's Tower.
   (C) Both men are interested in rock climbing.
   (D) The men are like brothers.

3. (A) The hot dogs are delicious.
   (B) She is still hungry.
   (C) She wants something to drink.
   (D) She does not want a hot dog.

4. (A) His involvement in sports is affecting his school work.
   (B) He has to study hard to do well in basketball.
   (C) He would rather play basketball than do anything else.
   (D) He is the greatest basketball player on the team.

5. (A) The bird will make her happy.
   (B) She should have paid less for the bird.
   (C) She has spent her money unwisely.
   (D) She needs to buy a new car.

6. (A) He might not need his sunglasses.
   (B) He might have left his sunglasses in the car.
   (C) He should be a more careful driver.
   (D) He will need his sunglasses for driving.

7. (A) He is changing his major to geology.
   (B) He will graduate next year.
   (C) He would rather take a different course.
   (D) He probably failed the exam.

8. (A) She is too busy to go look at cars.
   (B) She cannot decide which car to buy.
   (C) She cannot afford to buy a car.
   (D) She will ask Bill what he thinks.

9. (A) His mother is very impatient.
   (B) His mother cannot hear very well on the telephone.
   (C) The man should let her read the letters from his mother.
   (D) The man should call or write his mother.

10. (A) She may have difficulty getting her paper done.
    (B) She must have been lying about having a paper due.
    (C) She will have more fun at the ocean than at home.
    (D) He wishes he could go to the ocean with her.

 *(STOP TAPE)*

Answers to Exercises 1.7.A through 1.7.B are on page 630.

1.7 EXTENSION

1. Working in pairs, students identify key words and phrases in the conversations in Exercises 1.7.A and 1.7.B that help you understand the implications made by the speakers.

2. Working in pairs, students choose one of the conversations from Exercise 1.7.A or 1.7.B and rewrite it so that one of the incorrect answer choices is now the correct answer. Use the tapescripts on pages 686 and 687. Each student takes the part of one of the speakers. Practice reading the conversation aloud, concentrating on pronunciation. Present the conversation and question to the class. Classmates take a "live TOEFL exam." Be prepared to explain the new correct answer!

Example:

M: Nathalie is taking two classes this summer.
W: Is that all? She is required to be a full–time student.
N: What does the woman imply about Nathalie?

Correct answer: (C) She should take more than two classes (Ex. 1.7.A, #1)
Explanation: She needs more than two classes to be a full–time student.

1.8 Making Inferences about People

FOCUS

LISTENING

Listen to a conversation and choose the best answer to the question.

(START TAPE)

- ◯ She does not want to assist the man.
- ◯ She will take the stairs down to the fifth floor.
- ◯ She works in a medical clinic.
- ◯ She will make an appointment with Dr. O'Brien.

(PAUSE TAPE)

What do you know about Kelly?

You know that Kelly is one of the speakers. You know that a man asks for her help with some blood samples. You know that Kelly agrees to help him because she says *Sure*. You also know that she must first *rush these charts up to Dr. O'Brien on the fifth floor*. You learn a lot about Kelly from this short conversation.

What can be inferred about Kelly? You can infer that *she works in a medical clinic*. Therefore, the best answer is the third choice. Certain key words and phrases lead you to this conclusion.

You can eliminate the first answer choice because it is not true. You can eliminate the second and fourth choices because neither speaker said anything that would support such conclusions.

Now, listen to another conversation and choose the best answer to the question.

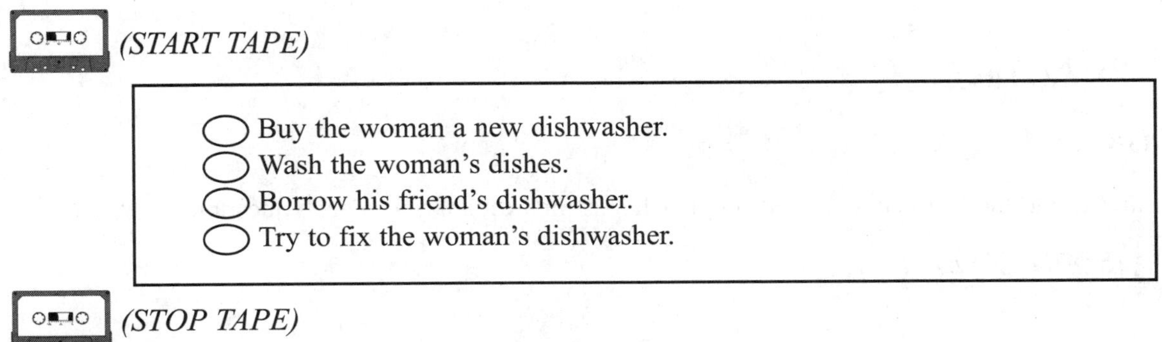

(START TAPE)

- ◯ Buy the woman a new dishwasher.
- ◯ Wash the woman's dishes.
- ◯ Borrow his friend's dishwasher.
- ◯ Try to fix the woman's dishwasher.

(STOP TAPE)

The conversation is about a dishwasher that is leaking water on the floor. The man says, *I think I know how to solve the problem*. What will the man probably do? The best answer to the question *What will the man probably do?* is the fourth choice, *Try to fix the woman's dishwasher.*

Both of these questions require you to make an inference about one of the people.

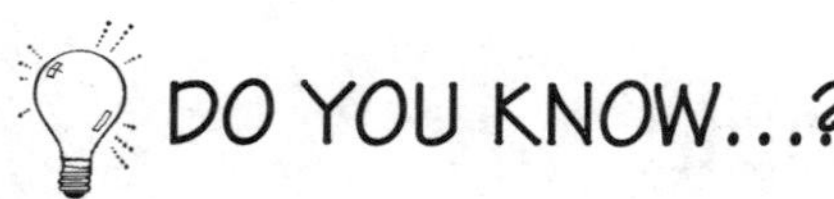

1. At least four questions on the paper–based TOEFL and two questions on the computer–based TOEFL will test your ability to make inferences about people in the short conversations you hear.

2. An ***inference*** is a conclusion that you can make based on what the speakers say. On the TOEFL, you will make inferences about either someone who is speaking or someone who is spoken about in the conversation.

   TOEFL questions about inferences sound like this:

   > What can be inferred from the conversation?
   > What can be inferred about _____?
   > What is the woman's job?

   Some inference questions ask you to make a ***prediction*** about what one of the speakers will probably do next. These questions sound like this:

   > What will the man probably do?
   > What will the speakers probably do next?

3. To make inferences and predictions, you must consider:
   - the meaning of key words, phrases, and idioms
   - the context and purpose of the conversation
   - the probable relationship of the speakers to each other

   In questions about inferences and predictions, some of the answer choices may try to trick you by:
   - not being supported by what the speakers say
   - repeating words and phrases from the conversation incorrectly
   - having words that sound similar to key words in the conversation

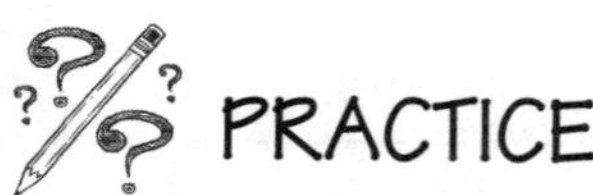

Exercise 1.8.A

Listen carefully to the following conversations. Choose the best answer to each question.

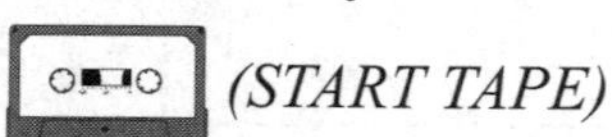
(START TAPE)

1. (A) Call in sick at work.
   (B) Go out for pizza.
   (C) Turn down the invitation.
   (D) Eat pizza at work.

2. (A) She is a dancer.
   (B) She is a professor.
   (C) She is a doctor.
   (D) She is a playwright.

3. (A) Drive to Fairville to find a motel.
   (B) Go to the convention in Fairville.
   (C) Drive to the airport in Fairville.
   (D) Demand to speak to the manager.

4. (A) Window cleaner.
   (B) Service station attendant.
   (C) Car mechanic.
   (D) Telephone solicitor.

5. (A) Go to a barbecue.
(B) Go on vacation.
(C) Work in a restaurant.
(D) Stay at her parents' beach house.

6. (A) He is a research scientist.
(B) He is a college student.
(C) He is a recording star.
(D) He is a good athlete.

7. (A) She is an excellent student.
(B) She is a business major.
(C) She will graduate at the end of next semester.
(D) She is a manager in a supermarket.

8. (A) He is missing.
(B) He is homesick.
(C) He is a poor student.
(D) He is in trouble.

9. (A) Pick up a plane ticket.
(B) Take a cruise.
(C) Travel by train.
(D) Speak to a travel agent.

10. (A) Hire an assistant.
(B) Quit his job.
(C) Work longer hours.
(D) Take a long vacation.

 *(STOP TAPE)*

Exercise 1.8.B

Listen carefully to the following conversations. Choose the best answer to each question.

 *(START TAPE)*

1. (A) Both the man and the woman missed biology class.
(B) Both the man and the woman went to the airport.
(C) The man is not doing well in biology.
(D) The woman never takes notes in class.

2. (A) He is unpopular with his students.
(B) He assigns a lot of busywork.
(C) He expects his students to work hard.
(D) His class is required for all students.

3. (A) Try the food in the deli.
(B) Eat something different in the cafeteria.
(C) Get sick from the food.
(D) Buy food in the bookstore.

4. (A) They are both pretty.
(B) They live far away.
(C) They are visiting their father.
(D) They are sisters.

5. (A) Go to a more expensive store.
(B) Ask the man to buy a scarf.
(C) Buy the less expensive scarf.
(D) Buy the blue scarf.

6. (A) He is looking for a job.
(B) He is a reference librarian.
(C) He is opening a checking account.
(D) He teaches physics.

7. (A) Study harder for the next chemistry test.
(B) Ask his chemistry professor for extra help.
(C) Drop his chemistry class.
(D) Change his major field of study.

8. (A) They work in a market.
(B) They are from Greece.
(C) They like Greek food.
(D) They were recently married.

9. (A) Ask someone else for advice.
(B) Choose one of the sushi bars.
(C) Walk to a supermarket.
(D) Take the woman out for pizza.

10. (A) Go to the drugstore.
(B) Buy the woman a poster.
(C) Send the woman a postcard.
(D) Go to the post office.

 *(STOP TAPE)*

Answers to Exercise 1.8.A through 1.8.B are on page 630.

1.8 EXTENSION

1. Working in pairs, students identify key words and phrases in the conversations in Exercises 1.8.A and 1.8.B that support the inferences you make.
2. In Exercises 1.8.A and 1.8.B, how many other inferences can be made from the same conversations? **Example:** In the conversation about Kelly in the Focus exercise at the beginning of this unit, you can also infer that (1) Kelly and the man are co–workers, (2) Kelly works for Dr. O'Brien, and (3) Kelly has some charts that Dr. O'Brien needs.
3. Working in pairs, students choose one of the conversations from Exercise 1.8.A or 1.8.B. Change part of the conversation and rewrite the answer choices. One must be the correct answer! Use the tapescripts on pages 687 and 688. Each student takes the part of one of the speakers. Practice reading the conversation aloud, concentrating on pronunciation. Write the new answer choices on the board. Present the conversation and question to the class. Classmates take a "live TOEFL exam." Be prepared to explain the correct answer!

Example:

W: Do you want to join me and Randy for pizza? We're meeting in fifteen minutes.
M: Sounds good, as long as you don't want anchovies.
N: What will the man probably do?

(A) Order anchovies.
(B) Go out for pizza.
(C) Invite another friend.
(D) Go to McDonald's.

Correct answer: (B).
Explanation: The man will probably go out for pizza because he said, "Sounds good."

1.9 Making Inferences about Context

Listen to a conversation and choose the best answer to the question.

(START TAPE)

- ◯ In a pharmacy.
- ◯ In a coffee shop.
- ◯ In a bank.
- ◯ At a gas station.

(PAUSE TAPE)

What words in the conversation are keys to understanding where the conversation takes place?

Some key words you may have heard are *prescription*, *refilled*, *label*. Where would people be talking about having a prescription refilled? You can infer that the conversation takes place in a pharmacy or drugstore. Therefore, the best answer is the first choice, *In a pharmacy*.

Listen to another conversation and choose the best answer to the question.

(START TAPE)

- ◯ Rinsing the dishes.
- ◯ Scrubbing the floor.
- ◯ Bathing a dog.
- ◯ Washing a car.

(STOP TAPE)

A key phrase spoken by the woman is *splashing water all over the floor*. Notice that all of the answer choices involve water. How can you eliminate some of these choices?

Another key phrase is *try to hold him*. Understanding this phrase is essential for understanding what the speakers are doing. This phrase helps you eliminate *rinsing the dishes*, *scrubbing the floor*, and *washing a car*.

Who are the speakers trying to hold? Anyone who has ever tried to give a dog a bath knows the best answer is the third choice, *Bathing a dog*.

Both questions require you to make an inference about the context of the conversation. In this type of question, listening for key words and phrases is essential.

You will see this type of question on the paper–based test only.

DO YOU KNOW...?

1. At least one question on the paper–based TOEFL will test your ability to make inferences about the context of the short conversations you hear.

2. The ***context*** is the situation in which a conversation takes place. The context can refer to both the ***setting*** of the conversation—*where* it takes place—and the ***purpose*** of the conversation—*why* it takes place.

   TOEFL questions about the context of conversations sound like this:

   > Where does this conversation probably take place?
   > In what kind of _____ does this conversation take place?
   > What are the speakers doing?
   > What are the speakers talking about?

   To make inferences about context, listen for ***key words*** which tell you:

   - the purpose of the conversation
   - the topic of the conversation
   - the relationship of the speakers to each other

PRACTICE

Exercise 1.9.A

Listen carefully to the following conversations. Choose the best answer to each question.

(START TAPE)

1. (A) In a coffee shop.
   (B) At a supermarket.
   (C) In a clothing store.
   (D) In an elevator.

2. (A) A math problem.
   (B) The woman's health.
   (C) An upcoming surgery.
   (D) The woman's car.

3. (A) Hardware store.
   (B) Supermarket.
   (C) Bookstore.
   (D) Drugstore.

4. (A) A wedding.
   (B) A play.
   (C) A concert.
   (D) A lecture.

5. (A) Preparing a speech.
   (B) Studying for a test.
   (C) Applying for a job.
   (D) Editing a book.

6. (A) In a restaurant.
   (B) At a shopping mall.
   (C) At a gas station.
   (D) In a bicycle repair shop.

7. (A) Tools.
   (B) Furniture.
   (C) Fruit.
   (D) Trees.

8. (A) In a dentist's office.
   (B) In a photography studio.
   (C) In a car wash.
   (D) In an airport.

(STOP TAPE)

Answers to Exercise 1.9.A are on page 631.

1.9 EXTENSION

1. Working in pairs, students identify key words and phrases in the conversations in Exercise 1.9.A that are clues to understanding the context.

2. Students create "TOEFL conversations" to test their classmates' ability to infer the context of a conversation. Working in pairs, follow this procedure:

   (1) Write a short conversation with two speakers. Make sure there are some key words and phrases that provide clues to the context.
   (2) Pass your conversation to the next pair of students.
   (3) With the conversation you now have (written by another pair of students), choose an appropriate "TOEFL question" from the list below. Then, pass the conversation and question to the next pair of students.
   (4) With the conversation and question you now have (written by others), write four answer choices. One must be the correct answer!
   (5) This conversation is now yours. Show your conversation, question, and answer choice to your teacher. The teacher may make suggestions and return the conversation to you.
   (6) Type the answer choices and give copies to the class.
   (7) Practice reading your conversation aloud, concentrating on pronunciation.
   (8) Present your conversation to the class. The teacher reads the questions, and the class takes a "live TOEFL exam."

TOEFL Questions

Where does this conversation probably take place?
In what kind of _____ does this conversation take place?
What are the speakers doing?
What are the speakers talking about?

ASSESSING PROGRESS — 1.7 through 1.9

QUIZ 3 *(Time – approximately 10 minutes)*

(START TAPE)

Directions: In this quiz you will hear short conversations between two people. After each conversation, you will hear a question about the conversation. The conversations and questions will not be repeated. After you hear a question, read the four possible answers and choose the best answer.

Here is an example.

On the recording, you hear:

In your book, you read:

(A) The man has an important form he must fill out.
(B) The man will inform the woman about the meeting.
(C) Neither speaker attended the meeting.
(D) An important announcement was made at the meeting.

The woman implies that she missed the meeting, and the man responds, *Didn't you go either?* which means he also did not go to the meeting. The best answer to the question, *What can be inferred from the conversation?* is (C), *Neither speaker attended the meeting.* Therefore, the correct choice is (C).

1. (A) They should take the Clairmont bridge.
(B) They should take the freeway bridge.
(C) They should avoid the bridges.
(D) They should drive as fast as they can.

2. (A) In a department store.
(B) In a laboratory.
(C) On a farm.
(D) In a florist's shop.

3. (A) Check the maps at the bus transfer station.
(B) Pick up a map at the train station.
(C) Get a bus transfer from the driver.
(D) Wait for the bus across the street at the park.

4. (A) He has a lot of experience.
(B) He starts work early each day.
(C) He is an excellent worker.
(D) He is new on the job.

5. (A) She doesn't mind if he smokes.
(B) Smoking should be allowed there.
(C) The man should smoke elsewhere.
(D) The man should quit smoking.

6. (A) A course catalog.
(B) A street map.
(C) A clothing catalog.
(D) A restaurant menu.

7. (A) He does not want to see his sisters.
(B) He has more sisters than brothers.
(C) He is from a large family.
(D) He is the youngest in his family.

8. (A) Dental assistant.
(B) Veterinary assistant.
(C) Animal trainer.
(D) Wildlife biologist.

9. (A) Arnold is more afraid of the water than the man is.
(B) Arnold should be more aware of water safety.
(C) Arnold should not be afraid of the water.
(D) Arnold is going to take sailing lessons.

10. (A) She must talk to Dr. Patel this weekend.
(B) She is going away for the weekend.
(C) She is not finished with her sociology paper.
(D) Her bibliography is not long enough.

11. (A) Not buy bagels.
(B) Go to Otto's Bakery.
(C) Go to Ralph's Thriftway.
(D) Drive to the lake.

12. (A) Tracy refused to give the woman a ride to work.
    (B) The woman did not ride to work with Tracy.
    (C) Tracy and the woman have the same job.
    (D) Tracy starts work at seven o'clock.

13. (A) Making tea.
    (B) Shopping for groceries.
    (C) Baking cookies.
    (D) Feeding a baby.

14. (A) She should invite him to meet her parents.
    (B) She should go with him to the Cajun restaurant.
    (C) She should try cooking Cajun food.
    (D) She should take her parents to the Cajun restaurant.

15. (A) Take Mr. Nolan's algebra class.
    (B) Drop Mr. Park's algebra class.
    (C) Ask Imelda about Mr. Park's class.
    (D) Ask Imelda to help her with algebra.

(Stop Tape)

Answers to Listening Quiz 3 are on page 631.

ASSESSING PROGRESS — 1.1 through 1.9

QUIZ 4 *(Time – approximately 15 minutes)*

(START TAPE)

Directions: In this quiz you will hear short conversations between two people. After each conversation, you will hear a question about the conversation. The conversations and questions will not be repeated. After you hear a question, read the four possible answers and choose the best answer.

Here is an example.

On the recording, you hear:

In your book, you read:

- (A) Peter will manage the project.
- (B) The project needs Peter's abilities.
- (C) The central problem is finding successful people.
- (D) Peter tolerates working with them.

You hear the man use the key words *talent* and *essential*. A synonym for *talent* is *ability*, and something that is *essential* is *needed*. The best answer to the question, *What does the man mean*? is (B), *The project needs Peter's abilities*. Therefore, the correct choice is (B).

1. (A) Receptionist.
   (B) Sales clerk.
   (C) Accountant.
   (D) Bank teller.

2. (A) He sees Brent often.
   (B) He detects that Brent is dishonest.
   (C) He usually agrees with Brent.
   (D) He sees that Brent is always right.

3. (A) Use the computerized catalog to find the information he needs.
   (B) Follow directions to the library.
   (C) Ask someone for directions to the library computer.
   (D) Scream if he has any trouble.

4. (A) She is obligated to help Sue move.
   (B) She can't make a choice about what to do.
   (C) She has no chance to help Sue.
   (D) She has chosen not to help Sue move.

5. (A) The speakers do not share Kaspar's taste in music.
   (B) The music at the party was too loud.
   (C) The woman felt awful at the party.
   (D) Kaspar knows more about music than the speakers.

6. (A) The man likes to shop.
   (B) The woman and man are going out together.
   (C) The man needs a haircut.
   (D) The man needs something for his garden.

7. (A) Jason is probably not angry.
   (B) Jason wants to know what the man said.
   (C) Jason is easily angered.
   (D) Jason doesn't like snow.

8. (A) Lucy is her best friend.
   (B) Lucy has a beautiful face.
   (C) Lucy can be deceitful.
   (D) Lucy is a little crazy.

9. (A) Her father prefers sweet desserts.
   (B) Her father thinks her roommate is very sweet.
   (C) Her father considers her roommate ill–bred.
   (D) Her father and her roommate share a lot of interests.

10. (A) He will plant a tree after class.
    (B) He is a science teacher.
    (C) He works in a factory.
    (D) He needs to rake leaves.

11. (A) She asks the man to repeat what he said.
(B) She didn't understand the man.
(C) She agrees with the man.
(D) She is surprised by the man.

12. (A) He will not borrow any more cassettes.
(B) He forgot about returning the cassette.
(C) He already returned the cassette.
(D) He hoped to keep the cassette.

13. (A) The man can't make a decision.
(B) Julie should work on the project.
(C) There is probably a better researcher than Julie.
(D) Julie might have a hard time deciding who should work on the project.

14. (A) Tina has never visited her.
(B) Tina must have moved.
(C) She will see Tina next year.
(D) She and Tina work in the same office building.

15. (A) The snow is too heavy for the man to drive.
(B) The man should drive to his neighbor's house.
(C) She would drive if she had a car.
(D) The man should drive home immediately.

16. (A) The man would be out of town on Friday.
(B) The man would pay for the woman's lunch.
(C) The man wanted to go to lunch on a different day.
(D) The man knew a good place to eat.

17. (A) His brakes can wait to be fixed.
(B) He will have to wait a little longer.
(C) He must remove his foot from the brake pedal.
(D) He must stop delaying repairing the brakes.

18. (A) Attendance at the workshop is required.
(B) She will give a computer workshop on Friday.
(C) She thinks the workshop is in Chicago.
(D) She has to commute to work on Friday.

19. (A) His coach asked him to wait before the game.
(B) His coach wants him to wait longer before playing.
(C) His coach thinks he is too heavy.
(D) He needs a new couch.

20. (A) In a hospital.
(B) In an elevator.
(C) In a hotel.
(D) In a dentist's office.

21. (A) The man should not speak so loud.
(B) She likes loud music.
(C) The man should not turn up the volume.
(D) The man should turn off the radio.

22. (A) Move to a new place.
(B) Try to find a parking space on the corner.
(C) Buy something new for the kitchen.
(D) Go out and buy something to eat.

23. (A) She cannot afford to have her roof fixed.
(B) She will have her roof fixed right away.
(C) The bill for her roof repair was incorrect.
(D) She has a question about her roof.

24. (A) The woman did not eat lunch with Gina.
(B) The woman will meet Gina for lunch.
(C) Gina skipped lunch.
(D) The woman ate lunch at Gina's house.

25. (A) What she should pack.
(B) Why the man called her.
(C) If she should call someone.
(D) If the trip was canceled.

26. (A) She doesn't want him to leave.
(B) She will be on vacation next week.
(C) She will call him right before he leaves.
(D) She agrees to take in his mail.

27. (A) She is not hungry.
(B) She needs time to think.
(C) She thought he was full.
(D) She thinks he is kind.

28. (A) The boys resemble their aunt.
(B) The boys are patient.
(C) The boys must walk behind their aunt.
(D) They should take the boys to see their aunt.

29. (A) The workers had an accident in the pickup.
(B) A worker attacked someone in the city.
(C) The workers stopped working.
(D) The workers were arrested for violent behavior.

30. (A) Frank didn't notice the cake.
(B) Frank never eats dessert.
(C) The cake was too hard to eat.
(D) Frank ate only a small amount of cake.

 *(STOP TAPE)*

Answers to Listening Quiz 4 are on page 631.

PART B/C — LONGER CONVERSATIONS AND TALKS

The Listening section of both the paper–based and computer–based test includes several longer conversations and talks.

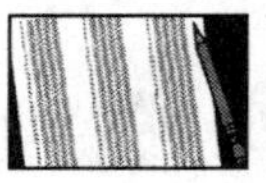

QUESTION TYPES ON THE PAPER TEST

Part B contains longer conversations followed by questions. Part C contains short talks and lectures followed by questions.

The conversations, talks, and questions will be presented only once. This means you must answer all questions as you go.

Multiple–Choice Questions

On the paper–based test, all of the questions in Parts B and C are multiple choice. After each conversation or talk, you will hear some questions and choose the one best answer of four possible choices, (A), (B), (C) or (D). Then, on your answer sheet, you will find the number of the question and fill in the space that corresponds to the letter of the answer you have chosen.

You will have twelve seconds to read the four answer choices and answer each question.

Part B – Longer Conversations

In Part B, you will hear a recording of a conversation like this one:

(Narrator) Questions 1 through 2. Listen to a conversation between a student and a professor.

(Woman) Excuse me, Dr. Gupta. May I speak with you?
(Man) Sure, what can I do for you, Lynne?
(Woman) I would like to change the topic of my paper. I was going to write about the history of trade, but I found something more interesting. My friend introduced me to her grandparents, who came from Japan. I'd like to write about Japanese immigration and interview some people in my friend's family. Is that OK?
(Man) Yes, that could be an interesting paper. But you'll want to be sure you have some historical facts. Use the interview material to illustrate the history.
(Woman) I found a couple of books on the *Issei* and *Nisei*.
(Man) Good. Also check out the web page for the Japanese American Historical Society. You may find some other useful resources there.
(Woman) I'll do that. Thank you, Dr. Gupta.

Then you will hear a question.

(Narrator) Why does the student go to see her professor?

In your book, you will read:

(A) She would like to introduce her grandparents.
(B) She wants to discuss the topic of her paper.
(C) She wants to show him some books she found.
(D) She is going to take a trip to Japan.

The best answer to the question, *Why does the student go to see her professor*? is (B), *She wants to discuss the topic of her paper.* Therefore, the correct choice is (B).

You will hear another question.

(Narrator) What does the professor recommend?

In your book, you will read:

(A) The student should look for information on the web.
(B) The student should interview people in Japan.
(C) The student should take photographs to illustrate her paper.
(D) The student should not change her topic.

The best answer to the question, *What does the professor recommend*? is (A), *The student should look for information on the web*. Therefore, the correct choice is (A).

Part C – Talks

In Part C, you will hear a recording of a talk or lecture like this one:

(Narrator) Listen to part of a talk in a geology class.

(Woman) Large caves such as Carlsbad Caverns in New Mexico are famous for their many underground chambers and varied and majestic landscapes. Delicate flowerlike and strawlike structures grow from the ceiling, as do massive curtains of stone. Among the most interesting and well–known formations are icicle–like stalactites, which hang from the ceiling, and stalagmites, which are found on the cave floor.

Groundwater seeping into a cave chamber contains carbon dioxide absorbed from the atmosphere or the soil. This carbon dioxide may unite with limestone to form calcium carbonate. Stalagmites are produced when water drops directly to the cave floor. The impact of the water striking the floor causes it to break into droplets or into a film, releasing the excess carbon dioxide, and the crystals begin to grow upward.

Then you will hear a question.

(Narrator) What is the talk mainly about?

In your book, you will read:

(A) Groundwater in caves
(B) The formation of Carlsbad Caverns
(C) Structures that form in caves
(D) Majestic landscapes

The best answer to the question, *What is the talk mainly about*? is (C), *Structures that form in caves*. Therefore, the correct choice is (C).

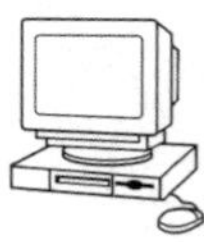

QUESTION TYPES ON THE COMPUTER TEST

On the computer test, longer conversations and talks are in Part B. There is no Part C on the computer test.

The conversations, talks, and questions will be presented only once. You will both *see* and *hear* the questions before the answer choices appear.

There are four types of questions in Part B. For each type of question, you will use the mouse to click on one or more answers or to move text.

You can take as much time as you need to answer each question; however, you should work as quickly as possible because the entire Listening section is timed. The amount of time you have left will appear on the computer screen. The time you spend listening to the conversations, talks, and questions is not counted in the total time.

You will be able to change your answer as many times as you like—*until you confirm your answer*. When you confirm your answer, the computer will give you the next question.

You will not be allowed to return to a previous question. This is because the answer you give helps the computer determine the difficulty level of your next question.

Part B – Longer Conversations and Talks

Here is an example of a talk and some questions:

(Narrator) Listen to part of a talk in a geology class.

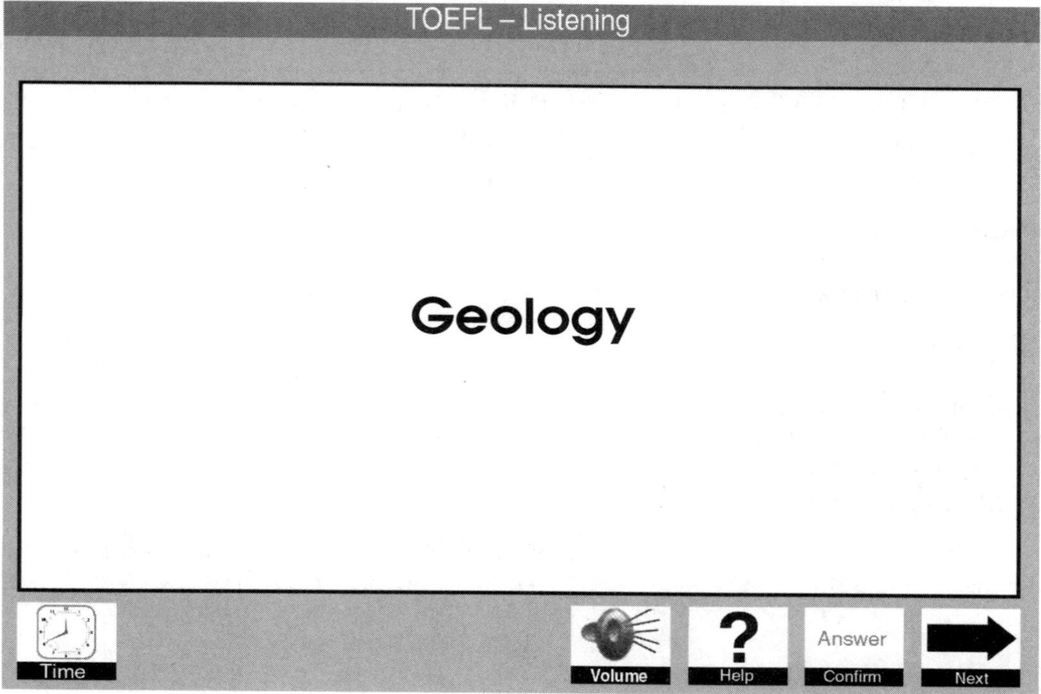

(Professor) Large caves such as Carlsbad Caverns in New Mexico are famous for their many underground chambers and varied and majestic landscapes. Delicate flowerlike and strawlike structures grow from the ceiling, as do massive curtains of stone. Among the most interesting and well–known formations are icicle–like stalactites, which hang from the ceiling, and stalagmites, which are found on the cave floor.

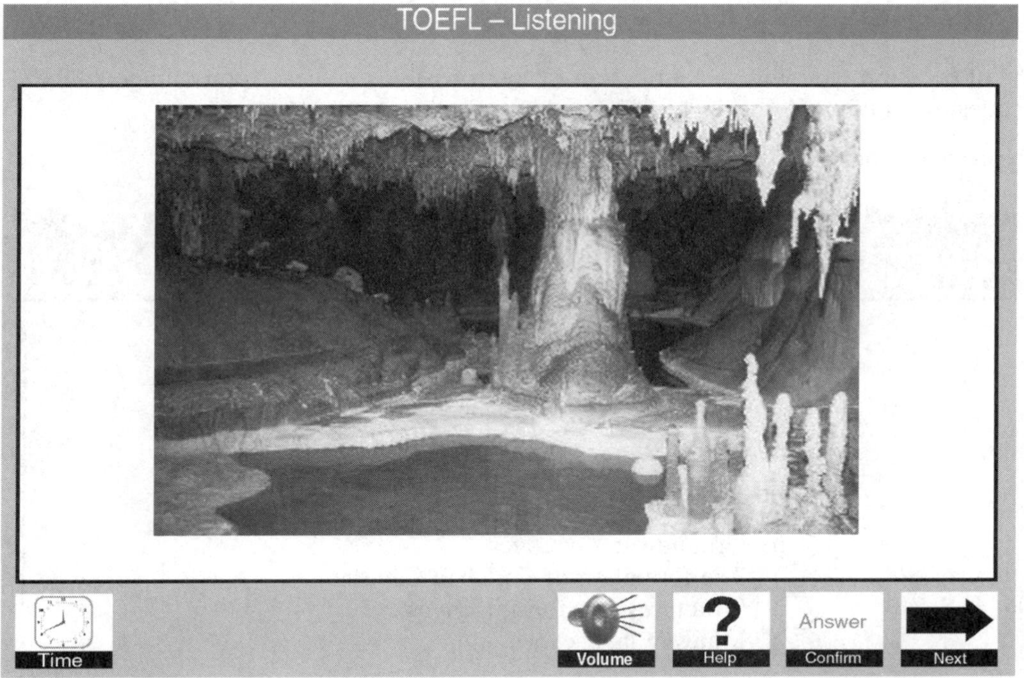

(Professor) Groundwater seeping into a cave chamber contains carbon dioxide absorbed from the atmosphere or the soil. This carbon dioxide may unite with limestone to form calcium carbonate. Stalagmites are produced when water drops directly to the cave floor. The impact of the water striking the floor causes it to break into droplets or into a film, releasing the excess carbon dioxide, and the crystals begin to grow upward.

Stalagmites usually have rounded tops and are large. Some are ten meters tall and up to ten meters in diameter. The rate of growth of stalagmites is not constant because it depends on water percolation from the surface.

After the talk you will read:

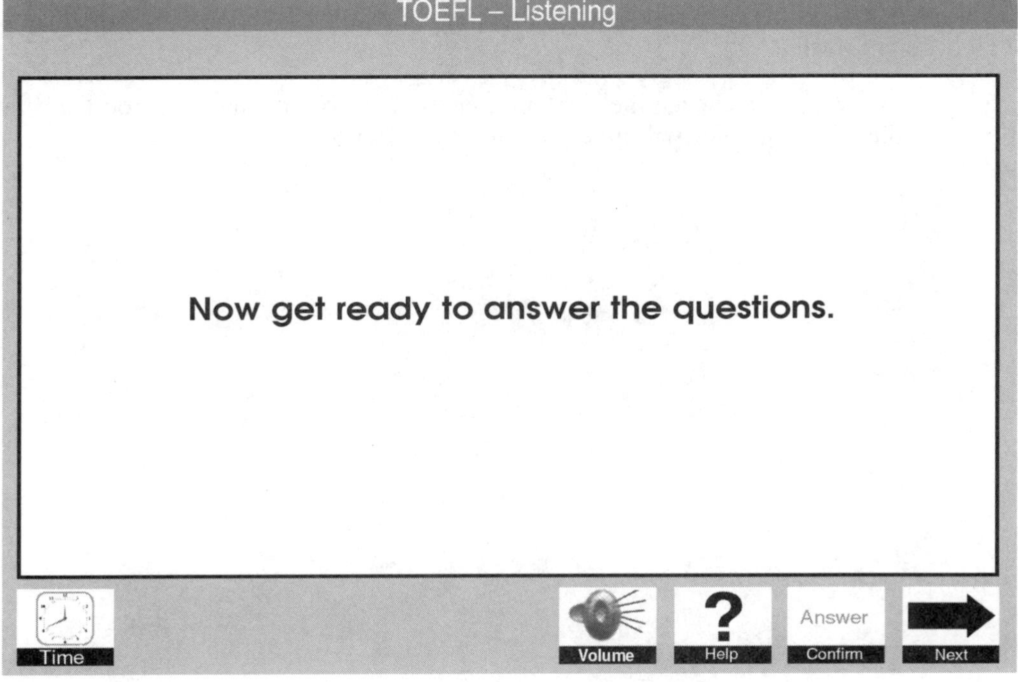

Question Type 1 – Multiple Choice

In the first type of question, you will select the best of four possible choices. Approximately 80 to 90 percent of the questions in Part B will be of this type.

For question type 1, the computer screen will look like this:

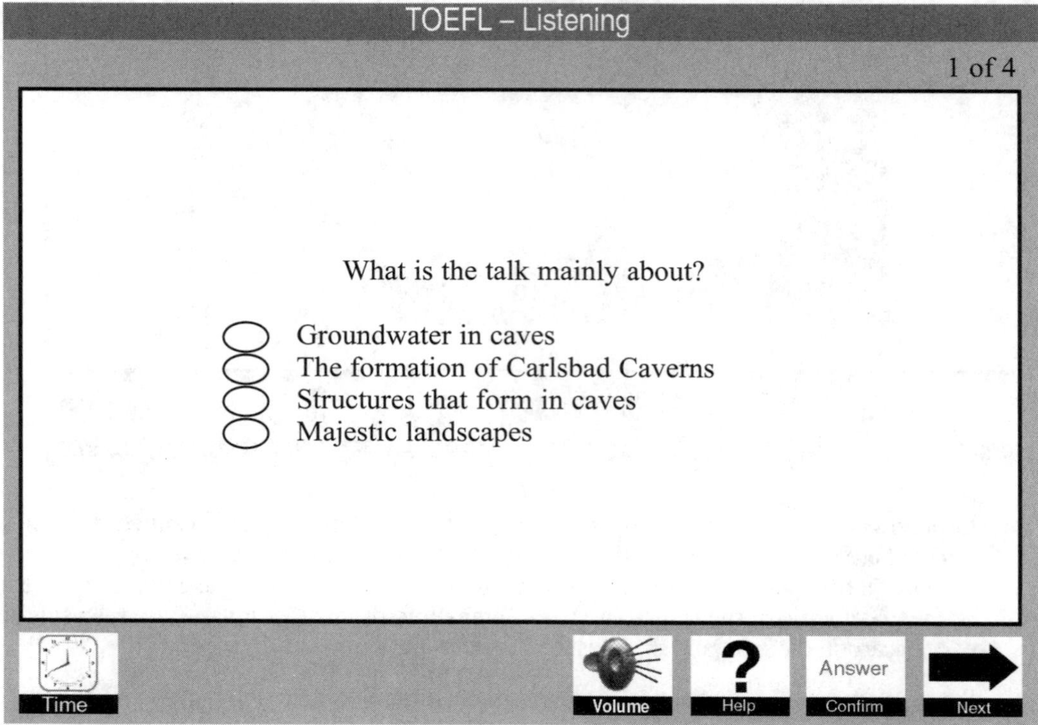

The topic of the talk is *Structures that form in caves*. Therefore, you should click on the third answer choice.

When you click on the oval next to one of the answer choices, the oval will darken. To change your answer, click on a different oval.

When you are satisfied that you have chosen the right answer, click on **Next**. Then click on **Confirm Answer**. When you do this, the computer will give you the next question.

Question Type 2 – Click on More than One Answer

In the second type of question, you will click on two answers. This type of question uses squares instead of ovals.

You must click on *both* correct answers to receive credit for answering the question correctly.

For question type 2, the computer screen will look like this:

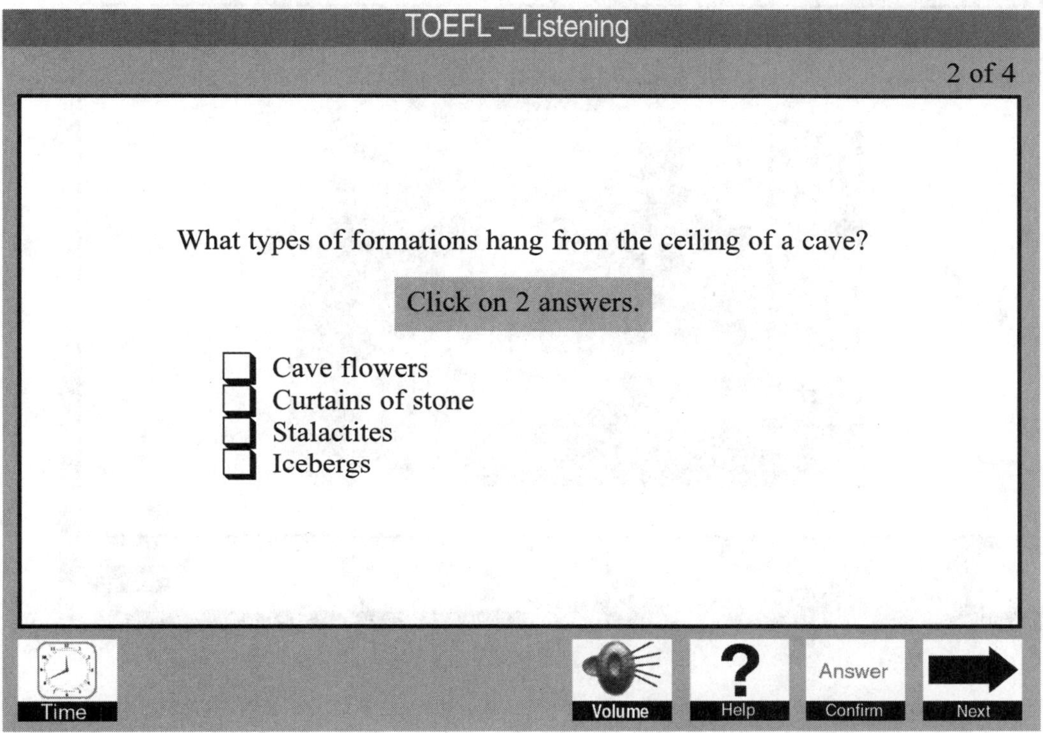

The professor says:

> Delicate flowerlike and strawlike structures grow from the ceiling, as do massive curtains of stone. Among the most interesting and well–known formations are icicle–like stalactites, which hang from the ceiling, and stalagmites, which are found on the cave floor.

Therefore, you should click on the second and third answer choices, *Curtains of stone* and *Stalactites*.

When you click on the answer choices, an ✗ will appear in each square. To change an answer, click on a different square.

When you are satisfied that you have chosen the right answer, click on **Next**. Then click on **Confirm Answer**. When you do this, the computer will give you the next question.

Question Type 3 – Click on a Picture

In the third type of question, you will click on a letter or a picture.

For question type 3, the computer screen will look like this:

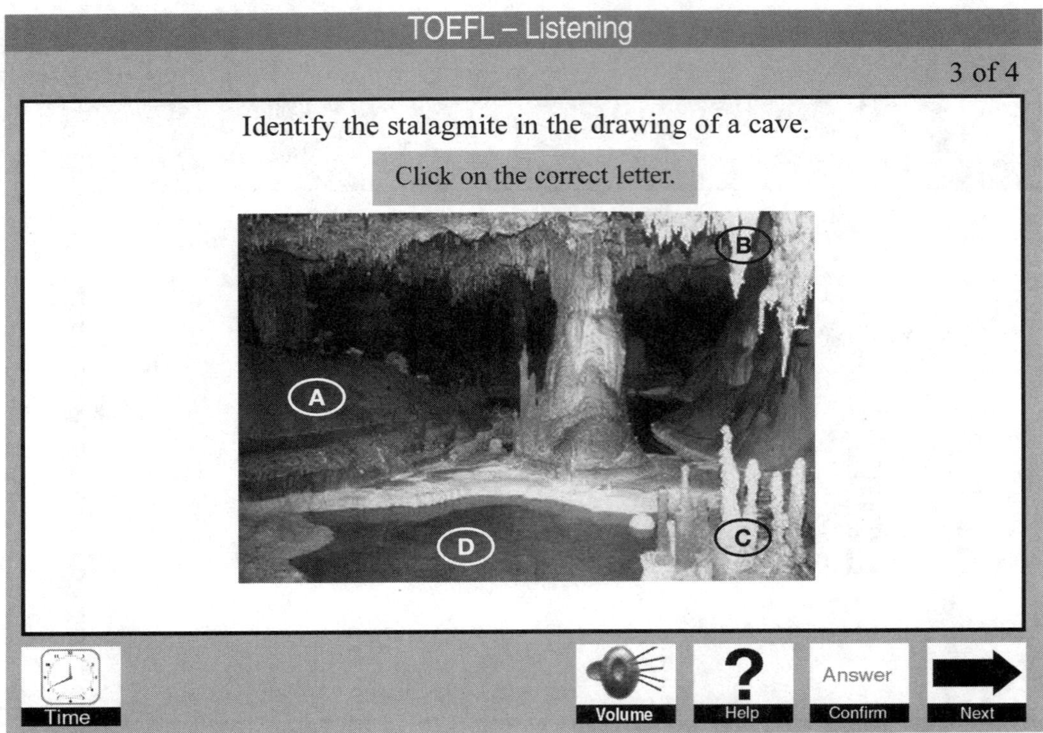

According to the professor, stalagmites are found on the cave floor. The part of the drawing that most closely represents a stalagmite is (C). Therefore, you should click on (C).

When you click on a letter in the drawing, the letter will be highlighted. To change your answer, click on a different letter.

When you are satisfied that you have chosen the right answer, click on **Next**. Then click on **Confirm Answer**. When you do this, the computer will give you the next question.

Question Type 4 – Match and Sequence Text

In the fourth type of question, you will match words and categories or put a set of words or statements in order.

For question type 4, the computer screen will look like this:

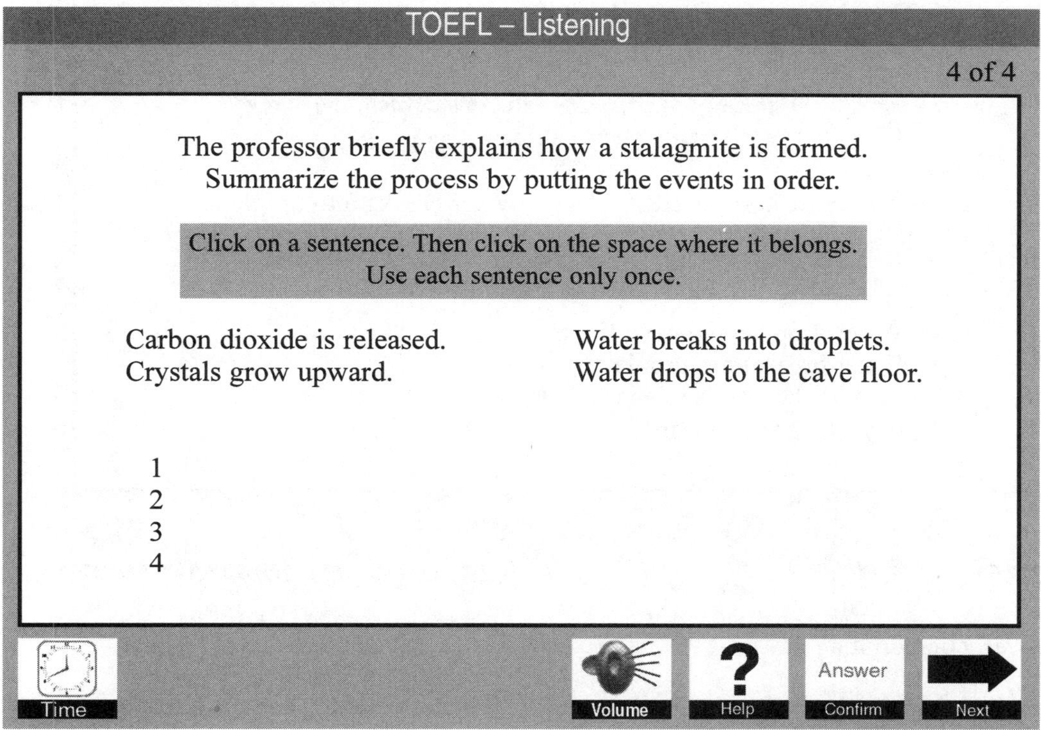

The professor says:

> Stalagmites are produced when water drops directly to the cave floor. The impact of the water striking the floor causes it to break into droplets or into a film, releasing the excess carbon dioxide, and the crystals begin to grow upward.

Therefore, the correct order of the events is:

1. Water drops to the cave floor.
2. Water breaks into droplets.
3. Carbon dioxide is released.
4. Crystals grow upward.

To choose your answers, click on each statement of the process and then click on the space where it belongs. As you do this, each statement will appear in the space you have selected.

The screen will then look like this:

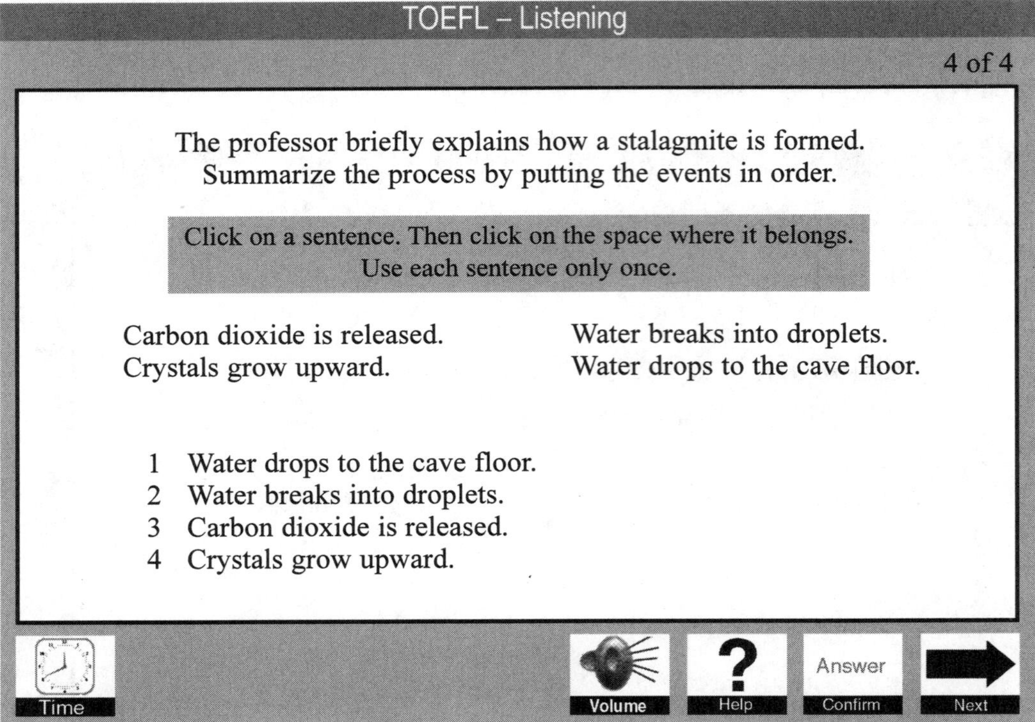

To change an answer, click on it again.

When you are satisfied that you have chosen the right answer, click on **Next**. Then click on **Confirm Answer**. When you do this, the computer will give you the next question.

STRATEGIES FOR PART B/C – LONGER CONVERSATIONS AND TALKS

Prepare before the Test

- Listen to a variety of academic talks, such as audiotapes of actual college lectures, videotaped documentaries, and educational television programs. A large number of the talks on the TOEFL deal with topics in the natural sciences, social sciences, and the arts. Listen to material in these subject areas to build comprehension.
- Work on building your vocabulary. Use the conversations and talks in this book to become familiar with the level of vocabulary on the TOEFL.
- For the computer test, be familiar with the instructions for the four different types of questions. Be familiar with the testing tools, such as **Time**, **Next**, and **Confirm Answer**. Practice using the mouse.

Pace Yourself during the Test

- On the paper test, you have only twelve seconds to read the four answer choices and answer each question. Work quickly and efficiently.
- On the computer test, you must answer each question before you can move on to the next question. You cannot skip questions. Confirm your answer only when you are certain you are ready to move on.

Listen for Meaning

- Listen to the short introductory sentence before each conversation and talk. The narrator will say something like "Questions _ through _. Listen to a talk in a _____ class. The professor is discussing _____." This introduction may provide key information about the context or topic.
- Focus on overall meaning and purpose. Listen for key words and concepts that are repeated throughout the conversation or talk.
- Listen for fact and inference questions. Fact questions ask about information that was mentioned by the speakers. Inference questions ask about information that was not directly mentioned but was implied by the speakers.

Concentrate

- Think only of the question you are currently working on. On the paper test, do not work on previous questions or try to read ahead to the next item. On the computer test, once you have moved on to the next question, forget the previous questions. You cannot go back and change them.
- Eliminate answer choices you know are incorrect. Then, if you are not sure of the correct answer, guess! On the paper test, your score is based on the number of questions you answer correctly, and wrong answers are not subtracted. On the computer test, if you answer a question incorrectly, the computer will make the next question easier.

Know the Tricks

- Be familiar with the various ways the TOEFL items try to trick you. This book gives you practice in noticing some of the common tricks in the Listening section of the TOEFL.

1.10 Identifying the Topic and Main Ideas

Listen to a conversation between a student and his tutor.

(START TAPE)

◯ Confusing signs. ◯ Musical scales. ◯ Diagrams on math tests. ◯ Solutions to math problems.

(STOP TAPE)

The question asks you to identify the topic of the conversation. What are the people talking about? What words and phrases help you understand the conversation?

The best answer is the third choice, *Diagrams on math tests*. Some phrases you may recall from the conversation are: *diagrams on the test*; *the base of a triangle*; *the picture*; *make your own drawing*.

The first and second choices try to trick you by repeating some words from the conversation—*confusing* and *scale*. However, these choices are inaccurate, or only partly correct. They are inaccurate because neither speaker mentions *signs* or *musical* scales.

The fourth choice mentions math problems. However, the conversation focuses more on the *drawings* for math problems and less on the *solutions* to math problems.

Sometimes the topic of a conversation or talk is stated directly by one of the speakers. Sometimes, as in the conversation you just heard, the topic is stated indirectly through key words and phrases.

DO YOU KNOW...?

1. Approximately three or four questions on the TOEFL will test your ability to identify the topic and main ideas in the conversations and talks you hear.

2. The ***topic*** is the subject of the conversation or talk. The topic is the most general answer to the question "What are the people talking about?" On the TOEFL, most of what the speakers say will relate to the topic.

   The ***main ideas*** form the general message of the conversation or talk. Main ideas are what is important about the topic, according to the speakers.

   TOEFL questions about the topic and main ideas of conversations and talks sound like this:

   What is the topic/subject of the conversation?
   What are the people discussing?
   What is the discussion/talk/lecture mainly about?
   What is the speaker describing?
   What is the purpose of the conversation/talk?
   What is the man's/woman's problem?
   What would be a good title for the lecture?
   What is the speaker's main point?
   What is the main idea of the talk?

3. In questions about the topic and main ideas, some of the answer choices may try to trick you by being:

   - too general: broader than what is mentioned by the speakers
   - too specific: details instead of main ideas
   - inaccurate: partly or wholly incorrect
   - about something not mentioned by the speakers

   When you answer questions about the topic and main ideas, think about the overall meaning of the conversation or talk. Try not to *overthink* this type of question; it is often best to trust your first impression.

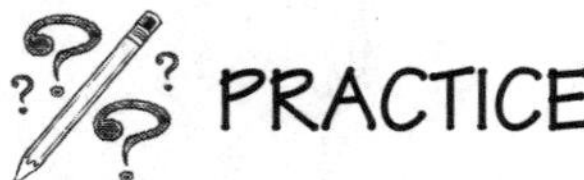

PRACTICE

Exercise 1.10.A

Listen to the following conversations and talks. Answer the questions based on the information you hear.

(START TAPE)

1. (A) He is confused by the professor's response to his paper.
   (B) He does not know what topic to write about.
   (C) He wants to write a paper about his family.
   (D) He received a poor grade on his paper.

2. (A) The man is asking for more salad.
   (B) The man forgot to pay for the soup.
   (C) The man is complaining about the soup.
   (D) The man is thanking the woman for making lunch.

3. (A) The Agricultural Cycle.
   (B) Religious Beliefs and Ceremonies.
   (C) The Gifts of Nature.
   (D) Planting and Harvesting Corn.

4. (A) To suggest ways to invest your money.
   (B) To give advice about borrowing money.
   (C) To explain why businesses either succeed or fail.
   (D) To explain how to start your own business.

5. (A) Problems with getting accurate survey results.
   (B) Problems between people from different ethnic backgrounds.
   (C) Attitudes about socializing with people from other groups.
   (D) Romantic relationships between people of different groups.

6. (A) Regionalism was neither honest nor admirable.
   (B) Regionalism expressed core American values.
   (C) Regionalism was the first truly American art movement.
   (D) Regionalism was less influential than modernism.

(STOP TAPE)

Answers to Exercise 1.10.A are on page 632.

1.10 EXTENSION

1. Working in pairs, students discuss why the three incorrect answer choices in Exercise 1.10.A are incorrect. How do they try to trick you?

2. After completing Exercise 1.10.A and checking answers, students listen to the cassette again. This time, write down key words and phrases that help reveal the topic and main ideas.

3. Students read the tapescripts for Exercise 1.10.A on page 691. Make a list of vocabulary words that are new or difficult. Make a class vocabulary list, with each student contributing 2 or 3 words. Use the list for a spelling quiz that is dictated by a student.

1.11 Comprehending Details

Listen to an instructor speak to a world history class.

(START TAPE)

1. (A) The following evening at nine o'clock.
   (B) Every Wednesday at eight o'clock.
   (C) Next Wednesday at eight o'clock.
   (D) Next Wednesday at ten o'clock.

2. Choose 2 answers.

   [A] How some inventions spread quickly.
   [B] How Native Americans grew wild grasses.
   [C] How the theory of evolution impacted history.
   [D] How geography and history are related.

(STOP TAPE)

Question 1 asks you about a specific detail, *when the program will be on television*. The instructor says:

> I'd like to tell you about an interesting program that will be shown on television next Wednesday. It's on channel 10, from eight until nine o'clock.

Therefore, you should check the third answer choice, *Next Wednesday at eight o'clock.*

Question 2 asks you about *what topics will be covered*. For this question you must choose two answers. The instructor says:

> The show will deal with how geography has impacted history. Topics will include how inventions such as the wheel spread quickly through Europe and Asia, and how the domestication of wild grass helped some societies evolve more rapidly than others.

Therefore, you should check the first choice, *How some inventions spread quickly*, and the fourth choice, *How geography and history are related.*

The above questions ask you about some of the details in the talk. What are some other details you can recall?

1.11 DETAILS

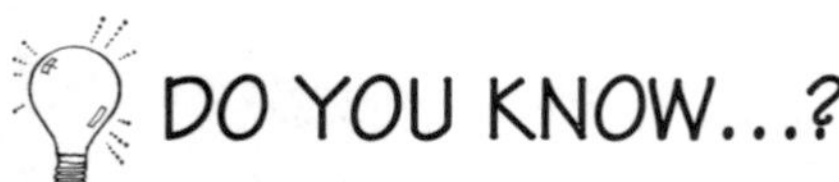

1. At least eight questions on the TOEFL will test your comprehension of the details you hear in conversations and talks.

2. ***Details*** are specific bits of information, such as facts, descriptions, definitions, and examples.

   TOEFL questions about the details in conversations and talks sound like this:

   > What does the man/woman/speaker say about _____?
   > What does the man/woman want?
   > What does the _____ want/suggest/advise the _____ to do?
   > What _____?
   > What type _____?
   > Who _____?
   > Where _____?
   > When _____?
   > Which _____?
   > How does the speaker describe _____?
   > How long/often _____?
   > How much/many _____?

   On the *computer test only*, detail questions may ask you to select one of three or four pictures or to identify one of three or four areas marked on a picture. Such questions sound like this:

   > Select the drawing that illustrates the concept of _____.
   > Select the diagram that shows/represents _____.
   > Which picture _____?
   > Identify the part of the diagram that represents _____.
   > Which area of the picture illustrates _____?

   Occasionally detail questions ask about what is NOT mentioned.

   > What is *not* mentioned/said about _____?
   > What does _____ *not* include?
   > What is *not* done by _____?

   Occasionally detail questions ask about specific terms.

   > What is a _____?
   > According to the speaker/professor, what does _____ mean?
   > what is the definition of _____?
   > In this conversation, what does _____ mean?

3. In questions about the details in conversations and talks, some of the answer choices may try to trick you by:

   - repeating words and phrases incorrectly
   - using words that sound similar to the words used
   - being inaccurate: partly or wholly incorrect
   - being about something not mentioned by the speakers

   Remember, you can answer all questions based on the information you hear in the conversation or talk. You do not need special knowledge of the topics to answer the questions correctly.

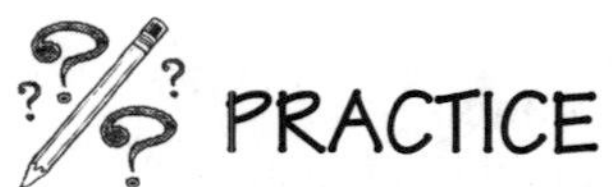

Exercise 1.11.A

Listen to the following conversations. Answer the questions based on the information you hear.

(START TAPE)

1. (A) Ice cubes.
   (B) Shrimp.
   (C) Crabs.
   (D) Clams.

2. (A) Go to the seafood counter at Charley's.
   (B) Go to the seafood store to buy more fish.
   (C) Call up Charley and ask him to dinner.
   (D) Invite five people to a party.

3. (A) A term paper.
   (B) A job interview.
   (C) A survey assignment.
   (D) A book report.

4. (A) Interview people of different ages.
   (B) Survey a large group of people.
   (C) Find three interesting opinions.
   (D) Ask her grandmother to help her.

5. (A) He doesn't want to give an oral report.
   (B) He cannot find enough people to survey.
   (C) He has difficulty expressing his opinion.
   (D) He cannot decide what to do.

6. (A) Read a story for English class.
   (B) Translate a story into English.
   (C) Write a story in Swedish.
   (D) Type a story.

7. (A) Norwegian.
   (B) English.
   (C) Swedish.
   (D) French.

8. (A) The next day.
   (B) In three days.
   (C) The following week.
   (D) In three weeks.

(STOP TAPE)

Exercise 1.11.B

Listen to the following talks. Answer the questions based on the information you hear.

(START TAPE)

1. (A) When a person has too little exercise.
   (B) When bone spurs appear on X–rays.
   (C) When the nose becomes inflamed.
   (D) When lumps form in the muscles.

2. (A) Swelling of the membrane lining a joint.
   (B) Difficulty in breathing.
   (C) Fracture of the hip joint.
   (D) Elevation of the blood pressure.

3. (A) Emotional stress.
   (B) Illegal drugs.
   (C) Hot weather.
   (D) Replacement surgery.

4. (A) With increased exercise.
   (B) With cool baths.
   (C) With vitamins.
   (D) With anti–swelling medication.

5. (A) As a music historian.
   (B) As a piano player.
   (C) As a bandleader and composer.
   (D) As a singer and songwriter.

6. (A) Symphonies.
   (B) Ballets.
   (C) Operas.
   (D) Marches.

7. (A) Disciplined.
   (B) Upbeat.
   (C) Solemn.
   (D) Mysterious.

8. (A) Listen to a Sousa recording.
   (B) Listen to Sousa talk about his music.
   (C) Look up information about Sousa.
   (D) Choose their favorite work by Sousa.

 *(STOP TAPE)*

Exercise 1.11.C

Listen to the following conversations or talks. Answer the questions based on the information you hear.

 *(START TAPE)*

1. (A) From midwinter until spring.
   (B) From fall until midwinter.
   (C) At the end of winter.
   (D) In early fall.

2. Choose 2 answers.

   [A] Lion.
   [B] Eagle.
   [C] Bear.
   [D] Moose.

3. (A) Managing the camps.
   (B) Snaring small animals.
   (C) Searching for game.
   (D) Making the bows and arrows.

4. Choose 2 answers.

   [A] Fishing.
   [B] Clan leadership.
   [C] Education.
   [D] Agriculture.

5. Choose 2 answers.

   [A] Architecture.
   [B] Marketing.
   [C] Railroad Engineering.
   [D] Industrial Design.

6.

7.

8. (A) Take an advanced course in drawing with perspective.
   (B) Draw their subject at eye level.
   (C) Sketch eye level and vanishing points in every drawing.
   (D) Do some quick sketches before beginning the actual drawing.

 *(STOP TAPE)*

Exercise 1.11.D

Listen to the following talk and answer the questions based on the information you hear.

 *(START TAPE)*

1. (A) Different types of lava.
   (B) Different types of volcanoes.
   (C) The formation of shield volcanoes.
   (D) The volcanoes of Hawaii and Iceland.

2. Choose 2 answers.

   [A] Hot gases.
   [B] Liquified rock.
   [C] Sedimentary rock.
   [D] Ice and rock.

3. (A)

(C)

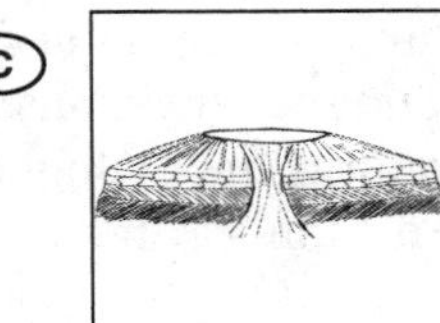

(B)

(D)

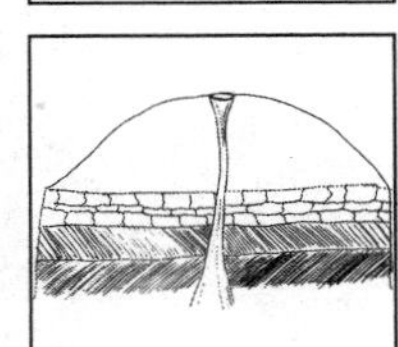

4. (A) As glowing cinders.
   (B) As solid particles.
   (C) As volcanic bombs.
   (D) As hot springs.

5. (A)

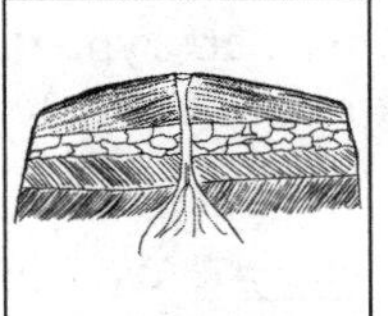

(C)

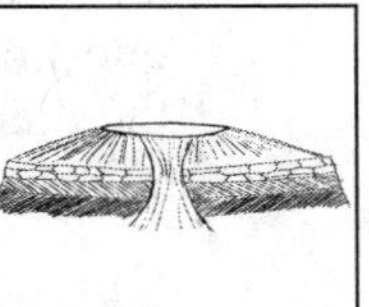

(B)

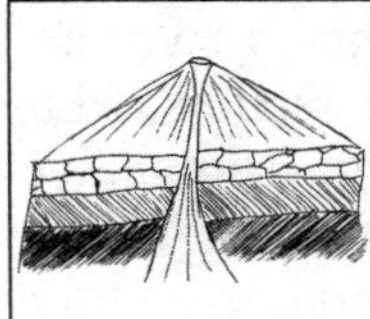

(D)

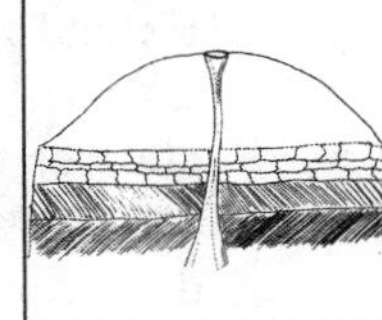

6. (A) Caldera.
   (B) Shield.
   (C) Cinder cone.
   (D) Bomb.

(STOP TAPE)

Answers to Exercises 1.11.A through 1.11.D are on page 632.

1.11 EXTENSION

1. Students create "TOEFL questions" to test their classmates' listening comprehension. Working in pairs, students choose one of the conversations from Exercise 1.11.A. Use the tapescript on page 692. Each student takes the part of one of the speakers. Practice reading the dialogue, concentrating on pronunciation. Write two new detail questions and four answer choices for each question. One must be the correct answer! Give your questions to the teacher. Type the answer choices and give copies to the class. Present the dialogue to the class. The teacher reads the questions, and the class takes a "live TOEFL exam."

2. Variation on activity #1. Working in pairs, students choose one of the short conversations from Exercises 1.1.A – 1.1.C (in Unit 1.1 – Key Words). Use the tapescript on page 681. Extend the dialogue by writing two or three more lines for each speaker. In other words, take a short conversation and make it longer. Write two detail questions and four answer choices for each question. Give your extended dialogue, questions, and answer choices to the teacher. The teacher makes suggestions and returns the dialogue. Practice reading the dialogue, concentrating on pronunciation. Proceed as in #1 above.

ASSESSING PROGRESS — 1.10 through 1.11

QUIZ 5 (Time – approximately 15 minutes)

(START TAPE)

Directions: In this quiz you will hear several conversations and talks. Each conversation or talk is followed by several questions. The conversations, talks, and questions will not be repeated.

For most of the questions, you will read four possible answers and choose the best answer. Some questions will have special directions.

Here is an example.

On the recording, you hear:

Now listen to a sample question.

In your book, you read:

(A) It is becoming more abundant.
(B) It normally does not attack people.
(C) It is a serious threat to domestic animals.
(D) It eats mainly deer and sheep.

The best answer to the question, *What does the instructor say about the cougar?* is (B), *It normally does not attack people.* Therefore, the correct choice is (B).

1. (A) Terms from a lecture.
   (B) Questions on a test.
   (C) Issues in property rights.
   (D) Topics for a term paper.

2. (A) A system in which one ruler owns all property.
   (B) Dividing property among several children.
   (C) A system of inheritance by the firstborn son.
   (D) Donating property to the state.

3. (A) A famous solar astronomer.
   (B) The number of stars in the universe.
   (C) The origin of the solar system.
   (D) The size and color of stars.

4. (A) A baseball.
   (B) An orange.
   (C) A marble.
   (D) An automobile.

5. Choose 2 answers.

   [A] Location.
   [B] Temperature.
   [C] Atmosphere.
   [D] Age.

6. (A)

(C)

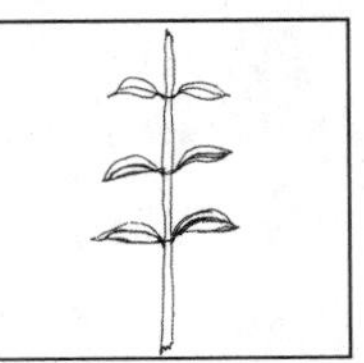

(B)

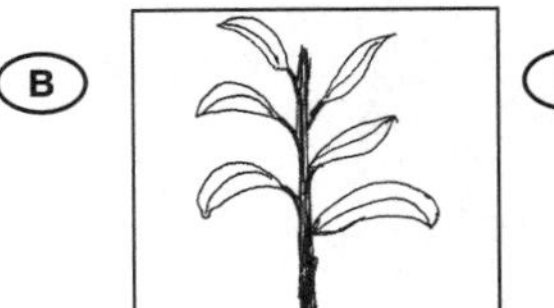

(D)

7. 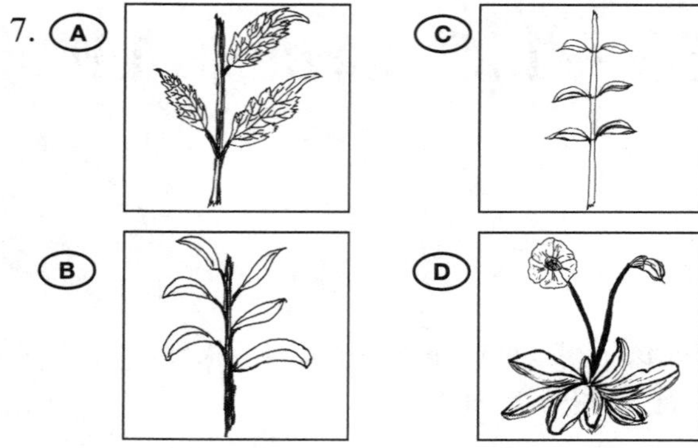

8. (A) Amaryllis.
   (B) Sunflower.
   (C) Daisy.
   (D) Basil.

9. (A) Look up some information.
   (B) Look at some flower samples.
   (C) Count the leaves of a flower.
   (D) Examine pictures of flowers.

10. Choose 2 answers.

   [A] Rich and brown.
   [B] With alternate leaves.
   [C] With opposite leaves.
   [D] Velvety.

11. (A) The benefits of planting trees.
   (B) An example of a forested park.
   (C) Landscape design in New York City.
   (D) The history of parks in North America.

12. (A) All of the trees in an urban park.
   (B) The trees planted along city streets.
   (C) The trees planted by landscape architects.
   (D) All of the trees in a city.

13. Choose 2 answers.

   [A] Romantic literature.
   [B] Landscape paintings.
   [C] European gardens.
   [D] European art.

14. (A) Land for crops.
   (B) Forests for research.
   (C) Pasture for animals.
   (D) Residential area for people.

15. (A) It is a beneficial extension of the urban forest.
   (B) It is the largest urban forest in the world.
   (C) It contrasts with the ugliness of the rest of the city.
   (D) It contributes to the wealth of the city.

 *(STOP TAPE)*

Answers to Listening Quiz 5 are on page 632.

1.12 Matching Words and Categories

Cover this page with a piece of paper. Then start the cassette.

Maple Narrow Broad Redwood

Evergreen Trees		Deciduous Trees	
Example	Leaf Shape	Example	Leaf Shape

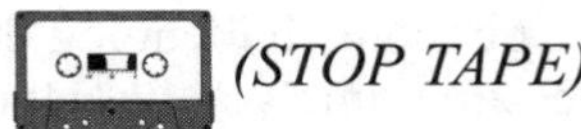

The question asks you to categorize each word—*Maple*, *Narrow*, *Broad*, *Redwood*—by putting it in the appropriate box.

One example of an evergreen tree mentioned by the speaker is a redwood. Therefore, you should put *Redwood* in the first box, starting on the left side.

The leaf shape of evergreen trees is narrow, so you should put *Narrow* in the second box.

One example of a deciduous tree given by the speaker is a maple. Therefore, you should put *Maple* in the third box.

The leaf shape of deciduous trees is broad, so you should put *Broad* in the fourth box.

You will see this type of question on the computer–based test only.

LISTENING

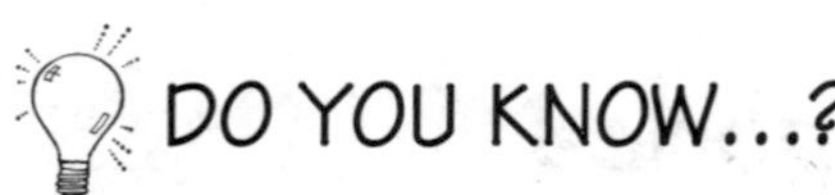

1. Approximately one or two questions on the computer–based TOEFL will ask you to match words and categories.

2. A ***category*** is a class or type of something. On the TOEFL, questions about matching words and categories will have three or four words to match with the correct category.

   TOEFL questions about category sound like this:

   > Match each word with the appropriate _____.
   > Which _____ is associated with each _____?
   > Based on the speaker's description, classify the following _____.
   > How did each word below _____?

   You will use the mouse to click on a word and then click on the box where the word belongs. The word will appear in that box. Use each word only once.

   Note: You must match *all* of the words with the correct category to receive credit for answering the question correctly.

3. On the actual test, questions about matching words and categories will be more challenging than can be shown in this book because you will not see the question at the same time you hear the information spoken. In other words, you will not see the boxes and categories until *after the speaker has finished talking.*

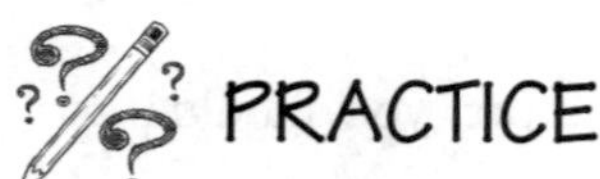

Exercise 1.12.A

For the questions about category, put the letter of each word in the correct box. For the rest of the questions, choose the best answer or answers.

To benefit most from this exercise, cover the boxes and answer choices until the end of the conversation or talk.

 *(START TAPE)*

1. (A) Cash a check.
   (B) Make a photocopy.
   (C) Buy coffee.

Near the bookstore	Near the computer lab	In the student union

2. (A) It is near the computer lab.
   (B) She doesn't know where it is.
   (C) The coffee there is bad.
   (D) No coffee is sold there.

3. (A) Shrimp.
   (B) Bats.
   (C) Early humans.

Entrance zone	Twilight zone	Dark zone

4. Choose 2 answers.

   [A] Abrupt temperature changes.
   [B] Blind creatures.
   [C] Little air movement.
   [D] Indirect sunlight.

5. (A) Native American religious customs.
(B) Changes in Native American life.
(C) Native American music and dance.
(D) The diversity of Native American cultures.

6. (A) Rain dance.
(B) War dance.
(C) Vision quest.

Hopi	Plains tribes	Apache

7. (A) Good and evil.
(B) Violence and corruption.
(C) Action and adventure.
(D) Compassion and dignity.

8. (A) Growing up.
(B) Failure and loss.
(C) Struggle against hardship.

First film	Second film	Third film

(STOP TAPE)

Answers to Exercise 1.12.A are on page 633.

1.13 Sequencing Events in a Process

FOCUS

Cover this page with a piece of paper. Then start the cassette.

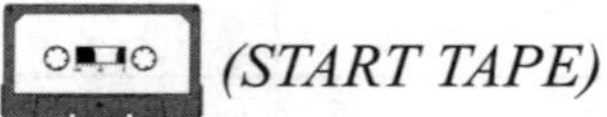

(START TAPE)

Go past the arts building.
Go into the recreation center.
Go left at the science building.
Turn right on State Street.

1	
2	
3	
4	

(STOP TAPE)

The question asks you to explain how the woman will get to the swimming pool by putting the steps in the correct order.

The man says:

> It's in the recreation center. Just turn right on the next street. Then go straight until you come to the science building. To the left of the science building, you'll see another street with a lot of trees along it. Turn there and go—oh a little ways—past the round arts building. The rec center will be right in front of you.

Therefore, the correct sequence of steps is:

> Turn right on State Street.
> Go left at the science building.
> Go past the arts building.
> Go into the recreation center.

Put each step in the correct space above.

You will see this type of question on the computer–based test only.

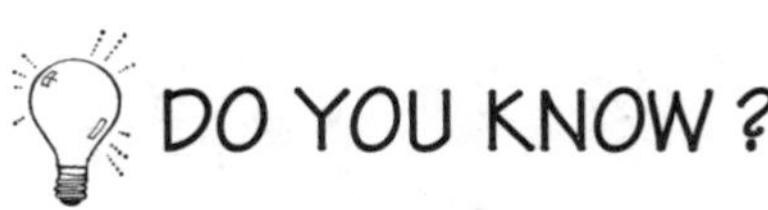

1. Approximately one or two questions on the computer–based TOEFL will ask you to put the events of a process in the correct sequence.

2. A ***sequence*** is an ordering of things or events. On the TOEFL, questions about sequences are usually about time order. You will hear a speaker describe a process, and then you will put three or four statements in the correct order.

   TOEFL questions about sequencing events sound like this:

   > The speaker briefly explains a process. Summarize the process by putting the events in order.
   > The speaker explains a sequence of events. Put the events in the correct order.
   > According to the speaker, what is the correct order of _____?
   > How does _____? Summarize the process by putting the steps in order.

   You will use the mouse to click on a statement and then click on the space where it belongs. The statement will appear in that space. Use each statement only once.

   Note: You must put *all* of the statements in the correct order to receive credit for answering the question correctly.

3. On the actual test, questions about sequencing events will be more challenging than can be shown in this book because you will not see the statements at the same time you hear the information spoken. In other words, you will not see the steps in the process until *after the speaker has finished talking*.

LISTENING

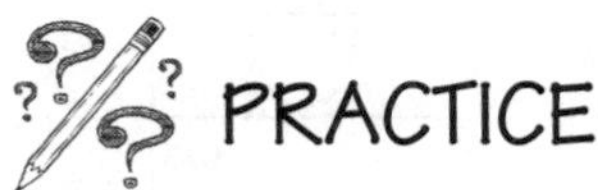

Exercise 1.13.A

For the questions about process, put the letters of the statements in the correct sequence. For the rest of the questions, choose the best answer.

To benefit most from this exercise, cover the boxes and statements until the end of the conversation or talk.

(START TAPE)

1. (A) They should choose their own subject.
   (B) They should start with a pencil sketch.
   (C) They should use erasable ink.
   (D) They should take a different class.

2. (A) Draw the outline of the violin.
   (B) Study the subject.
   (C) Add the details.
   (D) Draw the shape of the chair.

1	
2	
3	
4	

3. (A) Selecting a subject for a speech.
   (B) Entertaining an audience.
   (C) Believing in what you say.
   (D) Preparing a speech.

4. (A) Realize the importance of the speech.
   (B) Organize and develop your ideas.
   (C) Choose your subject.
   (D) Decide on your purpose.

1	
2	
3	
4	

5. (A) Give a speech.
   (B) Write down ideas they think of.
   (C) Choose from a list of possible topics.
   (D) Think of ways to make people laugh.

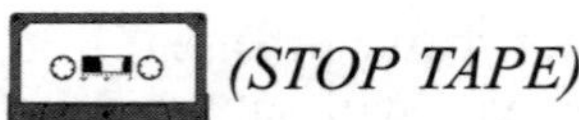
(STOP TAPE)

Exercise 1.13.B

For the questions about process, put the letter of each statement in the correct sequence. For the rest of the questions, choose the best answer.

To benefit most from this exercise, cover the boxes and statements until the end of the conversation or talk.

(START TAPE)

1. (A) Complex engines.
   (B) The production of energy.
   (C) How trees manufacture food.
   (D) Uses of the sun's energy.

2. (A) In the leaves of a tree.
   (B) On a tree's trunk.
   (C) In carbon dioxide molecules.
   (D) On the sun.

3. (A) Solar energy is used to combine carbon dioxide and water.
   (B) A leaf takes in water and carbon dioxide.
   (C) Carbohydrates move throughout the tree.

1	
2	
3	

4. (A) The bill is signed by the president.
   (B) The bill is passed by the House of Representatives.
   (C) Hearings are held to hear opinions on the bill.
   (D) The bill is approved by the Senate.

1	
2	
3	
4	

5. (A) The second reading of a bill.
   (B) The president's approval of a bill.
   (C) The president's signing of a bill.
   (D) The president's refusal to sign a bill.

6. (A) Business Law.
   (B) Accounting.
   (C) American Government.
   (D) Information Systems.

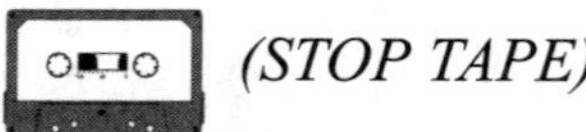
(STOP TAPE)

Answers to Exercises 1.13.A through 1.13.B are on page 633.

 ASSESSING PROGRESS — 1.10 through 1.13

QUIZ 6 (Time – approximately 15 minutes)

(START TAPE)

Directions: In this quiz you will hear several conversations and talks. Each conversation or talk is followed by several questions. The conversations, talks, and questions will not be repeated.

For most of the questions, you will read four possible answers and choose the best answer. Some questions will have special directions.

Here is an example.

On the recording, you hear:

Now listen to a sample question.

In your book, you read:

Ⓐ Agriculture and industry expanded.
Ⓑ Conservation laws were passed.
Ⓒ Forests covered North America.
Ⓓ Old–growth forests were half gone.

The correct order of events given by the professor is:

1	Ⓒ Forests covered North America.
2	Ⓐ Agriculture and industry expanded.
3	Ⓓ Old–growth forests were half gone.
4	Ⓑ Conservation laws were passed.

Therefore, the correct answer is Ⓒ–Ⓐ–Ⓓ–Ⓑ.

1. Ⓐ He wants to tell her about his illness.
   Ⓑ He wants her to get the materials from class.
   Ⓒ He wants to thank her for dropping by.
   Ⓓ He is inviting her to come visit him.

2. Ⓐ Make an extra copy of her notes.
   Ⓑ Get a book for the man.
   Ⓒ Drive the man to class.
   Ⓓ Drive to the mall after class.

3. Ⓐ Turn right on Harrison.
   Ⓑ Turn right on Lake Boulevard.
   Ⓒ Go over the freeway.
   Ⓓ Go past the mall.

1	
2	
3	
4	

4. Ⓐ The formation of wetlands.
   Ⓑ The plant and animal life of marshes.
   Ⓒ The diversity of animal life.
   Ⓓ How the food chain functions in marshes.

5. Ⓐ Trees.
   Ⓑ Shrubs.
   Ⓒ Grasses.
   Ⓓ Everglades.

LISTENING

6. (A) Snapping turtle. (B) Dragonfly. (C) Leopard frog. (D) Great blue heron.

Aquatic Insect	Amphibian	Reptile	Wading Bird

7. (A) Decaying vegetation turns the water dark brown.
(B) Bacteria and fungi break down the biomass.
(C) Plants and animals die in the marsh.

1	
2	
3	

8. Choose 2 answers.

[A] Laying the eggs.
[B] Defending the colony.
[C] Gathering pollen.
[D] Stinging the queen.

9. (A) The egg hatches into a larva.
(B) The larva enters the pupa state.
(C) The adult worker emerges.
(D) The egg is put into the worker cell.

1	
2	
3	
4	

10. (A) Eight days after laying the eggs.
(B) Eight hours after leaving the pupa.
(C) Eight days after leaving the pupa.
(D) Twenty–one days after leaving the pupa.

11. (A) Flying.
(B) Stinging.
(C) Working on the hive.

Head	Thorax	Abdomen

12. (A) Children think a lot about their inner feelings.
(B) Children need guidance in developing their social skills.
(C) Children become more egocentric as they enter adolescence.
(D) Children go through stages in developing social reasoning.

13. (A) Four.
(B) Eight.
(C) Ten.
(D) Fifteen.

14. (A) He cannot distinguish between thoughts and actions.
(B) He can understand only his own perspective.
(C) He can follow and give directions.
(D) He can comprehend social expectations in a variety of situations.

15. (A) Children develop an analytical and societal perspective.
(B) Children can understand two perspectives, but not at the same time.
(C) Children have an egocentric perspective.
(D) Children can take a third–person perspective.

1	
2	
3	
4	

(STOP TAPE)

Answers to Listening Quiz 6 are on page 633.

1.14 Determining Reasons

Listen to a conversation.

 *(START TAPE)*

1.	(A)	She must have her car repaired.
	(B)	She has an algebra test.
	(C)	She broke her arm and must see a specialist.
	(D)	She has a fever and a cough.
2.	(A)	She has a meeting.
	(B)	She has a class.
	(C)	She has an appointment.
	(D)	She has a cold.

 *(STOP TAPE)*

Question 1 asks you to identify the reason *why the student must reschedule her appointment*. The student says:

> I'm sorry, but I can't make my advising appointment at ten o'clock. My car broke down and I have to see my mechanic.

The student uses an idiomatic expression, *broke down*, to mean that her car stopped working. She has to see her mechanic, who will repair the car. Therefore, you should check the first answer choice, *She must have her car repaired.*

The second and third choices try to trick you by repeating some words from the conversation—*algebra* and *broke*—but inaccurately. The fourth choice is about something not mentioned at all.

Question 2 asks you *why the student can't meet at eight o'clock the next day*. The student says:

> Oh, no, I'm sorry. I have algebra at eight.

The student means that she has algebra class at eight o'clock. Therefore, you should check the second choice, *She has a class*.

The other answer choices try to trick you either by being inaccurate or by not being mentioned in the conversation.

LISTENING

DO YOU KNOW...?

1. Approximately four or five questions on the TOEFL will test your ability to determine reasons in the conversations and talks you hear.

2. A ***reason*** is the answer to the question "Why?" A reason is the cause for some action, belief, statement, fact, or event. Sometimes reasons are stated directly by one of the speakers. Sometimes reasons are stated indirectly through key words and phrases.

   TOEFL questions about reasons sound like this:

   Why is _____?
   Why does _____?
   Why can't _____?
   Why does the man/woman think _____?
   Why does the man/woman want _____?
   Why is the man/woman concerned?
   According to the speaker, why _____?
   Why does the speaker mention _____?
   Why are _____ known as _____?
   What reasons are given for _____?

3. In questions about reasons, some of the answer choices may try to trick you by:

   - repeating words and phrases incorrectly
   - using words that sound similar to the words used
   - being illogical or unrelated to the question
   - being inaccurate: partly or wholly incorrect
   - being about something not mentioned by the speakers

   Remember, you can answer all questions based on the information you hear in the conversation or talk. You do not need special knowledge of the topics to answer the questions correctly.

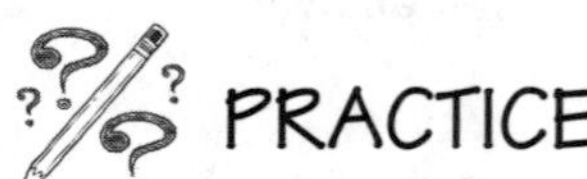

PRACTICE

Exercise 1.14.A

Listen to the following conversations and talks. Answer the questions based on the information you hear.

(START TAPE)

1. (A) It is an excellent introduction to photography.
   (B) It has beautiful photography of snow.
   (C) It reviews material that the students need to know.
   (D) It explains how to use the library reserve system.

2. (A) The viewing rooms there are the best on campus.
   (B) Items on reserve cannot be checked out.
   (C) Videotapes cannot be checked out.
   (D) It contains sensitive material.

3. (A) Factors influencing oil prices.
   (B) Consumer education.
   (C) The history of inflation.
   (D) Causes and effects of inflation.

4. (A) To compare prices in the United States with prices in other countries.
   (B) To explain how companies set the price of an item.
   (C) To show how a price increase for one item contributes to inflation.
   (D) To encourage students to tell stories about their families.

5. (A) The price of oil rose sharply.
(B) The population rose sharply.
(C) People wanted to buy more things.
(D) People spent too much money.

6. (A) Workers were not trained.
(B) Companies were hurt by inflation.
(C) Companies needed fewer workers.
(D) Companies could not find good workers.

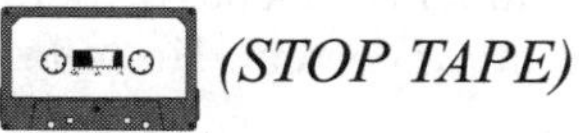
(STOP TAPE)

Exercise 1.14.B

Listen to the following conversations and talks. Answer the questions based on the information you hear.

(START TAPE)

1. (A) He doesn't like adventure stories.
(B) He thinks the main character was immoral.
(C) He thinks the film was too violent.
(D) He thinks the film was unbelievable.

2. Choose 2 answers.

[A] She likes films with a lot of action.
[B] She admires one of the characters.
[C] She considers it a classical hero story.
[D] She knows some of the people in the film.

3. (A) The soldier killed a lot of his enemies.
(B) The soldier survived going over a waterfall.
(C) The soldier died to save someone he loved.
(D) The soldier was the narrator in the film.

4. (A) They each have a different definition of "hero."
(B) They disagree over whether the story was true.
(C) They disagree over which character killed more people.
(D) One of the men did not see the end of the film.

5. (A) It is where companies research and develop new products.
(B) It is where companies can cut costs.
(C) It is where employees can update their computer skills.
(D) It provides jobs for college graduates.

6. (A) To advertise a new product.
(B) To show how companies set the price of an item.
(C) To explain why companies must keep costs down.
(D) To illustrate how the distribution process works.

7. (A) It is essential for controlling costs.
(B) It can lead to an executive position.
(C) It helps companies overproduce.
(D) It requires little or no training.

8. Choose 2 answers.

[A] They can accurately report on inventory.
[B] They provide good entry–level jobs for programmers.
[C] They make it easier for managers to supervise people.
[D] They train people for executive positions.

(STOP TAPE)

Answers to Exercises 1.14.A through 1.14.B are on page 634.

1.14 EXTENSION

1. Working in pairs, students discuss why the incorrect answer choices in Exercise 1.14.A and 1.14.B are incorrect. How do they try to trick you?

2. Students create "TOEFL questions" to test their classmates' ability to determine reasons for actions, beliefs, statements, or facts in conversations and talks. Working in pairs, students choose one of the conversations or talks from Exercises 1.10 through 1.13. Use the tapescripts beginning on page 691. Divide the conversation or talk so that each student takes a part. Each student practices reading aloud his or her part, concentrating on pronunciation. Write two questions about reasons in the conversation or talk. Use the list of reason questions on page 118 for examples of how to word the questions. For each question, write four answer choices. One must be the correct answer! Give your questions and answer choices to the teacher so that he or she can make suggestions. Then, type the answer choices and give copies to the class. Present your conversation or talk to the class, with each student reading his or her part and one of the questions. The class takes a "live TOEFL exam."

1.15 Making Inferences and Predictions

Listen to a lecture.

 *(START TAPE)*

1. Choose 2 answers.

   [A] Women are naturally inferior to men.
   [B] The American Revolution gave women full civil rights.
   [C] American women formerly could not own land.
   [D] By 1815 some traditional customs had changed.

2. (A) Changes in the position of women.
   (B) The American Revolution.
   (C) Women as housekeepers and mothers.
   (D) The feminist movement today.

 *(STOP TAPE)*

Question 1 asks you *what can be inferred from the lecture*. In other words, what conclusion can you make after hearing the lecture? For this question you must choose two answers.

The professor says:

> American women had been trained from childhood to assume the role of housekeepers, taught that they were naturally inferior to men, and denied the right to hold property.

and:

> The appearance of a feminist movement that would demand civil rights for women depended on the disappearance of some of the customs that had kept women in a position of inferiority. The first signs of this process were apparent well before 1815.

From this information, you can infer the third and fourth answer choices, *American women formerly could not own land*, and *By 1815 some traditional customs had changed.*

Question 2 asks you *what the professor will probably discuss next*. You must make a prediction.

The best answer is the first choice, *Changes in the position of women*. Some key phrases supporting this prediction are: *appearance of a feminist movement*, *disappearance of some of the customs*, and *the first signs of this process*.

The other answer choices cannot reasonably be predicted from the information in the lecture.

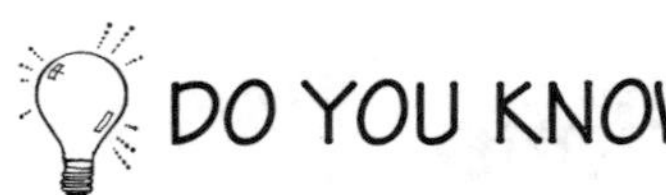

DO YOU KNOW?

1. Approximately four or five questions on the TOEFL will test your ability to make inferences and predictions based on the information you hear in conversations and talks.

2. An ***inference*** is a conclusion that you can make from the information given by the speakers. An inference is a "hidden" idea. To make an inference, you must interpret a message that is not stated directly by the speakers. One of the speakers *implies* or suggests something, and you *infer* the meaning.

   A ***prediction*** is a type of inference in which you must determine what will probably happen next or what a speaker will probably discuss next.

   To make inferences and predictions, use key ideas and your overall understanding of the conversation or talk, as well as reason, logic, and common sense.

   TOEFL questions about inferences and predictions sound like this:

   > What does the man/woman/speaker imply about _____?
   > What can be concluded about _____?
   > What can be inferred from the talk?
   > What do we learn about the man/woman from this conversation?
   > What is probably the speaker's job?
   > What is probably true about _____?
   > To what group of people was this talk most likely given?
   > In what course was this lecture probably given?
   > What will the man/woman/speaker probably do?
   > What will the speaker probably discuss next?
   > What will the next lecture probably be about?

3. In questions about inferences and predictions in conversations and talks, some of the answer choices may try to trick you by:

   - not being supported by what is stated or implied by the speakers
   - repeating words and phrases incorrectly
   - being inaccurate: partly or wholly incorrect
   - being about something not mentioned by the speakers

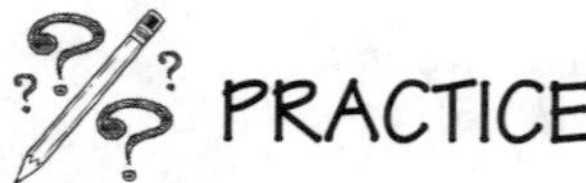

PRACTICE

Exercise 1.15.A

Listen to the following conversations and talks. Answer the questions based on the information you hear.

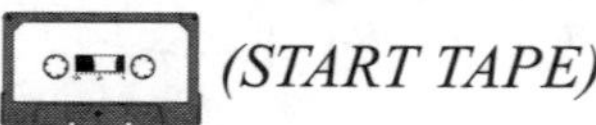

(START TAPE)

1. (A) Meatloaf.
   (B) Potatoes and gravy.
   (C) Chicken.
   (D) Vegetables.

2. (A) Chicken.
   (B) Meatloaf.
   (C) Pineapple.
   (D) Salad.

3. (A) He needs to change his registration.
(B) He will miss the beginning of the next term.
(C) He wants to join a student group.
(D) He wants to discuss his term project.

4. (A) It is not a good idea to miss class time.
(B) It is a good class for gaining valuable experience.
(C) The course assignments are flexible.
(D) The course will conclude on January 15.

5. (A) Take the class at another time.
(B) Turn in his paper on the due date.
(C) Join a different learning group.
(D) Cancel his trip to California.

6. (A) A textbook.
(B) A college course.
(C) A television program.
(D) A government agency.

7. (A) There were few large cities.
(B) A great natural disaster occurred.
(C) Baltimore was founded.
(D) The population grew rapidly.

8. Choose 2 answers.

[A] It was originally five cities.
[B] It was originally part of Baltimore.
[C] It is a progressive city.
[D] It has a borough called Brooklyn.

(STOP TAPE)

Exercise 1.15.B

Listen to the following conversations and talks. Answer the questions based on the information you hear.

(START TAPE)

1. (A) Philosophy.
(B) Computer Programming.
(C) Computer Languages.
(D) Architectural Design.

2. (A) Usefulness cannot be measured accurately.
(B) A design is more useful when many people create it.
(C) A design is more useful if it is simple.
(D) Architects find software design useful.

3. (A) Architecture and software design share certain concepts.
(B) Architecture requires knowledge of computer programming.
(C) Function is more important than beauty in architecture.
(D) Large buildings should be well–constructed and complex.

4. (A) The professor is an architect.
(B) The professor values simplicity in software design.
(C) Conceptual unity is difficult in software design.
(D) Software design is a growing field.

5. (A) Several different personality types.
(B) The psychology of motivation.
(C) The character traits of extroverted people.
(D) The type preferences of extroversion–introversion.

6. Choose 2 answers.

[A] Painter.
[B] Social worker.
[C] Philosopher.
[D] Politician.

7. (A) Reflective journal writing.
(B) Large group discussion.
(C) Oral presentation.
(D) Competitive team game.

8. (A) Some type preferences are better than others.
(B) Type preferences represent physical health.
(C) Type preferences cannot be changed.
(D) Type preferences can be worked on and changed.

(STOP TAPE)

Answers to Exercises 1.15.A through 1.15.B are on page 634.

1.14 EXTENSION

1. Working in pairs, students discuss why the incorrect answer choices in Exercise 1.15.A and 1.15.B are incorrect. How do they try to trick you? What key phrases support the inferences?

2. Obtain a videotape of a documentary or educational television program. Students listen to 2 or 3 minutes of the *audio only*, without watching the video portion. Working in small groups, make a list of *facts* (what is known) and a list of *inferences* (what can be concluded) based on what is heard in the audio portion. Groups share their lists with the class. Discuss what information in the recording supports each inference. Then, play the videotape again, this time with *both the audio and video*. How does watching the video affect your understanding of the material? Are facts confirmed? Are inferences confirmed?

3. Obtain an audiotape of an actual university lecture. Students listen to 2 or 3 minutes of the tape. Working in small groups, listen for the following in the lecture: (1) topic/main ideas, (2) details/facts, and (3) reasons. Then, write a list of statements that can be inferred or concluded from this information. Each group shares its inferences with the whole class.

4. Students create "TOEFL questions" to test their classmates' ability to make inferences. Working in pairs, students choose one of the talks or lectures from Exercises 1.10 through 1.14. Use the tapescripts beginning on page 691. Divide the talk into two parts. Each student practices reading aloud his or her part, concentrating on pronunciation. Write four questions about the talk. *At least two questions must be inference questions.* Use the list of inference questions on page 122 for examples of how to word the questions. For each question, write four answer choices. One must be the correct answer! Give your questions and answer choices to the teacher so that he or she can make suggestions. Then, type the answer choices and give copies to the class. Present your talk to the class, with each student reading his or her part and two of the questions. The class takes a "live TOEFL exam."

 ASSESSING PROGRESS — 1.14 through 1.15

Quiz 7 *(Time – approximately 15 minutes)*

 *(START TAPE)*

LISTENING

Directions: In this quiz you will hear several conversations and talks. Each conversation or talk is followed by several questions. The conversations, talks, and questions will not be repeated.

For most of the questions, you will read four possible answers and choose the best answer. Some questions will have special directions.

Here is an example.

On the recording, you hear:

Now listen to a sample question.

In your book, you read:

Choose 2 answers.

[A] They supported the reintroduction of the wolf.
[B] Their hunting decreased deer and elk populations.
[C] They were experienced soldiers.
[D] They viewed the wolf as a competitor.

The best two answers to the question, *What does the instructor imply about the early settlers in the region?* are [B], *Their hunting decreased deer and elk populations*, and [D], *They viewed the wolf as a competitor.* Therefore, the correct choices are [B] and [D].

Now listen to another question.

In your book, you read:

(A) They believe it will threaten livestock.
(B) They believe it will kill people.
(C) They think it will be expensive for the government.
(D) They are afraid the wolves will starve.

The best answer to the question, *Why do some people oppose the reintroduction of the wolf?* is (A), *They believe it will threaten livestock.* Therefore, the correct choice is (A).

1. (A) She is teaching him how to get around campus.
   (B) He is applying for a job.
   (C) He wants to park on the west campus.
   (D) She wants to buy his bicycle.

2. (A) Parking a bicycle is free on the west campus.
   (B) It can be sold for a lot of money.
   (C) It is more convenient than a car.
   (D) It will be useful on the job.

3. (A) Raymond will return to the student employment office.
(B) Raymond will show Ms. Kinney the bicycle.
(C) Ms. Kinney will offer Raymond the job.
(D) Ms. Kinney will borrow Raymond's bicycle.

4. (A) She feels very tired.
(B) She is concerned about the man's health.
(C) Her dog is ill.
(D) She has to see Dr. Adams.

5. (A) The woman cannot take care of Tippy.
(B) Dr. Adams wants to observe Tippy.
(C) Dr. Adams found Tippy when he ran away.
(D) Dr. Adams wants to adopt Tippy.

6. (A) He tries to reassure the woman.
(B) He provides fluids and antibiotics.
(C) He promises to call her tomorrow.
(D) He tries to help Tippy.

7. (A) Stop thinking about Tippy.
(B) Develop a fever of unknown origin.
(C) Sleep for a couple of days.
(D) Call Dr. Adams the next day.

8. Choose 2 answers.

[A] It grows in caves.
[B] It provides vitamins and minerals.
[C] It grows very quickly.
[D] It keeps for a very long time.

9. (A) Beans were not eaten in his culture.
(B) He thought beans contained blood.
(C) He thought only vegetarians should eat beans.
(D) He believed only the gods should eat beans.

10. Choose 2 answers.

[A] Beans have inspired the human imagination.
[B] Some types of beans can hold the souls of the dead.
[C] Beans have played an important role in world trade.
[D] Beans have been celebrated in festivals around the world.

11. (A) Perform a ritual bean dance.
(B) Pass around a beancake baked the night before.
(C) Teach the class some bean recipes.
(D) Teach the class how to grow beans.

12. Choose 2 answers.

[A] They were true.
[B] They were adventurous.
[C] They were superbly told.
[D] They were scary.

13. (A) He is handsome.
(B) He is mischievous.
(C) He is stupid.
(D) He is a good storyteller.

14. (A) They examine human nature in an amusing way.
(B) They are complex and mysterious.
(C) They portray animal behavior accurately.
(D) They stereotype animal and human behavior.

15. (A) Journalism.
(B) American History.
(C) Animal Behavior.
(D) American Literature.

(STOP TAPE)

Answers to Listening Quiz 7 are on page 635.

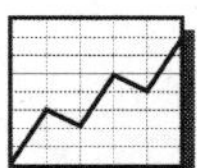

ASSESSING PROGRESS – 1.10 through 1.15

QUIZ 8 (Time – approximately 25 minutes)

(START TAPE)

Directions: In this quiz you will hear several conversations and talks. Each conversation or talk is followed by several questions. The conversations, talks, and questions will not be repeated.

For most of the questions, you will read four possible answers and choose the best answer. Some questions will have special directions.

Here is an example.

On the recording, you hear:

Now listen to a sample question.

In your book, you read:

(A) Groundwater in caves.
(B) The formation of Carlsbad Caverns.
(C) Structures that form in caves.
(D) Majestic landscapes.

The best answer to the question, *What is the talk mainly about*? is (C), *Structures that form in caves*. Therefore, the correct choice is (C).

Now listen to another sample question.

In your book, you read:

Choose 2 answers.

[A] Cave flowers.
[B] Curtains of stone.
[C] Stalactites.
[D] Icebergs.

The best two answers to the question, *What types of formations hang from the ceiling of a cave*? are [B], *Curtains of stone*, and [C], *Stalactites*. Therefore, the correct choices are [B] and [C].

1. (A) A customer is returning an item she bought.
   (B) A customer is complaining about an item she bought.
   (C) A customer is looking for a cotton sweater.
   (D) A customer is exchanging a sweatshirt.

2. (A) Put the cotton sweaters on the wall shelves.
   (B) Help another customer.
   (C) Buy a wool sweater from one of the tables.
   (D) Exchange the sweater she bought for another one.

3. (A) Look at the pullover sweaters.
   (B) Look at the cardigans.
   (C) Try on different styles of sweaters.
   (D) Complain to the manager.

4. (A) Houses.
   (B) Fruit.
   (C) Birds.
   (D) Stars.

5. (A) House finch (B) Sparrow (C) Starling

Brown	Red	Black

6. Choose 2 answers.

[A] They live in rural and urban areas.
[B] They are a nuisance to fruit growers.
[C] They have a beautiful song.
[D] They have been the subject of much study.

7. Choose 2 answers.

[A] Tea was cheap and easy to ship.
[B] Tea was a product of the mysterious East.
[C] Europeans wanted to learn commercial preparations of herbal tea.
[D] Europeans liked the healthful properties of tea.

8. (A) As a commercial success.
(B) As a poison.
(C) As an aid in the art of war.
(D) As a divine medicine.

9. (A) Herbs are sometimes poisonous.
(B) Herbs allow people to stay awake and work.
(C) Herbs help cure many diseases.
(D) Herbs have ceremonial significance.

10. (A) How to Prepare Herbal Tea.
(B) Tea: A Giant of the Herbal World.
(C) The Japanese Tea Ceremony.
(D) Witch's Brews and Mysterious Cures.

11. (A) To explain the causes of cancer.
(B) To compare skin cancer with other diseases.
(C) To describe a dangerous form of skin cancer.
(D) To discuss treatments for skin cancer.

12. (A) Avoiding sun exposure might prevent skin cancer.
(B) Increasing vitamin C might prevent skin cancer.
(C) Reducing smoking might prevent skin cancer.
(D) Medical experts do not know how to prevent skin cancer.

13. (A) Moles are a sign of beauty.
(B) A change in a mole could be a sign of melanoma.
(C) Some kinds of moles can irritate the skin.
(D) Melanoma causes moles to disappear.

14. (A) (B) (C) (D)

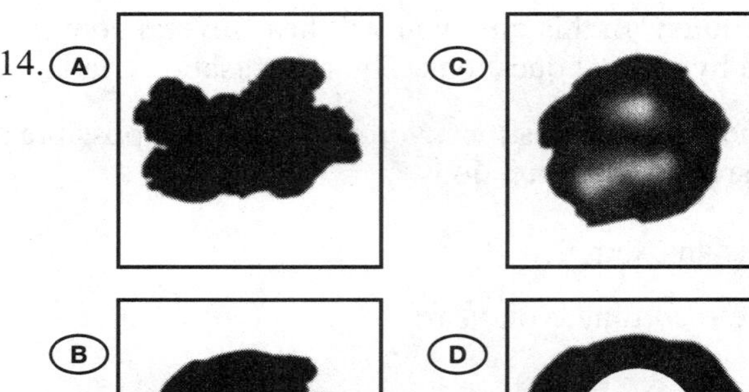

15. (A) (B) (C) (D)

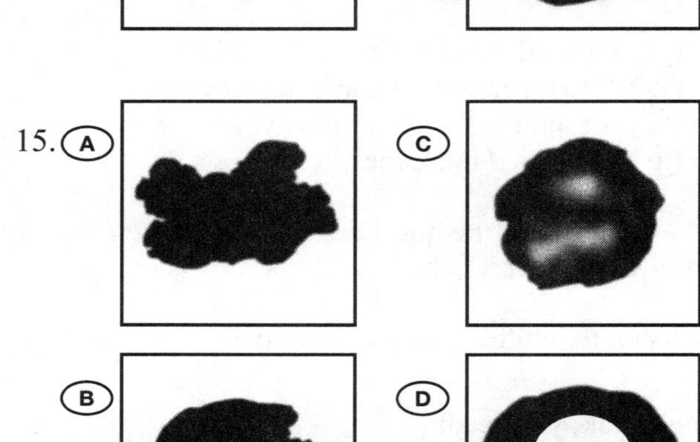

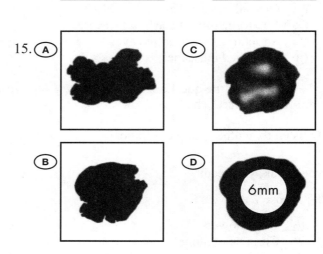

16. Choose 2 answers.

[A] Age.
[B] Talent.
[C] Training.
[D] Emotion.

17. (A) Wealth.
(B) Leadership skill.
(C) Writing skill.
(D) Optimism.

18. (A) Tastes in art change frequently.
(B) Employment can be uncertain.
(C) Training is long and difficult.
(D) Talent cannot be measured fairly.

19. (A) Photography.
(B) Acting.
(C) Graphic design.

Do paste–up for school newspaper.	Appear in local productions.	Take pictures for family wedding.

20. Choose 2 answers.

[A] A career in art will make you famous.
[B] Art alone may not provide an adequate income.
[C] A career in art should not be combined with other kinds of work.
[D] Artists sometimes must teach to support their art.

21. (A) How diseases change over time.
(B) Epidemiology as a profession.
(C) Experimental studies in epidemiology.
(D) The ways in which epidemiologists gather data.

22. Choose 2 answers.

[A] Level of education.
[B] Environment.
[C] Opinions.
[D] Occupation.

23. (A) To determine why some people get a disease and others do not.
(B) To compare different attitudes towards work.
(C) To explain why some people take better care of their health.
(D) To understand the social and cultural attitudes about disease.

24. (A) Descriptive.
(B) Observational.
(C) Experimental.

Observe what people do.	Compare treatment and nontreatment groups.	Look at trends of diseases over time.

25. (A) Descriptive.
(B) Observational.
(C) Experimental.
(D) Occupational.

26. (A) Americans aged 15 to 25.
(B) Americans aged 20 to 50.
(C) Demographers.
(D) Black and Asian immigrants.

27. (A) To describe characteristics of different groups.
(B) To measure diversity in colleges.
(C) To assess attitudes about race relations.
(D) To determine how people view themselves.

28. (A) There will be less racial diversity.
(B) There will be no majority racial group.
(C) Race relations will have worsened.
(D) People will identify strongly with their race.

29. (A) They feel that race is an important factor in judging someone.
(B) They are generally optimistic, with some differences between groups.
(C) They are not concerned with racial issues.
(D) They believe that racial differences will continue to be a problem.

30. Choose 2 answers.

[A] Native Americans.
[B] Whites.
[C] Asians.
[D] Blacks.

 *(STOP TAPE)*

Answers to Listening Quiz 8 are on page 635.

LISTENING

LISTENING COMPREHENSION REVIEW TEST 1

(Time – approximately 35 minutes)

 *(START TAPE)*

In the Listening section of the test, you will have an opportunity to demonstrate your ability to understand conversations and talks in English. Answer all the questions on the basis of what is stated or implied by the speakers you hear. Do not take notes or write during the test.

PART A

Directions: In Part A you will hear short conversations between two people. After each conversation, you will hear a question about the conversation. The conversations and questions will not be repeated. After you hear a question, read the four possible answers and choose the best answer.

Here is an example.

On the recording, you hear:

In your book, you read:

(A) She doesn't want to buy a printer.
(B) She would rather buy something else.
(C) She doesn't want to pay a lot for a printer.
(D) She wants to shop at a better place.

You learn from the conversation that the woman hopes to find a printer at a better price. The best answer to the question, *What does the woman mean*? is (C), *She doesn't want to pay a lot for a printer*. Therefore, the correct choice is (C).

LISTENING

1. (A) He fell and hurt his right foot.
   (B) He didn't feel like going skiing.
   (C) He could not get a ride to go skiing.
   (D) His driver fell while skiing.

2. (A) The man and woman like to meet at the club.
   (B) The man should have studied for the geometry exam.
   (C) The man went to the meeting without the woman.
   (D) Neither the woman nor the man went to the club meeting.

3. (A) Change his vacation plans.
   (B) Go on a great vacation.
   (C) Postpone the meeting.
   (D) Thank Mr. Maddox for a great meeting.

4. (A) Write a paper for her history class.
   (B) Attend a lecture given by Dr. Marcus.
   (C) Study for an examination.
   (D) Take Dr. Jarrett's history class.

5. (A) The man is a slow typist.
   (B) The man doesn't know when his paper is due.
   (C) The man has plenty of time to finish.
   (D) The man will not be able to finish.

6. (A) He doesn't always enjoy fixing gadgets.
   (B) He would like to spend more time fixing gadgets.
   (C) He has more gadgets than the woman.
   (D) He actually hasn't fixed many gadgets.

7. (A) He did not have time to eat dinner before his class.
   (B) He had to eat dinner earlier than usual.
   (C) He missed the train because he had to go to class.
   (D) He ate dinner during his evening class.

8. (A) She is becoming ill.
   (B) She fell down.
   (C) She will come downstairs.
   (D) She wants to sit down.

9. (A) She has just finished talking to her family.
   (B) Her mother often visits her.
   (C) She would rather talk on the phone than write her mother.
   (D) She doesn't talk to her mother very often.

10. (A) The announcement was made by e–mail.
    (B) The man should get a new e–mail account.
    (C) She did not know the boat trip was canceled.
    (D) She did not want to go on the boat trip.

11. (A) He will meet the woman after the ball game.
    (B) He will not be able to join the woman for dinner.
    (C) He must have a physical examination in order to join the ball team.
    (D) He is not going to take an exam.

12. (A) Melissa interrupts her conversations.
    (B) Melissa probably dislikes John.
    (C) Melissa likes to argue with John.
    (D) Melissa is very opinionated.

13. (A) Dawn shouldn't leave her book bag in the lounge.
    (B) He will look for Dawn's book bag in the lounge.
    (C) Dawn might have left her book bag in the lounge.
    (D) He can't help look for Dawn's book bag.

14. (A) She thinks the man used to be a good golf player.
    (B) She doesn't enjoy golf.
    (C) She prefers watching other people play golf.
    (D) She is accustomed to having others watch her play golf.

15. (A) He had to find a telephone after he stepped on a snake.
(B) He called for help when he saw a snake.
(C) He narrowly escaped being bitten by a snake.
(D) He had an imaginary conversation with a snake.

16. (A) It took her a long time to finish the book.
(B) She does not have enough time to read before class.
(C) She is sorry the man did not enjoy the book.
(D) She is surprised the man took so long to read the book.

17. (A) The woman should close the window.
(B) The man has a stuffy nose.
(C) The room will become uncomfortable.
(D) He is trying to study.

18. (A) He is polite and generous.
(B) He has some kind of jaundice.
(C) He is very intelligent.
(D) He is a gentleman.

19. (A) He can't eat his roommate's cooking.
(B) He is disgusted with his roommate.
(C) He is afraid of his roommate.
(D) He is worried about his roommate.

20. (A) The man should do the assignment later.
(B) The man should finish the assignment.
(C) The man should try to get a different assignment.
(D) The man should not do the assignment.

This is the end of Part A.

PART B

Directions: In this part of the test, you will hear several conversations and talks. Each conversation or talk is followed by several questions. The conversations, talks, and questions will not be repeated.

For most of the questions, you will read four possible answers and choose the best answer. Some questions will have special directions.

Here is an example.

On the recording, you hear:

Now listen to a sample question.

In your book, you read:

(A) It helped scientists see the atmosphere more clearly.
(B) It made it easier for scientists to send messages.
(C) It made data collection from weather stations faster.
(D) It helped airplanes fly higher.

The best answer to the question, *How did the telegraph improve the science of meteorology*? is (C), *It made data collection from weather stations faster*. Therefore, the correct choice is (C).

Now listen to another sample question.

In your book, you read:

Choose 2 answers.

[A] Forecast the weather.
[B] Study trends in rocket science.
[C] Solve air pollution problems.
[D] Study costs of building satellites.

The best two answers to the question, *What do meteorologists do today*? are [A], *Forecast the weather*, and [C], *Solve air pollution problems*. Therefore, the correct choices are [A] and [C].

Remember, you should not take notes during the test.

21. (A) He had studied a lot about the labor movement.
(B) There were no questions on material he had not studied.
(C) There was nothing on the test that he didn't know.
(D) He always does well on history tests.

22. (A) Play pool with the man.
(B) Go swimming.
(C) Skip her botany class.
(D) Take a botany test.

23. (A) He wants to apply for a job.
(B) He wants to discuss his assignment.
(C) He must miss class that day.
(D) He enjoyed her lecture.

24. (A) She is attending a conference off–campus.
(B) She is giving a lecture at two o'clock.
(C) She is visiting Professor Strong's class.
(D) She will answer his message tomorrow.

25. (A) Call Dr. Owada.
(B) Cancel his appointment with Dr. Owada.
(C) Write a note to his professor.
(D) Miss a lecture at two o'clock.

26. (A) He has too much work to do.
(B) He is worried that he can't do his job very well.
(C) He doesn't understand his boss's behavior.
(D) His boss is too strict.

27. (A) Mr. Jackson allows too many breaks.
(B) Mr. Jackson doesn't know Ben works fast.
(C) Mr. Jackson doesn't like the workers.
(D) Mr. Jackson wants to fire Ben.

28. (A) Ask his boss for advice.
(B) Look for a different job.
(C) Try to work faster.
(D) Ask his boss for more work.

29. (A) Abrupt Shifts in the World's Climate.
(B) The Climate of Northern Europe.
(C) Scientists Who Have Drilled for Ice.
(D) The Causes of Global Warming.

30. (A) The North Pole.
(B) Iceland.
(C) The United States.
(D) Greenland.

31. Choose 2 answers.

[A] Temperatures fell to minus 11 degrees every five years.
[B] Temperatures rose and fell several times.
[C] The melting of ice caused the sea level to rise.
[D] The deep chill lasted thousands of years.

32. (A) It occurred ten centuries ago.
(B) It might have taken less than a human lifetime.
(C) Scientists disagree about what happened.
(D) Snowfall gradually increased.

33. (A) Snow builds up as glacial ice.
(B) The sun's heat is reflected.
(C) More snow falls each winter.
(D) There is more moisture in the air.

1	
2	
3	
4	

34. (A) Education is important in American society.
(B) American society can be described as having four social classes.
(C) A stratified society has many disadvantages.
(D) Women are ranked below men in some societies.

35. (A) Similarity in age, race, and sex.
(B) Success or failure in business.
(C) Differences in inherited property.
(D) Similarity in education, income, and values.

Go on to the next page

LISTENING

36. (A) The upper class.
(B) The lower class.
(C) The lower–middle class.
(D) The professional class.

37. (A) Its members have many disadvantages.
(B) It is the largest social class.
(C) Its members have little chance of improving their lives.
(D) Its income is from jobs in factories.

38. (A) Upper. (C) Lower–middle.
(B) Upper–middle. (D) Lower.

Irregular work	Manual work	Refined living	Professional work

39. (A) Labels are generally accurate.
(B) Labels ignore people in the lowest classes.
(C) Labels can be misleading.
(D) Labels explain why people are rich or poor.

40. (A) The absorption of water into the atmosphere.
(B) The movement of water through the earth and atmosphere.
(C) The variety in vegetation from moist to dry climates.
(D) The changes in rain and snowfall throughout the seasons.

41.

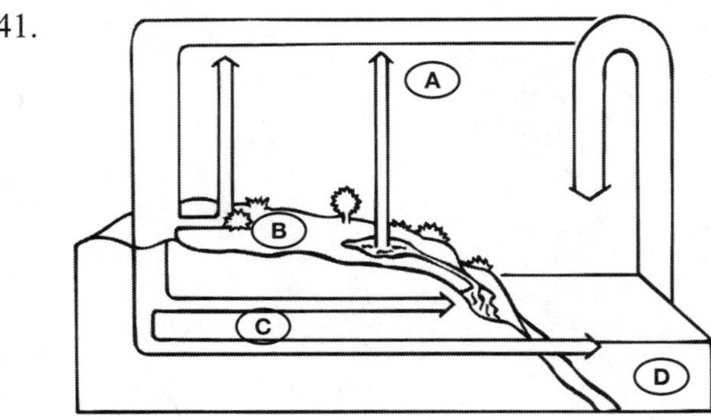

42.

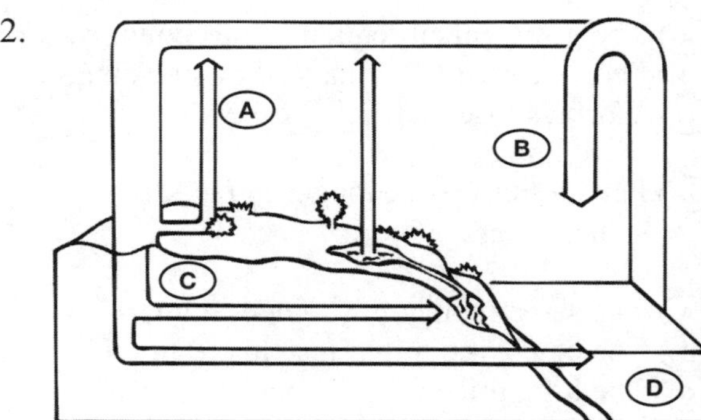

43. Choose 2 answers.

[A] It is stored in rivers and lakes.
[B] It causes changes in the climate.
[C] It penetrates the surface of the earth.
[D] It lowers the temperature of the soil.

44. (A) The loss of trees would affect the cycle.
(B) Trees take large quantities of water from the cycle.
(C) The growth of trees draws water from the atmosphere.
(D) More water is stored in trees than in lakes.

45. (A) As precipitation.
(B) As water vapor.
(C) As rain.
(D) As springs.

46. (A) To list the major problems in the economy.
(B) To describe some effects of inflation.
(C) To explain why bread prices increase.
(D) To classify the types of inflation.

47. (A) To compare prices of different kinds of bread.
(B) To illustrate the effect of price changes.
(C) To define standard of living.
(D) To explain social and political turmoil.

48. (A) The government regulates the economy.
(B) People save money instead of spending it.
(C) Workers lose their jobs if they buy more things.
(D) People must work longer to buy the same things.

49. (A) The same money buys fewer things.
(B) The employee might lose his or her job.
(C) The high price of bread means many people are hungry.
(D) The crime rate goes up.

50. (A) Moderate inflation.
(B) Galloping inflation.
(C) Hyperinflation.

Severe	Mild	Rapid

This is the end of the Listening Comprehension Review Test.

Answers to the Listening Comprehension Review Test are on page 636.

SECTION 2 – STRUCTURE

The Structure section of the TOEFL measures your ability to recognize language that is appropriate for standard written English. The language in this section is more formal than the conversational language in the Listening section. The topics usually relate to academic subjects.

Vocabulary is not directly tested in the Structure section, but knowledge of vocabulary and word forms makes it easier to answer many of the questions.

THE PAPER–BASED TEST

STRUCTURE

The paper–based TOEFL will continue to be administered in certain parts of the world and by certain educational institutions in North America.

There are 40 questions in the Structure section of the paper test. You have 25 minutes to complete this section. This time includes your reading of the directions.

QUESTION TYPES ON THE PAPER TEST

There are two types of questions in this section, with special directions for each type:

Question Type 1 – Complete the Sentence (15 questions)

In the first type of question, you will see an incomplete sentence. Beneath the sentence, you will see four words or phrases, marked (A), (B), (C), and (D). You must choose the one word or phrase that best completes the sentence. Then, on your answer sheet, find the number of the question and fill in the space that corresponds to the letter of the answer you have chosen.

Question type 1 will look like this:

Although Chicago is not ---------- New York, it has many attractions for visitors.

(A) as large as
(B) larger
(C) larger city
(D) the larger city is

The sentence should read, *Although Chicago is not as large as New York, it has many attractions for visitors*. Therefore, you should choose (A).

Question Type 2 – Identify the Error (25 questions)

In the second type of question, you must recognize the error in a sentence. You will see a sentence with four underlined words or phrases, marked A, B, C, and D. You must choose the one underlined word or phrase that must be changed for the sentence to be correct. In other words, you are looking for the part of the sentence that is *incorrect*.

Question type 2 will look like this:

Guglielmo Marconi, <u>the son of</u> (A) a wealthy Italian landowner, <u>made</u> (B) the first <u>successfully</u> (C) transmission <u>using</u> (D) radio waves.

The sentence should read, *Guglielmo Marconi, the son of a wealthy Italian landowner, made the first successful transmission using radio waves*. Therefore, you should choose (C).

THE COMPUTER–BASED TEST

The Structure section of the computerized TOEFL is *computer–adaptive*. This means that the computer will give you test questions that are aimed at your ability level.

How does the computer–adaptive test work? The first question will be of average difficulty.

- If you answer it correctly, the computer will then give you a slightly harder question.
- If you answer it incorrectly, the computer will then give you an easier question.

The second question will match your performance on the first question. In other words, the computer adapts the questions to your ability level.

You will be able to change your answer as many times as you like—*until you confirm your answer*. When you confirm your answer, the computer will give you the next question.

The computer will give you one question at a time.

You will not be allowed to go back to a previous question. This is because the answer you give helps the computer determine the difficulty level of your next question.

There are 20 to 25 questions in the Structure section of the computer test. You have 15 to 20 minutes to complete this section.

QUESTION TYPES ON THE COMPUTER TEST

There are two types of questions in this section. The two question types will be mixed up randomly. You must be able to quickly recognize the two different types because they ask you to do different things.

Question Type 1 – Complete the Sentence

In the first type of question, you will see a sentence with a blank space where part of the sentence is missing. Beneath each sentence, there are four words or phrases. You must choose the one word or phrase that best completes the sentence. In other words, you are looking for the *correct* answer.

For question type 1, the computer screen will look like this:

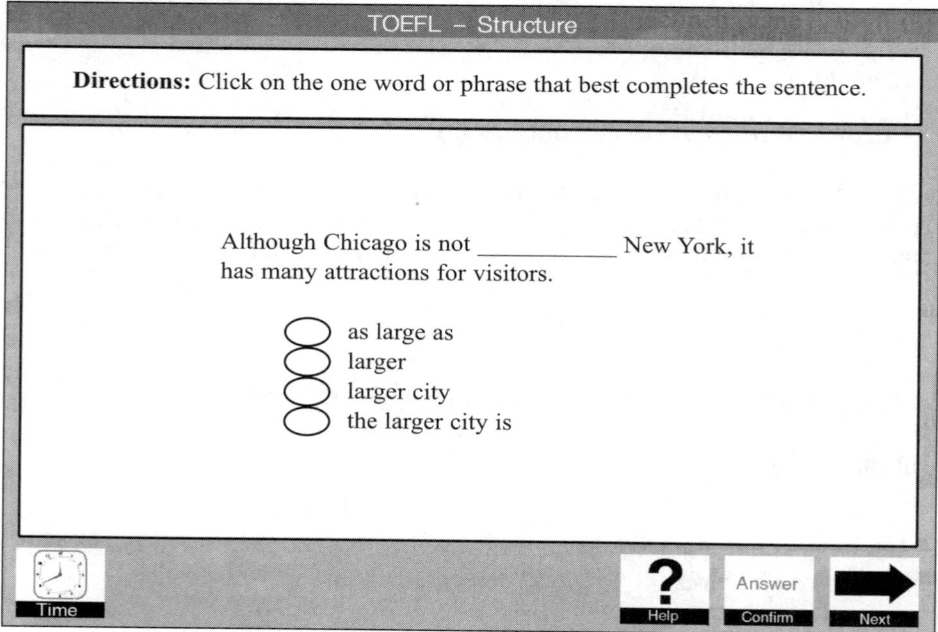

The sentence should read, *Although Chicago is not as large as New York, it has many attractions for visitors*. Therefore, you should click on the oval next to *as large as*, the first answer choice.

When you click on the oval next to one of the answer choices, the oval will darken. To change your answer, click on a different oval.

When you are satisfied that you have chosen the right answer, click on **Next**. Then click on **Confirm Answer**. When you do this, the computer will present the next question.

Question Type 2 – Identify the Error

In the second type of question, you will see a sentence with four underlined words or phrases. You must choose the one underlined word or phrase that must be changed for the sentence to be correct. In other words, you are looking for the part of the sentence that is *incorrect*.

For question type 2, the computer screen will look like this:

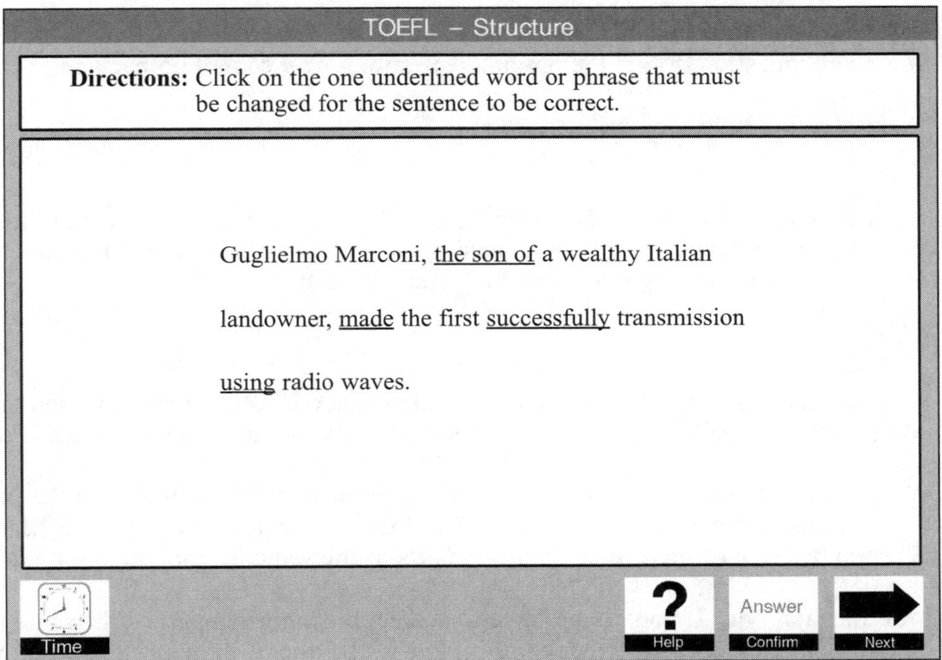

The sentence should read, *Guglielmo Marconi, the son of a wealthy Italian landowner, made the first successful transmission using radio waves*. Therefore, you should click on the word *successfully*.

When you click on one of the underlined answer choices, that word or phrase will darken. To change your answer, click on a different word or phrase.

When you are satisfied that you have chosen the right answer, click on **Next**. Then click on **Confirm Answer**. When you do this, the computer will present the next question.

 STRATEGIES FOR THE STRUCTURE SECTION

Pace Yourself

- Pay attention to the number of questions and the amount of time you have during the test. You have approximately 40 seconds to spend on each question, on both the paper test and the computer test. Use your time wisely. Do not spend too much time on a single question. When you take the quizzes in this book, time yourself. This will give you a good idea of how to pace yourself during the test.

- On the computer test, you must answer each question in this section before you can move on to the next question. You cannot skip questions. If you are not sure of the answer, eliminate the choices that you know are incorrect. Then, guess! Confirm your answer only when you are certain you are ready to move on to the next question.

Concentrate

- Think only of the question you are currently working on. On the computer test, once you have moved on to the next question, forget the previous questions. You cannot go back and change them.

Follow Directions

- Make sure you understand exactly what you are being asked to do. Are you choosing the *correct* answer to complete the sentence, or are you choosing the one word or phrase that is *incorrect*? Remember to change tactics for the two different types of questions.

Identify the Problem

- For question type 1, ask yourself, "What does this sentence need?" Read the whole sentence carefully and thoroughly. Read all of the answer choices. Only *one* of the choices is correct.

- For question type 2, ask yourself, "What is wrong with this sentence?" Only *one* of the underlined parts is incorrect. Look at the rest of the sentence for clues to help you find the error. Many of the errors are incorrect because of their relationship to parts of the sentence that are not underlined.

- Remember, for question type 2, you do not have to correct the incorrect part of the sentence! You only have to identify it. The incorrect part will always be one of the four underlined words or phrases.

- Try to identify the grammar point being tested in each question. Look for subjects and verbs in each clause of the sentence. Look for agreement among the various parts of the sentence. Notice any incorrect word forms.

Know the Tricks

- Be familiar with the various ways the TOEFL items try to trick you. This book gives you practice in noticing some of the common tricks in the Structure section of the TOEFL.

GRAMMAR CATEGORIES ON THE TEST

On the paper test, the content of the 40 questions in the Structure section is distributed over several grammar categories, as shown below. The computer test covers the same content; however, since there are fewer items on the computer test, the number for each category will be slightly lower.

CATEGORY	APPROXIMATE NUMBER
Subjects and Objects	1–2
Appositives	1
Plurals	1–2
Articles	1–2
Verbs and Auxiliaries	2+
Passives	1–2
Infinitives and Gerunds	2
Main and Subordinate Clauses	1
Noun Clauses	1
Adjective Clauses and Phrases	1–2
Adverb Clauses and Phrases	1
Conditionals	1
Inverted Subjects and Verbs	1
Subject–Verb Agreement	2
Pronoun Agreement	2
Adjective Word Order	1
Participial Adjectives	1
Negative Modifiers	1
Equatives, Comparatives, Superlatives	2
Conjunctions	1
Prepositions	2+
Word Form	2+
Word Choice	1–2
Redundancy	0–1
Parallel Structure	2+

OVERVIEW OF THIS SECTION

2.1 Checking Subjects and Objects

FOCUS

Consider the following TOEFL item:

> ------- sprang from the dissatisfaction of a handful of great performing artists.
>
> ◯ Why the Arts Theater Movement
> ◯ That the Arts Theater Movement
> ◯ The Arts Theater Movement which
> ◯ The Arts Theater Movement

What does this sentence need? Choose the answer that best completes the sentence.

Every sentence must have a ***subject***. A subject is a noun, pronoun, or other structure used as a noun. The subject is the person, object, or idea being discussed. The above sentence needs a subject for the verb *sprang*.

The fourth choice, *The Arts Theater Movement*, is a noun phrase that could be the subject of the sentence. Therefore, it is the correct answer.

Now, read another TOEFL item. What does this sentence need?

> A cataract blocks the passage of light to the retina, the tissue at the back of the eye that transmits ------- to the brain.
>
> ◯ visual
> ◯ visual impulses
> ◯ visual impulse
> ◯ an impulse visual

This sentence needs a direct object for the verb *transmits*. A ***direct object*** is a noun, pronoun, or other noun structure. The direct object receives the action of the verb.

The second choice, *visual impulses*, could be the object of *transmits*. Therefore, it is the correct answer.

Why are the other three answer choices incorrect?

DO YOU KNOW...?

1. Approximately one or two items on the TOEFL will test your ability to recognize where subjects and objects are needed in sentences. You must be able to identify both correct and incorrect noun structures used as subjects and objects.

2. Noun structures that will be tested include:

Noun:

Except during rush–hour periods, commuter trains seldom run at full capacity.

Noun Phrase:

Silicon Valley provides a good example of the expanding electronics industry and its importance.

Pronoun:

When a liquid turns to vapor, it loses heat and gets colder.

Subject of a Sentence:

In a short and simple musical instrument, such as the recorder, the fingers can cover all the holes directly.

Subject of a Subordinate Clause:

An ionizing smoke detector contains a chamber in which a low electric current flows through the air.

Subject Complement:

Andrew Jackson was the first president who was from the western frontier.

Passive Subject:

The global temperature balance is maintained by the movement of maritime air.

Direct Object:

Chemical reactions often involve the production or consumption of heat.

Indirect Object:

The art critic Lawrence Alloway, who said Pop was the culture of the mass media, gave us the term "Pop Art" in the 1950s.

Object Complement:

In 1782 King George III appointed William Pitt prime minister of Great Britain.

Object of a Preposition:

The General Assembly of the newly–formed United Nations first met in London in 1946, but later assemblies met at the permanent headquarters in New York City.

Other types of noun structures will be reviewed later in this book, including:

Infinitive (2.7):

Social animals, all North American canids tend to travel in packs.

Gerund (2.7):

Pressing the "play" button brings the playback head and drive mechanism into contact with the tape.

Noun Clause (2.9):

Cognitive psychologists are concerned with how people learn.

Noun Word Form (2.22):

Sometimes in childhood there seems to be a war between reality and imagination.

3. On the TOEFL, some of the answer choices will try to trick you by substituting some other type of structure where a noun structure is needed. Look at this example:

------- of the water withdrawn by industry is used for cooling.

- ◯ In ninety percent
- ◯ Ninety percent is
- ◯ Ninety percent
- ◯ That ninety percent

The first and second choices try to trick you by substituting a prepositional phrase (See 2.21) and a subject + verb structure (See 2.8) where a noun structure is needed. The fourth choice has the subordinating word *That*, which would make the sentence incomplete (See 2.9). The third choice, *Ninety percent*, best completes the sentence.

4. A test item may try to trick you by having a duplicate subject. Look at this example:

The octopus, a bottom–dwelling animal, it makes its home in a hole or rock crevice in shallow water.

Which underlined word must be changed for the sentence to be correct? If you chose *it*, you were correct. The subject of this sentence is *the octopus*. *It* is an incorrect duplicate subject. All of the other underlined words are correct and do not need to be changed.

By the way, the noun phrase *a bottom–dwelling animal* is an appositive (See 2.2), which gives you more information about the subject, *the octopus*. Don't let an appositive distract you from recognizing the subject of the sentence.

5. A test item may try to trick you with a distracting introductory phrase or clause. Look at this example:

> No matter how multicolored prints or slides may appear, ------- are made of only the three secondary colors arranged in layers.
>
> ◯ they
> ◯ and they
> ◯ so that they
> ◯ provided that they

What does this sentence need? If you chose the pronoun *they*, you were correct. *They* is the passive subject of the verb *are made*. (You will review passives in 2.6.) The important thing to know is that the sentence needs a subject. Don't let introductory phrases or clauses distract you.

Why are the other three answer choices incorrect?

6. A test item may try to trick you by having the "false" subject *it* or *there*. Look at this example:

> It is usually ------- in a middle school classroom who demand more attention from the teacher.
>
> ◯ the boys are
> ◯ for the boys
> ◯ the boys
> ◯ the boys whose

It is the "false" subject. What is the true subject? The subject must be a noun structure. Which of the answer choices is a noun?

The third choice, *the boys*, is the true subject of the sentence—this is the only choice that is a noun structure. You can check this by rewriting the sentence without *it* and *who*: *Usually, the boys in a middle school classroom demand more attention from the teacher*.

How do the other answer choices try to confuse you?

Look at another example:

> While it is difficult for some people to change unhealthy habits, there are ------- for exercising frequently and eating fewer fatty foods.
>
> ◯ an excellent reason
> ◯ excellent reasons
> ◯ excellent to reason
> ◯ much excellent reasons

There is the "false" subject of this sentence. What is the true subject? If you chose *excellent reasons*, you were correct. When *there* is the false subject, you can rewrite the sentence by using the verb *exist*. You can rewrite part of the above sentence like this: *Excellent reasons exist for exercising frequently and eating fewer fatty foods*.

Why are the other three answer choices incorrect?

PRACTICE

Exercise 2.1.A

Choose the one word or phrase that best completes the sentence.

1. In order to sustain a snowfall, there must be ------- to feed the growing ice crystals.

   (A) a constant inflow of moisture is
   (B) of a constant inflow of moisture
   (C) a constant inflow of moisture
   (D) moisture constantly flowed in

2. ------- who prides herself on her athletic ability may face an adjustment by the time she enters high school.

   (A) An elementary school girl
   (B) Why an elementary school girl
   (C) Elementary school girls
   (D) Because the elementary school girl

3. When a husband and wife decide to buy a specific house, ------- make an offer to the seller.

   (A) to
   (B) then
   (C) should they
   (D) they

4. People often overlook ------- of ice cream.

   (A) valuable nutrition
   (B) that is the nutritional value
   (C) the nutritional value
   (D) a nutritional value

5. It was ------- during the Civil War that inspired President Lincoln to issue the Emancipation Proclamation in 1863.

   (A) when a series of Union defeats
   (B) because a series of Union defeats
   (C) a series of Union defeats
   (D) the Union was defeated

6. The Isthmus of Panama, colonized by the Spanish in the early 1500s, became ------- of Spanish America with the conquest of the Incan empire by Francisco Pizzaro.

   (A) crossroad was
   (B) the crossroad
   (C) for the crossroad
   (D) its crossroad

7. Active mainly in the early morning and late afternoon, ------- often sleeps in a hole rooted in the earth or takes shelter in a cave.

   (A) the peccary
   (B) as the peccary
   (C) so that the peccary
   (D) and the peccary

8. In 1860 voters elected a candidate of the anti–slavery Republican Party ------- of the United States.

   (A) to the president
   (B) was the president
   (C) whom the president
   (D) president

STRUCTURE

Choose the one underlined word or phrase that must be changed for the sentence to be correct.

9. In 1841 America's best–known novelist (A), James Fenimore Cooper, he (B) published (C) *The Deerslayer*, the last and most (D) idyllic of the five "Leatherstocking Tales."

10. That (A) the diesel engine is similar to the (B) gasoline engine, but it (C) runs on a heavier grade of fuel (D).

Answers to Exercise 2.1.A are on page 637.

2.1 EXTENSION

1. Working in pairs, students explain why the three incorrect answer choices in Exercise 2.1.A are not acceptable. In what ways are the test items tricky?

2. In reading done outside class, students look for examples of sentences with various noun structures. Bring examples of sentences to share in class.

3. Students create "TOEFL sentences" to test their classmates' understanding of nouns. Students write their own sentences, or change sentences they find in print, so that each sentence substitutes some other type of structure where a noun structure is needed. Write the sentences either on the board or on cards. Classmates identify the error and make the correction.

2.2 Recognizing Appositives

Read the following sentences:

> A proven man–eater, the tiger shark is one of the most feared sharks in the world.
>
> Innumerable images of the bodhisattvas, the Buddha's early incarnations, have appeared in Indian art throughout the centuries.
>
> The first pictures of the moon's far side were taken by Russia's Luna 3, the first successful space probe.

What is similar about the sentences?

Each of the sentences contains an ***appositive***. An appositive is a noun or noun phrase that is placed just before or just after another noun structure. An appositive renames, defines, explains, or gives important information about the other noun structure. Sometimes an appositive is called a ***noun in apposition*** because its position is near another noun.

In the first sentence above, the appositive *A proven man–eater* gives important information about the *tiger shark*, the subject of the sentence. In the second sentence, the appositive *the Buddha's early incarnations* defines the noun *bodhisattvas*. In the third sentence, the appositive *the first successful space probe* explains *Russia's Luna 3*.

Notice that commas are a clue that can help you recognize appositives.

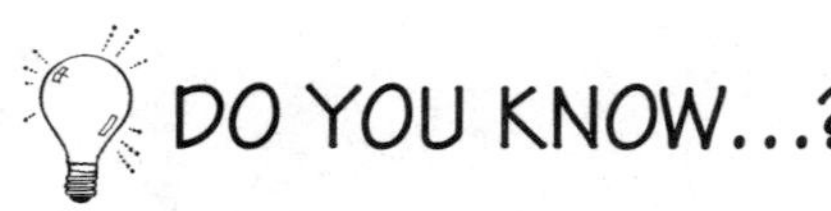

1. Approximately one item on the TOEFL will test your understanding of appositives and the noun structures they rename, define, or explain.

2. Appositives are noun structures. They are placed near the nouns they rename and are separated from the rest of the sentence by commas.

   To check if a noun is an appositive, try adding *who is/are* or *which is/are* before the noun (See 2.10).

   In the following sentence, *a cone–shaped organ* is an appositive because you can add *which is* before it.

   > The heart, a cone–shaped organ, pumps blood throughout the body.
   > The heart, which is a cone–shaped organ, pumps blood throughout the body.

   In the following sentence, *blue* is not an appositive because you cannot add *which is* and still make sense.

   > The color blue is rare in food.
   > The color which is blue is rare in food. *(Incorrect)*

   Can you identify the appositives in the following sentences? Underline the appositives and circle the nouns they rename.

   a. The sermons of Jonathan Edwards, an American–born preacher, sparked a religious movement known as the Great Awakening.
   b. To increase profits, supermarket chains are using two main strategies, both of which involve building bigger stores—super supermarkets.

   (***Answers:*** In (a) *an American–born preacher* is an appositive; it renames *Jonathan Edwards*. In (b) there are two appositives. *Both of which involve building bigger stores* is an appositive that gives information about *two main strategies*. *Super supermarkets* is an appositive that renames *bigger stores*. Here, a dash (—) helps you recognize the appositive.)

3. Not all commas indicate an appositive. In which of the following sentences do the commas indicate an appositive? Underline the appositives and circle the nouns they rename.

   a. Elephants eat a wide variety of grasses, foliage, and fruits.
   b. Young bulls, male elephants, are driven from the family when they reach puberty.
   c. An organ for breathing and smelling, the trunk is also an extra limb for picking up objects.
   d. After bathing, elephants coat their skin with dust for protection against insects.

   (***Answers:*** Only (b) and (c) contain appositives. In (b) *male elephants* is an appositive that renames *bulls*. In (c) *An organ for breathing and smelling* is an appositive that defines *trunk*.)

4. On the TOEFL, some of the answer choices will try to trick you by substituting some other type of structure where a noun structure is needed in an appositive. Look at this example:

> Without engineers, ------- of the world, modern technology would collapse.
>
> ○ they are the problem solvers
> ○ for the problem solvers
> ○ their problem solvers
> ○ the problem solvers

The commas after *engineers* and after *world* are clues that an appositive is needed. The first answer choice substitutes a clause. The second choice is a prepositional phrase. In the third choice, the possessive *their* does not make sense in this context.

The fourth choice, *the problem solvers*, is a noun phrase that best completes the sentence. The appositive *the problem solvers of the world* renames the noun *engineers*.

In the above example, *engineers* is the object of a preposition. What is the subject of the sentence?

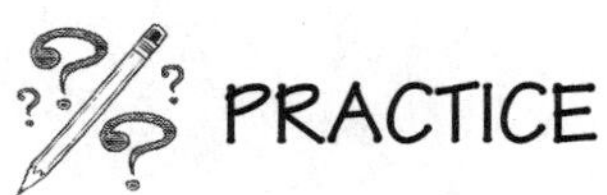

PRACTICE

Exercise 2.2.A

Choose the one word or phrase that best completes the sentence.

1. Between 3,000 and 2,000 B.C., the Egyptians started using papyrus, ------- which they dried into strips and then glued together in two layers to form a sheet.

   (A) a type of grass
   (B) it was a type of grass
   (C) as if a type of grass
   (D) of a grass type

2. -------, Edgar Allan Poe became known as the father of the modern detective story.

   (A) The son of actors was
   (B) He was the son of actors
   (C) The son of actors
   (D) Acted as the son of

3. In Asia's great central land mass, -------, the Mongols, had been pressing eastward into northern China for many years.

   (A) whose a vast group of horse–mounted nomads
   (B) a vast group of horse–mounted nomads were called
   (C) a vast group of horse–mounted nomads
   (D) they were a vast group of horse–mounted nomads

4. Barbara Tuchman, -------, won the Pulitzer Prize for general nonfiction in 1963 and 1972.

   (A) she was an American historian
   (B) an American historian who
   (C) an American historian
   (D) was an American historian

5. Persons who have taken a cold remedy containing -------, a narcotic, may feel drowsy and should not operate machinery or drive a vehicle.

   (A) codeine
   (B) the codeine
   (C) codeine is one type of
   (D) is codeine

6. African–American dance, ------- blend of elements derived from diverse traditions, has been attracting ever wider attention on the professional dance scene.

   (A) to
   (B) it's a
   (C) which a
   (D) a

7. -------, all with true horns, includes bison, mountain goats, and bighorn sheep.

   (A) It is the family of bovids
   (B) In the family of bovids
   (C) The family of bovids are
   (D) The family of bovids

8. Ichthyology, ------- of zoology dealing with fishes, has made important discoveries about the effects of pollution on the world's fish resources.

   (A) there is a branch
   (B) is branching
   (C) which a branch
   (D) a branch

9. The first airship to rise into the sky was a steam–powered machine invented by Henri Giffard, -------.

   (A) he was a French engineer
   (B) a French engineer
   (C) by a French engineer
   (D) whose a French engineer

10. The value placed on the pelt of the marten, ------- mammal of Canada, has led to its near extinction in many areas.

   (A) whom a
   (B) that is a
   (C) a
   (D) as a

Answers to Exercise 2.2.A are on page 637.

2.2 EXTENSION

1. For each sentence in Exercise 2.2.A, students underline the appositive and circle the noun that it renames. Identify the type of noun structure for each appositive and renamed noun. Use the list of noun structures on page 144.

2. In reading done outside class, students look for examples of appositives. Bring examples to share in class. Identify the nouns that are renamed, defined, or explained by the appositives.

3. Working in pairs, students write sentences about people or objects in the classroom. Add appositives to rename, define, explain, or provide information about the people or objects. Use commas correctly! **Example:** *Ali, a businessman from Kuwait, is sitting next to Solomon, an engineering student from Ethiopia.* Write the sentences on the board. Classmates must identify the appositives.

2.3 Checking Plurals

FOCUS

What is wrong with this sentence?

> Soybeans are a valuable subsistence crops, and the meal is used as a source of protein for humans and animals.

Soybeans are one type of crop. The singular article *a* in *a valuable subsistence crops* tells you that *crops* is incorrect because it is plural. It should be changed to its singular form, *crop*. (You will review articles in 2.4.)

What is wrong with this sentence?

> At eleven to fourteen inches, the pygmy rabbit is the smallest of the North American member of the leporidae family.

The pygmy rabbit is the smallest one of the many members of the leporidae family. *Member* is a countable noun, and this context requires its plural form, *members*.

What is wrong with this sentence?

> Most airlines allow no more than two carry–on luggages for each passenger.

You cannot have *two carry–on luggages*. *Luggage* is a noun that does not have a plural form. You can, however, have two *pieces of carry–on luggage*.

What is wrong with this sentence?

> When Rip Van Winkle came out of the forest after sleeping for twenty years, many news awaited him in his native village.

Rip could hear *much news* or *a lot of news*, but he could not hear *many news*. Why? *News*, although it looks like a plural, is an uncountable noun that does not have a plural form.

All of the above examples are similar to the types of sentences you will see on the TOEFL.

DO YOU KNOW...?

1. Approximately one or two items on the TOEFL will test your ability to check singular and plural forms of nouns. You must be able to identify correct and incorrect usage of singular and plural forms.

2. ***Countable nouns*** refer to people or things that can be counted. Countable nouns have ***singular*** forms for one person or thing. They have ***plural*** forms for two or more persons or things. Plural forms usually have the *–s/–es* word ending.

   Uncountable nouns are nouns that cannot be counted. Uncountable nouns refer to activities, ideas, qualities, or substances. Uncountable nouns are considered to be *wholes* that are made up of parts.

   Uncountable nouns usually do not have plural forms. You cannot have *several researches*. Why? Research is an activity. You cannot count research. However, you can have *several research studies* or *several research reports*. Why? You can count studies and reports.

   Sometimes countable nouns are called ***count nouns***. Sometimes uncountable nouns are called ***noncount nouns***.

COMMON UNCOUNTABLE NOUNS			
advice	importance	mail	scenery
baggage	information	money	soap
cash	jewelry	music	snow
clothing	knowledge	news	traffic
damage	laughter	peace	violence
equipment	leisure	rain	water
furniture	luggage	recognition	wind
homework	machinery	research	work

   Sometimes you can express an uncountable noun in the singular by preceding it with a countable noun + *of*:

an article of clothing	a piece of information	an act of violence

   Sometimes there are other ways to express uncountable nouns in the singular:

a news story	a raindrop	a homework assignment

   The countable nouns in these expressions can be pluralized, but the uncountable nouns can not be pluralized:

four articles of clothing	two pieces of information	several news stories

3. Countable and uncountable nouns are used with different expressions for showing quantity. Look at some examples:

EXPRESSIONS OF QUANTITY

COUNTABLE NOUNS	UNCOUNTABLE NOUNS
a/an, one, two, three...	—
another	—
few	little
a few	a little
fewer	less
a/the number of	amount of
many	much
several	—
a lot of	a lot of
some	some
any	any
no	no
each	—
every	—
all	all
other	other

A TOEFL item may try to trick you by using an incorrect expression of quantity. Look at this example:

> College enrollment figures for the past fifteen years show that less students are now choosing to major in fields such as sociology and history.

Which underlined word or phrase must be changed for the sentence to be correct? If you chose *less students*, you were correct. Since you can count students, you must use the correct expression of quantity: *fewer students*.

4. Other structures that may be tested include:

type of	kind of	one of	the --- of the

Countable nouns:

The hosta is a type of flowering plant that thrives in the shade.
Mark Twain said there are three kinds of lies: lies, damned lies, and statistics.
John Dewey is regarded as one of the twentieth century's great thinkers.
The Siberian tiger is the fiercest of the world's big cats.

Uncountable nouns:

Currency is a type of money that bears no interest.
A giggle and a chuckle are two kinds of laughter that mean quite different things.

5. Some TOEFL items contain numbers used as nouns or adjectives. When numbers are used as nouns, they can be plural, taking the *–s/–es* ending. In general, adjectives do not have plural forms. When numbers are adjectives, they do not take the *–s/–es* ending.

Look at some examples of correct and incorrect plurals in phrases involving numbers:

CORRECT You can have…	**INCORRECT** but you can't have…
NOUNS	
hundreds of examples	hundred of examples, hundreds of example
ADJECTIVES	
three feet	three foot
an eight–foot–long tail	an eight–feet–long tail
ten thousand people	ten thousands people
two million years ago	two millions years ago, two millions year ago
fifty percent of the inhabitants	fifty percents of the inhabitants
a fifty–percent decrease	a fifty–percents decrease, a fifties–percent decrease

Note: When a number is used with *percent*, such as in *fifty percent* or *one hundred percent*, *percent* takes the singular form.

A TOEFL item may test you by having an incorrect singular or plural form in a phrase involving numbers. Look at this example:

> Generally, twelve–years–old girls are taller and heavier than boys of that age.

Which underlined word or phrase must be changed for the sentence to be correct? If you chose *twelve–years–old*, you were correct because it is an adjective modifying *girls*. Adjectives do not have plural forms. Correction: *twelve–year–old girls*.

Note: The following are correct:

The girls are twelve years old.
They are twelve–year–old girls.

Look at another example:

> With a wing span of almost nine foot, the majestic California condor is the largest of the western birds of prey.

Which underlined word or phrase must be changed for the sentence to be correct? If you chose *almost nine foot*, you were correct because *foot* is a noun in this context. The noun *foot* has an irregular plural. Correction: *almost nine feet*.

PRACTICE

Exercise 2.3.A

Choose the one underlined word or phrase that must be changed for the sentence to be correct.

1. Research has shown that in North American society, less boys than girls are socialized to
   A B
   seek jobs in which they can help others, such as nursing.
   C D

2. A four–years–old child has difficulty focusing his eyes on small objects; therefore, his eye–hand
   A B C
   coordination may be imperfect.
   D

3. Much of the tropical storms and hurricanes are likely to occur in the late summer along the Atlantic
   A B C
   and Gulf of Mexico coasts.
   D

4. In the 1940s, Langston Hughes published the first of the satirical "Simple" story that later
   A B C
   were collected in five volumes.
   D

5. Every year, tornadoes cause a lot of damages to property and a tremendous loss of human and
   A B C
   animal life.
   D

6. The Miocene Period, lasting from 25 to 11 millions years ago, saw the further elaboration of
   A B
   mammals and the development of the anthropoid ape.
   C D

Choose the one word or phrase that best completes the sentence.

7. Florida, always a popular tourist destination, is well–known for its abundance of -------.

   (A) beautiful sceneries
   (B) beautifuls scenery
   (C) sceneries of beautiful
   (D) beautiful scenery

8. In 1872 Chicago merchant Montgomery Ward began sending copies of a 280–page catalog to ------- in the Midwest.

   (A) thousand farmers
   (B) a thousand of farmers
   (C) thousands of farmers
   (D) thousands of farmer

Exercise 2.3.B

Choose the one underlined word or phrase that must be changed for the sentence to be correct.

1. Dandelion wine is another kinds of beverage that is becoming increasingly popular among home
A B
wine makers, especially those in the West.
C D

2. The largest of the terrestrial carnivore, bears have massive, densely–furred bodies, moderate–sized
A B
heads with small ears, close–set eyes, and tiny tails.
C D

3. Counselors will be available to give students advices before they register for classes.
A B C D

4. The addition of a bicycle lane along five miles of the freeway has resulted in fewer bicycle traffic
A B C
on the two main routes through town.
D

5. Psychologist Erik Erikson defined the terms "generativity" as the concern for establishing and
A B
guiding the next generation.
C D

6. Between five and six thousands year ago, men developed the first writing and began to work
A B C
in metal—first in copper, then in bronze.
D

7. Each furniture on display in the central mall is on sale for thirty percent off the regular price.
A B C D

8. The Alien Land Law of 1920, one of several discriminatory acts of the period, reduced the number
A B
of Japanese American in agriculture.
C D

9. In the 1800s there were about 1,000 million people on the earth, and until recently there was
A B C
few increase in world population.
D

10. Potatoes require a temperate climate with a regular and plentiful supplies of rain.
A B C D

Answers to Exercises 2.3.A through 2.3.B are on page 638.

2.3 EXTENSION

1. Card game for groups of 2 to 5. Teachers or students prepare two sets of cards. On each card of the first set, write an expression of quantity from the list on page 155 or an expression such as *an item of* or *a bit of*. On each card of the second set, write a countable or uncountable noun. Combine the sets and mix up the cards. Divide the class into several teams. Deal the cards so that each team has the same number of cards (at least 8 per team). The object is to see how quickly teams can match all of their cards into correct pairs. If a team has a surplus of one type of card, it can trade with another team. The first team to correctly pair all of their cards wins the game.

2. Students create "TOEFL sentences" to test their classmates' understanding of numbers used as nouns and adjectives. Students write their own sentences, or change sentences they find in print, so that a number has an incorrect singular or plural form. Write the sentences either on the board or on cards. Classmates identify the error and make the correction.

3. Discuss rare exceptions to the rule that uncountable nouns do not have plural forms. For example: *foods from around the world*, *paying for damages*, *doing good works*.

2.4 Checking Articles

FOCUS

What is wrong with this sentence?

> A hailstorm is product of the updrafts and downdrafts that develop inside the clouds of a thunderstorm.

The singular countable noun *product* needs an article. Either *a product* or *the product* could be correct in this sentence.

What is wrong with this sentence?

> The Altamira cave paintings show several animals and some figures of men in the act of the hunting.

The article *the* in *the hunting* is unnecessary. *Hunting* is a gerund (verb + *–ing* used as a noun), and gerunds generally do not take an article. (You will review gerunds in 2.7.)

What is wrong with this sentence?

> A flat mirror reflects the light rays which strike it so that the rays leave the surface of the mirror at exactly a same angle that they meet it.

This sentence has a lot of nouns and articles. Are they all correct?

Most of the nouns—*the light rays, the surface, the mirror*—are definite. This means they are specific and known to you, the reader. The indefinite article *a* in *a same angle* is incorrect. The noun phrase *same angle* is made specific by its use in the sentence. The light rays meet the surface of the mirror at an angle—some angle, any angle—which then becomes specific—*the angle*. The phrase should be changed to *the same angle*.

All of the above examples are similar to the types of sentences you will see on the TOEFL.

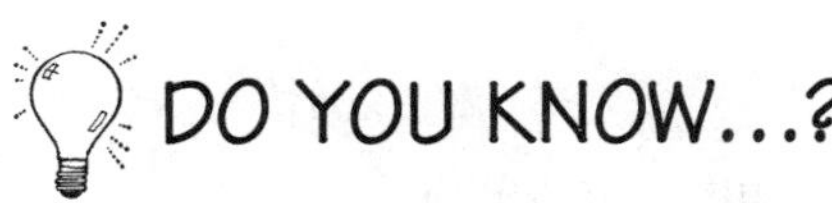

DO YOU KNOW...?

1. Approximately one or two items on the TOEFL will test your ability to recognize correct and incorrect usage of articles.

2. Article usage depends on whether a noun is:

   - indefinite or definite
   - singular or plural
   - countable or uncountable

3. The ***indefinite articles*** *a* and *an* are used with indefinite nouns. An ***indefinite noun*** refers to a thing that is not specifically identified. An indefinite noun is unknown either to you, the reader, or to the writer of the text. An indefinite noun is general rather than specific.

   A and *an* mean *one*. Use *a/an* only with singular countable nouns. Never use *a/an* with plural nouns. Never use *a/an* with uncountable nouns.

   Singular countable nouns:

   When an object moves in a circle, it is always changing direction.
   Leaves can be an important aid to identifying a wildflower.

   Nouns that represent a whole class or type of things:

   The chill of an ice storm can be felt inside as well as outside.
   An ophthalmologist is a doctor who specializes in the structure and diseases of the eye.

   ***A* or *An*?**

   Use *a* before a consonant sound. Use *an* before a vowel sound:

a hurricane	an American	an oil derrick
a wild animal	an invention	an uprising
a year ago	an economics professor	an unusual request

   Some words are spelled with a vowel but are pronounced with a consonant sound:

a European	a university	a useful example
a eulogy	a uniform	a utility vehicle

   Some words are spelled with a consonant but are pronounced with a vowel sound:

an honor	an heir	an hourly wage

4. The ***definite article***, *the*, is used with definite nouns. A ***definite noun*** refers to a thing that is known to you, the reader. A definite noun can be made known by being mentioned in the sentence. A definite noun is specific rather than general.

   Use *the* with singular and plural countable nouns and with uncountable nouns.

STRUCTURE

Singular countable nouns:

The gearbox of a gasoline engine lies between the clutch and the differential.

Plural countable nouns:

The crankshaft always turns faster than the wheels.
The different ratios of teeth on the gears produce different speeds.

Uncountable nouns:

It was four o'clock before the police received the information about the suspect.
Good teachers care about the progress made by their students.

Note: A noun may be indefinite the first time it is mentioned and later become definite. After a noun is mentioned, it is then specific and known to the reader. Look at this example:

The size of a perennial border can vary, but if the garden setting is large, the border should also be large.

In the above sentence, *a perennial border* is changed to *the border* because it becomes known.

Use *the* with other nouns and structures:

Specific species of animals and plants:

Despite its tiny size, the hummingbird migrates great distances every year.
The desert cactus has the most slender stems of all southwestern chollas.

Inventions, instruments, models, and types of buildings:

The elevator was invented just in time to lend itself to the new architecture of the urban–industrial age, the skyscraper.
The mandolin has been used widely by composers in many genres.

Superlatives and *one of*:

The great gray owl is the largest owl in North America.
A ripe apricot is one of the most pleasurable rewards from an orchard.

The only one of something:

Infrared photographs show variations in surface temperature across the moon.
Poet Lucy Larcom was the seventh daughter of ten children in a seafaring family.

Body parts:

Asthma attacks cause the airways of the lungs to constrict and the linings of the windpipe to swell.

Names of large bodies of water, regions, and groups of mountains, islands, and lakes:

the Arctic Ocean	the Panama Canal	the Ural Mountains
the Columbia River	the West	the Philippines
the Caribbean	the Pacific Rim	the Great Lakes

5. No article is used with some nouns. Look at some examples:

Plural countable nouns that are indefinite:

Capitol Reef National Park is a rock wilderness of massive domes, cliffs, and canyons.
In headlights and flashlights, a concave mirror is located behind the light bulb.

Generalizations about uncountable nouns:

Land, labor, and capital are essential for the production of goods.
Economics is the study of money, interest rates, capital, and wealth.

Gerund (verb + *ing*):

Copper mining is one of Chile's largest industries.

Note: Gerunds are usually uncountable and indefinite, with a notable exception. A gerund + *of* structure is made specific and therefore takes the definite article *the*:

The mining of copper accounts for nearly 40% of Chile's export revenues.

No article is used when a noun has a possessive or a demonstrative (*this*, *that*, *these*, *those*):

Abraham Lincoln delivered his famous Gettysburg address at the dedication of a cemetery.
Many engineers obtain master's degrees, which is desirable for promotion in this field.

6. A TOEFL item may test you by having:

- no article where one is needed
- an article where one is not needed
- an incorrect article

If you think that a TOEFL question is testing your understanding of articles, check all of the answer choices to see if the noun structures have the correct articles where they are needed.

7. A TOEFL item may try to trick you by having no article where one is needed. Look at this example:

> After it was introduced in the Middle East around 3,500 B.C., plow freed some people from the necessity of growing their food.

Which underlined word or phrase must be changed for the sentence to be correct? If you chose *plow*, you were correct because it is an invention, which takes the definite article. Correction: *the plow.*

Look at another example:

> Edgar Varese was ------- major composers to embrace the possibilities of electronic music.
>
> ◯ first
> ◯ a first
> ◯ one of the first
> ◯ one of first

STRUCTURE

What does this sentence need? The subject, *Edgar Varese*, needs a complement after the verb *was*. The first answer choice is incorrect because *first* is the only one of something and therefore needs the definite article. The second choice, *a first*, is incorrect because *a* would not be used with the plural *composers*.

The answer is the third choice, *one of the first*, a *one of*–expression. Why is the fourth choice incorrect?

8. A TOEFL item may try to trick you by having an article where one is not needed. Look at this example:

> Individuals can now purchase technology for the home because an electronic equipment is becoming less expensive.

Which underlined word or phrase must be changed for the sentence to be correct? If you chose *an electronic equipment*, you were correct. *Equipment* is uncountable. Remember, never use *a/an* with an uncountable noun! Omit the article.

Look at another example:

> Identical twins have the identical bloodtypes, eye and skin colors, and fingerprints.

Which underlined word or phrase must be changed for the sentence to be correct? If you chose *the identical*, you were correct. This is a general statement about *identical twins* and *identical bloodtypes*. These nouns are plural, countable, and indefinite. Therefore, no article should be used before *identical bloodtypes*.

9. A TOEFL item may try to trick you by using an incorrect article. Look at this example:

> Although not every engineer has a outdoor job, there are combinations of indoor–outdoor jobs within many of the engineering fields.

Which underlined word or phrase must be changed for the sentence to be correct? If you chose *a outdoor job*, you were correct because *outdoor* begins with a vowel sound. Correction: *an outdoor job*.

PRACTICE

Exercise 2.4.A

Choose the one underlined word or phrase that must be changed for the sentence to be correct.

1. In analog recording, the recording medium (A) varies continuously in a way (B) that is similar to (C) or analogous to incoming signal (D).

2. Humanitarian idealism (A) mixed with the need for a workforce (B) to man expanding economy (C) made America an immigrant society (D) in the nineteenth century.

3. Many of greatest floods occur when excessive rains fall during winter storms over river basins that
A B C
are already saturated because of previous wet periods.
D

4. By the middle of the nineteenth century, Americans needed to forge a sense of the nationalism to
A B C
unify their growing country.
D

5. Issues surrounding the distribution of income are among most controversial in economics.
A B C D

6. Sometimes an English word is derived from an association with a place; for example, the kind of
A B C
the cheese we know as cheddar originated in Cheddar, England.
D

7. Over half of all mammal species are rodents, and the nearly three thousand species of rodents
A B C
form a largest mammalian order.
D

Choose the one word or phrase that best completes the sentence.

8. When the first gummed postage stamp was introduced, some Americans humorously called ------- stamp a "lick–and–stick."

(A) a such adhesive
(B) such a adhesive
(C) such adhesive
(D) such an adhesive

9. Louis Moreau Gottschalk, the first American–born composer of -------, made his reputation with a series of piano pieces based on folk music from Louisiana and the Caribbean.

(A) international importance
(B) the international importance
(C) an important international
(D) an international importance

10. Nimbus clouds generally have ------- and are amorphous in appearance.

(A) an uniform dark color
(B) a uniformly dark color
(C) uniformly the dark color
(D) uniform dark color

Answers to Exercise 2.4.A are on page 638.

2.4 EXTENSION

1. Students clip a short article (1–3 paragraphs) from a newspaper or magazine and bring it to class. Students underline all of the nouns in the text and then exchange papers with a classmate. Classmates circle all of the articles and identify whether the nouns are: (a) singular or plural, (b) countable or uncountable, and (c) definite or indefinite. Discuss why some of the nouns have no articles.

2. Students create "TOEFL sentences" to test their classmates' understanding of articles. Students write their own sentences, or change sentences they find in print, so that each sentence has an article error. Write the sentences either on the board or on cards. Classmates identify the error and make the correction.

ASSESSING PROGRESS – 2.1 through 2.4

QUIZ 1 *(Time – 10 minutes)*

STRUCTURE

Choose the one underlined word or phrase that must be changed for the sentence to be correct.

1. In a survey of suburban homeowners, a lawn mower was rated one of the most important and
   A B C
   necessary equipments.
   D

2. The desert pocket mouse, common in the American Southwest, it is active mainly at night.
   A B C D

3. Many of color images we see are not composed of all the colors we perceive but are made of
   A B C
   three primary colors mixed together.
   D

4. There are at least two prominent historians who believe that President Nixon's resignation was
   A B
   a result of a well–known eighteen–minutes gap in a tape recording.
   C D

Choose the one word or phrase that best completes the sentence.

5. Although sunlight appears white, ------- is actually a combination of all the colors of the spectrum.

   (A) that it
   (B) because it
   (C) it
   (D) he

6. In 1962 the American Telephone and Telegraph Company launched Telstar, ------- communications satellite to transmit telephone and television signals.

   (A) it was a first
   (B) that was the first
   (C) first it was a
   (D) the first

7. ------- in the Black Muslim religion until ousted in 1963, Malcolm X founded a rival church and was soon afterward shot to death.

   (A) Preached
   (B) He preached
   (C) He was a preacher
   (D) A preacher

Quiz 1

Choose the one underlined word or phrase that must be changed for the sentence to be correct.

8. As soon as (A) psychologists developed ways to measure human attributes (B), they discovered that most characteristics of the human beings (C) seem to be distributed in the form (D) of a bell–shaped curve.

9. There are two kinds of (A) magnetic disks (B): floppy disks, which are portable, and hard disks, which can store many (C) more information than (D) floppy disks.

10. There are life situations (A) that tend to cause a individual (B) to want to know how to make the best (C) nutritional decisions (D).

11. Many (A) historians would agree that there are a number of reason (B) for the American Civil War, but the two main causes (C) are the disagreement over states' rights and the conflict (D) over slavery.

12. The (A) fractional rig is preferred for all sizes of racing craft (B), from The Lightning all the way up to the highly (C) complex, fifty–feet–long (D) offshore racing dinghies.

Choose the one word or phrase that best completes the sentence.

13. -------, set in her native South, spring from her long familiarity with the thoughts and feelings of ordinary people.

(A) The stories of Eudora Welty are
(B) The stories of Eudora Welty
(C) In the stories of Eudora Welty
(D) Not only are the stories of Eudora Welty

14. Prejudice is a set of rigid and ------- toward a particular group that is formed in disregard of facts.

(A) an unfavorable attitude
(B) unfavorable attitudes
(C) attitudes unfavorable
(D) unfavorably attitude

15. Scott Joplin, -------, composed several works in the style known as "ragtime."

(A) an excellent piano player
(B) was an excellent piano player
(C) to play a piano
(D) the excellent piano player who

Answers to Structure Quiz 1 are on page 639.

2.5 Checking Verbs and Auxiliaries

FOCUS

Consider the following TOEFL item. What does this sentence need?

> The escallonia plant ------- popular because of the many varieties available.
>
> ◯ especially
> ◯ is especially
> ◯ especially it is
> ◯ being especially

Every sentence must have a subject and a verb. The above sentence has a subject, *the escallonia plant*, but it needs a verb.

The answer is the second choice. The sentence should read: *The escallonia plant is especially popular because of the many varieties available.*

Now, read another TOEFL item. What does this sentence need?

> When a vampire bat drinks the blood of farm animals, it ------- with the deadly rabies disease.
>
> ◯ their infection
> ◯ to infect them
> ◯ can infecting them
> ◯ can infect them

Every clause in a sentence must have a subject and a verb. The above sentence has two clauses. (You will review clauses in 2.8.) The main clause needs a verb for the subject *it*.

The fourth choice is a verb phrase that would be correct in this context; therefore, it is the answer. The main clause should read: *it can infect them with the deadly rabies disease.*

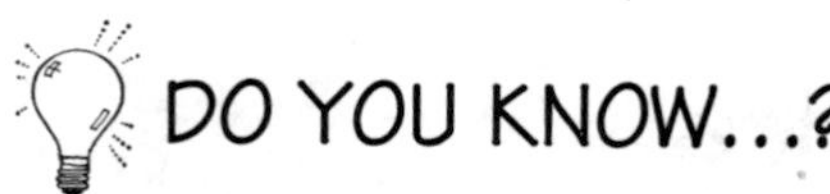

1. At least two items on the TOEFL will test your ability to recognize correct and incorrect usage of verbs, auxiliary verbs, modals, and verb phrases.

2. A ***verb*** shows action, possession, or state of being. It also may indicate the time of the action. What is the time—present, past, future—of the action or being in the following sentences?

   a. Lava Butte *formed* seven thousand years ago when gas–charged magmas *erupted*.
   b. There certainly *will be* more volcanic eruptions in central Oregon.

   (***Answers:*** a. past; b. future)

   An ***auxiliary verb*** accompanies another verb and "helps" the verb by expressing:

   - person: first, second, third
   - number: singular, plural
   - tense: present, past, future

   The most common auxiliary verbs are: *be*, *have*, *do*. What person, number, and tense are expressed by the auxiliaries in the following sentences?

   c. We *are* only beginning to be able to predict when earthquakes will occur.
   d. Central Oregon *has* experienced a large earthquake once every ten thousand years.
   e. Geologists *did* not fully understand where the magma came from.

   (***Answers:*** c. first person, plural, present; d. third person, singular, present; e. third person, plural, past)

   A ***modal*** is a special kind of auxiliary verb. A modal auxiliary expresses mood or attitude. A modal can express that an action is intended, certain, possible, probable, advisable, or necessary.

   Modals are always followed by the base form of a verb. The most common modals on the TOEFL are:

will would can could may might should must

   What mood does the writer express in the following sentences?

   f. Each cubic meter of rock *can* store the equivalent of one firecracker.
   g. The next eruption of South Sister *might* occur in the next thousand years.
   h. Every home *should* have an emergency kit in an accessible location.

   (***Answers:*** f. possibility; g. probability; h. advisability)

   A ***verb phrase*** is a group of words that always contains a verb. It may also include words that:

   - are closely related to the verb: auxiliaries, direct and indirect objects
   - modify the verb: adverbs, prepositional phrases

   In the following sentences, identify: verbs, auxiliaries, objects, adverbs, prepositional phrases:

   i. Changes in the caldera floor have presumably accompanied each eruption.
   j. The lava from Lava Butte dammed the Deschutes River in many places and permanently altered the river's course.

(***Answers:*** i. verb: *accompanied*; auxiliary: *have*; object: *each eruption*; adverb: *presumably*; j. verbs: *dammed, altered*; objects: *the Deschutes River, the river's course*; adverb: *permanently*; prepositional phrase: *in many places*.)

3. Verbs have five forms or ***principal parts***. Look at some examples:

BASE FORM	PRESENT FORM	PAST FORM	PRESENT PARTICIPLE	PAST PARTICIPLE
be	am/is/are	was/were	being	been
call	call(s)	called	calling	called
take	take(s)	took	taking	taken

Verbs have several tenses to indicate the time of the action, possession, or state of being.

The ***continuous tenses***—also called the ***progressive tenses***—are formed with *be* + present participle. The present participle is never used as a verb unless it has an auxiliary.

The ***perfect tenses*** are formed with *have* + past participle. The past participle is never used as a verb unless it has an auxiliary.

The ***perfect progressive tenses*** are formed with *have* + *been* + present participle.

Verb tenses that you will see on the TOEFL include:

Simple Present:

Thunderstorms form when an air parcel becomes buoyant and rises.

Present Continuous:

Theorists are now looking for a new planet X, which they believe is beyond Pluto.

Present Perfect:

Sophisticated detection devices have brought the extent of pollution to the public's attention.

Present Perfect Continuous:

Since 1979, Anna Deavere Smith has been writing and performing one–woman plays that expose the American character.

Simple Past:

Each time the money changers of ancient Greece made an exchange, they charged a fee.

Past Continuous:

Between 1945 and 1980, the U. S. government was spending 75 percent of its transportation budget on highways.

Past Perfect:

Before the two Germanies reached accords in 1972, East Germany had built the Berlin Wall to keep East Berliners from crossing the border into the west.

Past Perfect Continuous:

Humans had been dreaming of flight for centuries before the Wright brothers built their glider.

Simple Future:

Global warming will cause flooding, windstorms, and killer heat waves.
A committee appointed by the president is going to examine race relations.

Future Continuous:

The number of U. S. teenagers will be steadily increasing until it peaks around 2008.

The time meaning of a sentence is often indicated by words or phrases that function as ***time markers***:

SIMPLE TENSES	CONTINUOUS TENSES	PERFECT TENSES
usually	for	for
during	during	since
sometimes	now (present)	already
yesterday (past)	while (past)	yet (negative)
ago (past)		so far
never		never

Dates often indicate time and determine tense. What are some other time markers you know that express past, present, and future time?

4. A TOEFL item may test you by having:

- no verb where one is needed
- an incorrect verb form or tense
- no auxiliary where one is needed
- an incorrect auxiliary
- incorrect word order

5. A test item may try to trick you by not having a verb where one is needed. Remember, every sentence must have at least one verb. Look at this example:

The flavor of coffee dependence largely on the characteristics of the bean.

Which underlined word must be changed for the sentence to be correct? If you chose *dependence*, you were correct. The sentence lacks a verb for the subject *the flavor of coffee*. *Dependence* is not a verb. It is a noun, and it must be changed to its verb form (See 2.22). What is the verb form of *dependence*?

6. A test item may try to trick you by having an incorrect verb form. Look at this example:

There is evidence that the formation of life is not an accidental occurrence but a process that taken place whenever a planet exists under the right conditions.

Which underlined word or phrase must be changed for the sentence to be correct? If you chose *taken place*, you were correct. Because this sentence makes a general statement of theory or belief, the simple present tense is appropriate. Correction: *takes place*.

Look at another example:

> European Americans had fighted several wars and made treaties with Native Americans before the nineteenth century ended.

Which underlined word or phrase must be changed for the sentence to be correct? If you chose *fighted*, you are correct because it is an incorrect form. *Fight* is an irregular verb, and the correct past participle is *fought*.

7. A test item may try to trick you by having an incorrect verb tense. Look at this example:

> When men first learned to hunt in groups and to use axes of chipped stone, they start to dominate the other creatures of the earth.

Which underlined word or phrase must be changed for the sentence to be correct? If you chose *start*, you were correct. In the introductory clause, the verb *learned* is simple past tense. However, in the main clause, the verb *start* is simple present, which does not agree in tense meaning with *learned*. Correction: *started*.

8. A test item may try to trick you by having no auxiliary where one is needed. Look at this example:

> By the time he was sixteen years old, Wolfgang Amadeus Mozart written several sonatas, symphonies, and operas.

Which underlined word or phrase must be changed for the sentence to be correct? If you chose *written*, you were correct because it lacks the necessary auxiliary for the past perfect tense. Correction: *had written*.

9. Some of the answer choices will try to trick you by having incorrect word order in the verb phrase. Look at this example:

> Warm, moist airstreams moving over the mountains ------- that eventually caused the 1976 Colorado flood.
>
> ○ quickly formed the thunderheads
> ○ quickly the thunderheads formed
> ○ the thunderheads quickly formed
> ○ the quickly forming thunderheads

This sentence needs a verb for the subject *airstreams*. Careful reading of the sentence shows that the blank space is followed by an adjective clause beginning with *that* (See 2.10). Therefore, the missing part is probably a verb phrase that includes a direct object. The first answer best completes the sentence because it has the correct word order: adverb + verb + noun.

How do the other answer choices try to confuse you?

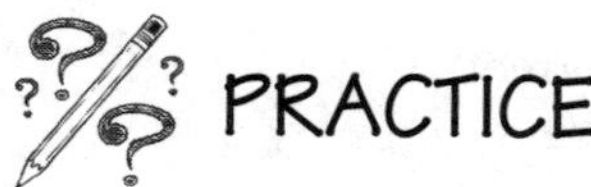

PRACTICE

Exercise 2.5.A

Choose the one word or phrase that best completes the sentence.

1. Millions of office workers ------- most of their time sitting in front of computer screens.

   (A) spend
   (B) spending
   (C) to spend
   (D) are spent

2. Mule deer ------- a wide variety of twigs, grass, berries, and fruit.

   (A) eating
   (B) has eaten
   (C) used to eating
   (D) are used to eating

3. Radio waves, traveling at the speed of light, have ------- their discoveries to Earth.

   (A) bringing
   (B) for bringing
   (C) to be brought
   (D) brought

4. The first punk rock ------- of the mid–sixties middle–American garage bands to the more genteel British Invasion.

   (A) the aggressive response
   (B) did the aggressive response
   (C) was the aggressive response
   (D) was responding aggressively

5. Thomas Paine's *Common Sense* was a brilliant piece of propaganda that ------- for breaking free of England.

   (A) eloquently the reasons state
   (B) were stated the reasons eloquently
   (C) was stating the reasons eloquent
   (D) eloquently stated the reasons

6. The production of a practical hydrofoil first ------- in Italy, where it was developed during the first decade of the twentieth century.

   (A) taking place
   (B) took place
   (C) taken place
   (D) to take place

7. In a retail store, consumers ------- the merchandise and compare brands.

   (A) could inspected
   (B) can be inspected
   (C) can inspecting
   (D) can inspect

8. By the end of the 1800s, the output of European artists, writers, and scientists ------- to the point where it dwarfed the productiveness of the 1700s.

   (A) accelerating
   (B) accelerates
   (C) had accelerated
   (D) have accelerated

9. The American "cocktail" ------- around the world, and many countries have adopted both the word and the drink.

   (A) spreads
   (B) spreading
   (C) has spread
   (D) to spread

10. In 1993 a consumer organization in Washington ------- and vegetables for their level of pesticide contamination.

    (A) rates forty fruits
    (B) rated forty fruits
    (C) forty fruits rated
    (D) forty were rating fruits

Exercise 2.5.B

Choose the one underlined word or phrase that must be changed for the sentence to be correct.

1. Many psychologists belief that it is young adulthood and not middle age that is the most
A B C
stressful period of adult life.
D

2. In 1867 Karl Marx, who was living in London, published the first volume of *Das Kapital*,
A B
which become the fundamental written work of world socialism.
C D

3. Fall is an excellent time to plant trees, but there were several points to consider in determining
A B C
which tree is best for a landscape.
D

4. One nineteenth–century writer observed that Americans considered nature inexhaustible, and
A B C
until recently, this is been true.
D

5. Old–growth forests are defined as being at least 250 years old, though some forests to be actually
A B C
far older, with a few approaching one thousand years.
D

6. Apes and gorillas can, like chimpanzees, communicate with a wide variety of vocal calls, but they
A B C
just could not speak.
D

7. Fighting break out between France and Vietnam in 1946, when the two nations could not
A B
reconcile their differences.
C D

8. The publication of *The Feminine Mystique* challenged the domesticity that had define women's
A B
lives since they were forced out of the workplace by soldiers returning from World War II.
C D

9. During the Jurassic Period, which extend from 180 million to 135 million years ago, reptiles
A B C
reached fantastic size.
D

10. Drawing upon natural body movements, Isadora Duncan gave her audiences dances that
A B
stressing emotional responses to symphonic music.
C D

Answers to Exercises 2.5.A through 2.5.B are on page 639.

2.5 EXTENSION

1. Students identify time markers in Exercises 2.5.A – 2.5.B.

2. In reading done outside class, students look for sentences with various verb forms and tenses. Bring examples to share in class. Underline all verb phrases. Identify auxiliaries, modals, direct and indirect objects, adverbs and prepositional phrases.

3. Students create "TOEFL sentences" to test their classmates' understanding of verbs. Students write their own sentences or change sentences they find in print so that each sentence contains one of the following errors: (a) incorrect verb form or tense, or (b) incorrect auxiliary. Write the sentences either on the board or on cards. Classmates identify the error and make the correction.

2.6 Recognizing Passives

FOCUS

Read the following sentences:

> The state of Texas was annexed by the United States in 1845.
>
> Venus, the second planet from the sun, is covered with a dense, white, cloudy atmosphere.
>
> The idea that everything is made up of elements was first studied by the ancient Greeks.

What is similar about the sentences?

Each of the sentences is in the ***passive voice***. This means that the subject of the sentence is not the doer of the verb's action but the receiver of the action.

Who or what is the subject of the first sentence? *The state of Texas* is the subject of the sentence, but it is not the doer of the action. Who or what does the action? *The United States* performs the action: The United States annexed the state of Texas in 1845. *The state of Texas* is the object of the action and the ***passive subject*** of the sentence.

Can you identify the passive subjects of the second and third sentences above?

Look at the following sentences. What do the verb structures have in common?

> A variety of health problems can be helped by stress management, proper nutrition, and exercise.
>
> Steps should have been taken to control garden pests before they damaged all the plants.

In each sentence above, the verb in the main clause is in the passive voice. Each passive verb also has a modal auxiliary: *can be helped, should have been taken.*

You must be able to recognize passive verbs and sentences. All of the above examples are similar to the types of sentences you will see on the TOEFL.

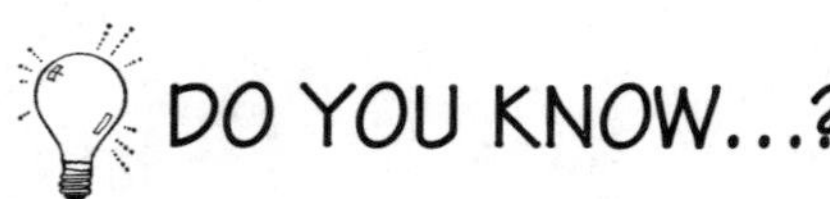

1. At least one or two items on the TOEFL will test your ability to recognize correct and incorrect usage of verbs that are in the passive voice.

2. ***Voice*** refers to the relationship between the verb and the subject of a sentence. In an ***active voice*** sentence, the subject is the doer of the action and is placed before the verb. This emphasizes who or what performs the action.

   Active Voice:

   A variety of chromatographic methods has simplified the separation of complex chemical mixtures. (doer of action placed before verb)

   In a ***passive voice*** sentence, the writer expresses that the action or the object of the action is more important than who or what performs the action. In a passive sentence, the doer of the action is either placed after the verb or omitted.

   Passive Voice:

   The separation of complex chemical mixtures has been simplified *by a variety of chromatographic methods*. (doer of action placed after verb)

   The separation of complex chemical mixtures has been simplified. (doer of action omitted)

   In passive sentences, the direct or indirect object of the verb is the passive subject of the sentence. For this reason, only transitive verbs (verbs that have an object) can be written in the passive voice. In the above examples, the direct object *the separation of complex chemical mixtures* becomes the passive subject when the sentence is rewritten in the passive voice.

3. The passive is formed with the appropriate tense of *be* + the past participle of the verb. Tenses commonly written in the passive voice include:

   Simple Present:

   A language is considered "dead" when it is no longer used for oral communication.

   Present Continuous:

   Algebra and physical science are now being taught in the eighth grade.

   Present Perfect:

   Cats have been kept as domestic animals ever since humans started harvesting and storing grains.

   Simple Past:

   The first thermometer was invented by the great Italian astronomer Galileo.

   Past Continuous:

   Theories of logic and binary numbers were being developed by Gottfried Leibniz in the 1600s.

Past Perfect:

By the seventeenth century, chemistry <u>had been recognized</u> as a science.

Simple Future:

The course Human Development <u>will be offered</u> only in fall semester.

Infinitive:

The innovative group of painters working in New York after the war came <u>to be known</u> as "abstract expressionists."

Note: The present perfect continuous, past perfect continuous, future continuous, and future perfect continuous tenses are not used in the passive voice.

Note: Adverbs are usually placed after the first auxiliary:

The woodchuck <u>has traditionally been called</u> a "groundhog" because it seldom travels far from its underground den.

Note: When a passive verb is negative, *not* is placed after the first auxiliary:

The savagery <u>had not been confined</u> to one side of the conflict.
Jupiter's smaller satellites <u>can not be seen</u> without a telescope.

4. Verbs with a modal auxiliary can be written in the passive voice.

For present and future meanings, *be* is in its base form: modal + *be* + past participle

Generalizations are scientific statements that <u>can be tested</u> and <u>verified</u> with data.
Any changes in the program <u>will be announced</u> before the first speaker begins.

For past meaning: modal + *have been* + past participle

It is now clear that the American Civil War <u>could not have been prevented</u> by another political compromise.
Stonehenge <u>must have been built</u> to serve a scientific or religious purpose.

5. Passive sentences can be rewritten in the active voice. When the doer of the action is omitted, you can usually infer who or what it is.

Passive voice:	The tides <u>are caused</u> mainly by the moon.
Active voice:	Mainly the moon <u>causes</u> the tides.
Passive voice:	Radar maps of several planets <u>have been produced</u>.
Active voice:	Scientists <u>have produced</u> radar maps of several planets. (doer of action inferred)

Passive sentences occur frequently in written English, especially in textbooks and in scientific, technical, business, and government publications. Writers use the passive voice when they want the action or the receiver of the action to be the focus of the sentence.

6. A TOEFL item may test your understanding of which voice to use. Look at this example:

> Ammonia ------- as the refrigerant in the first practical refrigerator, made by Karl von Linde in 1876.
>
> ◯ used
> ◯ had been using
> ◯ to use
> ◯ was used

Should the missing verb be in the active or passive voice? *Ammonia* is not the doer of the action because ammonia cannot *use* anything. In this sentence, *ammonia* is a passive subject of the verb *use*.

The first two answer choices are in the active voice and are therefore incorrect. The third choice is an infinitive, which does not function as a verb. (You will review infinitives in 2.7.) The fourth choice best completes the sentence: *Ammonia was used as the refrigerant in the first practical refrigerator*.

How would you rewrite the above sentence in the active voice?

Look at another example:

> The coastal and mountain <u>regions</u> of Peru are frequently <u>shaken</u> by earthquakes, and the major quake of 1970 <u>was killed</u> fifty <u>thousand</u> people.

Which underlined word or phrase must be changed for the sentence to be correct? If you chose *was killed*, you were correct. In this context, the quake performed the action, so the verb must be in the active voice: *the major quake of 1970 killed fifty thousand people*.

How would you rewrite the above sentence entirely in the passive voice?

7. A test item may try to trick you by using an incorrect verb form in a passive sentence. Look at this example:

> The great apes are being <u>force</u> out of their natural habitat by poverty–stricken farmers <u>who</u> seize the land <u>to grow</u> crops and <u>raise</u> cattle.

Which underlined word or phrase must be changed for the sentence to be correct? If you chose *force*, you were correct because it is a passive, which takes the past participle of the verb. Correction: *forced*.

How would you rewrite the above sentence in the active voice?

8. A test item may try to trick you by having an incorrect or missing auxiliary verb in a passive sentence. Look at this example:

> In <u>colonial</u> America, conformity in <u>many</u> facets of daily living <u>enforced</u> upon the members <u>of society</u>.

Which underlined word or phrase must be changed for the sentence to be correct? If you chose *enforced*, you were correct. The passive subject, *conformity in many facets of daily living*, needs a passive verb. Correction: *was enforced*.

How would you rewrite the above sentence in the active voice?

Look at another example:

Snowflakes ------- single ice crystals or multi–crystal aggregates.

- ◯ be composed of
- ◯ could be composing a
- ◯ can be composed of
- ◯ can are composed of

The third choice best completes the sentence, which should read: *Snowflakes can be composed of single ice crystals or multi–crystal aggregates.*

Why are the other three answer choices incorrect?

STRUCTURE

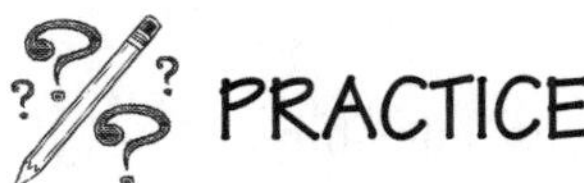

Exercise 2.6.A

Choose the one word or phrase that best completes the sentence.

1. The U. S. Constitution ------- by the vote of each state, but it was not ratified by North Carolina until the Bill of Rights was added in 1789.

   (A) was adopting
   (B) was adopted
   (C) adopted
   (D) to be adopted

2. Construction augers ------- drill holes in soft ground for the piers of large buildings.

   (A) for
   (B) used to
   (C) are used by
   (D) are used to

3. Conference planners are advised to include more than one workshop format so that a wide range of styles -------.

   (A) can accommodate
   (B) can accommodated
   (C) can be accommodated
   (D) could accommodate

4. A rack–and–pinion gear was used in a water clock that was ------- by the Greek inventor Ctesibius in about 250 B.C.

   (A) build
   (B) building
   (C) built
   (D) been built

5. A robot may ------- an action such as paint spraying by guiding its hand through the movements.

   (A) be taught
   (B) taught
   (C) is taught
   (D) to teach

6. Two epic poems, the *Iliad* and the *Odyssey*, ------- by the blind poet Homer.

   (A) were probably written
   (B) probably wrote
   (C) probably written
   (D) be written probably

7. Each word in our mental dictionaries ------- with its unique sound and meaning.

   (A) must store
   (B) must be stored
   (C) must is stored
   (D) must to be stored

8. Tuition and fees ------- if a student withdraws after the fifteenth day of the term.

   (A) not refunded
   (B) will be not refunded
   (C) will not be refunded
   (D) will not to be refunded

Exercise 2.6.B

Choose the one underlined word or phrase that must be changed for the sentence to be correct.

1. The great majority of Kenyans engage in subsistence farming, but several crops—including
   A B C
   coffee, tea, and sisal—be exported.
   D

2. In 1826 Joseph Niepce found a way of fixing an image created in a camera "dark room,"
   A B C
   a device which had used for many years as a drawing aid for artists.
   D

3. The changes needed for healthy living can be attain by stress control, which replaces unhealthy
   A B C
   ways of dealing with anxiety with simple techniques that help us relax.
   D

4. After the gas–charged lava foam was been expelled from the volcano, liquid lava broke through
   A B C
   the south side of the cone, spreading over five miles to the west.
   D

5. The American eel is being studied in the hope that information about its migration and feeding
   A B
   habits will be explained why its numbers are decreasing.
   C D

6. Because they left no written records, little known about the Tainos, a group of Indians who
   A B
   inhabited Puerto Rico when the Spanish came in the fifteenth century.
   C D

7. The road test for the first Ford automobile had to been postponed because the finished car was
   A B
   wider than the door of the shed in which it was built.
   C D

8. The first writing ink was made from pigment find in the octopus's ink sac, which also helps
   A B C
   the animal avoid being attacked.
   D

Answers to Exercises 2.6.A through 2.6.B are on page 640.

2.6 EXTENSION

1. Students identify the tense for each verb in Exercises 2.6.A and 2.6.B. For all passive verbs, who/what is the passive subject? Who/what is the doer of the action?

2. Students rewrite sentences in Exercises 2.6.A and 2.6.B so that all verbs are in the active voice. If the doer of the action is not stated directly, it must be inferred.

3. In reading done outside class, students look for examples of sentences written in the passive voice. Bring examples to share in class. Discuss why the writer probably used the passive voice. Would the sentences be better if they were written in active voice?

4. Students create "TOEFL sentences" to test their classmates' understanding of passive voice verbs. Students write their own passive voice sentences or change sentences they find in print so that each sentence contains an incorrect verb structure. Students write the sentences either on the board or on cards. Classmates identify the error and make the correction.

ASSESSING PROGRESS – 2.5 through 2.6

QUIZ 2 *(Time – 10 minutes)*

Choose the one word or phrase that best completes the sentence.

1. The female hummingbird ------- with lichen and other soft plants.

   (A) to make the nest
   (B) making the nest
   (C) makes the nest
   (D) the nest made

2. No one living during the nineteenth century ------- the changes which would take place in the next century.

   (A) can predict
   (B) could a prediction
   (C) could have been predicted
   (D) could have predicted

3. When elephants are foraging for food out of sight of one another, they ------- by making rumbling noises similar to gargling.

   (A) communicating
   (B) were communicating
   (C) to communicate
   (D) communicate

4. Autumn is the time to take care of any outside chores that ------- in the garden before the first frost.

   (A) must to do
   (B) must have been done
   (C) must be doing
   (D) must be done

5. The ten–minute carpal tunnel surgery ------- snipping the carpal ligament to temporarily relieve pressure that is damaging the nerve.

   (A) involves
   (B) involving
   (C) is involved
   (D) to involve

6. The successful trial of John Peter Zenger ------- an end to prosecutions for sedition in colonial America.

   (A) hardly brought
   (B) bringing hardly
   (C) hardly to bring
   (D) was hardly brought

7. Polar bears ------- throughout the polar region, but they spend most of their time on coastal land near open water.

   (A) find
   (B) are finding
   (C) be found
   (D) are found

Choose the one underlined word or phrase that must be changed for the sentence to be correct.

8. As a source of power, electricity had no rival because it is clean, silent, can be turned on and off
A B
instantly, and can be fed easily to where it is needed.
C D

9. The American Jewish community in the 1800s was characterize by the multitude and variety of
A B
self–help organizations that it established.
C D

10. The Colosseum, finished in A.D. 80, could seat fifty thousand spectators, far too great a number
A B C
to be entertaining by the intimacy of plays.
D

11. Most shrubs should fertilized early in the summer; moreover, late fertilizing or using the wrong
A B C
type of fertilizer can damage the evergreen plants.
D

12. Between 1914 and 1932, T. S. Eliot taught school in England, became a London bank clerk,
A B
wrote poems, and assistant in editing a literary journal.
C D

13. Air pollution and smog may appear yellow or brown, but sometimes they do not easily distinguished
A B C
from haze, which usually is blue to white.
D

14. Most people know what they should been doing to live a healthy lifestyle, but sometimes they fail
A B C
to measure up to the perfectly balanced picture of health.
D

15. The United States entered World War II more unified than it ever been or ever would be again, and
A B
Congress granted the president new powers to wage war.
C D

Answers to Structure Quiz 2 are on page 640.

2.7 Checking Infinitives and Gerunds

FOCUS

What is wrong with this sentence?

> The cougar likes hunt under the cloak of darkness, using its keen binocular vision to spy its prey of deer and other small mammals.

The cougar likes something—what does it like? The verb *likes* needs a noun object. *Hunt* is a verb form that must be changed to a noun. A suitable noun form of *hunt* is either the infinitive *to hunt* or the gerund *hunting*. The clause should be changed to either *the cougar likes to hunt* or *the cougar likes hunting.*

What is wrong with this sentence?

> Some linguists believe that women use conversation to creating equality between the speakers, and men use it establishment hierarchy.

This sentence has two errors: *to creating*, an incorrectly formed infinitive, and *establishment*, an incorrect part of speech. Each error should be changed to the correct infinitive form: *to create, to establish.*

The writer is making a statement about *how* women and men use conversation. Therefore, in this case, the infinitives function as adverbs because they modify the verb phrase *use conversation.*

What is wrong with this sentence?

> Most Americans believe in allow their children the freedom to be independent and self–reliant.

This sentence uses an incorrect gerund form. The verb *believe in* (a verb + preposition combination) can not be followed by a verb. The verb *allow* must be changed to a noun form, which in this case is the gerund *allowing.*

You must be able to recognize where infinitives and gerunds are needed in sentences. All of the above examples are similar to the types of sentences you will see on the TOEFL.

DO YOU KNOW...?

1. Approximately two items on the TOEFL will test your ability to recognize correct and incorrect usage of infinitives and gerunds.

2. ***Infinitives*** and ***gerunds*** are two examples of verbals. A ***verbal*** is a verb form that functions as another part of speech in a sentence. Both infinitives and gerunds are used as nouns. Infinitives can also be used as adjectives or adverbs.

   Infinitives and gerunds that come from transitive verbs (verbs that have an object) can have objects. Infinitives and gerunds can also have adverb and adjective modifiers. An ***infinitive phrase*** consists of an infinitive and its objects and modifiers. A ***gerund phrase*** consists of a gerund and its objects and modifiers.

   Infinitive Phrase:

   The Roman abacus used pebbles to represent numbers.

   Gerund Phrase:

   Frequently checking your rear view mirror is a good tip for safe freeway driving.

   In the above infinitive and gerund phrases, what are the objects of the verbals? What are the modifiers?

   (***Answers:*** Objects: *numbers*, *your rear view mirror*; adverb: *frequently*; adjectives: *safe*, *freeway*.)

3. An ***infinitive*** is formed with *to* + the base form of a verb. Infinitives and infinitive phrases can serve these functions in a sentence:

   Subject:

   To own a home has always been part of the American dream.

   Subject Complement:

   The main purpose of the Federal Reserve System is to control the money supply.

   Direct Object:

   Jane Addams strived to put her education to use in social work.

   Adverb:

   Sensors are designed to detect the presence of specific substances.
   To focus on an image, a photographer looks through the camera's viewfinder.

   Adjective:

   The McCarran–Walter Act of 1952 had the power to end discrimination against Asian immigrants.

STRUCTURE

Adjective Complement:

It is becoming common to see office workers dressing casually on Fridays.

Infinitives can be in the passive voice:

Most teenagers want to be taken seriously by adults.

Infinitives are frequently used with the "false" subject *it*:

It is important to check the oil in your car once a month.

Note: When an infinitive is compound, you can omit *to* after the first infinitive:

The liver manages to process proteins, produce bile, and cleanse the blood.

Note: For infinitives that follow the verb *help*, you can either omit *to* or use *to*. For infinitives that follow *have*, *let*, and *make*, use only the base form of the verb, omitting *to*:

The World Bank helps member nations develop their economies.
The World Bank helps member nations to develop their economies.
Depression can make people say things they would not ordinarily say.

4. An infinitive can be a direct object following these verbs:

VERB + INFINITIVE

advise*	claim	fail	need**	seem
afford	come	forbid*	neglect	serve
agree	compel*	force*	offer	strive
allow*	consent	get**	order*	struggle
appear	convince*	help**	permit*	teach*
appoint*	decide	hesitate	persuade*	tell*
arrange	dare**	hire*	plan	tend
ask**	demand	hope	prepare	threaten
be	deserve	intend**	pretend	urge*
beg**	direct*	invite*	proceed	volunteer
care	enable*	learn	promise**	wait
cause*	encourage*	manage	refuse	want**
challenge*	exist	mean**	remind*	warn*
choose**	expect**	motivate*	require*	wish

Note: With verbs marked *, you need: verb + indirect object + infinitive.

President Jefferson appointed Meriwether Lewis to lead the expedition into Louisiana.
V IO Infin

Note: With verbs marked **, you can have either: verb + infinitive
or: verb + indirect object + infinitive.

Most parents want to set a good example for their children.
V Infin

Most parents want their children to receive a good education.
V IO Infin

An infinitive can be an adjective complement following these adjectives:

ADJECTIVE + INFINITIVE				
afraid	dangerous	eager	important	relieved
anxious	delighted	easy	motivated	strange
careful	determined	essential	necessary	surprised
common	difficult	hesitant	prepared	usual
content	disappointed	honored	ready	willing

Project plans should include the steps that are necessary to ensure the project's success.

5. A ***gerund*** is formed by adding *–ing* to the base form of a verb. Gerunds and gerund phrases can serve these functions in a sentence:

Subject:

Writing the introduction may be easier after the body of the essay is finished.

Subject Complement:

The largest professional occupation in the United States is teaching.

Direct Object:

Marian Anderson began singing opera to help support her mother and sisters.

Object of a Preposition:

In the 1950s, the U.S. government was responsible for developing communications satellites.

Note: Infinitives cannot be the object of a preposition, but gerunds frequently function as the object of a preposition.

Note: Gerunds are uncountable nouns and do not usually take an article. An exception is the gerund + *of* structure, which takes the definite article *the*:

Historically, the primary responsibility for the rearing of children belonged to the parents.

6. A gerund can be a direct object following these verbs:

VERB + GERUND				
admit	consider	give up	object to	report
aid in	count on	imagine	postpone	resent
anticipate	delay	insist on	practice	resist
appreciate	deny	involve	prevent	resume
approve of	depend on	keep (on)	put off	risk
avoid	discuss	look forward to	recall	succeed in
believe in	enjoy	mention	recollect	suggest
call for	finish	mind	recommend	think about/of
complete	forgive	miss	rely on	tolerate

After a six–month delay, the company resumed importing raw materials from Asia.

Either an infinitive or a gerund can be a direct object following these verbs:

VERB + INFINITIVE OR GERUND				
advise	begin	forbid	prefer	start
allow	continue	forget*	regret*	stop*
attempt	dislike	like	remember*	try

Note: These two sentences have the same meaning:

People began to use the waterwheel in the first century B.C.
People began using the waterwheel in the first century B.C.

Note: With verbs marked *, infinitives and gerunds convey a different meaning:

You must remember to use your turn signal. (*Meaning*: *Remembering* occurs before *using*.)
You must remember using your turn signal. (*Meaning*: *Using* occurs before *remembering*.)

7. The verb *use* is frequently followed by either an infinitive or *for* + gerund (the gerund is the object of the preposition *for*). These two sentences have the same meaning:

Men use conversation to establish hierarchy.
Men use conversation for establishing hierarchy.

In the following sentences, change infinitives to *for* + gerund, and change gerunds to infinitives:

a. A scalpel is used to cut tissue during surgery and dissection.
b. Retailers are now using computers for making sales presentations in stores.
c. Chimpanzees use sticks and other tools to obtain food.
d. Traffic signs are used for controlling the flow of traffic.

(***Answers:*** a. *for cutting* b. *to make* c. *for obtaining* d. *to control*)

8. A TOEFL item may test you by:

- having an incorrect form of infinitive or gerund
- using an infinitive where a gerund is needed
- using a gerund where an infinitive is needed

9. A test item may try to trick you by using an incorrect form of infinitive or gerund. Look at this example:

> To becoming airborne and begin soaring, a glider is pulled behind a motor vehicle by a cable attached to a tow hook.

Which underlined word must be changed for the sentence to be correct? If you chose *becoming*, you were correct because it is an incorrect infinitive form. Correction: *become*.

Look at another example:

> Beginning around 1830, the Underground Railroad helped thousands of escaped slaves ------- their way north to freedom.
>
> ○ find
> ○ finding
> ○ found
> ○ to be found

The sentence needs a direct object for the verb *helped*. Following *help*, you may use an infinitive with or without *to*. Therefore, the first answer choice, *find*, best completes the sentence.

10. A test item may try to trick you by substituting a gerund for an infinitive, or vice versa. Look at this example:

> There are a number of different strategies for to discourage squirrels from eating food set out for wild birds.

Which underlined word or phrase must be changed for the sentence to be correct? If you chose *to discourage*, you were correct because only a gerund can be the object of a preposition. Correction: *discouraging*.

PRACTICE

Exercise 2.7.A

Choose the one underlined word or phrase that must be changed for the sentence to be correct.

1. Dogs tend establish (A) a regular path through the yard, and repellents should be used (B) in those paths (C) when attempting to discourage (D) them.

2. A (A) recent study shows that selenium, a mineral found in (B) seafood, is (C) linked to reduce (D) the human cancer risk.

3. Not only does (A) personality affect (B) specific occupations and life successes, but it (C) also helps shaping (D) the emotional fabric of adult life.

4. A nation can have (A) a major impact on its economic performance through its (B) economic policies: spending, taxing (C), and change (D) the money supply.

5. When walking over the ice, polar bears appear (A) bow–legged, but the purpose of this strange walk is enable (B) these massive animals to maintain (C) their balance without slipping (D).

Choose the one word or phrase that best completes the sentence.

6. In 1954 Dr. Jonas Salk began ------- a killed–virus vaccine for polio.

   (A) tested
   (B) had tested
   (C) test
   (D) testing

7. Many mechanical machines exist ------- one form of movement into another.

   (A) to convert
   (B) to be converted
   (C) with which conversion
   (D) are converted

8. We cannot understand the life of someone without ------- of the world in which he or she lived and the great events of that time.

   (A) have knowledge
   (B) to have knowledge
   (C) having knowledge
   (D) be having knowledge

9. Motivation is a difficult subject ------- because so many different factors influence the inclination to act.

   (A) be analyzed
   (B) to analyze
   (C) for analyze
   (D) analyzing

10. Almost everyone has trouble ------- at one time or another.

   (A) sleeping
   (B) for sleeping
   (C) sleep
   (D) slept

Exercise 2.7.B

Choose the one underlined word or phrase that must be changed for the sentence to be correct.

1. In one type of coffee maker, a plunger is pushed down over the wet coffee grounds to separated
   A B C
   the beverage from the grounds.
   D

2. On days of extreme heat, the keeping cool for just a few hours each day, even in an air–conditioned
   A B
   building lobby or a movie theater, can save lives.
   C D

3. Because of their high rate of predation, it is not unusual for rabbits producing more than six litters
   A B C D
   of young per year.

4. The purpose of a screwdriver's handle is not only to enable you to hold it but also to amplify the
   A B C
   force with which you turn the screwdriver for drive a screw.
   D

5. A "marked deck" is one in which the backs of the playing (A) cards have been (B) altered slightly to allow (C) a player read (D) their values illegally.

6. The upstop wheels of a roller coaster lock (A) the cars to the track, and the (B) guide wheels are used (C) for to glide (D) on straightaways and hills.

7. Chromatographic devices generate (A) so much data that chemists frequently must use (B) computers to (C) help analyzing (D) the results.

8. Investment (A) money means to put it (B) into some business project such as operating (C) a mine, building a housing complex, or doing (D) medical research.

STRUCTURE

Answers to Exercises 2.7.A through 2.7.B are on pages 640 and 641.

2.7 EXTENSION

1. In reading done outside class, students look for sentences with infinitives and gerunds. Bring examples to share in class. Determine whether each infinitive and gerund is used as a subject, object, adverb, adjective, or object of a preposition. Can any of the infinitives be rewritten as gerunds, or vice versa?

2. Students practice speaking and writing sentences using verbs from the verb + infinitive and verb + gerund lists on pages 188 and 189.

3. Discuss the difference in meaning between:

   (a) *forget to say*, *forget saying* (b) *stop to listen*, *stop listening*.

2.8 Recognizing Main and Subordinate Clauses

FOCUS

Read the following TOEFL item. What does this sentence need?

> Cardiac muscle is found only in the heart, where ------- that organ's thick walls.
>
> ◯ it forms
> ◯ forms
> ◯ is forming
> ◯ formation of

This sentence has two clauses. A ***clause*** is a group of words that has a subject and a verb. The first clause is *Cardiac muscle is found only in the heart*. The second clause, beginning with *where*, needs a subject and a verb.

The answer is the first choice. The clause should read: *where it forms that organ's thick walls.*

Now, read another TOEFL item. What does this sentence need?

> ------- of deuterium and tritium are fused, they produce a nucleus containing two protons and three neutrons.
>
> ◯ The nuclei
> ◯ In the nuclei
> ◯ Which the nuclei
> ◯ When the nuclei

This sentence also has two clauses. Every clause must have a subject and a verb. The first clause has a verb, *are fused*, but it needs a subject.

The answer is the fourth choice. The sentence should read: *When the nuclei of deuterium and tritium are fused, they produce a nucleus containing two protons and three neutrons.*

Why are the other three answer choices incorrect?

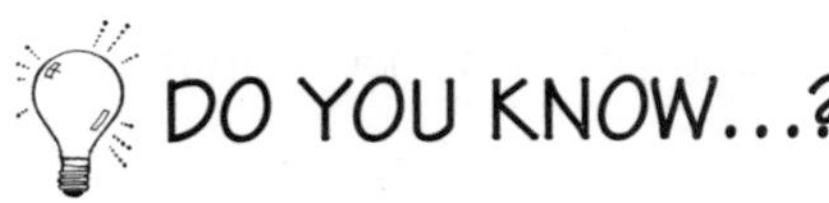

1. At least one item on the TOEFL will test your ability to recognize main and subordinate clauses. You must be able to determine where subjects, verbs, and subordinators are needed in clauses and sentences.

2. The ***main clause*** of a sentence is also called an ***independent clause*** because it can stand alone as a sentence, without the help of another clause. A main clause contains a subject and a verb and expresses a complete idea. All complete sentences have at least one main clause.

   Main Clause:

   The steam turbine was invented by Charles Parsons in 1884.

   A sentence with only one clause is called a ***simple sentence***. The above sentence is a simple sentence. A sentence with two or more independent clauses is called a ***compound sentence***. In a compound sentence, you can join the independent clauses with a comma and a conjunction such as *and*, *but*, *or*, *so*, and *yet*.

   Compound Sentence:

   The first mercury thermometer was invented by the German physicist Gabriel Fahrenheit, <u>and</u> the Fahrenheit temperature scale bears his name.

   Can you identify the subject + verb structures in the above sentence?

   (***Answers:*** *The first mercury thermometer was invented*; *the Fahrenheit temperature scale bears*)

3. A ***subordinate clause*** contains a subject and a verb but does not express a complete idea. A subordinate clause is an incomplete sentence; it cannot stand alone. You must connect it to a main clause by using a ***subordinating word***, which is also called a ***subordinator***. Because a subordinate clause depends on a main clause to express a complete idea, it is sometimes called a ***dependent clause***.

   Subordinate Clauses:

   that a boat displaces water
   who governed the ancient Nile lands
   because it is hollow

   In the subordinate clauses above, the subordinators are: *that*, *who*, and *because*. Can you identify the subject + verb structure in each clause?

   (***Answers:*** *a boat displaces*; *who governed*; *it is*)

   A sentence with at least one subordinate clause is called a ***complex sentence***.

   Complex Sentence:

   As electronic technology rapidly developed, the transistor gave way to the integrated circuit.

   Note: When the subordinate clause comes first, it is followed by a comma.

Subordinators signal the beginning of a subordinate clause. In the following sentences, circle the words that are subordinators.

a. In 1924 Congress passed the Johnson–Reed Act, which severely restricted immigration.
b. Because sunglasses filter light, they are absolutely essential for snow travel.
c. People who speak to animals are apparently under the impression that the animal understands what is being said.

(***Answers:*** a. *which*; b. *Because*; c. *who*, *that*, *what*)

Can you see why subordinators are sometimes called ***clause markers***?

There are three kinds of subordinate clauses, and each will be reviewed later in this book:

Noun Clause (2.9):

What predicts life satisfaction in middle adulthood has been the subject of much research on young adults.

Adjective Clause (2.10):

The discovery of fire, which happened in Africa about a million years ago, provided heat for cooking and warmth.

Adverb Clause (2.11):

As the Yellowstone River moves eastward through the prairies, it picks up the waters of three other rivers.

4. One clause can contain another clause. This means that a subordinate clause can be part of another clause. Look at the underlined clause in this sentence:

Economists believe that investment takes place because investors decide that the economy will get more consumption tomorrow if it sacrifices consumption today.

The underlined clause contains two other subordinate clauses:

that the economy will get more consumption tomorrow
if it sacrifices consumption today

In the underlined part of the above sentence, circle the subordinator and underline the subject + verb structure in each clause.

(***Answers:*** Subordinator: *because*; S + V: *investors decide*; subordinator: *that*; S + V: *the economy will get*; subordinator: *if*; S + V: *it sacrifices*)

5. Every clause in a sentence must have a subject and a verb. A test item may try to trick you by having a main or subordinate clause in which the subject or verb is missing. Look at this example:

> Telescopes and microscopes <u>upgrade</u> the lenses in our eyes <u>to reveal</u> the extraordinary <u>amount</u> of fine detail that <u>actually present</u> in light rays.

Which underlined word or phrase must be changed for the sentence to be correct? If you chose *actually present*, you were correct. Why? The word *that* is a subordinator. It tells you *that actually present in light rays* is a subordinate clause. All clauses must have a verb. Correction: *actually is present* or *is actually present.*

6. A test item may try to confuse you by having the "false" subject *it* or *there* (See 2.1). Look at this example:

> Although the jaguar has a reputation as a man–eater, ------- numerous stories about people being followed by jaguars for long distances without being attacked.
>
> ◯ in the
> ◯ there
> ◯ there are
> ◯ and

In this sentence, *Although the jaguar has a reputation as a man–eater* is a subordinate clause. The main clause needs a subject and a verb. The first answer choice would turn the clause into a prepositional phrase. The second and fourth choices do not contain a verb. Only the third choice contains a subject and a verb: *there are.*

If *there* is the "false" subject of a clause, you can rewrite the clause by using the verb *exist.* For example: *numerous stories exist about people being followed by jaguars for long distances without being attacked.*

Look at another example:

> ------- recessions and high unemployment are extremely costly to a nation's economy.
>
> ◯ Apparent that now
> ◯ Now it apparent
> ◯ That is apparent now
> ◯ It is now apparent that

If you chose none of the above answers, the clause could stand alone as a complete sentence because it is an independent clause. However, the TOEFL will expect you to choose from among the answer choices.

The first choice, *Apparent that now*, is an adjective + subordinator structure, which cannot begin a sentence. The second choice, *Now it apparent*, is an incomplete clause because it has a subject but no verb. The third choice, *That is apparent now*, is a main clause; if you chose it, the sentence would have two incorrectly joined main clauses.

The answer is the fourth choice, *It is now apparent that*, which becomes the main clause and turns the other clause, *recessions and high unemployment are extremely costly to a nation's economy*, into a subordinate clause.

On the TOEFL, *there* or *it* will often appear as the subject of a clause.

7. A test item may try to trick you with a distracting introductory phrase or appositive (See 2.2). Look at this example:

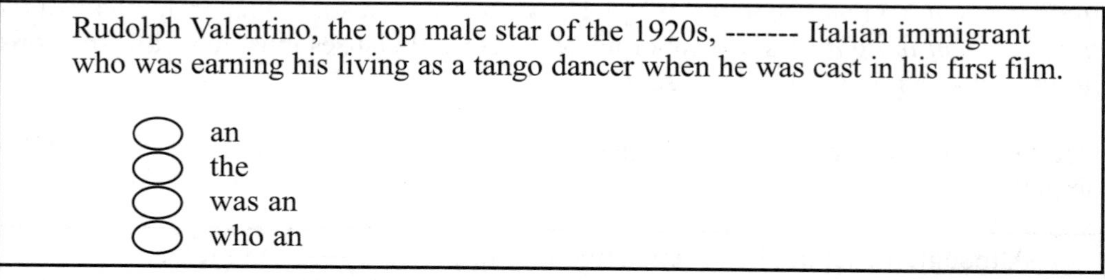

Rudolph Valentino, the top male star of the 1920s, ------- Italian immigrant who was earning his living as a tango dancer when he was cast in his first film.

- an
- the
- was an
- who an

You must check that every clause has a subject and verb. The main clause of this sentence is *Rudolph Valentino ----- Italian immigrant*. This clause also contains an appositive, *the top male star of the 1920s*, which describes the subject, *Rudolph Valentino*. When you are careful not to let the appositive distract you, you can easily see that the main clause needs a verb. Only the third answer choice, *was an*, contains a verb.

PRACTICE

Exercise 2.8.A

Choose the one word or phrase that best completes the sentence.

1. The Harvest Moon, the full moon nearest the autumnal equinox, ------- a period of several days when the moon rises soon after sunset.

   (A) it brings
   (B) bringing
   (C) for bringing
   (D) brings

2. Like the end of the Paleozoic era, ------- marked by widespread extinction of species.

   (A) of the Mesozoic was
   (B) was the end of the Mesozoic
   (C) the end of the Mesozoic was
   (D) the end was of the Mesozoic

3. On some sailboats ------- a tiller instead of a wheel for steering.

   (A) there is
   (B) having
   (C) in which
   (D) with

4. Even before -------, Spain had begun to devise an administrative system to control its empire in the New World.

   (A) to be over the heroic age
   (B) it the heroic age
   (C) was the heroic age over
   (D) the heroic age was over

5. After banks have determined how much the money of one country is worth in another, ------ people from both places exchange one type of money for another.

(A) helping
(B) to help
(C) and they help
(D) they help

6. ------- limits on the dollar amount of contributions taxpayers can deduct on their income tax return.

(A) There
(B) There may be
(C) Maybe there
(D) Why there may be

7. The terminus of the Northeast Passage, ------- a major ice–free port and base for naval and fishing vessels.

(A) Murmansk
(B) at Murmansk
(C) Murmansk is
(D) is Murmansk

8. -------, founded in 1837, that was the first institution of higher education for women in the United States.

(A) Mount Holyoke College
(B) Mount Holyoke College was
(C) Because Mount Holyoke College
(D) It was Mount Holyoke College

Choose the one underlined word or phrase that must be changed for the sentence to be correct.

9. Fixed bridges do not (A) moving parts, while movable bridges, such as (B) lift bridges and drawbridges, either (C) lift or swing open (D).

10. A jointed–arm robot can perform (A) complex actions because the various sections of its arm around (B) six joints, each of which (C) is driven (D) by an electro–hydraulic system.

Answers to Exercise 2.8.A are on page 641.

2.8 EXTENSION

1. In Exercise 2.8.A, students identify main and subordinate clauses. In clauses where *it* or *there* is the "false" subject, identify the true subject.

2. Students create "TOEFL sentences" to test their classmates' understanding of where subjects and verbs are needed in clauses. Students write their own sentences or use sentences they find in print. Include a lot of sentences with more than one clause. Omit the subject of a clause and leave a blank space where it should be. Classmates must complete the sentences by supplying an appropriate subject.

3. Do activity #2 again, but this time omit a verb, and leave a blank space where it should be. Write four possible "answers" (one of them must be correct!). Each student contributes one "TOEFL item" to a student–made quiz that can be given to the whole class.

ASSESSING PROGRESS – 2.7 through 2.8

QUIZ 3 *(Time – 10 minutes)*

Choose the one word or phrase that best completes the sentence.

1. The first engine ------- heat to drive a machine was the steam engine.

   (A) made use of
   (B) to make use of
   (C) of using
   (D) of making use

2. The enormous size of full–grown mammoths meant that ------- to attack them.

   (A) most fearless men dared the only
   (B) only the most fearless men dared
   (C) to dare the most fearless men only
   (D) dared only the most fearless men

3. Traditional religious beliefs are dominant in Cameroon, but ------- large minorities of Christians and Muslims.

   (A) there
   (B) why there are
   (C) there are
   (D) are

4. An important function of banks ------- international trade and investments.

   (A) promote
   (B) to promote
   (C) is to promote
   (D) to be promoted

5. ------- crude hydrocarbons into such products as gasoline and petrochemicals is at the heart of the petroleum industry.

   (A) Refine
   (B) Refined
   (C) To refining
   (D) Refining

6. ------- slow changes in the distribution of the earth's magnetic field.

   (A) The
   (B) How the
   (C) Do the
   (D) There are

7. The hummingbird's agility in flight lets it ------- from flower to flower like an insect.

   (A) flit
   (B) flitting
   (C) to flit
   (D) flitted

8. Though built on a bend in the Mississippi River, ------- protected by a series of levees.

   (A) New Orleans is
   (B) is New Orleans
   (C) New Orleans
   (D) New Orleans has

Choose the one underlined word or phrase that must be changed for the sentence to be correct.

9. Although Nathaniel Ward remained in the American colonies only thirteen years before return to
A B
England, he left his mark by writing the first code of laws for Massachusetts.
C D

10. Mozart's genius was evident during his lifetime, and his compositions continue exert a particular
A B C
fascination for musicians and music lovers.
D

11. The gray whale feeds by stirring up mud in shallow water, sucking in the water, and use its baleen
A B C
as a filter to trap prey while forcing the mud and water back out of its mouth.
D

12. In 1920 the U. S. Census revealed that more people in cities than on farms, and usually they left
A B
the former and reached the latter by automobile.
C D

13. In the liquid–fuel rocket, the purpose of the valves is control the flow of the propellants, enabling
A B C
the engine to work at different degrees of power.
D

14. Although pocket gophers damage crops, their tunneling aerates the soil, which helps conserve
A B C
ground water and preventing erosion.
D

15. The British began setting up new industries in India such as mills to process cotton and factories
A B C
for extract indigo for dye.
D

Answers to Structure Quiz 3 are on page 641.

ASSESSING PROGRESS – 2.1 through 2.8

QUIZ 4 – REVIEW *(Time – 15 minutes)*

Choose the one underlined word or phrase that must be changed for the sentence to be correct.

1. In an experiment, octopuses were [A] trained to distinguished [B] between shapes and also to recognize [C] objects by touch [D].

2. Because of the increasing amount [A] of panhandling on city streets, travelers are advised [B] not to carry many [C] cash but to rely on [D] traveler's checks or credit cards.

3. The first part of a plant's scientific name always [A] capitalized and is usually assigned to [B] a number [C] of species with many [D] characteristics in common.

4. As a zipper is opened [A], the triangular upper wedge in slide [B] detaches the teeth [C] and forces [D] them apart.

Choose the one word or phrase that best completes the sentence.

5. Because their instructors are highly trained professionals, ------- many efforts at innovative teaching within community colleges.

   (A) there
   (B) there are
   (C) that there are
   (D) and are

6. One purpose of the African elephant's enormous ears is ------- a stream of air over the animal's body, like a fan.

   (A) create
   (B) created
   (C) to create
   (D) creation

7. The ancient Egyptians constructed the Great Pyramid by using -------, the first principle of technology to be put to work.

   (A) inclined plane
   (B) the inclined plane
   (C) an inclined plane was
   (D) with the inclined plane

8. While some monarchs tried to prohibit coffee, Frederick the Great of Prussia ------- it.

   (A) had decide to simply tax
   (B) to decide simply taxing
   (C) simply decided to tax
   (D) simply deciding to tax

9. People ------- how light behaves thousands of years ago.

(A) must have begun observing
(B) must began to observe
(C) must to begin to observe
(D) must begin observing

10. It is ------- rather than moderate inflation that distorts prices and sends economies tumbling.

(A) a galloping inflation rate
(B) because a galloping inflation rate
(C) by a galloping inflation rate
(D) an inflation rate is galloping

11. If everybody liked the same kind of tea, ------- only one kind of tea.

(A) that
(B) it would
(C) there would be
(D) would be

12. Within three years of the first commercial radio broadcast, ------- of radio stations in North America had reached nearly six hundred.

(A) had the amount
(B) for the amount
(C) that the number
(D) the number

13. In typical four–year engineering curricula, the first two years ------- basic sciences, and the last two years are devoted to specialized engineering courses.

(A) to spend studying
(B) to be spent studying
(C) were spent to study
(D) are spent studying

14. While most Americans ------- their parents "mama" and "papa," today these terms are seldom heard in urban America outside the South.

(A) used to be called
(B) used to call
(C) used to calling
(D) are used to being called

15. Since 1954, ------- the polio vaccine was introduced, infantile paralysis has diminished but not disappeared.

(A) it was the year
(B) a year
(C) the year of
(D) the year

STRUCTURE

Choose the one underlined word or phrase that must be changed for the sentence to be correct.

16. "Lost Generation" was the first term (A) for to identify (B) a young generation considered (C) separate from the general population by its age (D) and special experience.

17. Scientists found that an (A) ice core taken (B) from a glacier in western China it (C) supports the idea that the world's climate is (D) more unstable than previously believed.

18. There was much (A) discrimination against Filipino immigrants (B), and one of the first (C) anti–Filipino riots broken (D) out in Yakima, Washington, in 1928.

19. At the age of twenty, "Babe" Zaharias <u>won</u> (A) the first of several golf <u>tournament</u> (B), and she later was <u>the first</u> (C) American <u>to win</u> (D) the British Women's Open Championship.

20. <u>Some</u> (A) retail stores have <u>experimented</u> (B) with <u>faster</u> (C) checkout counter belts and a device <u>call</u> (D) a *spectrophysic scanner*.

21. A study by the Harvard School of Public Health shows <u>that</u> (A) everyday measures <u>to avoid</u> (B) heart disease—such as <u>exercising more</u> (C) and eating less fat—<u>saving</u> (D) about 32,000 lives each year.

22. <u>The</u> (A) British governor of India <u>established a code</u> (B) which reformed the judicial system of India but <u>excluding</u> (C) native Indians from all <u>high posts</u> (D).

23. Besides <u>causing</u> (A) shortages in water <u>supply</u> (B) and inflicting <u>damage</u> (C) on crops, drought can also <u>leading</u> (D) to dust storms and forest fires.

24. A bird bath that <u>is kept full</u> (A) of clean water is <u>the perfect place</u> (B) for <u>a wild birds</u> (C) <u>to perform</u> (D) their cold weather ablutions.

25. A great <u>amount</u> (A) of recent <u>researches</u> (B) <u>has focused</u> (C) on the role of single fathers in <u>raising</u> (D) their children.

Answers to Structure Quiz 4 are on page 642.

2.9 Recognizing Noun Clauses

FOCUS

Read the following TOEFL item. What does this sentence need?

> Effective journalists can predict ------- respond to a story.
>
> ○ do their readers
> ○ how will their readers
> ○ how their readers will
> ○ of their readers

This sentence needs a direct object for the verb *can predict*. A direct object must be a noun structure.

Look at the part of the sentence after the blank space: *respond to a story*, a verb phrase. It suggests that the direct object of the sentence is a clause, and *respond* is the verb of this clause. The missing part, then, is the beginning of a noun clause.

A ***noun clause*** is a type of subordinate clause that functions as a noun in a sentence. Like all subordinate clauses, a noun clause has a subordinator, a subject and a verb.

The third choice, *how their readers will*, has all the necessary parts of a noun clause: subordinator + subject + verb. Therefore, it is the correct answer.

The sentence should read: *Effective journalists can predict how their readers will respond to a story.*

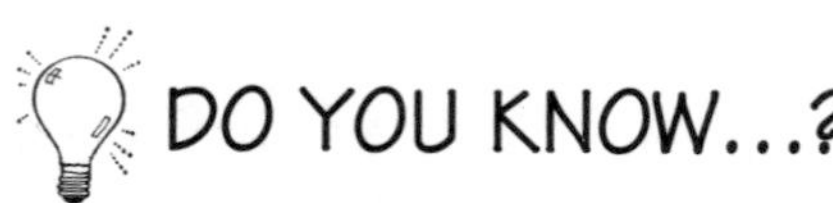

1. Approximately one item on the TOEFL will test your ability to recognize a noun clause in a sentence. You must be able to recognize the parts of a noun clause and to understand what function the noun clause serves in the sentence.

2. A noun clause is formed with subordinator + subject + verb (+ rest of clause). A noun clause can serve these functions in a sentence:

Subject:

How life began has been a topic of debate for many centuries.

Subject Complement:

A little mass gives a lot of energy, and this is why nuclear power is so abundant.

Direct Object:

In 1978 scientists discovered that the planet Pluto has a satellite.

Object of a Preposition:

Microeconomics is concerned with how wheat prices rise while cotton prices fall.

Noun clauses usually begin with words called ***subordinating conjunctions*** or ***subordinators***.

SUBORDINATORS IN NOUN CLAUSES			
how	how soon	whenever	who
however	if	where	whoever
how long	that	wherever	whom
how many	what	whether (or not)	whomever
how much	whatever	which	whose
how often	when	whichever	why

Note: In some sentences, the subordinator is also the subject of the noun clause.

Whoever bothers to read junk mail is probably wasting a lot of time.

In the following sentences, underline the noun clauses and circle their subjects and verbs.

a. What one person considers a wildflower may be a weed to another.
b. Psychiatrists have concluded that stress–related changes contributed to major illness in 79 percent of the persons studied.
c. Scholars disagree over who really wrote some of Shakespeare's sonnets.

(***Answers:*** a. Noun clause: *What one person considers a wildflower*; subject: *one person*; verb: *considers*; b. Noun clause: *that stress–related changes contributed to major illness in 79 percent of the persons studied*; subject: *stress–related changes*; verb: *contributed*; c. Noun clause: *who really wrote some of Shakespeare's sonnets*; subject: *who*; verb: *wrote*)

3. When a noun clause is the subject of a sentence, there must be a verb in the main clause.

> That goods are scarce is the central fact behind the science of economics.
> NC V

When a noun clause is the direct object of a sentence, there must be a subject and a verb in the main clause.

> Children usually imitate whatever their parents do.
> S V NC

You must be careful to check that both the main clause and the noun clause contain a subject and a verb.

In the following sentence, what are the subject and verb of the main clause? What are the subject and verb of the noun clause?

> That secondhand smoke, like active smoking, can cause serious health problems has been shown by several studies.

(***Answers:*** The subject of the main clause is the noun clause: *That secondhand smoke can cause serious health problems*. Verb of main clause: *has been shown*. Subject of noun clause: *secondhand smoke*. Verb of noun clause: *can cause*.)

Beware! Sometimes a TOEFL sentence will try to trick you by separating the subject and verb with a modifying phrase, such as *like active smoking* in the above example.

Note: When a noun clause begins with *that* and is used as a direct object in a sentence, you can omit *that*, with no change in meaning.

> Most astronomers believe that some form of life must exist on other planets.
> Most astronomers believe some form of life must exist on other planets.

4. Some noun clauses can be reduced to infinitive phrases (See 2.7). Look at some examples:

Noun Clause:

> How society should distribute scarce goods is a central economic problem in any society.

Infinitive Phrase:

> How to distribute scarce goods is a central economic problem in any society.

Noun Clause:

> In children's games, the leader tells the others what they must do.

Infinitive Phrase:

> In children's games, the leader tells the others what to do.

5. A TOEFL item may test your ability to recognize when a noun clause is needed in a sentence. Look at this example:

> Sharks were once thought to be instinctive killing machines, but it is now believed -------.
>
> ◯ they learn to hunt by experience
> ◯ that learn to hunt by experience
> ◯ learning to hunt by experience
> ◯ that their learning to hunt by experience

The second clause of this sentence needs direct object for the verb *believed*. This direct object is also the true subject of the clause; *it* is the "false" subject (See 2.1).

The first answer choice, *they learn to hunt by experience*, is a clause because it has a subject and a verb—but is it a noun clause? Yes, it is. Remember, if a noun clause is a direct object, and if the noun clause begins with *that*, sometimes *that* is omitted. In this case, *that* has been omitted, but this does not change the fact that *they learn to hunt by experience* is a noun clause. It is also the choice that best completes this sentence.

Why are the other three answer choices incorrect?

Look at another example:

> There are a number of organizations and books that can help you learn more about ------- indoor air quality.
>
> ◯ to improve
> ◯ how to improve
> ◯ how improve the
> ◯ improvement

This sentence needs an object for the preposition *about*. The object of a preposition must be a noun. (You will review prepositions in 2.21.) In this case, you can see the missing part must be a noun clause with *indoor air quality* as its direct object.

Which answer choice is a noun clause? The second choice, *how to improve*, is a noun clause that has been reduced to an infinitive phrase. It is the choice that best completes the sentence.

Why are the other three answer choices incorrect?

6. A TOEFL item may test your ability to choose the correct subordinator for a noun clause. Look at this example:

> ------- standardized tests discriminate against certain types of students has been argued since the 1970s.
>
> ◯ There are
> ◯ Unless
> ◯ That
> ◯ The

You can recognize that the verb of the main clause, *has been argued*, must have a subject. Its subject must be a noun clause whose subject + verb is *standardized tests discriminate*. This noun clause must begin with a subordinator.

The first and fourth answer choices are not subordinators. The second choice, *Unless*, is a subordinator, but it introduces adverb clauses (See 2.11). The third choice best completes the sentence. The sentence should read: *That standardized tests discriminate against certain types of students has been argued since the 1970s.*

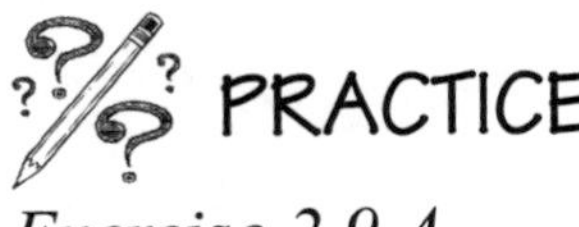

PRACTICE

Exercise 2.9.A

Choose the one word or phrase that best completes the sentence.

1. A good college history textbook includes ------- about history.

   (A) every student knowing
   (B) should every student know
   (C) in that every student should know
   (D) what every student should know

2. The Counseling and Career Center provides academic and career advising, and it also will tell students ------- for other community resources.

   (A) where to go
   (B) where go
   (C) they can go where
   (D) wherever

3. How vines climb, -------, and what special needs they have all make a big difference when deciding where to put which vine.

   (A) when they can be planted
   (B) they can be planted
   (C) can they be planted
   (D) when were they being planted

4. A female tiger signals ------- ready to mate by leaving her scratch marks and scent on trees.

   (A) her
   (B) that she is
   (C) is she
   (D) she

5. A study found that men in discussion groups spent a lot of time finding out ------- about politics and current events.

   (A) who was best informed
   (B) best informed who was
   (C) best informed by whom
   (D) was who informed best

6. When changing lanes, a driver should use his turn signal to let other drivers know -------.

   (A) he is entering which lane
   (B) which lane he is entering
   (C) where lane he is entering
   (D) into lane he is entering

7. The architects of the grand Palace at Fontainebleau did not seem to know ------- with the building's exterior.

   (A) doing it
   (B) to do what
   (C) what to do
   (D) they did what

8. ------- Abraham Lincoln was the greatest American president was the unanimous vote of a group of prominent historians.

   (A) It was
   (B) As
   (C) That
   (D) Because

9. Before paper was invented, people wrote on ------- could lay their hands on: silk, palm leaves, or clay tablets.

   (A) which they
   (B) what
   (C) whatever
   (D) whatever they

10. It is believed ------- seasonal variation is the change in the wind patterns of the Northern and Southern Hemispheres.

   (A) the principal cause to be
   (B) of the principal cause
   (C) that the principal cause of
   (D) the principal cause is

Answers to Exercise 2.9.A are on page 642.

2.9 EXTENSION

1. For each sentence in Exercise 2.9.A, students identify (a) the subject and verb of the main clause and (b) the subject and verb of the noun clause.

2. Students create "TOEFL sentences" to test their classmates' understanding of noun clauses as the subject of a sentence. Students write their own sentences or change sentences they find in print. Omit the subject of the sentence, and leave a blank space where it should be. Classmates must complete the sentences with a noun clause. Use the list of subordinators on page 206.

3. Do activity #2 again, but this time omit the direct object of the sentence and leave a blank space where it should be. Classmates must complete the sentences with a noun clause.

2.10 Recognizing Adjective Clauses and Phrases

FOCUS

Read the following sentences:

> Air pollution is a hazard to human, plant, and animal health as well as to physical structures.
>
> When hiking, you should carry a map of the area where you plan to be.
>
> A mountain range, from which many swift rivers flow, forms the backbone of the Malay Peninsula.
>
> A form of electric engine called a linear induction motor drives the maglev train.

STRUCTURE

What is similar about the underlined parts of the sentences? All of the underlined parts work as adjectives. The first sentence has several single–word adjectives.

Both the second and third sentences contain an adjective clause. An ***adjective clause*** is a subordinate clause that functions in the same way that a single–word adjective does. An adjective clause describes, defines, modifies, or gives information about a noun.

The fourth sentence has an ***adjective phrase***, which is an adjective clause that has been reduced. The adjective phrase *called a linear induction motor* modifies the noun *engine*.

All of the above examples are similar to the types of sentences you will see on the TOEFL.

DO YOU KNOW...?

1. One or two items on the TOEFL will test your ability to recognize adjective clauses and adjective phrases. You must be able to recognize correct and incorrect usage of all of the parts of adjective clause and phrases.

2. Adjective clauses come after the nouns they modify. Adjective clauses are sometimes called ***relative clauses*** because they begin with words called ***relative pronouns***.

RELATIVE PRONOUNS		
	People	**Animals and Things**
Subject	who, that	which, that
Object	whom, that	which, that
Possessive	whose	whose

Adjectives clauses can also begin with these subordinators:

when	where	whereby	why

Like all clauses, an adjective clause must have a subject and a verb. Sometimes the subject is the relative pronoun. Within an adjective clause, the relative pronoun can serve these functions:

Subject of an Adjective Clause:

Frederick Douglass was a former slave <u>who became a leader in the anti–slavery movement</u>.

Direct Object:

Abraham Lincoln is the president <u>whom historians believe was the greatest</u>.
The cat is the animal <u>that many Americans choose as their pet</u>.

Note: When *whom*, *that*, or *which* functions as the direct object of the adjective clause, you can omit it, with no change in meaning:

Abraham Lincoln is the president <u>historians believe was the greatest</u>.
The cat is the animal <u>many Americans choose as their pet</u>.

Object of a Preposition:

Bermuda is an area of islands and coral rocks <u>to which thousands of tourists are attracted every year</u>.

Note: The preposition before the relative pronoun is part of the adjective clause. Use a preposition if it is needed with the verb or if you want to communicate a specific meaning. Look at the above sentence written in a different way:

Thousands of tourists <u>are attracted</u> <u>to</u> an area of islands and coral rocks, Bermuda.

The verb *are attracted* needs the preposition *to*, so the preposition must come before *which* in the adjective clause:

(an area) <u>to which</u> thousands of tourists are attracted every year.

Note: *Who*, *that*, *where*, *when*, and *why* never follow a preposition at the beginning of an adjective clause.

3. When an adjective clause is needed to identify a noun, it is called a ***necessary*** or ***restrictive*** adjective clause. No commas are used around necessary adjective clauses.

   Of all living things, the chimpanzee has a genetic make–up that is most similar to ours.

   When an adjective clause gives extra information and is not necessary to identify the noun, commas are placed around the adjective clause. Commas are a clue that can help you recognize some adjective clauses.

   Elizabeth Cady Stanton, who was born in Johnstown, New York, was an early American feminist.

   Note: When commas are used around an adjective clause, *that* cannot begin the clause.

4. Adjective clauses appear frequently in written and spoken English. A sentence might contain several adjective clauses. An adjective clause can contain other adjective clauses.

   In the following sentence, underline the adjective clauses. Circle the nouns they modify:

   There are social situations where people who give information are higher in status than those who need information.

   (***Answers:*** The adjective clause *where people who give information are higher in status than those who need information* modifies the noun *situations*. The adjective clause *who give information* modifies the noun *people*. The adjective clause *who need information* modifies the pronoun *those*.)

5. Some adjective clauses can be reduced to adjective phrases, with no change in meaning. An adjective clause can be reduced to an adjective phrase only when the clause has *who*, *which*, or *that* as its subject.

   Adjective Clause:

   The general who had led the Union Army to victory was Ulysses S. Grant.

   Adjective Phrase:

   The general leading the Union Army to victory was Ulysses S. Grant.

   Adjective Clause:

   A proton is one of two kinds of particles that make up the nucleus of an atom.

   Adjective Phrase:

   A proton is one of two kinds of particles making up the nucleus of an atom.

   To reduce an adjective clause to an adjective phrase:

   - omit the subject of the clause (the relative pronoun)
   - omit the auxiliary verbs, if there are any
   - change the verb to its *–ing* form

Note: Use the *–ing* form (present participle) when the adjective phrase is in the active voice. Use the *–ed* form (past participle) when the adjective phrase is in the passive voice (See 2.6). These rules apply to verbs in any tense.

Active Voice:

The technology that impacts us most is what we use in our homes.
The technology impacting us most is what we use in our homes.

Passive Voice:

Yellowstone, which was authorized by Congress in 1872, is the oldest national park in the United States.
Yellowstone, authorized by Congress in 1872, is the oldest national park in the United States.

Note: If the adjective clause needs commas, the adjective phrase also needs commas:

Crater Lake, which was formed by a volcano, is a superb setting for day hikes.
Crater Lake, formed by a volcano, is a superb setting for day hikes.

6. Some adjective clauses can be reduced to appositive phrases. An ***appositive*** is a noun phrase that is placed near another noun to define or explain it (See 2.2). Appositives do not have verbs.

Adjective Clause:

One application of the laser is holography, which is the production of three–dimensional images.

Appositive Phrase:

One application of the laser is holography, the production of three–dimensional images.

7. A TOEFL item may test you by having:

- no adjective clause where one is needed
- an incomplete adjective clause
- an incorrect relative pronoun
- no preposition where one is needed before a relative pronoun
- an incorrect participle in an adjective phrase

8. A TOEFL item may test your ability to recognize when an adjective clause is needed. Look at this example:

> The fat–soluble vitamins are stored in body fat and may therefore accumulate in quantities -------.
>
> ○ can be toxic
> ○ that can be toxic
> ○ they can be toxic
> ○ can they be toxic

All of the answer choices contain a verb. Therefore, you know that the missing part of the sentence must be an adjective clause that will modify the noun *quantities*.

Only the second choice, *that can be toxic*, has the correct form and necessary parts of an adjective clause: subject (relative pronoun) + verb. The other three choices are incorrect because they either lack a relative pronoun or have incorrect word order.

9. A test item may try to trick you by having an incorrect relative pronoun. Look at this example:

> Benefits of a credit account, what may change from time to time, typically include certain kinds of insurance coverage.

Which underlined word or phrase must be changed for the sentence to be correct? If you chose *what*, you were correct because *what* makes a noun clause (See 2.9), not an adjective clause. Correction: *which*.

10. Some of the answer choices may test you by not having a preposition where one is needed before the relative pronoun. Look at this example:

> For today's astronomers, constellations are simply areas of the sky ------- interesting objects await observation.
>
> ◯ in that
> ◯ which
> ◯ in which
> ◯ are

Interesting objects await observation *in* areas of the sky. A preposition is needed before the relative pronoun to communicate this location. The third answer choice, *in which*, best completes the sentence, which should read: *For today's astronomers, constellations are simply areas of the sky in which interesting objects await observation.*

Why are the other three answer choices incorrect?

11. A TOEFL item may test your ability to recognize the correct participle in an adjective phrase. Look at this example:

> Bobsleds, ------- by two– or four–man crews, have a metal brake with several teeth.
>
> ◯ driven
> ◯ are driven
> ◯ they are driven
> ◯ driving

The commas are a clue that the missing part of the sentence is the beginning of an adjective clause or phrase to modify *bobsleds*. Because the answer choices contain a participle but not a relative pronoun, you know the correct answer is an adjective phrase.

You can see that *by two– or four–man crews* indicates passive voice (See 2.6). The first answer choice, *driven*, best completes the sentence because it is the past participle, which passive voice requires.

Why are the other three answer choices incorrect?

Look at another example:

> A great amount of unemployment is the simple turnover of people either ------- for the first time or reentering it.
>
> ◯ enter the labor force
> ◯ entered the labor force
> ◯ are entering the labor force
> ◯ entering the labor force

In this sentence, *people* needs an active voice verb because people are doing the action; they are entering or reentering the labor force. Therefore, you must use the present participle. The fourth choice, *entering the labor force*, best completes the sentence.

How would you rewrite the above adjective phrase as an adjective clause?

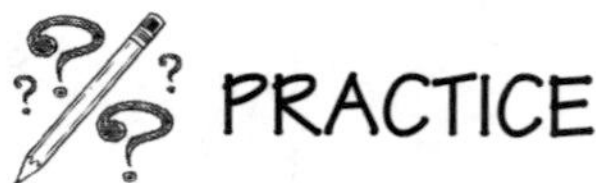

PRACTICE

Exercise 2.10.A

Choose the one underlined word or phrase that must be changed for the sentence to be correct.

1. The vacuum coffee maker is a complicated (A) device which (B) steam is generated (C) in a glass bowl connected (D) to a holding container of coffee grounds and hot water.

2. Although he is not the scientist he invents (A) the new process, the innovator (B) is the one who (C) successfully introduces it (D) to the public.

Choose the one word or phrase that best completes the sentence.

3. Hammurabi, ------- his capital at Babylon, issued a famous code of laws for the management of his large empire.

   (A) who had
   (B) had
   (C) whose
   (D) he had

4. Composer Maurice Ravel based some of his finest works on the Oriental scales ------- he was introduced at the Paris Exhibition of 1889.

   (A) at which
   (B) to which
   (C) which
   (D) that

5. When changing banks, credit card companies may assign a cash advance limit that is less than the full credit line -------.

   (A) to a client's account assigned
   (B) assigned to a client's account
   (C) assigning to a client's account
   (D) is assigning to a client's account

6. Large, fast–moving trucks have been known to create wind blasts ------- a motorcyclist.

   (A) for can startle
   (B) can that startle
   (C) that can startle
   (D) can startle

7. Mount Vernon, George Washington's mansion, has wide lawns, fine gardens, and several smaller buildings, ------- with attention to Washington's detailed notes.

   (A) restoring all
   (B) all were restored
   (C) all restored
   (D) all restoration

8. Cubism was an art movement, primarily in painting, ------- in 1907.

   (A) originated in Paris
   (B) it originated in Paris
   (C) in Paris was originated
   (D) that originated in Paris

9. Australia's first penal colony, -------, was at Sydney.

   (A) it was often called Botany Bay
   (B) often called Botany Bay
   (C) Botany Bay was often called
   (D) often calling Botany Bay

10. The aromatic herb tarragon has long been cultivated for its leaves, ------- for flavoring vinegar, sauces, and soups.

   (A) that are used
   (B) which are used
   (C) been used
   (D) they are used

STRUCTURE

Exercise 2.10.B

Choose the one word or phrase that best completes the sentence.

1. A capo, a movable device ------- to a guitar neck, is used to raise the pitch of the strings.

   (A) that attaching
   (B) attached
   (C) is attached
   (D) where is attached

2. The Tarascans, ------- were traditionally known for their hummingbird–feather mosaics, are still noted for their weaving, music, and lacquerware.

   (A) they
   (B) who
   (C) that
   (D) which

3. Interest is a device ------- two functions in the economy.

   (A) that serves
   (B) that it serves
   (C) serves
   (D) can be served

4. Gravity dams, ------- of concrete, use their own weight to provide resistance to the pressure of water.

   (A) usually to make
   (B) they are usually made
   (C) are usually made
   (D) usually made

5. Edouard Daladier, ------- over France in the early months of World War II, was overthrown when he failed to aid Finland.

   (A) was presided
   (B) presided
   (C) who presided
   (D) that presided

6. Nathaniel Currier and James Ives were American lithographers and publishers ------- highly popular hand–colored prints of nineteenth–century scenes.

   (A) production of
   (B) produced
   (C) they produced
   (D) who produced

7. ------- at Montreux Casino Hall on Lake Geneva, the Montreux International Jazz Festival showcases leading jazz artists and jazz–rock performers.

   (A) Held
   (B) Holding
   (C) It is held
   (D) Which is held

8. The principles of Dada, ------- Max Ernst and Marcel Duchamp, were eventually modified to become the basis of Surrealism.

   (A) were carried to New York by
   (B) carried to New York by
   (C) they were carried to New York by
   (D) carried them to New York

Answers to Exercises 2.10.A through 2.10.B are on page 643.

2.10 EXTENSION

1. For each sentence in Exercises 2.10.A and 2.10.B, students identify (a) the subject and verb of the main clause and (b) the subject and verb of the adjective clause. Which sentences have adjective phrases?

2. In reading done outside class, students look for examples of adjective clauses and phrases. Bring examples to share in class. Identify the nouns that are modified by the adjective clauses and phrases.

3. Students create "TOEFL sentences" to test their classmates' understanding of adjective clauses. Students write their own sentences with adjective clauses, or use sentences they find in print. Change the relative pronoun in each adjective clause so that it is incorrect. Write the sentences either on the board or on cards. Classmates must identify the error and make the correction.

ASSESSING PROGRESS – 2.9 through 2.10

QUIZ 5 (Time – 10 minutes)

Choose the one word or phrase that best completes the sentence.

1. Companies buy information from marketing analysts to help characterize their customers and learn -------.

   (A) finding more of them
   (B) that finding more of them
   (C) they find more of them
   (D) how to find more of them

2. Babism, ------- elements of Sufism and other religions, is centered on a belief in the coming of the Promised One.

   (A) incorporated
   (B) incorporating
   (C) it incorporates
   (D) incorporation

3. Some mountains are cones of volcanoes or intrusions of igneous rock -------.

   (A) form the domes
   (B) that form domes
   (C) where form domes
   (D) form domes

4. Some people may not realize ------- a memory unit and a processing unit similar to those in a computer.

   (A) a pocket calculator has
   (B) a pocket calculator it has
   (C) in a pocket calculator
   (D) that is a pocket calculator

5. During the Boston Massacre of 1770, five members of a rioting crowd were killed by British soldiers ------- to maintain order.

   (A) sending to Boston
   (B) sent to Boston
   (C) they were sent to Boston
   (D) to be sent to Boston

STRUCTURE

Choose the one underlined word or phrase that must be changed for the sentence to be correct.

6. The rising water flooded (A) the citrus groves, eventually rising to the point why (B) villagers used boats to harvest (C) dates from the (D) tallest palms.

7. Trade is mutually beneficial (A) between two countries in where (B) one is more efficient in making one good (C) and the other (D) is more efficient in producing another good.

8. Base (A) in part on the experience of a real man (B), Daniel Defoe's *Adventures of Robinson Crusoe* is often considered (C) the first true novel in English (D).

Quiz 5

Choose the one word or phrase that best completes the sentence.

9. ------- is a question that concerns the researchers who have been studying the owl since it was listed as a threatened species.

(A) Because the spotted owl's survival
(B) Whether the spotted owl can survive
(C) Can the spotted owl it survive
(D) The spotted owl can survive

10. Rome was built around an open marketplace into which main roads converged and ------- buildings were grouped.

(A) near
(B) in order that
(C) around which
(D) as though

11. Igor Stravinsky, ------- the Bach of the twentieth century, represented the best of the "old" as well as the "new" music.

(A) be considered
(B) he was considered
(C) considered
(D) considering

12. ------- anthropologists found the fossil of a human ancestor in the Olduvai Gorge is well–known among scientists who study the origins of the human race.

(A) The
(B) That
(C) Because
(D) Some

13. Niels Bohr's atomic theory ------- the hydrogen atom consisted of a positive massive nucleus and an electron traveling in orbits around it.

(A) to
(B) that
(C) stated that
(D) it stated that

14. The great civilization which had prospered for over a thousand years along the Indus River was destroyed around 1500 B.C. by nomads -------.

(A) came from Persia probably
(B) from Persia probably were coming
(C) probably came from Persia
(D) probably coming from Persia

15. Milton Avery is known for figurative paintings ------- display bold massing of forms.

(A) for
(B) in that
(C) to which
(D) that

Answers to Structure Quiz 5 are on page 643.

2.11 Recognizing Adverb Clauses and Phrases

FOCUS

Read the following TOEFL item. What does this sentence need?

------- common usage among economists, the term "natural rate" is misleading.

- It has gained
- That it has gained
- Although it has gained
- Has it gained

This sentence needs an introductory clause or phrase before the main clause, *the term "natural rate" is misleading*. Since the sentence has a main clause, you know the missing part of the sentence must be a subordinate clause.

In the third choice, the subordinator *Although* makes an adverb clause. An ***adverb clause*** is a subordinate clause that functions in the same way that a single–word adverb does. An adverb clause modifies a verb or a main clause.

The third choice best completes the sentence, which should read: *Although it has gained common usage among economists, the term "natural rate" is misleading.*

Now, read another TOEFL item. What does this sentence need?

Jack McAuliffe had been the undefeated amateur boxing champion ------- the professional champion in 1885.

- and becoming
- before becoming
- became
- before became

This sentence needs a subordinate clause after the main clause, *Jack McAuliffe had been the undefeated amateur boxing champion*. Notice, however, that none of the answer choices has a subject! How can one of them be a clause?

Like adjective clauses (See 2.10), some adverb clauses can be reduced to phrases. The answer is the second choice, *before becoming*, which is an ***adverb phrase*** that has been reduced from the adverb clause *before he became*.

STRUCTURE

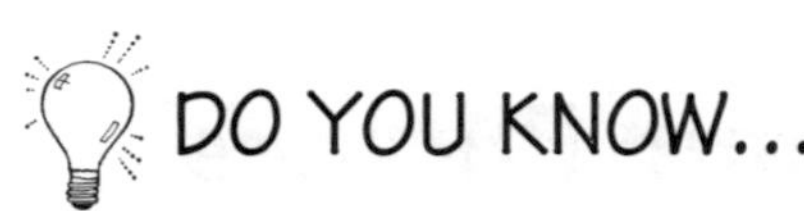

1. At least one item on the TOEFL will test your ability to recognize correct usage of adverb clauses and phrases.

2. An ***adverb clause*** modifies a main clause or the verb in a main clause. Like all subordinate clauses, an adverb clause must have a subject and a verb. An adverb clause cannot stand alone as a sentence. It must be connected to a main clause to make a complete sentence.

   Adverb clauses begin with words called ***subordinators*** or ***subordinating conjunctions***.

   Subordinators in Adverb Clauses

Time	after	as	as long as	as soon as
	before	by the time	now that	since
	until	when	whenever	while
Place	where	wherever		
Cause/Result	because	since	so that	in order that
	so...that	such...that		
Contrast	although	even if	even though	despite the fact that
	though	whereas	while	in spite of the fact that
Manner	as	as if	as though	just as
	like			
Condition	as long as	if	in case	whether or not
	provided	unless		

   > Martin Luther King was <u>such</u> a powerful orator <u>that his speeches continue to inspire people many years afterward</u>.
   > <u>Even though it appears to help some people</u>, doctors disagree on melatonin's safety.
   > The raccoon rubs and tears its food underwater, <u>as if the food needed washing</u>.

   Note: Sentences with adverb clauses of condition are called ***conditional sentences***. (You will review conditional sentences in 2.12.)

   The order of the adverb clause and the main clause can be reversed without a change in meaning. These two sentences have the same meaning:

   > Malcolm X had been assassinated <u>by the time his autobiography was published</u>.
   > <u>By the time his autobiography was published</u>, Malcolm X had been assassinated.

   Note: When the adverb clause comes first, it is followed by a comma.

3. Some adverb clauses can be reduced to adverb phrases, with no change in meaning. An adverb clause can be reduced to an adverb phrase only when the subject of the adverb clause is the same as the subject of the main clause.

   Adverb clauses that begin with *after*, *before*, *since*, *when*, and *while* are frequently reduced to phrases.

Adverb Clause:

When a substance undergoes a slow oxidation, the substance can burst into flame.

Adverb Phrase:

When undergoing a slow oxidation, a substance can burst into flame.

Adverb Clause:

Benjamin Franklin invented many things while he was working as a printer.

Adverb Phrase:

Benjamin Franklin invented many things while working as a printer.

To reduce an adverb clause to an adverb phrase:

- omit the subject of the clause
- omit the auxiliary verbs, if there are any
- change the verb to its *–ing* form

Note: Use the *–ing* form (present participle) when the adverb phrase is in the active voice. Use the *–ed* form (past participle) when the adverb phrase is in the passive voice (See 2.6). These rules apply to verbs in any tense.

Active Voice:

Frank Sprague developed the elevator after he had improved the electric motor.
Frank Sprague developed the elevator after improving the electric motor.

Passive Voice:

Since it was discovered, penicillin has been used to treat bacterial infections.
Since discovered, penicillin has been used to treat bacterial infections.

Note: When reducing adverb clauses that begin with *because*, *when*, or *while*, you can sometimes omit the subordinator as well as the subject.

Adverb Clause:

Because it was once considered a dangerous predator, the wolf has been hunted to near–extinction.

Adverb Phrase:

Once considered a dangerous predator, the wolf has been hunted to near–extinction.

Adverb Clause:

When she returned to her native city, Kate Chopin began to write the stories for which she is noted.

Adverb Phrase:

Returning to her native city, Kate Chopin began to write the stories for which she is noted.

Note: An adverb clause cannot be reduced if the adverb clause and main clause have different subjects. The following sentence cannot be reduced:

Wherever ornamental grasses are used, the garden will have a finished look.

4. Some of the answer choices may try to trick you by having an incorrect subordinator. Look at this example:

> The art of yoga began in India more than 2,000 years ago, ------- people discovered they could use a breathing exercise to develop focus.
>
> ◯ some
> ◯ that
> ◯ as if
> ◯ when

This sentence needs a word to connect the main clause to the second clause, which is an adverb clause. The first answer choice, *some*, is not a connecting word. The second choice, *that*, is an incorrect subordinator because it would make a noun clause (See 2.9).

The third and fourth choices, *as if* and *when*, can introduce adverb clauses. Which one is more appropriate for this context? The fourth choice, *when*, best completes this sentence because it introduces adverb clauses of time.

5. Some of the answer choices may try to trick you by having an incorrectly formed adverb phrase. Look at this example:

> ------- Becquerel's work with radioactivity, Marie Curie began to study uranium.
>
> ◯ She followed
> ◯ Followed
> ◯ Following
> ◯ It follows

This sentence begins with an adverb phrase that is in the active voice. Therefore, the adverb phrase needs the *–ing* form of the verb. The third answer choice, *Following*, best completes the sentence, which should read: *Following Becquerel's work with radioactivity, Marie Curie began to study uranium.*

Why are the other three answer choices incorrect?

PRACTICE

Exercise 2.11.A

Choose the one word or phrase that best completes the sentence.

1. ------- golf became increasingly accessible to Americans after World War II, the game achieved popularity with both average people and professional players.

   (A) So
   (B) As if
   (C) As
   (D) That

2. The spider called "daddy longlegs" is omnivorous, ------- plant fluids, animal tissue, and other daddy longlegs.

   (A) feeding on
   (B) feeds on
   (C) is fed
   (D) to feed

3. Customers are entitled to receive additional credit services ------- maintain their account in good standing.

   (A) because of
   (B) they can
   (C) do they
   (D) as long as they

4. Brasses are musical instruments that produce tones -------.

   (A) are lips buzzing the mouthpiece
   (B) if buzz the mouthpiece
   (C) lips buzz the mouthpiece
   (D) when lips buzz the mouthpiece

5. ------- songs in a wild falsetto, Little Richard became a seminal figure in the birth of rock and roll.

   (A) Pounding the piano and howling
   (B) To be pounding the piano and howling
   (C) He pounded the piano and howled
   (D) The piano was pounded and howling

6. Prehistoric men hunted the hairy mammoth with spears and axes, ------- the animal's body to a variety of uses.

   (A) later they put
   (B) to be later put
   (C) later putting
   (D) they were putting later

7. ------- a surgeon in 1811, sixteen–year–old John Keats soon met the writer Leigh Hunt and gave up surgery for poetry.

   (A) To be apprenticed
   (B) Apprenticed to
   (C) He was apprenticed to
   (D) Apprenticeship to

8. Claude Debussy started the modern harmonic revolution in France, ------- not without help from other musical impressionists.

   (A) although it was
   (B) because of
   (C) since
   (D) unless he did

9. ------- to within thirty feet of its victim, the Siberian tiger pounces and grabs its prey by the neck, with its back feet still firmly planted on the ground.

   (A) It creeps
   (B) When crept
   (C) Crept
   (D) Creeping

10. The Aztecs underwent a considerable period of tutelage to the Toltecs, ------- the agriculture and irrigation practiced by these people.

    (A) learned much of
    (B) learning much of
    (C) were learning much
    (D) much was learned

Answers to Exercise 2.11.A are on page 644.

2.11 EXTENSION

1. Oral or written exercise. In Exercise 2.11.A, students identify which sentences contain adverb phrases (reduced clauses). Restate the adverb phrases as adverb clauses by adding a subordinator and a subject and changing the verb, as necessary.

2. In reading done outside class, students look for examples of adverb clauses and phrases. Bring examples to share in class. Can any of the adverb clauses be reduced? If so, how?

3. Students create "TOEFL sentences" to test their classmates' understanding of adverb clauses. Students write their own sentences, or use sentences they find in print. Omit the subordinator in each adverb clause, and leave a blank space where it should be. Write the sentences either on the board or on cards. Classmates must complete the sentences with an appropriate subordinator. Use the list of subordinators on page 222.

2.12 Recognizing Conditionals

FOCUS

Read the following sentences:

> If you study a foreign language, you have to learn both word meanings and how to combine them into sentence meanings.
>
> The aurora borealis may appear as a soft glow along the northern horizon if the base of its arc is beneath the horizon.
>
> A seedling will grow into a large, healthy tree as long as it can extend its roots to a nearby soil pocket in the rocky landscape.

What is similar about the sentences?

Each of the sentences discusses a condition that will or may lead to a certain result. In conditional sentences, the condition is sometimes called the *if*–clause.

In the first sentence, the condition is *if you study a foreign language*. The result is *you have to learn both word meanings and how to combine them into sentence meanings*. This is a statement of general truth.

In the second sentence, notice the location of the *if*–clause. What is the condition? The condition is *if the base of its arc is beneath the horizon*. The result is the *aurora borealis may appear as a soft glow along the northern horizon*. This is a statement of probable truth.

What is the condition in the third sentence? Here, the condition is not an *if*–clause; it is indicated by *as long as*, which in this context has a similar meaning to *if*. The condition is *as long as it can extend its roots to a nearby soil pocket in the rocky landscape*. What is the probable result?

All of the above examples are similar to the types of sentences you will see on the TOEFL.

STRUCTURE

2.12 Conditionals

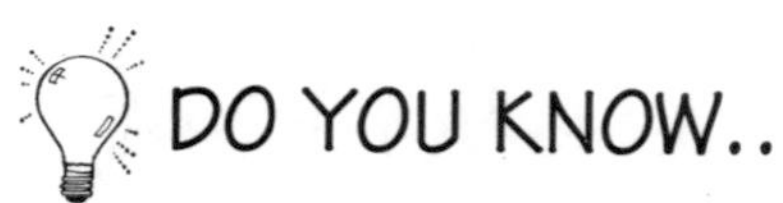

DO YOU KNOW...?

1. Approximately one item on the TOEFL will test your ability to recognize a conditional sentence. You must be able to recognize correct and incorrect usage of the verbs, auxiliaries, and subordinators in conditional sentences.

2. A ***conditional sentence*** is a complex sentence with a ***subordinate clause*** (the condition or *if*–clause) and a ***main clause*** (the result clause). *If* is a subordinator, and the *if*–clause is a type of adverb clause (See 2.11).

   The order of the *if*–clause and the result clause can be reversed without a change in meaning. These two sentences have the same meaning:

   > If a submarine's ballast tanks are flooded with water, its weight increases.
   > The weight of a submarine increases if its ballast tanks are flooded with water.

   Note: When the *if*–clause comes first, it is followed by a comma.

3. There are different types of conditional sentences to express differences in time (present, future, past) and degree of reality or truth. A situation is ***real*** if it is certain, probable or possible, and ***unreal*** if it is unlikely or not true.

   Tense is important in conditional sentences. Certain tenses and modals are commonly used with the different types of conditional sentences.

   Types of conditional sentences:

   Present Real:

   Use the present real for scientific facts and general truths. In present real conditionals, you can change *if* to *when* without a change in meaning.

	Subordinate Clause	Main Clause
If +	simple present present continuous present perfect present perfect continuous	simple present

> If something vibrates faster than twenty times a second, we can hear it.
> Today, if Americans are traveling cross–country, they usually choose to fly.
> Today, when Americans are traveling cross–country, they usually choose to fly.

Future Real:

Use the future real for situations that will certainly, probably or possibly happen in the present or future.

	Subordinate Clause	Main Clause	
If +	simple present present continuous present perfect present perfect continuous	*will* *can* *may* *might* *should* *have to*	+ base form of verb

If a project makes money, the investors will receive some of the profits.
The patient may need to consult an allergist if medicines have no effect.

Past Real:

Use the past real for general truths or common occurrences in the past.

	SUBORDINATE CLAUSE	MAIN CLAUSE
	simple past	
If +	past continuous	simple past

Before 1950, Americans took the train if they were traveling cross–country.

Present Unreal:

Use the present unreal for situations that are not real or are unlikely to happen in the present or future.

	SUBORDINATE CLAUSE	MAIN CLAUSE	
	simple past	*would*	
If +	past continuous	*could*	+ base form of verb
		might	
		should	

If energy decreased as machines worked, the machines would eventually slow down and stop.
(*Meaning:* Energy does not decrease as machines work, and machines will not slow down and stop.)

Note: On the TOEFL, the *were* form of *be* is used in the *if*–clause for all persons (first, second, third):

If this patient were over sixty and overweight, he could have a heart attack in the next five years.

Past Unreal:

Use the past unreal for situations that did not happen.

	SUBORDINATE CLAUSE	MAIN CLAUSE	
	past perfect	*would*	
If +	past perfect continuous	*could*	+ *have* + past participle
		might	
		should	

If their supply ship had arrived on time, the colonists at Roanoke might not have perished.
(*Meaning:* The ship did not arrive on time, and the colonists perished.)

4. Conditional sentences can be in the passive voice:

If a sore throat is accompanied by a fever and swollen glands in the neck, it may be caused by the streptococcus bacteria.
If the principle of conservation of energy were suddenly erased from the rule–book governing machines, then nothing would work.

5. Sometimes a conditional sentence on the TOEFL will have a subordinator other than *if*:

as long as	in case	provided (that)	unless	whether or not

Banks will make a profit provided that they collect more interest than they pay out in loans.
Unless the eggs are kept warm in a nest of vegetation, the young alligators will die.

Note: *unless* + affirmative verb = *if* + negative verb

The above sentence could also be written like this:

If the eggs are not kept warm in a nest of vegetation, the young alligators will die.

6. A TOEFL item may test you by having an incorrect form of the verb or auxiliary in a conditional sentence. Look at this example:

> If she was not attached to a static line, which automatically opens the parachute, a sky diver can free–fall before pulling her rip cord.

Which underlined word or phrase must be changed for the sentence to be correct? If you chose *was not*, you were correct because the auxiliary *was* is incorrect. The main clause has a modal + base–form verb: *can free–fall*, which tells you this situation is possible in the present or future (future real). The *if*–clause should be in the present tense. Correction: *is not*.

7. A TOEFL item may test your ability to choose the correct subordinator in a conditional sentence. Look at this example:

> ------- a predator approaches, the plover performs a distraction display, pretending to have a broken wing.
>
> ○ There is
> ○ That
> ○ Why
> ○ If

You should be able to recognize this as a conditional sentence. The simple present tense tells you this is a statement of scientific fact—something that happens when a predator approaches (present real).

The first answer choice has no subordinator. The second and third choices have subordinators that introduce noun clauses (See 2.9). The fourth choice best completes the sentence, which should read: *If a predator approaches, the plover performs a distraction display, pretending to have a broken wing.*

PRACTICE

Exercise 2.12.A

Choose the one word or phrase that best completes the sentence.

1. If thunder is the atmosphere's noisiest production, lightning ------- its most dazzling.

   (A) is certainly
   (B) certainly
   (C) certain to be
   (D) was certainly

2. ------- information is encoded effectively in the memory, it may not be easily recalled when necessary.

   (A) The
   (B) Unless
   (C) That
   (D) So that

3. Soil–covered lava lands usually support a normal forest ------- enough water.

   (A) if there is
   (B) or if there is
   (C) there has been
   (D) there is also

4. If teachers communicate the "prophecy" that certain students ------- in a certain manner, those students may behave in the expected manner.

   (A) to behave
   (B) behaved
   (C) will behave
   (D) behavior

5. Unless skill standards ------- as the basis for hiring employees, they will serve no role in helping people move from school to work.

   (A) accepted
   (B) been accepted
   (C) were accepted
   (D) are accepted

STRUCTURE

Choose the one underlined word or phrase that must be changed for the sentence to be correct.

6. If you have already <u>plant</u> (A) your vegetable garden, you <u>may want</u> (B) to make some changes in subsequent <u>plantings</u> (C) to take <u>advantage</u> (D) of natural companions for your vegetables.

7. A balloon will rise <u>as long as</u> (A) the weight of <u>the</u> (B) balloon and the air it contains <u>was</u> (C) less than the upthrust of the air <u>it displaces</u> (D).

8. <u>If</u> (A) you <u>are living</u> (B) on a mile–wide comet in the Kuiper Belt, <u>another</u> (C) large comet would pass within <u>a million miles</u> (D) of you once a month.

9. In 1838 New York State passed (A) the Free Banking Act, which (B) allowed anyone to start (C) a bank—as long as that person has made (D) certain promises.

10. If the goal of education is to enhance (A) both (B) individual achievement and social progress, then the "shopping mall colleges" should been (C) replaced with colleges that are (D) true learning communities.

Answers to Exercise 2.12.A are on page 644.

2.12 EXTENSION

1. In Exercise 2.12.A, students determine whether each situation is (a) present, future, or past, (b) real (certain, probable, possible) or unreal (unlikely or untrue).

2. In reading done outside class, students look for examples of conditional sentences. Bring examples to share in class. Identify the condition clauses. Discuss whether the situations are certain, probable, possible, unlikely, or untrue.

3. Conditional chain. Each student writes a condition clause (begin with *if* or *as long as*) using the verb in (a) below. Pass your paper to the person on your left. On the paper you now have, finish the sentence. Then, write a condition clause with verb (b). Pass your paper to the person on your left. Continue through (f). When you finish the last sentence, pass your paper to the person on your left. Choose a sentence from your paper and read it to the class.

   (a) see (b) don't like (c) feel (d) felt (e) changed (f) had changed

4. Spoken conditional chain. Perform activity #3 as an oral exercise. Students can use the verbs above in #3 or generate their own list of verbs. One student recites an *if*–clause, and a different student completes the sentence orally. A third student changes the sentence from real to unreal, or vice versa, and then begins a new sentence by reciting an *if*–clause.

2.13 Recognizing Inverted Subjects and Verbs

FOCUS

Read the following sentences:

> At the North Pole is a massive sheet of permanent ice.
>
> In the Amazon Basin live more than two million species of insects.
>
> Never had the submarine been used so effectively until the First World War.
>
> Hardly ever does the black bear attack humans.

What is similar about the subject–verb structures in the sentences?

In all of these sentences, the verb comes before the subject. This is unusual because in standard word order the subject comes before the verb.

Notice that the first two sentences begin with a prepositional phrase: *At the North Pole*, *In the Amazon Basin*. Both of these phrases refer to a location.

In the third sentence, notice that the sentence begins with a negative word, *Never*. The fourth sentence begins with the phrase *Hardly ever*. Why is the order of the subject and verb inverted in these sentences? You can probably guess that the word order changes when a sentence begins with certain expressions.

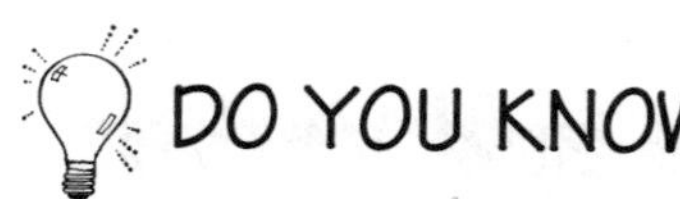

DO YOU KNOW...?

1. Approximately one item on the TOEFL will test your ability to recognize a situation where the word order of the subject and verb is inverted.

2. The standard word order of a sentence is: subject + verb (+ object). Use standard word order in main clauses and in subordinate clauses that begin with question words:

   When the bear hibernates, its temperature drops.

   Invert the subject and verb in direct questions:

   When does the bear hibernate?

   Inverted subject–verb word order is sometimes called ***question word order***.

   Invert the subject and verb in the following situations:

   - after prepositional phrases of location
   - after certain negative expressions
   - after the special expressions *so* and *neither*

   Note: When inverting a subject and verb with one or more auxiliaries, the subject comes after the first auxiliary:

   Never had the submarine been used so effectively until the First World War.

3. When a statement begins with a prepositional phrase of location, the subject and verb are inverted. (You will review prepositional phrases in 2.21.)

   Along the Mississippi are forty–one dams to regulate the flow of the river.

   When *there* is the subject, use standard word order:

   Along the Mississippi, there are forty–one dams to regulate the flow of the river.
   There are forty–one dams along the Mississippi to regulate the flow of the river.

PREPOSITIONS OF LOCATION

above	around	beneath	in/inside	on
along	at	beside	near	over
among	below	between	next to	under

Note: In some sentences, an introductory prepositional phrase expresses position in a group instead of physical location:

Among the best–loved fairy tales are *Cinderella* and *Snow White*.

A test item may try to trick you by using standard word order where inverted word order is needed. Look at this example:

> Among central Asia's oldest cities Tashkent is, the economic heart of Uzbekistan and leading manufacturer of textiles and machinery.

Which underlined word or phrase must be changed for the sentence to be correct? If you chose *Tashkent is*, you were correct because the order of the subject and verb should be inverted. The prepositional phrase *Among central Asia's oldest cities* expresses Tashkent's position in a group of cities. Correction: *is Tashkent.*

Also, in the above sentence, notice the appositive (See 2.2) following the comma: *the economic heart of Uzbekistan and leading manufacturer of textiles and machinery*. The appositive is a clue that a noun, not a verb, must be placed before it.

4. When a sentence or main clause begins with certain negative or "almost negative" expressions, the subject and verb are inverted.

NEGATIVE EXPRESSIONS

hardly ever	not once	only
neither	not only…but also	rarely
never	not until	scarcely
no sooner…than	nowhere	seldom
not often	on no account	under no circumstances

Not until the 1840s could women own property in the United States.

Note: When the negative expression comes at the beginning of a subordinate clause, invert the subject and verb in the main clause, not the subordinate clause:

Only when you see no oncoming traffic should you make a left turn.

Look at this TOEFL item:

Rarely ------- the company of others of its species.

- ◯ seeks the adult jaguar
- ◯ does the adult jaguar seek
- ◯ the adult jaguar seeks
- ◯ the adult jaguar is seeking

For the missing part of the sentence, standard word order would be *the adult jaguar seeks*. However, *Rarely* is an "almost negative" word, which means that you should invert the subject and verb (use question word order). Both the first and second answer choices have inverted subject–verb order, but which best completes the sentence?

In question word order, if there is no auxiliary, you must add the correct form of *do* as the first part of the verb. In the above example this is: *does the adult jaguar seek*. Therefore, the second choice best completes the sentence.

5. With the special expressions *so* and *neither*, the subject and verb are inverted to avoid unnecessary repetition.

The gull is a cliff–dweller, and the common murre is a cliff–dweller.
The gull is a cliff–dweller, and so is the common murre.

A test item may try to trick you by having *so* or *neither* in only some of the answer choices. Look at this example:

> In the early 1990s, the endangered peregrine falcon was not often seen, and -------.
>
> ◯ neither the upland sandpiper
> ◯ neither was the upland sandpiper
> ◯ the upland sandpiper neither was seen
> ◯ does not the upland sandpiper

All of the answer choices contain a negative expression. The first choice lacks a verb. The second and third choices have *neither*, but only the second choice has an inverted subject and verb: *neither was the upland sandpiper*. The fourth choice has an incorrect auxiliary.

The second choice best completes the sentence, which should read: *In the early 1990s, the endangered peregrine falcon was not often seen, and neither was the upland sandpiper.*

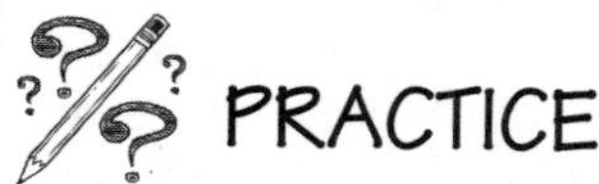

Exercise 2.13.A

Choose the one word or phrase that best completes the sentence.

1. Not only ------- the fall of the czar, it also destroyed the short–lived Provisional Government of Aleksandr Kerenski.

   (A) did World War I bring about
   (B) World War I brought about
   (C) it was brought about by World War I
   (D) bring World War I about

2. On the Galapagos Islands ------- the forty thousand breeding pairs of the blue–footed booby.

   (A) half live
   (B) the half live
   (C) live half of
   (D) half are living

3. The coyote prefers to hunt at night, and so -------.

   (A) the leopard also
   (B) the leopard does hunt
   (C) is the leopard
   (D) does the leopard

4. Under no circumstances ------- without looking carefully to the rear.

   (A) should one back up a motor vehicle
   (B) should a motor vehicle one back up
   (C) one should back up a motor vehicle
   (D) a motor vehicle should back up

5. Among Italo Calvino's works ------- about World War II, *The Path to the Nest of Spiders*.

   (A) a realistic novel
   (B) it is a realistic novel
   (C) a realistic novel is
   (D) is a realistic novel

6. In the very center of the flower -------.

   (A) one or more pistils are
   (B) or one more pistil
   (C) is one or more pistils
   (D) one or more is a pistil

7. Nowhere in the United States ------- grizzly bear attacks than in Glacier National Park.

(A) are there more
(B) are more
(C) there are more
(D) more are there of

8. The sea fig's scientific name means "blooming at midday," and seldom ------- unless it receives full sun.

(A) flowers
(B) does it flower
(C) it flowers
(D) flowering

Choose the one underlined word or phrase that must be changed for the sentence to be correct.

9. <u>In the</u> (A) Cascade Range <u>the mountain bluebird lives</u> (B), which <u>is sometimes seen</u> (C) in <u>snags and open areas</u> (D).

10. Only after <u>the Civil War had started</u> (A) <u>Lincoln issued</u> (B) the Emancipation Proclamation, <u>which put an end</u> (C) to slavery <u>in the South</u> (D).

Answers to Exercise 2.13.A are on page 644.

STRUCTURE

2.13 EXTENSION

1. In reading done outside class, students look for sentences with inverted subject–verb order. Bring examples to share in class. Discuss why the subject and verb are inverted.

2. Students create "TOEFL sentences" to test their classmates' understanding of inverted subject–verb order. Students write sentences that begin with a prepositional phrase of location. Use the list of prepositions on page 234. Omit the subject and verb, and leave a blank space where they should be. Classmates must provide an appropriate subject and verb in the correct order.

3. Students create "TOEFL sentences" that begin with a negative expression from the list on page 235. Omit the subject and verb, and leave a blank space where they should be. Write the subject and verb (+ auxiliaries) below the sentence, but mix up the order. Classmates must provide the subject and verb in the correct order.

ASSESSING PROGRESS – 2.11 through 2.13

QUIZ 6 (Time – 10 minutes)

Choose the one word or phrase that best completes the sentence.

1. The tasks of preparing project budgets and marketing plans can have disastrous effects on the program -------.

   (A) they not be done well
   (B) and they are not done well
   (C) if they are not done well
   (D) if they were not done well

2. Not often ------- fatal today, but immediate medical attention is essential.

   (A) a rattlesnake bite's
   (B) by a rattlesnake's bite
   (C) a rattlesnake bite is
   (D) is a rattlesnake bite

3. ------- opportunities for irrigation are few in New Mexico, most farmland is used for the grazing of cattle and sheep.

   (A) Because of
   (B) Because
   (C) That
   (D) Instead

4. ------- a living plant, animal, or bacterial cell, they make use of the host cell's chemical energy.

   (A) Viruses enter
   (B) Viruses entering
   (C) When entered
   (D) When viruses enter

Choose the one underlined word or phrase that must be changed for the sentence to be correct.

5. Many of the early American settlers thought that unless they do their jobs well and believed in God, they would not be rewarded.

   A: Many — B: they do — C: believed — D: be rewarded

6. Between mountains and desert Damascus lies, which is the largest city in Syria and perhaps the oldest continuously occupied city in the world.

   A: Between — B: Damascus lies — C: which — D: continuously occupied

Choose the one word or phrase that best completes the sentence.

7. Until recently, Cleveland has had no viable tourism industry, and -------.

   (A) Toledo has not had
   (B) Toledo has neither
   (C) neither Toledo has had one
   (D) neither has Toledo

8. Buckminster Fuller, the maverick engineer and social planner, criticized the wasteful procedures that were usually followed -------.

   (A) that building a house
   (B) when building a house
   (C) a house was being built
   (D) build a house

9. If you ------- something cold, the molecules in your fingers slow down as they lose heat.

(A) touch
(B) touched
(C) to touch
(D) were to touch

10. ------- in tree cavities, but the mated pair often perches in trees, especially when searching for a nesting site.

(A) If the wood duck nests
(B) Because the wood duck nests
(C) How does the wood duck nest
(D) Not only does the wood duck nest

11. Botulism causes disturbances in swallowing and paralysis of respiratory muscles, -------.

(A) ultimately leading to suffocation
(B) led ultimately to suffocation
(C) ultimately it leads to suffocation
(D) was ultimately led to suffocation

Choose the one underlined word or phrase that must be changed for the sentence to be correct.

12. If the front <u>teeth</u> (A) of a rodent <u>were</u> (B) not continue <u>growing</u> (C), they would be <u>worn</u> (D) away.

13. Physicians now <u>believe that</u> (A) even if <u>a person</u> (B) is genetically predisposed to a certain disease, <u>although changes</u> (C) in lifestyle <u>can alter</u> (D) the course of his or her health.

Choose the one word or phrase that best completes the sentence.

14. West of the Appalachian Mountains ------- and rolling plains of the Pennyroyal, the famous Bluegrass region of Kentucky.

(A) the rocky hills
(B) the rocky hills are
(C) are the rocky hills
(D) of the rocky hills

15. In 1988 an earthquake struck northern Armenia, ------- over fifty thousand people.

(A) killing
(B) it killed
(C) killed
(D) would kill

Answers to Structure Quiz 6 are on page 645.

2.14 Checking Subject–Verb Agreement

FOCUS

What is wrong with this sentence?

> The slender bristles of "cotton" on the stems of cotton grass is actually the tiny petals of the plant's flowers.

In this sentence, the subject and verb are not in agreement. ***Agreement*** is a correct match between two parts of a sentence. In this example, the verb does not fit, or agree with, the subject.

The subject of the sentence, *The slender bristles*, is plural. It needs a plural verb; therefore, the verb *is* must be changed to *are*. The sentence should read: *The slender bristles of "cotton" on the stems of cotton grass are actually the tiny petals of the plant's flowers.*

What is wrong with this sentence?

> Haze from pollen and forest fires have always been present in the Grand Canyon, but the recent increase comes from outside the national park.

The subject of this sentence, *Haze*, is an uncountable noun (See 2.3). Uncountable nouns take singular verbs. The plural verb in this sentence, *have always been* must be changed to the singular *has always been*.

Beware! Sometimes a TOEFL sentence will try to trick you by separating the subject and verb with a modifying phrase or clause. Finding the subject and verb is sometimes tricky, but you have to be able to find them in order to check their agreement.

1. Approximately two items on the TOEFL will test your ability to check the agreement of subjects and verbs. You must be able to recognize errors in subject–verb agreement in main and subordinate clauses.

2. Subjects and verbs must agree in number. A singular subject takes a singular verb. A plural subject takes a plural verb.

   Singular Subject and Verb:

   An amplifier increases the voltage of a weak signal from a microphone.

   Plural Subject and Verb:

   Sensors detect the presence of something and often are used to measure it.

   Note: A singular verb takes the *–s* or *–es* ending, but a plural verb does not. Use *–s*/*–es* when:

   - the subject is third person singular

   and

   - the verb is in the present tense

   An element contains only one kind of atom.
   When one catches a cold, resting and drinking fluids are the best cure.

   Note: Use *has* with third person singular subjects in the present perfect tense:

   Washington has been the site of political demonstrations for two centuries.

   The verb *be* has its own special singular forms (*am*, *is*, *was*) and plural forms (*are*, *were*). Use these forms when *be* is the main verb and when *be* is auxiliary to another verb.

   Singular Subject + *Be*:

   The polar bear is one of the largest carnivores in the world.
   In the last four years of his life, Mozart was writing his best operas.

   Plural Subject + *Be*:

   Floods are caused by excessive rain and poor drainage.
   Laurel and Hardy were famous comedians of films made in the 1920s.

3. Phrases and clauses that come between the subject and verb do not change the number of the subject. These phrases and clauses modify the subject noun, and are therefore part of the subject, but they do not affect the verb. You must look at the subject noun and the main verb when you check subject–verb agreement.

In the following sentences, circle the subjects and verbs. Underline phrases and clauses that separate the subjects and verbs.

a. All devices and machines powered by electricity contain an electric circuit.
b. Invasion of the lungs by plague bacteria causes a fatal form of the disease.
c. A substance that kills plants or inhibits their growth is called a "herbicide."

(***Answers:*** a. subject: *All devices and machines*; verb: *contain*; adjective phrase: *powered by electricity*; b. subject: *Invasion*; verb: *causes*; prepositional phrases: *of the lungs*, *by plague bacteria*; c. subject: *A substance*; verb: *is called*; adjective clause: *that kills plants or inhibits their growth*)

4. Singular verbs are used with singular nouns, uncountable nouns, and certain other nouns and pronouns. Use a singular verb with the following subjects:

Uncountable Noun:

Research has shown that men speak more than women in meetings.

Gerund:

Preparing a budget translates planned activities into monetary terms.

Noun Clause:

How animals interact with each other interests their trainers.

"False" Subject *It*:

It is the hormones produced in the pancreas that regulate blood–sugar levels.

Some pronouns take singular verbs, even though they may seem to have plural meanings:

anybody	each	everyone	nobody	somebody
anyone	either	everything	no one	someone
anything	everybody	neither	nothing	something

Each of the climate zones has its own patterns of weather.
Everything alive on earth is composed of cells.

Expressions of groups of people, animals, or things take singular verbs, even though the nouns with them are plural:

a collection of	a colony of	a family of	a flock of	a pair of

A pair of electrodes conducts the current in a battery.

Some nouns appear plural but really are singular and take singular verbs:

economics	mathematics	news	physics	politics

Physics, one of the natural sciences, deals with energy and matter.

5. Plural verbs are used with plural nouns, compound subjects, and certain pronouns.

Use a plural verb with compound subjects joined by *and* or *both...and*:

Both Spain *and* France were major colonial powers of the Americas.

Use a plural verb when certain words are used as pronouns:

both	few	many	several

Of all the states, few have as much open space as Montana.

6. Sometimes other parts of the sentence determine whether the verb is singular or plural.

In an adjective clause with a relative pronoun as the subject of the clause (See 2.10), the verb agrees with the noun referred to by the relative pronoun.

A hiker can go to places in Sequoia National Park that are far from any road.

In the above sentence, the verb in the adjective clause, *are*, agrees with the noun referred to by *that*. The verb agrees with the noun *places*.

Some pronouns take either a singular or a plural verb, depending on the noun that comes after them:

all	any	most	none	some

Some of the news on television distorts the truth. (singular)
Some of the endangered species are disappearing rapidly. (plural)

In sentences with the "false" subject *there*, the verb agrees with the true subject, which comes after the verb:

Until 1977, *there* was no Department of Energy at the federal level. (singular)
There were creatures who were living on earth long before humans. (plural)

With compound subjects joined by the following expressions, the verb agrees with the subject that it is closer to:

either...or	neither...nor	not only...but also

Either work references or a school certificate is necessary to get a job. (singular)
Not only the grizzly bear *but also* many birds are becoming endangered. (plural)

A number of (meaning *several*) is plural and needs a plural verb. *The number of* is singular and needs a singular verb.

A number of department stores are developing a specialty–store look. (plural)
The number of people who go to college has been increasing steadily. (singular)

STRUCTURE

7. Some structures that show importance or necessity have special rules for subject–verb agreement.

Following certain verbs of importance, noun clauses with *that* + subject + verb take the base form of the verb, even when the subject is third person singular:

ask	insist	propose	request	suggest
demand	prefer	recommend	require	urge

Doctors *recommend* that a young adult have at least seven hours of sleep every night.

Note: For the passive voice, use the base form of *be*:

The company *requires* that each employee be evaluated once a year.

With certain adjectives of importance, noun clauses that come after *It is* + adjective + *that* take the base form of the verb, even when the subject is third person singular:

essential	important	necessary	recommended	required

It is necessary that the mining industry have safety regulations that are enforced.

8. A TOEFL item may test you by:

- using a singular subject with a plural verb
- using a plural subject with a singular verb
- making the subject and verb difficult to find
- using an expression that has special subject–verb agreement rules

9. A test item may try to trick you by making the words that must agree—the subject and verb—difficult to find. Sometimes they are separated by other words, phrases or clauses. Look at this example:

> A minnow, which is usually small and drab, is a member of the family of freshwater fish that include brightly colored carp and goldfish.

Which underlined word or phrase must be changed for the sentence to be correct? If you chose *include*, you were correct because it is the verb of an adjective clause and must agree with the noun referred to by *that*. *That* refers *to the family of freshwater fish*, or simply *family*, a singular noun. Correction: *includes*.

The sentence should read: *A minnow, which is usually small and drab, is a member of the family of freshwater fish that includes brightly colored carp and goldfish.*

Look at another example:

> In a capitalist economy, what will be produced are determined by the marketplace, which is considered the center of the system.

Which underlined word or phrase must be changed for the sentence to be correct? If you chose *are*, you were correct because the subject of this verb is *what will be produced*, which is a noun clause (See 2.9). Noun clauses are singular and need singular verbs. Correction: *is*.

Look at another example:

> Strip mining and quarrying both start from the earth's surface and maintains exposure to it.

This sentence has a compound subject, *Strip mining and quarrying*, which needs a plural verb. However, the verb is also compound (two verbs joined by *and*): *start...and maintains*. One is plural and the other is singular. One of them is incorrect.

Which verb must be changed so that there is subject–verb agreement? If you chose *maintains*, you were correct because both verbs in a compound verb phrase must agree with the subject. Correction: *maintain*.

10. A test item may try to trick you by using an expression that has special subject–verb agreement rules. Look at this example:

> It is essential that each hiker carries a flashlight, matches, and extra food and clothing, even though only a day hike is planned.

Which underlined word or phrase must be changed for the sentence to be correct? If you chose *carries*, you were correct. This sentence has an *It is* + adjective–of–importance structure. It must be followed by a noun clause with a base–form verb, even though the subject is third person singular. Correction: *carry*.

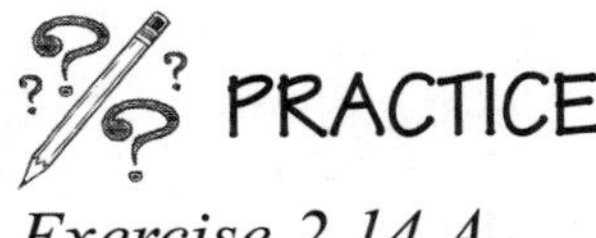

PRACTICE

Exercise 2.14.A

Choose the one underlined word or phrase that must be changed for the sentence to be correct.

1. Ocean currents, moisture–bearing winds, and air temperature all contributes (A) to rainfall, which is (B) one of (C) the primary factors (D) of climate.

2. A few months after they are (A) born, babies start (B) looking into the eyes of adults, and adult facial expressions—very basic ones (C) such as smiling—draws (D) responses from the infants.

3. Macroeconomics deal with (A) the behavior (B) of the economy as a whole (C), the overall level of a nation's output, employment, and prices (D).

4. Adding extra passengers cause (A) a boat to settle deeper in the water (B), but the boat must not be loaded (C) so that the water marks on its side go (D) below the surface of the water.

5. Archaeologists have found (A) records over two thousand years (B) old that shows (C) the amount of precious metal people deposited (D) in a temple in Babylon.

6. A number of (A) important services (B) for individuals and corporations is (C) provided by a bank, which is (D) more than just a safe place to store money.

7. An association of producers or manufacturers are called (A) a "cartel" if it is formed (B) to regulate (C) prices and production in some field (D) of business.

Choose the one word or phrase that best completes the sentence.

8. *The Book of Changes*, a classic Chinese book of wisdom, ------- eight trigrams that correspond to the powers of nature.

(A) consist of
(B) consists of
(C) are consisting of
(D) consisting

9. Everyone who reads the newspaper or watches the news ------- American health care is changing.

(A) who knows
(B) know that
(C) knows that
(D) have known

10. The physical environment in which educational activities take place -------.

(A) learning is affected
(B) to affect learning
(C) affect learning
(D) affects learning

Exercise 2.14.B

Choose the one underlined word or phrase that must be changed for the sentence to be correct.

1. Much (A) information about (B) cross–cultural facial expressions have (C) been published (D) recently in psychological journals.

2. The best known of the mimosas are (A) the sensitive plant, whose (B) leaves fold up (C) and collapse under such stimuli as touch, darkness (D), or drought.

3. If you (A) want to start (B) an exercise program, remember that (C) either swimming or cycling are excellent (D) for aerobic conditioning and muscle strengthening.

4. The number of women <u>who enter</u> (A) nontraditional <u>fields</u> (B) such as engineering <u>have been</u> (C) increasing steadily <u>since the 1970s</u> (D).

5. Forensic scientists, <u>who work</u> (A) in crime laboratories, <u>carry out</u> (B) testing that <u>help</u> (C) law enforcement agencies <u>solve</u> (D) crimes.

6. <u>Many</u> (A) health care specialists recommend that an adult <u>consumes</u> (B) no more than twenty <u>percent</u> (C) of <u>his or her</u> (D) daily calorie intake in the form of fat.

7. The 1892 trial of Lizzie Borden <u>for the murder</u> (A) of her parents <u>have become</u> (B) legendary, and this case <u>remains</u> (C) one of the most famous unsolved <u>crimes</u> (D) in American history.

8. In <u>an escalator</u> (A), the descending half of the stairs <u>act</u> (B) as a counterweight to the ascending half, and the motor <u>moves</u> (C) only the weight of the people who <u>are riding</u> (D).

9. In the early 1900s, there <u>were</u> (A) experimentation among painters <u>who</u> (B) were attempting <u>to express</u> (C) ideas that could not <u>be explained</u> (D) through conventional methods.

10. A college graduate who <u>is trained</u> (A) in one of the natural sciences or <u>mathematics</u> (B) usually <u>qualify</u> (C) for a beginning–level <u>engineering job</u> (D).

Answers to Exercises 2.14.A through 2.14.B are on pages 645 and 646.

2.14 EXTENSION

1. For each sentence in Exercises 2.14.A and 2.14.B, students cross out any words, phrases, or clauses that separate the subject and verb and make them difficult to find.

2. In reading done outside class, students look for sentences where the subject includes a word such as *both*, *few*, *many*, *several*, *all*, *any*, *most*, *none*, or *some*. Bring examples to share in class. Are the subjects singular or plural? Are the verbs singular or plural?

3. Students create "TOEFL sentences" to test their classmates' understanding of subject–verb agreement. Students write their own sentences or use sentences they find in print. In some but not all of the sentences, change the verb so that it does not agree with the subject. Keep some of the sentences correct. Write either on the board or on cards. Classmates must determine whether there is an error in subject–verb agreement. If there is an error, classmates make the correction.

2.15 Checking Pronoun Agreement

FOCUS

What is wrong with this sentence?

> Retailers use a strategy called "one–stop shopping" to draw in busy consumers, and many supermarkets now have its own restaurants and delicatessens.

Whose restaurants and delicatessens are mentioned? *Many supermarkets* have restaurants and delicatessens. Because *many supermarkets* is plural, the possessive word referring to it must also be plural. The singular *its* before *own restaurants* is incorrect. It should be changed so that the clause reads: *many supermarkets now have their own restaurants and delicatessens.*

What is wrong with this sentence?

> If you are planning to travel in a foreign country, one should learn to use the tools of nonverbal communication of that culture.

The first part of this sentence has a second person pronoun, *you*. The second part of the sentence shifts to third person with the pronoun *one*. Which is correct? Either would be correct, but the two parts of the sentence must match. One of the pronouns must be changed.

The sentence could say either *If you are planning to travel..., you should learn to use...* or *If one is planning to travel..., one should learn to use....* Both are correct. Which seems more formal?

What is wrong with this sentence?

> Orville and Wilbur Wright were the first Americans which achieved flight in a mechanically propelled plane.

This sentence has an incorrect relative pronoun, *which*. *Which* refers only to things or animals and never refers to people (See 2.10). The pronoun in this sentence refers to *the first Americans*. *Which* should be changed to *who*, the correct relative pronoun for people.

1. Approximately two items on the TOEFL will test your ability to check the agreement of pronouns and their noun referents. You must be able to recognize errors in pronoun agreement.

2. Pronouns agree in form, person, number, and gender with the nouns they refer to or replace.

   - form: subject, object, possessive, reflexive
   - person: first, second, third
   - number: singular, plural
   - gender: masculine, feminine, neuter

A pronoun's form depends on its function in a sentence:

SUBJECT PRONOUN	OBJECT PRONOUN	POSSESSIVE ADJECTIVE	POSSESSIVE PRONOUN	REFLEXIVE PRONOUN
I	me	my	mine	myself
we	us	our	ours	ourselves
you	you	your	yours	yourself(ves)
he	him	his	his	himself
she	her	her	hers	herself
one	one	one's	—	oneself
it	it	its	—	itself
they	them	their	theirs	themselves

Because they are honest, some people are able to examine their own faults.
If you asked them to speak honestly, some people would be uncomfortable.
Some people find your mistakes more forgivable than theirs.
Some people are able to view themselves honestly, and others are not.

Pronouns referring to things are ***neuter gender***. The neuter pronouns are *it* (singular) and *they* (plural). *They* also refers to people, but *it* never refers to people.

First person refers to the person or persons who are speaking (*I*, *we*). ***Second person*** is the person or persons spoken to (*you*). ***Third person*** is the person(s) or thing(s) spoken about (*he*, *she*, *one*, *it*, *they*).

Note: On the TOEFL, most of the sentences are third person, but occasionally you will see first or second person.

In the following sentences, underline the pronouns and circle the nouns they refer to. What person, number, and gender are expressed by the pronouns?

a. Willa Cather grew up in Nebraska, where she placed many of her novels.
b. The cat keeps itself clean with its paws and barbed tongue.
c. Although songbirds have no commercial value, they freely give us their music.

(***Answers:*** a. *she (Willa Cather)*: third person, singular, feminine; *her (Willa Cather)*: third person, singular, feminine; b. *itself (the cat)*: third person, singular, neuter; *its (the cat)*: third person, singular, neuter; c. *they (songbirds)*: third person, plural, neuter; *us (humans)*: first person, plural, masculine and feminine; *their (songbirds)*: third person, plural, neuter)

3. Relative pronouns in adjective clauses agree with the nouns that the adjective clauses modify (See 2.10). The relative pronouns are:

who	whom	which	that	whose

Different relative pronouns are used for people and things.

Who and *whom* refer only to people.

> Archimedes, who first defined the principle of levers, also developed the pulley.
> Judges are professionals in whom fairness is an essential quality.

Which refers only to animals and things.

> The thyroid gland, which is part of the endocrine system, regulates the body's metabolic rate.

That can refer to people, animals, and things.

> Workers that are analytical, confident, and sociable often make good supervisors.
> Constrictors are snakes that wrap and squeeze their prey.

Whose, the possessive form, can refer to people, animals, and things.

> Sonja Henie was a figure skater whose skill brought her three Olympic medals.
> Electrons, whose movement causes electricity, are the smallest atomic particles.

4. Demonstrative pronouns and adjectives agree in number with the nouns they refer to, replace, or modify. The demonstratives are:

this	that	these	those

Demonstrative Pronoun:

> Western maples do not turn as red in autumn as those in eastern North America.

Demonstrative Adjective:

> These parts of your car need to be checked regularly: oil, fluids, brakes, and tires.

Note: Demonstrative adjectives are the only adjectives that agree in number with their nouns.

In the following sentences, underline the demonstrative pronouns. Are they singular or plural? What nouns do they refer to?

a. Linking a store's computer to that of the supplier helps automate the processes of ordering, shipping, and billing.
b. Eugene O'Neill's plays have been compared to those of the ancient Greeks.
c. Driving while intoxicated is illegal, but this is not the only reason to avoid doing it.

(***Answers:*** a. *that*: singular; refers to *computer*; b. *those*: plural; refers to *plays*; c. *this*: singular; refers to the illegality of *driving while intoxicated*)

5. A TOEFL item may test you by:

   - using an incorrect form of pronoun
   - mixing up pronouns for people and things
   - having a pronoun that does not agree with its noun in person, number, or gender

6. A test item may try to trick you by using an incorrect form of pronoun. Look at this example:

   > We laugh during moments of anxiety because we feel a loss of control, and our laughter reassures ours that we can cope with the situation.

   Which underlined word must be changed for the sentence to be correct? If you chose *ours*, you were correct. *Ours* is the possessive form, but the object form is needed because it is the object of the verb *reassures*. Correction: *us*.

7. A test item may try to trick you by having a pronoun that does not agree with its noun in person, number, or gender. Look at this example:

   > There is little evidence that men who are more successful in their careers are a great deal happier or better adjusted than that who are less successful.

   Which underlined word must be changed for the sentence to be correct? If you chose *that*, you were correct. *That* does not agree in number with the noun it replaces.

   This sentence discusses two kinds of men: men who are more successful and men who are less successful in their careers. The demonstrative *that* is used to avoid repetition of *men*. Since *men* is a plural noun, the demonstrative must also be plural. Correction: *those*.

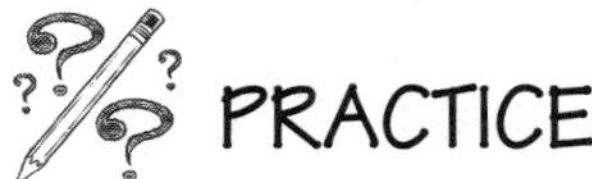

PRACTICE

Exercise 2.15.A

Choose the one underlined word or phrase that must be changed for the sentence to be correct.

1. Memory begins to diminish in some (A) people as early as their (B) forties, but this (C) does not mean their (D) will develop Alzheimer's disease.

2. Gutzon Borglum, whose (A) first work was (B) a statue of Abraham Lincoln, is famous for the figures he carved (C) on mountainsides, especially that (D) on Mount Rushmore.

3. In 1609 Galileo constructed (A) the first telescope, whom (B) he used to discover (C) the four largest satellites (D) of Jupiter.

4. When applying for admission to a university, one generally must submit an application form and
A B C
transcripts of all of your previous college–level work.
D

5. A hurricane is a tropical storm who is formed over the North Atlantic Ocean in which the winds
A B
reach speeds of greater than 75 miles per hour.
C D

6. When a chimpanzee is frightened, it touches another chimpanzee, just like a child who is watching
A B C
a scary movie takes their mother's hand.
D

7. A galaxy is held together by the gravitational attraction between its parts, and its rotational motion
A B
prevents them from collapsing on itself.
C D

8. Mary Pickford, an actress known as "America's Sweetheart," was most famous for his roles in
A B C D
films such as *The Poor Little Rich Girl* and *Rebecca of Sunnybrook Farm.*

9. The Hurons, who numbered about twenty thousand in the 1600s, were a confederation of Native
A B
American groups whom spoke Wyandot, which was an Iroquoian language.
C D

10. Although the two are similar in size and behavior, the red squirrel can be identified by its coat,
A
which is brighter and redder than those of its cousin, the Douglas squirrel.
B C D

Exercise 2.15.B

Choose the one underlined word or phrase that must be changed for the sentence to be correct.

1. In 1290 the government at Delhi, which was made up of ex–slaves, was replaced by that of the Turks,
A B C
it ruled for the next thirty years.
D

2. If one wants to observe the planets Venus and Mars together, you should look in the southwestern sky
A B C
just after sunset during the month of December.
D

3. Political theorists Thomas Hobbes and John Locke thought of society as a compact among people,
A
in which the state's primary duty was to protect the interests of their citizens.
B C D

4. Many employers are unable to express any opinion about <u>which</u> (A) local schools prepare <u>they</u> (B) students best or about <u>what</u> (C) changes <u>they</u> (D) would make in educational programs.

5. <u>During</u> (A) the Civil War, the North's population, industrial capacity, and financial resources <u>were</u> (B) much <u>greater</u> (C) than <u>that</u> (D) of the South.

6. Ernest Hemingway, <u>whose</u> (A) many people <u>consider</u> (B) to be among the great storytellers, <u>wrote</u> (C) novels about people <u>who</u> (D) lived essential and dangerous lives.

7. In ancient times there <u>were</u> (A) people <u>who</u> (B) exchanged coins from different cities and traded coins for gold and silver, and each time <u>they</u> (C) made an exchange, <u>it</u> (D) charged a fee.

8. The black rosy finch builds <u>its nest</u> (A) in a place predators cannot reach, such as a rocky crevice or hidden ledge, similar to <u>these</u> (B) often <u>chosen</u> (C) by the <u>other types</u> (D) of finches.

Answers to Exercises 2.15.A through 2.15.B are on page 646.

2.15 EXTENSION

1. In reading done outside class, students look for sentences with pronouns and demonstratives. Bring examples to share in class.

2. <u>Card game for groups of 2 to 5</u>. Teachers or students prepare two sets of cards: one with sentences, one with pronouns. On each card of the first set, write a sentence that uses a pronoun, but omit the pronoun and leave a blank space where it should be. On each card of the second set, write one of the missing pronouns. Combine the sets and mix up the cards. Divide the class into several teams of 2 to 5 people. Deal the cards so that each team has the same number of cards (at least 8 per team). The object is to see how quickly the teams can match all of their sentence cards with pronoun cards. Pronoun agreement is essential! A team can trade with another team. The first team to correctly match all of their cards wins the game.

3. Discuss why some nonliving things are often referred to by masculine or feminine pronouns. For example, some people refer to their car or boat as *she*. Also, why do you think animals are sometimes referred to by *it* or *which*, and sometimes by *he*, *she*, or *who*?

ASSESSING PROGRESS – 2.14 through 2.15

QUIZ 7 (Time – 10 minutes)

Choose the one underlined word or phrase that must be changed for the sentence to be correct.

1. Despite the differences [A] between the speaking styles [B] of boys and girls, there is [C] some similarities in their [D] styles and concerns.

2. Benjamin Franklin, who was [A] an author, scientist, and statesman, built an international reputation which [B] made his [C] the most valuable [D] American diplomat during the Revolution.

3. Periods of currency overvaluation and recession is [A] when [B] countries are [C] likely to establish [D] protective tariffs.

4. Some research suggests [A] that personality differences are [B] more strongly related [C] to social role than it is [D] to age.

5. It [A] is important that a corporate trainer obtains [B] the input of both [C] managers and workers when developing [D] training for new employees.

6. The National Geographic Society's lectures have [A] offered its [B] members the opportunity to meet explorers and scientists, and in the past they were [C] the only means of presenting his [D] work to the public.

7. Since the 1980s, several [A] studies in the Netherlands have reported [B] that there is [C] a lower risk of heart disease among fish eaters than among people which [D] eat no fish.

Choose the one word or phrase that best completes the sentence.

8. Employing fourteen million workers in the U. S., ------- the largest employment sector in marketing and one of the nation's largest industries.

   (A) retail sales is
   (B) retail sales are
   (C) are retail sales
   (D) retail sales being

9. A demonstration of the link between long life and health practices ------- a study that took place in California.

   (A) from
   (B) come from
   (C) comes from
   (D) are coming from

Choose the one underlined word or phrase that must be changed for the sentence to be correct.

10. If one wants to keep up with the rapid advances in workplace technology, they must plan to take
A B C D
frequent refresher courses.

11. A pair of binoculars are basically two small telescopes that produce a stereoscopic view which the
A B C
brain perceives as an image with depth.
D

12. The U. S. social security system, which provides unemployment compensation and retirement
A
insurance, was established much later than those of Great Britain.
B C D

13. Role changes, such as marriage, the birth of a child, and a change in job, causes the stress that all
A B
adults experience in their lives.
C D

14. Enforcing minimum wages are the economic responsibility of the government, which also has the
A B C
duty to regulate business and protect the environment.
D

15. The first studio to train architects was founded by Richard Morris Hunt, most of whom work
A B C
imitated styles that had been popular in earlier periods.
D

Answers to Structure Quiz 7 are on page 646.

 ASSESSING PROGRESS – 2.1 through 2.15

Quiz 8 – Review (Time – 15 minutes)

Choose the one underlined word or phrase that must be changed for the sentence to be correct.

1. There are several good <u>reasons</u> (A) <u>for</u> (B) to include <u>a lot</u> (C) of fruits and vegetables in your diet—especially <u>those</u> (D) that are rich in beta carotene.

2. <u>When</u> (A) Halley's Comet appeared in 1986, <u>they</u> (B) could <u>be seen</u> (C) clearly <u>only</u> (D) by people in the southern half of the United States.

3. Most of the Kenyan coffee crop <u>goes</u> (A) to European dealers, <u>who</u> (B) pay the top price, but a small share <u>available</u> (C) for Americans who are particular about <u>their</u> (D) coffee.

Choose the one word or phrase that best completes the sentence.

4. The greatest weather disaster in American history occurred on the Great Plains in the 1930s, ------- the Dust Bowl Days.

   (A) it was known as a period
   (B) that period was
   (C) to know a period of
   (D) a period known as

5. A female leopard is an extremely good hunter, and -------.

   (A) a lioness is
   (B) so is a lioness
   (C) does a lioness
   (D) so be a lioness

6. ------- of the three primary colors of light, it is possible to produce all other colors.

   (A) Combine the light sources
   (B) The light sources combining
   (C) Combining the light sources
   (D) It is combining the light sources

7. Recent linguistic research has shed light on the role played by -------, regardless of their gender.

   (A) how people speak
   (B) how people were spoken
   (C) how do people speak
   (D) people are speaking

8. The westerly flow of the North American air is ------- by local storm circulation over the United States and southern Canada.

   (A) regular interruption
   (B) regularly interrupted
   (C) interrupting regularly
   (D) interrupted regular

Choose the one underlined word or phrase that must be changed for the sentence to be correct.

9. When planning (A) workplace policies, it is necessary that a manager considers (B) the politics of the organization, such as how (C) decisions are made and who makes them (D).

10. The French and Indian War was the (A) final phase of a long struggle between France and England to win (B) control of North America, and its (C) was also a part of the greater war taking place (D) in Europe.

11. The beads on the stem of the ice plant (A) are swollen (B) with a water (C) and give the plant a moist feel (D).

12. It is when (A) the ratio of angry exchanges (B) compared to more positive expressions gets high that couples are likely report (C) serious dissatisfaction with their (D) marriage.

Choose the one word or phrase that best completes the sentence.

13. *Autoimmune disease* is a general term for several disorders ------- the body produces antibodies against its own substances.

(A) in which
(B) which
(C) in that
(D) how

14. It is ------- rather than shortfalls of precipitation alone that cause water shortages.

(A) deficits in the net amount of water
(B) because deficits in the net amount of water
(C) with deficits in the net amount of water
(D) deficits in the net amount of water are

15. If the subduction zone along the coast were to break, the inhabitants of that area -------.

(A) felt an earthquake
(B) an earthquake had been felt
(C) will feel an earthquake
(D) would feel an earthquake

16. Any of a variety of unconscious reactions ------- to satisfy emotional needs is called a "defense mechanism."

(A) to use by individuals
(B) used by individuals
(C) that used by individuals
(D) individuals using

17. ------- both a fluid core and rapid rotation were necessary to generate a planetary magnetic field.

(A) It was formerly believed that
(B) To be believed that formerly
(C) Formerly believing that
(D) That formerly

18. Among George Gershwin's best–known pieces ------- "Summertime" and "I Got Rhythm."

(A) of the songs
(B) the songs are
(C) to be the songs
(D) are the songs

Quiz 8

Choose the one underlined word or phrase that must be changed for the sentence to be correct.

19. In October 1962, President Kennedy announced (A) in a special television broadcast that (B) the Soviet Union had building (C) nuclear missile bases (D) in Cuba.

20. The two standard procedures have been (A) replaced, and instruction in these (B) classical techniques occupy (C) a very small part (D) of today's chemistry curriculum.

21. If (A) a million electrons (B) were lined up, they will (C) scarcely reach across the head (D) of a pin.

22. Swimming is becoming (A) the sport of choice because (B) it not only tones every muscle in the body, it also requires (C) fewer (D) equipment than skiing, cycling, or tennis.

23. The octopus does (A) most of its hunting at night, when it (B) emerges from its rocky lair to seek (C) crabs, crayfish, and mollusks, which its (D) favorite foods.

24. Silver, one of the first metal (A) used by humans, (B) is an excellent (C) conductor of heat and electricity (D).

25. In (A) face–to–face communication, it is (B) the expression in the eyes that do (C) the most important communicating (D).

Answers to Structure Quiz 8 are on page 647.

2.16 Checking Adjective Word Order

What is wrong with this sentence?

> A *steppe* is a grassland temperate of Eurasia, but sometimes the term is applied to the pampas of South America and the high veld of South Africa.

This sentence has incorrect word order in the phrase *grassland temperate*. Single–word adjectives, such as *temperate*, come before the nouns they modify. In this sentence, the word order should be changed so that the adjective comes before the noun: *A steppe is a temperate grassland of Eurasia.*

What is wrong with this sentence?

> When examining biological specimens, it is necessary to stain the material and cut it into samples enough thin for a light beam to penetrate them.

This sentence has incorrect word order in the phrase *samples enough thin*. When *enough* is used with an adjective, it means *sufficiently* and comes after the adjective. Here, the word order should be changed so that *enough* comes after the adjective *thin*: *it is necessary to stain the material and cut it into samples thin enough for a light beam to penetrate them.*

Why does *thin enough* come after *samples* in the above example? This is a situation where an adjective clause has been reduced (See 2.10). *Samples* is modified by a clause, *that are thin enough*, which has been reduced to *thin enough*. Reduced adjective clauses come after the nouns they modify.

2.16 Adjective Word Order

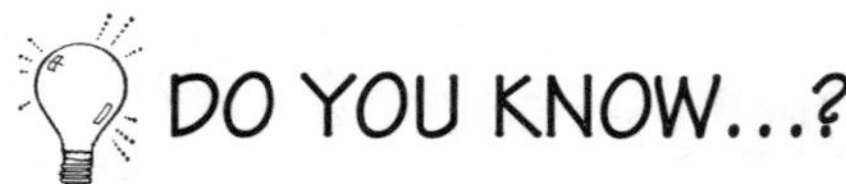

DO YOU KNOW...?

1. At least one item on the TOEFL will test your ability to check the word order of adjectives and the words around them.

2. The standard word order of adjectives and nouns is: adjective + noun. An article comes before the adjective.

    Floods claim an annual toll of two hundred lives.
    (annual = Adj, toll = N, two hundred = Adj, lives = N)

    More than one adjective can come before a noun:

    The warbler lays its eggs in a loose, shallow, grass–lined nest in a small tree.
    (loose = Adj, shallow = Adj, grass–lined = Adj, nest = N)

    Note: When an adjective comes after the verb *be*, it is not always followed by a noun. When there is no noun, the adjective modifies the subject:

    The fruit of the eggplant is purple, white, or striped.
    (fruit = S, purple = Adj, white = Adj, striped = Adj)

    Adjective phrases and clauses come after the nouns they modify (See 2.10).

    The winds blowing around mountain ridges are a form of dust devil.
    (winds = N, blowing around mountain ridges = Adj Phrase)

3. Adjectives can be modified by adverbs. The standard word order is: adverb + adjective + noun. An article comes before the adverb.

    Electronically controlled robots are a fairly recent invention.
    (Electronically = Adv, controlled = Adj, robots = N, fairly = Adv, recent = Adj, invention = N)

    Note: When an adverb + adjective structure comes after the verb *be*, it is not always followed by a noun. When there is no noun, the adjective modifies the subject:

    The jack rabbit's ears are characteristically long.
    (ears = S, characteristically = Adv, long = Adj)

4. A TOEFL item may test your ability to recognize the correct word order of adjectives, adverbs, and nouns. Look at this example:

    > Caracas is -------, major industrial center, and capital of Venezuela.
    >
    > ○ an extremely cosmopolitan city
    > ○ extreme city cosmopolitan
    > ○ a cosmopolitan city extremely
    > ○ extreme is a cosmopolitan city

    This sentence describes Caracas as *major industrial center* and *capital of Venezuela*, which are both noun phrases. The missing part is also a noun phrase.

The first answer choice, *an extremely cosmopolitan city*, has the correct word order for a noun phrase: article + adverb + adjective + noun. Therefore, it is the choice that best completes the sentence.

Why are the other three answer choices incorrect?

5. There are special rules for the word order of adjectives used with *enough* or *too* and an infinitive (See 2.7). When *enough* and *too* are used with infinitives, there is a cause–result relationship.

Adjective + *enough* + infinitive:

The water must be hot enough to steep the tea leaves.

In the above sentence, *hot enough* is the cause, and *to steep the tea leaves* is the result.

Note: Sometimes *for* + noun comes after *enough* and before the infinitive:

The specimens must be thin enough *for a light beam* to penetrate them.

***Too* + adjective + infinitive:**

Some systems for checking blood glucose levels are too inaccurate to be reliable.

In the above sentence, *too inaccurate* is the cause. *To be reliable* is the result.

Note: When *too* is used with an adjective, it means *excessively or more than necessary.*

A TOEFL item may test your ability to recognize the correct word order of an adjective with *enough* or *too* and an infinitive. Look at this example:

On moonless nights, it is ------- without some form of artificial light.

- ○ very dark to see
- ○ too dark to see
- ○ seeing too dark
- ○ enough dark to see

You can see that all of the answer choices have an adjective, *dark*, and three choices have an infinitive, *to see*. Which is the correct answer?

This sentence expresses a cause–result relationship between *dark* and *to see*. The first choice, *very dark to see*, is incorrect because *very* is not used with infinitive phrases that show result. In the second choice, *too* stresses the cause–result relationship between *dark* and *to see without some form of artificial light.*

The second choice best completes the sentence, which should read: *On moonless nights, it is too dark to see without some form of artificial light.*

Why are the third and fourth answer choices incorrect?

PRACTICE

Exercise 2.16.A

Choose the one word or phrase that best completes the sentence.

1. The novels of Truman Capote often reflect a world of grotesque and -------.

   (A) innocence people strangely
   (B) strangely innocent people
   (C) strange innocently people
   (D) strange people innocent

2. When transplanting a rhododendron, make sure the hole is ------- for the roots to spread out.

   (A) wide enough
   (B) widely enough
   (C) enough wide
   (D) enough wider than

3. Spray cans produce an aerosol, which is -------.

   (A) spraying of very fine
   (B) a spray very fine
   (C) very a fine spray
   (D) a very fine spray

4. Kites come in all shapes and sizes, some ------- a person.

   (A) large enough carrying
   (B) enough large to carry
   (C) large enough to carry
   (D) large to carry enough

Choose the one underlined word or phrase that must be changed for the sentence to be correct.

5. When (A) the sun is setting in Shanghai, on the directly side opposite (B) of the earth New York is just emerging (C) into sunlight (D).

6. The early tall masonry buildings (A) of the nineteenth century (B) required walls very thick (C) in the lower stories (D), limiting floor space.

7. Water particles carried (A) to a great height (B) freeze into ice particles and are swept upward and refrozen repeatedly (C) until enough heavy (D) to fall as hail.

8. The tremendously popular (A) entertainment known as *vaudeville* consisted of (B) songs unrelated (C), dances, acrobatic and magic acts, and humorous skits (D).

9. <u>During</u> the Spanish–American War, the U. S. realized the <u>strategic importance</u> of Hawaii and
   A B
<u>made it a territory</u> in 1900, with Sanford Dole as the <u>governor territorial</u>.
   C D

10. Trenches in the ocean floor are of <u>great interest</u> because they are lines <u>where</u> the earth's crust often
   A B
is <u>so weak</u> to resist the impact of <u>frequent earthquakes</u>.
   C D

Answers to Exercise 2.16.A are on page 647.

2.16 EXTENSION

1. Students create "TOEFL sentences" to test their classmates' understanding of adjective word order. Students write their own sentences, or use sentences they find in print. Each sentence should have an (a) adjective + noun or (b) adverb + adjective structure. Change the order of the adjectives, nouns, and adverbs so that the word order is incorrect. Write the sentences either on the board or on cards. Classmates must identify the error and make the correction.

2. Students practice speaking and writing sentences with adjective + *enough* + infinitive structures. **Example:** *I feel hungry enough to eat a bear.*

3. <u>Variation on #2.</u> Students practice speaking and writing sentences with *enough* + noun + infinitive structures. **Example:** *There is not enough bear to satisfy me.*

2.17 Checking Participial Adjectives

FOCUS

What is wrong with this sentence?

> The main sources of typhoid fever are contaminate water and milk and food handlers who are carriers of the bacteria.

This sentence has an incorrect adjective form—*contaminate*—describing the nouns *water* and *milk*. *Contaminate* is a verb, but verbs do not usually modify nouns.

Think of the meaning of the sentence. First, water and milk *are contaminated* by typhoid bacteria. Then, people get the disease by drinking the *contaminated water and milk.*

The correct adjective form is *contaminated*, which is called a ***participial adjective*** because it comes from the *past participle* of a verb.

What is wrong with this sentence?

> The exterior of Hagia Sophia is not elaborately decorating, and so nothing distracts from the mosque's basic form.

This sentence discusses a mosque, a building. But can the exterior of a building perform an action such as *decorating*? Of course, it cannot! However, people can decorate (or not decorate). Hagia Sophia *was decorated* by people.

The sentence should read: *The exterior of Hagia Sophia is not elaborately decorated, and so nothing distracts from the mosque's basic form.*

What is wrong with this sentence?

> Sam Cooke's pure, clear vocals were widely imitated, and his appealed image influenced the style of soul singing for the next two decades.

The phrase *appealed image* is incorrect. An *–ed* adjective conveys a passive meaning, but Sam Cooke's image was not passive. His image was active because it influenced other singers. An *–ing* adjective is needed.

An *–ing* adjective is a ***participial adjective*** that comes from the *present participle* of a verb. In the above sentence, Sam Cooke's *appealing* image influenced the style of soul singing.

DO YOU KNOW...?

1. Approximately one item on the TOEFL will test your ability to check participial adjectives. You must be able to recognize both correct and incorrect usage of these adjectives.

2. Participial adjectives are formed from verbs. They are extreme reductions of adjective clauses (See 2.10). Look at these examples:

Adjective Clause:

Toes that are frozen by sub–zero temperatures sometimes must be amputated.

Adjective Phrase:

Toes frozen by sub–zero temperatures sometimes must be amputated.

Participial Adjective:

Frozen toes sometimes must be amputated.

Participial adjectives come before the nouns they modify.

Freezing temperatures cause a lot of damage to fingers, toes, and orange trees.
Adj N

Note: When a participial adjective comes after the verb *be*, it is not always followed by a noun. The adjective modifies the subject.

Most of China is ideally suited for growing tea.
S Adj

Note: Participial adjectives can be modified by adverbs. In the above sentence, the adverb *ideally* modifies the adjective *suited*.

3. Active participial adjectives describe the doer of an action. Active participial adjectives come from active–voice verbs (See 2.6) and take the *–ing* form (present participle) of the verb.

Active Participial Adjective:

A magnifying glass makes objects appear larger than they really are.

In the above sentence, *a glass* performs the action: a glass magnifies objects.

4. Passive participial adjectives describe the receiver of an action. Passive participial adjectives come from passive–voice verbs (See 2.6) and take the *–ed* form (past participle) of the verb.

Passive Participial Adjective:

The U. S. Constitution is required reading for American high school students.

In the above sentence, *reading* does not perform the action; it receives the action. Reading the Constitution *is required* by teachers and school officials.

STRUCTURE

Note: Adjectives that come from irregular verbs have irregular past participles. Look at some examples:

broken arm	fallen branches	forbidden fruit	well–kept secret

5. A TOEFL item may test your ability to choose the correct form of an adjective. Look at this example:

> The toga worn by the Etruscan kings was decorated with embroidered or ------- designs.
>
> ○ sew
> ○ to sew
> ○ sewing
> ○ sewn

Two adjectives modify the noun *designs*. The first is *embroidered*, a passive participial adjective. You can see that the missing adjective probably is also a passive adjective. Which answer choice is a passive adjective? If you chose *sewn*, you were correct. *Sewn* is the past participle of *sew*, an irregular verb.

PRACTICE

Exercise 2.17.A

Choose the one underlined word or phrase that must be changed for the sentence to be correct.

1. Nine out of ten Americans recognized (A) a man's expression (B) in a photograph as fear (C), yet six out of ten Japanese thought the man was sad or surprise (D).

2. One of the best publicized (A) and lavishly praising (B) architectural projects of the twentieth century was Habitat, the experimental housing (C) complex created (D) for Expo 67 in Montreal.

3. Tragic actors in ancient times (A) were respected (B) citizens, and the more gift ones (C) were in great demand, being paid well to travel to distant places (D) for festivals.

4. If one lives in a disorganized (A), pollution (B), crime–ridden world, one's (C) energies will be directed (D) at simple survival.

5. Lipids, one of the principle components (A) of living cells (B), have a specialize role (C) as the main structural component (D) of membranes.

Choose the one word or phrase that best completes the sentence.

6. Preparations for the potlatch ceremony required the accumulation of blankets, animal skins, fish oil, -------, and berries.

   (A) dried fish
   (B) fish dried
   (C) fish drying
   (D) dry the fish

7. That all ------- is made up of cells is a unifying concept in modern biology.

   (A) living material
   (B) lived material
   (C) material is living
   (D) material to live

8. In 1851 Isaac Singer received a patent for the first continuous–stitch -------.

   (A) machine it sewed
   (B) sew machine
   (C) sewing machine
   (D) machine sewing

9. The belief that a man in his early twenties ought to have a firm occupational choice reflects ------- that development is complete by the end of adolescence.

   (A) the prevailing view
   (B) the prevailed view
   (C) the view prevailed
   (D) this view is prevailing

10. Henri Rousseau was the first ------- painter to enter the history of painting.

   (A) self to teach
   (B) to teach himself
   (C) self–teaching
   (D) self–taught

Answers to Exercise 2.17.A are on page 648.

2.17 EXTENSION

1. Discuss whether the participial adjectives in Exercise 2.17.A are active or passive. Who or what is the doer of the adjective's action?

2. In reading done outside class, students look for examples of participial adjectives. Bring examples to share in class. Are the adjectives active or passive?

3. Students create "TOEFL sentences" to test their classmates' understanding of participial adjectives. Students write their own sentences with participial adjectives, or use sentences they find in print. In some but not all of the sentences, change the adjective so that it is the incorrect participle (change *–ing* to *–ed,* and vice versa). Keep some of the adjectives correct. Write the sentences either on the board or on cards. Classmates must determine whether there is an error in the participial adjective. If there is an error, classmates make the correction.

2.18 Checking Negative Modifiers

FOCUS

Read the following TOEFL item. What does this sentence need?

> Most people seem to think ------- form of home heating is as convenient as electricity.
>
> ○ nothing
> ○ not
> ○ never
> ○ no

This sentence needs a modifier before the noun phrase *form of home heating*. Nouns are modified by adjectives. Which answer choice is an adjective?

The fourth choice, *no*, best completes this sentence because it can be used as an adjective. The sentence should read: *Most people seem to think no form of home heating is as convenient as electricity.*

Now, read another TOEFL item. What does this sentence need?

> Insurance agents may work for ------- one company or may act as independent agents.
>
> ○ only
> ○ not only
> ○ the only
> ○ an only

This sentence needs a modifier before the noun phrase *one company*.

The first answer choice, *only*, would be correct in this context. The sentence should read: *Insurance agents may work for only one company or may act as independent agents.*

The above examples are similar to the types of sentences you will see on the TOEFL.

DO YOU KNOW...?

1. Approximately one item on the TOEFL will test your ability to check negative modifiers. You must be able to recognize correct and incorrect usage of these modifiers.

2. The following negative expressions are used to modify nouns:

no	not any	not many
not all	not every	not much

<u>No</u> smoking is allowed in government buildings.
There are <u>not any</u> poisonous snakes that are native to New Zealand.
<u>Not many</u> members of the Republican Party call themselves "liberals."

Note: When *no* is used as an adjective, it means *not any*.

Note: In the above sentences, *not* is an adverb. *Any* and *many* are adjectives. These sentences have standard word order: adverb + adjective + noun.

The following "almost negative" expressions also modify nouns:

barely any	hardly any	scarcely any

Women in the United States had <u>barely any</u> civil rights until the 1860s.

Note: *Barely*, *hardly*, and *scarcely* are adverbs that modify the adjective *any*.

3. The modifier *only* can be either an adjective or an adverb. *Only* comes immediately before the word or structure it modifies:

The bat is the <u>only</u> mammal that can fly. (modifies the noun *mammal*)

Of all the mammals, <u>only</u> the bat can fly. (modifies the noun phrase *the bat*)

Most bears hunt <u>only</u> at night. (modifies the prepositional phrase *at night*)

4. The following negative expressions are adverbs:

not	never

Some people think we may <u>never</u> discover evidence of life on other planets.

Adverbs modify verbs or adjectives. In the following sentence, *not* modifies an adjective:

<u>Not</u> <u>all</u> clouds produce rain or snow.

Beware! *Not* and *never* sometimes appear as incorrect answers on TOEFL items where adjectives are needed. You must be careful to check how these words are being used.

STRUCTURE

The following negative expressions are nouns or pronouns:

neither	none	nothing

Neither of the proposals will satisfy the requirements of the contract.
There is nothing that can be done to prevent an earthquake.

Note: Nouns and pronouns function as subjects and objects. They are usually not modifiers. However, sometimes *neither* functions as an adjective modifying a singular noun:

Neither proposal will satisfy the requirements of the contract.

The following negative expressions are conjunctions:

neither	not only

When used as a conjunction, *neither* is usually accompanied by *nor*. *Not only* is usually accompanied by *but also*.

Neither Millard Fillmore nor Franklin Pierce is a well–known ex–president.
Rats are not only agricultural pests but also carriers of disease.

Note: Conjunctions are not modifiers; they are connecting words (See 2.20). *Neither* and *not only* sometimes appear as incorrect answers on TOEFL items where adjectives are needed. You must be careful to check how these words are being used.

5. A test item may try to trick you by using the incorrect word form of a negative modifier. Look at this example:

> No every reduction in visibility is necessarily man–made, and natural haze is known to have been present centuries ago in humid regions.

Which underlined word or phrase must be changed for the sentence to be correct? If you chose *No*, you were correct. *No* is an adjective that is used to modify nouns, but here an adverb is needed to modify the adjective *every*. Correction: *Not.*

In the above example, *not every* modifies *reduction*. Remember the standard word order: adverb + adjective + noun.

Look at another example:

> Why a person has ------- friendships is something that cannot be adequately determined by a survey.
>
> ◯ not
> ◯ none
> ◯ neither
> ◯ no

The first choice is incorrect because *not* is an adverb, which does not modify a noun. The second choice, *none*, is a pronoun, which does not modify a noun. The third choice is incorrect in this context because *neither* is used as an adjective only with singular nouns, but *friendships* is plural.

The fourth choice is correct. *No* is an adjective that modifies *friendships*.

6. Some of the answer choices will try to trick you by having modifiers with incorrect word order. Look at this example:

> People who work in an office in their home spend ------- on transportation and work clothing.
>
> ◯ money hardly any
> ◯ hardly any money
> ◯ hardly money
> ◯ money is hardly

This sentence needs a direct object for the verb *spend*. The direct object must be a noun structure. Which answer choice is a noun structure with correct word order?

The second choice, *hardly any money*, is a noun phrase with adverb + adjective + noun word order. It is the choice that best completes the sentence.

Why are the other three answer choices incorrect?

STRUCTURE

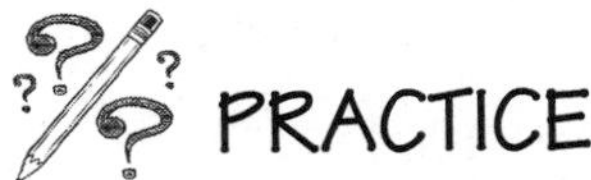

PRACTICE

Exercise 2.18.A

Choose the one word or phrase that best completes the sentence.

1. Of all the planets of the solar system, ------- known to support life.

   (A) only Earth is
   (B) Earth is not only
   (C) the only one is Earth
   (D) Earth only to be

2. The first steam engine was invented by Hero, an engineer of ancient Greece, but it was of -------.

   (A) no practical use
   (B) none practical use
   (C) not only the practical use
   (D) practically not used

3. ------- types of investments go up or down in value at the same time.

   (A) Not
   (B) Not only
   (C) Not all
   (D) None

4. Of all the poisonous snakes of the Americas, ------- is as deadly as the brightly–colored coral snake.

   (A) no
   (B) none
   (C) not only
   (D) never

5. Although sometimes there is not ------- before an avalanche, there are some basic signs of avalanche danger.

   (A) warn nothing
   (B) neither warning
   (C) any warning
   (D) no warning

6. The chewable substance called *chicle* had ------- until Thomas Adams added licorice and sold it as gumballs.

   (A) hardly any flavor
   (B) any flavor hardly
   (C) flavor hardly not
   (D) hardly not flavor

7. In fourth gear, ------- are engaged, and transmission goes directly from the clutch to the differential.

   (A) not only gear wheels
   (B) no gear wheels
   (C) not gear wheels
   (D) gear wheels not

8. Of every one hundred new U. S. residents in 1997, ------- sixty–four were born in the United States.

   (A) only of the
   (B) the only
   (C) not only
   (D) only

Choose the one underlined word or phrase that must be changed for the sentence to be correct.

9. In a capitalist system, <u>not person</u> (A) or group of persons can control the marketplace, <u>which</u> (B) means <u>that power</u> (C) cannot be monopolized <u>by a party</u> (D) or a clique.

10. In <u>sixteenth–century</u> (A) Europe, it was <u>none</u> (B) accident that witchcraft came into <u>increasing</u> (C) prominence along with protests <u>against</u> (D) social and economic inequities.

Answers to Exercise 2.18.A are on page 648.

2.18 EXTENSION

1. In reading done outside class, students look for examples of negative modifiers. Bring examples to share in class.

2. Students create "TOEFL sentences" to test their classmates' understanding of negative expressions. Students write sentences, using expressions from this list: *no, not all, not any, not every, not many, not much, hardly any, only, not, never, neither, none, nothing.* Omit the negative expression, and leave a blank space where it should be. Write the sentences either on the board or on cards. Classmates must complete the sentences with an appropriate word or phrase from the list.

3. Discuss how the meanings of the following sentences are similar or different:

   Not all students carry a backpack.
   Not any students carry a backpack.
   Not every student carries a backpack.
   Not many students carry a backpack.

2.19 Checking Equatives, Comparatives, and Superlatives

FOCUS

Read the following TOEFL item. What does this sentence need?

> At the spring and autumn equinoxes, day has the same amount of sunlight ------- of darkness.
>
> ◯ and night has
> ◯ as night has
> ◯ for night it has
> ◯ night has also

This sentence discusses a similarity between day and night. At the equinoxes, day and night are of equal length. In other words, *day has the same amount of sunlight as night has of darkness*. The second answer choice best completes the sentence.

This is an example of the ***equative degree***. The equative shows how two things are equal.

Now, read another TOEFL item. What does this sentence need?

> In the United States, household water consumption is ------- than that in Europe.
>
> ◯ slightly high
> ◯ highest
> ◯ as high
> ◯ slightly higher

The word *than* is a clue that two things are being compared. This sentence compares household water consumption in the United States and household water consumption in Europe. When two things are compared, the ***comparative degree*** is used.

The fourth choice, *slightly higher*, is the correct comparative form. The sentence should read: *In the United States, household water consumption is slightly higher than that in Europe.*

2.19 EQUATIVES, COMPARATIVES, AND SUPERLATIVES

DO YOU KNOW...?

1. Approximately two items on the TOEFL will test your ability to check expressions of the equative, comparative, and superlative degrees of adjectives and adverbs. You must be able to recognize correct and incorrect usage of these expressions.

2. The ***equative degree*** expresses equality between two things. The equative degree has the same form for short and long words:

SHORT ADJECTIVE OR ADVERB	LONG ADJECTIVE OR ADVERB
as...as	**as...as**
as large as	as successful as
as fast as	as interesting as
as early as	as consistently as

A banana contains as many calories as a half–cup of noodles.
Manila has almost as much annual rainfall as Hong Kong has.
A smoker's risk of heart attack is twice as high as that of a nonsmoker.

Note: The equative degree can be used to show complex equalities.

The song of the lark is just as beautiful as its color is dull.
Crater Lake is seven times as deep as the Giant Sequoia Tree is tall.

Note: *Not* can be used with the equative form to show inequality.

Quinine is not as effective as new anti–malarial drugs, such as primaquine.

3. The ***comparative degree*** compares two things that are not equal. One thing is more or less of something than the other.

The comparative degree has different forms for short and long words:

SHORT ADJECTIVE OR ADVERB	LONG ADJECTIVE OR ADVERB
–er than	**more/less...than**
larger than	more successful than
faster than	more interesting than
earlier than	less consistently than

Puerto Rico has higher average January temperatures than Hawaii has.
Quinine is less effective than new anti–malarial drugs, such as primaquine.

4. A ***double comparative*** is formed when two comparatives are used together. In double comparatives, *the* comes before each comparative.

The longer the treatment for snakebite is delayed, the greater one risks losing a limb.

The first comparative usually expresses *cause*, and the second comparative expresses *result*. In the above sentence, the cause is *the longer the treatment for snakebite is delayed*. The result is *the greater one risks losing a limb*.

Note: In some double comparatives, the verb is omitted. Look at this example:

The farther a car moves away from a radar speed trap, the lower the frequency of the radar signal.

In the above example, the verb is omitted from the second comparative. In conversation, people often omit the verbs in double comparatives such as the expression *the sooner, the better*.

5. The ***superlative degree*** compares three or more things that are not equal.

The superlative degree has different forms for short and long words:

SHORT ADJECTIVE OR ADVERB	LONG ADJECTIVE OR ADVERB
the –est	**the most/least...**
the largest	the most successful
the fastest	the least interesting
the earliest	the most consistently

Jamaica produces some of the finest coffees in the world.
Mark Twain is probably the most frequently quoted American humorist.

Note: *The* is omitted if there is a possessive before the superlative:

Great Smoky Mountains National Park is America's busiest national park.

6. Some common adjectives have irregular comparative and superlative forms:

BASE FORM	COMPARATIVE	SUPERLATIVE
bad	worse	worst
good	better	best
little	less	least
many	more	most
much	more	most

Some common adverbs have irregular comparative and superlative forms:

BASE FORM	COMPARATIVE	SUPERLATIVE
badly	worse	worst
well	better	best

7. Some of the answer choices will try to trick you by having incorrectly formed degree structures. Look at this example:

Because some insurance agents work on commission, they must work ------- to earn higher pay.

- ◯ more the long hours
- ◯ hours more long
- ◯ longer hours
- ◯ as longer hours

This sentence needs a comparative to balance the comparative *to earn higher pay*. Which of the answer choices has the correct comparative form?

The first and second choices have incorrectly formed comparatives and incorrect word order. *Long* is a short adjective; its comparative form is *longer*. The third and fourth choices have *longer*, but the fourth choice is incorrect because *as* is used with the equative, not the comparative degree.

The third choice best completes the sentence: *Because some insurance agents work on commission, they must work longer hours to earn higher pay*. This sentence has parallel comparative structures. (You will review parallel structure in 2.25.)

Look at another example:

> Longest river in the world, the Nile nourished the most long–lived of the great ancient civilizations and now supports agriculture in Egypt and the Sudan.

This sentence has two superlatives. Which underlined word must be changed for the sentence to be correct? If you chose *Longest*, you were correct because it is an incorrectly formed superlative. Correction: *The longest.*

8. A test item may try to trick you by using one degree where another is needed. Look at this example:

> Tribal–owned enterprises of the Navaho Indians include the larger tribal newspaper in the United States and the first Indian–operated college.

Which underlined word or phrase must be changed for the sentence to be correct? If you chose *larger*, you were correct because the comparative degree is incorrect here.

Two clues tell you the superlative is needed. The first clue is *the*, which comes before a superlative. The second clue is *in the United States*, which tells you that many tribal newspapers—certainly more than two—are being compared. Correction: *largest*.

9. A test item may try to trick you by separating the parts of a comparative with a phrase or clause. Look at this example:

> People are ------- the need for health insurance than for life insurance.
>
> ◯ more likely to see
> ◯ likely to see
> ◯ seeing more like
> ◯ seeing most

The word *than* is a clue that two things are being compared. The parts of the comparative are separated by the phrase *the need for health insurance*.

The first answer choice best completes the sentence because it is the only choice with correct comparative form. The sentence should read: *People are more likely to see the need for health insurance than for life insurance*.

PRACTICE

Exercise 2.19.A

Choose the one word or phrase that best completes the sentence.

1. An air conditioner works in the same way ------- a refrigerator.

   (A) by
   (B) as
   (C) as if
   (D) to be

2. ------- falls in Seattle per year than in any city on the east coast of North America.

   (A) Less rain
   (B) Lesser rain
   (C) Little rain
   (D) A little rain

3. In most species of seal, the females are not -------.

   (A) as large as the males
   (B) as larger than the males
   (C) larger the males
   (D) the males as large

4. Many people find the collie as beautiful -------.

   (A) than the bulldog is ugly
   (B) that the bulldog is ugly
   (C) as the bulldog is ugly
   (D) as ugly as the bulldog

5. All bonds are graded, and -------, the higher the yield, because lower–grade bonds involve more risk.

   (A) lower grade
   (B) the lower the grade
   (C) if a low grade
   (D) the lowest grade

6. Dinah Washington's style of blues was ------- complex than that of Chicago blues singers.

   (A) the most
   (B) much was
   (C) much
   (D) much more

7. The booby's brown feathers are ------- its blue feet are bright.

   (A) very dull
   (B) duller
   (C) as dull as
   (D) dull as

8. Since snowshoes are considerably ------- the the bottom of your foot, you must adjust the way you walk.

   (A) bigger
   (B) as big
   (C) bigger than
   (D) biggest

STRUCTURE

Exercise 2.19.B

Choose the one underlined word or phrase that must be changed for the sentence to be correct.

1. Australia is the flattest <u>and dry</u> (A) of the continents, <u>as well as</u> (B) the <u>oldest</u> (C) and most <u>isolated</u> (D).

2. The cat's eyes, perhaps <u>its most distinctive</u> (A) feature, can function just as well in almost <u>total darkness</u> (B) <u>as if they can</u> (C) in <u>bright daylight</u> (D).

3. The corporation is the formalest business arrangement, and the sole proprietorship is the least complex.
A B C D

4. The crocodile is slightly smaller and least bulky than the alligator, and it has a larger, narrower snout.
A B C D

5. The influence and skills of the Sumerians spread to lands far as Egypt in Mediterranean Africa and
A B C
the Indus River in the Indian subcontinent.
D

6. When an object is heated, the molecules move faster, and the faster they move, the hot the object.
A B C D

7. There is much cross–cultural misunderstanding about facial expressions, and misunderstanding is
A
likely to be more greater for more subtle expressions.
B C D

8. Thomas Edison's the most significant contributions were his development of the first practical light
A B
bulb and his design for a complete electrical distribution system for lighting.
C D

Answers to Exercises 2.19.A through 2.19.B are on pages 648 and 649.

2.19 EXTENSION

1. In reading done outside class, students look for examples of equatives, comparatives, and superlatives. Bring examples to share in class.

2. Students create "TOEFL sentences" to test their classmates' understanding of the equative and comparative degrees. Students write their own sentences with equatives and comparatives, or use sentences they find in print. Write either on the board or on cards. In each sentence, omit the equative or comparative expression, and leave a blank space where it should be. Write the base form of the adjective or adverb below the sentence. **Example:** *Dogs make —— pets —— cats.* Write below: *good.* One classmate must provide an appropriate equative. Another classmate must provide a comparative. Decide which statement is closer to the truth!

ASSESSING PROGRESS – 2.16 through 2.19

QUIZ 9 (Time – 10 minutes)

Choose the one word or phrase that best completes the sentence.

1. The relatively small ocelot is ------- a hunter as the larger panther.

   (A) as just more efficient
   (B) as just efficient
   (C) just as efficient
   (D) it has just efficiency

2. A study showed that most men reported fatherhood is ------- for them.

   (A) extreme importantly
   (B) extreme important
   (C) extremely important
   (D) importance extremely

3. Prehistoric tribes had ------- of men over age forty to serve in positions of leadership.

   (A) only a small number
   (B) a small number only
   (C) an only number small
   (D) the small number was only

Choose the one underlined word or phrase that must be changed for the sentence to be correct.

4. Because (A) its molecular order is not as fixed that (B) of a solid crystal, a liquid crystal can be easily modified by (C) radiation, stress, or temperature (D).

5. According to the *New York Times*, a person average (A) who has a high school diploma (B) will earn the equivalent of thirty percent less (C) on a job in 2001 than his counterpart (D) earned in 1979.

6. Anthropologists discovered that certain tribes (A) practiced (B) public consumption and waste to a degree unmatched (C) by most wasteful (D) of consumer economies.

7. To a young adult, inadequate support and poor mentoring can be (A) just as damaging (B) be (C) poor parenting in childhood (D).

QUIZ 9

Choose the one word or phrase that best completes the sentence.

8. Everglades National Park, an area of ------- and saw grass, is rich in wildlife.

   (A) mud packing solid
   (B) solidly mud packing
   (C) solidly pack mud
   (D) solidly packed mud

9. More military technological innovations happened during World War I ------- war in history.

   (A) as another
   (B) by any other
   (C) than in any other
   (D) than others

10. The raccoon's fingers are ------- to turn doorknobs and open refrigerators.

   (A) nimbly for enough
   (B) nimble enough
   (C) enough nimble
   (D) more nimble than

11. In any vibrating object, the stronger the vibrations, -------.

   (A) the loudest sound
   (B) louder being the sound
   (C) the sound is louder
   (D) the louder the sound

12. Chippewa National Forest in Minnesota has one of ------- bald eagle populations outside Alaska.

   (A) the largest
   (B) largest
   (C) the largest one
   (D) larger than

13. If it were not for the jet engine, many people would have ——— experience of flight.

   (A) any
   (B) no
   (C) not
   (D) none

Choose the one underlined word or phrase that must be changed for the sentence to be correct.

14. The ancient Egyptians made <u>basic discoveries</u> (A) in geometry and the natural sciences, and their art was <u>colorful</u> (B) and <u>appealed</u> (C) and their literature <u>very human</u> (D).

15. The "baby boom" generation, <u>which makes up</u> (A) <u>the largest generation</u> (B) in recent history, has had <u>much influence</u> (C) on the birth rate than the generation <u>that followed</u> (D).

Answers to Structure Quiz 9 are on page 649.

2.20 Checking Conjunctions

What is wrong with this sentence?

> Rice needs either plains and terraces which can be flooded, as well as abundant water in the growing season.

This sentence contains some words that join other words and phrases. These connecting words are called ***conjunctions***.

Can you identify the conjunctions in this sentence? One conjunction is *either*. *Either* is usually paired with *or*; however, in the above sentence it is incorrectly paired with *and*. *And* should be changed so that the clause reads: *Rice needs either plains or terraces which can be flooded.*

Either…or is a two–part conjunction. There is also another conjunction in the above sentence: *as well as*, which shows addition.

What is wrong with this sentence?

> Businesses use workers, managers, machinery, and land, well as the services and products of other organizations, to produce and deliver what consumers want.

Businesses use many things. Some of these things are listed above, with some conjunctions that show addition. One of the conjunctions is incomplete. Which one? If you chose *well as*, you were correct. It should be changed to *as well as*, which adds more things that businesses use: *the services and products of other organizations*.

What other conjunction shows addition in the above sentence?

STRUCTURE

DO YOU KNOW...?

1. At least one item on the TOEFL will test your ability to check conjunctions. You must be able to recognize both correct and incorrect usage of conjunctions.

2. ***Conjunctions*** are words and expressions that join other words, phrases, or clauses.

   Coordinating conjunctions connect structures of the same value: single words, phrases, or main clauses. The most common coordinating conjunctions are:

and	but	or	so	yet

   Words:

   The flower known as "baby's–breath" begins to bloom in June *or* July.

   Phrases:

   A jet engine takes in air at the front *and* ejects it from the back.

   Main Clauses:

   Lincoln had a lot of political enemies, *yet* he managed to preserve the Union.

3. ***Correlative conjunctions*** have two parts and connect structures of the same value: single words, phrases, or main clauses. Correlative conjunctions are sometimes called ***paired expressions***. The most common correlative conjunctions are:

ADDITION	ALTERNATIVE	EXCLUSION/INCLUSION
and...as well as	either...or	not...but
both...and	neither...nor	
not only...but also		

   Words:

   Thomas Jefferson was a farmer *and* architect, *as well as* a statesman.

   Phrases:

   Many people learn about job openings *not* by reading the newspaper *but* by talking to people who work.

   Main Clauses:

   Not only is Kobe a major port and industrial center, *but* it is *also* a cultural center, with several colleges, universities, temples, and shrines.

Note: *As well as* is usually paired with *and*, *both...and*, or *either...or*. However, sometimes you will see *as well as* by itself:

The Salish Indians developed their wood arts as well as their mythology.

Note: *Not...but* excludes the structure after *not* (makes it not true) and includes the structure after *but* (makes it true). In the following sentence, it is true that a groundhog is *a large rodent*:

A groundhog is actually not a hog but a large rodent.

Note: *Also* can be omitted from *not only...but also* and *as well* used instead.

Astronomers are beginning to understand not only the physical make–up of stars, but their origins and life cycles as well.

In the following sentences, identify the conjunctions. What types of structures do the conjunctions connect?

a. Neither the cat's teeth nor its digestive system is suited for anything but an all–meat diet.
b. The poetry of Emily Dickinson was focused on both material and spiritual values.
c. The scorpion's poison is not in its bite but in the sting of its tail.

(***Answers:*** a. *Neither...nor* connects noun phrases *(the cat's teeth*, *its digestive system*); *but* connects noun phrases (*anything*, *an all–meat diet*); b. *both...and* connects adjectives (*material*, *spiritual*); c. *not...but* connects prepositional phrases (*in its bite*, *in the sting of its tail*)

STRUCTURE

4. Two other types of conjunctions appear on the TOEFL: *subordinating conjunctions* and *conjunctive adverbs*. These types of conjunctions join clauses.

Subordinating conjunctions connect a main clause and a subordinate clause and express a relationship between the ideas in the clauses. (See 2.11 and the list of subordinating conjunctions on page 222.)

Contrast:

Some artists are just beginning to work with computers, while others have readily accepted this tool.

Cause/Result:

The disk plate is exposed to the air so that heat generated by braking is released.

Conjunctive adverbs connect main clauses and express a relationship between the ideas in the clauses.

ADDITION	CONTRAST	CAUSE/RESULT
also	however	as a result
besides	instead	consequently
furthermore	nevertheless	hence
in addition	still	therefore
moreover	on the contrary	thus
on the other hand		

Computer graphics contributes to productivity and creativity; moreover, it is a vital part of the computer–human interface.
A black pigment absorbs all three primary colors; therefore, it appears black.

Note: *On the one hand* is a conjunctive adverb that must be paired with *on the other hand*:

> On the one hand, the majority of Americans take their main vacation in July or August; on the other hand, a number of people prefer taking a winter vacation.

Note: Notice the use of semicolons (;) and commas (,) with conjunctive adverbs in the above sentences.

5. A TOEFL item may test your ability to recognize where a conjunction is needed. Look at this example:

> ------- Mother Teresa and Martin Luther King, Jr., won the Nobel peace prize.
>
> ○ Either
> ○ As
> ○ Both
> ○ They

This sentence needs a conjunction that agrees with *and*, which joins the two subjects. The first answer choice, *either*, cannot be paired with *and*. The second choice, *as*, would make the sentence incomplete.

The third choice best completes the sentence. *Both...and* is a paired expression.

Why is the fourth choice incorrect?

6. A test item may try to trick you by incorrectly pairing the different parts of a two–part conjunction. Look at this example:

> Not only are rhododendrons known for their dramatic, colorful flowers, and they are also very valuable as landscape plants.

Which underlined word or phrase must be changed for the sentence to be correct? If you chose *and they*, you were correct because it does not agree with the first part of the conjunction, *not only*. Correction: *but they*.

Look at another example:

> On the one hand, earth was lifeless for its first two billion years; on the contrary, it was a seething mass of volcanic and geologic activity.

Which underlined word or phrase must be changed for the sentence to be correct? If you chose *on the contrary*, you were correct because *on the one hand* must be paired with *on the other hand*. Change *on the contrary* to *on the other hand*.

PRACTICE

Exercise 2.20.A

Choose the one word or phrase that best completes the sentence.

1. Combustion produces ------- heat.

   (A) light and of
   (B) both light and
   (C) light also
   (D) as enough light as

2. In the early 1980s, some economists called for a return to the gold standard, ------- others urged a more broadly based standard.

   (A) or
   (B) the
   (C) that
   (D) while

3. Birds not only bring song, color, and activity to a garden ------- are vitally needed by plants.

   (A) but also
   (B) as well as
   (C) and
   (D) and they

4. A new kind of civilization came into being around 3,000 B. C., based not on superior agricultural lands ------- superior location for trade.

   (A) but on
   (B) but also
   (C) based on having
   (D) having

5. Two–thirds of Australia is -------.

   (A) desert either semiarid
   (B) either desert or semiarid
   (C) either desert nor it is semiarid
   (D) either desert and semiarid

Choose the one underlined word or phrase that must be changed for the sentence to be correct.

6. Many (A) astronomers agreed with Harlow Shapley's *big galaxy hypothesis*; therefore (B), others disputed the idea that there was (C) nothing (D) beyond the Milky Way.

7. Columbia University includes not only (A) the Teachers College but also schools of (B) journalism, mining, and (C) international affairs, as well (D) a geological laboratory.

8. In summer, the tiger shark may follow (A) warm water currents as far south (B) as New Zealand, or north to Japan (C) nor (D) the northern United States.

9. Examples of minimal art are the structures of such sculptors as Carl Andre and Donald Judd,
A B
as well the hard–edge paintings of such artists as Frank Stella.
C D

10. Unlike early capitalism, modern capitalism is dependent on the state, and the government
A B
is expected to take measures to fight either unemployment and inflation.
C D

Answers to Exercise 2.20.A are on page 649.

2.20 EXTENSION

1. In reading done outside class, students look for examples of different kinds of conjunctions. Bring examples to share in class. Identify the types of structures joined by the conjunctions.

2. Students create "TOEFL sentences" to test their classmates' understanding of correlative conjunctions (paired expressions). Students write sentences with: *and...as well as*, *both...and*, *not only...but also*, *either...or*, *neither...nor*, and *not...but*. Write the sentences either on the board or on cards. Omit both parts of the conjunction, and leave blank spaces where they should be. Classmates must complete the sentences with appropriate conjunctions.

3. Students create "TOEFL sentences" to test their classmates' understanding of conjunctive adverbs. Students write sentences with the conjunctive adverbs from the list on page 283. In each sentence, omit the conjunctive adverb, and leave a blank space where it should be. Classmates must complete the sentences with appropriate expressions.

2.21 Checking Prepositions

FOCUS

What is wrong with this sentence?

> Supermarkets depend high volume and low overhead to keep prices below the average for stores.

This sentence has a missing preposition. Certain prepositions follow some verbs. The verb *depend* is usually followed by *on*. *Depend on* is one of many common verb + preposition structures. The sentence should read: *Supermarkets depend on high volume and low overhead to keep prices below the average for stores*.

What is wrong with this sentence?

> Alchemy, which aimed to change base metals into gold, arrived to Europe through Sicily and Spain between the eleventh and sixteenth centuries.

This sentence has an incorrect preposition between *arrived* and *Europe*. The verb *arrive* is never followed by *to*. In this context, alchemy *arrived in Europe*. *To* should be changed to *in*.

There are several other prepositions in the above sentences. Can you identify them? Hint: prepositions are always followed by noun structures.

The prepositions are: *below*, *for*, *into*, *through*, and *between*.

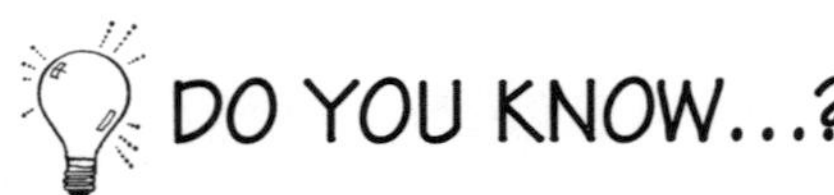

DO YOU KNOW...?

1. At least two items on the TOEFL will test your ability to check usage of prepositions and prepositional phrases.

2. A ***preposition*** is a word that shows how a noun structure is related to another word in a sentence. Prepositions can express relationships of space, time, direction, and position.

   A ***prepositional phrase*** is a preposition joined with a noun structure. The noun is the object of the preposition. The object of a preposition can be one of the following noun structures:

   Noun:

   > The cause *of* malnutrition is a lack of essential vitamins, minerals, and proteins.

   Noun Phrase:

   > Civil conflict characterized much of Asia *in* the mid–twentieth century.

   Pronoun:

   > Most energy waves pass *by* us or *through* us without having any harmful effect *on* us.

   Gerund:

   > Bank tellers are responsible *for* recording all of the transactions they perform.

   Noun Clause:

   > Physical health has a definite effect *on* how people cope with emotional crises.

   Note: Infinitives cannot be objects of prepositions. In infinitives, such as *to plan* and *to control*, *to* is not a preposition; it is part of the infinitive structure (See 2.7).

3. Prepositional phrases are modifiers. They can function as adjectives or adverbs.

   Prepositional phrases used as adjectives come after the nouns they modify:

   > The rise (N) of science (PP) challenged the authority (N) of the old order (PP).

   Prepositional phrases used as adverbs modify verbs or clauses. These prepositional phrases can come at different places in a sentence:

   > Many of the institutions of capitalism existed (V) in ancient times (PP).

   > Due to rapid deforestation (PP), timber towns have experienced economic depression (MAIN CLAUSE).

4. Words that are commonly used as prepositions are:

PREPOSITIONS				
about	at	despite	of	toward
above	before	down	off	under
across	behind	during	on	unlike
after	below	for	out	until
against	beneath	from	over	up
along	beside	in	since	upon
among	between	into	through	with
around	beyond	like	throughout	within
as	by	near	to	without

Several ***compound prepositions*** are made up of two or more words:

COMPOUND PREPOSITIONS				
according to	aside from	except for	in favor of	out of
ahead of	because of	in addition to	in spite of	prior to
along with	contrary to	in case of	instead of	regardless of
as a result of	due to	in contrast to	next to	together with

Note: Some prepositions resemble words that perform other functions:

Immunization for measles is recommended because of the possibility of secondary infection.
Measles is a serious disease because it can lead to secondary infection.

In the first sentence above, the preposition *because of* is followed by a noun object, *the possibility of secondary infection*. In the second sentence, the subordinating conjunction *because* is followed by a clause, *it can lead to secondary infection*.

Remember, you can identify a preposition by looking for its noun object. If some structure other than a noun follows a word, then that word is probably not a preposition.

5. Certain verb + preposition combinations are commonly used. Sometimes they are called ***phrasal verbs*** or ***two–word verbs***. A verb + preposition structure sometimes has a meaning that is different from the verb alone. Such structures are *idiomatic* (See 1.2).

VERB + PREPOSITION STRUCTURES				
agree with	deal with	grow up	prepare for	succeed in
approve of	depend on	keep on	refer to	think about
bring about	differ from	listen to	rely on	think of
communicate with	divide into	object to	reply to	turn off/on
consist of	find out	point out	respond to	worry about

The Steller's jay differs from the eastern bluejay mainly in appearance.

STRUCTURE

Certain adjectives are commonly followed by prepositions:

ADJECTIVE + PREPOSITION STRUCTURES

associated with	common in/to	confused about	interested in	qualified for
aware of	composed of	conscious of	made (out) of	related to
based on	concerned with	different from	pleased with	satisfied with
capable of	confined to	equal to	prejudiced against	similar to

Diabetes is associated with high blood sugar and altered protein metabolism.

6. Certain structures with prepositions may appear on the TOEFL:

***by + –ing* (gerund):**

A primary color cannot be formed by mixing other colors.

***–ed + by* (passive):**

The common cold is caused by a viral infection of the upper respiratory tract.
Romeo and Juliet was written by Shakespeare around 1595. (irregular passive)

***from…to* (paired expression):**

Shoppers can have funds transferred automatically from their bank account to that of a store.

***between…and* (paired expression):**

Between 1940 and 1945, scientists in Britain developed radar.

7. A TOEFL item may test you by having:

- no preposition where one is needed
- a preposition where one is not needed
- an incorrect preposition

8. A TOEFL item may test your ability to recognize where a preposition is needed. Look at this example:

> Research into the chemical complexities of the human body may reveal new insights ------- variety of diseases.
>
> ◯ into a
> ◯ a
> ◯ but
> ◯ that a

This sentence needs a preposition to show the relationship between *variety of diseases* and *insights*. Only the first answer choice, *into a*, would make a prepositional phrase. The prepositional phrase *into a variety of diseases* modifies *insights*.

The second choice, *a*, does not show any relationship. The third choice, *but*, is a conjunction that does not make sense in this context. The fourth choice, *that a*, would introduce a noun clause (See 2.9), but *variety of diseases* is not a clause.

Look at another example:

> A man of twenty is ------- his bodily vigor and is ready to take his place as a man in the society of adults.
>
> ◯ that the height
> ◯ at the height of
> ◯ height of
> ◯ the height

This sentence needs a preposition before *his bodily vigor*. Only the second and third answer choices have a preposition in that position. Which is correct?

The second choice, *at the height of*, best completes the sentence. It makes two prepositional phrases: *at the height of his bodily vigor*. The third choice does not make sense in this context.

The wrong answer choices do not make sense. This shows how important prepositions are. They are little words that make meaningful connections between nouns and other words.

9. A test item may try to trick you by having a preposition where one is not needed. Look at this example:

> The law outlines the requirements for operating under each of the three main for ways of organizing a business.

Which underlined word or phrase must be changed for the sentence to be correct? If you chose *for*, you were correct because a preposition is not needed here. How do you know this? *Main* is an adjective that modifies *ways*. Prepositions do not come between adjectives and the nouns they modify. Correction: omit *for*.

10. A TOEFL item may test you by having an incorrect preposition. Look at this example:

> The first animals that lived on land were amphibians, which lived part of their lives of water and part on land.

Which underlined word must be changed for the sentence to be correct? If you chose *of*, you were correct because it is the incorrect preposition before *water* in this context. Amphibians live part of their lives *in water* and part *on land*. Correction: *in*.

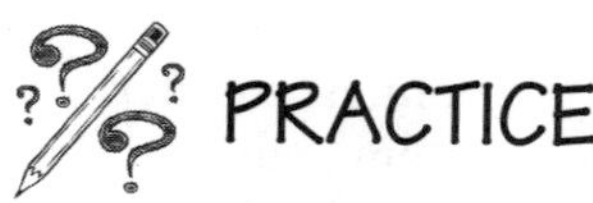

PRACTICE

Exercise 2.21.A

Choose the one word or phrase that best completes the sentence.

1. Earthquakes cause vibrations to pass ------- around the earth in wave form.

   (A) through
   (B) through the
   (C) through an
   (D) through and

2. Psychologists believe that women are not very ------- men and that they have the same desires and can develop the same skills as men.

   (A) different
   (B) differ from
   (C) to differ
   (D) different from

3. Amelia Earhart was the first woman to fly across the Atlantic and the first person to fly alone ------- to California.

   (A) Hawaii
   (B) from Hawaii
   (C) of Hawaii
   (D) that Hawaii

4. A range manager helps ranchers improve and increase livestock production ------- of animals to raise.

   (A) determine the kind
   (B) for determine the kind
   (C) when is the kind determined
   (D) by determining the kind

5. Sensory cells ------- impulses by producing electrical signals.

   (A) responding
   (B) to respond
   (C) respond to
   (D) respond

Choose the one underlined word or phrase that must be changed for the sentence to be correct.

6. The edelweiss is found at high altitudes in the mountains for Europe, Asia, and South America.
   (A: at; B: in; C: for; D: and)

7. An exponent is a number or algebraic expression written above and to the right another number or algebraic expression called the base.
   (A: a number; B: written above; C: to the right; D: called)

8. Because fingerprints have ridges that form a pattern that is unique to each person, fingerprint identification is used extensively to criminal investigation and banking.
   (A: Because; B: to; C: is used; D: to)

9. Immanuel Kant never left the town of his birth and taught at the university of there, where he became professor of logic and metaphysics in 1770.
   (A: at; B: of; C: where; D: of)

10. The term *nightmare* is used by dreams in which a series of events is associated with anxiety.
    (A: by; B: in; C: of; D: with)

Exercise 2.21.B

Choose the one underlined word or phrase that must be changed for the sentence to be correct.

1. Many studies of brain function come from research on animals, whose behavior we can study, but
A B C
who cannot communicate us very fluently.
D

2. Agricultural economists deal of problems related to producing, financing, pricing, and marketing
A B
farm products, and they provide information to many sectors of the agriculture industry.
C D

3. In the 1500s, civil unrest led to the breakup of Vietnam for several smaller states.
A B C D

4. Inventor James Watt sold his steam engine to the industrialists, most of whom had been farmers,
A B
of describing its ability to work in terms of "horsepower."
C D

5. Bitter feelings among the American colonists were caused of the Stamp Act of 1765, which required
A B C
that all legal documents bear stamps that were bought from the government.
D

6. Oil varnishes are made out hard gum or resin dissolved in oil, and they dry to a thin, hard, glossy film.
A B C D

7. In the early 1900s, investigations were made of the role played chromosomes, bodies discovered to
A B
exist in the nucleus of all living cells.
C D

8. Using carbolic acid as an antiseptic together with heat sterilization of instruments, Joseph Lister
A B C
dramatically decreased the number deaths following surgery.
D

9. Artificial selection, the selection of individuals that are best suited for a specific purpose, is common
A B C
of plant and animal breeding.
D

10. The undersea mountains off the coast of Oregon resemble the Hawaiian Islands, which are volcanoes
A B
that grew up the ocean floor to eventually break the surface.
C D

Answers to Exercises 2.21.A through 2.21.B are on pages 649 and 650.

2.21 EXTENSION

1. In reading done outside class, students look for examples of verb + preposition structures (phrasal verbs) and adjective + preposition structures. Bring examples to share in class.

2. Students create “TOEFL sentences” to test their classmates’ understanding of prepositions. Students write their own sentences or use sentences they find in print. Write either on the board or on cards. In each sentence, omit all prepositions, and leave blank spaces where they should be. Classmates must complete the sentences with appropriate prepositions. ***Note:*** In many places, more than one preposition may be correct.

3. Students practice speaking and writing sentences with verb + preposition structures and adjective + preposition structures from the lists on pages 289 and 290.

 ASSESSING PROGRESS – 2.20 through 2.21

QUIZ 10 *(Time – 10 minutes)*

Choose the one underlined word or phrase that must be changed for the sentence to be correct.

1. The immediate cause by (A) most shallow earthquakes is the sudden release of (B) stress along (C) a fault, or fracture, in (D) the earth's crust.

2. The Sanctuary of Fortuna Primigenia is notable not only for its grand size also (A) for what it reveals about (B) the Romans' idea of the relationships between (C) architecture and (D) landscape.

3. Poison gas, because its (A) stealth and murderous fumes, is the most (B) fear–inspiring of all (C) weapons of war (D).

4. In 1889 (A) President Harrison issued a formal declaration (B) making both Montana or (C) Washington new states in (D) the Union.

5. The music group known as (A) the Commodores picked their name out of (B) a dictionary at (C) placing a finger on the page (D).

6. Before (A) World War II, the coal–tar industry was by (B) the basis of organic chemistry, but after (C) the war petroleum became the major source of (D) organic compounds.

Choose the one word or phrase that best completes the sentence.

7. The seeds of the peanut are eaten fresh or roasted, ------- oil is used for industrial purposes.

   (A) the
   (B) while the
   (C) for the
   (D) that the

8. By the end of the sixth century, Indian mathematicians were using the symbol for zero ------- the decimal point.

   (A) both
   (B) also using
   (C) as was
   (D) and also

9. Philosophers have traditionally distinguished ------- "simple" ideas and "complex" ideas.

   (A) either
   (B) among
   (C) between
   (D) but

10. The first use of the principle of the airfoil was ------- but in water, when Thomas Moy tested the hydrofoil in 1861.

   (A) in air
   (B) in neither air
   (C) either in air
   (D) not in air

STRUCTURE

Quiz 10

Choose the one underlined word or phrase that must be changed for the sentence to be correct.

11. Buddhism was brought <u>of</u> (A) China to Japan <u>during</u> (B) the middle years <u>of</u> (C) the <u>sixth</u> (D) century.

12. On the one hand, the use of synthetic chemical products <u>is increasing</u> (A); on the <u>contrary</u> (B), vegetable oilseeds and oils <u>are rising</u> (C) in value and <u>importance</u> (D).

13. The flexible magnetic disk <u>known</u> (A) as a *floppy disk* is used <u>to the disk drive</u> (B) of a computer <u>to store or</u> (C) retrieve information <u>and</u> (D) programs.

14. The earth <u>is divided to</u> (A) climatic zones <u>that are based</u> (B) <u>on average annual</u> (C) temperature <u>and rainfall</u> (D).

15. The classes <u>of</u> (A) steroids differ <u>to</u> (B) one another <u>only</u> (C) in the additional atoms attached <u>to</u> (D) their central structure.

Answers to Structure Quiz 10 are on page 650.

 ASSESSING PROGRESS – 2.16 through 2.21

QUIZ 11 – REVIEW (Time – 15 minutes)

Choose the one word or phrase that best completes the sentence.

1. Georgia O'Keeffe's works are marked ------- that are painted in clear, strong colors.

   (A) the organic forms
   (B) by organic forms
   (C) organic forms by
   (D) of the organic forms

2. The chipmunk lives mostly on the ground but builds its nest in either an underground burrow -------.

   (A) and a hollow limb
   (B) or a hollow limb
   (C) or it built in a hollow limb
   (D) a hollow limb

STRUCTURE

Choose the one underlined word or phrase that must be changed for the sentence to be correct.

3. *Commedia dell' arte* was a popular form (A) of comedy in Italy (B) from the sixteenth in the eighteenth (C) century which greatly (D) influenced French pantomime.

4. The higher a bond is rated (A), the less (B) chance the issuer will default on the bond, and the much (C) chance you have of getting (D) your periodic interest payments.

5. Economists study the effects of (A) technology on (B) the supply of and demand for farm products and the resulted (C) impact on costs and (D) prices.

6. The effect of the Industrial Revolution on (A) architecture was much little (B) direct than was the effect of (C) the political revolutions of the eighteenth (D) century.

7. With the rise (A) of the global economy, businesses must compete worldwide with industries (B) that have different costs with (C) capital, labor, and materials (D).

8. Early calculators only (A) did arithmetic and could neither store results but (B) be given (C) instructions to perform (D) different tasks.

9. In sixteenth–century Korea, <u>none faction</u> among those fighting <u>for control</u> of the country was <u>strong enough</u> to unify the Korean people <u>under its rule</u>.
A: none faction; B: for control; C: strong enough; D: under its rule

10. The development <u>of a cell</u> is determined <u>of</u> the chemical products <u>of</u> neighboring cells and an internal program that is <u>genetically controlled</u>.
A: of a cell; B: of; C: of; D: genetically controlled

Choose the one word or phrase that best completes the sentence.

11. *Star Wars* and *The Empire Strikes Back* were space odyssey movies in which ------- entered a new dimension.

(A) effects specials
(B) especially effects
(C) special effects
(D) the effects were special

12. The genet is not only very cat–like in appearance ------- about the size of a domestic cat.

(A) as well as
(B) also
(C) and
(D) but also

13. In the eighth century, the calendar used in Europe was not as ------- used by the Mayans in Central America.

(A) that was accurate as
(B) accurate than
(C) accurate as that
(D) accurately as

14. The work of middle age is ------- that of youth.

(A) different from
(B) different
(C) differently than
(D) difference

15. Silicon, a nonmetallic element, is ------- abundant element of the earth's surface.

(A) most the second
(B) the more second
(C) second most
(D) the second most

Choose the one underlined word or phrase that must be changed for the sentence to be correct.

16. A comet is a <u>mostly gaseous body</u> of small mass and <u>volume enormous</u> that can be seen <u>from earth</u> for periods ranging <u>from a few days</u> to several months.
A: mostly gaseous body; B: volume enormous; C: from earth; D: from a few days

17. Steel, <u>which</u> is basically iron mixed <u>with</u> carbon, <u>depends</u> combustion at several points <u>in its</u> manufacture.
A: which; B: with; C: depends; D: in its

18. Johann Bach wrote <u>instrumental music</u> (A) for the organ and clavichord, <u>as well</u> (B) group compositions <u>featuring</u> (C) the violin, flute, oboe, and <u>other instruments</u> (D).

19. <u>Because</u> (A) their locations on trade routes <u>between</u> (B) Europe and the Mediterranean, Venice, Genoa, and Florence flourished <u>as</u> (C) trade <u>with</u> (D) China and India expanded.

20. A ripe apricot bulging <u>with</u> (A) sweet juices is <u>considered</u> (B) one of <u>most</u> (C) pleasurable rewards <u>from</u> (D) the fruit orchard.

Choose the one word or phrase that best completes the sentence.

21. Paul Cezanne was ------- to devote all his life to art without having to worry about selling his paintings.

(A) enough wealthy
(B) wealthy enough
(C) he had enough wealth
(D) having enough of wealth

22. The Puerto Rico deep ocean trench is almost ------- as Venezuela's Angel Falls is high.

(A) ten times deep than
(B) as ten times deeper
(C) as deep ten times
(D) ten times as deep

23. As people get older, they usually become ------- by ambition and more concerned with the value of their efforts.

(A) driving less
(B) less driving
(C) less driven
(D) to drive less

24. The world's largest deserts lie in regions where mountains block the trade winds creating a condition where there is ------- precipitation.

(A) no hardly
(B) not hardly
(C) hardly any
(D) hardly none

25. Computers can be used in stores to check inventory and tell the store which products are selling well and which are -------.

(A) less popular
(B) less popularly
(C) leastly popular
(D) as popular as

Answers to Structure Quiz 11 are on page 650.

2.22 Checking Word Form

What is wrong with this sentence?

> The question of whether computers can have minds is rapid becoming a significant issue.

This sentence has a word with the incorrect form. *Rapid* is an adjective, which is incorrect in this context because an adjective cannot modify a verb. An adverb is needed to modify *is becoming*. You must change *rapid* to its adverb form, *rapidly*.

The sentence should read: *The question of whether computers can have minds is rapidly becoming a significant issue.*

What is wrong with this sentence?

> The skin of mammals is a complexity organ that serves vital protective and metabolic functions.

The word form of *complexity* is incorrect. In this sentence, *complexity* modifies the noun *organ*, which means it should be an adjective. *Complexity* is a noun form. You must change it to its adjective form, *complex*.

The sentence should read: *The skin of mammals is a complex organ that serves vital protective and metabolic functions.*

There are three other adjectives in the above sentence. Can you identify them?

The adjectives are: *vital*, *protective*, and *metabolic*. All three of these adjectives modify the noun *functions*. All three of these adjectives have other word forms:

vital	protective	metabolic
vitality	protection	metabolism
vitalize	protect	metabolize
vitally	protectively	metabolically

The form of a word must agree with its function in a sentence.

DO YOU KNOW...?

1. At least two items on the TOEFL will test your ability to recognize correct and incorrect word forms in sentences.

2. A word may have several related forms. The form of a word depends on how it is used in a sentence. Sometimes a word's function is called its ***part of speech***. Different parts of speech—*nouns*, *verbs*, *adjectives*, and *adverbs*—take different word forms.

   Look at how the form of *success* changes in the following sentences:

   Paul Newman has known much success throughout his long acting career.
   Paul Newman succeeded in making numerous award–winning films.
   Paul Newman is a successful American film actor, director, and producer.
   Paul Newman successfully directed *The Glass Menagerie* in 1987.

   Can you identify the function of each underlined word in the above sentences?

   (***Answers:*** *success*, noun; *succeeded*, verb; *successful*, adjective; *successfully*, adverb)

3. Different word forms are made by adding different endings to a word. These word endings are called ***suffixes***. A suffix can help you identify a word's form and function.

   A ***noun*** names a person, place, thing, activity, or idea.

NOUN SUFFIXES

Suffix	Example	Suffix	Example
–acy, –cy	sufficiency	–ing	building
–age	postage	–ion	champion
–al	rehearsal	–ism	socialism
–ance, –ence	appearance	–ist	biologist
–ant, –ent	correspondent	–ite	dynamite
–ate	primate	–ity	similarity
–dom	kingdom	–ment	establishment
–ee	employee	–ness	darkness
–er, –or	professor	–ship	relationship
–hood	childhood	–ster	youngster
–ic, –ics	mathematics	–tion, –sion	concentration
–ide	chloride	–ure	moisture

A ***verb*** expresses action, possession, or state of being.

VERB SUFFIXES

Suffix	Example	Suffix	Example
–ate	compensate	–ify	qualify
–en	liken	–ing	experiencing
–ed	installed	–ize	capitalize

STRUCTURE

An ***adjective*** modifies a noun or other noun structure. Adjectives describe or define nouns by answering the question *what kind of*?

Adjective Suffixes

Suffix	Example	Suffix	Example
–able, –ible	edible	–ic	economic
–al, –ial, –ical	physical	–ile	mobile
–an, –ian	Canadian	–ing	captivating
–ant, –ent	relevant	–ish	reddish
–ar	spectacular	–ive	active
–ary	ordinary	–less	hairless
–ate	literate	–like	lifelike
–ed	recommended	–ly	deadly
–en	golden	–ous, –eous, –ious	anxious
–ese	Japanese	–some	lonesome
–ful	careful	–y	tricky

Note: Adjectives made from numbers (except *first*, *second*, and *third*) take the suffix *–th*; for example: *fifth*, *nineteenth*.

An ***adverb*** modifies a verb, an adjective, a main clause, or another adverb. Adverbs express *how*, *when*, *where*, or *how often*.

Adverb Suffixes

Suffix	Example	Suffix	Example
–ly	precisely	–wise	clockwise
–ward	forward		

Note: The suffix *–ly* is used with both adverbs and adjectives. Adjectives with *–ly* usually come from nouns; for example: *friendly*, *yearly*. Adverbs with *–ly* usually come from adjectives; for example: *commonly*, *clearly*.

Some adjectives and adverbs have the same form:

early	fast	high	low
far	hard	late	much

To check word form on the TOEFL, look at how words function in sentences. Check suffixes to see if word form agrees with word function.

In the following sentence, identify the function of each underlined word:

> Jewish American history, from Biblical times to the settlement of the first Jews in America, is a vast story, woven into nearly four thousand years of civilization.

(***Answers:*** *Jewish*, adjective; *Biblical*, adjective; *settlement*, noun; *woven*, adjective (from past participle of verb; see 2.10); *nearly*, adverb; *civilization*, noun)

4. A TOEFL item may try to trick you by using an incorrect form of a word. Look at this example:

> Possibly the easiest and most enjoyably way to become a weather watcher is simply to observe the clouds.

Which underlined word or phrase must be changed for the sentence to be correct? If you chose *enjoyably*, you were correct. It is an adverb, but an adjective is needed to modify the noun *way*. Correction: *enjoyable*.

PRACTICE

Exercise 2.22.A

Choose the one word or phrase that must be changed for the sentence to be correct.

1. Today Thomas Jefferson's elegance home is a national shrine, visited yearly by thousands of people.
   A B C D

2. Business and labor leaders sometimes join in a cooperatively effort to improve job training.
   A B C D

3. The modern skyscraper original in the United States, and many nineteenth–century technological improvements contributed to its development.
   A B C D

4. Edison's workshop at Menlo Park was a forerunner of the modern industrial research laboratory, in which teams of workers systematic investigate a problem.
   A B C D

5. An autistic child usually appearance to go through his early development normally, but a break in development usually occurs by the age of three.
   A B C D

6. The largest technically occupation in the United States, engineering, has twenty–five professional societies.
   A B C D

7. By the end of the 1970s, Patti Smith had proved remarkable influential, releasing what may be the first punk–rock record.
   A B C D

8. The radiator removes heat from the cooling water that circulation through the engine of a car.
   A B C D

9. In 1877 Romania proclaimed <u>independent</u> (A) from Turkey and <u>became</u> (B) an <u>independent</u> (C) state <u>by</u> (D) the Treaty of Berlin in 1878.

10. The forget–me–not, the <u>state</u> (A) flower of Alaska, has a long <u>traditional</u> (B) in the <u>east</u> (C), west, and south <u>as well as</u> (D) the cold north.

Exercise 2.22.B

Choose the one word or phrase that must be changed for the sentence to be correct.

1. Raoul Dufy is an artist <u>whose</u> (A) paintings are easily <u>recognized</u> (B): a few pure colors <u>skillful</u> (C) applied, combined with <u>free</u> (D), evocative drawing.

2. The soles of the polar bear's feet <u>are covered</u> (A) <u>with</u> (B) fur, which <u>provides</u> (C) stability on slippery, <u>freeze</u> (D) ground.

3. The development of new building materials and <u>mass–produce</u> (A) techniques brought <u>significant</u> (B) changes to <u>architecture</u> (C) in the first quarter of the <u>twentieth</u> (D) century.

4. When flares <u>are used as</u> (A) distress <u>signals</u> (B), <u>they contain</u> (C) chemicals that produce <u>intensely</u> (D) colors.

5. In <u>the late</u> (A) 1990s, the U. S. birth rate had <u>fallen to</u> (B) a <u>historically</u> (C) low, matching a record <u>set in the</u> (D) mid–1970s.

6. The <u>six–thousand–year–old</u> (A) Nubian civilization disappeared <u>beneath</u> (B) Lake Nasser, <u>created</u> (C) in the 1960s by the <u>built</u> (D) of the Aswan High Dam on the Nile River.

7. A group of <u>historians</u> (A) judged the computer to be <u>the most</u> (B) <u>influence</u> (C) invention of the <u>twentieth</u> (D) century.

8. There is a <u>different</u> (A) between income <u>and wealth</u> (B); people can have a <u>large income</u> (C) and <u>no wealth</u> (D).

9. The Hyksos warriors rode across the desert in highly <u>maneuver</u> (A) war chariots <u>from which</u> (B) <u>they</u> (C) could send deadly <u>flights</u> (D) of arrows.

10. <u>The primary</u> (A) <u>vertically</u> (B) element in the Gothic cathedral was <u>the pier</u> (C), a cluster of <u>slender</u> (D) pillars.

Answers to Exercise 2.22.A through 2.22.B are on page 651.

2.22 EXTENSION

1. For each underlined word in Exercises 2.22.A and 2.22.B, students work with a partner to identify the word's function (noun, verb, adjective, adverb). List other forms of each word. **Example:** *elegance*, noun; other forms: *elegant*, adjective; *elegantly*, adverb.

2. Students create "TOEFL sentences" to test their classmates' understanding of word forms. Students write their own sentences, or use sentences they find in print. In each sentence, change one word so that its form does not agree with its function. For example, change an adverb to an adjective, or a noun to a verb. Write the sentences either on the board or on cards. Classmates must identify the error and make the correction.

3. On the board or on paper, make a grid with four columns and twelve rows. Label the columns: *noun*, *verb*, *adjective*, *adverb*. Students write the following words in the correct column on the grid: *analytic*, *comfort*, *consider*, *decision*, *depend*, *easy*, *efficient*, *frequently*, *possess*, *prevention*, *quick*, *respond*. Students complete the grid with other forms of each word. Use the lists of suffixes on pages 301 and 302 or a dictionary. There may be more than one example, or no examples, of some word forms.

2.23 Checking Word Choice

FOCUS

What is wrong with this sentence?

> Sign language comes from gestures and facial expressions that accompany to speak.

In this sentence, *to speak* is not a correct word form or choice. The verb *accompany* needs a noun object. *To speak* is a noun structure, an infinitive (See 2.7). However, *accompany* never takes an infinitive as its object. What other noun is similar in meaning to *to speak*?

A correct word choice is the noun *speech*. The sentence should read: *Sign language comes from gestures and facial expressions that accompany speech.*

What is wrong with this sentence?

> The industrial sector of Cambodia centers on the processing of agricultural producers such as rice, peanuts, and tobacco.

The noun *producers* is an incorrect word choice for this context. *The processing of agricultural producers* does not make sense. *Producers* are people who produce things. Producers cannot be processed! Also, *such as* tells you that *rice*, *peanuts*, and *tobacco* are examples of *agricultural* something—not *producers* but *products*.

You must change *producers* to *products*. The sentence should read: *The industrial sector of Cambodia centers on the processing of agricultural products such as rice, peanuts, and tobacco.*

DO YOU KNOW...?

1. Approximately one or two items on the TOEFL will test your ability to recognize incorrect word choice in sentences.

2. Incorrect word choice sometimes occurs when two words are similar. Some pairs or groups of words are confusing because they are similar in sound. Look at some examples:

advice, advise

When starting a business, one should seek the advice of other people. (noun)
Counselors advise their clients in how to cope with life changes. (verb)

alike, like

The gray jay and Steller's jay are alike in their camp–robbing behavior. (adjective)
Like the gray jay, the Steller's jay steals food from campsites. (preposition)

Note: The adjective *alike* shows similarity between two or more nouns and usually follows these nouns. *Like* is a preposition and must be followed by a noun object.

almost, most

Almost all sports clothing is designed for a specific activity. (adverb)
Most sports clothing is designed for a specific activity. (adjective)

Note: The adverb *almost* means *nearly* or *not entirely*. The adjective *most* means *the greatest amount or number.*

another, other, others, the other

One type of thunderstorm is caused by local conditions; another type is caused by the arrival of a cold front. (adjective)
Other equipment will be necessary to complete the job. (adjective)
There are other types of precipitation besides rain and snow. (adjective)
Some birds perch on branches, while others cling to tree trunks. (pronoun)
One spouse likes to get up early; the other one likes to stay up late. (adjective)
One spouse likes to get up early; the other likes to stay up late. (pronoun)

Note: *Another* is used only with singular nouns. *Other* means *more of the group* and can modify either uncountable nouns or plural nouns. The plural pronoun *others* means *different members of a group*. The adjective or pronoun *the other* means *the rest of the group.*

beside, besides

Many small towns have a wooded park beside a lake or stream. (preposition)
Inflation is hard on the individual; besides, it can be a serious threat to a nation's economic health. (conjunctive adverb)
Besides being hard on the individual, inflation can be a serious threat to a nation's economic health. (preposition)

Note: The preposition *beside* means *next to*. The conjunctive adverb *besides* means *also* or *in addition to. Besides* can also function as a preposition when it has a noun object.

especially, special

Some people are <u>especially</u> sensitive to dust and pollen. (adverb)
The solstices held a <u>special</u> significance for early agricultural societies. (adjective)

hard, hardly

Obsidian, a <u>hard</u> volcanic glass, was used for making arrowheads. (adjective)
When rain or hail falls <u>hard</u>, crops can be damaged. (adverb)
Some couples <u>hardly</u> know each other before they are married. (adverb)

Note: *Hard* can be either an adjective or an adverb. The adverb *hard* usually comes after the verb it modifies. The adverb *hardly* means *scarcely* and usually comes before the verb it modifies.

lay, lie

At the end of some card games, the players must <u>lay</u> their cards on the table.
People suffering from insomnia may <u>lie</u> awake all night.
Most societies teach their children not to <u>lie</u>.

Note: *Lay* (*lay*, *laid*, *laid*, *laying*) means *put* or *set* and must be followed by a direct object. *Lie* has two meanings. *Lie* can mean *repose* (*lie*, *lay*, *lain*, *lying*), or it can mean *not tell the truth* (*lie*, *lied*, *lied*, *lying*).

near, nearly

Most settlements thrived only if they were <u>near</u> a source of water. (preposition)
There are <u>nearly</u> enough people present to start the meeting. (adverb)

Note: The preposition *near* means *not far from*. The adverb *nearly* means *almost*.

raise, rise

The development of cloning <u>raises</u> several moral and ethical issues.
If fog <u>rises</u> above the surface of the earth, it forms a cloud.

Note: *Raise* must be followed by a direct object. *Rise* cannot be followed by a direct object.

than, then

The Lena River is only slightly longer <u>than</u> the Mackenzie River. (conjunction)
If two angles of a triangle are equal, <u>then</u> the sides opposite them are also equal. (adverb)

their, there

Babies get <u>their</u> first teeth around the age of six months. (possessive adjective)
In 1789, <u>there</u> were only thirteen states in the United States. (pronoun)

3. Some pairs or groups of words are confusing because they are similar in meaning. Look at some examples:

amount, number, quantity

Paris and London have almost the same amount of rain each year.
An increasing number of women are choosing to attend law school.
A generous quantity of luck is required to win a lottery.

Note: *Amount* and *quantity* are used with uncountable nouns. *Number* is used with countable nouns (See 2.3).

and, also

Rubber is composed chiefly of carbon and hydrogen. (conjunction)
Sapporo is a food processing center; it is also a tourist mecca. (adverb)

as, like

Ernest Hemingway served as an ambulance driver during World War I.
Like other members of his generation, Hemingway wrote about the loss of hope.

Note: The preposition *as* means *in the role or function of.* The preposition *like* means *similar to.*

between, among

Relationships between parents and their adult children are often very complex.
Yellowstone is among the best–loved of America's national parks.

Note: *Between* shows a relationship of two things. *Among* shows a relationship of three or more things.

do, make

A study showed that most people would rather play sports than do housework.
The ability to make decisions is a necessary skill for managers.

Note: *Do* means *perform* or *finish*. *Make* means *create*, *produce*, or *cause.*

during, while

Food shortages may occur during extended periods of drought. (preposition)
Many Americans have part–time jobs while they are going to college. (adverb)

Note: The preposition *during* is followed by a noun object. The adverb *while* is followed by a clause.

too, very

If a person's body temperature drops too low, he will get hypothermia. (adverb)
Daytime temperatures on the planet Mercury are very hot. (adverb)

Note: *Too* usually expresses a negative result caused by something excessive. *Very* means *excessively* but does not always express a cause–result relationship.

4. Some groups of nouns are confusing because their meanings are related. Some of these nouns refer to people, and others refer to activities, things, or ideas. Look at some examples:

PEOPLE	ACTIVITIES AND THINGS
employer, employee	employment
farmer	farming
inventor	invention
photographer	photograph, photography
realist	reality

5. A TOEFL item may test you by using an incorrect word that:

- is similar in sound to the correct word
- is similar in meaning to the correct word
- refers to activities or things instead of people
- refers to people instead of activities or things

6. A TOEFL item may try to trick you by using an incorrect word that is similar in sound to the correct word. Look at this example:

> Some students choose to live in a dormitory, other likes apartments, and still others prefer to live in a house.

Which underlined word or phrase must be changed for the sentence to be correct? If you chose *other likes*, you were correct. *Other* usually modifies a noun, but there is no noun following it. Correction: *other students like* or *others like* (*others* is a pronoun).

7. A TOEFL item may try to trick you by using an incorrect word that is similar in meaning to the correct word. Look at this example:

> The orca is a very intelligent and efficient predator that is special skilled at finding and catching harbor seals.

Which underlined word must be changed for the sentence to be correct? If you chose *special*, you were correct. An adverb must modify the adjective *skilled*. Correction: *especially*.

Look at another example:

> When bird–watching, you must do much walking because the more you walk, the more birds you are likely to look.

Which underlined word must be changed for the sentence to be correct? If you chose *to look*, you were correct. *Look* must be followed by a preposition, such as *at* or *for*. In this context, however, when bird–watchers walk a lot, they are more likely *to see* many birds. A better word choice is *to see*.

8. A TOEFL item may try to trick you by substituting an activity noun for a person noun, or vice versa. Look at this example:

> Both artist and engineer, Louis Sullivan followed the simple maxim "form follows function" and became known as the father of modern American architect.

Which underlined word must be changed for the sentence to be correct? If you chose *architect*, you were correct. An *architect* is a person, but this sentence needs a word for the field or profession of which Louis Sullivan was the father. Correction: *architecture*.

PRACTICE

Exercise 2.23.A

Choose the one word or phrase that must be changed for the sentence to be correct.

1. A caricature is a portrait in art or literature (A) that does (B) its subject (C) appear ridiculous (D).

2. Before the coming (A) of railways, the well–to–do traveled only (B) to visit friends or improve their (C) education, and the poor traveled hard (D) at all.

3. Securities brokers advice (A) customers who want to make (B) financial investments and arrange for the purchase or (C) sale of stocks, bonds, and other (D) securities.

4. A snowstorm consists of a most (A) infinite number (B) of ice crystals formed (C) in the below–freezing environment (D) of the middle and upper atmosphere.

5. Tax preparers must enjoy contact with (A) the public, because (B) an important aspect of there (C) work involves (D) face–to–face consultations with clients.

6. Many (A) pens work by capillary action, which occurs in too (B) narrow tubes in which (C) liquid flows up because (D) the pressure inside is lowered.

7. Speeding (A) stars near the center (B) of the Milky Way give strong prove (C) that a huge black hole is acting (D) like an anchor at the center of the galaxy.

8. The area with the greatest (A) average amount (B) of thunderstorms each year is (C) the interior of the Florida peninsula, where (D) the Atlantic and Gulf airstreams meet.

9. Making an electrocardiograph recording requires the patient to lay quietly on his or her back on a table.
A B C D

10. Because of the cold climate in which it lived, the mammoth's ears were many smaller than those of
A B C D
today's elephant.

Exercise 2.23.B

Choose the one word or phrase that must be changed for the sentence to be correct.

1. Most precious opals come from South Australia; others sources include Mexico and parts of the
A B C D
United States.

2. Air heated on the surface of the earth tends to raise as an invisible column through surrounding cooler air.
A B C D

3. Sometimes lying is an essential weapon for self–protection, especially while war.
A B C D

4. Cellular phones and laptop computers are becoming increasingly distracting to drives on North
A B C
America's highways.
D

5. There is no need to travel to find the weather; to experience it, you need only to step outdoors or view
A B C D
out a window any day of the year.

6. Alike the bald eagle, the osprey's nesting success has decreased in many areas because the fish it eats
A B C
are contaminated with toxic chemicals.
D

7. If ice were denser then liquid water, it would sink, and if ice did not float, some large bodies of water
A B C
might freeze up completely.
D

8. Carson McCullers was born in Georgia, where almost of her stories and novels are set.
A B C D

9. A hailstorm can be the most damaging part of a thunderstorm, causing injury to people and destroying
A B C
crops and property as a giant pounding machine.
D

10. Beside killing and eating prairie dogs, the ferret also occupies its victim's home, often enlarging and
A B C
redecorating it.
D

Answers to Exercises 2.23.A through 2.23.B are on page 651.

2.23 EXTENSION

1. Students write a list of nouns referring to people and to related activities or things. **Example:** *swimmer*, *swimming*. Students use this list to create "TOEFL sentences" to test their classmates' ability to check word choice. In some but not all of the sentences, change the noun so that it is incorrect. For example, change *swimmer* to *swimming*. Keep some of the sentences correct. Write either on the board or on cards. Classmates must determine whether there is an error. If there is an error, classmates make the correction.

2. Students create "TOEFL sentences" by using words from the lists of confusing words starting on page 307. In some but not all of the sentences, change the word so that it is incorrect. Keep some of the sentences correct. Classmates must determine whether there is an error. If there is an error, classmates make the correction.

3. Students write a list of their own confusing pairs of words. Compile a class list. Use words from this list to create more "TOEFL sentences" for practice and review.

2.24 Recognizing Redundancy

FOCUS

Read the following pair of sentences. Which is better?

> It is vital and very important that everyone drink at least eight glasses of water each day.
>
> It is vital that everyone drink at least eight glasses of water each day.

In the first sentence, there are two expressions with the same meaning. *Vital* means *very important*. Therefore, *very important* adds nothing to the sentence. It is excessive, or ***redundant***.

Now, read another pair of sentences. Which is better?

> Because nitroglycerin decomposes violently when disturbed, it must be handled cautiously in a careful manner.
>
> Because nitroglycerin decomposes violently when disturbed, it must be handled cautiously.

If you chose the second sentence, congratulations! You are able to recognize redundancy. The phrase *in a careful manner* is redundant because it has the same meaning as *cautiously*.

In general, *the fewer words, the better*! Redundancy is poor writing style.

DO YOU KNOW...?

1. Approximately one item on the TOEFL may test your ability to recognize redundant words or phrases in sentences.

2. ***Redundancy*** occurs when words and phrases exceed what is necessary. One type of redundancy occurs when a sentence has two words with the same meaning. Redundant words add no new information. Look at this example:

   The first original packaged breakfast cereal was introduced in 1894.

   First and *original* have almost the same meaning; therefore, one of them is redundant.

   Look at some other examples of redundancy:

advance forward	nearly almost	reread again
ancient old	precede before	return back
enter into	proceed forward	same identical
follow after	progress forward	sufficient enough
join together	repeat again	tiny little

   Can you add any redundant expressions to the above list?

3. Redundancy occurs when words are repeated unnecessarily. Look at this example:

   By 1970 Japan produced half of the world's ships, ranked second in automobile manufacturing, and Japan was known to be third in steel production.

   It is redundant to repeat the subject, *Japan*. You, the reader, already know that Japan is being discussed. Also, *known to be* is unnecessary because it adds no new information. To improve the sentence, omit both underlined expressions.

   In the following sentences, cross out redundant words and phrases:

   a. People generally do not like to repeat their mistakes again.
   b. Driver inattention is a factor in contributing to half of all auto accidents, and things are expected to get worse.
   c. The Black Mesa serves as a huge, giant water reservoir, collecting rainwater from its extensive surface.

   (***Answers:*** a. *again*; b. *contributing to*; c. either *huge* or *giant*)

   Remember, redundancy makes poor writing! In your own writing, beware of using redundant words and phrases.

STRUCTURE

4. A TOEFL item may test you by having a redundant word or phrase. Look at this example:

> Chimpanzees have a wide range of calls which serve to communicate and convey some types of information.

The phrase *and convey* is redundant because it has the same meaning as *communicate*; therefore, it adds no new information. Correction: omit *and convey*.

PRACTICE

Exercise 2.24.A

Choose the one word or phrase that must be changed for the sentence to be correct.

1. The use of machine guns in World War I led to (A) a long stalemate in the trenches, with neither (B) side being able to advance its (C) lines ahead (D).

2. Unlike (A) a roller, a wheel requires an axle on which (B) to turn, so (C) the potter's wheel was the first earliest (D) true wheel.

3. It is necessary and required (A) that dental technicians and others who (B) work with X–rays limit their (C) exposure to these highly (D) penetrating rays.

4. Because of (A) the crowded and (B) filthy conditions on the slave ships, fatal (C) diseases that took many (D) lives were rampant.

5. Puerto Ricans in the United States are a young and (A) growing population whose numbers are increasing (B), and the Puerto Rican community is becoming (C) more politically active (D).

6. Once you have finished (A) an article and identified its (B) main ideas, it may not be necessary (C) to reread it again (D).

7. Under (A) Otto von Bismarck, Germany joined together with (B) Austria–Hungary and (C) Italy to create (D) the Triple Alliance.

8. After a method was invented for amplifying recorded (A) dialogue and music so it could (B) be heard throughout a theater, technology (C) for sound films progressed forward (D).

9. If the air is sufficiently unstable enough, the upward currents will draw in warm, moist air and cause water vapor to condense into raindrops.
(A: If; B: unstable enough; C: moist; D: to condense)

10. In addition to oil refining and international banking, Panama is also known for growing bananas, pineapples, and sugar.
(A: refining; B: also; C: growing; D: pineapples)

Answers to Exercise 2.24.A are on page 652.

STRUCTURE

2.24 EXTENSION

1. Students create "TOEFL sentences" to test their classmates' ability to recognize redundancy. Students write sentences with redundant words and phrases. Use a student–generated list or the list of redundant expressions on page 315. Write the sentences either on the board or on cards. Classmates must identify the redundancy and improve the sentence.

2. Redundancy contest for teams of 2 to 3. The object is to see which team can write the best redundant sentence! Begin with this sentence: *People eat and sleep*. Now, add to it! Be creatively redundant! Teams share their sentences with the class. Decide which team should win an award for the sentence that is (a) the funniest, (b) the strangest, and (c) the most redundant.

ASSESSING PROGRESS – 2.22 through 2.24

QUIZ 12 *(Time – 10 minutes)*

Choose the one underlined word or phrase that must be changed for the sentence to be correct.

1. The U. S. Environmental Protection Agency consistent ranks indoor air pollution among the top
A B
five environmental risks to public health.
C D

2. Whenever the early Chinese seismograph picked up tremors from an earthquake, balls would roll
A B
off the instrument, indicating from which director the vibrations had come.
C D

3. A read–only memory chip stores data even when the power is off, and alike a random–access
A B
memory chip, it contains a grid of cells connected by data lines.
C D

4. Esteemed in Europe as a symbol of pure, the woolly–white edelweiss flower is protected by law
A B C D
in Switzerland.

5. A founding member of Roxy Music, Brian Eno went on to work as a solo artistic and a collaborator
A B C
with David Bowie, Devo, and others.
D

6. A flashing yellow traffic signal means one must slow down and proceed forward with caution,
A B
watching for pedestrians, vehicles, or other hazards.
C D

7. The balance of international payments reference to all the transactions between a nation and the
A B C
rest of the world.
D

8. Six tribal groups make up almost of the population of Mali, an African nation where sixty–five percent
A B C D
of the population is Muslim.

9. Unlikely the mobile crane, the tower crane does not expand like a telescope; instead, it extends itself
A B C D
section by section.

10. During the eighth century, the Mayan Empire to achieve magnificent cultural and economic heights.
A B C D

11. Showroom models wear clothes the manufacturers hope to sell to buyers who come to the showroom,
A B C
while another fashion models work in department stores.
D

12. Between 1900 and 1910, almost nine million immigrants entered into the United States, most of whom
A B C D
came from southern and eastern Europe.

13. The autopilot of an aircraft keeps it on the same course by correcting for any drifting that occurrence
A B C
during the flight.
D

14. The formation of the United Nations was an attempt to unite the nations of the world in a single,
A B
cooperate, deliberative forum for the peaceful resolution of disputes.
C D

15. Some Americans stay in a single occupation while the period from seventeen to thirty–five years
A B
of age, but the majority make at least a few job changes.
C D

Answers to Structure Quiz 12 are on page 652.

STRUCTURE

2.25 Recognizing Parallel Structure

FOCUS

Read the following pair of sentences. Which is better?

> The beaver is a large rodent with dark brown fur, a black scaly tail, and it also has large front teeth.
>
> The beaver is a large rodent with dark brown fur, a black scaly tail, and large front teeth.

These sentences describe the beaver by listing some of its characteristics: *dark brown fur*, *a black scaly tail*, and *large front teeth*.

In the first sentence, the phrase *it also has* is redundant and also interferes with parallel structure. Sentences have ***parallel structure*** when they contain structures that are similar in form and position.

The second sentence has parallel structure. Here, three noun phrases are parallel: *dark brown fur*, *a black scaly tail*, and *large front teeth*.

Now, read another pair of sentences. Which is better?

> Bob Marley's songs not only inspired his followers in Jamaica but also an audience all over the world.
>
> Bob Marley's songs not only inspired his followers in Jamaica but also found an audience all over the world.

Both sentences have the two–part conjunction, *not only...but also*. The structures following the two parts of this conjunction should be similar in form and function.

In the first sentence, these structures are *inspired his followers in Jamaica* and *an audience all over the world*. These structures are not parallel.

The second sentence has two verb phrases that are parallel:

inspired (V) his followers (O) in Jamaica

found (V) an audience (O) all over the world

Sentences with parallel structure are less redundant, more balanced, and easier to read.

DO YOU KNOW...?

1. At least two items on the TOEFL will test your ability to recognize parallel structure. You must be able to recognize structures that are parallel and those that are not parallel.

2. The structures in a list or series should be parallel. Parallel structures have the same *value*, that is, the same form (part of speech) and position (function in the sentence).

   Use parallel structures in lists that are joined with *and*, *but*, and *or*. Look at some examples:

   Nouns:

   Inertia is a resistance to motion, exertion, *or* change.

   Gerunds:

   Writing, editing, *and* proofreading involve skills that can be improved by training.

   Adjectives:

   The best buys are low in price *but* high in value.

   Verb Phrases:

   Some of the biggest problems a gardener experiences are plants that grow out of bounds, become misshapen, *or* remain sparse.

   Prepositional Phrases:

   The great blue heron is frequently seen along harbors *or* near suburban lakes.

   Adverb Clauses:

   Friction appears when a solid object rubs against another, *or* when it moves through a gas or liquid.

   Note: Main clauses that are related in meaning should be parallel in structure whenever possible. Look at these examples:

   The wolf is highly social, but the fox is relatively solitary.
   Single life offers more freedom of choice; marriage provides more security.

   In the following sentences, underline the structures that are parallel.

   a. After locating prey by scent or sound, the cougar slinks forward slowly and silently.
   b. *Kinetics* is the study of the forces that produce, stop, or modify motions of the body.
   c. Jogging, riding a bicycle, and walking briskly all provide an aerobic workout.
   d. Some travelers like to plan where to go, what to do, and how much to spend before they leave home.

   (***Answers:*** a. parallel: *scent*, *sound*; *slowly*, *silently*; b. parallel: *produce*, *stop*, *modify*; c. parallel: *jogging*, *riding a bicycle*, *walking briskly*; d. parallel: *where to go*, *what to do*, *how much to spend*)

STRUCTURE

A TOEFL item may try to trick you by having a list with structures that are not parallel. Look at this example:

> Many native plants have been depleted because of lumbering, to farm, and grazing.

To farm is not parallel to the other items in the list, *lumbering* and *grazing*. Correction: *farming*.

3. The structures following the parts of two–part conjunctions should be parallel (See 2.20). Use parallel structures with these conjunctions:

and...as well as	either...or	not only...but also
both...and	neither...nor	not...but

Both the physical environment *and* the social structure of the South were changed by the Civil War.
When the beaver fells a tree, it *either* eats the bark *or* stores it for winter use.

A TOEFL item may try to trick you by having structures that are not parallel after the parts of a conjunction. Look at this example:

> When Guglielmo Marconi demonstrated his wireless telegraph, he was thinking not about broadcasting but he thought about rapid communication.

Which underlined word or phrase must be changed for the sentence to be correct? If you chose *he thought*, you were correct. The structure following *not* is a prepositional phrase, *about broadcasting*. The structure following *but* must be parallel. Correction: omit *he thought*.

The sentence should read: *When Guglielmo Marconi demonstrated his wireless telegraph, he was thinking not about broadcasting but about rapid communication.*

Look at another example:

> Humidity not only determines what kind of weather we have, it also -------.
>
> ○ regulates our comfort
> ○ our comfort is regulated
> ○ the regulation of our comfort
> ○ regulated the comfort

The structures that follow the two parts of *not only...(but) also* should be parallel. The first answer choice, the verb phrase *regulates our comfort*, best completes the sentence because it is parallel to *determines what kind of weather we have*.

Why are the other answer choices incorrect?

4. In equative and comparative expressions (See 2.19), the structures being compared should be parallel.

 The Olmec art of Yucatan is believed to be *as old as* the Chavin art of Peru.
 As much misunderstanding exists between people from the same culture *as* it does between people from different cultures.
 Gold is *softer* and *more malleable than* other precious metals.
 Human error causes *more problems* in the workplace *than* computer malfunction does.

 Note: The two things being compared must also be parallel in *meaning*. Consider these sentences:

 The temperature on Mars is lower than on Earth. (not parallel)
 The temperature on Mars is lower than that on Earth. (parallel)

 Two things are being compared: *the temperature on Mars* and *the temperature on Earth*. The pronoun *that* is used to avoid repeating *the temperature*. Here, *that* is necessary for parallel meaning and structure.

 A TOEFL item may test you by having structures that are not parallel in an equative or comparative. Look at this example:

 > Presenting yourself well in a job interview is as important as to learn about the organization.

 Which underlined word or phrase must be changed for the sentence to be correct? If you chose *to learn*, you were correct. This sentence has an equative expression, *as important as*. In equatives, the two things being equated must be parallel in structure.

 Here, *to learn* must be changed so that it is parallel to *presenting yourself well in a job interview*. Correction: *learning*.

PRACTICE

Exercise 2.25.A

Choose the one word or phrase that best completes the sentence.

1. A study found that suicides increase after earthquakes, hurricanes, and -------.

 (A) is flooding
 (B) it happens after a flood
 (C) floods
 (D) to flood

2. In the 1980s there was a tremendous expansion of the Western economies and the emergence -------.

 (A) of a global economy
 (B) global economy
 (C) globally economic
 (D) there is now a global economy

3. Spiders stay out of each other's way by partitioning off their hunting grounds and ------- different strategies for catching food.

 (A) the use of
 (B) to use
 (C) usefulness
 (D) using

4. Nuclear fusion not only powers the sun ------- in thermonuclear weapons.

 (A) but also occurs
 (B) also does it occur
 (C) but it also occurs
 (D) it also has occurred

5. In small companies, the same human resource workers may interview and hire as well as ------- employees.

(A) training
(B) train
(C) to train
(D) they train

6. Marilyn Monroe's story is well–known: an unhappy childhood, -------, several marriages and divorces, and eventual suicide.

(A) a struggle to become a star
(B) she was struggling to become a star
(C) she became a star
(D) then a star she became

7. ------- a unicycle usually requires more practice than learning to swim.

(A) To learn riding
(B) When you learn to ride
(C) Learning to ride
(D) That riding

8. California has not only ------- but also the most productive economy of any state in the United States.

(A) the larger a population
(B) population that is very large
(C) it has the largest population
(D) the largest population

9. Blood from the veins, high in carbon dioxide but -------, returns to the right atrium of the heart.

(A) being low in oxygen
(B) low in oxygen it is
(C) is it low in oxygen
(D) low in oxygen

10. Store layout and merchandise presentation, as well as -------, help shoppers find items more quickly.

(A) to have appropriate signs
(B) appropriate signs are necessary
(C) appropriate signs which
(D) appropriate signs

Exercise 2.25.B

Choose the one underlined word or phrase that must be changed for the sentence to be correct.

1. Walking (A) reduces depression (B) and anxiety, lessens stress (C), self–esteem is raised (D), and increases energy.

2. Every (A) organization that produces goods or (B) services needs (C) a wide variety of people managing (D) the operation and handle the clerical work.

3. An (A) emergency campfire not only for providing (B) warmth but also has a calming effect (C) on most (D) people.

4. The electronics (A) technology program prepares students for employment (B) in industries that involve the repair, fabrication, to install (C), and maintenance (D) of electronic systems.

5. Garlic has been hailed for its ability (A) to lower (B) cholesterol, reducing (C) the risk of cancer, boost immunity, and curb high (D) blood pressure.

6. Contract law determines which contracts are <u>enforceable</u> (A) in court and defines <u>the steps</u> (B) must be <u>taken</u> (C) to comply with the obligations <u>of a contract</u> (D).

7. A <u>balanced</u> (A) diet contains all of the <u>essential</u> (B) nutrients in adequate <u>amounts</u> (C) needed by the body for growth, energy, <u>to repair</u> (D), and maintenance of normal health.

8. <u>For the</u> (A) waterwheel is <u>basically</u> (B) the same machine as the windmill, but it <u>is driven</u> (C) by air <u>instead of</u> (D) water.

9. The north magnetic pole is <u>where</u> (A) <u>the magnetic force is</u> (B) vertically downward, and the <u>magnetic pole for the south</u> (C) is where the magnetic force is <u>vertically upward</u> (D)

10. Entry–level jobs in retail sales <u>include</u> (A) marking <u>prices</u> (B), stocking shelves, <u>to operate</u> (C) a cash register, and some types of <u>selling</u> (D).

Answers to Exercises 2.25.A through 2.25.B are on page 652.

2.25 EXTENSION

1. In reading done outside class, students look for examples of sentences with parallel structure. Bring examples to share in class. What types of structures are parallel: words, phrases, or clauses?

2. Students create "TOEFL sentences" to test their classmates' understanding of parallel structure. Students write sentences with parallel words or phrases in a series. Change one item in the series so that it is not parallel. Write the sentences either on the board or on cards. Classmates identify the error and make the correction.

3. Students create "TOEFL sentences" with parallel structures following two–part conjunctions. Use the list of conjunctions on page 322. Change one of the structures so that it is not parallel. Classmates identify the error and make the correction.

ASSESSING PROGRESS – 2.22 through 2.25

QUIZ 13 (Time – 10 minutes)

Choose the one underlined word or phrase that must be changed for the sentence to be correct.

1. Most of the European immigrants to the United States settled in cities because they had neither the
   A B
   means nor did they desire to settle in rural areas.
   C D

2. Socialism is a middle ground between capitalism and communism, stressing government ownership
   A B C
   of the means of production and plan by the state.
   D

3. The nerve endings in the skin respond to various stimuli, including light touch, pressure, painful,
   A B C
   heat, and cold.
   D

4. John Muir founded the Sierra Club, the nation's first group of people who were environmental activities.
   A B C D

5. Macroeconomics is a vital subject today because macroeconomic perform is central to the success
   A B C
   or failure of nations.
   D

6. While periods of drought, unusual and severe dust storms can arise, most frequently on the Great
   A B C D
   Plains of North America.

7. Dams may be built for multiple purposes: providing water for irrigation, aid flood control, furnish
   A B
   hydroelectric power, and improve the passability of waterways.
   C D

Choose the one word or phrase that best completes the sentence.

8. The German contribution to the American sandwich is seen in hamburgers and hot dogs, as well as ------- on rolls and buns.

   (A) of some other sandwiches
   (B) another sandwich
   (C) sandwiches also that one sees
   (D) other sandwiches

9. Heat is transferred from one substance to another by three means: conduction, convection, -------.

   (A) and radiation
   (B) also by radiation
   (C) it radiates
   (D) by radiating

Choose the one underlined word or phrase that must be changed for the sentence to be correct.

10. The securities broker is (A) an essential (B) link among (C) the consumer and (D) the stock market.

11. Business law includes (A) the branches of law that affect (B) the formation, operate (C), and termination (D) of a business firm.

12. Having quiet time by yourself (A) may be just as good for emotional (B) well–being as to spend (C) time with (D) friends and family.

13. The bird drawings (A) and paintings of John James Audubon remain among (B) the greatest (C) achievements of American intellectually (D) history.

14. Most (A) ducks and geese (B) have webbed toes for swimming and to stand (C) on soft mud, while perching birds have feet designed (D) for grasping branches.

15. Since cross–country skiing (A) includes to climb (B) slopes as well as sliding down them (C), ski tourers apply climbing (D) waxes to their skis.

Answers to Structure Quiz 13 are on page 653.

ASSESSING PROGRESS – 2.16 through 2.25

QUIZ 14 – REVIEW *(Time – 15 minutes)*

Choose the one underlined word or phrase that must be changed for the sentence to be correct.

1. As heat is added to a liquid, some molecules nearly the surface gain enough energy to evaporate
A B
from the liquid and change to a gaseous state.
C D

2. Because of its ability to land and take off in small areas, the helicopter is used in a wide range of
A B
services, such as fire fighting, crop sowing, and to control traffic.
C D

3. Range managers must deal constantly with the public, ranchers, government agencies, and persons
A B
who specialization in other areas of conservation.
C D

4. The essential basic ingredient in the creation of a thunderstorm is a warm, moist, unstable atmosphere.
A B C D

5. Cell division depends the replication of DNA molecules and the separation of the products of
A B C
this replication.
D

6. Slang, which is not generally acceptable in formal usage, is notable for its liveliness, humor, and
A B C
it exaggerates.
D

7. An endoscope, a tube that can be inserted into the throat, contains air and water pipes as well a
A B C D
channel for small surgical instruments.

8. Yosemite Falls is the most high waterfall in North America, with a total drop of over seven hundred
A B C D
meters in two stages.

9. Insurance companies prefer that claim adjusters have either college training or they have work
A B
experience in a related field.
C D

Choose the one word or phrase that best completes the sentence.

10. In the early twentieth century, American art and literature remained ------- it had been in the explosive 1800s.

(A) as productive as
(B) to be productive as
(C) productive as
(D) productive than

11. In a lawn sprinkler, ------- extra source of power is needed because the mechanism is driven by the movement of the water through the sprinkler.

(A) not
(B) not only
(C) nothing
(D) no

12. Architecture in the United States was transformed through ------- of Henry Richardson, Louis Sullivan, and Frank Lloyd Wright.

(A) their work was related
(B) the related work
(C) the relationship working
(D) they are relating the work

Choose the one underlined word or phrase that must be changed for the sentence to be correct.

13. The gigantic carve heads (A) of Easter Island, some weighing (B) more than (C) fifty tons, have been the subject of much speculation (D) by psychologists and ethnologists.

14. The Republic of the Philippines consists of (A) over seven thousand (B) islands that to stretch (C) eleven hundred miles from north (D) to south.

15. The spleen, an organ that filters foreign organisms from (A) the bloodstream, lies (B) on the left side of (C) the abdominal cavity, besides (D) the diaphragm.

16. Bonds can provide a steady flow (A) of income (B) to help of living expenses (C), which makes them especially suitable for retired people (D).

17. As early (A) as 1699, money was referred to (B) as "currency" in England because it (C) was the current, accepted generally (D) medium of exchange.

Choose the one word or phrase that best completes the sentence.

18. It was Alessandro Volta who discovered that electricity came not from a dead frog ------- the metals that touched the leg of the frog.

    (A) but from
    (B) but also
    (C) and from
    (D) nor

19. The field of electronics has become ------- on inorganic chemistry.

    (A) to depend highly
    (B) depending highly
    (C) highly dependent
    (D) depends higher

20. Humans were not alone in their ability to build a home; neither their use of native materials nor ------- was unique.

    (A) their structures were complex
    (B) theirs were complex structures
    (C) they built complex structures
    (D) the complexity of their structures

Choose the one underlined word or phrase that must be changed for the sentence to be correct.

21. The height of the ozone layer varies from approximately (A) twelve to (B) twenty miles above (C) the earth, but traces exist as low as six miles and its height as (D) thirty–five miles.

22. Robert Peary, Roald Amundsen, and Robert Scott are the best known (A) along (B) the early legion of men from many (C) nations who explored (D) the two polar regions.

23. The skin (A) provides a barrier against to invade (B) from outside organisms and protects underlying tissues (C) from injury (D).

24. As a parachute opens, it (A) develops a large amount of (B) friction with (C) the air, and because this friction is great than (D) gravity, the parachutist slows down.

25. Almost (A) thunderstorms occur in the late afternoon and evening hours, when the effect of (B) the heated earth (C) is at its (D) maximum.

Answers to Structure Quiz 14 are on page 653.

STRUCTURE REVIEW TEST 

(Time – 25 minutes)

The Structure section of the TOEFL measures your ability to recognize language that is appropriate for standard written English. There are two types of questions in this section.

In the first type of question, there are incomplete sentences. Beneath each sentence, there are four words or phrases. Choose the one word or phrase that best completes the sentence.

Example I

Although Chicago is not ------- New York, it has many attractions for visitors.

(A) as large as
(B) larger
(C) larger city
(D) the larger city is

Sample Answer
● (B) (C) (D)

The sentence should read, *Although Chicago is not as large as New York, it has many attractions for visitors*. Therefore, you should choose (A).

The second type of question has four underlined words or phrases. Choose the <u>one</u> underlined word or phrase that must be changed for the sentence to be correct.

Sample Answer
(A) (B) ● (D)

Example II

Guglielmo Marconi, <u>the son of</u> a wealthy Italian landowner, <u>made</u> the
A B
first <u>successfully</u> transmission <u>using</u> radio waves.
C D

The sentence should read, *Guglielmo Marconi, the son of a wealthy Italian landowner, made the first successful transmission using radio waves*. Therefore, you should choose (C).

Now begin work on the questions.

Go on to the next page

2 2 2 2 2 2 2 2 2

1. The high mesa of Canyonlands National Park, known as the Island of the Sky, ------- above the river.

   (A) it rises 2,000 feet
   (B) rising 2,000 feet
   (C) is risen 2,000 feet
   (D) rises 2,000 feet

2. The screw is a ------- form of inclined plane, one which is wrapped around a cylinder.

   (A) disguise heavily
   (B) heavy disguise
   (C) heavily disguised
   (D) disguising heavy

3. Many individuals view death ------- a time of sorrow but as a time to celebrate the life of someone.

   (A) not
   (B) not only
   (C) no
   (D) not as

4. The exhaust gases of a gasoline engine would produce intolerable noise ------- directly.

   (A) and allow to escape
   (B) by allowing to escape
   (C) allowing to escape
   (D) if allowed to escape

5. The parachute was one of several (A) inventions that were (B) forecast by Leonardo da Vinci, who drawn (C) one (D) in 1485.

6. When Rosa Parks was arrested for refusing (A) to give up her seat to a white man on a city bus, the African American community did the (B) decision to organize (C) a boycott of the (D) bus system.

7. The first bicycles were pushed along by the feet (A), and it was not until (B) 1839 that Kirkpatrick Macmillan, a British (C) blacksmith, inventor (D) the pedal–operated bicycle.

8. Though (A) the sweet potato is native to the New World, what we now call (B) simply a *potato* was first been brought (C) to Boston by the Irish (D) around 1719.

9. The great central plateau of Bolivia lies between (A) two great mountain (B) ranges with three of highest (C) peaks in South America (D).

10. A couturier <u>who</u> works <u>in</u> the field of women's fashion <u>designed</u> original models for his customers and also produces a <u>fairly</u> limited number of copies.
(A: who, B: in, C: designed, D: fairly)

11. <u>The first</u> European stock exchange <u>was established</u> in Belgium in 1531, but not until the period of 1620–1700 <u>did</u> English merchants and bankers begin <u>develop</u> our modern stock market terms.
(A: The first, B: was established, C: did, D: develop)

12. The sounds of <u>speaking</u> language <u>do</u> not <u>always</u> match up with <u>the symbols of</u> written language.
(A: speaking, B: do, C: always, D: the symbols of)

STRUCTURE

13. When plants or animals are "indicator" species, ------- indicate the health of an ecosystem.

(A) should
(B) so that they
(C) to
(D) they

14. Storms, floods, -------, and erosion uproot many trees, which eventually wash up on shore.

(A) the rocks sliding
(B) rock slides
(C) the rocks slid
(D) the rocks which are sliding

15. In 1884 Mark Twain published the *Adventures of Huckleberry Finn*, ------- in American literature.

(A) an important work
(B) it has been an important work
(C) he was importantly working
(D) as important as work

16. <u>Much</u> of the 41 million members of Generation X—people <u>born</u> <u>from</u> 1965 to 1979—are turning <u>to</u> a new mixture of liberalism and conservatism.
(A: Much, B: born, C: from, D: to)

17. <u>Almost</u> hurricanes <u>are</u> <u>accompanied</u> by heavy rain and <u>powerful</u> winds.
(A: Almost, B: are, C: accompanied, D: powerful)

Go on to the next page

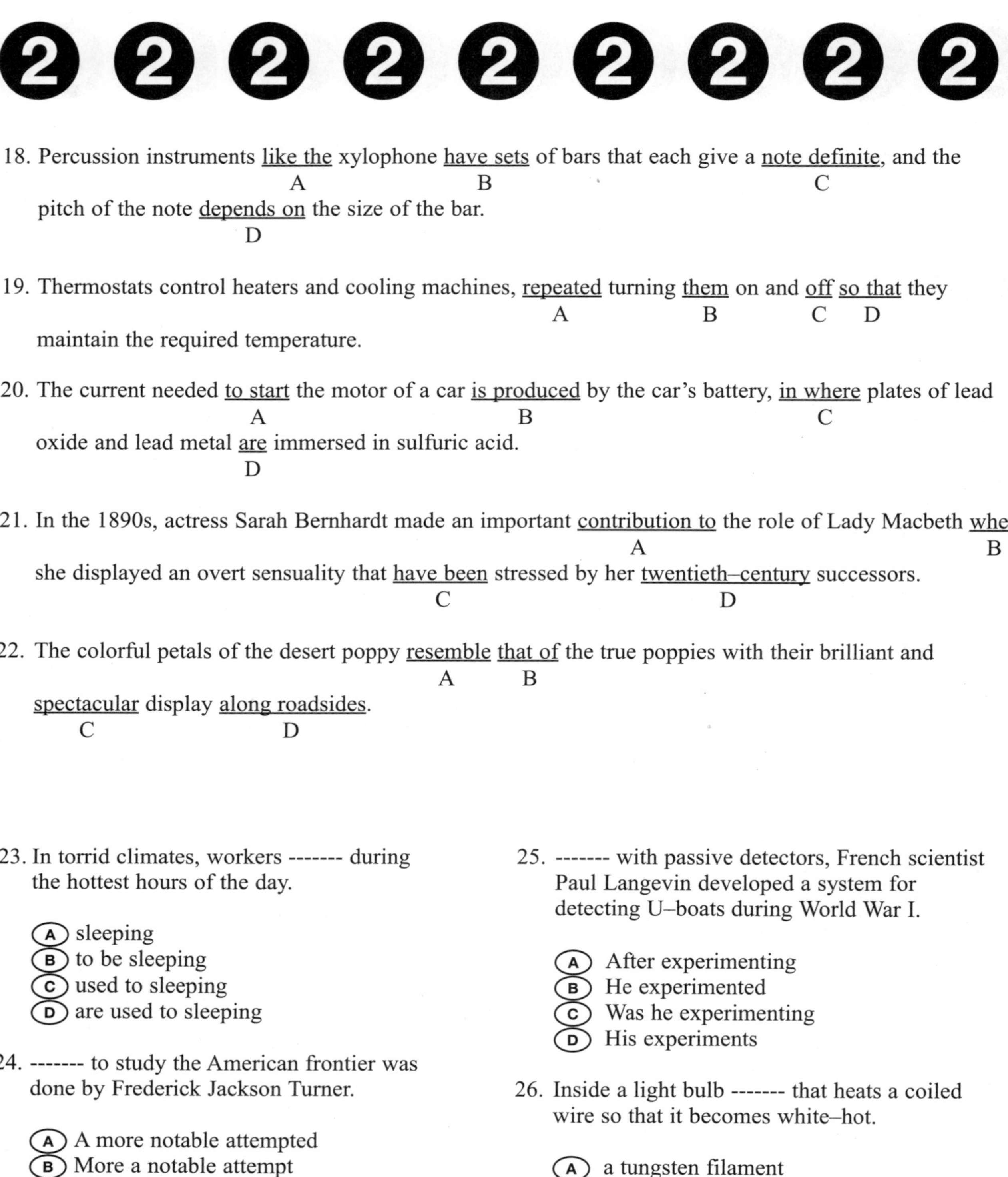

18. Percussion instruments like the [A] xylophone have sets [B] of bars that each give a note definite [C], and the pitch of the note depends on [D] the size of the bar.

19. Thermostats control heaters and cooling machines, repeated [A] turning them [B] on and off [C] so that [D] they maintain the required temperature.

20. The current needed to start [A] the motor of a car is produced [B] by the car's battery, in where [C] plates of lead oxide and lead metal are [D] immersed in sulfuric acid.

21. In the 1890s, actress Sarah Bernhardt made an important contribution to [A] the role of Lady Macbeth when [B] she displayed an overt sensuality that have been [C] stressed by her twentieth–century [D] successors.

22. The colorful petals of the desert poppy resemble [A] that of [B] the true poppies with their brilliant and spectacular [C] display along roadsides [D].

23. In torrid climates, workers ------- during the hottest hours of the day.

(A) sleeping
(B) to be sleeping
(C) used to sleeping
(D) are used to sleeping

24. ------- to study the American frontier was done by Frederick Jackson Turner.

(A) A more notable attempted
(B) More a notable attempt
(C) The most notable attempt
(D) The most notable by attempting

25. ------- with passive detectors, French scientist Paul Langevin developed a system for detecting U–boats during World War I.

(A) After experimenting
(B) He experimented
(C) Was he experimenting
(D) His experiments

26. Inside a light bulb ------- that heats a coiled wire so that it becomes white–hot.

(A) a tungsten filament
(B) a tungsten filament is
(C) is a tungsten filament
(D) that a tungsten filament

Go on to the next page

27. Ice storms can damage a tree's branches -------.

(A) a cause for breaking
(B) when breaking it causes
(C) by causing them to break
(D) causing to break them

28. Of the five social classes identified by sociologists, most Americans fall into either the middle class
A B C
and the working class.
D

29. Some species of bats have spoon–shaped bristles on the hind toe of their feet with grooming themselves.
A B C D

30. A laser is a device that produces a narrow beam of very bright light or infra–red rays in which all the
A B
waves have exactly the same frequency, are in phase, and to move exactly together.
C D

31. The first American to be worth the equivalent of one million dollars was probably plantation owner and
A B
banker Robert "King" Carter, whom father arrived in Virginia in 1635 and began buying land.
C D

32. Psychologist Abraham Maslow argued that humans have unique desires to discover and understand,
A B
the giving of love to others, and to fulfill their inner potential.
C D

33. North America has experienced periods of heavy rain that ------- to the flood stage.

(A) was rising its rivers
(B) have raised its rivers
(C) its rivers are rising
(D) has been raised by its rivers

34. ------- the formation of the universe began with an enormous explosion called the Big Bang.

(A) Believed that
(B) That is believed
(C) It is believed that
(D) It believed that

35. Hydrofoils ------- employ the same principles that keep airplanes in the air.

(A) fly through the waves
(B) flying through the waves
(C) were flying through the waves
(D) flew through the waves

2 2 2 2 2 2 2 2 2

36. Electronic mail to describe an upcoming workshop should used (A) only if (B) potential participants use this (C) form of communication regularly (D).

37. Like (A) many electronic devices, solar cells depend (B) semiconductors, materials in which (C) the flow of electrons can be controlled (D).

38. Many (A) ancient cities had fire watchers, but as late as 1666 England's largest (B) city had nothing (C) organized fire protection system when the Great Fire of London destroyed much (D) of that city.

39. Most plants (A) need more humidity is normally found (B) in the average home—especially during (C) the dry winter season, when homes are heated (D).

40. It is essential that commercial (A) fishing has (B) large shoals of fish of one species (C) within (D) reach of markets.

Answers to the Structure Review Test are on page 654.

SECTION 3 – READING

The Reading Comprehension section of the TOEFL measures your ability to understand a variety of non–technical reading materials. The language in this section is more formal than the conversational language in the Listening section. The topics are taken from general and academic subjects.

You will read four or five passages of 250 to 350 words in length and answer questions about them. There will be approximately 8 to 13 questions about each passage. The questions based on the passages do not require you to have outside knowledge of the topics. All of the information you need to answer the questions is either stated or implied in the passages.

Some of the questions will ask you to identify the topic, major ideas, and supporting details in the passages. Some questions will require you to make inferences, to analyze the organization of the passage, or to identify the author's purpose. Some questions will ask you about the meaning of certain words and phrases as they are used in the context of the passage.

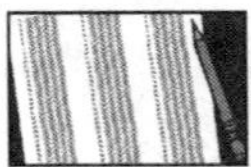

THE PAPER–BASED TEST

The paper–based TOEFL will continue to be administered in certain parts of the world and by certain educational institutions in North America.

There are five reading passages and 50 questions in the Reading Comprehension section. You have 55 minutes to complete this section. This time includes your reading of the directions.

Multiple–Choice Questions

On the paper TOEFL, all of the questions in the Reading section are multiple choice. For each question, you will choose the one best answer of four answer choices, (A), (B), (C), or (D). Then, on your answer sheet, find the number of the question and fill in the space that corresponds to the letter of the answer you have chosen.

A reading passage and question will look like this:

> The coffees of Central America profit from the area's steady climate and wealth of mountains. The mountains of the Pacific Cordillera, which stretch in a virtually unbroken line from Guatemala to the middle of Panama, provide the best combination of climate, altitude, and soil.
>
> Guatemala was a relative latecomer to the commercial coffee business, exporting beans only since 1875. This mountainous country is ideally suited for coffee production, and its exports now surpass those of much larger countries. European merchants still take about 50 percent of the Guatemalan beans, with most of the best beans today being exported to England.

It can be inferred from the passage that coffee grows well

(A) in the northern hemisphere
(B) in mountainous regions
(C) in small countries
(D) near the Pacific Ocean

This passage implies that the mountainous regions of Central America are ideally suited for coffee production. The other answer choices cannot be inferred from the information given. Therefore, you should choose (B).

You are allowed to skip questions and return to them later. You may also change your answers to previous questions by erasing and then filling in a different space on your answer sheet.

THE COMPUTER-BASED TEST

On the computerized TOEFL, you must read the passages before you begin to answer the questions. The computer will not present the questions until you have scrolled through the passage.

The computer will give you one question at a time. You will be able to refer to the passage while you are answering the questions. The passage will appear on the left side of the screen, and the questions will appear on the right side.

The Reading section is not computer–adaptive. This means that the way in which the computer gives you passages and questions is not based on your performance.

You are allowed to skip questions and return to them later. You may also change your answers to previous questions. You can go back to any previous questions in the Reading section by clicking on **Prev**. However, this process is very slow.

There are four to five reading passages and 44 to 60 questions in the Reading section.

You have 70 to 90 minutes to complete this section. Before you begin the test, there is extra time to spend on a tutorial that teaches you how to answer the different types of reading questions.

QUESTION TYPES ON THE COMPUTER TEST

There are three types of questions in the Reading Comprehension section. For each type of question, you will use the mouse to click on one answer.

Question Type 1 – Multiple Choice

In the first type of question, you will select one of four answer choices. Approximately 60 percent of the questions will be of this type.

For question type 1, the computer screen will look like this:

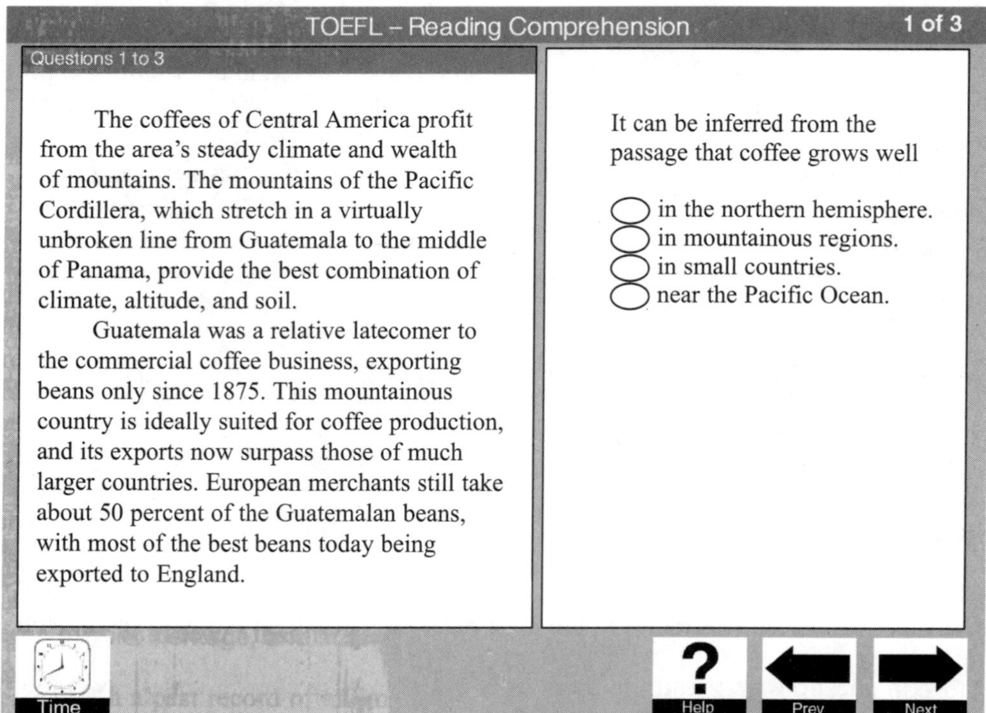

This passage implies that the mountainous regions of Central America are ideally suited for coffee production. Therefore, you should click on *in mountainous regions*, the second answer choice.

When you click on the oval next to one of the answer choices, the oval will darken. To change your answer, click on a different oval.

When you are satisfied that you have chosen the right answer, click on **Next**. When you do this, the computer will give you the next question.

Question Type 2 – Click on a Word, Phrase, or Sentence

In the second type of question, you will click on a word, phrase, or sentence. Sometimes you may be asked to click on a whole paragraph.

For question type 2, the computer screen will look like this:

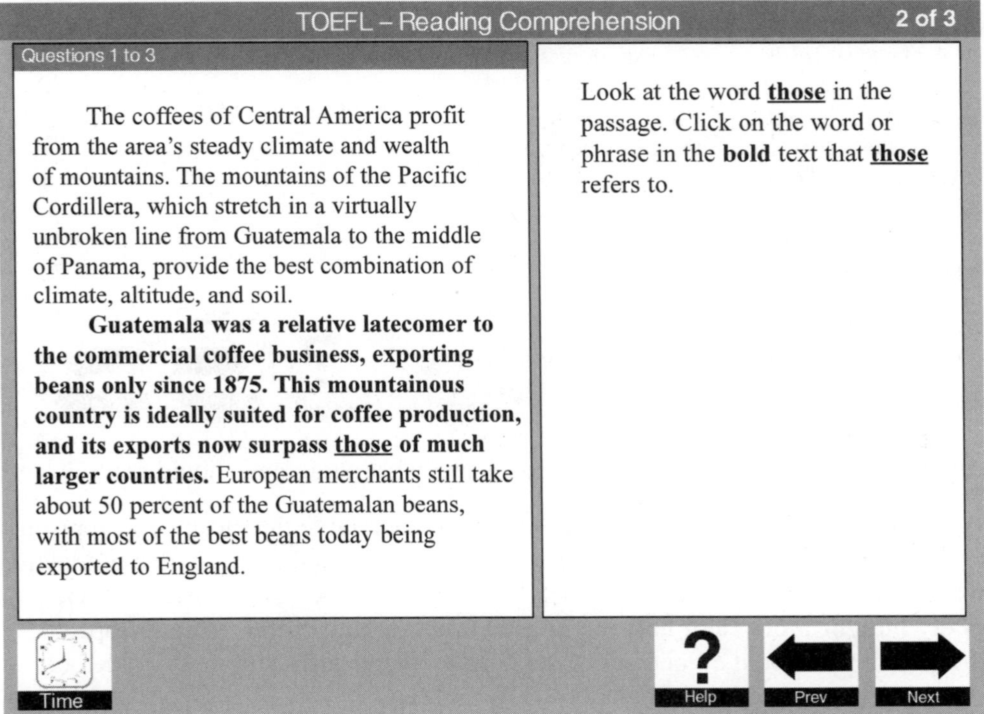

The correct answer is found in the bold text in the passage.

In this passage, *those* refers to *exports*. You should use the mouse to click on *exports*.

To answer this type of question, you can click on any part of the word or phrase in the bold text of the passage. The word or phrase you have chosen will darken. To change your answer, click on a different word or phrase.

When you are satisfied that you have chosen the right answer, click on **Next**. Then, the computer will give you the next question.

Question Type 3 – Add a Sentence

In the third type of question, you will click on a square to add a sentence to the passage.

For question type 3, the computer screen will look like this:

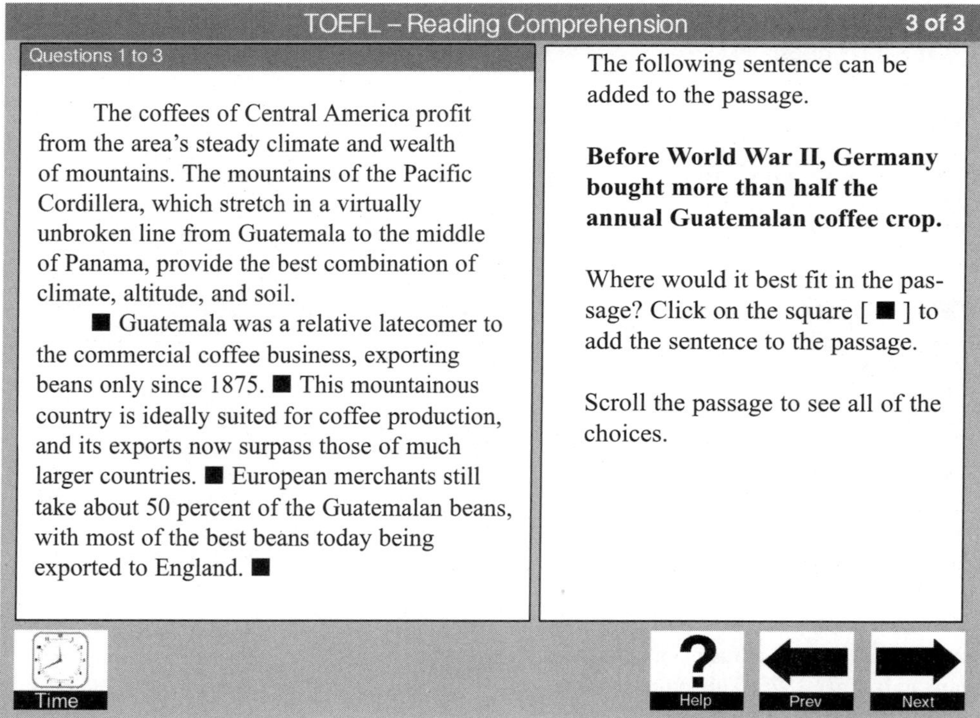

In this passage, the sentence would best fit at the third square. That paragraph should read:

> Guatemala was a relative latecomer to the commercial coffee business, exporting beans only since 1875. This mountainous country is ideally suited for coffee production, and its exports now surpass those of much larger countries. **Before World War II, Germany bought more than half the annual Guatemalan coffee crop.** European merchants still take about 50 percent of the Guatemalan beans, with most of the best beans today being exported to England.

When you click on a square, the sentence will appear in the passage at the place you have chosen. To change your answer, click on a different square. The sentence will then appear at this new location. The sentence will be highlighted.

When you are satisfied that you have chosen the right answer, click on **Next**. Then, the computer will give you the next question.

STRATEGIES FOR THE READING COMPREHENSION SECTION

Prepare before the Test

- Read on a variety of topics to build your English vocabulary. A large number of the passages on the TOEFL deal with topics in the natural sciences, the social sciences, and history. A smaller number relate to culture and the arts. Read as much as you can in these subject areas, particularly from textbooks, magazines, and newspapers.

- Practice trying to guess the meaning of unfamiliar words from the way they are used in sentences. Use other words in the sentence, your understanding of the passage, and your knowledge of the world as clues to the meanings of unfamiliar words.

- Be familiar with the testing tools used on the computer test. Practice using the mouse and the scroll bar. Practice reading from a computer screen and scrolling through a passage.

Pace Yourself

- Work as quickly as you can. Pay attention to the number of questions and the amount of time you have during the test. On the paper test, you have 55 minutes to read all of the passages and answer 50 questions. This means you have only 10 or 11 minutes to spend on each passage and its questions.

- You can leave questions unanswered on both the paper test and the computer test. Later, you can go back to answer, review, or change your answers to previous questions. This is easier to do on the paper test because you can see and mark the questions. On the computer test, you have to remember which questions you skip because you are not allowed to write on anything.

- Eliminate answer choices you know are incorrect. Then, if you are not sure of the correct answer, guess!

- Answer all questions about one passage before you move on to the next passage. On the computer test, although you are allowed to return to previous passages, this process takes a lot of time. It is better to finish each passage before going on.

Begin by Skimming

- On both the paper and computer tests, begin a passage by skimming it. *Skimming* is reading quickly for a general understanding of the meaning and organization. Frequently the first question about a passage asks about its topic or main idea.

- Read the first one or two sentences in each paragraph to get an idea of its content. Notice key words and phrases that are repeated throughout the passage. Read the last sentence in the last paragraph.

- On the computer test, you must use the scroll bar to skim the passages because most of them are too long to fit on a single screen.

Identify What the Question Wants

- Identify exactly what each question wants to know. Does it ask about information that is mentioned in the passage? Or does it ask about something that is NOT in the passage? Does it ask you to identify something the author stated, or does it ask you to make an inference based on something the author implied? Does it ask you about the meaning of a word or phrase?

- When you know what you are looking for, you can scan the passage to find the information you need. *Scanning* means looking for key words and phrases. On the computer test, sometimes the computer will tell you which paragraph to look in and will mark that paragraph with an arrow.

- Think carefully about questions that ask you to make an inference or prediction based on what you read. Eliminate answer choices that cannot be inferred from the information given in the passage.

- In questions about vocabulary, look for context clues in the passage. Use your knowledge of sentence structure, punctuation, and other words and ideas in the passage.

Know the Tricks

- Be familiar with the various ways the answer choices try to trick you. This book gives you practice in noticing some of the common tricks in the Reading section of the TOEFL.

READING SKILLS ON THE TEST

Six reading skills are tested in the Reading Comprehension section of the TOEFL. On the paper test, with a total of 50 questions, these skills are distributed as shown below. The computer test has a similar distribution of these skills, with the additional skill of recognizing coherence.

READING SKILL	APPROXIMATE NUMBER
Identifying the Topic and Main Ideas	4
Comprehending Details and Supporting Ideas	12+
Locating Referents	5+
Understanding Vocabulary in Context	12+
Making Inferences	10
Identifying Organization and Purpose	4
Recognizing Coherence (computer test only)	4

OVERVIEW OF THIS SECTION

3.1 Identifying the Topic and Main Ideas

FOCUS

Read the following paragraph quickly. What key words and phrases are clues to the paragraph's meaning?

> The colonial delegates assembled at Albany, New York, in the summer of 1754 to attempt a common peace with all of the Native American tribes. The most important result of the conference was the acceptance by the delegates of a plan to unite the colonies. This plan for intercolonial union was drawn up by Benjamin Franklin. Thus, the roots of the United States are in the Indian–white relations of the mid–eighteenth century. Men like Franklin saw the confederacy of Native tribes as a model to build upon.

Some key words and phrases are below. What others did you find?

colonial delegates	most important result
plan to unite the colonies	intercolonial union

Now, answer a question:

> What does the paragraph mainly discuss?
>
> ○ Colonial policies of the eighteenth century
> ○ The end of war with the Native American tribes
> ○ A plan to unite the American colonies
> ○ The roots of Indian–white relations

The correct answer is the third choice, *A plan to unite the American colonies.*

A key sentence is: *The most important result of the conference was the acceptance by the delegates of a plan to unite the colonies.*

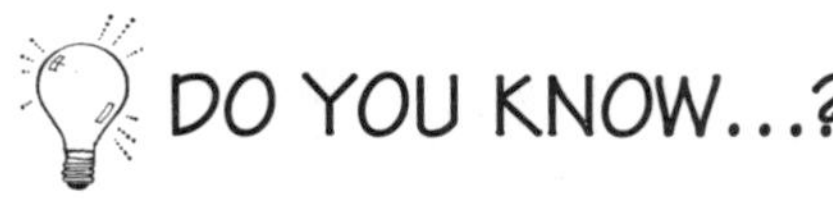

1. Approximately four items on the TOEFL will test your ability to identify the topic and main ideas in the passages you read. Questions of this type are often first after each reading passage.

   Success in college and university depends on being able to read effectively. Students in North America are required to do a lot of reading in their courses. Identifying main ideas is an essential academic skill. You will be expected to read material and discuss the ideas in class. You will also be required to summarize ideas when you write term papers.

2. The ***topic*** of a passage is the answer to the question, "What is this passage about?" The topic is the main subject of the passage. It is the passage's most general idea and can usually be stated in a few words or phrases.

   TOEFL questions about the topic of a passage look like this:

   > What does the passage mainly discuss?
   > What is the topic/subject of the passage?
   > Which of the following is the main topic of the passage?
   > The passage primarily discusses _____.
   > The passage deals mainly with _____.
   > The passage mainly discusses _____ in terms of _____.
   > With what topic is paragraph __ mainly concerned?

3. The ***main idea*** of a passage answers the question, "What is important about the topic?" The main idea is the general message. It may be stated directly in a ***topic sentence***, often appearing near the beginning or end of the passage. Sometimes it is not stated directly but implied through key words and phrases.

   The main idea is sometimes called the ***controlling idea*** because it guides both the writer and the reader through discussion of the topic. It is the one idea that is present throughout the entire passage.

   Identifying the main idea of a passage is one of the most useful reading skills you can develop. It is a skill you can apply to any kind of reading.

   TOEFL questions about the main idea of a passage look like this:

   > What is the main idea of the passage?
   > What is the main purpose of the passage?
   > What is the main point the author makes in the passage?

4. ***Supporting ideas*** answer the question, "What makes the main idea believable?" Most of the sentences in a well–written passage contain supporting ideas that explain, illustrate, describe, or develop the main idea. These ideas strengthen and support the main idea.

   Some TOEFL questions ask you to recognize how supporting ideas relate to the main idea. Look at some examples:

   > Which of the following statements does the passage support?
   > The passage supports all of the following statements EXCEPT

Reading

The above questions are really asking you to identify the main idea. You are likely to get this type of question when the main idea is not stated directly in the passage.

Note: In a question like *The passage supports all of the following statements EXCEPT...*, three of the answer choices will be true according to the passage. However, the *correct* answer is the one choice that is *not true* or *not dealt with* in the passage.

Look at main and supporting ideas in the following passage:

> Snow consists of large and often complex crystals that originate in clouds. When snowflakes form in significant number and become heavy enough to fall from the clouds, a snowstorm is born. Although <u>snowstorms</u> can cause damage, they also <u>help sustain human, animal, and plant life</u>.
>
> Snow is of tremendous *importance in air–climate patterns*, and it has a major effect on our daily lives. Perhaps the best way to appreciate the significance of snow is to consider what happens when it fails to fall in places that rely on it. Snow *provides water for forests, agriculture, industry, and drinking.* In California, for instance, most of the *water for irrigation* comes from snow melt. Also, *insulating and reflective snow cover* on the ground can *affect the global climate and the local weather.*

The main idea is *snowstorms help sustain human, animal, and plant life.* Ideas that support this statement are shown in italics.

There are other ideas in the passage—snow originates in clouds, snow can cause damage—but these ideas do not control the passage. Rather, they provide background about the topic.

5. ***Skimming*** is the skill of reading quickly to get a general idea of a passage. Skimming involves looking for information and clues that give you an idea of a passage's topic, main ideas, and overall organization.

   When you take the TOEFL, begin each new passage by skimming it. Read only the key sentences to get the main idea. Read the first and the last sentence of each paragraph. Skim the rest of the passage for key words. You do not have to read every word—at least not at first.

   On the computer test, you *must* skim the passage before the computer will present the first question.

   Skim for key words. Read the following paragraphs quickly. Underline key words and phrases that are clues to the meaning of each paragraph.

   a. Noxious weeds are aggressive, non–native plants that invade an area, displace native plants, and cause long–lasting problems. Noxious weeds increase fire hazards, replace valuable wildlife food, poison livestock, and reduce the quality of recreational experiences. Many are toxic to humans as well as animals. They reduce plant diversity and threaten the health of the forest and the community.

   b. There are three categories of insurance: life, health, and property–liability. Each protects its policyholder against possible financial loss. Life insurance pays the customer's family a certain sum upon the holder's death. Health insurance protects its policyholders against large medical expenses. By paying premiums to an insurance company, the policyholder can ensure payment of medical bills. Property–liability insurance, sometimes called casualty insurance, covers accidents such as auto crashes, fire, and theft.

With your classmates and teacher, discuss the key words you identified. Use them to answer these questions:

What does each paragraph mainly discuss?

What is the main idea of each paragraph?

6. In topic and main idea questions, some of the answer choices may try to trick you by being:

- too general: broader than what is covered in the passage
- too specific: supporting ideas and details instead of main ideas
- inaccurate or untrue according to the passage
- irrelevant or not dealt with in the passage

Look at an example:

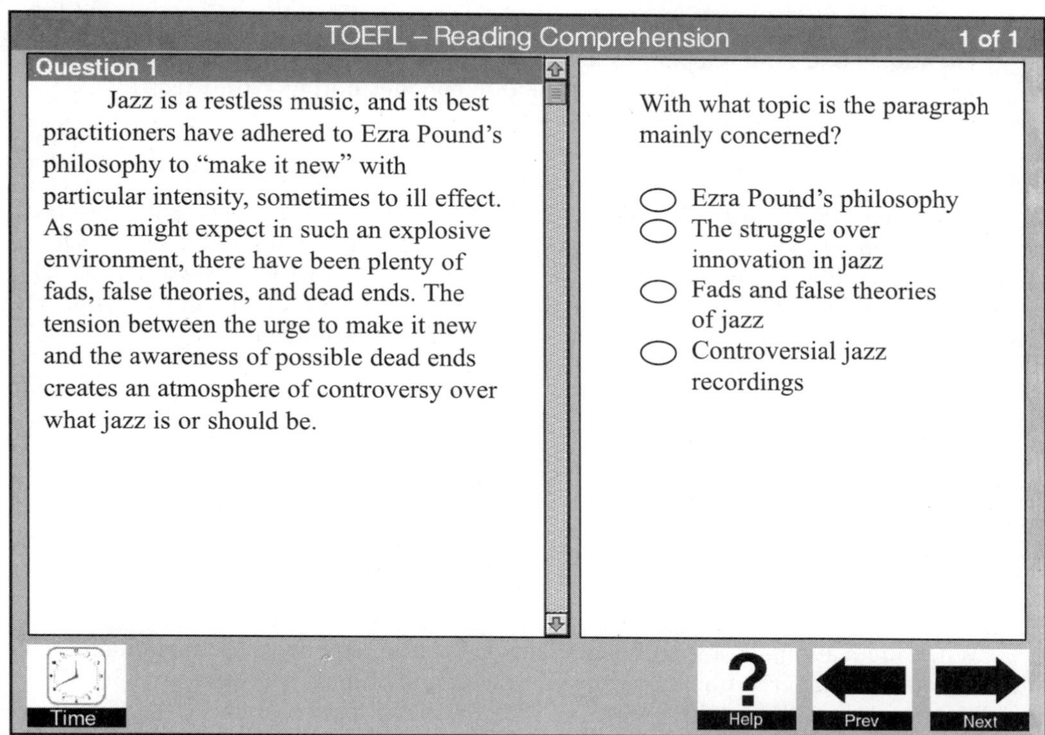

The first answer choice, *Ezra Pound's philosophy*, is too general to be the topic of the paragraph. The third choice, *Fads and false theories of jazz*, is too specific; it is a supporting detail. The fourth choice, *Controversial jazz recordings*, is not dealt with here.

The answer is the second choice, *The struggle over innovation in jazz*. Innovation is creativity. Some key phrases are "*make it new*," *explosive environment*, *tension*, *urge to make it new*, and *atmosphere of controversy*.

READING

PRACTICE

Exercise 3.1.A

Read the following passages and choose the one best answer to each question.

1. During World War I, a new means of electronic communication appeared, barely ten years after its invention—radio. Radio permitted much more rapid installation of communications, at far longer ranges, than was possible with field telephones. Also, its invisible signals could not be stopped by artillery fire or wire cutters, as telephone lines could. Few improvements have been made in field telephones since World War I, but improvements in radio transmission have been continuous.

   What is the main idea of the paragraph?

   (A) Radio was the newest technology during World War I.
   (B) The radios and field telephones used during World War I were primitive.
   (C) Radio was more advantageous than field telephones during World War I.
   (D) Radio has improved greatly since World War I.

2. Rangelands cover more than one billion acres of the United States, mostly in the Western states and Alaska. They contain many natural resources—grass and shrubs for animal grazing, habitats for livestock and wildlife, water from vast watersheds, facilities for water sports and other kinds of recreation, and valuable mineral and energy resources. Rangelands also serve as areas for scientific study of the environment.

   What is the main idea of the paragraph?

   (A) The United States has vast areas of rangelands.
   (B) There are many benefits derived from rangelands.
   (C) The natural resources of rangelands are becoming threatened.
   (D) Rangelands are the subject of much scientific study.

3. When the National Football League decided to end expensive bidding among teams for the best college players, it held a draft. The first football draft was held in 1936. The Philadelphia Eagles, as the weakest team, had the first draft choice. It chose the University of Chicago's Jay Berwanger, then sold the rights to him to the Chicago Bears. The Bears and Berwanger could not come to contract terms; thus, the first player drafted by the pros never played professional football.

   The paragraph primarily discusses

   (A) the origins of the National Football League
   (B) the short football career of Jay Berwanger
   (C) the contract dispute between the Chicago Bears and Jay Berwanger
   (D) the first National Football League draft

4. *Dust devils* and *sand devils*, familiar sights in dry, desert country, are spiraling columns of dust– or sand–filled air, often several hundred feet high, that perform their antics for a few minutes. Devils differ in their origin from true tornadoes. They are caused by intense local heating of the surface of the earth, whereas tornadoes are caused by clashing warm and cold air currents aloft that lead to atmospheric instability and severe turbulence.

Which of the following statements does the paragraph support?

(A) Dust devils and tornadoes look similar but are different in origin.
(B) Dust devils and sand devils are small tornadoes.
(C) Dust devils are dangerous to human and animal life.
(D) There are many fascinating natural phenomena in the desert.

5. Marian Anderson, the first in a succession of black divas at the Metropolitan Opera, was the first African–American woman to break the barriers which kept blacks from the concert stage. She encountered many racial slights, the most famous being the refusal of the Daughters of the American Revolution to allow her to appear in Constitution Hall in Washington, D. C. This insult was publicly confronted by first lady Eleanor Roosevelt, who arranged for Anderson to sing from the steps of the Lincoln Memorial on Easter Sunday of 1939.

The paragraph mainly discusses Marian Anderson in terms of her

(A) success at the Metropolitan Opera
(B) appearance in Constitution Hall in Washington, D. C.
(C) role in breaking barriers of racial prejudice
(D) confrontation with first lady Eleanor Roosevelt

6. In 1965 the United States Congress created Medicaid and Medicare as amendments to the Social Security Act. Medicaid uses federal, state, and local money to underwrite medical care for low–income persons. Medicare is the first U. S. government–operated health insurance system for persons aged 65 and over. It provides basic hospital insurance and assistance with doctors' and other health–care bills. Although these two programs have assisted millions of people, the United States remains the only Western industrial nation without some form of comprehensive national health insurance.

The paragraph deals mainly with

(A) two existing health insurance programs
(B) the funding of Medicaid
(C) amendments to the Social Security Act
(D) the need for comprehensive national health insurance

Exercise 3.1.B

Read the following passages and choose the one best answer to each question.

QUESTIONS 1–2

A middle ear infection (*otitis media*) usually starts when a cold causes the eustachian tube between the ear and throat to swell and close. When the tube closes, fluid seeps into the ear and bacteria start to grow. As the body fights the infection, pressure builds up, causing pain. Young children get more ear infections because they get more colds, and their eustachian tubes are more easily blocked.

Symptoms of a bacterial ear infection include earache, dizziness, ringing or fullness in the ears, hearing loss, fever, headache, and runny nose. Children who cannot yet talk may tug on the ear as a sign of pain.

Antibiotic treatment stops bacterial growth, relieving pressure and pain. Left untreated, the pressure can cause the eardrum to rupture. A single eardrum rupture usually does not have long–term consequences. However, repeated ruptures may cause hearing loss.

1. What does the passage mainly discuss?

Ⓐ The body's response to bacterial infection
Ⓑ The symptoms of middle ear infections
Ⓒ Why young children get more ear infections
Ⓓ The causes and effects of middle ear infections

2. What is the main purpose of paragraph 2?

Ⓐ To explain the causes of middle ear infection
Ⓑ To point out the signs of middle ear infection
Ⓒ To warn parents about the dangers of colds in young children
Ⓓ To compare colds and bacterial ear infections

QUESTIONS 3–5

Few families have made more contributions to mathematics than the Bernoullis of Basel, Switzerland. Eight Bernoullis, over three generations spanning the years from 1680 to 1800, were distinguished mathematicians. Several helped build the new mathematics of probability.

James (1654–1705) and John (1667–1748) were sons of a prosperous Swiss merchant and studied mathematics against the will of their father. Both were among the finest mathematicians of their times. James was the first to see clearly the idea of a long–run proportion as a way of measuring chance. His *law of large numbers* helped connect probability to the study of sequences of chance outcomes observed in human affairs.

Nicholas (1687–1759) and Daniel (1700–1782) also studied probability. Nicholas saw that the pattern of births of male and female children could be described by probability. Daniel studied mainly the mathematics of flowing fluids that was later applied to designing ships and aircraft. In the field of probability, he gave evidence for the effectiveness of inoculation against smallpox.

The Bernoulli family in mathematics, like their contemporaries the Bachs in music, are an unusual example of talent in one field appearing in successive generations. Their work helped probability grow from its birthplace in the gambling hall to a respectable tool with worldwide applications.

3. Which of the following is the main topic of the passage?

(A) The origins of the new mathematics of probability
(B) Mathematical developments in the period from 1680 to 1800
(C) Contributions of one family to the study of probability
(D) Past and present applications of probability theory

4. What is the main idea of the passage?

(A) The Bernoullis developed several practical applications of probability.
(B) James Bernoulli's *law of large numbers* influenced the study of human affairs.
(C) The Bernoulli and Bach families were the finest mathematicians of their times.
(D) Probability grew from its questionable origins in the gambling hall.

5. The passage supports all of the following statements EXCEPT

(A) some families show evidence of talent in one field
(B) probability has several useful applications
(C) the Bernoulli family was prominent in the field of mathematics
(D) studying mathematics was popular in the time of the Bernoullis

QUESTIONS 6–8

Packaging plays an important role in marketing. With the variety of goods for sale, packages must use every trick of color and design to attract the attention of shoppers. In many cases the appearance of the package is more important than the product. An example is facial tissues. If a supermarket carries different brands of tissues that are similar in price and quality, a shopper will probably pass up the plain box and choose a decorator box that matches the decor of the shopper's home.

Packaging influences consumer choices in other ways, too. With food products, medicines, and household cleaning products, many consumers look for safety features in packaging. They want to be sure that the product has not been tampered with or that it is childproof. Packaging that makes a product more convenient or functional is also important. No–drip spouts, handles, or non–breakable containers can be decisive in selling a product.

Customers who have a favorite brand of shampoo or soap must be able to recognize their brand on the supermarket shelf immediately; otherwise, they may be tempted to look around and choose another brand. Packages convey brand images, and package designers seek to create a recognizable identity for a product.

6. What does the passage mainly discuss?

(A) Why consumers prefer attractive packaging
(B) What consumers look for when they buy a product
(C) How packaging tricks customers
(D) The role of packaging in selling products

7. What is the main point the author makes in the passage?

(A) Customers are influenced by the packaging of products.
(B) Customers can not always recognize misleading packaging.
(C) Customers will buy their favorite brand despite its packaging.
(D) Package designers must know about human psychology.

8. The passage supports all of the following statements EXCEPT

(A) packaging is an essential part of marketing products
(B) shoppers like packaging that is convenient and attractive
(C) most customers read the label before they buy a product
(D) packaging influences which product a customer will choose

Answers to Exercises 3.1.A through 3.1.B are on page 655.

3.1 EXTENSION

1. Working in pairs, students discuss why the three incorrect answer choices in Exercises 3.1.A and 3.1.B are incorrect. How do they try to trick you?

2. In reading done outside class, preferably from a textbook for another class, students select a short passage of 1 to 3 paragraphs. Make 3 or 4 photocopies and bring them to class. In groups of 3 or 4, students pass out the copies of their passages. Students work as a team to identify key words and sentences that are clues to the main ideas in each passage. Write a main idea sentence for each passage. This can also be done as a whole–class exercise or quiz if students write the passage on a transparency for an overhead projector.

3. Students create "TOEFL questions" to test their classmates' ability to identify the topic and main ideas of a passage. Students select a short passage from a textbook for another class. Working in pairs, students write one or two questions for each passage. Use the list of topic and main idea questions on page 345 for examples of how to word the questions. Then write four answer choices for each question. One must be the correct answer! Three choices must be incorrect because they are (a) too general, (b) too specific, or (c) not dealt with in the passage.

For activity #3, the teacher collects the passages with questions and answer choices, edits them, and uses them in a student–made "TOEFL exam."

Assessing Progress – 3.1

Quiz 1 *(Time – 15 minutes)*

Read the following passages and choose the one best answer to each question. Answer all questions on the basis of what is stated or implied in that passage.

1. The tiger shark has good eyesight, but it relies mostly on other senses to track and catch its prey. It has an acute sense of smell, which enables it to pick up even the faintest traces of blood in the water and follow them to their source. It is also sensitive to low–frequency pressure waves produced by movements in the water. Even tiny nerve and muscle twinges reach its sensitive electroreceptors, enabling the shark to pinpoint prey in the darkest, murkiest water.

   What is the main idea of the paragraph?

   (A) The tiger shark depends on its keen eyesight to track and catch prey.
   (B) The tiger shark has many features that help it find food.
   (C) The tiger shark relies on its electroreceptors for navigating in dark water.
   (D) The tiger shark is an endangered species.

2. The earth is considered a solid, rigid mass with a dense core of magnetic material. The outer part of the core is probably liquid. Around the core is a thick mantle of heavy rock which is covered by a thin crust forming the solid granite and basalt base of the continents and ocean basins. Over broad areas of the earth's surface, the crust has a thin cover of sedimentary rock such as sandstone, shale, and limestone formed by weathering of the earth's surface and deposit of sands, clays, and plant and animal remains.

   With what topic is the paragraph mainly concerned?

   (A) The magnetic core of the earth
   (B) The evolution of life on earth
   (C) How the continents were formed
   (D) The structure and composition of the earth

3. Folklorists and anthropologists have recorded and studied women's laments in the villages of Greece. Laments are ritualized oral poems that some Greek women chant to express grief over the loss of loved ones. Women typically recite laments in the company of other women and even feel that they need the participation of other women for the lament to be successful. Each woman's expression of grief reminds the others of their own suffering, and communal expression of pain bonds the women to each other.

   What is the main idea of the paragraph?

   (A) Laments have a long history among women in Greek villages.
   (B) Laments have been the subject of much anthropological study.
   (C) Laments are a traditional communal form of expressing grief.
   (D) Women in Greece face unique problems surrounding the loss of loved ones.

Reading

Questions 4–5

A handful of almonds may be your ticket to health. Investigators found that munching on 3 1/2 ounces of almonds a day reduced LDL cholesterol by 10 to 15 percent. In a Loma Linda University study, vegetarians who ate nuts at least five times a week cut their risk of a heart attack by 50 percent.

Almonds are low in saturated fat and high in unsaturated fats that can lower cholesterol. Compared with other snack foods like potato chips, pretzels and peanuts, almonds are rich in vitamin E and in the amino acid arginine. Arginine relaxes blood vessels and inhibits the proliferation of cells in blood vessel walls—steps important in blocking heart disease. Almonds also contain high amounts of magnesium and copper—two minerals that make the blood vessels less prone to plaque attack.

4. What does the passage mainly discuss?

   (A) A study of vegetarians who ate nuts
   (B) The nutritional benefits of almonds
   (C) Steps in blocking heart disease
   (D) The importance of reducing cholesterol

5. Which of the following statements does the passage support?

   (A) Eating almonds can reduce the risk of heart disease.
   (B) Vegetarians have a lower risk of heart attack than meat eaters.
   (C) Most snack foods contain saturated fat.
   (D) Almonds are a high–energy, low–calorie snack food.

Questions 6–7

It was not until enterprising sea captains imported exotic animals to sell to traveling showmen that words such as *lion* or *polar bear* had much meaning to Americans. In 1789 the first large collection of exotic wild animals was put on permanent exhibit in New York. By the 1830s, most circuses had a collection of animals that generally included elephants, camels, lions, tigers, kangaroos, and apes. These *animal shows* served as traveling zoos where many Americans saw their first exotic animal. The creatures made such an impression that American English began to acquire new phrases.

To monkey around and *monkey business* are expressions of the early 1800s, and *to make a monkey out of someone* is from 1899, all being terms based on the increasing number of monkeys seen in circuses and zoos. A large or uncouth man was called a *big ape* by 1831, and *gorilla* was used to mean a hairy, tough man by the 1860s and a thug by 1926.

6. What is the main idea of the passage?

   (A) Americans did not know about exotic animals until they were imported.
   (B) Traveling zoos were popular entertainments in the nineteenth century.
   (C) Americans have always been concerned about animal welfare.
   (D) Americans responded to imported animals creatively through language.

7. With what topic is paragraph 2 mainly concerned?

   (A) Terms inspired by monkeys and apes
   (B) The early history of circuses and zoos in America
   (C) Similarities between monkeys and humans
   (D) Vulgar terms to describe certain men

QUESTIONS 8–10

The developmental period known as the Early Adult Transition usually begins at age twenty–two, give or take two years, and lasts about six years. In entering the adult world, a young person has to fashion and test out an initial life structure that provides a viable link between the self and the adult society. He or she must now shift the center of gravity from the position of child in the family of origin to the position of novice adult with a new home base that is more truly his or her own.

The young adult faces two major tasks. First, he or she has to discover and generate alternative options. To varying degrees, the external world provides multiple possibilities and invites the young person to try different choices before making final commitments. Second, the young adult must create a stable life structure, taking on adult responsibilities and making something of his or her life. Externally, there are pressures to "grow up," get married, enter an occupation, and lead a more organized life. Internally, there are desires for stability and order, for roots, membership in the tribe, lasting ties, and fulfillment of core values.

8. What does the passage mainly discuss?

(A) Difficulties of the Early Adult Transition
(B) Building a life structure that will last a lifetime
(C) The transition from youth to adulthood
(D) The transition from external to internal values

9. What is the main purpose of paragraph 2?

(A) To point out alternative options for young adults
(B) To describe two tasks of early adulthood
(C) To criticize societal pressures on young adults
(D) To compare external and internal pressures on young adults

10. The passage supports all of the following statements EXCEPT

(A) young adults must face the Early Adult Transition on their own
(B) the Early Adult Transition involves forming an initial life structure
(C) young adults usually seek options and try different choices
(D) young adults must find a way to link the self with the adult society

Answers to Reading Quiz 1 are on page 655.

READING

3.2 Comprehending Details and Supporting Ideas

FOCUS

Read the following passage and answer the question.

> Diabetes affects millions of people in North America, almost half of whom do not realize they have the disease. At risk are people who have a family history of diabetes, are obese, have a history of large birth weight, and are over age forty.
>
> People with diabetes do not convert food into energy the same way most people do. If a person without diabetes eats a piece of candy, for example, the pancreas will produce insulin which then converts those carbohydrates into glucose, or sugar. That glucose is then used by the cells for energy. However, glucose is not automatically accepted into the cells. It requires a specific key—insulin—to be converted into energy. Without insulin, glucose is locked out of the cells, causing the body to build up extra supplies of it. In people with diabetes, who do not produce insulin, this can eventually lead to hyperglycemia or diabetic coma, also known as high blood sugar.
>
> What substance does the body require to convert food into energy?
>
> ◯ Glucose
> ◯ Insulin
> ◯ Candy
> ◯ Carbohydrates

This question asks about a specific detail in the passage. The second answer choice, *insulin*, is the correct answer. What key words and phrases in the passage help you determine this?

Now, read a question about what is NOT in the passage:

> Which of the following sentences should NOT be included in a summary of the passage?
>
> ◯ People with a family history of diabetes are at risk of getting the disease.
> ◯ People with diabetes do not produce insulin.
> ◯ A lack of insulin can result in diabetic coma or high blood sugar.
> ◯ There are several methods for monitoring and treating diabetes.

A ***summary*** includes the important points made in a passage. This question asks you to recognize which *three* ideas are important—and which *one* is not.

The fourth answer choice, *There are several methods for monitoring and treating diabetes*, is not mentioned in the passage. Therefore, it should NOT be included in a summary.

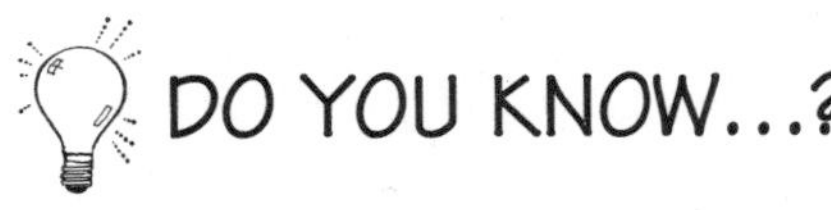

DO YOU KNOW...?

1. Approximately twelve items on the TOEFL will test your understanding of details and supporting ideas in the passages you read. For each individual passage, approximately two to four questions will ask you about details and supporting ideas.

   On the paper test, the detail questions are usually asked in the same order that the information appears in the passage.

   On the computer test, the detail questions are also asked in the order that the information appears in the passage. The computer may scroll automatically to the section in the passage where the answer is to be found. If you want to review the whole passage, you can use the scroll bar to move up and down on the screen.

2. A ***detail*** is a specific bit of information, such as a fact, statistic, example, reason, or illustration. Details are like ***supporting ideas*** because they support other ideas in a passage. Details and supporting ideas make main ideas stronger and more convincing.

   TOEFL questions about the details and supporting ideas in a passage look like this:

   According to the passage, who _____?
   what _____?
   why _____?
   where _____?
   when _____?
   which _____?
   how _____?
   According to the author, _____?
   The passage/author states that _____.
   The author makes the point that _____.
   The author indicates that _____.
   What was one of the main reasons for _____?
   The author compares _____ with _____.
   The author mentions _____ as an example of _____.

3. Another kind of detail question on the TOEFL asks about information that is NOT in the passage. These questions look like this:

   According to the passage, which of the following does NOT _____?
   Which of the following is NOT mentioned as/about _____?
   The author mentions all of the following EXCEPT
   The passage discusses all of the following EXCEPT
   Which of the following is NOT stated in the passage?
   Which of the following sentences should NOT be included in a summary of the passage?

READING

Note: In TOEFL questions with *NOT* or *EXCEPT*, look for the *one* answer choice with information that is:

- not in the passage

or

- not true according to the passage

4. ***Scanning*** is the skill of reading quickly to locate specific information. Unlike ***skimming***, which is reading quickly to get a general idea of a passage (See 3.1), ***scanning*** is searching for details.

   When you scan a passage for information, you know what kind of information you need because the TOEFL question tells you what you are looking for. The question gives you key words and phrases to help you scan the passage for the answer.

   On the computer test, a skill that is related to scanning is ***scrolling***, which is moving through the text quickly. Scrolling is necessary when the passage is too long to fit on one computer screen.

5. Certain key expressions are clues that can help you understand the relationships between ideas within sentences and paragraphs. These words and phrases are sometimes called ***transitions*** or ***connectors***.

TRANSITIONS

Illustrate	for example such	for instance such as	next
Explain	at this point in this case	furthermore	in fact
Compare	both like	equally important similarly	in the same way similar to
Contrast	in contrast unlike	instead whereas	on the other hand while
Add	also in addition	first, second, third… moreover	furthermore not only…but also
Limit	although however	but yet	except for
Emphasize	certainly surely	indeed	most importantly
Show Result	as a result otherwise	accordingly therefore	consequently thus
Conclude	at last in summary	finally to sum up	in conclusion

Can you add any expressions to this list?

6. In detail and supporting idea questions, some of the answer choices may try to trick you by:
   - restating information with synonyms and other words (***paraphrasing***)
   - repeating words and phrases from the passage in incorrect ways
   - being inaccurate or untrue according to the passage
   - being irrelevant or not mentioned in the passage

   Look at an example:

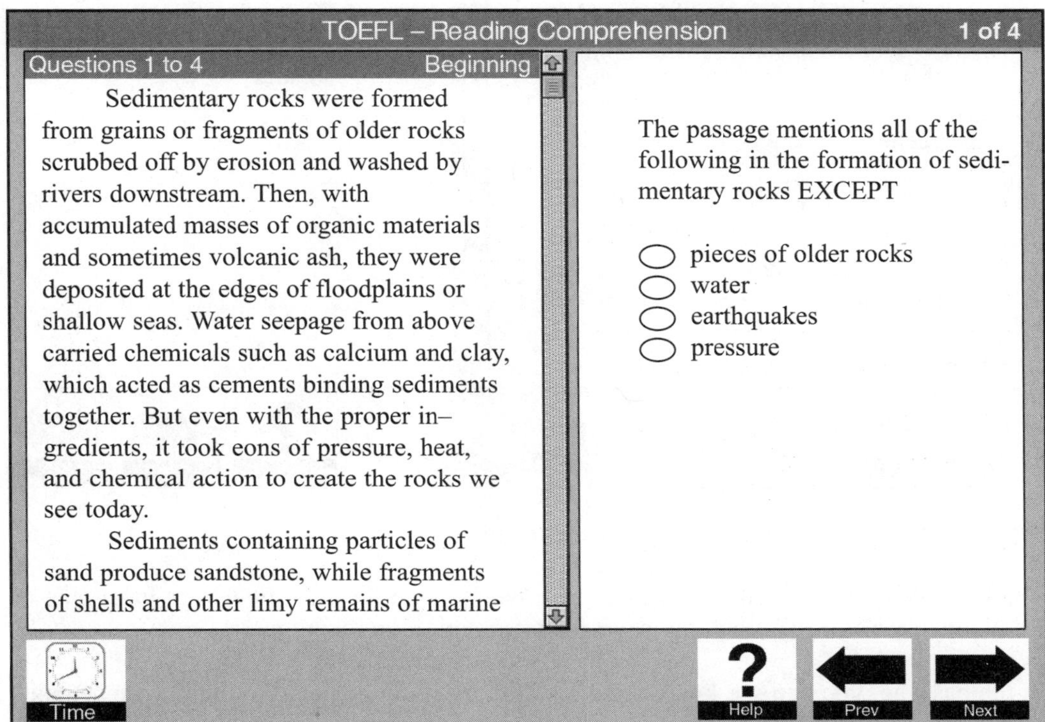
TOEFL – Reading Comprehension 1 of 4

Questions 1 to 4 Beginning

Sedimentary rocks were formed from grains or fragments of older rocks scrubbed off by erosion and washed by rivers downstream. Then, with accumulated masses of organic materials and sometimes volcanic ash, they were deposited at the edges of floodplains or shallow seas. Water seepage from above carried chemicals such as calcium and clay, which acted as cements binding sediments together. But even with the proper in–gredients, it took eons of pressure, heat, and chemical action to create the rocks we see today.

Sediments containing particles of sand produce sandstone, while fragments of shells and other limy remains of marine

The passage mentions all of the following in the formation of sedimentary rocks EXCEPT

- pieces of older rocks
- water
- earthquakes
- pressure

A key phrase in the question is *the formation of sedimentary rocks*. This enables you to scan the text for the needed information. As you scan the first paragraph, you can see similar words, *Sedimentary rocks were formed*. This tells you the answer is probably in the first paragraph.

Another very important word in the question is *EXCEPT*. It tells you that you are looking for the one answer that is *not* in the passage.

The correct answer is the third choice, *earthquakes*, because it is the only choice that is not mentioned in the formation of sedimentary rocks.

Look at another example:

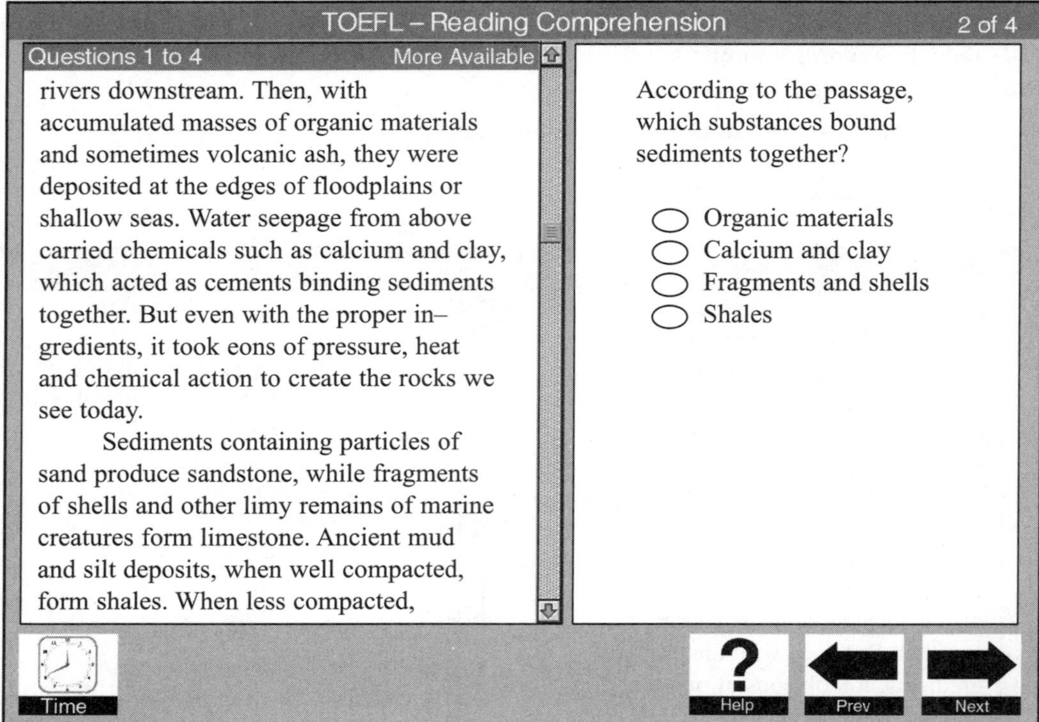

A key phrase in the question is *bound sediments together.*

The left side of the screen shows that you have scrolled through the text to locate the answer. Remember, ***scrolling*** is how you ***scan*** for information on a computer!

In the passage, you can see key words from the question repeated in the phrase cements *binding sediments together*. Thus, the correct answer is the second choice, *Calcium and clay.*

The three incorrect answer choices are all mentioned in the passage, but not in relation to the question.

Look at another example:

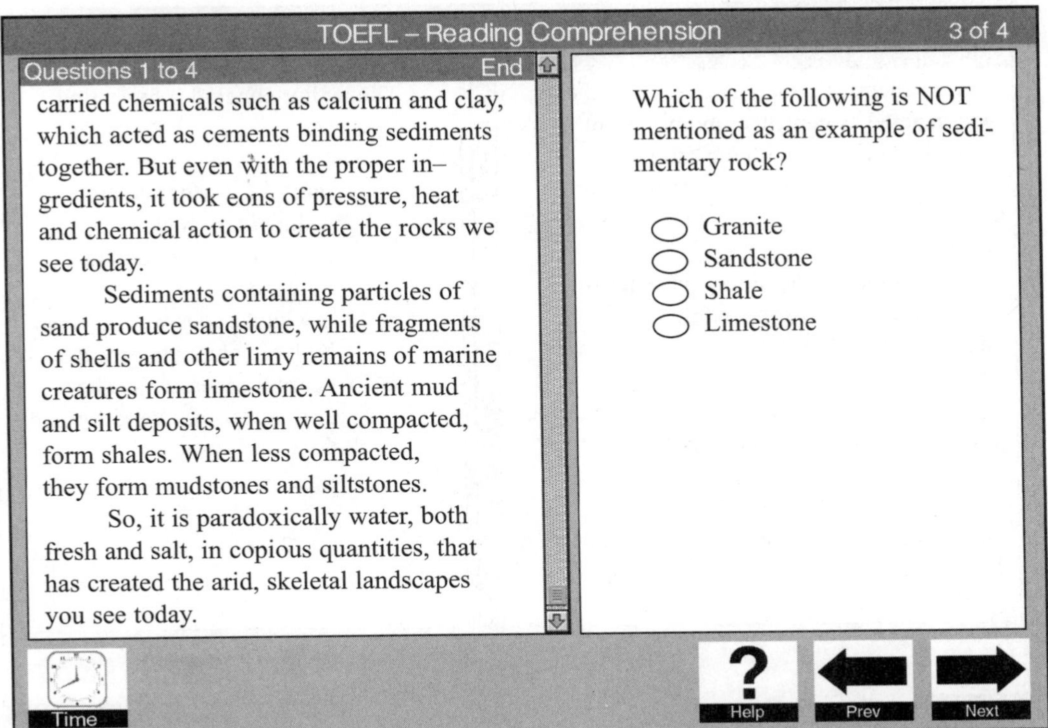
TOEFL – Reading Comprehension 3 of 4

Questions 1 to 4 End

carried chemicals such as calcium and clay, which acted as cements binding sediments together. But even with the proper in–gredients, it took eons of pressure, heat and chemical action to create the rocks we see today.

Sediments containing particles of sand produce sandstone, while fragments of shells and other limy remains of marine creatures form limestone. Ancient mud and silt deposits, when well compacted, form shales. When less compacted, they form mudstones and siltstones.

So, it is paradoxically water, both fresh and salt, in copious quantities, that has created the arid, skeletal landscapes you see today.

Which of the following is NOT mentioned as an example of sedimentary rock?

- Granite
- Sandstone
- Shale
- Limestone

Time Help Prev Next

An important word in the question is *NOT*. It tells you that you are looking for the one answer that is *not* mentioned as an example of sedimentary rock.

Reading the answer choices tells you what words to scan for in the passage.

The middle paragraph gives several examples of sedimentary rocks. By scanning this paragraph, you can find three of the answer choices: *sandstone*, *limestone*, and *shale*.

Granite is not mentioned. Therefore, the correct answer is the first choice, *Granite*.

Look at another example:

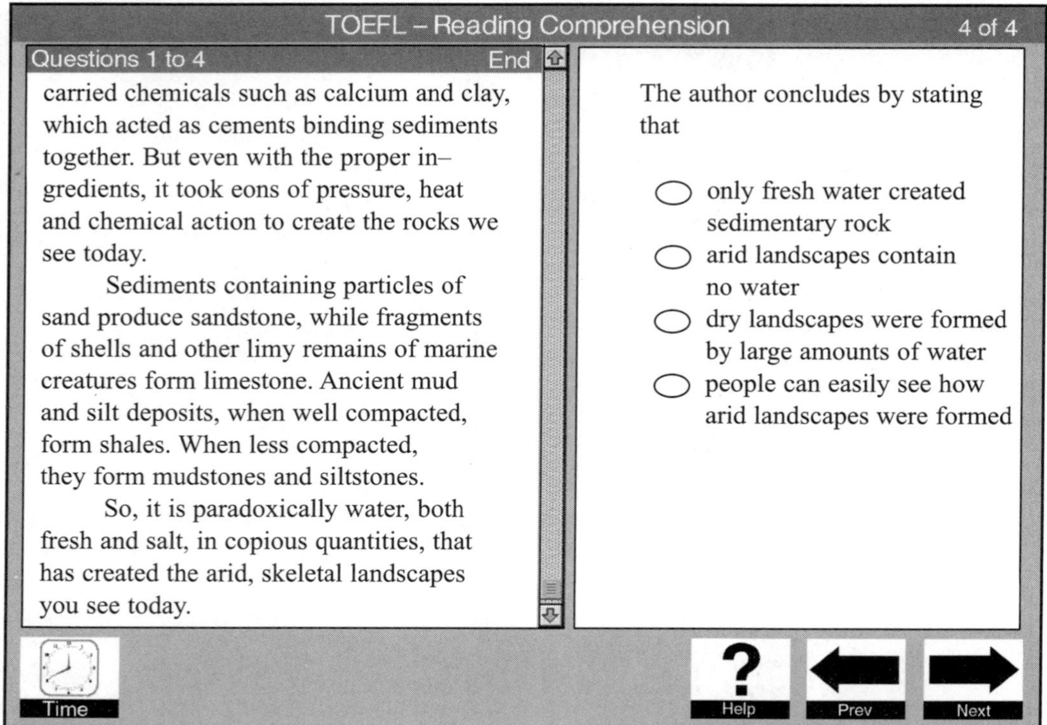
TOEFL – Reading Comprehension 4 of 4

Questions 1 to 4 End

carried chemicals such as calcium and clay, which acted as cements binding sediments together. But even with the proper in–gredients, it took eons of pressure, heat and chemical action to create the rocks we see today.

Sediments containing particles of sand produce sandstone, while fragments of shells and other limy remains of marine creatures form limestone. Ancient mud and silt deposits, when well compacted, form shales. When less compacted, they form mudstones and siltstones.

So, it is paradoxically water, both fresh and salt, in copious quantities, that has created the arid, skeletal landscapes you see today.

The author concludes by stating that

- only fresh water created sedimentary rock
- arid landscapes contain no water
- dry landscapes were formed by large amounts of water
- people can easily see how arid landscapes were formed

The author concludes tells you to look at the last part of the passage. *End* in the upper left screen shows that you have scrolled to the end of the text.

In this type of question, the correct answer is usually a paraphrase of what is stated in the text. Look for words with the same meaning as the words in the answer choices.

The first choice is incorrect because *only fresh water* does not agree with *water, both fresh and salt* in the passage. The second choice, although true, is not the conclusion of the passage. The fourth choice is incorrect because *people can easily see how* is not an idea in the passage.

The third choice, *dry landscapes were formed by large amounts of water*, is the correct answer. It restates the last sentence of the passage. Notice that synonyms are used: *dry* instead of *arid; large amounts of water* instead of *water...in copious quantities*.

On the TOEFL many correct answers will be restatements, or paraphrases, of information from the passage.

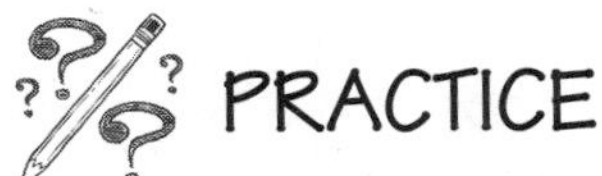

PRACTICE

Exercise 3.2.A

Read the following passages and choose the one best answer to each question.

QUESTIONS 1–3

Because all dramatic productions begin with a script, there is a constant need for playwrights and scriptwriters. Beginning writers may work on "spec," or speculation; they do not know if their play or screenplay will find a buyer. Playwrights generally submit their work to a theater. The theater may produce the play or hold readings of it. A few theaters have regular positions for playwrights in residence, but in general, even established playwrights work on a freelance, or job–by–job, basis.

This is also true of scriptwriters who write screenplays and teleplays for film and television production companies. Established writers in the broadcasting industry may work steadily for a particular television program, but many writers work on a script–by–script basis.

Stage and screen writers may initially learn their trade in colleges and universities that offer degree programs in play and screenplay writing. Requirements of the programs usually include reading the works of other writers and writing an original play or screenplay.

1. According to the passage, "spec" writers sell their plays or scripts by

   (A) working for a specific theater or production company
   (B) submitting their work to a theater or production company
   (C) first becoming established writers
   (D) holding readings of their work

2. The author makes the point that both playwrights and scriptwriters

   (A) usually begin working on a freelance basis
   (B) usually begin working for one theater or production company
   (C) are required to earn a college degree
   (D) usually begin by writing plays and later writing screenplays

3. Which of the following sentences should NOT be included in a summary of the passage?

   (A) Many writers work on a job–by–job basis.
   (B) Some universities have degree programs in writing for the stage and screen.
   (C) It is difficult to get established as a film or television writer.
   (D) There is always a need for new writers and new dramatic material.

READING

QUESTIONS 4–6

What made Native American and European subsistence cycles so different from one another in colonial America had less to do with their use of plants than with their use of animals. Domesticated grazing animals and the plow were the most distinguishing characteristics of European agricultural practices. The Native Americans' relationship to the deer, moose, and beaver they hunted was far different from that of the Europeans to the pigs, cows, sheep, and horses they owned.

Where Natives had contented themselves with burning the woods and concentrating their hunting in the fall and winter months, the English sought a much more total and year–round control over their animals' lives. The effects of that control could be seen in most aspects of New England's rural economy, and by the end of the colonial period were responsible for a host of changes in the New England landscape: the endless miles of fences, the silenced voices of the vanished wolves, the system of country roads, and the new fields covered with grass, clover, and buttercups.

4. What is the main point the author makes?

   (A) Native Americans and Europeans competed over plants and animals.
   (B) Native Americans and Europeans tried to control animals in New England.
   (C) Europeans had to learn how to hunt the deer, moose, and beaver.
   (D) Native Americans and Europeans differed in their use of animals.

5. The author mentions cows and sheep as examples of

   (A) European subsistence cycles
   (B) animals owned by European settlers
   (C) animals hunted by Native Americans
   (D) animals eaten by wolves

6. Which of the following is NOT mentioned as an agricultural practice of Europeans in New England?

   (A) Burning the woods
   (B) Building fences
   (C) Plowing fields
   (D) Growing grass and clover

QUESTIONS 7–10

A tornado undergoes considerable changes in size, shape, and behavior during its life cycle. The tornado usually develops within a cumulonimbus cloud and subsequently extends toward the ground. We see this stage as a rotating funnel cloud that descends from the cloud base. When the rotating column of air reaches the ground, it becomes a tornado by definition. Sometimes dust and debris begin whirling on the ground before the funnel actually touches down. In weak tornadoes, particularly in dry climates, this ground–level dust whirl may be visible before the funnel cloud.

During the tornado's mature stage, the funnel reaches its greatest width. It is usually nearly vertical, and most of the time is touching the ground, though skipping may occur along a lengthy path. At this time, the tornado causes severe damage to whatever it encounters.

During the tornado's shrinking stage, the funnel narrows and tilts away from its vertical position. Now the path of damage becomes smaller. As the tornado decays, the funnel stretches into a rope shape, and the visible portion becomes contorted and finally dissipates. This stage is often called the *rope stage* because of its appearance.

7. According to the passage, a rotating funnel cloud is defined as a tornado when it

   (A) develops in a cumulonimbus cloud
   (B) is observed by humans
   (C) touches the ground
   (D) causes dust and debris to begin whirling

8. During which stage is a tornado the most dangerous?

   (A) The formation stage
   (B) The mature stage
   (C) The shrinking stage
   (D) The rope stage

9. In its final stage, a tornado resembles

   (A) a dust whirl
   (B) a funnel
   (C) a rope
   (D) a vertical cloud

10. The passage discusses all of the following EXCEPT

    (A) how to recognize a tornado
    (B) the life cycle of a tornado
    (C) the appearance of a tornado
    (D) how to avoid a tornado

Exercise 3.2.B

Read the following passages and choose the one best answer to each question.

QUESTIONS 1–2

About 300 genera and 3,000 species of the *Apiaceae* family exist in the Northern Hemisphere. Nearly a quarter of these genera are native to the United States, with several large genera in the West.

Members of this family are usually aromatic herbs with hollow stems, fern–like leaves, and small flowers in umbels that are further grouped into a compound cluster. The family is important for such foods as carrots, parsnips, and celery and such spices and seasonings as coriander, caraway, anise, parsley, and dill. However, some species are very poisonous.

1. Approximately how many genera of the *Apiaceae* family are native to the United States?

   (A) 25
   (B) 75
   (C) 300
   (D) 3,000

2. Which of the following is NOT mentioned as a member of the *Apiaceae* family?

   (A) Parsnips
   (B) Potatoes
   (C) Carrots
   (D) Parsley

QUESTIONS 3–5

Erik Erikson believed that personality development is a series of turning points, which he described in terms of a tension between desirable qualities and dangers. He emphasized that only when the positive qualities outweigh the dangers does healthy psychosocial development take place.

An important turning point occurs around age six. A child entering school is at a point in development when behavior is dominated by intellectual curiosity and performance. He or she now learns to win recognition by producing things. The child develops a sense of industry. The danger at this stage is that the child may experience feelings of inadequacy or inferiority. If the child is encouraged to make and do things, allowed to finish tasks, and praised for trying, a sense of industry is the result. On the other hand, if the child's efforts are unsuccessful, or if they are criticized or treated as bothersome, a sense of inferiority is the result. For these reasons, Erikson called the period from age six to eleven *Industry vs. Inferiority*.

3. According to Erikson's theory, what desirable quality should develop in a child six to eleven years old?

   (A) A liking for school
   (B) A feeling of inadequacy
   (C) An ability to finish tasks
   (D) A sense of industry

4. According to Erikson's theory, what will happen if a child's efforts are criticized?

   (A) The child will dislike his teacher.
   (B) The child will avoid other children.
   (C) The child will try harder to win recognition.
   (D) The child will feel inferior.

5. *Industry vs. Inferiority* is an example of

   (A) a tension between a positive quality and a danger
   (B) intellectual curiosity
   (C) the difference between a child of six and a child of eleven
   (D) an educational theory

QUESTIONS 6–10

It is not known exactly when people first came to the Americas. However, archaeologists have ruled out the possibility that men and women evolved in the Western Hemisphere because no fossils of pre–*Homo sapiens* have been found there. No remains of the closest cousins of human beings, the great apes, have been found in the Americas, either. Despite these theories, however, many Native American groups believe that they evolved in the Americas. These beliefs must be respected until archaeological findings are more conclusive.

Archaeologists believe that Native Americans originally came from Asia. Estimates of when they came to this continent vary greatly. However, some archaeologists believe that people may have been in the Western Hemisphere as long as 35,000 years.

Most archaeologists use the Bering Strait theory to explain how the first people reached the Western Hemisphere. The Bering Strait is the body of water separating Siberia from Alaska. Archaeologists believe that at various points in prehistory this water receded and a land bridge connected present–day Siberia and Alaska. The early ancestors of Native Americans crossed this stretch of land while hunting animals and plants to eat. Archaeologists do not believe that these immigrants looked like present–day Asian peoples. If we accept this theory, we can think of the ancestors of Native Americans as physically "pre–Asian."

6. Why do many archeologists believe that humans did not evolve in the Americas?

   (A) No studies have been done on this topic.
   (B) Only fossils of the great apes have been found there.
   (C) No fossils of human ancestors have been found there.
   (D) Archaeological findings have not been conclusive.

7. According to the passage, many Native American groups today

   (A) believe they originated in the Americas
   (B) believe their ancestors came from Asia
   (C) are recent immigrants from Asia
   (D) are involved in archaeological study

8. The author makes the point that

   (A) Native American culture began 35,000 years ago
   (B) Native American culture is older than Asian culture
   (C) the history of Native Americans is well–known
   (D) the beliefs of Native Americans must be respected

9. The passage discusses all of the following EXCEPT

   (A) estimates of when people first arrived in the Americas
   (B) proof that Native Americans originally came from Asia
   (C) belief that ancestors of Native Americans came from Asia
   (D) a theory of how the first people arrived in the Americas

10. Which of the following is NOT part of the Bering Strait theory?

   (A) A land bridge used to join what is now Siberia and Alaska.
   (B) The ancestors of Native Americans were hunters.
   (C) The first people who came to the Americas resembled present–day Asian peoples.
   (D) The first people who came to the Western Hemisphere traveled by land.

Exercise 3.2.C

Read the following passages and choose the one best answer to each question.

QUESTIONS 1–4

The youngest child of a prosperous Midwestern manufacturing family, Dorothy Reed was born in 1874 and educated at home by her grandmother. She graduated from Smith College and in 1896 entered Johns Hopkins Medical School. After receiving her M. D., she worked at Johns Hopkins in the laboratories of two noted medical scientists. Reed's research in pathology established conclusively that Hodgkin's disease, until then thought to be a form of tuberculosis, was a distinct disorder characterized by a specific blood cell, which was named the *Reed cell* after her.

Marriage in 1906 to Charles Mendenhall took Reed away from the research laboratory. For ten years, she remained at home as the mother of young children before she returned to professional life. She became a lecturer in Home Economics at the University of Wisconsin, where her principal concerns were collecting data about maternal and child health and preparing courses for new mothers.

Dorothy Reed Mendenhall's career interests were reshaped by the requirements of marriage. Her passion for research was redirected to public health rather than laboratory science. Late in life, she concluded that she could not imagine life without husband and sons, but she hoped for a future when marriage would not have to end a career of laboratory research.

1. Which of the following should NOT be included in a summary of Dorothy Reed Mendenhall's life?

Ⓐ She earned a medical degree at Johns Hopkins Medical School.
Ⓑ Marriage and motherhood left her confused about her career.
Ⓒ The *Reed cell* was named after her.
Ⓓ The latter part of her career was devoted to the health of mothers and children.

2. What was Dorothy Reed's area of research at Johns Hopkins?

Ⓐ Manufacturing
Ⓑ Pathology
Ⓒ Tuberculosis
Ⓓ Maternal health

3. Why did she stop working in the research laboratory?

Ⓐ Marriage required that she remain at home.
Ⓑ She became more interested in public health.
Ⓒ Johns Hopkins did not accept women as laboratory scientists.
Ⓓ Her work on Hodgkin's disease was completed.

4. What did Dorothy Reed Mendenhall conclude about marriage?

Ⓐ It inspired her passion for research.
Ⓑ She would have preferred not to marry and have a family.
Ⓒ It need not prevent women from having careers in laboratory research.
Ⓓ It should be the greatest source of joy for women.

QUESTIONS 5–10

Most early Americans were farmers. As people moved inland, they continued to hunt and farm and supply most of their own needs. However, there were some things they could not produce themselves; for these they relied on traveling peddlers. Peddlers brought pots and pans, scissors, ribbons and lace, spices and medicines.

With the Industrial Revolution in the first half of the nineteenth century, people moved to cities to work in factories. Immigrants from Europe helped swell the population of cities. With so many people clustered together, merchants could set up stores to supply residents' needs.

Before the Civil War, store owners made their own buying trips, or manufacturers visited store owners. Travel by stagecoach, canal boat or steamer was slow and crude, and it was difficult to keep stores stocked. Store owners could not visit every manufacturer, nor could manufacturers visit every store owner. The rise of the wholesaler, who bought large quantities of manufacturers' goods and sold them to store owners, provided an essential link in the distribution process.

After the Civil War, the expansion of railroads had a tremendous impact on marketing and distribution. There was now a speedy and low–cost way to move large quantities of goods over great distances. Railroads could bring goods to markets previously unreachable. Chain stores and mail–order houses flourished as a result of the railroad.

Traveling salespeople multiplied to take merchants' orders. New inventions were coming into the marketplace. Then, as now, sales workers had to sell the public on the ideas behind the new inventions. For instance, people reacted strongly against the typewriter because they thought it would depersonalize correspondence and ruin business. The sewing machine, elevator, and insurance met with similar resistance initially.

5. What does the passage mainly discuss?

(A) The history of marketing and distribution in America
(B) The impact of the Industrial Revolution on American cities
(C) The history of transportation in America
(D) The causes and results of the Civil War

6. The author makes the point that in early America

(A) traveling peddlers made a good living
(B) traveling peddlers bought what they needed from farmers
(C) farmers had to buy things they could not produce on the farm
(D) most people worked in factories in cities

7. By the time of the Civil War, an essential link in the distribution system was

(A) the farmer
(B) the immigrant
(C) the manufacturer
(D) the wholesaler

8. According to the passage, what was one effect of the railroad?

(A) Manufacturers could easily visit every store.
(B) Goods could reach new markets.
(C) The price of goods rose.
(D) Traveling salespeople were no longer necessary.

9. The author mentions the typewriter as an example of

(A) an item supplied by traveling peddlers
(B) a machine people could order by mail
(C) a way to ruin business
(D) an invention people resisted at first

10. The author mentions all of the following EXCEPT

(A) European immigration to America
(B) transportation difficulties before the Civil War
(C) supermarkets and convenience stores
(D) chain stores and mail–order houses

Answers to Exercises 3.2.A through 3.2.C are on page 656.

READING

3.2 EXTENSION

1. Working in pairs, students identify comprehension clues in the passages in Exercises 3.2.A to 3.2.C. Circle transitions and other expressions that help readers understand the ideas within sentences and paragraphs.

2. In reading done outside class, preferably from a textbook, students select a short passage of 1 to 3 paragraphs. Make a photocopy and bring it to class. Working in pairs, students identify main ideas in their passages. Circle details, facts, and other ideas that support the main ideas.

3. Students create "TOEFL questions" to test their classmates' understanding of supporting details in a passage. Select a short passage from a textbook for another class. Working in pairs, students write two questions for each passage. Use the list of detail and supporting idea questions on page 357 for examples of how to word the questions. Then write four answer choices for each question. One must be the correct answer! Use synonyms and paraphrasing in some of the answer choices.

4. Working in pairs, students create "TOEFL questions" with *EXCEPT* and *NOT* to test their classmates' understanding of information that is not in the passage selected in activity #3 above. Use the list of this type of question on page 357. Then write four answer choices. Be careful! This time, three of the answers must be correct and only one incorrect according to the information given in the passage.

Activities #3 and #4 may also be done individually as homework. For both activities, the teacher collects the passages with questions and answer choices, edits them, and uses them in a student–made "TOEFL exam."

ASSESSING PROGRESS – 3.1 through 3.2

QUIZ 2 *(Time – 13 minutes)*

Read the following passages and choose the one best answer to each question. Answer all questions on the basis of what is stated or implied in that passage.

QUESTIONS 1–5

At the turn of the twentieth century, people's attitudes toward money were far more conservative than they are today. Borrowing and being in debt were viewed as a moral failing, almost as a disgrace. Thrift and saving were highly prized, and people who needed to borrow to make ends meet were seen as careless, unreliable, or extravagant. The focus in the economy as a whole was on developing large corporations like railroads, oil companies, and other companies that produced basic goods and services.

Then, in the 1920s, the economy changed. A huge network of banks and financial institutions developed, helping money to move more quickly and easily through the economy. At the same time, the economy was increasing its focus on consumer goods—clothing, cars, household appliances, and other things that individuals buy. To help promote the sale of these items, consumers were encouraged to buy *on credit*. If they could not afford an item right away, a store or a bank might lend them the money, which they could pay back in installments.

With the development of consumer credit and installment purchases, people's attitudes toward debt and spending changed. The model citizen was no longer someone who was thrifty, buying only what he or she needed. People were respected less for being thrifty than for knowing how to use their money to buy as many things as possible—an attitude that persists at the turn of the twenty–first century.

1. What is the main point the author makes in the passage?

   (A) People are generally less conservative than they were in the past.
   (B) Being thrifty is a value that persists at the turn of the twenty–first century.
   (C) In the 1920s, the economy focused more on consumer goods than on corporations.
   (D) Changes in the economy and consumer credit have altered attitudes toward money.

2. According to the passage, which of the following is NOT a belief that was commonly held in the early twentieth century?

   (A) Owing someone money is a moral failing.
   (B) People who save their money are respectable.
   (C) People who buy as many things as possible are respectable.
   (D) People who borrow money for necessities are careless and unreliable.

3. What helped money move more quickly through the economy in the 1920s?

   (A) The growth of railroads
   (B) The growth of banks and financial institutions
   (C) The rate at which people paid back their loans
   (D) The increase in installment purchases

READING

4. The author mentions cars as an example of

(A) a consumer good
(B) a household appliance
(C) an extravagant purchase
(D) a new invention

5. According to the passage, how did the rise of consumer credit change people's attitudes toward debt and spending?

(A) Attitudes toward debt and spending became more conservative.
(B) People used credit to buy only what they needed.
(C) Extravagant borrowing and spending became highly prized.
(D) Spending wisely became more respectable than being thrifty.

Questions 6–10

Range managers—sometimes called range scientists, range ecologists, or range conservationists—manage, improve, and protect range resources to maximize their use without damaging the environment. For example, range managers help ranchers improve livestock production by determining the grazing system to use and the best season for grazing. At the same time, however, they conserve the soil and vegetation for other uses, such as wildlife habitat, outdoor recreation, and timber. While in the field, they may evaluate the water supply and types of vegetation available, take soil samples, and estimate the number of deer and other wildlife on the land.

An essential part of the job is restoring rangelands through controlled burning, reseeding, and biological, chemical, or mechanical control of undesirable plants. For example, some rangelands that have been invaded by sagebrush or other shrubs may be plowed and reseeded with more desirable plants. Range managers also determine the need for, and carry out, range conservation and development plans that provide water for grazing animals, erosion control, and fire prevention.

Range managers usually begin their careers on the range. They often spend considerable time away from home and work outdoors in all kinds of weather. Employers generally supply cars, small planes, or, in rough country, four–wheel–drive vehicles or horses for range managers to get around.

6. The passage primarily discusses

(A) why people become range managers
(B) what range managers do
(C) where range managers work
(D) how to get a job as a range manager

7. Which of the following is NOT mentioned as a duty of a range manager?

(A) Enforcing laws relating to rangelands
(B) Protecting natural resources
(C) Assisting ranchers
(D) Evaluating the water supply

8. According to the passage, restoring rangelands is done by

(A) grazing livestock
(B) hunting undesirable wildlife
(C) chemical fertilization
(D) controlled burning and reseeding

9. If rangeland is invaded by sagebrush or other shrubs,

(A) it may be used for grazing animals
(B) it may need erosion control or fire prevention
(C) it may be reseeded with more desirable plants
(D) it may be sold to a rancher

10. The author makes the point that range managers

(A) need a college degree
(B) prefer working outdoors over working in an office
(C) work outdoors in all kinds of weather
(D) must own a four–wheel drive vehicle or horse

Answers to Reading Quiz 2 are on page 656.

3.3 Locating Referents

FOCUS

Read the following paragraph.

> In looking at a hologram, each eye sees many points formed by different sets of layers in the interference pattern. This gives an image of an object. The two eyes look at different parts of the hologram and therefore see separate images of the object. The brain combines them to give a three–dimensional image.

Look at the underlined word *them* in the last sentence. What word or phrase could replace *them* and still have the sentence make sense?

When you reread the sentence before that, you can see that *them* refers to *separate images of the object*. You can check this by replacing *them* in the sentence: *The brain combines separate images of the object to give a three–dimensional image.*

Now, read another paragraph. Look at the underlined word *its* in the first sentence.

> An aggressive bird, the eagle will often steal the catch of an osprey or other bird in favor of finding its own. Occasionally, a pair of eagles will team up to catch a gull or diving bird, with each eagle taking a turn at striking the bird when it surfaces from its dive and following above as it attempts to escape underwater.

What word or phrase could replace *its* and still have the sentence make sense?

If you change *its* to *the eagle's* the sentence will have the same meaning. You can rewrite the sentence like this: *An aggressive bird, the eagle will often steal the catch of an osprey or other bird in favor of finding the eagle's own.*

The eagle's is the ***referent*** of *its*. *Its* is used to avoid repetition of the *eagle's*.

Now, look at the other underlined words in the paragraph. What word or phrase could replace each word?

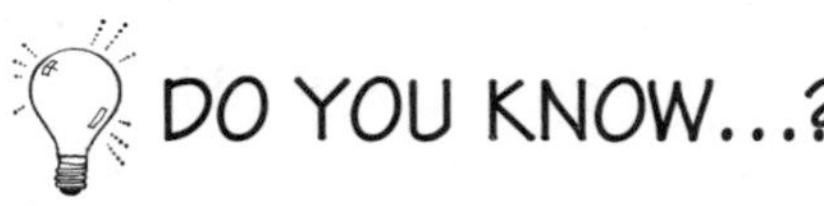

1. Approximately five items on the TOEFL will test your ability to locate words and phrases that are the referents of pronouns and other words.

2. ***Referents*** are words in a passage that other words refer to. Pronouns such as *they* and *it* have noun referents; the referents are the nouns that are replaced by the pronouns (See 2.15). Words such as *that*, *these*, and *some* also have referents. The referents are other words or phrases appearing in the same passage.

   Usually, the referent is mentioned before the referring word in the passage, often immediately before it, but sometimes the referent appears later. The referent may be in the same sentence or in another sentence.

   Look at some examples. The referent for each underlined word is shown in italics.

   The refraction of light by <u>its</u> internal layers causes *the moonstone's* milky sheen.

   The tallest peak of the Rockies is twice as high as <u>that</u> of the Appalachians.

   Most *daisies* are perennials, but <u>some</u> bloom for only one or two seasons.

   Some words that have referents are:

Subject Pronouns	he	she	it	they
Object Pronouns	him	her	it	them
Possessive Adjectives	his	her	its	their
Possessive Pronouns	his	hers	—	theirs
Demonstratives	this	that	these	those
Indefinite Pronouns	all each one	another many others	any most several	both none some

3. The most common type of referent question on the TOEFL asks you to locate the referent of a pronoun or possessive adjective. However, sometimes you must identify the referent of a specified term or phrase.

   Look at the underlined phrase in the following passage:

   > Like the gray and fox squirrels, the Eastern chipmunk often feeds on acorns and hickory nuts. Essentially a ground species, <u>this pert rodent</u> does not hesitate to climb large oak trees when the acorns are ripe.

   This pert rodent refers to *the Eastern chipmunk*, which is the subject of both sentences in the passage.

   Use both the function and the meaning of the referring words and referents to determine the correct answer to referent questions on the TOEFL.

READING

Check to see if your answer choice is correct by putting it in the sentence. If the both the structure and the meaning of the sentence still make sense, your answer is correct.

In the following sentences, circle the words or phrases that the underlined words refer to. Draw a line to connect the two.

a. A study of 500 people undergoing outpatient surgery found that those who smoked within 24 hours of having general anesthesia were much less likely to receive enough oxygen to their heart during surgery.

b. Some elements, such as hydrogen and oxygen, are gases at normal temperatures, others are solids, and only two, bromine and mercury, are liquids.

c. Electromagnetism is the relationship between electricity and magnetism; either can be used to produce the other.

d. Despite the vampire bat's tiny size—its body is no larger than that of a mouse—this blood–sucking creature is a threat to cattle in its native Latin America.

(***Answers***: a. *Those* refers to *people undergoing outpatient surgery*. b. *Others* refers to *elements*; *two* refers to *elements*, specifically *bromine and mercury*. c. *Either* refers to *electricity* or *magnetism*. d. *That* refers to *body*; *this blood–sucking creature* refers to *the vampire bat*.)

4. On the paper test, questions about referents look like this:

> The word "_____" in line __ refers to _____.
> The phrase "_____" in line __ refers to _____.

Look at these examples:

QUESTIONS 1–2

Parasites such as viruses, bacteria, and fungi—the causes of most disease—specialize in breaking into cells, either to eat them, as fungi and bacteria do, or, like viruses, to subvert their genetic machinery for the purpose of making new viruses. Either way, they must get into cells. To do that, they employ protein molecules that fit into, or bind to, other molecules on cell surfaces. The struggle between parasites and their hosts is all about these binding procedures.

1. The word "their" in line 3 refers to

(A) parasites
(B) viruses
(C) fungi
(D) cells

2. The word "they" in line 4 refers to

(A) parasites
(B) diseases
(C) cells
(D) protein molecules

The correct answer to question 1 is (D), *cells*, because it is *the cells'* genetic machinery that viruses subvert. *Parasites*, *viruses*, and *fungi* all specialize in breaking into cells.

You can check the answer by replacing *their* with *cells'* in the sentence.

The correct answer to question 2 is (A), *parasites*. It is *parasites* such as viruses, bacteria, and fungi that specialize in breaking into cells. *Parasites* is the subject of the first sentence, and *they* is the subject of the next the two sentences (line 4). This parallel position is a structural clue that helps you see that *they* refers to *parasites*.

You can check the answer by replacing *they* with *parasites*.

5. On the computer test, questions about referents look like this:

> Look at the word _____ in the passage. Click on the word or phrase in the **bold** text that _____ refers to.

To answer, use the mouse to click on the word or phrase in the passage that is the referent of the word or phrase specified in the question.

Look at an example:

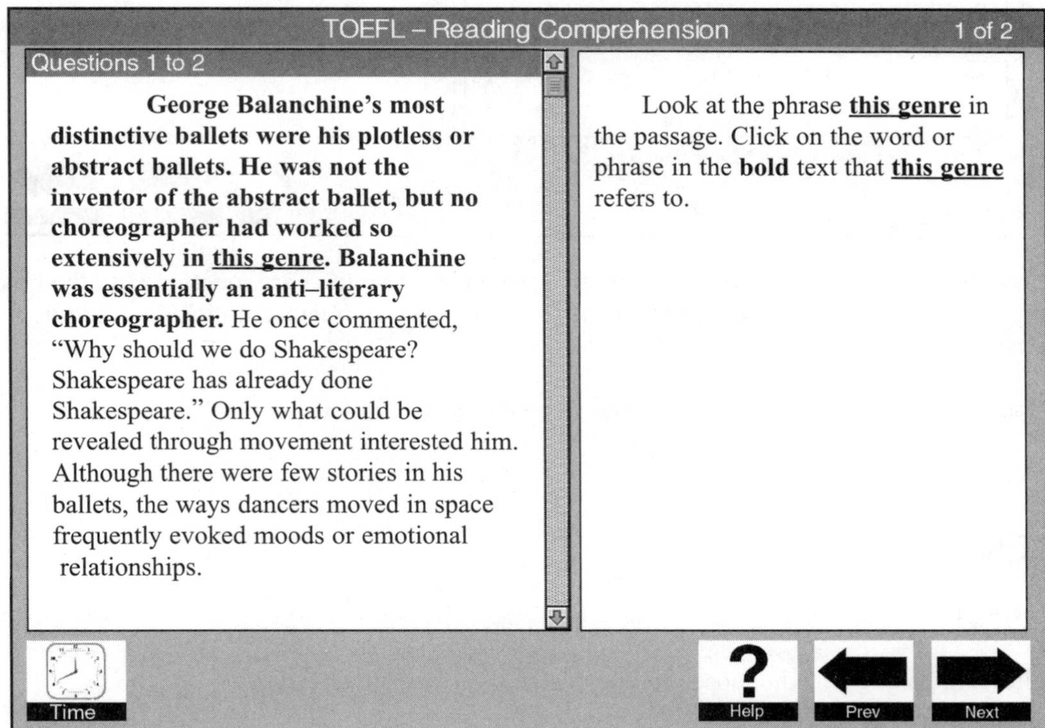

TOEFL – Reading Comprehension
1 of 2
Questions 1 to 2
George Balanchine's most distinctive ballets were his plotless or abstract ballets. He was not the inventor of the abstract ballet, but no choreographer had worked so extensively in this genre. Balanchine was essentially an anti–literary choreographer. He once commented, "Why should we do Shakespeare? Shakespeare has already done Shakespeare." Only what could be revealed through movement interested him. Although there were few stories in his ballets, the ways dancers moved in space frequently evoked moods or emotional relationships.
Look at the phrase this genre in the passage. Click on the word or phrase in the **bold** text that this genre refers to.
Time
Help
Prev
Next

The correct answer is found in the bold text in the passage.

Key phrases in the first sentence—*most distinctive ballets*, *plotless or abstract ballets*— tell you the subject of the passage is George Balanchine's abstract ballets.

The referent of *this genre* is found in the second sentence: *He was not the inventor of the abstract ballet, but no choreographer had worked so extensively in this genre*. Notice that both *the abstract ballet* and *this genre* are objects of prepositions and are in parallel positions in their clauses—a structural clue that helps you find the answer.

The abstract ballet is a type of ballet. *Genre* is a synonym for *type*.

You should click on *the abstract ballet* as the phrase that *this genre* refers to.

Look at another example:

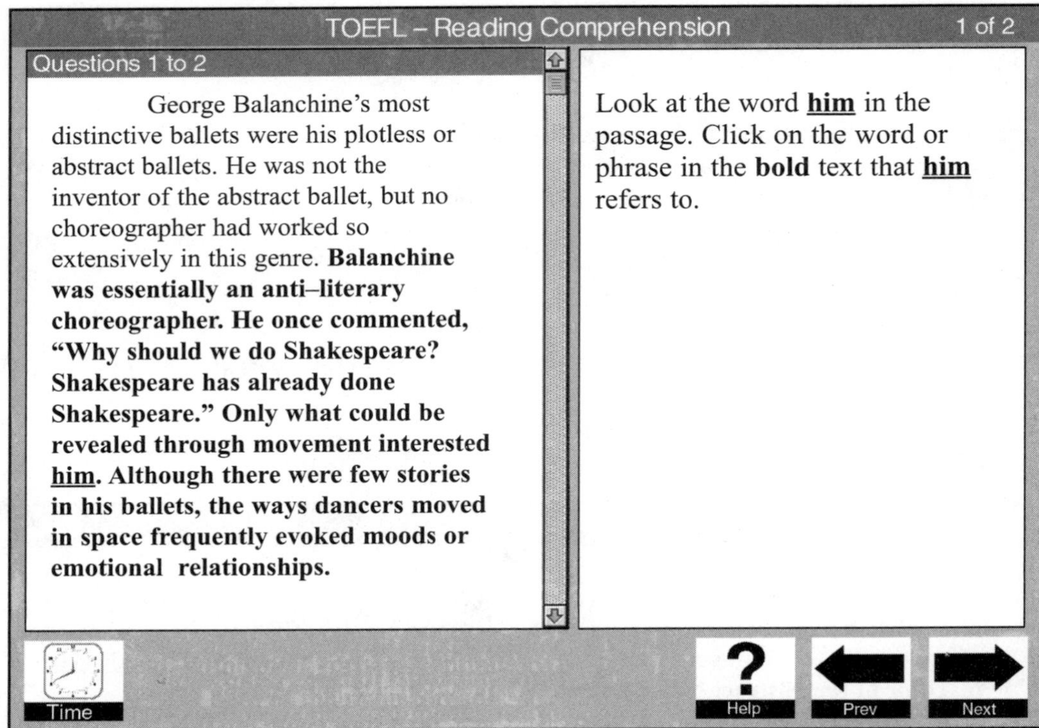
TOEFL – Reading Comprehension
1 of 2
Questions 1 to 2
George Balanchine's most distinctive ballets were his plotless or abstract ballets. He was not the inventor of the abstract ballet, but no choreographer had worked so extensively in this genre. **Balanchine was essentially an anti–literary choreographer. He once commented, "Why should we do Shakespeare? Shakespeare has already done Shakespeare." Only what could be revealed through movement interested him. Although there were few stories in his ballets, the ways dancers moved in space frequently evoked moods or emotional relationships.**
Look at the word **him** in the passage. Click on the word or phrase in the **bold** text that **him** refers to.
Time
Help
Prev
Next

You know that the pronoun *him* refers to a man. Only two men are mentioned in the bold text of the passage: *Balanchine* and *Shakespeare*. Which one was interested in *what could be revealed through movement*?

You should click on *Balanchine* as the word that *him* refers to.

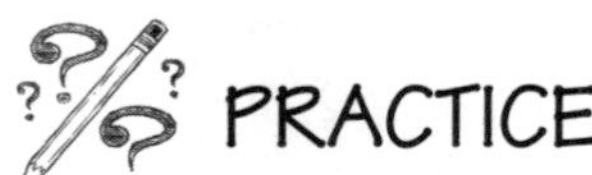
PRACTICE

Exercise 3.3.A

Read the following passages and choose the one best answer to each question.

QUESTION 1

In the highlands of Ethiopia in the first century, the kingdom of Axum, apparently founded by Asian emigrants from the Arabian Peninsula, was approaching a high cultural level. Around the year 50, it had established extensive trade with neighboring Kush, and had become the center of the ivory market, linked by trade to other African communities as well as to the Arabian Peninsula.

1. The word "it" in line 3 refers to

(A) Ethiopia
(B) the kingdom of Axum
(C) the Arabian Peninsula
(D) Kush

QUESTION 2

When you raise vegetables, you become acutely aware of the sun, rain, and most of all, the life–giving soil. You work with these natural elements and sometimes battle them to produce nutritious food for your table. Success brings an age–old satisfaction that goes back to the days when there were no supermarkets. The rhythm of sowing, growing, and harvesting can be just as valuable to your well–being as the vitamin– and mineral–rich harvest you eat, freeze, or can.

2. The phrase "these natural elements" in line 2 refers to

(A) vegetables
(B) sun, rain, and soil
(C) sowing, growing, and harvesting
(D) vitamins and minerals

QUESTIONS 3–4

A revolution currently taking place in the field of mathematics is the successful use of mathematics as a fundamental tool to study human beings: their behavior, values, interactions, conflicts, organizations, and decision making, as well as their interface with technology. This revolution could eventually prove to be as far reaching as the turning of mathematics to study physical objects and their motion three centuries ago. As mathematics and computers play an increasingly important role in understanding our social institutions, a new profession is emerging that is devoted to thinking mathematically about human affairs.

3. The word "their" in lines 2 and 3 refers to

(A) mathematics
(B) fundamental tools
(C) human beings
(D) revolutions

4. The word "their" in line 5 refers to

(A) human beings
(B) physical objects
(C) computers
(D) human affairs

QUESTIONS 5–6

He was never called an exciting actor, but "Duke"—the strong, silent cowboy who stood for all that was good and solid about America—is recognized today as the biggest moneymaker in movie history. John Wayne had been in films since 1928 and had made literally hundreds of cheap Westerns and adventure epics before director John Ford starred him in *Stagecoach* in 1939. His box–office status climbed throughout the next decade, but he did not break through as a top star until the late 1940s, when he appeared in the Westerns *Fort Apache* and *Red River*, as well as the World War II epic *Sands of Iwo Jima*.

5. The word "Duke" in line 1 refers to

(A) an exciting actor
(B) John Wayne
(C) the name of a film
(D) John Ford

6. The phrase "the next decade" in lines 5 and 6 refers to

(A) ten Westerns
(B) several epics
(C) the 1930s
(D) the 1940s

READING

Exercise 3.3.B

Read the following passages and choose the one best answer to each question.

QUESTIONS 1–2

Digital record players and digital audio discs, or *compact discs*, were introduced in the United States in 1983. The initial sales were small, but as discs and players came down in price, their sales increased dramatically. The compact disc, or CD, is less than five inches in diameter and has only one playable side. It can, however, hold more than 60 minutes of music. It is played on a digital record player that uses a laser beam to scan the recorded surface.

In digital recording, a computer samples 44,000 bits of sound per second and assigns each a numerical value. The numbers are then recorded in pits imbedded in the disc. It is these numbers that are read by the laser beam and changed back into sound.

1. The word "their" in line 3 refers to

(A) compact discs
(B) discs and players
(C) new recordings
(D) laser beams

2. The word "each" in line 8 refers to

(A) compact disc
(B) computer
(C) bit of sound
(D) number

QUESTIONS 3–6

When England's Charles II granted to William Penn the entire tract of land west of the Delaware River between New York and Maryland, Penn became the proprietor of an immense and fertile domain. Penn insisted on religious toleration and welcomed all races and creeds into Pennsylvania. Foreseeing the economic possibilities of the region, he offered attractive terms to settlers and soon large numbers of immigrants came. To the original Swedes, Dutch, and English were added Welsh, Irish, Swiss, and Germans. The population of Pennsylvania jumped from 2,000 in 1682 to 200,000 by 1750. Philadelphia was by then the greatest center of population, wealth, and culture in the American colonies.

Penn planned his capital city of Philadelphia well. He appointed a commission to choose the site and lay out a regular pattern of streets. There were nine broad streets between the two rivers, and these were crossed by 21 shorter streets to divide the town into rectangular blocks. Five areas were set aside as public squares, which in time were planted in grass. Penn also desired that each house be placed in the middle of its lot and surrounded by gardens and shade trees.

3. The phrase "the region" in line 4 refers to

(A) New York
(B) Maryland
(C) Pennsylvania
(D) Philadelphia

4. The word "these" in line 12 refers to

(A) the commissioners
(B) the patterns
(C) nine broad streets
(D) two rivers

5. The word "its" in line 14 refers to

(A) Philadelphia
(B) a public square
(C) the grass
(D) each house

6. The passage supports all of the following statements EXCEPT

(A) William Penn wanted Pennsylvania to be settled only by religious people.
(B) William Penn encouraged the economic development of Pennsylvania.
(C) Pennsylvania's population grew rapidly in the early eighteenth century.
(D) Philadelphia was an important city in colonial America.

QUESTIONS 7–10

Saturn, last of the planets visible to the unaided eye, is almost twice as far from the sun as Jupiter. It is second in size to Jupiter, but its mass is much smaller. Saturn's specific gravity is less than that of water. Its diameter is about 71,000 miles at the equator; its rotational speed spins it completely around in a little more than ten hours. Saturn's atmosphere is much like that of Jupiter, except that the temperature at the top of its cloud layer is at least 100 degrees F. lower. Saturn's theoretical construction resembles that of Jupiter; it is either all gas, or it has a small dense center surrounded by a layer of liquid and a deep atmosphere.

Saturn's ring system begins about 7,000 miles above the visible disk of Saturn, lying above its equator and extending about 35,000 miles into space. The diameter of the ring system visible from Earth is about 170,000 miles; the rings are estimated to be no thicker than ten miles. The ring particles are large chunks of material averaging a meter on each side.

7. The word "its" in lines 3 and 4 refers to

(A) Saturn
(B) the sun
(C) Jupiter
(D) Earth

8. The word "that" in line 5 refers to

(A) the diameter
(B) the rotational speed
(C) the atmosphere
(D) the temperature

9. The word "it" in line 7 refers to

(A) Saturn's atmosphere
(B) Saturn's theoretical construction
(C) Jupiter's cloud temperatures
(D) Saturn's ring system

10. According to the passage, which of the following is NOT a characteristic of Saturn's ring system?

(A) It reaches 35,000 miles into space.
(B) It can be seen from Earth.
(C) The rings are more than ten miles thick.
(D) Most of the ring particles are around a meter thick.

READING

Exercise 3.3.C

Read each passage and follow the directions on the right side of the screen.

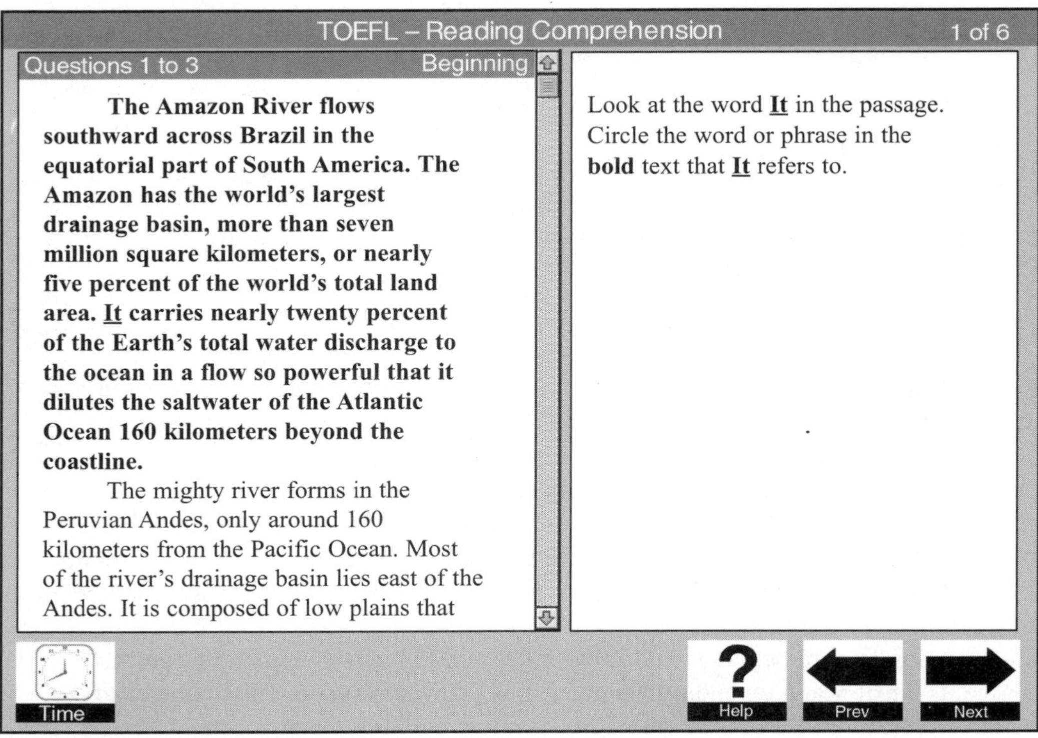

TOEFL – Reading Comprehension
1 of 6
Questions 1 to 3
Beginning
The Amazon River flows southward across Brazil in the equatorial part of South America. The Amazon has the world's largest drainage basin, more than seven million square kilometers, or nearly five percent of the world's total land area. It carries nearly twenty percent of the Earth's total water discharge to the ocean in a flow so powerful that it dilutes the saltwater of the Atlantic Ocean 160 kilometers beyond the coastline.
The mighty river forms in the Peruvian Andes, only around 160 kilometers from the Pacific Ocean. Most of the river's drainage basin lies east of the Andes. It is composed of low plains that
Look at the word It in the passage. Circle the word or phrase in the **bold** text that It refers to.
Time
Help
Prev
Next

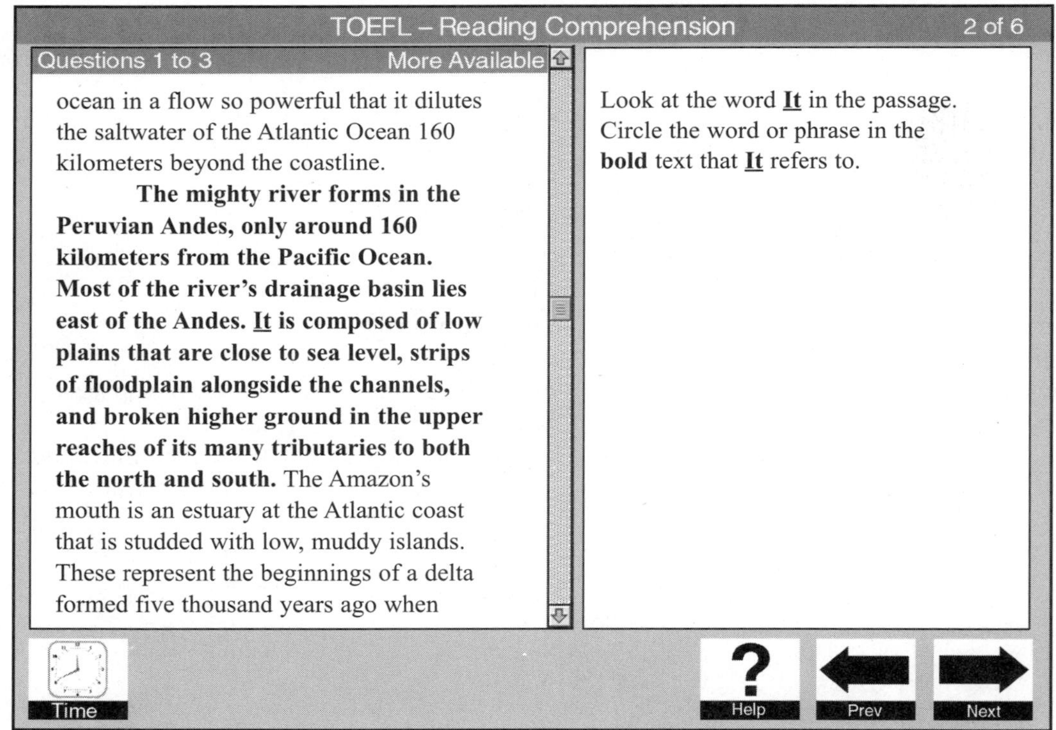

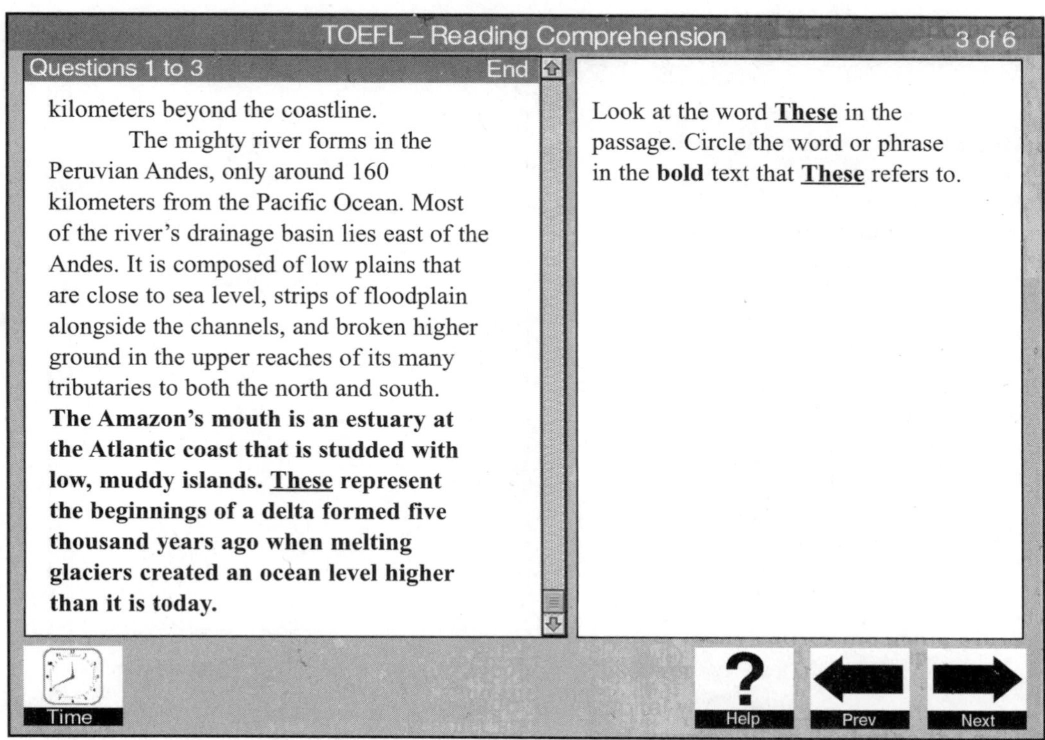
TOEFL – Reading Comprehension 3 of 6

Questions 1 to 3 End

kilometers beyond the coastline.

The mighty river forms in the Peruvian Andes, only around 160 kilometers from the Pacific Ocean. Most of the river's drainage basin lies east of the Andes. It is composed of low plains that are close to sea level, strips of floodplain alongside the channels, and broken higher ground in the upper reaches of its many tributaries to both the north and south. **The Amazon's mouth is an estuary at the Atlantic coast that is studded with low, muddy islands. <u>These</u> represent the beginnings of a delta formed five thousand years ago when melting glaciers created an ocean level higher than it is today.**

Look at the word **<u>These</u>** in the passage. Circle the word or phrase in the **bold** text that **<u>These</u>** refers to.

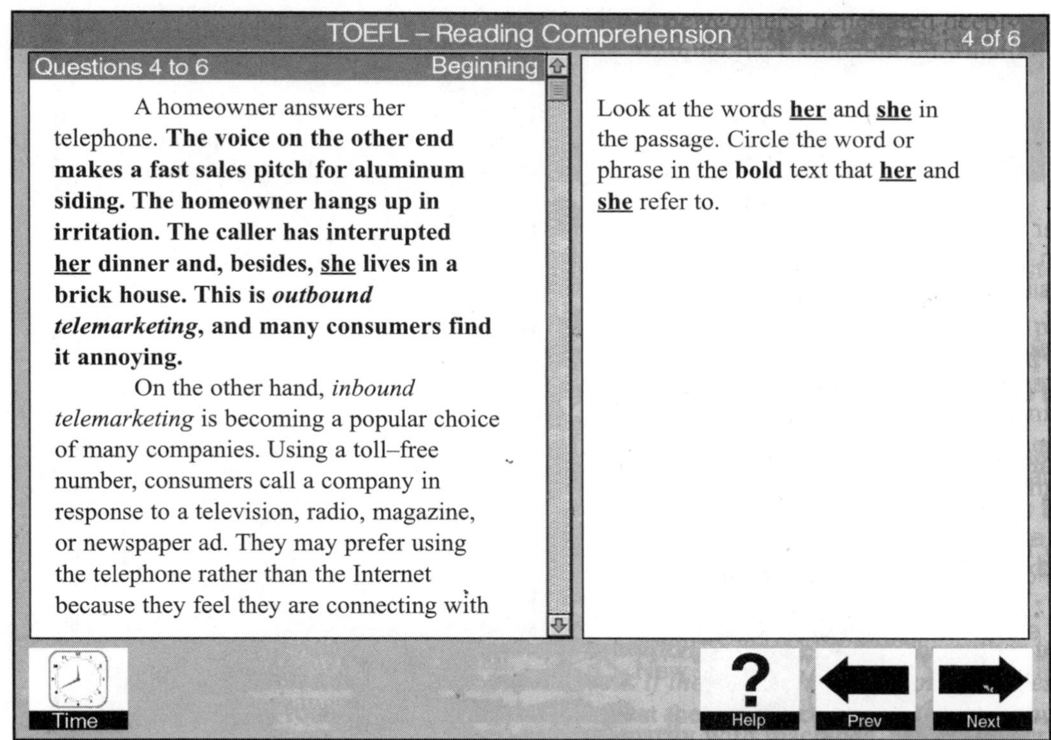
TOEFL – Reading Comprehension 4 of 6

Questions 4 to 6 Beginning

A homeowner answers her telephone. **The voice on the other end makes a fast sales pitch for aluminum siding. The homeowner hangs up in irritation. The caller has interrupted <u>her</u> dinner and, besides, <u>she</u> lives in a brick house. This is *outbound telemarketing*, and many consumers find it annoying.**

On the other hand, *inbound telemarketing* is becoming a popular choice of many companies. Using a toll–free number, consumers call a company in response to a television, radio, magazine, or newspaper ad. They may prefer using the telephone rather than the Internet because they feel they are connecting with

Look at the words **<u>her</u>** and **<u>she</u>** in the passage. Circle the word or phrase in the **bold** text that **<u>her</u>** and **<u>she</u>** refer to.

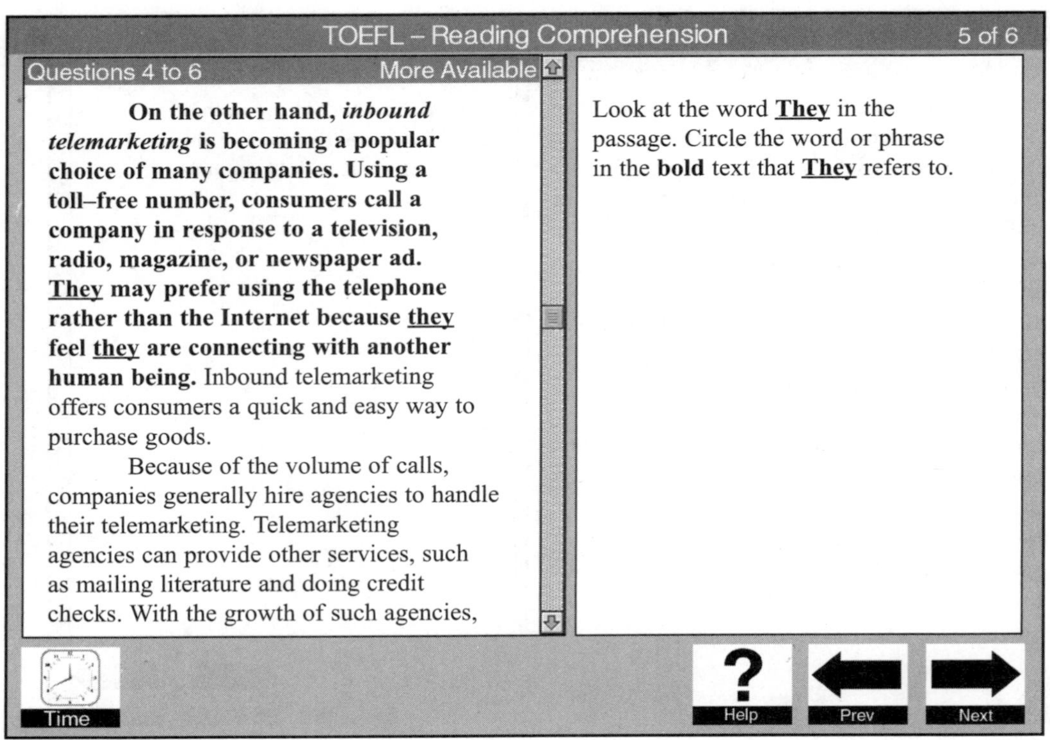

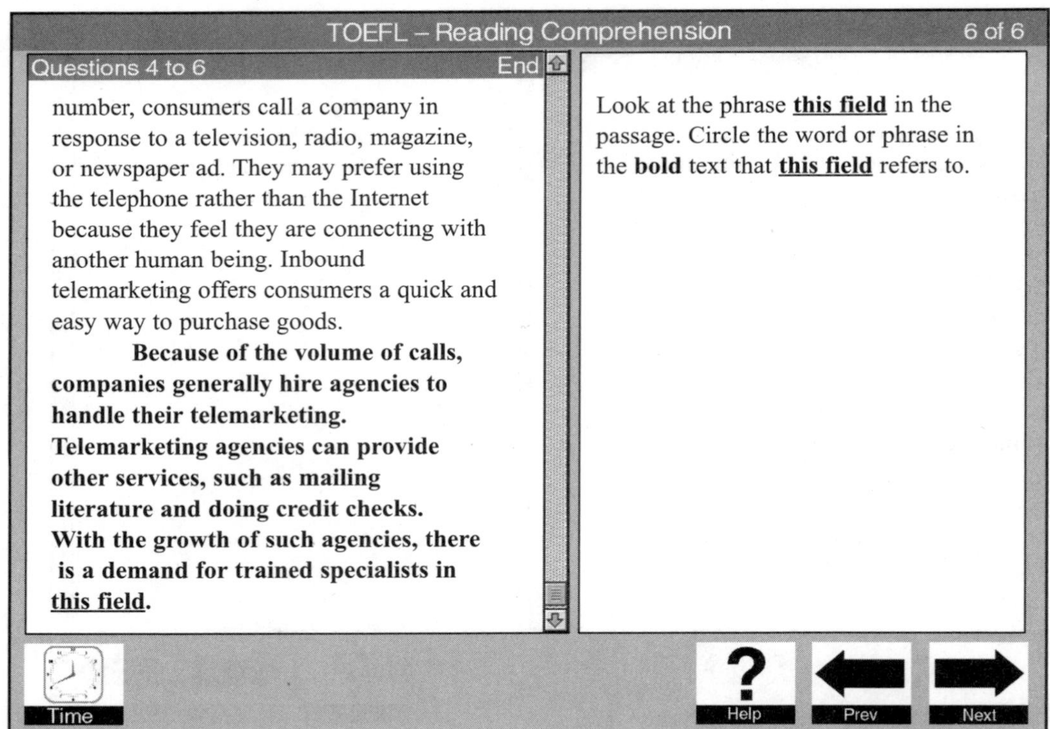

Answers to Exercises 3.3.A through 3.3.C are on pages 656 and 657.

3.3 EXTENSION

1. In reading done outside class, students select a short passage of 1 to 3 paragraphs. In the passage, students circle all pronouns and words that refer to other words. Draw a line to connect referring words with their referents.

2. Students create "TOEFL questions" to test their classmates' understanding of referents. Select a short passage from a textbook or magazine. Working in pairs, students locate one pronoun or other word that refers to another word or phrase in the passage. For each pronoun/referring word, locate the true referent and three false referents nearby. Use these to write a TOEFL item and four answer choices. Make the three incorrect answers agree in number (singular/plural) so that classmates must work harder to find the correct answer!

3. In reading done outside class, students select a short passage (the passage selected for #1 above may be used). In the passage, students locate 2 or 3 pronouns/referring words and their referents. On a sheet of paper, an overhead projector transparency, or a computer, rewrite the passage, omitting pronouns and referents and leaving blank spaces where they should be. Below the passage, write the missing words in mixed–up order. Classmates must fill in the blanks correctly. Look at the example below:

> _____ burn uncontrolled in a forested, wooded, or scrubby area. Forest fires occur chiefly in old–growth or second–growth forest. Brush fires are _____ that occur in scrub areas. Fires inject tremendous amounts of microscopic _____ into the atmosphere. _____ may be considered pollutants by people living downwind from a fire, but _____ are essential to the generation of clouds and precipitation.

ASH PARTICLES THEY WILDFIRES THESE PARTICLES THOSE

READING

ASSESSING PROGRESS – 3.1 through 3.3

QUIZ 3 (Time – 22 minutes)

Read the following passages and choose the one best answer to each question. Answer all questions on the basis of what is stated or implied in that passage.

QUESTIONS 1–6

Depression is the term used to describe the most severe type of recession in an economy. During the Great Depression that began in 1929, for example, almost one–third of the United States work force was unemployed. Hundreds of thousands of people were suddenly poor. Many were thrown out of their apartments because they could not pay their rent, or they had their homes taken away when they could not pay their mortgages. Farmers lost their farms, small business owners lost their businesses, and many big business owners had trouble selling their products and keeping their companies going.

A topic on which economists disagree is how to stop a depression. Many people believe that President Ronald Reagan was successful in stopping the recession of the 1970s by cutting taxes on corporations, removing other restrictions on businesses, increasing military spending, and cutting back on government social programs. Other people believe that, although some people benefited from Reagan's policies, many others fell into severe poverty as a result. Furthermore, critics charge, the prosperity that Reagan created lasted only a short time, and was followed by more severe economic problems.

1. With what topic is paragraph 1 mainly concerned?

   (A) Causes of economic recession
   (B) Effects of the Great Depression
   (C) Economic hardship and unemployment
   (D) The economy since 1929

2. The word "Many" in line 4 refers to

   (A) recessions
   (B) farmers
   (C) big business owners
   (D) unemployed people

3. The word "their" in line 7 refers to

   (A) farmers
   (B) small business owners
   (C) big business owners
   (D) customers

4. The word "others" in line 12 refers to

   (A) policies
   (B) social programs
   (C) people
   (D) businesses

5. According to the passage, critics of President Reagan believe

   (A) Reagan's policies resulted in more serious economic problems
   (B) the recession of the 1970s ended when Reagan became president
   (C) Reagan cut taxes and increased military spending to stimulate the economy
   (D) Reagan's policies created more wealth for a large number of people

6. Which of the following should NOT be included in a summary of the passage?

   (A) The Great Depression caused unemployment and business failures.
   (B) President Reagan's childhood during the Great Depression shaped his philosophy.
   (C) The most serious type of recession is a depression.
   (D) People disagree over the success of President Reagan's economic policies.

Questions 7–12

The old–time merchant in a village store used the power of persuasion to get people to buy. Today the continued growth of self–service has resulted in the decline of personalized selling in many retail outlets. Retailers and manufacturers rely more and more on other means to induce customers to buy. Merchandising is one of these means.

Today's retailers use a number of persuasive merchandising techniques such as displays and the positioning of goods in the store. Retailers put goods they are trying to move at eye level because items placed there sell faster than those placed either too high or too low. Retailers also favor jumbled displays that customers can root through and examine instead of neatly constructed pyramids that buyers dare not touch for fear of knocking them down.

Department stores and specialty shops employ display workers to plan and construct displays. Many display workers have training in design and business. Window displays draw consumers into the store. In–store displays of merchandise encourage shoppers to stop and look. In the process of looking, they are likely to pick up and buy additional items they had not planned on buying.

7. What is the main idea of the passage?

   (A) Self–service has caused a decline in the number of retail stores.
   (B) The old–time merchant has been replaced by the display worker.
   (C) Merchandising is a growing area of specialization.
   (D) Merchandising is a way for retail stores to persuade shoppers to buy goods.

8. The author mentions the positioning of goods in the store as an example of

   (A) self–service
   (B) a merchandising technique
   (C) a pyramid
   (D) training in design

9. The word "there" in line 7 refers to

   (A) at eye level
   (B) in a retail store
   (C) on a pyramid
   (D) in a store window

10. The word "those" in line 7 refers to

   (A) retailers
   (B) displays
   (C) items
   (D) techniques

11. The passage mentions all of the following as merchandising techniques EXCEPT

   (A) shopping carts
   (B) placement of goods
   (C) jumbled arrangements
   (D) window displays

12. The word "they" in lines 14 and 15 refers to

   (A) retailers
   (B) display workers
   (C) in–store displays
   (D) shoppers

QUESTIONS 13–20

Active primarily at night, and at dusk and dawn, muskrats nonetheless may be seen at any time of day in all seasons, especially spring. Excellent swimmers, these aquatic rodents spend much of their time in water. Propelled along by their slightly webbed hind feet and using their rudderlike tail for guidance, they can swim backward or forward with ease. They dislike strong currents and avoid rocky areas.

Their mouths close behind protruding incisors, thus allowing them to chew underwater. They can remain submerged for long periods, traveling great distances underwater. One muskrat was filmed underwater for 17 minutes, coming to the surface for air for 3 seconds, then submerging for another 10 minutes.

Their large houses commonly contain one nesting chamber with one or more underwater entrances. Houses constructed along banks may have several chambers, each with one or more tunnels leading underwater. The houses and feeding platforms are added to as long as they are used; they usually house only one individual, though several muskrats may live together harmoniously. Food is commonly towed out to the feeding platforms, which can be distinguished from the houses by plant cuttings and other scattered debris from eating. Houses are kept immaculately clean, with litter deposited on logs and rocks outside.

Droughts and flooding are common hazards faced by these rodents, causing periodic population fluctuations. Overcrowding, especially when it occurs during fall or winter, causes fighting among individuals, forcing many to travel several miles overland to seek a new place to live.

13. What does the passage mainly discuss?

(A) Animals that live near water
(B) Physical characteristics of the muskrat
(C) The living habits of the muskrat
(D) Muskrat houses

14. Which of the following is NOT mentioned as a characteristic of the muskrat?

(A) Bushy tail
(B) Webbed feet
(C) Swimming ability
(D) Ability to stay underwater

15. The author makes the point that the construction of the muskrat's mouth

(A) makes it a plant eater
(B) allows it to stay underwater a long time
(C) allows it to eat underwater
(D) allows it to catch fish easily

16. The word "They" in line 7 refers to

(A) muskrats
(B) incisors
(C) webbed feet
(D) mouths

17. The word "they" in line 13 refers to

(A) plant cuttings and debris
(B) underwater entrances
(C) nesting chambers
(D) houses and feeding platforms

18. How can one tell the difference between muskrat houses and feeding platforms?

(A) Houses have more chambers than feeding platforms.
(B) Houses are cleaner than feeding platforms.
(C) Feeding platforms can hold several muskrats.
(D) Houses are underwater.

19. The phrase "these rodents" in line 18 refers to

(A) muskrat houses
(B) food
(C) muskrats
(D) enemies of muskrats

20. The author mentions overcrowding as

(A) being rare in muskrat houses
(B) the reason many muskrats must relocate
(C) the reason litter surrounds the muskrat's house
(D) a cause of flooding during fall or winter

Answers to Reading Quiz 3 are on page 657.

3.4 Understanding Vocabulary in Context

Read the following paragraph and answer the question.

> Thomas Edison's staff began making films for the peep shows in 1893. A special tarpaper studio, affectionately called the Black Maria, was built in East Orange, New Jersey. It stood on a revolving platform and could be turned to take maximum advantage of the sunlight.
>
> What was the "Black Maria?"
>
> ◯ Thomas Edison's first film
> ◯ A peep show
> ◯ A film studio
> ◯ A revolving platform

First, scan the paragraph to find *Black Maria*. It appears in an adjective phrase, *affectionately called the Black Maria* (See 2.10). This phrase modifies *studio*—a structural clue that helps you see the Black Maria was *a film studio*, the third answer choice.

By the way, tarpaper is a kind of paper that has been coated with tar, which makes it black!

Now, read another paragraph and answer the question.

> Tobacco was grown and much prized by the Native Americans, not only for smoking but also for religious purposes. Masks used in ceremonials were consecrated by attaching bags of tobacco to them. Tobacco was also burned as an incense, and the rising smoke was a visible prayer.
>
> The word "consecrated" in line 3 is closest in meaning to
>
> ◯ made heavy
> ◯ made sacred
> ◯ made beautiful
> ◯ smoked

Scan the third line to find *consecrated*. You can see it is a verb expressing something that is done to masks used in ceremonials. What other clues are there in the paragraph?

The correct meaning of *consecrated* is *made sacred*, the second answer choice. This meaning best fits the context of the paragraph.

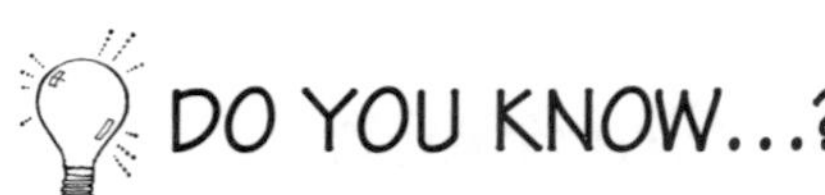

DO YOU KNOW...?

1. Approximately twelve items on the TOEFL will test your comprehension of words and phrases in the context of the passages you read. For each individual passage, two or three questions will ask you about the meaning of vocabulary.

2. The ***context*** is the setting—the sentence and paragraph—in which a word or phrase appears. The meaning of a word or phrase ***in context*** is its meaning in the particular sentence and paragraph in which it is used. A single English word can have many different meanings. Its precise meaning always depends on the context in which it is used.

   To understand the meaning of a word in context, you must use different types of ***context clues***—that is, your knowledge of structure, punctuation, and the meaning of other words in the same sentence or paragraph.

   In the reading you do in class and the real world, there may not always be context clues to help you. However, sometimes you can guess the probable meaning of an unfamiliar word by using your overall understanding of the ideas in a passage as well as your common sense and knowledge of the world.

3. ***Structural clues*** are a type of context clue. Structural clues are certain words, phrases, and grammatical structures that point to the relationships among the various parts of a sentence. These clues help you understand the meaning of unfamiliar words by showing you how they relate to other words and ideas in the sentence.

   Words and phrases can be defined by these structural clues:

   Be:

   > Everyone faces times when one goal or another has to come first; deciding which goals are most important *is* setting <u>priorities</u>.

   The meaning of *priorities* is given by the information that comes before the verb *is*. *Priorities* are the most important goals.

   Or:

   > A <u>skyscraper</u>, *or* building more than twenty stories high, is built on a foundation of reinforced concrete piers supported by piles driven into the ground.

   The meaning of *skyscraper* is given by the information following *or*. A *skyscraper* is a building more than twenty stories high.

   Appositive:

   > Thermal power stations are designed to pass as much energy as possible from the fuel to the <u>turbines</u>, *machines whose blades are turned by the movement of the steam.*

   The meaning of *turbines* is given by the appositive (See 2.2), the noun phrase following the comma. *Turbines* are machines with blades that are turned by the movement of the steam.

Adjective clause or phrase:

> The sun crosses the equator twice a year at the equinoxes, *when day and night are nearly equal in length.*
>
> Prescribed fire, *ignited by forest rangers under controlled conditions to restore balance in the forest*, is a safe way to mimic natural fire conditions.

The meaning of *equinoxes* is given in the adjective clause *when day and night are nearly equal in length* (See 2.10). *Equinoxes* are the times when day and night are almost equal.

The meaning of *prescribed* is given in the adjective phrase *ignited by forest rangers under controlled conditions to restore balance in the forest* (See 2.10). *Prescribed* describes something done or recommended as a treatment to make something better.

List or series:

> Because of their similar teeth, seals and walruses are believed to have evolved from the same ancestral groups as *the weasels, badgers, and other* mustelids.

The meaning of *mustelids* is given by the other words in the list: *the weasels, badgers, and other*. Things in a list or series are related in some way. *Mustelids* are animals like weasels and badgers.

Example:

for example	for instance	like	such as

> Several personnel managers complain about the lag of business colleges in eliminating obsolete skills. *For instance*, shorthand is still taught in many secretarial programs although it is rarely used.
>
> Intangible assets, *such as* a company's recognized name and its goodwill, are neither physical nor financial in nature.

The meaning of *obsolete* is given by the information following *for instance*. Shorthand is an example of an obsolete skill. *Obsolete* describes something that is no longer useful.

The meaning of *intangible* assets is given by the information following *such as*. A company's name and goodwill are examples of intangible assets. More information is provided following the verb *are*. *Intangible assets* are such non–physical values as one's name and relationship with others.

Contrast:

but	in contrast	on the contrary	unlike
despite	in spite of	on the other hand	whereas
however	instead	rather than	while

> *Unlike* sun pillars, which are caused by reflection of light, arcs and haloes are caused by refraction of light through ice crystals.
>
> "Twilight" rays are nearly parallel, *but* because of the observer's perspective, they appear to diverge.

The meaning of *refraction* is given by *unlike* and *reflection*. From this, you know that *refraction* is different from *reflection*.

The meaning of *diverge* is given by *but* and *parallel*. From this, you know that *diverge* is different from *parallel*.

4. ***Punctuation clues*** can help you understand the meaning of unfamiliar words. Punctuation marks sometimes show that one word identifies, renames, or defines another word.

Punctuation marks:

comma	,	parentheses	( )
dash	—	quotation marks	" "
colon	:	brackets	[ ]

Folate supplementation before and during pregnancy can prevent certain defects of the brain and spine, such as anacephaly (absence of a major part of the brain).

Crepuscular rays—alternating bright and dark rays in the sky—appear to radiate from the sun.

The meaning of *anacephaly* is given by the information inside the parentheses. *Anacephaly* is the absence of a major part of the brain.

The meaning of *crepuscular rays* is given by the information between the dashes. *Crepuscular rays* are alternating bright and dark rays in the sky.

Scan for structural and punctuation clues. In the following sentences, circle structural and punctuation clues that help you understand the meaning of each underlined word. There are no single right answers.

a. Accessories add interest to a room. They can accent or highlight an area and give a room beauty and personality. A painting, for example, is pleasing to the eye.

b. Songbirds are early risers and remain active throughout the day, except during the warmest hours in summer. Owls, on the other hand, are primarily nocturnal.

c. Virtually every community college now offers contract education: short–term programs, ranging from a couple of hours to several days, for employees of specific companies, which pay a large share of the cost.

d. The inclination or tilt of the earth's axis with respect to the sun determines the seasons.

e. The radiating surface of the sun is called the photosphere, and just above it is the chromosphere, which is visible to the naked eye only at times of total solar eclipses, appearing then to be a pinkish–violet layer.

f. If someone is said to have "a chip on his shoulder," he is angry, pugnacious, sullen, and looking for trouble.

With your classmates and teacher, discuss the clues you identified. What types of context clues are they? Discuss probable meanings of the underlined words.

5. ***Key words*** in a sentence or passage can be context clues. Use the meanings of key words in a sentence and your understanding of the sentence as a whole to help you guess the meaning of an unfamiliar word.

   Look at this example:

   > Light output, measured in lumens, depends on the amount of electricity used by a bulb.

   The meaning of *lumens* is given by other words and phrases in the sentence: *light output*, *measured*, *electricity*. From these key words, you know that a *lumen* is a unit of measurement of light output.

   Scan for key words. In the following passages, circle key words that help you understand the meaning of the underlined words. There are no single right answers.

   a. Like the other giant planets, Neptune emits more energy than it receives from the sun. These excesses are thought to be the cooling from internal heat sources and from the formation of the planet.

   b. Most people think spring has begun when average daily temperatures are above freezing. By this definition, spring generally starts about March 1 in the northern states. Some people think that the threshold of spring should be the date when the daily normal temperature reaches 10 degrees Celsius, about which time most plant life has revived from its winter dormancy. Such temperatures occur about February 15 in the Deep South, but not until April 1 in the area from Virginia to Kansas.

   With your classmates and teacher, discuss the key words you identified. Use them to write a short definition or description of each underlined word.

6. ***Word parts*** are clues that can help you understand the meaning of unfamiliar words. Many English words are made up of parts of older English, Greek, and Latin words. If you know the meanings of some of these word parts, you can usually get a general understanding of some unfamiliar words, especially in context.

   There are three types of word parts: *prefixes*, *stems*, and *suffixes*. A ***prefix*** is a word beginning. A prefix affects the meaning of a word. A ***stem*** is the basic, underlying form of a word. Groups of words that have the same stem are related in meaning. A ***suffix*** is a word ending. A suffix affects the function of a word, for example, making it a noun or a verb (See 2.22).

PREFIX	STEM	SUFFIX	WORD
con	feder	ate	confederate
intro	duc	tion	introduction
syn	chron	ize	synchronize

   On the TOEFL, use both context clues and word parts to help you understand the meaning of unfamiliar words and phrases.

READING

Study the following lists of common prefixes and stems. Can you add any more examples?

PREFIX	MEANING	EXAMPLES
ab–	away, from	abolish, abnormal, abstract
ad–	to, toward	advance, admire, adhere
anti–	against	antiwar, antipathy, antibiotic
auto–	self, same	autobiography, autoimmune
bene–, bon–	good	benefit, benevolence, bonus
bi–	two	bilingual, binary, bilateral
co–, com–, con–	with, together	cooperate, compose, convene
contra–, counter–	against	contrary, contradict, counteract
de–	down, from, away	descend, derive, dehydration
dia–	through, across	dialogue, diagram, diagonal
dis–	not, take away	disease, disability, disappear
e–, ec–, ex–	out	emigrate, ecstasy, export
fore–	front, before	forehead, foresee, foreshadow
in–, im–	in, into, on	invade, immigrate, impose
in–, im–, il–, ir–	not	inequality, illegal, irrational
inter–	between	international, intersect
intro–, intra–	within, inside	introspection, intravenous
micro–	small	microchip, microscope
mis–	bad, wrong	misprint, misunderstand
mono–	one	monopoly, monotonous
multi–	many	multiply, multinational
out–	beyond	outlive, outgain, outspend
over–	too much	overbearing, overcompensate
para–	beside, alongside	parallel, paraphrase, paradox
post–	after	postwar, posterior, postpone
pre–	before	prepare, prevent, preview
pro–	forward	process, promote, produce
re–	back, again	return, replay, reunite
se–	apart, aside	separate, secede, segregate
sub–, sup–, sus–	below, after	subsidize, suppose, suspend
syn–, sym–, syl–	with, together	synthesis, symbol, syllabus
tele–	far, distant	telephone, telepathy
trans–	across	translate, transmit, transaction
un–	not	unable, unreal, unreasonable
uni–	one	unit, uniform, universe

STEM	MEANING	EXAMPLES
–bio–	life	biology, biodiversity, antibiotic
–cap–, –capit–	head, chief	captain, capital, decapitate
–cede–, –ceed–, –cess–	go, move	concede, proceed, success
–chron–	time	chronicle, anachronism
–cred–	believe	credit, incredible, creed
–dic–, –dict–	say, speak	dictator, predict, jurisdiction
–duc–, –duct–	lead	duct, introduce, reduction
–fact–, –fect–	make, do	factory, manufacture, effect
–fid–, –feder–	trust, faith	confidence, federation
–geo–	earth	geology, geothermal
–graph–, –gram–	write, draw	graphic, photography, grammar
–hydro–	water	hydroelectric, dehydrate
–log–, –ology–	word, study	logic, catalog, psychology
–man–, –manu–	hand	manual, manager, manuscript
–mit–, –miss–	send	transmit, omit, mission
–mort–	death	mortality, immortal, mortify
–phon–, –son–	sound	microphone, supersonic
–polis–, –polit–	city	metropolis, politics, police
–pon–, –pos–	put, place	postpone, position, deposit
–port–	carry	portable, reporter, import
–rect–	right, straight	correct, rectangle, rectify
–scrib–, –script–	write	describe, script, inscription
–secut–, –sequ–	follow	consecutive, sequence
–spect–	look at	spectator, spectacle, inspector
–struct–	build	structure, instruct, destructive
–therm–	heat	thermometer, hypothermia
–ven–, –vene–	come	convention, intervene
–ver–	true	verify, conversation, universal
–vid–, –vis–	see	video, visit, invisible
–voc–, –vok–	call, voice	vocal, vocabulary, revoke

7. On the paper test, questions about vocabulary in context look like this:

> The word/phrase "_____" in line __ is closest in meaning to _____.
> The word/phrase "_____" in line __ could best be replaced by _____.
> The word/phrase "_____" in line __ means that _____.
> The word/phrase "_____" in line __ refers to a type of _____.
> According to the passage, what is "_____?"

Look at these examples:

Questions 1–2

By the early 1900s, factories were churning out goods for an affluent middle class. No longer self–sufficient farmers, the American people depended on manufactured products. With so many goods in the marketplace, competition among manufacturers accelerated. They came to realize the importance of advertising.

In the 1920s, radio started a trend of mass marketing. Everybody in America heard about and wanted the same products. Since World War II, television has had a great impact on marketing. No other advertising medium can present so much information to so many people in so short a time. Television enables an advertiser to show to millions of people at once what a product can do. Moreover, it can repeat its sales message over and over again.

1. The word "self–sufficient" in line 2 is closest in meaning to

(A) selfish
(B) efficient
(C) independent
(D) poor

2. The phrase "mass marketing" in line 6 means that

(A) efforts were made to reach a large number of people
(B) supermarkets were all advertising and selling the same products
(C) more middle–class people were buying radios and televisions
(D) a large amount of money was spent on advertising

For question 1, you must scan line 2 to find *self–sufficient*. Some context clues in that sentence are *no longer* and *depended*. *No longer* indicates change or contrast. From this context, you know that *self–sufficient* is different from *depended*.

The correct answer to question 1 is (C), *independent*, which means not dependent.

For question 2, you must scan line 6 to find *mass marketing*. Some context clues in that paragraph are the key words *radio*, *everybody*, *television*, *so much information*, *so many people*, and *millions of people*.

The correct answer to question 2 is (A), *efforts were made to reach a large number of people*. This description of mass marketing best fits the context of the paragraph.

8. On the computer test, questions about vocabulary in context look like this:

> Look at the word _____ in the passage. The word _____ is closest in meaning to _____.
> Look at the word _____ in the passage. Click on the word or phrase in the **bold** text that is closest in meaning to _____.
> Look at the word _____ in the passage. Click on the word or phrase in the **bold** text that has the same meaning as _____.

Look at an example:

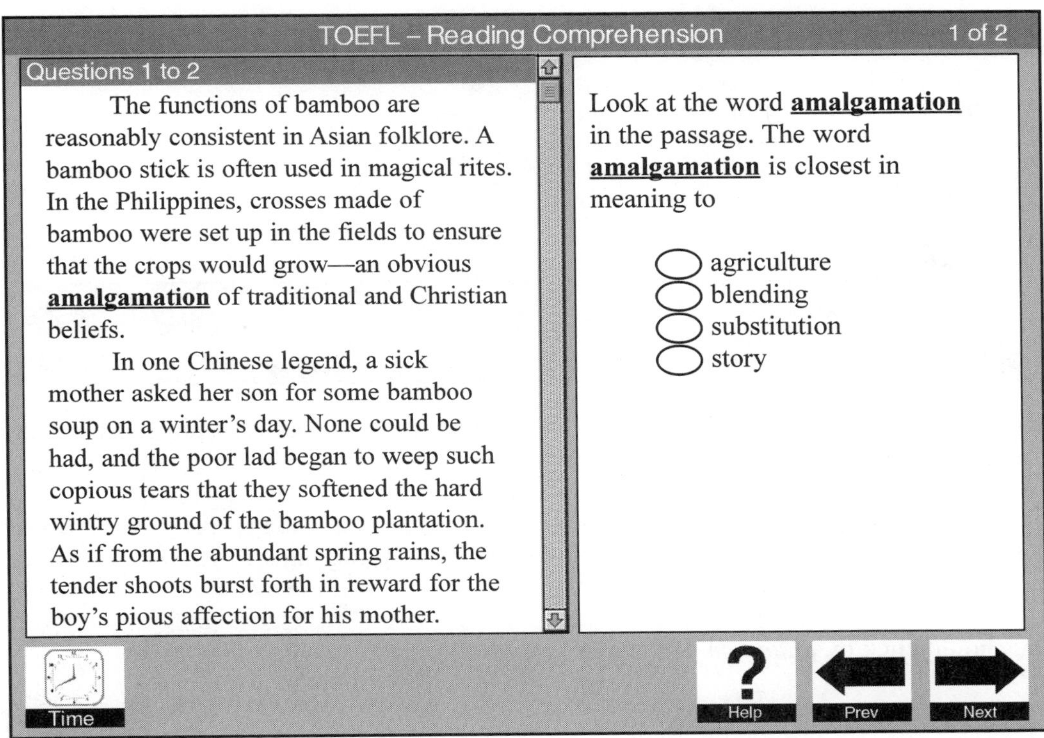

The word is highlighted to make it easier to find. In that sentence, a context clue is *of traditional and Christian beliefs*.

The answer is the second choice, *blending*, which indicates a mixing of two things. In this context, the crosses made of bamboo are *an obvious amalgamation*, or *blending*, of traditional and Christian beliefs.

Look at another example:

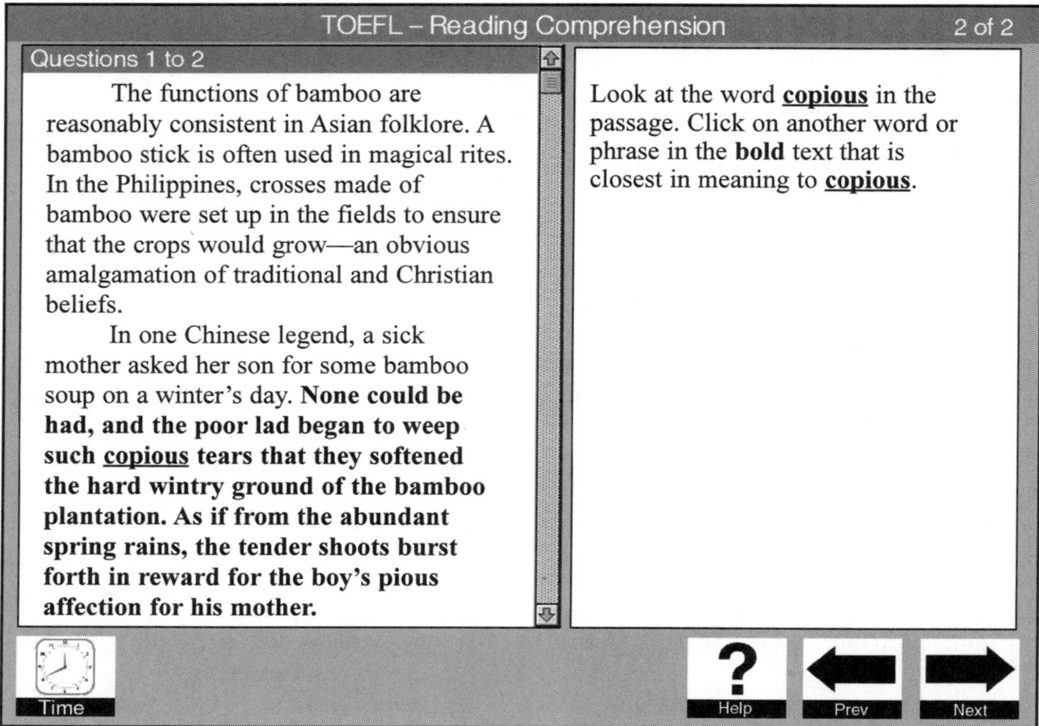

From the context, you know that *copious* is an adjective that modifies *tears*. This is a structural clue that tells you to look for another adjective.

The author is making a comparison between the boy's tears and the spring rains. The boy's *copious* tears softened the ground, just as the *abundant* spring rains soften the ground and cause the bamboo shoots to grow every year. *Abundant* and *copious* are synonyms.

You should click on *abundant* as the word that is closest in meaning to *copious*.

PRACTICE

Exercise 3.4.A

Read the following passages and choose the one best answer to each question.

QUESTION 1

A study found that children wore bicycle helmets close to 90 percent of the time when their parents made it a strict rule, but only about 20 percent of the time if their parents did not insist on it.

1. The phrase "insist on it" in line 3 is closest in meaning to

(A) recommend it
(B) care about it
(C) demand it
(D) know it

QUESTION 2

In 1652, Massachusetts issued the first American coins, which were known as shillings (worth about 12 cents each), sixpences (worth six "pennies" or "pence"), and threepences. These coins were in the same denominations, or amounts, as British money.

2. A word in the passage that has the same meaning as the word "denominations" in line 3 is

(A) shillings
(B) cents
(C) pennies
(D) amounts

QUESTION 3

You can make a homemade rain gauge easily from a glass tumbler or a metal can with straight sides and a sharp–edged open rim at the top to split the raindrops. You need only leave this receptacle outside to collect rain and then measure the catch with a ruler to get a rough approximation of the amount of precipitation.

3. The word "precipitation" in line 4 could best be replaced by

(A) rain
(B) glass
(C) metal
(D) energy

QUESTIONS 4–5

In the late seventeenth century, a transformation began that would make coffee one of the most popular drinks in Europe. The coffeehouse—meeting place of bankers, dissidents, artists, merchants, poets, wits, and rogues—was in some ways the cradle of modern Europe. Coffee would change, in less than a century, from the drink of a few princes and a few paupers to the chief social beverage of the rising middle class.

4. The word "transformation" in line 1 is closest in meaning to

(A) trend
(B) event
(C) change
(D) custom

5. The word "rogues" in line 3 refers to a type of

(A) beverage
(B) person
(C) book
(D) coffee

QUESTIONS 6–8

Exercise and vitamin D increase the amount of calcium in your bones. You can get all the vitamin D you need from simply being outdoors for thirty minutes. Milk is fortified with vitamin D, and drinking nonfat milk gives you calcium, vitamins, and energy. However, if you decide to take supplemental vitamin D, 400 to 800 IU per day will safely prevent any deficiencies.

6. The word "fortified" in line 3 is closest in meaning to

   (A) blended
   (B) flavored
   (C) irradiated
   (D) enhanced

7. The word "supplemental" in line 4 is closest in meaning to

   (A) additional
   (B) special
   (C) natural
   (D) concentrated

8. The word "deficiencies" in line 5 is closest in meaning to

   (A) abnormalities
   (B) insufficiencies
   (C) illnesses
   (D) excesses

Exercise 3.4.B

Read the following passages and choose the one best answer to each question.

QUESTIONS 1–4

Since the 1980s, the biggest influence on business has been electronic technology. Computers are being used for inventory control, sales analysis and forecasting, distribution control, and budget analysis. At–home electronic shopping is becoming commonplace. With this system, consumers view merchandise on a computer monitor and then use a modem, which links the computer to a telephone line, to signal the goods they want to order. Just as traveling salesmen once brought wares to the home, electronic technology makes it possible for modern consumers to see and select from an array of goods in their homes.

1. The word "forecasting" in line 2 is closest in meaning to

   (A) prediction
   (B) efficiency
   (C) accounting
   (D) decision making

2. The word "modem" in line 5 refers to a type of

   (A) electronic shopping
   (B) electronic device
   (C) telephone
   (D) computer screen

3. The word "wares" in line 6 is closest in meaning to

   (A) clothing
   (B) items for sale
   (C) messages
   (D) household appliances

4. The word "array" in line 7 is closest in meaning to

   (A) pair
   (B) container
   (C) category
   (D) collection

QUESTIONS 5–10

So much sentimentality is attached to the rose in popular feeling that it is difficult to separate the original mythological and folkloric beliefs from the sentimental dross that surrounds the flower. Yet if we look into the beliefs, we find that the rose is much more than the mere symbol of romantic love invoked by every minor poet and painter. One of its most common associations in folklore, for example, is with death. The Romans often decked the tombs of the dead with roses; in fact, Roman wills frequently specified that roses were to be planted on the grave. To this day, in Switzerland, cemeteries are known as rose gardens. The Saxons believed that when a child died, the figure of death could be seen plucking a rose outside the house.

The rose has a long association with female beauty. Shakespeare mentions the rose more frequently than any other flower, often using it as a token of all that is lovely and good. For the Arabs, on the other hand, the rose was a symbol not of feminine but of masculine beauty.

Later it became a sign of secrecy and silence. The expression *sub rosa*, "under the rose," is traced to a Roman belief. During the sixteenth and seventeenth centuries, it was common practice to carve or paint roses on the ceilings of council chambers to emphasize the intention of secrecy.

5. The word "dross" in line 2 is closest in meaning to

(A) confusion
(B) scent
(C) excess
(D) popularity

6. The word "invoked" in line 4 is closest in meaning to

(A) believed
(B) called on
(C) looked for
(D) thought about

7. The word "decked" in line 6 could best be replaced by

(A) filled
(B) lined
(C) covered
(D) disguised

8. The word "plucking" in line 9 could best be replaced by

(A) planting
(B) killing
(C) wearing
(D) picking

9. The word "token" in line 11 is closest in meaning to

(A) symbol
(B) acceptance
(C) justification
(D) contradiction

10. The phrase "sub rosa" in line 14 means

(A) beautifully
(B) intentionally
(C) secretly
(D) emphatically

Exercise 3.4.C

Read the following passage and choose the one best answer to each question.

QUESTIONS 1–10

According to the ancient Greek philosophers, the stars were "fixed and immutable," the constant, changeless, and immortal inhabitants of the heavens, appearing nightly in all their brilliance and beauty, yet forever unknowable. But the stars are, in fact, neither fixed, immutable, nor unknowable. Like humans, they are born, they live and change, they grow old, and they die—it just takes them a long time to do so. Some stars have life spans of millions of years, others hundreds of millions, and still others billions of years. Inevitably, however, they all burn out and shine no longer.

Stars are created when vast interstellar clouds of gas and dust come together through gravitational attraction. As this matter coalesces, a protostar—a loose, globular mass of the stuff—results. Gravitational forces cause the protostar to condense and heat up. Eventually, the contraction causes tremendous pressure and heat in the core of the protostar, igniting a process of fusion reaction in which hydrogen, the most abundant element in the protostar, is converted to helium. This process causes the protostar to "switch on," to begin radiating energy—to shine.

When its energy output equals the pressure exerted on it by gravity, a balance is achieved and the protostar stabilizes and stops contracting. It is now a star; in effect, a gigantic thermonuclear reactor in outer space. It now enters what is known as the main sequence, the prime of a star's life, burning hydrogen and radiating energy steadily. A star remains in its main sequence for about 80 percent of its lifetime. Our sun, which is an estimated 5 billion years old, is right in the middle of its main sequence.

Inevitably, however, a star exhausts its supply of hydrogen fuel. Its outer layers begin to cool, and the star swells tremendously and turns red, becoming what is known as a red giant. Star death comes in a variety of forms: the red giant may become unstable and explode violently in a supernova; or it may simply collapse, becoming a kind of fading stellar cinder, known as a white dwarf, or a small, cold, burned–out black dwarf.

1. What does the passage mainly discuss?

   (A) The brilliance and beauty of stars
   (B) The life span of stars
   (C) The formation of stars
   (D) Similarities between stars and humans

2. The word "immutable" in lines 2 and 4 could best be replaced by

   (A) everlasting
   (B) irresistible
   (C) unchangeable
   (D) mysterious

3. The phrase "interstellar clouds" in line 8 means

   (A) magnetic particles
   (B) loose, dark clouds
   (C) clouds inside an old star
   (D) clouds between stars

4. The word "coalesces" in line 9 is closest in meaning to

   (A) unites
   (B) cools
   (C) burns
   (D) explodes

5. The word "protostar" in paragraph 2 describes

   (A) a star–shaped object
   (B) a heavy star
   (C) the earliest form of a star
   (D) an extremely hot star

6. The phrase "This process" in line 13 refers to

   (A) gravitational force
   (B) contraction
   (C) fusion reaction
   (D) radiation

7. The word "exerted" in line 15 is closest in meaning to

   (A) forced
   (B) dropped
   (C) spread
   (D) created

8. Which of the following is NOT true about the main sequence of a star?

   (A) A star contracts during its main sequence.
   (B) Our sun is about halfway through its main sequence.
   (C) The main sequence is the longest part of a star's existence.
   (D) A star in its main sequence gives off energy.

9. The word "swells" in line 22 could best be replaced by

   (A) spins
   (B) heats up
   (C) vibrates
   (D) enlarges

10. The word "cinder" in line 25 is closest in meaning to

   (A) gaseous substance
   (B) burned object
   (C) dense cloud
   (D) fine dust

Exercise 3.4.D

Read each passage and follow the directions on the right side of the screen.

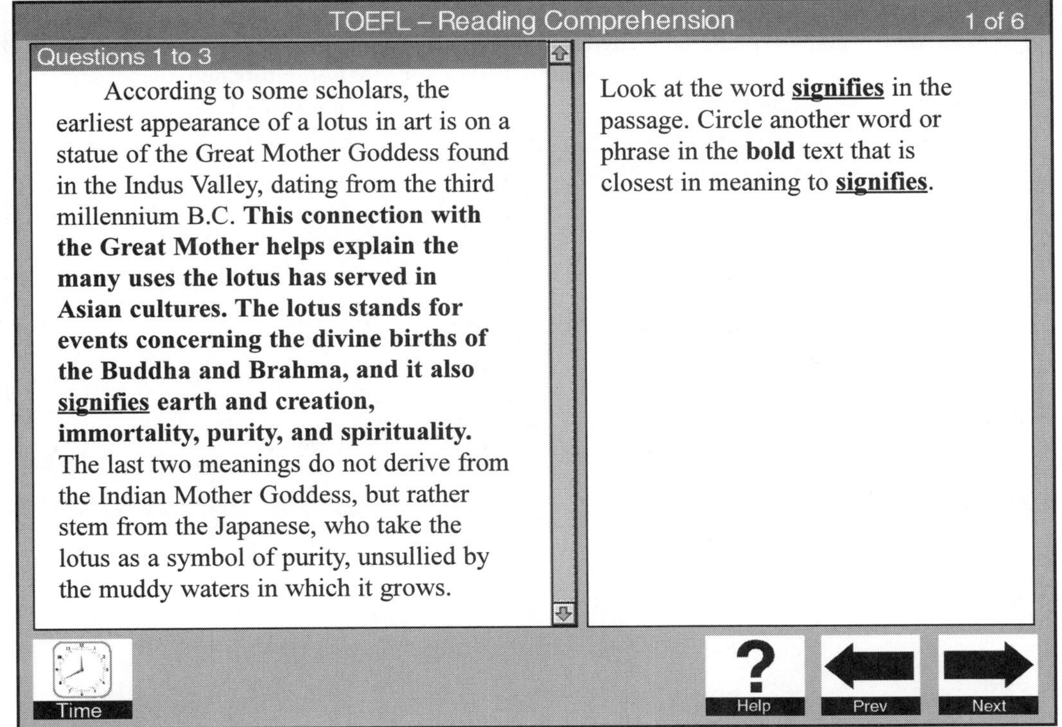
TOEFL – Reading Comprehension 1 of 6

Questions 1 to 3

According to some scholars, the earliest appearance of a lotus in art is on a statue of the Great Mother Goddess found in the Indus Valley, dating from the third millennium B.C. **This connection with the Great Mother helps explain the many uses the lotus has served in Asian cultures. The lotus stands for events concerning the divine births of the Buddha and Brahma, and it also <u>signifies</u> earth and creation, immortality, purity, and spirituality.** The last two meanings do not derive from the Indian Mother Goddess, but rather stem from the Japanese, who take the lotus as a symbol of purity, unsullied by the muddy waters in which it grows.

Look at the word **<u>signifies</u>** in the passage. Circle another word or phrase in the **bold** text that is closest in meaning to **<u>signifies</u>**.

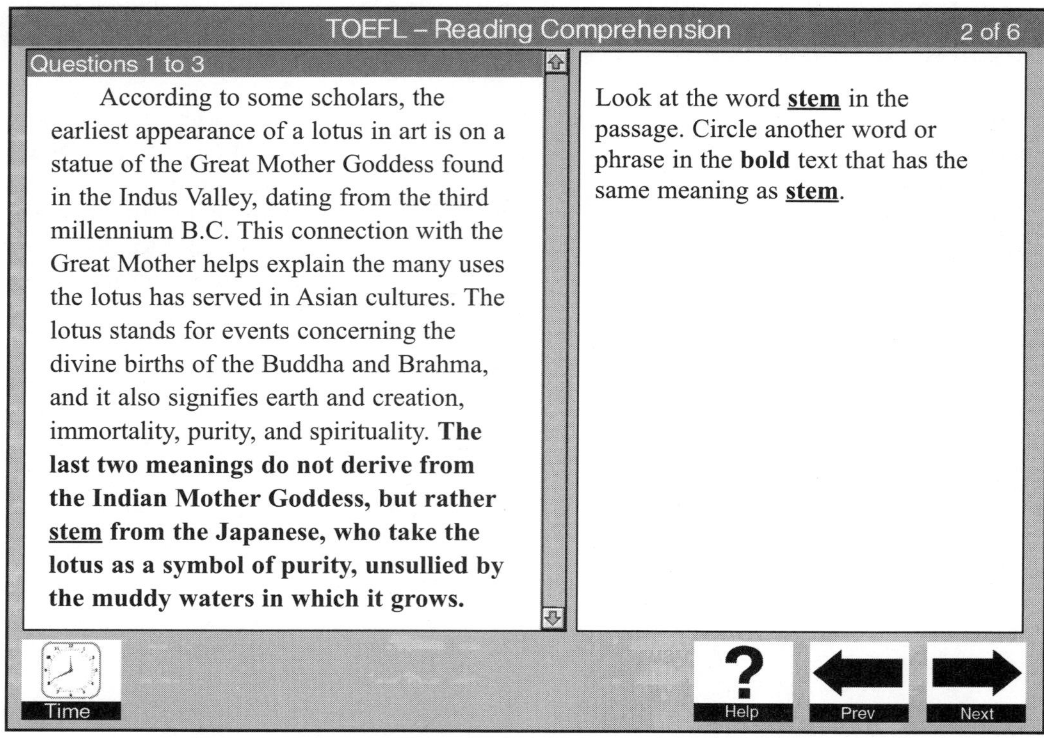
TOEFL – Reading Comprehension
2 of 6
Questions 1 to 3
According to some scholars, the earliest appearance of a lotus in art is on a statue of the Great Mother Goddess found in the Indus Valley, dating from the third millennium B.C. This connection with the Great Mother helps explain the many uses the lotus has served in Asian cultures. The lotus stands for events concerning the divine births of the Buddha and Brahma, and it also signifies earth and creation, immortality, purity, and spirituality. **The last two meanings do not derive from the Indian Mother Goddess, but rather stem from the Japanese, who take the lotus as a symbol of purity, unsullied by the muddy waters in which it grows.**
Look at the word **stem** in the passage. Circle another word or phrase in the **bold** text that has the same meaning as **stem**.
Time
Help
Prev
Next

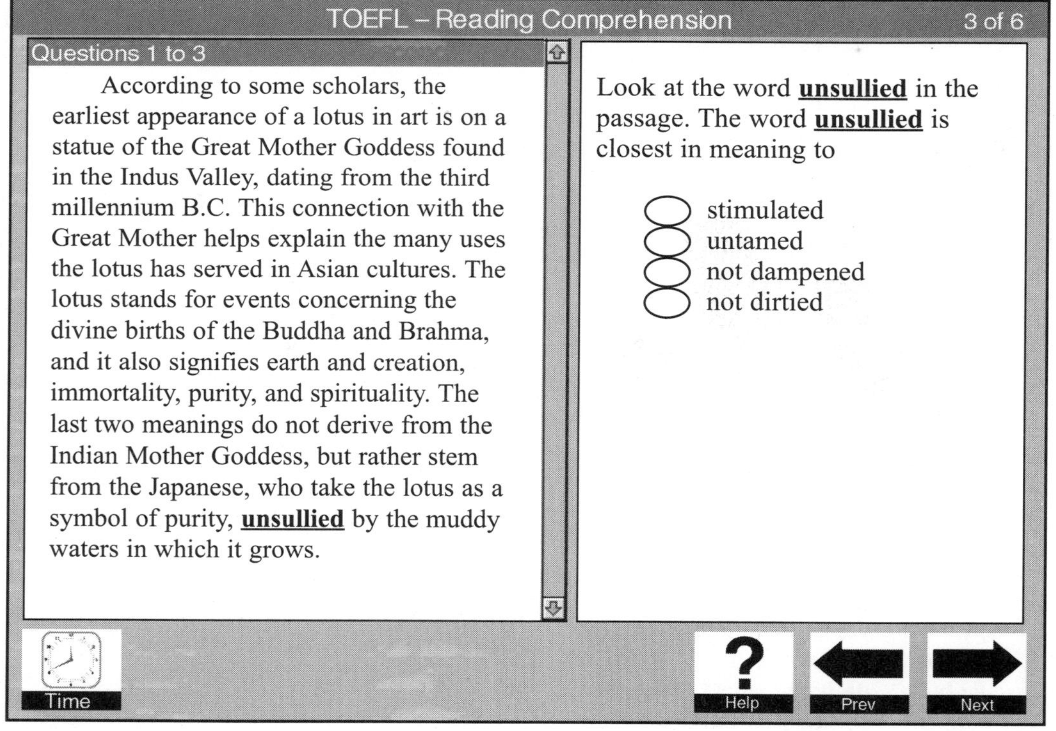
TOEFL – Reading Comprehension
3 of 6
Questions 1 to 3
According to some scholars, the earliest appearance of a lotus in art is on a statue of the Great Mother Goddess found in the Indus Valley, dating from the third millennium B.C. This connection with the Great Mother helps explain the many uses the lotus has served in Asian cultures. The lotus stands for events concerning the divine births of the Buddha and Brahma, and it also signifies earth and creation, immortality, purity, and spirituality. The last two meanings do not derive from the Indian Mother Goddess, but rather stem from the Japanese, who take the lotus as a symbol of purity, **unsullied** by the muddy waters in which it grows.
Look at the word **unsullied** in the passage. The word **unsullied** is closest in meaning to
stimulated
untamed
not dampened
not dirtied
Time
Help
Prev
Next

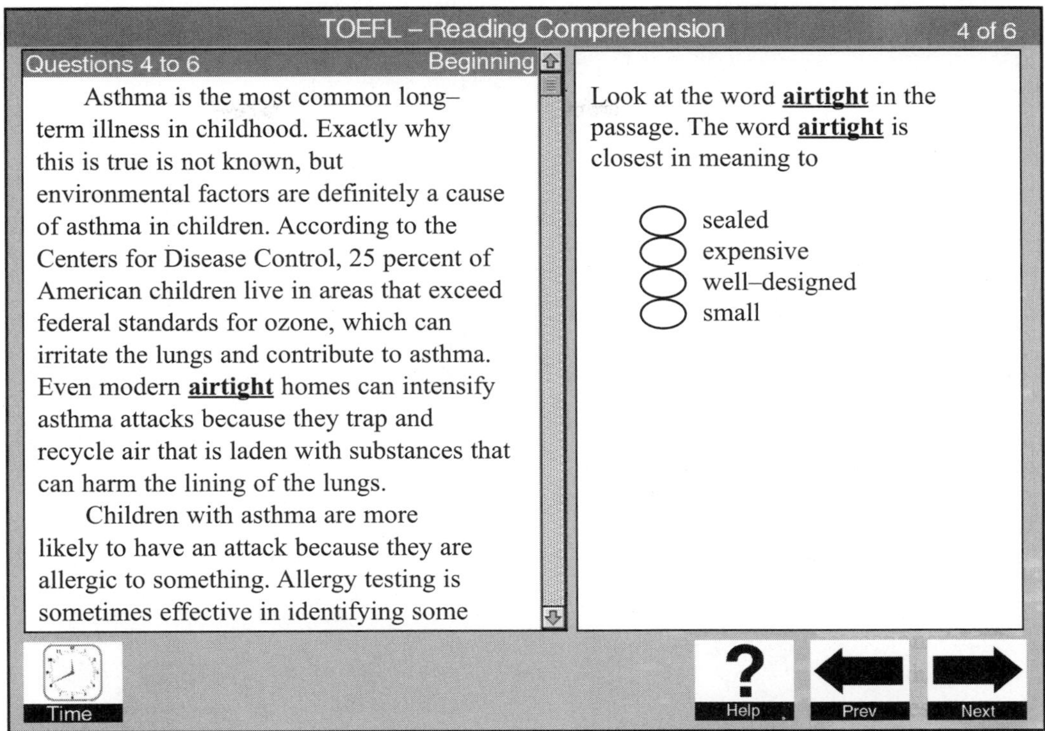
TOEFL – Reading Comprehension
4 of 6
Questions 4 to 6
Beginning
Asthma is the most common long–term illness in childhood. Exactly why this is true is not known, but environmental factors are definitely a cause of asthma in children. According to the Centers for Disease Control, 25 percent of American children live in areas that exceed federal standards for ozone, which can irritate the lungs and contribute to asthma. Even modern **airtight** homes can intensify asthma attacks because they trap and recycle air that is laden with substances that can harm the lining of the lungs.
Children with asthma are more likely to have an attack because they are allergic to something. Allergy testing is sometimes effective in identifying some
Look at the word **airtight** in the passage. The word **airtight** is closest in meaning to
sealed
expensive
well–designed
small
Time
Help
Prev
Next

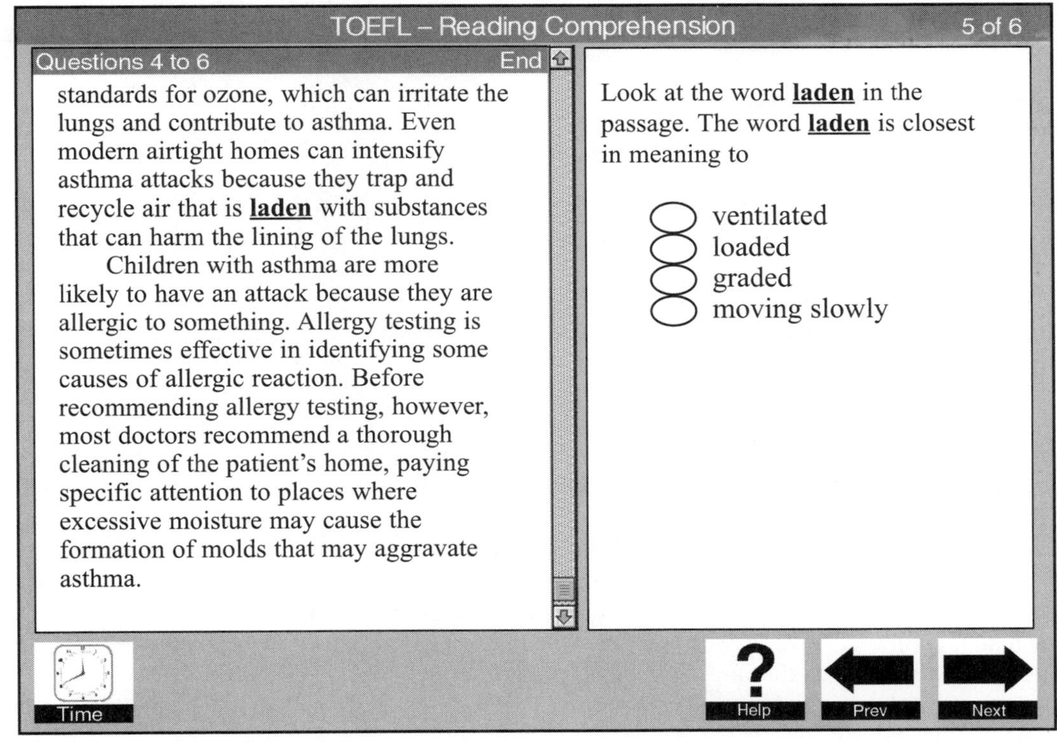
TOEFL – Reading Comprehension
5 of 6
Questions 4 to 6
End
standards for ozone, which can irritate the lungs and contribute to asthma. Even modern airtight homes can intensify asthma attacks because they trap and recycle air that is **laden** with substances that can harm the lining of the lungs.
Children with asthma are more likely to have an attack because they are allergic to something. Allergy testing is sometimes effective in identifying some causes of allergic reaction. Before recommending allergy testing, however, most doctors recommend a thorough cleaning of the patient's home, paying specific attention to places where excessive moisture may cause the formation of molds that may aggravate asthma.
Look at the word **laden** in the passage. The word **laden** is closest in meaning to
ventilated
loaded
graded
moving slowly
Time
Help
Prev
Next

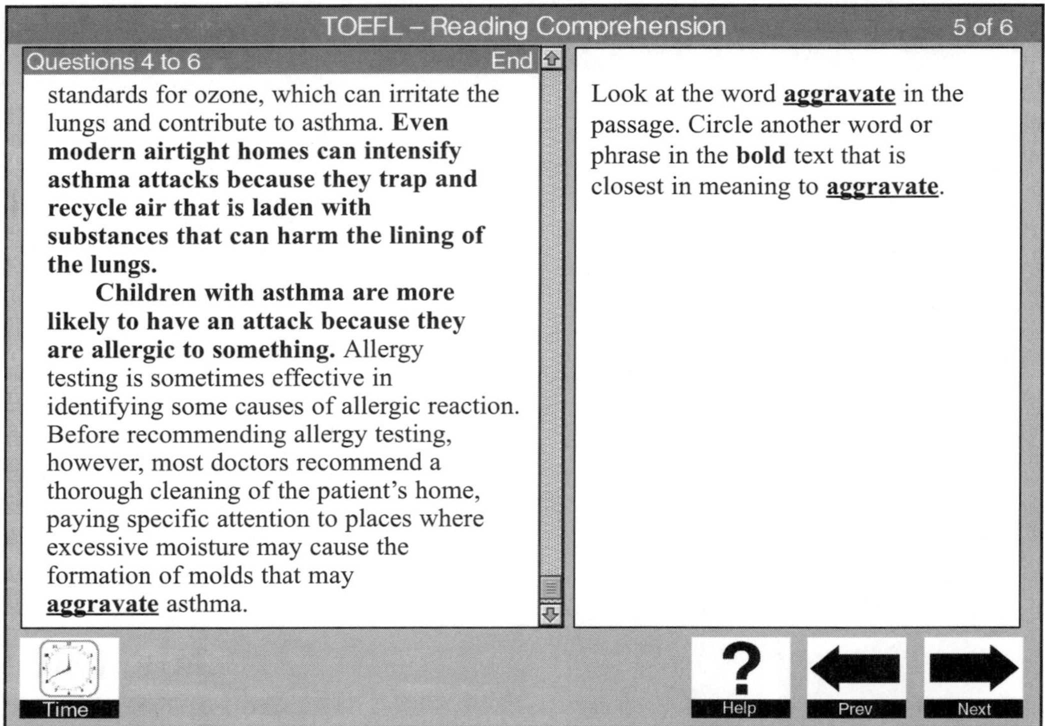

Answers to Exercises 3.4.A through 3.4.D are on page 658.

3.4 EXTENSION

1. Working in pairs, students identify context clues in the reading passages in Exercises 3.4.A to 3.4.D. What types of context clues do you find? Structural clues? Punctuation clues? Key words?

2. In reading done outside class, students select a paragraph in which they have learned at least one new word. Copy the paragraph and underline the new word. Bring 3 or 4 photocopies to class. In groups of 3 to 4, pass out the copies of the paragraphs. Work as a team to identify context clues and/or word parts that help you understand the meaning of each underlined word. Use the clues to write a short definition or description of each word. Then, look up the words in a dictionary. Are your definitions accurate?

3. Students begin a vocabulary notebook to help prepare for the TOEFL. In the notebook, write new words learned through reading. Include sentences showing the new words in context. Determine a way to organize the notebook. Suggestions: words by subject area (science, business, music); words from your major field of study; words with the same prefix or stem; words that are difficult to remember.

4. Discuss these questions: What is the best way to acquire new English vocabulary? How did you learn in the past? What works best for you now? (Possible answers: listen to lectures; write down three new words every day; memorize word lists; translate words into your native language; read a lot of different types of material; read in your major field of study; try using new words in conversation; watch television and movies.)

 ASSESSING PROGRESS – 3.4

QUIZ 4 (Time – 13 minutes)

Read the following passages and choose the one best answer to each question. Answer all questions on the basis of what is stated or implied in the passage.

QUESTIONS 1–4

In reading rocks for clues to their identity, one must look beyond their beauty and focus on their physical characteristics. One of the most important features is rock shape. Water is instrumental in shaping rocks, but the precise shape sculpted by the water is determined by several factors within the rock layer itself. These include its thickness, as well as its hardness or softness. Harder rock layers contain more of the natural elements, such as iron oxide or calcium carbonate, while softer rocks contain fewer of these agents. In some rock layers, the quantity of these elements varies throughout the rock so that some portions which are softer than others erode at a different rate, producing a variety of interesting shapes and, in some instances where the rock is very soft, creating pockets in the rock.

The shape of a particular rock layer is also affected by the hardness or softness of the rock layers immediately above and below it in the rock stack. These exposed alternating layers of hard and soft rock are visible along the walls of canyons and on the steep slopes of plateaus and mesas, either formed by faulting and uplifting of the land or by the action of a river cutting down on all sides of a land mass, leaving it elevated above the surrounding land. If the top of one of these elevated land masses is composed of soft rock, it will erode until a layer of erosion–resistant harder rock under it emerges to the surface, forming a flat protective cap over the rock layers below it.

1. The word "instrumental" in line 3 is closest in meaning to

   (A) tool–like
   (B) unnecessary
   (C) required
   (D) speedy

2. The word "erode" in lines 8 and 17 could best be replaced by

   (A) accumulate
   (B) move forward
   (C) wear away
   (D) develop

3. The word "alternating" in line 13 is closest in meaning to

   (A) fascinating
   (B) light and dark
   (C) thick and thin
   (D) successive

4. The word "faulting" in line 14 is closest in meaning to

   (A) rising
   (B) breaking
   (C) blaming
   (D) building

READING

QUESTIONS 5–10

Human decision making is being influenced profoundly by modern mathematics, and several particular mathematical subjects have been created primarily to assist in arriving at good decisions. Many aspects involved in arriving at a decision are, of course, nonquantitative in nature. These may relate to history, past experience, instinct, judgment, morality, and so forth. As a consequence, one often refers to decision making as an art. On the other hand, many ingredients in contemporary decision making are mathematical in nature, and one can also view this activity as a science.

A decision maker will begin by listing the options over which he or she has some control and the likely outcomes resulting from these choices. The person may attempt to identify all relevant variables and the relationships among them and may associate quantitative measures when possible. Moreover, the decision maker must clarify his or her own values, identify desired goals, and spell out explicitly any limiting resources or social constraints. One then seeks the best possible result obtainable.

The situation is typically confounded by a variety of different uncertainties involving data and forecasting that typically cannot be completely resolved in advance. The effect that other decision makers may have on the outcome, and the best responses to their moves, should be predetermined. Various ethical concerns such as fairness may well need consideration, and ways to ascertain group opinions may be necessary. Finally, decision makers must study the social and political context in which the decision will be implemented.

5. The word "nonquantitative" in line 4 is closest in meaning to

(A) not numerical
(B) immeasurable
(C) difficult
(D) unimportant

6. The word "outcomes" in line 9 could best be replaced by

(A) decisions
(B) calculations
(C) consequences
(D) numbers

7. The phrase "spell out explicitly" in line 12 is closest in meaning to

(A) express clearly
(B) try to avoid
(C) count carefully
(D) write neatly

8. The word "constraints" in line 13 has the same meaning as

(A) goals
(B) results
(C) resources
(D) limitations

9. The phrase "confounded by" in line 14 is closest in meaning to

(A) clarified by
(B) made up of
(C) confused by
(D) solved by

10. The word "implemented" in line 20 is closest in meaning to

(A) carried out
(B) announced
(C) tried out
(D) evaluated

Answers to Reading Quiz 4 are on page 658.

 ASSESSING PROGRESS – 3.1 through 3.4

QUIZ 5 *(Time – 22 minutes)*

Read the following passages and choose the one best answer to each question. Answer all questions on the basis of what is stated or implied in the passage.

QUESTIONS 1–10

Most Americans still get married at some point in their lives, but even that group is shrinking. Among current generations of adult Americans—starting with those born in the 1920s—more than 90 percent have married or will marry at some point in their lives. However, based on recent patterns of marriage and mortality, demographers calculate that a growing share of the younger generations are postponing marriage for so long that an unprecedented number will never marry at all.

More Americans are living together outside of marriage. Divorced and widowed people are waiting longer to remarry. An increasing number of single women are raising children. Put these trends together with our increasing life expectancy, and the result is inevitable: Americans are spending a record low proportion of their adult lives married.

Marriage rates for unmarried men and women have dropped from their post–1950s highs to record lows. Part of this fall is due to the change in the age at which people first marry. The median age at first marriage is the age by which half the men or women who will ever marry have done so. It fell almost continuously from the time it was first measured, in 1890, at 22.0 years for women and 26.1 for men, to a low of 20.3 for women and 22.6 for men between 1947 and 1962. Since then, it has risen at a rapid pace, to a record high of 23.8 for women and 26.2 for men in 1994.

The length of time between marriages is also increasing, and more divorced people are choosing not to remarry. In 1990, divorced women had waited an average of 3.8 years before remarrying, and divorced men had waited an average of 3.5 years, an increase of more than one year over the average interval in 1970.

Data on cohabitation and unmarried childbearing suggest that marriage is becoming less relevant to Americans. 2.8 million of the nation's households are unmarried couples, and one–third of them are caring for children, according to the Census Bureau.

1. The passage supports all of the following statements EXCEPT

   (A) almost all Americans get married at least once
   (B) Americans are spending fewer years married than they did in the past
   (C) divorced Americans are waiting longer to remarry
   (D) Americans are having fewer children than they did in the past

2. The word "those" in line 2 refers to

   (A) adult Americans
   (B) married Americans
   (C) American men
   (D) younger generations

3. The word "unprecedented" in line 6 is closest in meaning to

   (A) impossible to count
   (B) decreasing
   (C) never before seen
   (D) unbelievable

4. According to the passage, recent demographic patterns suggest that

(A) an increasing number of young people will never marry
(B) most young people delay marriage for personal reasons
(C) 90 percent of the younger generations will marry
(D) young people prefer to marry in order to have children

5. The word "inevitable" in line 10 is closest in meaning to

(A) incredible
(B) unavoidable
(C) surprising
(D) serious

6. The phrase "median age" in line 13 means

(A) most common age for marrying
(B) age by which half have married
(C) youngest age for marrying
(D) half of the marriage age

7. Between 1890 and the 1950s, the age at which men first married

(A) remained about the same
(B) increased by almost 2 years
(C) decreased by less than 2 years
(D) decreased by more than 3 years

8. In paragraph 3, the author shows that the median age at first marriage

(A) rose and then fell between 1890 and 1962
(B) reached a record high for women in the early 1960s
(C) rose between the 1960s and the 1990s
(D) fell continuously between 1947 and 1962

9. A word or phrase in paragraph 4 that has the same meaning as the word "interval" in line 21 is

(A) length of time
(B) divorced people
(C) increase of more than one
(D) 3.5 years

10. The word "them" in line 24 refers to

(A) Americans
(B) single women
(C) unmarried couples
(D) divorced women

Questions 11–20

American humor and American popular heroes were born together. The first popular heroes of the new nation were comic heroes, and the first popular humor of the new nation was the antics of its hero–clowns. The heroic and the comic were combined in novel American proportions in popular literature.

The heroic themes are obvious enough and not much different from those in the legends of other times and places: Achilles, Beowulf, Siegfried, Roland, and King Arthur. The American Davy Crockett legends repeat the familiar pattern of the Old World heroic story: the pre–eminence of a mighty hero whose fame in myth has a tenuous basis in fact; the remarkable birth and precocious strength of the hero; single combats in which he distinguishes himself against antagonists, both man and beast; vows and boasts; pride of the hero in his weapons, his horse, his dog, and his woman.

Davy Crockett conquered man and beast with a swaggering nonchalance. He overcame animals by force of body and will. He killed four wolves at the age of six; he hugged a bear to death; he killed a rattlesnake with his teeth. He mastered the forces of nature. Crockett's most famous natural exploit was saving the earth on the coldest day in history. First, he climbed a mountain to determine the trouble. Then he rescued all creation by squeezing bear–grease on the earth's frozen axis and over the sun's icy face. He whistled, "Push along, keep movin'!" The earth gave a grunt and began moving.

Neither the fearlessness nor the bold huntsman's prowess was peculiarly American. Far more distinctive was the comic quality. All heroes are heroic; few are also clowns. What made the American popular hero heroic also made him comic. "May be," said Crockett, "you'll laugh at me, and not at my book." The ambiguity of American life and the vagueness which laid the continent open to adventure, which made the land a rich storehouse of the unexpected, which kept vocabulary ungoverned and the language fluid—this same ambiguity suffused both the comic and the heroic. In a world full of the unexpected, readers of the Crockett legends were never quite certain whether to laugh or to applaud, or whether what they saw and heard was wonderful, awful, or ridiculous.

11. What is the main point the author makes in the passage?

    (A) American popular literature was based on the legends of other times and places.
    (B) American popular heroes were characteristically comic.
    (C) Davy Crockett wrote humorous stories about mastering the forces of nature.
    (D) The Davy Crockett stories reflected the adventurous spirit of early America.

12. The word "those" in line 5 refers to

    (A) popular heroes
    (B) heroic themes
    (C) legends
    (D) comic heroes

13. Which of the following is NOT mentioned as a heroic theme?

    (A) Fluid use of language
    (B) Pride in the hero's woman
    (C) Boasting by the hero
    (D) Superior physical strength

14. The word "antagonists" in line 10 could best be replaced by

    (A) opponents
    (B) heroes
    (C) forces
    (D) wild animals

15. Davy Crockett is an example of

    (A) a popular writer
    (B) an Old World hero
    (C) a heroic theme
    (D) a hero–clown

16. In paragraph 3, the author mentions a story in which Davy Crockett

(A) ate a rattlesnake
(B) killed a wild boar
(C) saved the earth
(D) saved a bear

17. The word "exploit" in line 15 is closest in meaning to

(A) character trait
(B) heroic act
(C) skill
(D) resource

18. The word "prowess" in line 19 is closest in meaning to

(A) caution
(B) goal
(C) bravery
(D) weapon

19. In paragraph 4, the author makes the point that

(A) American writers strove to create a distinctively American literature
(B) Americans enjoyed laughing at other people
(C) Americans valued comic qualities more than heroic qualities
(D) American life was open to adventure and full of the unexpected

20. The word "ambiguity" in lines 22 and 25 is closest in meaning to

(A) uncertainty
(B) quality
(C) ridiculousness
(D) richness

Answers to Reading Quiz 5 are on page 658.

3.5 Making Inferences

Read the following passage.

> Ever since people discovered the importance of exchanging information, communications have been vital to society. Improvements in communication have broadened people's knowledge of the world. Today it is possible to follow events taking place around the globe simply by turning on a television or logging onto the Internet. Yet, for much of human existence, communications moved only as fast as a person could move.
>
> A breakthrough occurred in the fifteenth century with the development of printing with movable type. In the 1830s, Samuel Morse's invention of the telegraph showed that messages could move at the speed of electricity. Since then, telephone, radio, television, and satellite relays have continued to revolutionize communications. Today the revolution is still going on.

How many of the following statements can you conclude from reading this passage? Check as many as you know to be true, based on the information in the passage.

____ Societies value the exchange of information.
____ The Internet is a form of communication.
____ Before the fifteenth century people had no technology.
____ The telegraph is a form of communication.
____ Samuel Morse invented electricity.
____ The passage was written during a war.

From the information given, you can conclude that *societies value the exchange of information*, *the Internet is a form of communication*, and *the telegraph is a form of communication*. The other statements cannot be concluded. While they might be true, there is nothing in the passage to support them.

Now, answer a question:

> What does the paragraph following this passage probably discuss?
>
> ◯ Improvements in our standard of living
> ◯ How satellite television has changed society
> ◯ Global events at the turn of the century
> ◯ Current breakthroughs in communications technology

The second paragraph discusses important developments in communications technology from the fifteenth century to the present. It concludes with *Today the revolution is still going on*. This implies that the next paragraph will discuss *Current breakthroughs in communications technology*.

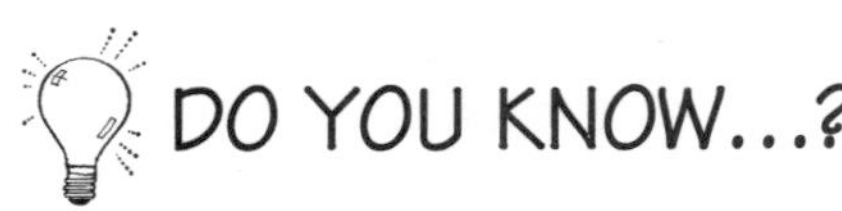

DO YOU KNOW...?

1. Approximately ten items on the TOEFL will test your ability to make inferences based on the information you read. For each individual passage, two or three questions will ask you to make an inference.

   On the paper test, the inference questions are usually asked in the same order that the information appears in the passage.

   On the computer test, the inference questions are also asked in the order that the information appears. The computer may scroll automatically to that part of the passage or point out in which paragraph you can find the answer.

2. An ***inference*** is a conclusion you can make from the information given in a passage. Some inferences can be made from a single sentence. Some inferences are based on a whole paragraph or on the entire passage.

   An inference is a "hidden" idea. To make an inference, you must understand an idea that is not stated directly by the author. To do this, you must interpret the information that is stated directly. What the author does not state directly, he or she may *imply* or *suggest* by mentioning certain details. When an author implies something, you must *infer* or *conclude* the meaning based on what the author does tell you.

3. A ***prediction*** is a type of inference in which you must determine what the author would probably say in the next paragraph or in a similar situation, or you may have to identify which statement the author would agree with.

   When you make an inference or prediction, use key words and ideas in the passage, your general understanding of the author's message, reason, logic, and common sense.

4. TOEFL questions about inferences and predictions look like this:

> It can be inferred from the passage that _____.
> Which of the following can be inferred about _____?
> It can be concluded from lines __ that _____.
> It can be inferred by the phrase "_____" that _____.
> The author of the passage implies/suggests that _____.
> In paragraph __, the author implies/suggests that _____.
> What does the author suggest was _____?
> What does the author mean by the statement __________?
> With which of the following statements would the author most probably agree?
> Which of the following is most probably _____?
> Which of the following would be most likely _____?
> What can be said/concluded about _____?
> What does the paragraph following the passage probably discuss?
> All of the following can be inferred from the passage EXCEPT
> Which of the following could NOT be said/concluded about _____?

Note: In TOEFL questions with *EXCEPT* or *NOT*, look for the *one* answer choice that is *not* supported by the information either stated directly or implied in the passage.

5. In inference questions, some of the answer choices may try to trick you by:

- not being supported by the information stated or implied in the passage
- being inaccurate or untrue according to the passage
- repeating words and phrases from the passage in incorrect ways
- being too general
- being irrelevant

Look at an example:

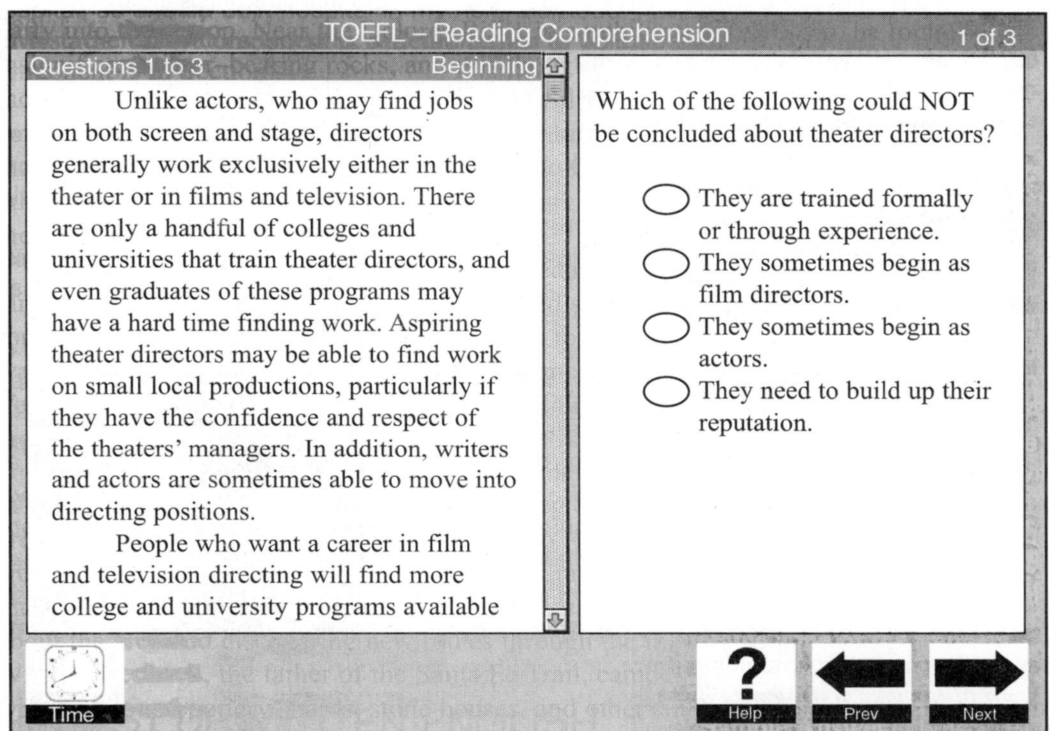

An important word in the question is *NOT*. It tells you to look for the *one* statement that is *not* supported by the information in the passage.

The first statement, *They are trained formally or through experience*, is supported in the passage. The author mentions that a handful of colleges and universities train theater directors and that aspiring theater directors may get experience by finding work on small local productions or by moving into directing after working as writers or actors.

The second statement, *They sometimes begin as film directors*, is neither supported nor implied in the passage.

The third statement, *They sometimes begin as actors*, is implied in paragraph 1.

The fourth statement, *They need to build up their reputation*, is implied when the author tells you that aspiring theater directors may be able to find work *if they have the confidence and respect of the theaters' managers*. From this, you can conclude that theater directors must work at building up their reputation.

The correct answer is the second choice: *They sometimes begin as film directors*. It is the only choice that is *not* implied in the passage.

Look at another example:

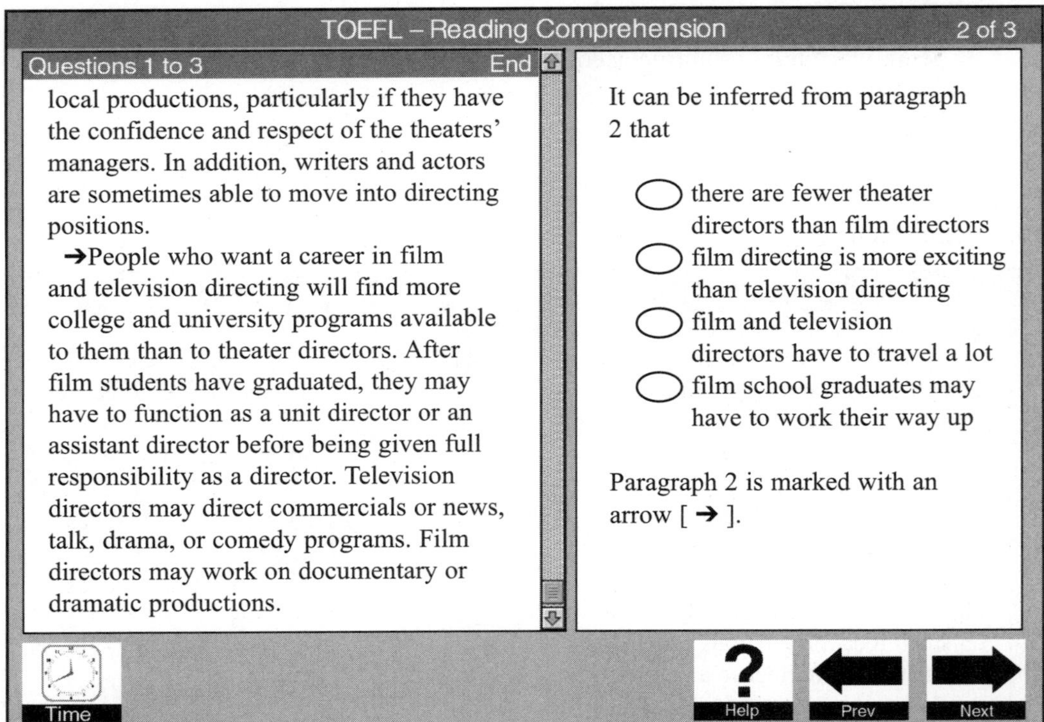

TOEFL – Reading Comprehension 2 of 3

Questions 1 to 3

local productions, particularly if they have the confidence and respect of the theaters' managers. In addition, writers and actors are sometimes able to move into directing positions.

➔People who want a career in film and television directing will find more college and university programs available to them than to theater directors. After film students have graduated, they may have to function as a unit director or an assistant director before being given full responsibility as a director. Television directors may direct commercials or news, talk, drama, or comedy programs. Film directors may work on documentary or dramatic productions.

It can be inferred from paragraph 2 that

- ◯ there are fewer theater directors than film directors
- ◯ film directing is more exciting than television directing
- ◯ film and television directors have to travel a lot
- ◯ film school graduates may have to work their way up

Paragraph 2 is marked with an arrow [➔].

The computer has identified paragraph 2 for you.

The first answer choice, *there are fewer theater directors than film directors*, is not supported in the passage. The second choice, *film directing is more exciting than television directing*, is irrelevant because excitement is neither mentioned nor implied in the passage. The third choice, *film and television directors have to travel a lot*, is also irrelevant. Nothing in the passage suggests this.

The fourth choice, *film school graduates may have to work their way up*, is implied in this sentence:

> After film students have graduated, they may have to function as a unit director or an assistant director before being given full responsibility as a director.

The correct answer is the fourth choice—the only choice you can infer from the passage.

Look at another example:

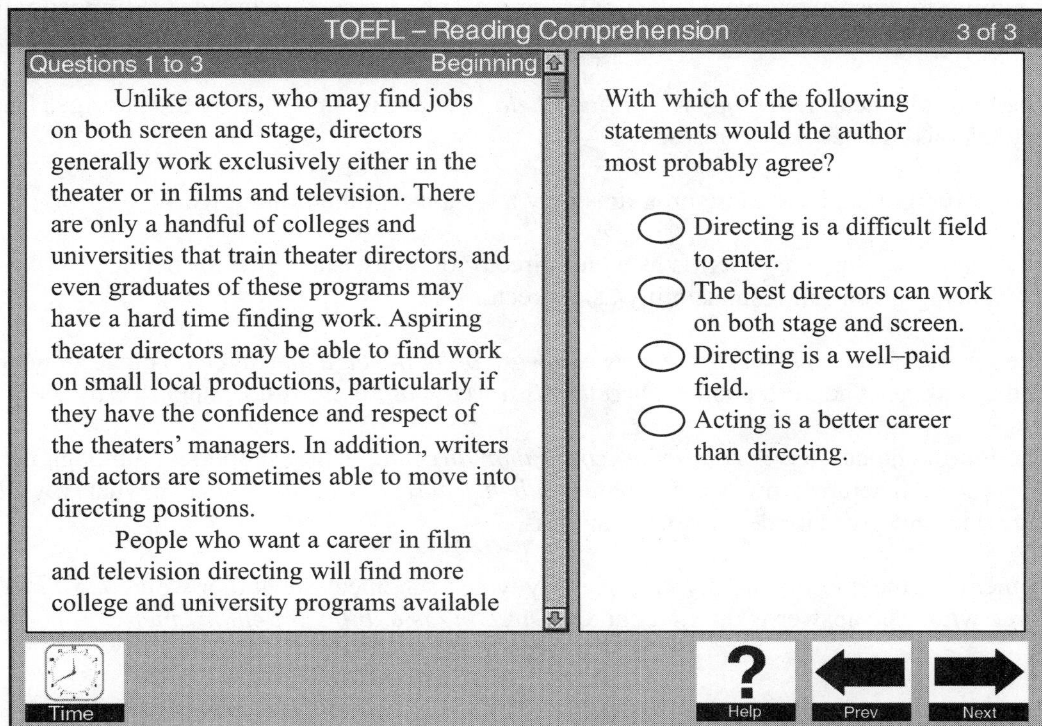

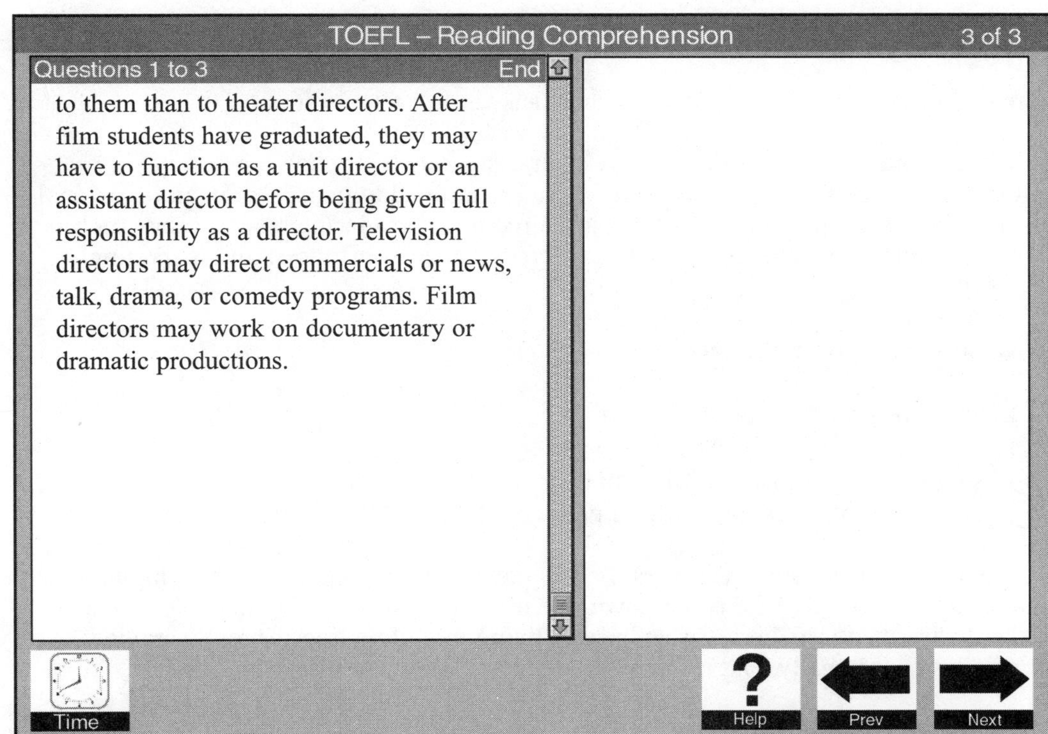

Use the scroll bar to read the whole passage if it does not fit on one screen.

The question requires you to draw a conclusion about the author's message. This type of question is similar to those about main and supporting ideas; however, here the idea is implied rather than stated directly.

The first statement, *Directing is a difficult field to enter*, is supported by the passage. The author implies this in a few key clauses:

> even graduates of these programs may have a hard time finding work
>
> they may have to function as a unit director or an assistant director before being given full responsibility as a director

The second choice, *The best directors can work on both stage and screen*, is inaccurate according to the passage. The third choice, *Directing is a well–paid field*, is not supported by the passage.

The fourth choice, *Acting is a better career than directing*, is not supported, although the passage does mention actors. However, the phrase *a better career* is vague. *Better* in what way? The passage does not give any details to explain this.

Remember, the question asks you to identify which statement the author would *most probably* agree with. The answer is the first choice, *Directing is a difficult field to enter*.

PRACTICE

Exercise 3.5.A

Read the following passages and choose the one best answer to each question.

1. Temporary workers often receive their assignments through temporary employment agencies. They work for firms that require additional help on an occasional basis. In other cases, temporary workers are hired by shops during busy seasons such as Christmas. Temporary workers include cashiers, sales demonstrators, and marketing researchers.

   It can be inferred from the paragraph that

   (A) temporary workers are well paid
   (B) some firms hire only temporary workers
   (C) shops need extra help at Christmas
   (D) temporary workers hope to find permanent jobs

2. Good climbers and swimmers, fishers have a large range in winter. Although the origin of their common name is unknown, the mink's habit of fishing may have been mistakenly ascribed to fishers. Fishers prefer living in hollow trees or rocky crevices, shifting sites occasionally, and if disturbed, they are known to hiss, snarl, or spit.

   It can be inferred that fishers

   (A) are athletic people
   (B) are rich from catching fish
   (C) are most active in winter
   (D) are wild animals

3. Middle age has been regarded as a vague interim period when one is no longer young and not quite old. The connotations of youth are vitality, growth, and the heroic; whereas old age connotes vulnerability, withering, and the brink of nothingness. This overly negative imagery of old age adds greatly to the burden of middle age. It is terrifying to go through middle age as though one were already very old, and it is a self–defeating illusion to live it as though one were still simply young.

The author of the paragraph implies that middle age

(A) is preparation for the nothingness of old age
(B) is when people have illusions about still being young
(C) is defined primarily in negative terms
(D) lasts several years

4. The telephone system makes contacting customers easier, and customers can also phone in orders. Personal computers and the Internet have revolutionized how people buy and sell. The nationwide system of highways, on which large trucks can travel, enables huge quantities of goods to be transported over great distances in a very short time. Sales workers, traveling by road or air, can visit numerous customers every week.

Which of the following can be concluded from the paragraph?

(A) The telephone will soon be superseded by personal computers and the Internet.
(B) Improvements in communications and transportation have influenced commerce.
(C) Changes in technology have made human society more complex.
(D) Traveling by road is less necessary because of telephones and the Internet.

5. About 750 million acres, or one–third of the land in the United States, is covered with forests. All fifty states have forest lands. The forests provide trees for building materials, paper, fuel, and a variety of other uses. They help clean the air, protect water supplies, and make a home for wildlife. They are a major source of recreational opportunities for people and are the basis of hundreds of thousands of jobs.

It can be inferred from the paragraph that

(A) forests in the United States have been replanted
(B) Americans prefer houses built from wood
(C) the number of jobs in forests is increasing
(D) industrialized and urbanized states have forests

6. The traditional English wooden house was built to insure strength and durability. The house was built on a sturdy frame of heavy timbers about a foot thick. These were held together by cutting down the end of one beam into a tongue which was then fitted into a groove in the adjoining beam. This kind of construction required shaping tongues and grooves, making wooden pegs, and fitting all these neatly together.

It can be inferred that traditional English houses

(A) required the tools and the training of a skilled carpenter
(B) took as long as a year to complete
(C) were sturdier and more durable than the houses built today
(D) are no longer being built

READING

Exercise 3.5.B

Read the following passages and choose the one best answer to each question.

QUESTIONS 1–3

The first European to set eyes on the Americas was probably a Norseman named Bjarni Herjulfsson in A.D. 986. He evidently sighted land but did not go ashore. A decade later, a Norse captain, Leif Ericson of Greenland, struck land in present–day Newfoundland, establishing the first European colony in North America. Ericson spent a winter in rough Viking huts thrown up in the area he named Vinland, after its abundant grapes or berries. He returned home in the spring, abandoning the rude settlement that, a few years later, would serve as home base for Thorfinn Karlsevni, another Greenlander.

Thorfinn passed two years in Vinland, exploring the Newfoundland coast and battling local tribes of Inuits, whom the Vikings called *skrelings*, old Norse for "dwarfs." Thorfinn was killed in an encounter with the natives, and continued threats discouraged the Norsemen from further settlement. The Viking explorations, which seemed to Norsemen to have resulted in the discovery of a new land, apparently struck the Inuits as an attempt to invade their homeland. What neither Viking nor Inuit could know, of course, was that it was only the first attack of the European invasion.

1. In lines 1–4 the author suggests that

(A) Bjarni Herjulfsson was born before Leif Ericson
(B) Herjulfsson left some record of seeing land
(C) Leif Ericson was the first European to see North America
(D) the Norsemen were from Newfoundland

2. It can be concluded from paragraph 2 that

(A) the Inuits were a rival group of Vikings
(B) the Vikings attempted to teach the Inuits the Norse language
(C) the relationship between the Vikings and Inuits was hostile
(D) the Vikings were the first Europeans to enslave Native Americans

3. In lines 11–14 the author implies that

(A) more Europeans invaded at a later date
(B) the Inuits declared war on the Vikings
(C) the Inuits would later welcome the Vikings to their homeland
(D) the Vikings intended to conquer the Inuits

QUESTIONS 4–7

Baseball fans have a love affair with statistics. There is absolutely no doubt about it: baseball is the greatest statistics game there is. Because baseball goes back so far in this country's history, it is embedded in most of the population. Fans really understand a home run, a batting average, and an earned run average—all those basics that have been with baseball throughout its history. The basics have never changed, so people know and love them.

In the last quarter century, many new statistics have evolved: hitting with runners in scoring position; the percentages of men driven in with runners on second and third base; a pitcher's saves, as opposed to the percentage of times he has the opportunity to make a save. These are the so–called sophisticated statistics.

There is a whole lore of baseball history involving statistics. One "game" is to compare the players of old with the players of today. Many times on talk shows people will say, "Could Ken Griffey Junior or Alex Rodriguez have played with Ty Cobb or Mickey Cochran or Joe Dimaggio?" What you have to argue with is statistics. You have to go back and examine Dimaggio's years in the big leagues. You look at what he did year by year: he was on average a .300–and some hitter; he drove in so many home runs; he did thus–and–so defensively in the outfield. The statistics are all that remain of the career of that star player. So, you lay them out and try to compare them with the statistics of a player of today. That is the fun of the game.

READING

4. It can be inferred from paragraph 1 that an earned run average is

   (A) a statistic
   (B) difficult to achieve
   (C) a baseball game
   (D) embedded in people's minds

5. In paragraph 2, the author suggests that

   (A) hitting with runners in scoring position was not accomplished until recently
   (B) hitting with runners in scoring position is a complex statistic
   (C) the pitcher is one of the most sophisticated players
   (D) new statistics will evolve in the next quarter century

6. In paragraph 3, the author implies that

   (A) baseball players are often guests on talk shows
   (B) Ken Griffey Junior could play baseball with Ty Cobb
   (C) Joe Dimaggio's career started a new kind of baseball statistics
   (D) Ty Cobb and Mickey Cochran were great baseball players

7. With which of the following statements would the author most probably agree?

   (A) Statistics will replace baseball as the greatest game there is.
   (B) Baseball provides a fascinating way to look at statistics.
   (C) Someone is always inventing a new statistics game.
   (D) Baseball statistics are too complex for many people to understand.

QUESTIONS 8–10

When Thomas Lincoln took his family across the Ohio River into Indiana in 1816, he was searching for a permanent homestead site. He found it near Little Pigeon Creek on a plot of land he had laid claim to earlier. Here the family settled down and remained for fourteen years, and it was here that Nancy Hanks Lincoln died from "milksick," an illness caused by milk from cattle that had eaten snakeroot.

Today the site of the Lincoln cabin is marked by bronze castings of sill logs and a stone hearth. Just beyond this, behind a split–rail fence, is a reconstruction of the little house. It contains the homely and convincing clutter of Abraham Lincoln's boyhood home: log table and benches, a trundle bed, spinning wheels, and a fireplace with iron pots. In a shed behind the cabin the tobacco crop is dried. A few horses, sheep, and chickens complete the pleasant pioneer farm scene. Interpreters in period dress are at hand—tending the crops, working the farm—and are happy to answer one's questions.

Five bas–relief panels depicting scenes from Abraham Lincoln's life decorate the visitor center. A walkway leads from the center to the small hill where the president's mother is buried. Another walk is the Trail of Twelve Stones. Each stone is from a site that played an important part in Lincoln's life.

8. It can be concluded from lines 4–5 that

   (A) "milksick" was a common illness on farms
   (B) snakes killed many cattle
   (C) snakeroot is a poisonous plant
   (D) both people and cattle died from "milksick"

9. It can be inferred from paragraphs 2 and 3 that

   (A) the site of the Lincoln homestead is now a museum
   (B) the Lincoln cabin was built of stone and bronze
   (C) the Lincolns raised mainly tobacco
   (D) the Lincoln farm was modest but beautiful

10. Which of the following is most likely true?

   (A) Thomas Lincoln was originally from Indiana.
   (B) The Lincoln farm produced crops for only fourteen years.
   (C) President Lincoln is buried on a small hill at the homestead.
   (D) Thomas and Nancy Hanks Lincoln were president Lincoln's parents.

Exercise 3.5.C

QUESTIONS 1–3

Read the following passages and choose the one best answer to each question.

Swamps are a type of wetland in which the water table is at or above the surface of the land. Plant growth in swamps is limited to species that can withstand having their roots submerged for long periods of time.

Swamps are dominated by woody plants, primarily trees and shrubs. In the northeastern United States, red maple is a distinctive swamp tree, and in the southeastern United States, the bald cypress and gums dominate. Forested wetlands often show a vertical stratification in vegetation structure, with tree, shrub, and herbaceous layers. Shrubs such as swamp azalea and sweet pepperbush may form a continuous layer. Beneath the shrubs, skunk cabbage may cover the ground, along with a diversity of wetland species, including cardinal flower, jewelweed, and marsh marigold.

1. It can be inferred from the passage that

   (A) the red maple can tolerate having its roots submerged in water
   (B) there are no swamps in the western United States
   (C) few species of animals can survive in a swamp
   (D) swamps should be drained so that more species of trees can grow there

2. The phrase "vertical stratification" in line 7 means that

   (A) the trees and shrubs in swamps do not grow very tall
   (B) swamp trees have three visible layers on their trunks
   (C) there are distinct layers from trees down to herbaceous plants
   (D) herbaceous layers grow alongside trees that have fallen over

3. Which of the following is most probably true about the cardinal flower, jewelweed, and marsh marigold?

   (A) They are rarely found in swamps.
   (B) They are herbaceous plants.
   (C) They grow on shrubs.
   (D) They have colorful, fragrant blooms.

QUESTIONS 4–10

The first balloon–frame building was probably St. Mary's Church in Chicago, which cost about forty dollars and was built in three months with the labor of three men. This was approximately half the expenditure of time and money required for a building of conventional design in 1833. Within twenty years, balloon–frame structures prevailed in the American urban West.

In the manner of other American innovations, balloon–frame construction arose as a solution to peculiar problems of the American upstart city. If the flood of people who poured into the cities was to be housed quickly, houses had to be built in a new way.

The "balloon–frame" was nothing more than the substitution of a light frame of two–by–fours held together by nails in place of the old heavy beams joined by mortise, tenon, and pegs. The wall plates and studs, floor joists, and roof rafters were all made of thin sawed timbers nailed together in such a way that every strain went in the direction of the fiber of the wood. "Basket–frame" was the name sometimes given it, because the light timbers formed a simple basketlike cage to which any material could be applied, inside and out. Usually, clapboards covered the outside. Nothing could be simpler.

It is appropriate that this great innovation should still be known by the derisive name that called attention to its flimsiness and contrasted it with the heaviness of the traditional house. "Balloon–frame" is what respectable builders first called it because the first strong wind, they said, would surely blow it away. However, the construction they were ridiculing would, within decades, become conventional. Into the twentieth century, this was the style that made possible the vast American housing developments. Without it, the quick–grown American city, the high standard of American housing, and the extensive American suburbs would be hard to imagine.

4. It can be inferred from the passage that balloon–frame construction is

(A) based on traditional methods
(B) flimsy and low standard
(C) fast and inexpensive
(D) heavy and solid

5. The author implies that St. Mary's Church in Chicago was

(A) built in a conventional design
(B) expensive to build
(C) not a permanent structure
(D) built in 1833

6. It can be inferred from paragraph 1 that

(A) there were many conventional building designs in the 1830s
(B) balloon–frame construction was common in western cities by the 1850s
(C) balloon–frame construction was the invention of three Chicago men
(D) several original balloon–frame structures have been preserved in Chicago

7. It can be inferred from paragraph 2 that

(A) American cities were growing rapidly
(B) American builders had peculiar ideas
(C) balloon–framing was problematic in cities
(D) balloon–framing was invented when a flood left many people homeless

8. The author implies that traditional construction

(A) was stronger and more long–lasting than balloon–framing
(B) was heavier and required more labor than balloon–framing
(C) was more beautiful than balloon–framing
(D) remained popular despite balloon–framing

9. Builders originally called this method "balloon–frame" because

(A) it allowed a lot of light into a building
(B) they compared it to a simple basket
(C) it did not withstand high winds
(D) they considered it ridiculously light

10. It can be concluded from lines 19–23 that balloon–frame construction

(A) was replaced by other styles in the twentieth century
(B) was a convention for a few decades
(C) has been used extensively in America
(D) has been used more in cities than in suburban development

Answers to Exercises 3.5.A through 3.5.C are on page 659.

3.5 EXTENSION

1. Working in pairs, students identify the parts of the passages in Exercises 3.5.A to 3.5.C from which each correct inference can be made. Underline key words and phrases. How do the incorrect answer choices try to trick you?

2. Working in teams of 3 to 4 people, students read the passage below. Each team writes a list of statements that can be inferred or concluded from the information in the passage. Work for five minutes. Then, each team shares its inferences with the whole class. Is there information in the passage to support each inference?

   A distinction between two kinds of intelligences—crystallized and fluid intelligence—has been widely studied by researchers studying adult learning. Crystallized intelligence is heavily dependent on education and experience. It consists of the set of skills and knowledge that we each learn as part of growing up in any culture. It includes such skills as vocabulary, the ability to reason clearly about real–life problems, and the technical skills we learn for our jobs. Crystallized abilities are "exercised" abilities.

   Fluid intelligence, in contrast, is thought to be a more "basic" set of abilities, not so dependent on specific education. These are the "unexercised" abilities. Most tests of memory tap fluid intelligence.

   Crystallized abilities generally continue to rise over our lifetime, while fluid abilities begin to decline much earlier, beginning perhaps at age 35 or 40.

3. Students create "TOEFL questions" to test their classmates' ability to make inferences. Students select a short passage from a textbook or magazine. Working in pairs, write one or two inference questions for each passage. Use the list of inference questions on page 414 for examples of how to word the questions. Then write four answer choices for each question. One must be a correct inference! Three choices must be incorrect because they are not supported by information that is either stated or implied in the passage.

For activity #3, the teacher collects the passages with questions and answer choices, edits them, and uses them in a student–made "TOEFL exam."

ASSESSING PROGRESS – 3.5

QUIZ 6 (Time – 13 minutes)

Read the following passages and choose the one best answer to each question. Answer all questions on the basis of what is stated or implied in that passage.

QUESTIONS 1–5

Culture refers to a group's program for survival in and adaptation to its environment. The cultural program consists of knowledge, concepts, and values that are shared by group members through their symbols and systems of communication.

The United States, like other nations, has a shared set of values and symbols that form the core culture. This culture is shared to some extent by all the various cultural and ethnic groups that make up the nation. This core culture is difficult to describe because the United States is such a complex nation; it is easier to identify the core culture within an isolated premodern society. However, it is possible to assert that the political institutions reflecting some of the nation's core values were heavily influenced not only by the British but also by the Native Americans, particularly those practices related to making group decisions.

A key concept in the U. S. core culture is the idea that "all men are created equal." When the nation's founding fathers expressed this idea in 1776, their conception of men was limited. White men without property, white women, and all African Americans and Native Americans were excluded. While the concept of equality had a limited meaning at that time, it has proven to be a powerful idea in the quest for civil rights in the United States. It remains an important part of the U. S. core culture and is still used by victimized groups to justify their struggles for equality.

1. With which of the following statements would the author most probably agree?

   (A) People generally view culture in terms of survival.
   (B) Americans believe their culture is superior to others.
   (C) The cultural program of a society is established by its political institutions.
   (D) Most people in a country share certain core values.

2. Which of the following would NOT be included under the definition of "culture" in paragraph 1?

   (A) Educational system
   (B) Concept of humor
   (C) Skin and eye color
   (D) Concept of human rights

3. In lines 6–8, the author suggests that

   (A) the United States is an isolated premodern society
   (B) the culture of a premodern society is simpler than the U. S. culture
   (C) the United States has no core culture
   (D) very little is known about societies that have developed in isolation

4. The author implies that the original idea that "all men are created equal"

   (A) applied only to white men who owned property
   (B) included only people who were born in the United States
   (C) was a value shared by most Americans in 1776
   (D) was not part of the core culture until 1776

5. In paragraph 3, the author implies that

(A) the struggle for equality is ongoing in the United States
(B) some people do not have to struggle for civil rights
(C) the idea that "all men are created equal" is not part of the core culture
(D) core values tend to victimize some groups of people

QUESTIONS 6–10

Before the 1960s, no one really knew if rockets would ever be able to carry humans into space. The first man's step onto the moon's surface was a triumph for science and technology, as well as the culmination of a national quest that had begun in 1961, when President Kennedy vowed to put a man on the moon before the decade was out.

In the eight years from 1961 to 1969, Americans moved from a president's vision to the reality of a lunar landing. Most people think of this achievement in terms of the tremendous scientific advances it represented in physics, engineering, chemistry, and associated technologies. However, there was another side to this far–reaching project. Someone had to set the objectives, commission the work, suffer the setbacks, overcome unforeseen obstacles, and tie together a project with thousands of disparate components. The kind of science responsible for such details is a branch of mathematics called *management science*.

NASA administrators faced many new problems in putting a man on the moon. They had to choose the best design for the spacecraft, design realistic ground simulations, and weigh the priorities of conducting experiments with immediate returns against those that would serve long–term goals. When NASA commissioned the Apollo module, it was asking several hundred companies to design, build, test, and deliver components and systems that had never been built before. Supporting these space age goals, however, was management science, which strove to find ways to make the operations as productive and economical as possible.

6. In lines 1–7 the author implies that

(A) no one believed a man could walk on the moon
(B) a man walked on the moon in 1969
(C) President Kennedy led the space program for eight years
(D) President Kennedy wanted to walk on the moon

7. Which of the following could NOT be inferred about management science?

(A) It is guided by systematic mathematical analysis.
(B) It developed before the invention of computers.
(C) It coordinates the details of complex projects.
(D) It attempts to manage problems that arise unexpectedly.

8. It can be inferred that NASA is

(A) a branch of mathematics
(B) a spacecraft
(C) a space organization
(D) a university

9. It can be inferred from the passage that

(A) President Kennedy was a management scientist
(B) there have been numerous successful moon landings
(C) a lunar landing would have been possible without management science
(D) management science played an important role in the space program

READING

10. What does the paragraph following the passage probably discuss?

(A) How management science promoted efficiency in the space program
(B) How space travel developed between 1961 and 1969
(C) NASA's space goals in the 1960s
(D) How management science has contributed to science and technology

Answers to Reading Quiz 6 are on page 659.

3.6 Identifying Organization and Purpose

Read the following paragraph and answer the question.

Most jazz is based on two short forms—the blues and the ballad. Blues traditionally have a twelve–bar chorus; ballads usually have 32 bars. Ballads that are worked over by successive generations of players become known as standards. "Going to Chicago" is a blues. "Autumn Leaves" is a standard. Both of these forms are short and quite simple, allowing for greater freedom in improvisation.

Which of the following best describes the organization of the paragraph?

- A definition of jazz
- An account of the origins of jazz
- A classification of types of jazz
- A comparison of two jazz forms

The paragraph describes two musical forms—the blues and the ballad—noting both similarities and differences and giving an example of each form.

The answer is the fourth choice, *A comparison of two jazz forms*. Why are the other three answer choices incorrect?

Now, read another paragraph and answer the question.

Among the growing number of alternative work styles is flextime. Flextime allows workers to adjust work hours to suit personal needs. The total number of hours in the week remains the same, but the daily schedule varies from standard business hours. Flextime can also mean a change in workdays, such as four 10–hour days or six short days. Workers on flextime schedules include employment agents, claim adjusters, mail clerks, and data entry operators.

What is the purpose of the paragraph?

- To describe flexible workers
- To define flextime
- To discuss alternative work styles
- To compare different jobs

The answer is the second choice, *To define flextime*. All of the sentences in the paragraph support this purpose. Why are the other three answer choices incorrect?

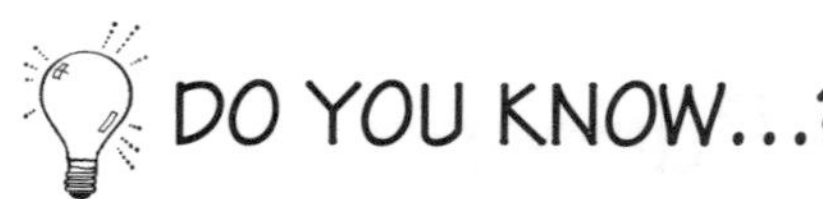

DO YOU KNOW...?

1. Approximately four items on the TOEFL will test your ability to analyze the organization of a passage or to identify the author's purpose in writing the passage.

2. The ***organization*** of a passage is the way the author presents the information and ideas. The organizational structure is the author's plan.

   TOEFL questions about organization look like this:

   > Which of the following best describes the organization of the passage?
   > Which of the following best describes the development of the passage?
   > The format of the passage could best be described as _____.
   > The passage discusses _____ in terms of _____.
   > Where in the passage does the author mention _____?
   > refer to _____?

   Some ways that passages or paragraphs can be organized include:

causes	contrast	explanation	narrative
cause and result	definition	history	process
classification	description	illustration	reasons
comparison	examples	instructions	summary

   On the TOEFL, some of the above words may appear in the answer choices for questions about organization.

3. The ***purpose*** of a passage is the reason the author wrote it. Every well–written passage has a purpose. The purpose may be to inform, define, explain, illustrate, compare, criticize, or so on. The author's purpose is closely related to the main idea (See 3.1).

   TOEFL questions about purpose can be about either a whole passage or part of a passage. Sometimes each paragraph in a passage serves a different purpose. For example, one paragraph may define a concept, another may give examples to illustrate the concept, and another may compare this concept to another concept.

   Some questions may ask what the author means by a specific sentence. Others may ask why the author mentioned a certain word or phrase.

   TOEFL questions about purpose look like this:

   > What is the purpose of the passage/paragraph __?
   > The purpose of the passage/paragraph __ is to _____.
   > Why does the author claim that _____?
   > What does the author mean by the statement __________?
   > Why does the author mention/suggest _____ in paragraph/line __?

Some key words you may see in answer choices for questions about purpose are:

analyze	criticize	illustrate	prove
caution	define	persuade	show
classify	describe	point out	summarize
compare	emphasize	praise	support
contrast	explain	predict	warn

TOEFL questions about both organization and purpose look like this:

Where in the passage does the author
describe _____?
compare _____?
explain _____?
give an example of _____?
give reasons for _____?

4. Some TOEFL questions ask you to describe the author's attitude toward something in the passage.

The author's attitude toward _____ could best be described as _____.

Some key words you may see in answer choices for questions about author's attitude are:

advisory	complimentary	explanatory	objective
approving	concerned	historical	persuasive
cautionary	critical	indifferent	sarcastic

5. On the paper test, questions about organization and purpose require you to scan the passage for specific information. Look at these examples:

Questions 1–2

The hydrologic cycle is the continual flow of water from the ocean to the atmosphere to the land and, after several days, back to the ocean again. The water in the atmosphere is extremely mobile, and the quantity of water in all phases of the cycle is interrelated. Any modification of the amount of water on, in, or above the land produces changes in other parts of the cycle. Actions by individuals in one place are balanced by changes in the cycle either at the same place or at some distant place.

Nearly every human enterprise has modified the hydrologic cycle in some way. Over the centuries, vast amounts of land have been converted from forest to arable fields and pasture. Overgrazing of livestock has changed many landscapes. Changes in vegetation types caused by human activity have resulted in the development of a drier climate and a change in the quantity of water in the different phases of the hydrologic cycle. By cutting forests, plowing land, building reservoirs, and creating urban complexes, people have greatly altered the exchange of moisture between land and atmosphere.

1. Why does the author claim that actions by individuals are balanced by changes in the hydrologic cycle somewhere?

   (A) To explain why the amount of water on Earth will decrease
   (B) To criticize the actions of individuals who use too much water
   (C) To point out that all water on Earth is part of a single system
   (D) To warn of the dangers of water pollution

2. Where in the passage does the author give an example of the human impact on the landscape?

   (A) Lines 1–2
   (B) Lines 2–4
   (C) Lines 5–7
   (D) Lines 10–12

For question 1, you have to scan the passage for key words and phrases from the question. In lines 5–6, you can see the key phrases *actions by individuals* and *changes in the cycle*. By rereading paragraph 1, you can see that an important idea is *the quantity of water in all phases of the cycle is interrelated.*

Choice (A) is incorrect because the passage does not specify a *decrease* in the amount of water. Choice (B) is incorrect because the passage does not focus on using too much water. Choice (D) is not dealt with here.

The correct answer to question 1 is (C), *To point out that all water on Earth is part of a single system*. This is also the main idea of the passage because everything in both paragraphs supports and develops this idea.

For question 2, you have to scan the passage to find information about the *human impact on the landscape*. Scan the lines specified in each of the answer choices to see which of these lines discusses the human impact on the landscape.

The correct answer to question 2 is (D), *Lines 10–12*, because it is here that the author states that overgrazing of livestock has changed many landscapes and that changes in vegetation types have resulted in the development of a drier climate.

6. On the computer test, questions about organization and purpose look like this:

> Click on the sentence in paragraph __ that discusses _____.
> Click on the paragraph that describes _____.
> compares _____.
> outlines _____.
> explains _____.
> Why does the author mention _____ in paragraph __?
> What does the author mean by the statement __________?

Look at an example:

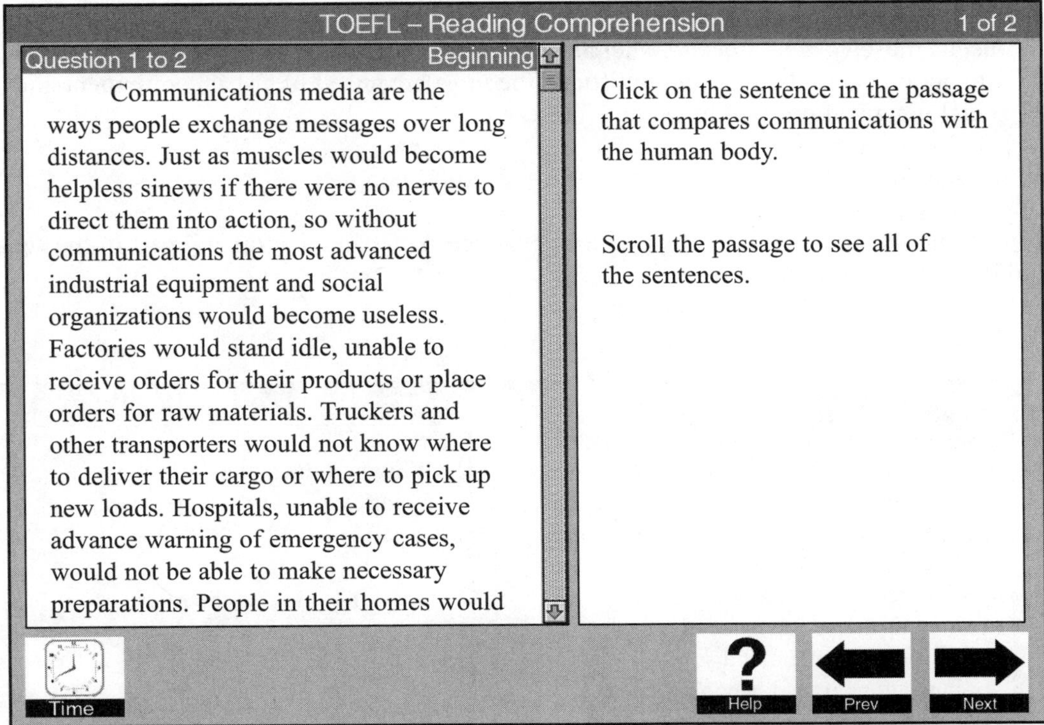

TOEFL – Reading Comprehension
1 of 2
Question 1 to 2
Beginning
Communications media are the ways people exchange messages over long distances. Just as muscles would become helpless sinews if there were no nerves to direct them into action, so without communications the most advanced industrial equipment and social organizations would become useless. Factories would stand idle, unable to receive orders for their products or place orders for raw materials. Truckers and other transporters would not know where to deliver their cargo or where to pick up new loads. Hospitals, unable to receive advance warning of emergency cases, would not be able to make necessary preparations. People in their homes would
Click on the sentence in the passage that compares communications with the human body.
Scroll the passage to see all of the sentences.
Time
Help
Prev
Next

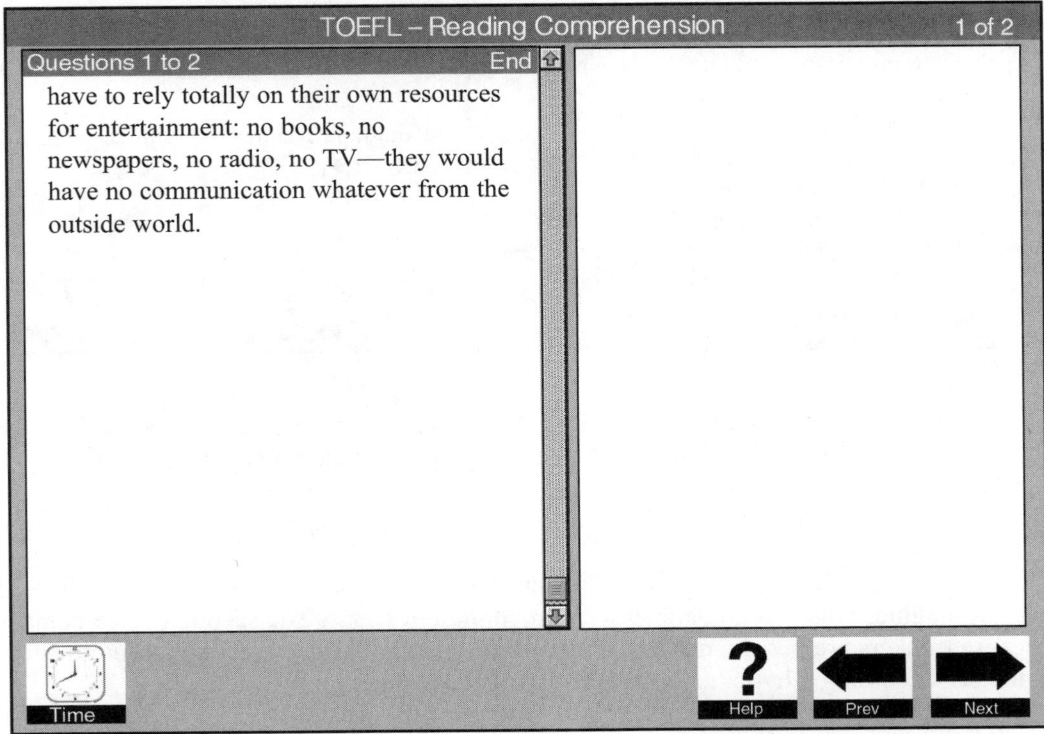

TOEFL – Reading Comprehension
1 of 2
Questions 1 to 2
End
have to rely totally on their own resources for entertainment: no books, no newspapers, no radio, no TV—they would have no communication whatever from the outside world.
Time
Help
Prev
Next

For this question, you must scan the passage for key words referring to the human body. You can find the key words *muscles*, *sinews*, and *nerves* in this sentence:

> Just as muscles would become helpless sinews if there were no nerves to direct them into action, so without communications the most advanced industrial equipment and social organizations would become useless.

In this sentence, you also find the comparative expression *just as*.

You should use the mouse to click on this sentence. You can click on any part of the sentence and it will darken on the screen.

Look at another example:

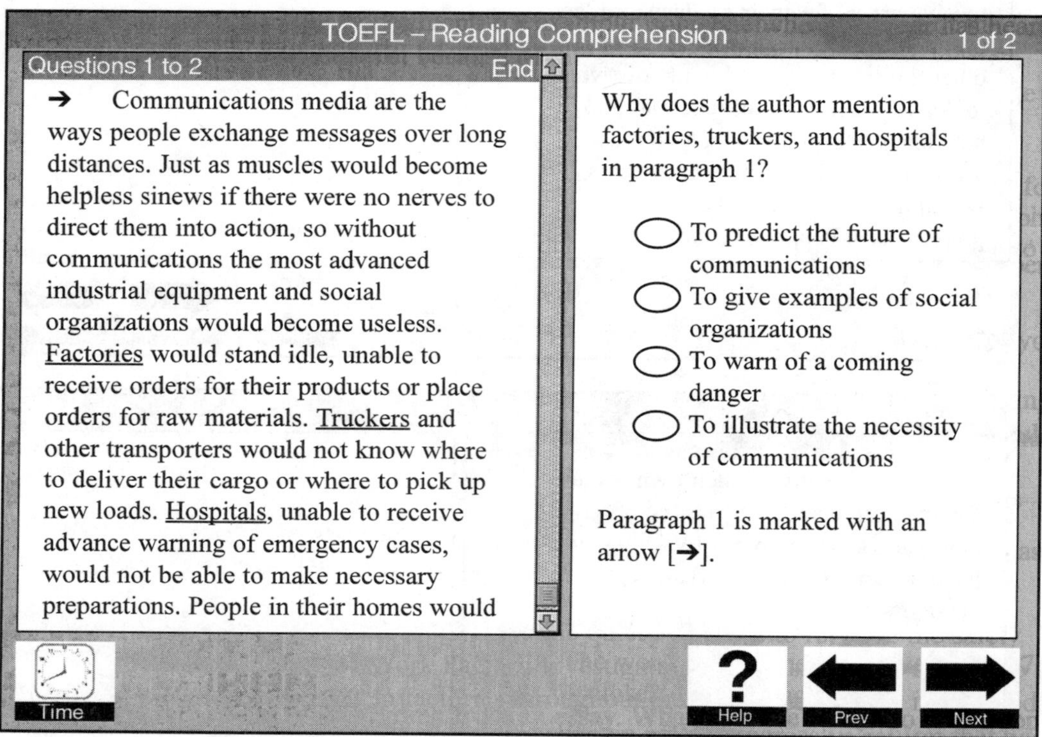

Scan the passage to find *factories*, *truckers*, and *hospitals*. In these sentences, you can see that the author is giving examples of people and things that depend on communications.

The answer is the fourth choice, *To illustrate the necessity of communications*.

The first choice is inaccurate because the author does not try to predict the future. Instead, the author imagines what *would* happen without communications. The second choice is incorrect because truckers are people, not social organizations. The third choice is inaccurate because the author is discussing a hypothetical rather than a real danger.

PRACTICE

Exercise 3.6.A

Read the following passages and choose the one best answer to each question.

Questions 1–3

Mary Cassatt was not only the best of the American Impressionists but the outstanding woman painter of the nineteenth century. Her insights as an artist, her originality of mind, and the rigor of design in her scenes of mothers and children all make her so. It is worth noting, however, that Cassatt was no more or less "American" than Whistler or Sargent were, although she spent less of her life in America than Whistler or Sargent, living almost all her long life in Paris.

Nevertheless, there are good reasons for seeing her in the American context. First, she was raised and educated in Philadelphia, and she never dropped her American citizenship. Second, her work had more impact in America than in France and was eagerly bought by American collectors. And thirdly, she was known as *une Americaine* by the painters in Paris. She never tried to redefine herself as French, and it was in the context of American expatriation that she was appreciated by other artists, both French and American.

1. The author's attitude toward Mary Cassatt could best be described as

   (A) advisory
   (B) critical
   (C) concerned
   (D) explanatory

2. Why does the author mention Whistler and Sargent in lines 4–6?

   (A) To show that Cassatt's work was appreciated by Americans
   (B) To criticize the work of Whistler and Sargent
   (C) To compare Cassatt with other American painters
   (D) To explain why Cassatt chose to live in Paris

3. What is the purpose of paragraph 2?

   (A) To explain why Cassatt should be considered an American painter
   (B) To summarize Cassatt's education and experience
   (C) To explain why Cassatt's paintings were popular in America and France
   (D) To compare American and French attitudes toward Cassatt's work

QUESTIONS 4–8

In 1781, William Herschel, a professional musician in Bath, England, was tired of simply reading about the stars, so he rented a small reflecting telescope, and began spending his nights reading the heavens. He soon came to the conclusion, much like Galileo and Newton, that he could build a better telescope himself, which he presently did. Then he built several more, each with a larger mirror. With each new mirror, he saw increasing numbers of stars. At night, he could be found in his backyard, sweeping the sky with his latest telescope. He would stay out until dawn, studying the stars and planets and recording their positions in what he called his "Book of Sweeps."

Herschel decided to build a telescope with a 36–inch–diameter mirror. Fortunately, the king of England was aware of his accomplishments as an astronomer, which included the discovery of the planet Uranus. Herschel was given a fellowship in the prestigious Royal Society and was also granted the money he needed to build his telescope. A team of craftsmen, under Herschel's supervision, constructed the world's largest telescope, with a 48–inch, 2,000–pound mirror housed within a 40–foot tube. On the night that the telescope was unveiled, the king, along with various members of the Royal Society and other dignitaries, watched as Herschel climbed a ladder and peered into the telescope's eyepiece. Then he climbed back down and wandered away, apparently stunned. "I have looked," he was heard to say, "farther into space than any human being did before me."

4. Which of the following best describes the organization of the passage?

   (A) A description of the reflecting telescope
   (B) An account of the development of the reflecting telescope
   (C) An explanation of how the reflecting telescope works
   (D) A statement supported by examples

5. Why does the author mention Galileo and Newton in lines 3–4?

   (A) To compare Herschel with great scientists
   (B) To praise the work of Galileo and Newton
   (C) To compare the telescopes of Galileo and Herschel
   (D) To show how scientists worked together

6. Why does the author mention the discovery of Uranus in line 11?

   (A) To illustrate the structure of the solar system
   (B) To give an example of Herschel's work
   (C) To prove that Herschel was more a scientist than a musician
   (D) To contrast Herschel with the king of England

7. Where in the passage does the author mention Herschel's writing?

   (A) Lines 1–3
   (B) Lines 3–5
   (C) Lines 7–8
   (D) Lines 11–12

8. Where in the passage does the author quote Herschel?

   (A) Lines 3–5
   (B) Lines 9–11
   (C) Lines 12–14
   (D) Lines 17–18

Exercise 3.6.B

Read the following passages and choose the one best answer to each question.

QUESTIONS 1–3

Several men have been responsible for promoting forestry as a career. Foremost was Gifford Pinchot, the father of professional forestry in America. He was chief of the Forest Service from 1898 until 1910, working with President Theodore Roosevelt to instigate sound conservation practices in American forests. Later he was professor of forestry and founder of the Pinchot School of Forestry at Yale University. Another great forester was Dr. Bernard E. Fernow, the very first head of the U. S. Forest Service. He organized the first collegiate school of professional forestry in the United States at Cornell University.

Foresters today, like Pinchot and Fernow in the past, plan and supervise the growth, protection, and utilization of trees. They make maps of forest areas, estimate the amount of standing timber and future growth, and manage timber sales. They also protect the trees from fire, harmful insects, and disease. Some foresters may be responsible for other duties, ranging from wildlife protection and watershed management to the development and supervision of camps, parks, and grazing lands. Others do research, provide information to forest owners and to the general public, and teach in colleges and universities.

1. Why does the author call Gifford Pinchot "the father of professional forestry in America"?

(A) To emphasize his contribution to the field
(B) To describe his family background
(C) To praise his management skills
(D) To illustrate his influence on the president

2. Where in the passage does the author mention the first university program in forestry?

(A) Lines 1–2
(B) Lines 4–5
(C) Lines 7–8
(D) Lines 14–16

3. Where in the passage does the author discuss the academic work of foresters?

(A) Lines 2–4
(B) Lines 9–10
(C) Lines 12–14
(D) Lines 14–16

READING

QUESTIONS 4–8

Telecommunications technology has created a new class of worker—telecommuters—employees who work at home using computer terminals, then send their work to the office by means of modems. A secretary may work at home four days a week, processing a large volume of routine business letters, and electronically transmitting copies of the letters to the office, where they can be printed out and mailed. The secretary goes to the office one day a week to meet with his or her supervisor to discuss the work. Many companies are experimenting with telecommuting because employees who work at home can save them money on office space, utilities, and parking.

Telecommuting offers several benefits. Telecommuters do not have to drive back and forth to work and do not have to keep a strict nine–to–five schedule. Telecommuting can be ideal for people with disabilities who cannot easily get out of the house or for parents who want to be at home when their children come home from school. Some telecommuters find that they are more productive at home because they are not distracted by other people.

Telecommuting has some disadvantages, however. Telecommuters must have enough self–discipline to work without supervision. Without the companionship of co–workers and the encouragement of supervisors, they may feel isolated. Since few telecommuters are represented by labor unions, they may be underpaid, and even superior workers may be overlooked for promotions and rewards. Also, many telecommuters are not covered by company medical and liability insurance, and many do not get other benefits such as sick pay and vacations.

4. What does the author mean by the statement "Telecommunications technology has created a new class of worker"?

(A) There is a growing demand for telecommunications technology.
(B) Workers must be trained in telecommuting.
(C) There are several problems with driving back and forth to the office.
(D) A number of people now work away from the office.

5. What is the purpose of paragraph 2?

(A) To describe the typical telecommuter
(B) To explain why some people telecommute
(C) To persuade people to try telecommuting
(D) To describe the process of telecommuting

6. What is the purpose of paragraph 3?

(A) To warn of the loneliness of telecommuting
(B) To discuss the drawbacks of telecommuting
(C) To criticize companies who take advantage of telecommuters
(D) To outline the financial disadvantages of telecommuting

7. What does the author mean by the statement "Telecommuters must have enough self–discipline to work without supervision"?

(A) Telecommuters often need to be disciplined by their supervisors.
(B) Supervisors cannot be telecommuters.
(C) Telecommuters must be motivated to work independently.
(D) Telecommuters and supervisors need to cooperate in planning the work.

8. Where in the passage does the author give an example of a telecommuter?

(A) Lines 3–5
(B) Lines 7–8
(C) Lines 9–10
(D) Lines 15–17

Exercise 3.6.C

Read the following passage and follow the directions on the right side of the screen.

TOEFL – Reading Comprehension

Questions 1 to 6

Small business owners manage their own companies. Small businesses include not only retail stores, such as gift shops and bookstores, but also real estate, advertising and employment agencies, self–service laundries, manufacturing firms and franchise operations such as fast food restaurants and gas stations. Many consultants in various fields run their own businesses. In general, companies are considered as small businesses if their yearly sales are below $9 million. However, different standards are applied in different industries.

The three most common types of small businesses are sole proprietorships, partnerships and corporations. In a sole proprietorship, one person owns the business. A partnership is an agreement involving two or more people who own a business together. In a sole proprietorship or partnership, the company's profits are kept by the owner or divided among the partners. The owners are also liable for the firm's debts. In a small corporation, the owners are usually the officers of the corporation and are paid a salary. One advantage of a corporation is that its officers cannot be held personally responsible for the firm's debts.

The responsibilities of small business owners depend on the nature of the company. Most frequently, their primary functions involve planning, money management, and marketing. To keep their companies in business, owners must know when to take financial risks. They must adapt to changing market conditions by creating new products, improving services, or promoting their company in innovative ways. In addition, they must buy services and equipment efficiently.

Some small business owners run the entire operation themselves. The owner of a bicycle shop may buy the inventory, make the repairs, and sell to customers. The owner may also unpack merchandise, build displays, and clean the shop.

1 of 6

Identify the paragraph that outlines the typical duties of most small business owners.

- ○ Paragraph 1
- ○ Paragraph 2
- ○ Paragraph 3
- ○ Paragraph 4

2 of 6

Identify the paragraph that discusses the different ways that small businesses can be organized.

- ○ Paragraph 1
- ○ Paragraph 2
- ○ Paragraph 3
- ○ Paragraph 4

Time Help Prev Next

READING

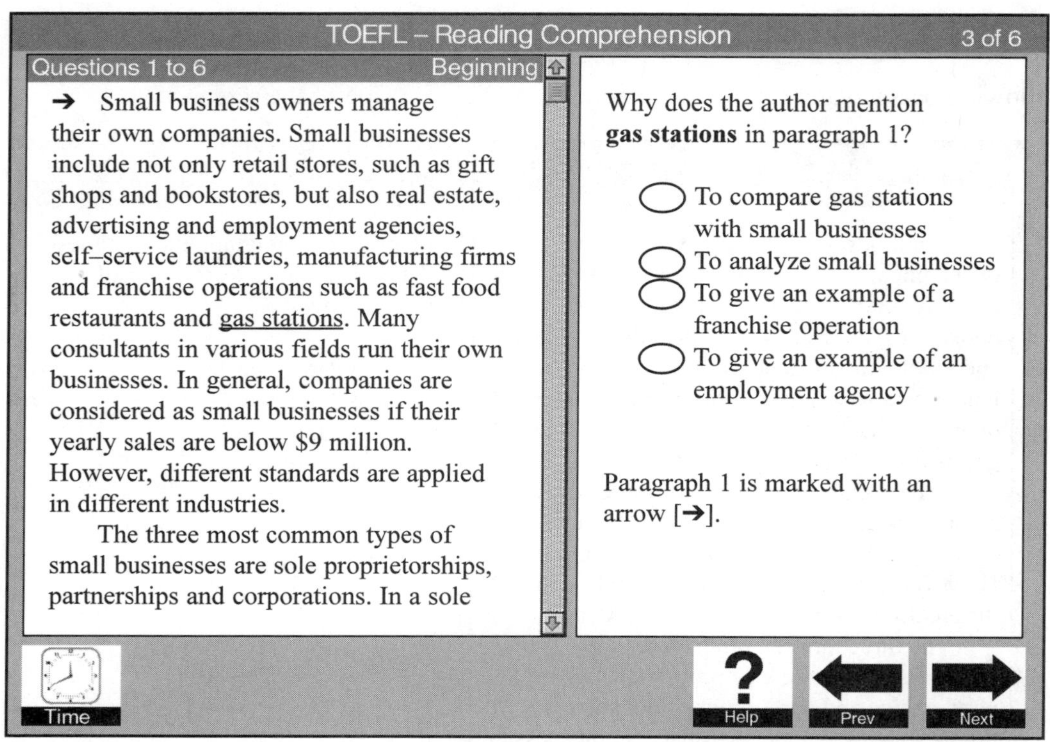
TOEFL – Reading Comprehension
3 of 6
Questions 1 to 6
Beginning
➔ Small business owners manage their own companies. Small businesses include not only retail stores, such as gift shops and bookstores, but also real estate, advertising and employment agencies, self–service laundries, manufacturing firms and franchise operations such as fast food restaurants and gas stations. Many consultants in various fields run their own businesses. In general, companies are considered as small businesses if their yearly sales are below $9 million. However, different standards are applied in different industries.
The three most common types of small businesses are sole proprietorships, partnerships and corporations. In a sole
Why does the author mention **gas stations** in paragraph 1?
To compare gas stations with small businesses
To analyze small businesses
To give an example of a franchise operation
To give an example of an employment agency
Paragraph 1 is marked with an arrow [➔].
Time
Help
Prev
Next

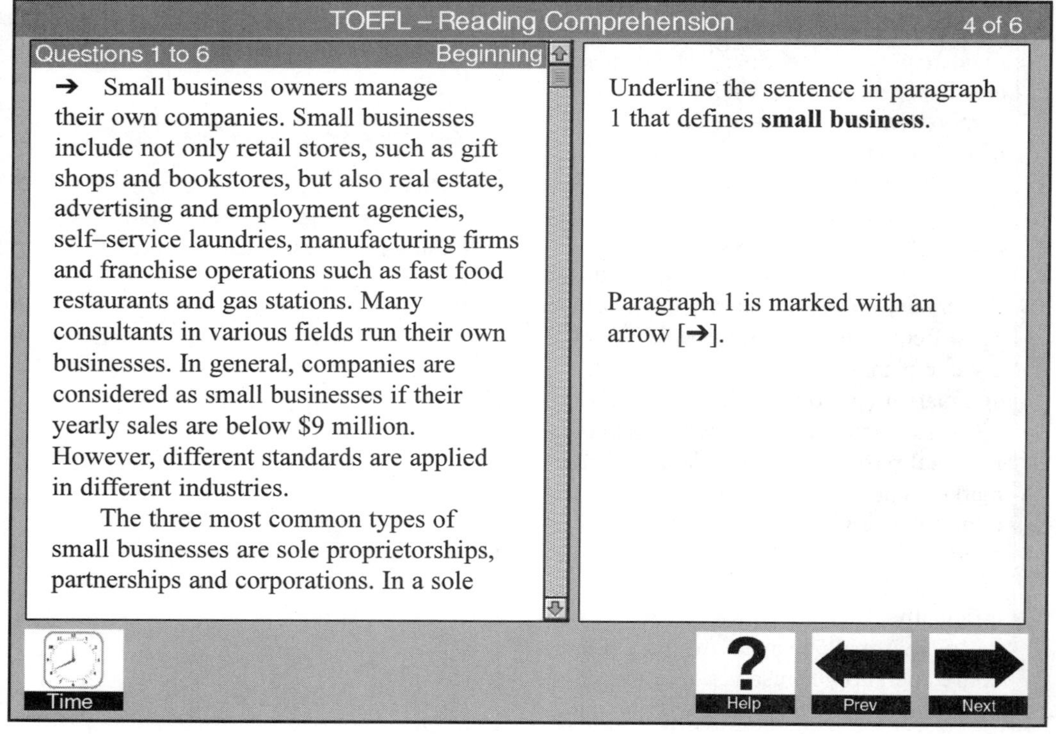
TOEFL – Reading Comprehension
4 of 6
Questions 1 to 6
Beginning
➔ Small business owners manage their own companies. Small businesses include not only retail stores, such as gift shops and bookstores, but also real estate, advertising and employment agencies, self–service laundries, manufacturing firms and franchise operations such as fast food restaurants and gas stations. Many consultants in various fields run their own businesses. In general, companies are considered as small businesses if their yearly sales are below $9 million. However, different standards are applied in different industries.
The three most common types of small businesses are sole proprietorships, partnerships and corporations. In a sole
Underline the sentence in paragraph 1 that defines **small business**.
Paragraph 1 is marked with an arrow [➔].
Time
Help
Prev
Next

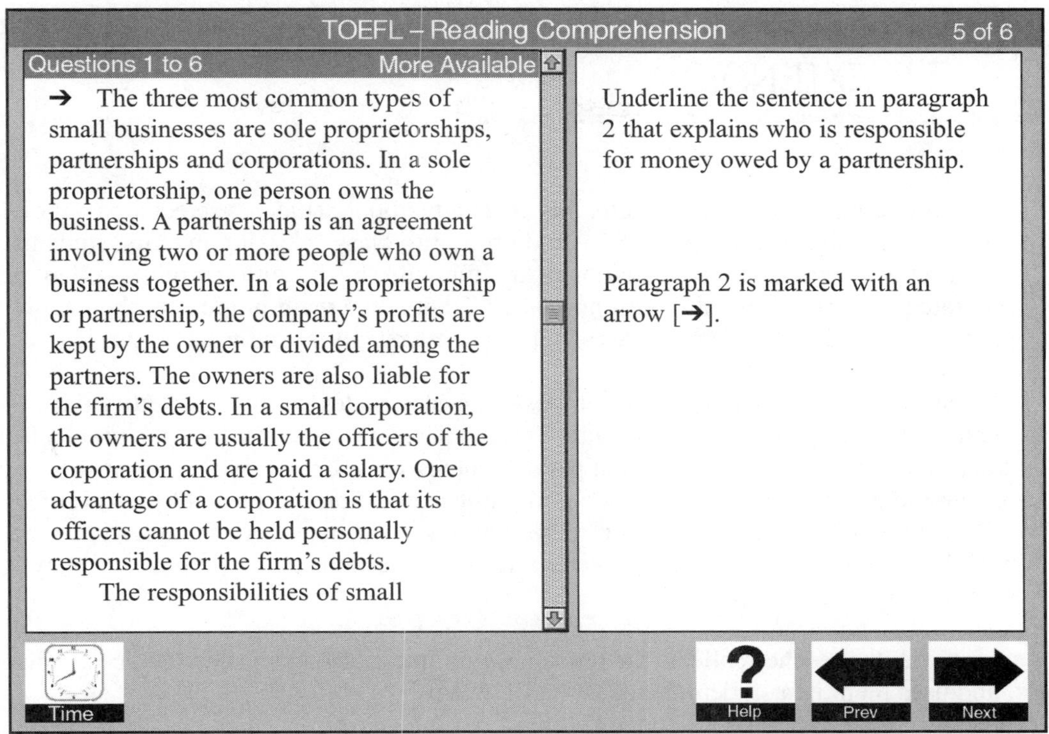
TOEFL – Reading Comprehension
5 of 6
Questions 1 to 6
More Available
➔ The three most common types of small businesses are sole proprietorships, partnerships and corporations. In a sole proprietorship, one person owns the business. A partnership is an agreement involving two or more people who own a business together. In a sole proprietorship or partnership, the company's profits are kept by the owner or divided among the partners. The owners are also liable for the firm's debts. In a small corporation, the owners are usually the officers of the corporation and are paid a salary. One advantage of a corporation is that its officers cannot be held personally responsible for the firm's debts.
The responsibilities of small
Underline the sentence in paragraph 2 that explains who is responsible for money owed by a partnership.
Paragraph 2 is marked with an arrow [➔].
Time
Help
Prev
Next

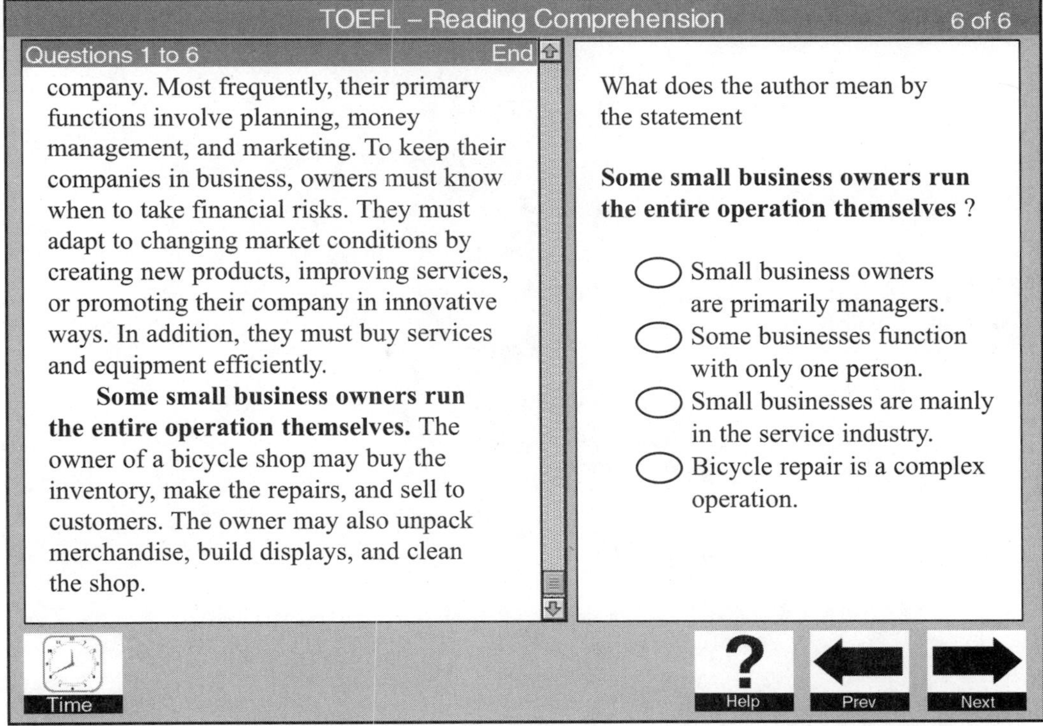
TOEFL – Reading Comprehension
6 of 6
Questions 1 to 6
End
company. Most frequently, their primary functions involve planning, money management, and marketing. To keep their companies in business, owners must know when to take financial risks. They must adapt to changing market conditions by creating new products, improving services, or promoting their company in innovative ways. In addition, they must buy services and equipment efficiently.
Some small business owners run the entire operation themselves. The owner of a bicycle shop may buy the inventory, make the repairs, and sell to customers. The owner may also unpack merchandise, build displays, and clean the shop.
What does the author mean by the statement
Some small business owners run the entire operation themselves ?
Small business owners are primarily managers.
Some businesses function with only one person.
Small businesses are mainly in the service industry.
Bicycle repair is a complex operation.
Time
Help
Prev
Next

Answers to Exercises 3.6.A through 3.6.C are on page 660.

READING

3.6 EXTENSION

1. In reading done outside class, preferably from a textbook, students select a passage of 3 to 5 paragraphs. Make a photocopy and bring it to class. Working in pairs, students identify (a) the passage's organizational structure and (b) the author's purpose. Do the separate paragraphs have different purposes? What is the main purpose of the whole passage? What key words or phrases help you understand the author's purpose?

2. Students create "TOEFL questions" to test their classmates' ability to identify the organization and purpose of a passage. Select a short passage of 1 to 3 paragraphs from a textbook or magazine. Working in pairs, students write one or two questions for each passage. Use the lists of organization and purpose questions on page 430 for examples of how to word the questions. Then write four answer choices for each question. One must be the correct answer! In answer choices for questions about purpose, use key words from the list on page 431.

For activity #2, the teacher collects the passages with questions and answer choices, edits them, and uses them in a student–made "TOEFL exam."

 ASSESSING PROGRESS – 3.5 through 3.6

Quiz 7 (Time – 13 minutes)

Read the following passages and choose the one best answer to each question. Answer all questions on the basis of what is stated or implied in that passage.

Questions 1–4

The mathematics of chance, the mathematical description of randomness, is called the *theory of probability*. Probability describes the predictable long–run patterns of random outcomes.

Toss a coin in the air. Will it land heads or tails? It lands sometimes heads and sometimes tails. We cannot say what the next fall will be. Perhaps you would argue that the coin has an equal chance of falling heads or tails on the next toss.

Suppose that we toss a coin not once but ten thousand times. John Kerrich, an English mathematician, actually did this while a prisoner of World War II. Kerrich's first ten tosses gave four heads, a proportion of 0.4. The proportion of heads increased to 0.5 after twenty tosses and to 0.57 after thirty tosses. In a small number of tosses, the proportion of heads fluctuates—it is still essentially unpredictable. However, many tosses will produce a smoothing effect. A proportion of 0.507 resulted after Kerrich threw the coin five thousand times. Moreover, in all ten thousand trials, he again scored 0.507 of the total. After many trials, the proportion of heads settled down to a fixed number. This number is the probability of a head.

1. What is the purpose of the passage?

    (A) To illustrate a theory
    (B) To compare a theory and an experiment
    (C) To outline a procedure
    (D) To explain why a coin toss favors heads

2. It can be inferred from paragraph 2 that

    (A) we cannot guess the result of a coin toss
    (B) how a coin lands depends on its monetary value
    (C) a coin has an equal chance of falling heads or tails
    (D) a coin has two sides: "heads" and "tails"

3. Where in the passage does the author summarize Kerrich's experiment?

    (A) Lines 1–3
    (B) Lines 4–5
    (C) Lines 7–9
    (D) Lines 13–15

4. With which of the following statements would the author most probably agree?

    (A) A coin toss is not an accurate way to predict probability.
    (B) John Kerrich's experiment was scientifically unreliable because he was a prisoner.
    (C) A large number of trials is necessary to determine the probability of an outcome.
    (D) Ten coin tosses will produce the same outcome as ten thousand tosses.

Questions 5–10

Benjamin Franklin said many things we still say today, did many things we still talk about today, and created many things that called forth new American words: *postmaster*, *rocking chair*, *lightning rod*, *bifocals*. This practical, tinkering, mobile American who had so many interests, was born in 1706, the fifteenth child of a Boston soap and candle maker. Apprenticed to a brother, a printer, Benjamin ran away to Philadelphia at seventeen, owned his own printing shop at twenty–four, and retired at forty–six to devote himself to science, philosophy, and politics.

Franklin was a problem solver. His passion was to make the large scientific theories of his day practical, to improve the daily lives of common people. He helped establish the first American hospital in Philadelphia in 1751, and that same year was widely talked about for his famous "kite–key experiment," which demonstrated that lightning is electricity. At a time when electricity was nothing more than a parlor trick, he used it to roast turkeys. He invented the bifocals that he himself wore. For his own home, he invented the lightning rod and that marvel of efficiency, the Franklin stove.

His *Pennsylvania Gazette* was the most valuable newspaper in the American colonies between 1730 and 1748, and his *Poor Richard's Almanac* was the most widely read and quoted almanac in the colonies at a time when the almanac served as a family guide, popular encyclopedia, and home entertainment center.

Franklin rose quickly in the political life of the colonies and is best known for his place in American history. He represented the colonies in England and France, was a member of the Second Continental Congress, helped Thomas Jefferson draft the Declaration of Independence, and was the elder statesman of the Constitutional Convention. He was a whole man, a man of the world who imagined the complete experience of American life, yet in his will, he listed himself first as "Printer."

5. The author's attitude toward Benjamin Franklin could best be described as

   (A) persuasive
   (B) complimentary
   (C) indifferent
   (D) emotional

6. In lines 1–3, the author suggests that

   (A) Franklin influenced American English
   (B) Franklin remains controversial today
   (C) many new words were created to describe Franklin
   (D) Franklin's writings are still well–read today

7. It can be inferred that the *Pennsylvania Gazette* and *Poor Richard's Almanac*

   (A) taught many people to read
   (B) influenced American politics
   (C) were printed by Franklin
   (D) made Franklin a rich man

8. Where in the passage does the author mention a scientific experiment?

   (A) Lines 8–9
   (B) Lines 11–12
   (C) Lines 13–14
   (D) Lines 19–20

9. Where in the passage does the author discuss Franklin's role in the government?

   (A) Paragraph 1
   (B) Paragraph 2
   (C) Paragraph 3
   (D) Paragraph 4

10. It can be inferred from lines 20–24 that

   (A) Franklin was a friend of the kings of England and France
   (B) Thomas Jefferson could not finish the Declaration of Independence alone
   (C) Franklin was a wealthy, materialistic man
   (D) Franklin considered printing his most important role

Answers to Reading Quiz 7 are on page 660.

 ASSESSING PROGRESS – 3.1 through 3.6

QUIZ 8 (Time – 22 minutes)

Read the following passages and choose the one best answer to each question. Answer all questions on the basis of what is stated or implied in that passage.

QUESTIONS 1–9

The house style that dominated American housing during the 1880s and 1890s was known as "Queen Anne." This may seem a curious name for an American style, and it was, in fact, a historical accident. The style originated with fashionable architects in Victorian England who coined the name with apparently no reason other than its pleasing sound. The style was loosely based on medieval buildings constructed long before 1702, the beginning year of Queen Anne's reign.

A distinctive characteristic found in most Queen Anne houses is the unusual roof shape—a steeply pitched, hipped central portion from which protrude lower front and side extensions ending in gables. It is often possible to spot these distinctive roof forms from several blocks away. Another feature usually found on this style is wood shingle siding cut into fanciful decorative patterns of scallops, curves, diamonds, or triangles. Queen Anne houses are almost always asymmetrical. If you draw an imaginary line down the middle of one, you will see how drastically different the right and left sides are, all the way from ground level to roof peak. A final common characteristic is the inviting wraparound porch—one that includes the front door area and then extends around to either the right or left side.

Queen Anne houses faded from fashion early in the twentieth century as the public's taste shifted toward the more "modern" prairie and craftsman houses. Today, however, Queen Anne houses are favorite symbols of the past, painstakingly and lovingly restored by old–house buffs. They are also being reproduced by contemporary builders, with faithful attention to the distinctive shapes and detailing which were first popularized more than one hundred years ago.

1. The passage primarily discusses

   (A) the history of American housing
   (B) a popular American house style
   (C) English influence on American architecture
   (D) why Queen Anne houses are being reproduced today

2. The word "This" in line 2 refers to

   (A) a house style
   (B) American housing
   (C) "Queen Anne"
   (D) a historical accident

3. Which of the following is NOT mentioned as a characteristic of a Queen Anne house?

   (A) Decorative windows
   (B) Wood shingle exterior
   (C) Large porch
   (D) Steep roof

4. From the phrase "fanciful decorative patterns" in line 11, it can be inferred that

   (A) Queen Anne houses were expensive to build
   (B) the wood shingles were hand–made
   (C) Queen Anne houses were ornate
   (D) bright colors were popular in the 1880s and 1890s

5. The word "asymmetrical" in line 12 is closest in meaning to

(A) inefficient
(B) bold
(C) unusual
(D) unbalanced

6. According to the passage, why did Queen Anne houses go out of style?

(A) They became seen as a symbol of the past.
(B) People started moving to the suburbs and prairies.
(C) People were more interested in newer styles.
(D) Queen Anne houses became too expensive to build.

7. The word "buffs" in line 20 is closest in meaning to

(A) sellers
(B) buyers
(C) painters
(D) fans

8. In paragraph 3, the author implies that

(A) old–fashioned styles are no longer being built
(B) the Queen Anne style is enjoying a new popularity
(C) one cannot distinguish reproductions of Queen Anne houses from real ones
(D) people's tastes in housing are always changing

9. Where in the passage does the author mention an architectural influence on the Queen Anne style?

(A) Lines 5–6
(B) Lines 7–9
(C) Lines 17–18
(D) Lines 20–22

QUESTIONS 10–20

After the Anasazi abandoned southwestern Colorado in the late 1200s or early 1300s, history's pages are blank. The Anasazi were masons and apartment builders who occupied the deserts, river valleys, and mesas of this region for over a thousand years, building structures that have weathered the test of time.

The first Europeans to visit southwestern Colorado were the ever–restless, ambitious Spanish, who sought gold, pelts, and slaves. In 1765, under orders from the Spanish governor in Santa Fe, Juan Maria Antonio Rivera led a prospecting and trading party into the region. Near the Dolores River in southwestern Colorado, he found some insignificant silver–bearing rocks, and it is thought that it was he who named the mountains nearby the Sierra de la Plata or the Silver Mountains. Rivera found little of commercial value that would interest his superiors in Santa Fe, but he did open up a route that would soon lead to the establishment of the Old Spanish Trail. This expedition and others to follow left names on the land which are the only reminders we have today that the Spanish once explored this region.

In 1776, one of the men who had accompanied Rivera, Andre Muniz, acted as a guide for another expedition. That party entered southwestern Colorado in search of a route west to California, traveling near today's towns of Durango and Dolores. Along the way, they camped at the base of a large green mesa which today carries the name Mesa Verde. They were the first Europeans to record the discovery of an Anasazi archaeological site in southwestern Colorado.

By the early 1800s, American mountain men and trappers were exploring the area in their quest for beaver pelts. Men like Peg–leg Smith were outfitted with supplies in the crossroads trapping town of Taos, New Mexico. These adventurous American trappers were a tough bunch. They, possibly more than any other newcomers, penetrated deeply into the mountain fastness of southwestern Colorado, bringing back valuable information about the area and discovering new routes through the mountains. One of the trappers, William Becknell, the father of the Santa Fe Trail, camped in the area of Mesa Verde, where he found pottery shards, stone houses, and other Anasazi remains.

10. What does the passage mainly discuss?

(A) Early exploration of Colorado
(B) The history of the Anasazi in Colorado
(C) The Spanish influence in Colorado
(D) Economic exploitation of Colorado

11. The phrase "weathered the test of time" in line 4 means that

(A) the Anasazi culture was very old
(B) the Anasazi abandoned Colorado because of the desert conditions
(C) Anasazi buildings can still be seen
(D) climatic conditions have changed since the time of the Anasazi

12. Why does the author mention "gold, pelts, and slaves" in line 6?

(A) To point out the wealth of the region
(B) To classify the natural resources
(C) To criticize the cruelty of the Spanish
(D) To show commercial interest in the region

13. The phrase "the region" in line 8 refers to

(A) Sierra de la Plata
(B) Santa Fe
(C) southwestern Colorado
(D) New Mexico

READING

14. It can be concluded from lines 12–14 that

(A) Rivera's expedition was unsuccessful
(B) many places in the area have Spanish names
(C) not much is known of the Spanish exploration of the region
(D) the Spanish culture quickly overtook the native culture

15. The purpose of the expedition of 1776 was

(A) to look for silver in the mountains
(B) to build the towns of Durango and Dolores
(C) to look for a way to reach California
(D) to study the archaeology of the region

16. The word "fastness" in line 25 is closest in meaning to

(A) wasteland
(B) stronghold
(C) desert
(D) starvation

17. In paragraph 4, the author suggests that

(A) mountain men and trappers survived in harsh conditions
(B) Peg–leg Smith owned a trading post in New Mexico
(C) American trappers traded with the Spanish
(D) beaver pelts were becoming scarce in Colorado in the 1800s

18. Which of the following is most likely true about William Becknell?

(A) He was wealthy from selling beaver pelts.
(B) He collected Anasazi pottery.
(C) He was well–educated about Anasazi culture.
(D) He built the Santa Fe Trail.

19. Which of the following best describes the organization of the passage?

(A) A comparison of Spanish and American expeditions
(B) A description of southwestern Colorado
(C) A historical account of southwestern Colorado
(D) An illustration of archaeological discovery

20. Which of the following sentences should NOT be included in a summary of this passage?

(A) The Anasazi were early inhabitants of Colorado.
(B) The discovery of gold and silver changed Colorado history.
(C) The Spanish were the first Europeans to explore Colorado.
(D) Economic interests influenced the exploration of Colorado.

Answers to Reading Quiz 8 are on page 661.

3.7 Recognizing Coherence

FOCUS

Read the sentences below. Put the sentences in order so that they form a paragraph. Which should come first? Beside each sentence, write 1, 2, or 3 to show its order in the paragraph.

___ The trunk's inner core consists of vertically oriented cells which are closely packed together in parallel rows.

___ Millions upon millions of such cells form the heartwood of the trunk—the nonliving central pillar on which the living tree hoists itself skyward.

___ The most distinguishing characteristic of a mature tree is its self–supporting woody spine, or trunk.

The most logical order for the sentences is:

> ■ The most distinguishing characteristic of a mature tree is its self–supporting woody spine, or trunk. ■ The trunk's inner core consists of vertically oriented cells which are closely packed together in parallel rows. ■ Millions upon millions of such cells form the heartwood of the trunk—the nonliving central pillar on which the living tree hoists itself skyward. ■

The following sentence can be added to the above paragraph.

All trees share certain growth characteristics that distinguish them from other members of the plant kingdom.

Where would it best fit? Choose the square [■] where the sentence could be added.

The sentence would best fit at the first square. In the revised paragraph below, notice how each sentence introduces the subject of the next sentence, helping the paragraph flow smoothly.

> **All trees share certain growth characteristics that distinguish them from other members of the plant kingdom.** The most distinguishing characteristic of a mature tree is its self–supporting woody spine, or trunk. The trunk's inner core consists of vertically oriented cells which are closely packed together in parallel rows. Millions upon millions of such cells form the heartwood of the trunk—the nonliving central pillar on which the living tree hoists itself skyward.

When a passage fits together logically and smoothly, it is ***coherent***.

READING

DO YOU KNOW...?

1. Approximately four items on the computer–based TOEFL will test your ability to recognize coherence in the order of the sentences in a passage. You must be able to identify where a sentence can be added to a passage.

2. ***Coherence*** is the quality of agreement and unity among the parts of a piece of writing. If a passage is coherent, there are logical connections among the ideas within sentences and among the sentences within paragraphs. Coherence is the quality of "making sense" because the various parts of a passage fit together logically.

   Sometimes you can eliminate an incorrect answer choice if it would separate two sentences that should appear consecutively.

3. Coherence is related to the organizational structure and purpose of a passage (See 3.6). Organization and purpose control the order of sentences. Look at this example:

   > *Two reasons* for government regulation of industry stand out. *First*, economists have traditionally stressed the importance of containing market power. *A second reason*, deriving from public–choice theories, is that the regulators are captured by the regulated.

4. ***Transitions***, or connecting expressions, create coherence (See 3.2).

   > Akira Kurosawa's masterful works burst on the international film scene in the 1950s with the sound of fireworks and epic battles. *In contrast*, the quiet dignity and unobtrusive techniques of Satyajit Ray's films also placed him among the world's great directors.

   Note: *In contrast* makes a logical connection between the two sentences above. This transition determines the order of the sentences. (See 3.2 for a list of useful transitions.)

5. Pronouns and other reference words create coherence (See 3.3).

   > The brain of a computer is its central processing unit. In the case of a microcomputer, *this* is a chip called the microprocessor. *It* is connected to the other units by groups of wires along which binary code signals pass.

   Note: The pronoun *this* refers back to *central processing unit* in the previous sentence. The pronoun *It* refers back to the *microprocessor*. The use of pronouns and referents is linked to the order of the sentences.

   Your knowledge of organization, purpose, transitions, and referents will help you determine where to add a sentence to a passage.

6. On the computer test, questions about coherence look like this:

   > The following sentence can be added to the passage/paragraph __.
   > **(Sentence)**
   > Where would it best fit in the passage/paragraph?
   > Click on the square [■] to add the sentence to the passage/paragraph.

Look at an example:

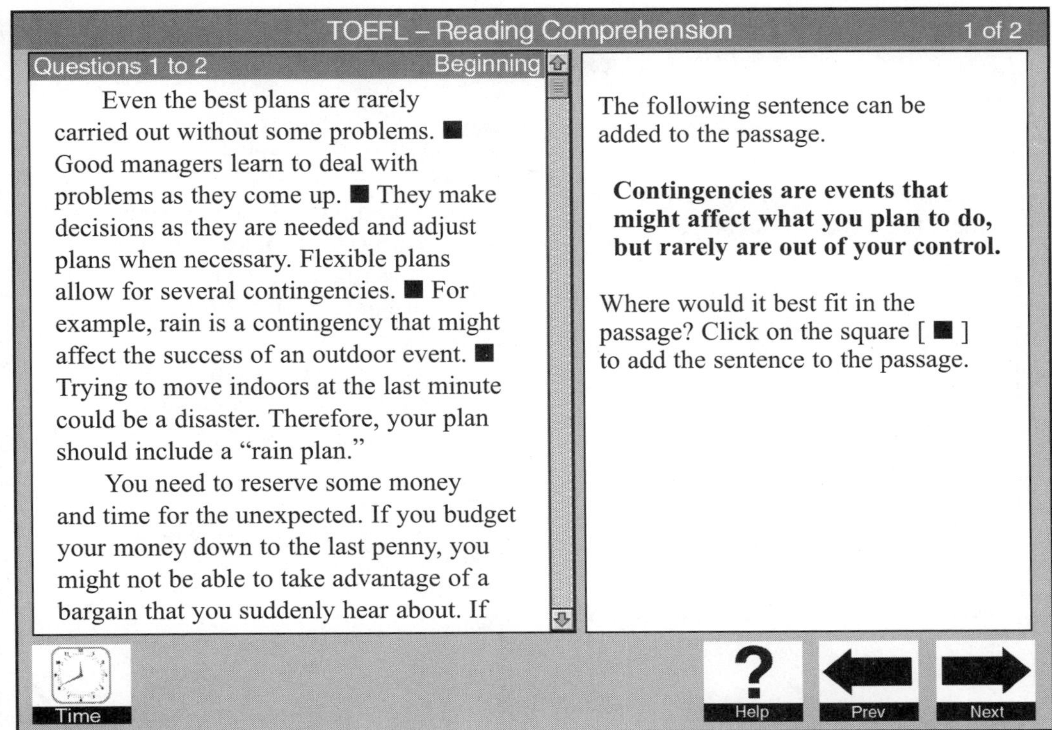

What is the purpose of the sentence to be added? It gives a definition of *contingencies*.

The author first mentions *contingency* in the sentence *Flexible plans allow for several contingencies.* The next sentence gives an example of a contingency: *For example, rain is a contingency that might affect the success of an outdoor event.*

The logical order would be to mention the new term, define it, and then give an example to illustrate it.

The sentence would best fit at the third square. That paragraph should read:

> Even the best plans are rarely carried out without some problems. Good managers learn to deal with problems as they come up. They make decisions as they are needed and adjust plans when necessary. Flexible plans allow for several contingencies. **Contingencies are events that might affect what you plan to do, but rarely are out of your control.** For example, rain is a contingency that might affect the success of an outdoor event. Trying to move indoors at the last minute could be a disaster. Therefore, your plan should include a "rain plan."

Adding the sentence at any of the other squares would result in a less coherent paragraph because it would interrupt the smooth flow of ideas between the sentences.

Look at another example:

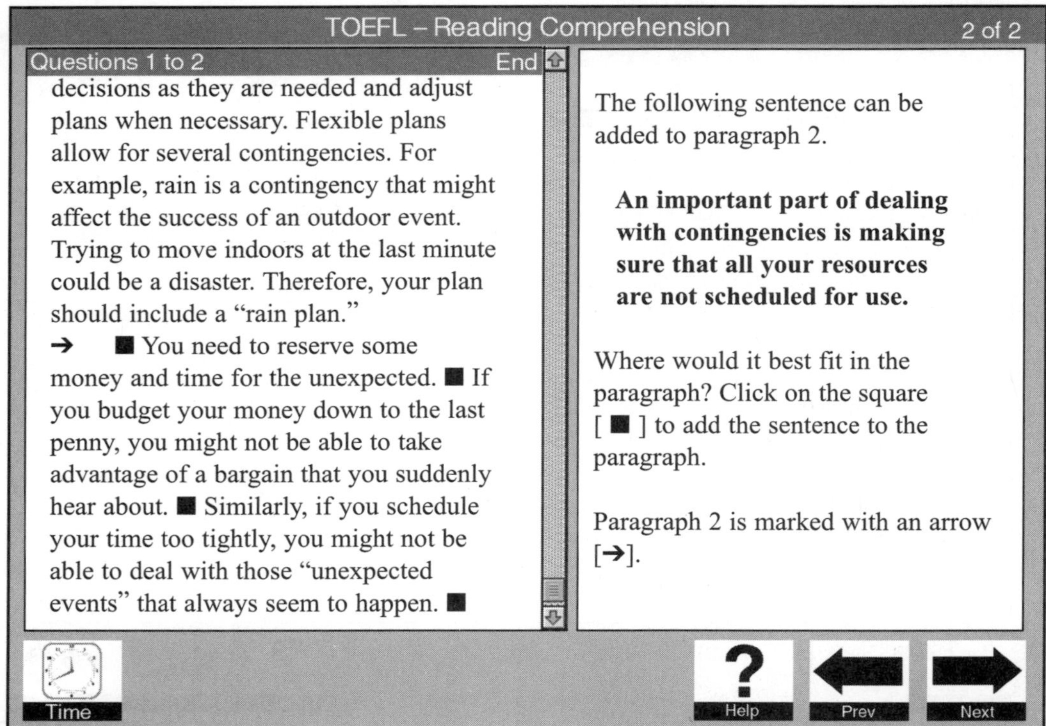

The purpose of the sentence to be added is to expand on the definition of *contingency* and introduce the topic of reserving resources to deal with contingencies. The purpose of paragraph 2 is to give reasons for reserving resources by discussing the consequences of not doing so.

The sentence would best fit at the first square. Here, it serves as the topic sentence of paragraph 2. It also serves as a transition between the definition of contingency in paragraph 1 and some real–life applications of the concept. That paragraph should read:

> **An important part of dealing with contingencies is making sure that all your resources are not scheduled for use.** You need to reserve some money and time for the unexpected. If you budget your money down to the last penny, you might not be able to take advantage of a bargain that you suddenly hear about. Similarly, if you schedule your time too tightly, you might not be able to deal with those "unexpected events" that always seem to happen.

Why would adding the sentence at any of the other squares be incorrect?

Note: On the TOEFL, when you click on a square, the sentence will appear in the passage at the place you have chosen. You can then check to see if this is the best place to add the sentence. To change your answer, click on a different square. You can try out the sentence at any square until you are satisfied.

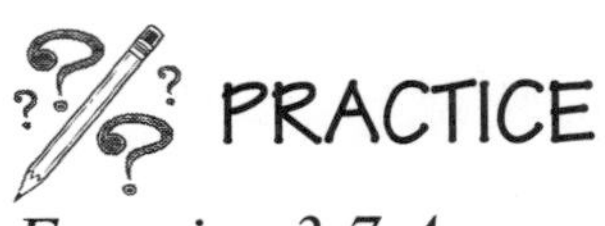

PRACTICE

Exercise 3.7.A

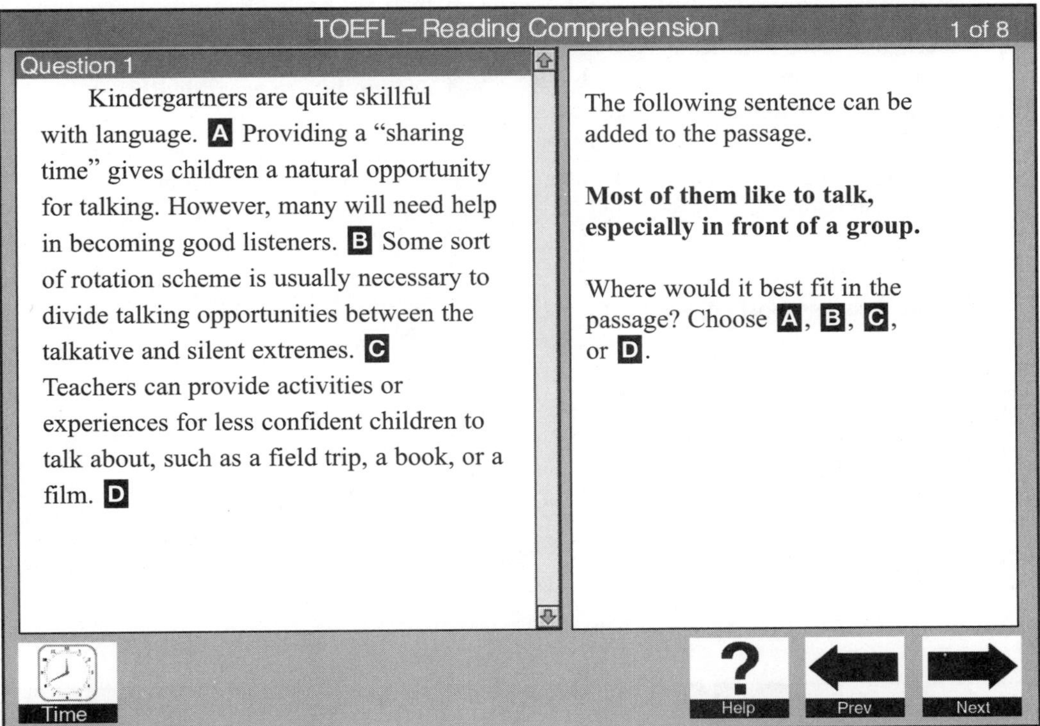

TOEFL – Reading Comprehension 1 of 8

Question 1

Kindergartners are quite skillful with language. **A** Providing a "sharing time" gives children a natural opportunity for talking. However, many will need help in becoming good listeners. **B** Some sort of rotation scheme is usually necessary to divide talking opportunities between the talkative and silent extremes. **C** Teachers can provide activities or experiences for less confident children to talk about, such as a field trip, a book, or a film. **D**

The following sentence can be added to the passage.

Most of them like to talk, especially in front of a group.

Where would it best fit in the passage? Choose **A**, **B**, **C**, or **D**.

Time | Help | Prev | Next

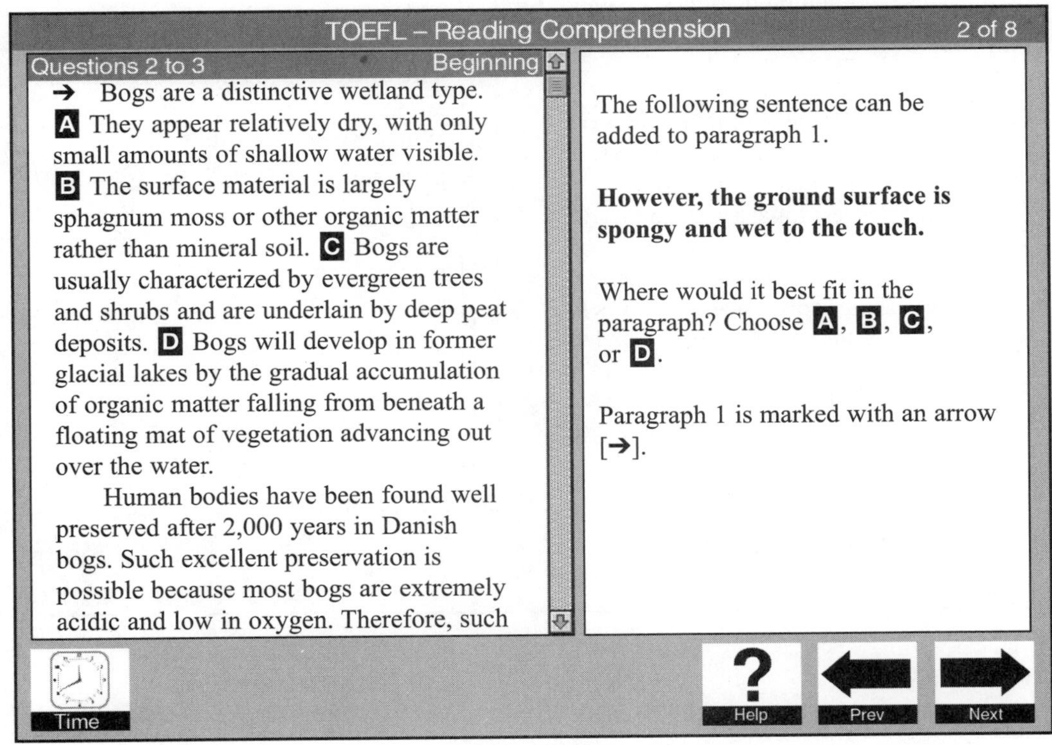

TOEFL – Reading Comprehension 2 of 8

Questions 2 to 3 Beginning

➔ Bogs are a distinctive wetland type. **A** They appear relatively dry, with only small amounts of shallow water visible. **B** The surface material is largely sphagnum moss or other organic matter rather than mineral soil. **C** Bogs are usually characterized by evergreen trees and shrubs and are underlain by deep peat deposits. **D** Bogs will develop in former glacial lakes by the gradual accumulation of organic matter falling from beneath a floating mat of vegetation advancing out over the water.

Human bodies have been found well preserved after 2,000 years in Danish bogs. Such excellent preservation is possible because most bogs are extremely acidic and low in oxygen. Therefore, such

The following sentence can be added to paragraph 1.

However, the ground surface is spongy and wet to the touch.

Where would it best fit in the paragraph? Choose **A**, **B**, **C**, or **D**.

Paragraph 1 is marked with an arrow [➔].

Time | Help | Prev | Next

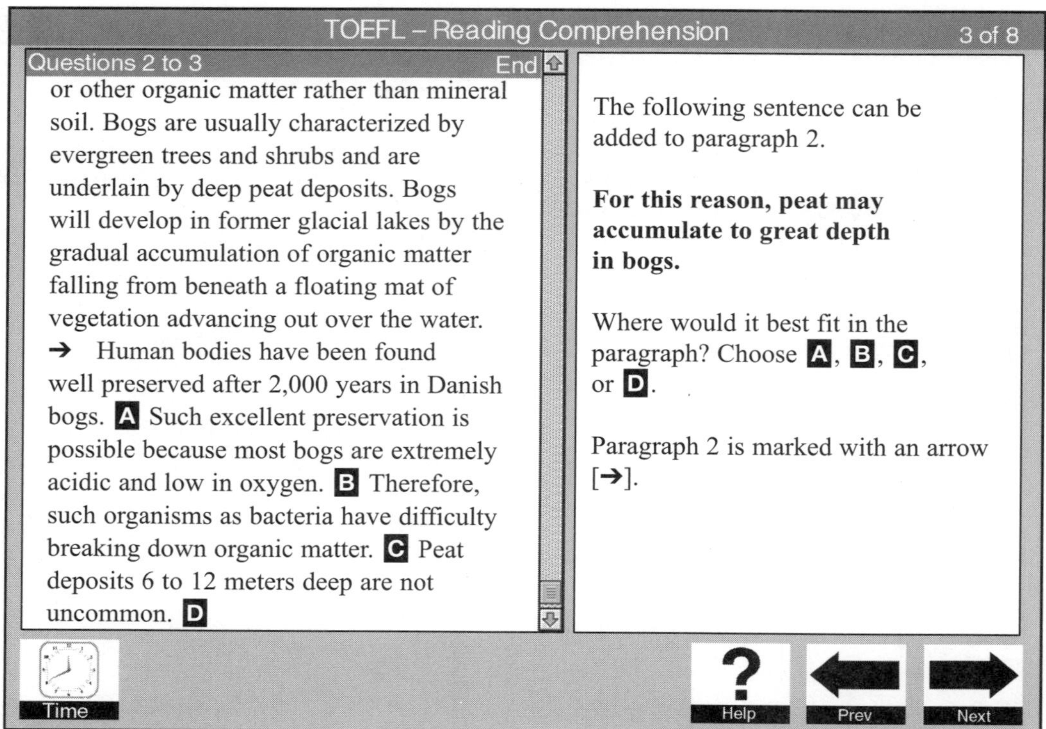
TOEFL – Reading Comprehension 3 of 8

Questions 2 to 3 End

or other organic matter rather than mineral soil. Bogs are usually characterized by evergreen trees and shrubs and are underlain by deep peat deposits. Bogs will develop in former glacial lakes by the gradual accumulation of organic matter falling from beneath a floating mat of vegetation advancing out over the water.

➔ Human bodies have been found well preserved after 2,000 years in Danish bogs. **A** Such excellent preservation is possible because most bogs are extremely acidic and low in oxygen. **B** Therefore, such organisms as bacteria have difficulty breaking down organic matter. **C** Peat deposits 6 to 12 meters deep are not uncommon. **D**

The following sentence can be added to paragraph 2.

For this reason, peat may accumulate to great depth in bogs.

Where would it best fit in the paragraph? Choose **A**, **B**, **C**, or **D**.

Paragraph 2 is marked with an arrow [➔].

Time Help Prev Next

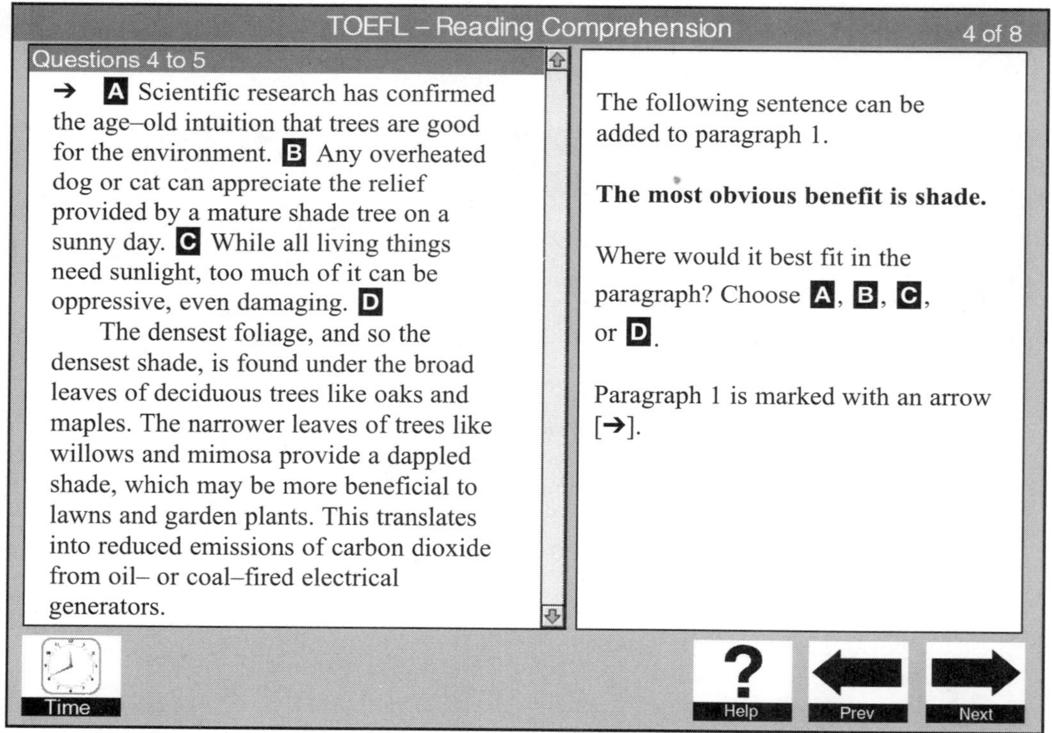
TOEFL – Reading Comprehension 4 of 8

Questions 4 to 5

➔ **A** Scientific research has confirmed the age–old intuition that trees are good for the environment. **B** Any overheated dog or cat can appreciate the relief provided by a mature shade tree on a sunny day. **C** While all living things need sunlight, too much of it can be oppressive, even damaging. **D**

The densest foliage, and so the densest shade, is found under the broad leaves of deciduous trees like oaks and maples. The narrower leaves of trees like willows and mimosa provide a dappled shade, which may be more beneficial to lawns and garden plants. This translates into reduced emissions of carbon dioxide from oil– or coal–fired electrical generators.

The following sentence can be added to paragraph 1.

The most obvious benefit is shade.

Where would it best fit in the paragraph? Choose **A**, **B**, **C**, or **D**.

Paragraph 1 is marked with an arrow [➔].

Time Help Prev Next

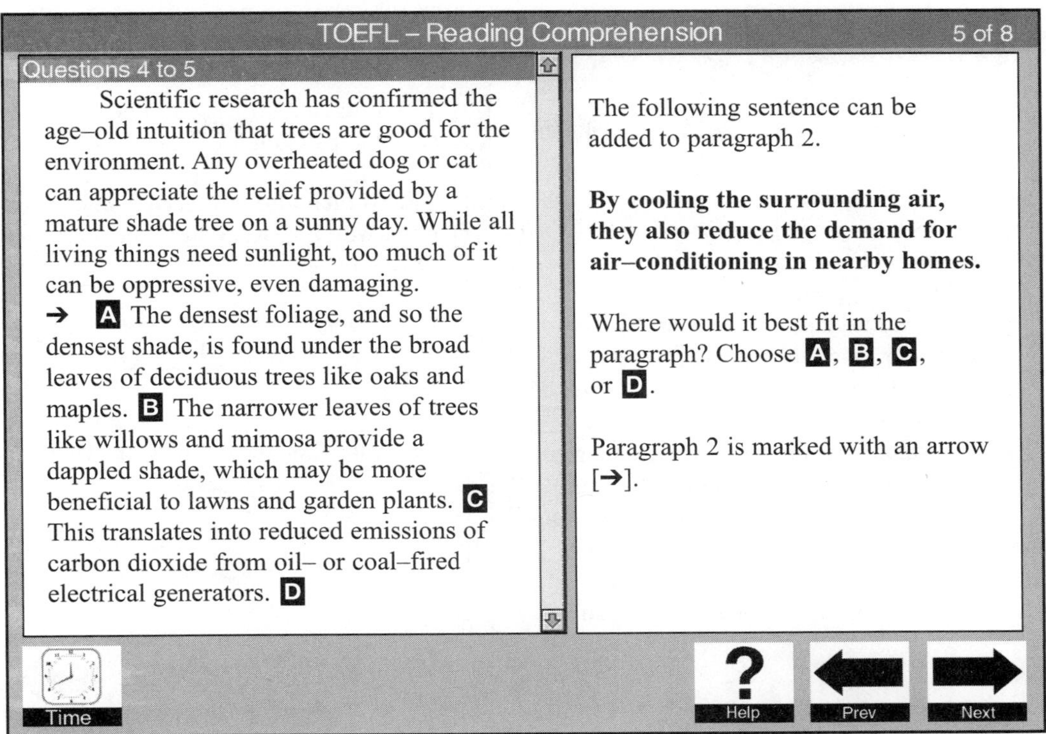
TOEFL – Reading Comprehension 5 of 8

Questions 4 to 5

Scientific research has confirmed the age–old intuition that trees are good for the environment. Any overheated dog or cat can appreciate the relief provided by a mature shade tree on a sunny day. While all living things need sunlight, too much of it can be oppressive, even damaging.

➔ **A** The densest foliage, and so the densest shade, is found under the broad leaves of deciduous trees like oaks and maples. **B** The narrower leaves of trees like willows and mimosa provide a dappled shade, which may be more beneficial to lawns and garden plants. **C** This translates into reduced emissions of carbon dioxide from oil– or coal–fired electrical generators. **D**

The following sentence can be added to paragraph 2.

By cooling the surrounding air, they also reduce the demand for air–conditioning in nearby homes.

Where would it best fit in the paragraph? Choose **A**, **B**, **C**, or **D**.

Paragraph 2 is marked with an arrow [➔].

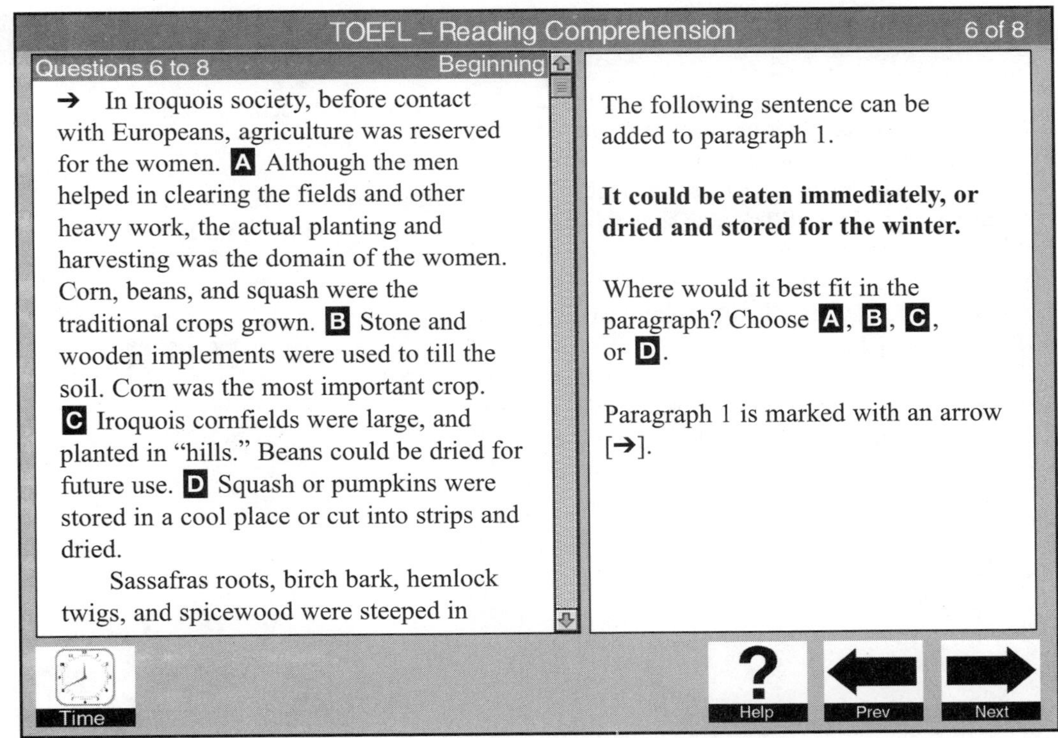
TOEFL – Reading Comprehension 6 of 8

Questions 6 to 8 Beginning

➔ In Iroquois society, before contact with Europeans, agriculture was reserved for the women. **A** Although the men helped in clearing the fields and other heavy work, the actual planting and harvesting was the domain of the women. Corn, beans, and squash were the traditional crops grown. **B** Stone and wooden implements were used to till the soil. Corn was the most important crop. **C** Iroquois cornfields were large, and planted in "hills." Beans could be dried for future use. **D** Squash or pumpkins were stored in a cool place or cut into strips and dried.

Sassafras roots, birch bark, hemlock twigs, and spicewood were steeped in

The following sentence can be added to paragraph 1.

It could be eaten immediately, or dried and stored for the winter.

Where would it best fit in the paragraph? Choose **A**, **B**, **C**, or **D**.

Paragraph 1 is marked with an arrow [➔].

READING

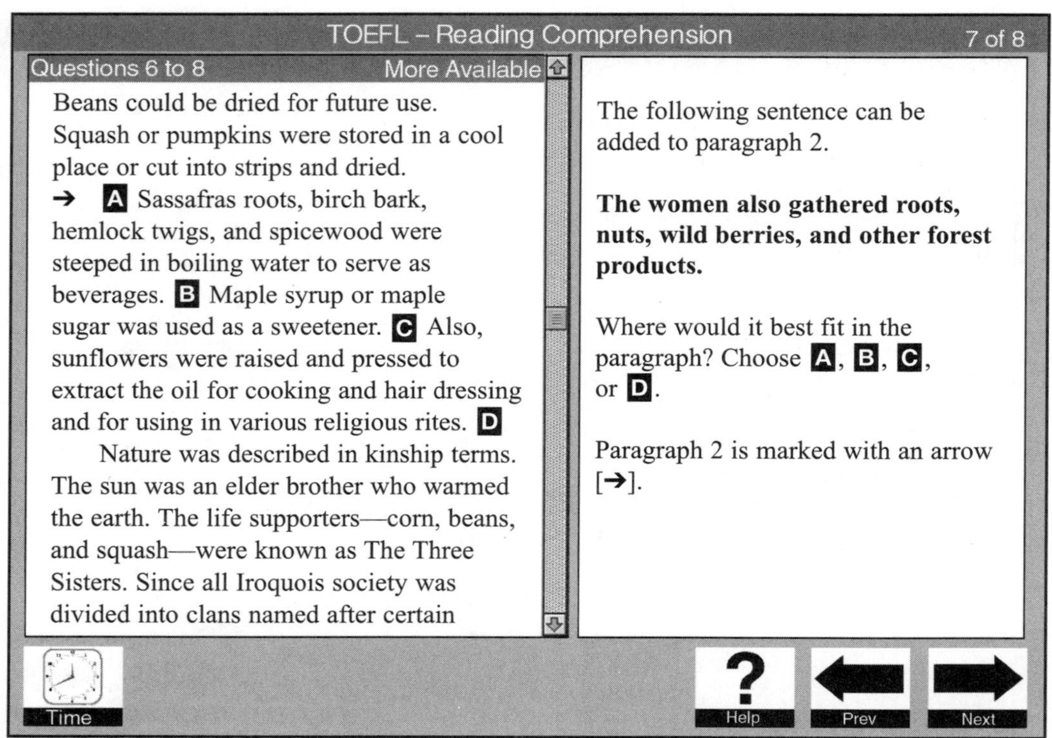

TOEFL – Reading Comprehension
7 of 8
Questions 6 to 8
More Available
Beans could be dried for future use. Squash or pumpkins were stored in a cool place or cut into strips and dried.
➔ A Sassafras roots, birch bark, hemlock twigs, and spicewood were steeped in boiling water to serve as beverages. B Maple syrup or maple sugar was used as a sweetener. C Also, sunflowers were raised and pressed to extract the oil for cooking and hair dressing and for using in various religious rites. D
Nature was described in kinship terms. The sun was an elder brother who warmed the earth. The life supporters—corn, beans, and squash—were known as The Three Sisters. Since all Iroquois society was divided into clans named after certain
The following sentence can be added to paragraph 2.
The women also gathered roots, nuts, wild berries, and other forest products.
Where would it best fit in the paragraph? Choose A, B, C, or D.
Paragraph 2 is marked with an arrow [➔].
Time
Help
Prev
Next

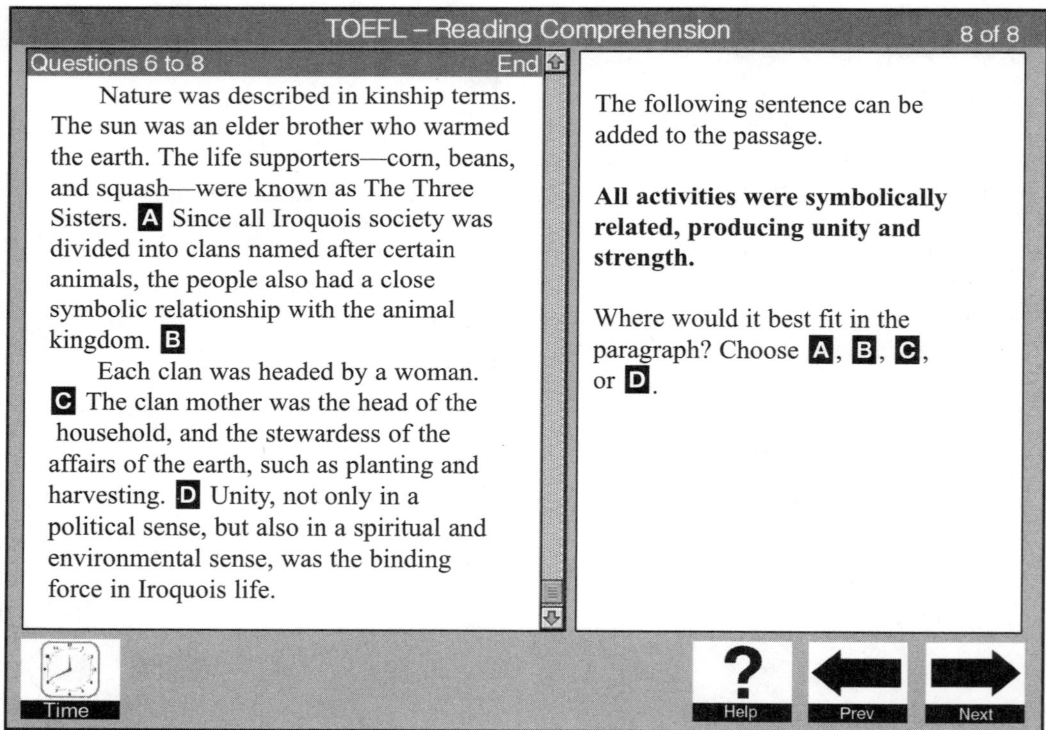

TOEFL – Reading Comprehension
8 of 8
Questions 6 to 8
End
Nature was described in kinship terms. The sun was an elder brother who warmed the earth. The life supporters—corn, beans, and squash—were known as The Three Sisters. A Since all Iroquois society was divided into clans named after certain animals, the people also had a close symbolic relationship with the animal kingdom. B
Each clan was headed by a woman. C The clan mother was the head of the household, and the stewardess of the affairs of the earth, such as planting and harvesting. D Unity, not only in a political sense, but also in a spiritual and environmental sense, was the binding force in Iroquois life.
The following sentence can be added to the passage.
All activities were symbolically related, producing unity and strength.
Where would it best fit in the paragraph? Choose A, B, C, or D.
Time
Help
Prev
Next

Answers to Exercise 3.7.A are on page 661.

3.7 EXTENSION

1. Working in pairs, students review the passages in Exercise 3.7.A. Identify the organization and purpose of each passage. Circle transitions, pronouns, and other key words and phrases that help make each passage coherent.

2. In reading done outside class, students select a paragraph of 4 to 5 sentences from a textbook or magazine. On a sheet of paper or an overhead projector transparency, list the sentences from the paragraph, *but mix up their order*. Classmates must arrange the sentences in a coherent order. Is there more than one possible order? Do transitions and pronouns make it easier or more difficult to arrange the sentences? Does changing the order of sentences change the meaning of the paragraph?

3. Students create "TOEFL items" to test their classmates' ability to correctly add a sentence to a paragraph. Students select a paragraph of 4 to 5 sentences from a textbook for another class. On a sheet of paper, an overhead projector transparency, or a computer, rewrite the paragraph, *but omit one sentence*. Write the omitted sentence in a box at the top. Draw squares in 4 or 5 spaces before, after, and between the other sentences in the paragraph. Classmates must add the omitted sentence at the correct square.

ASSESSING PROGRESS – 3.7

QUIZ 9 (Time – 13 minutes)

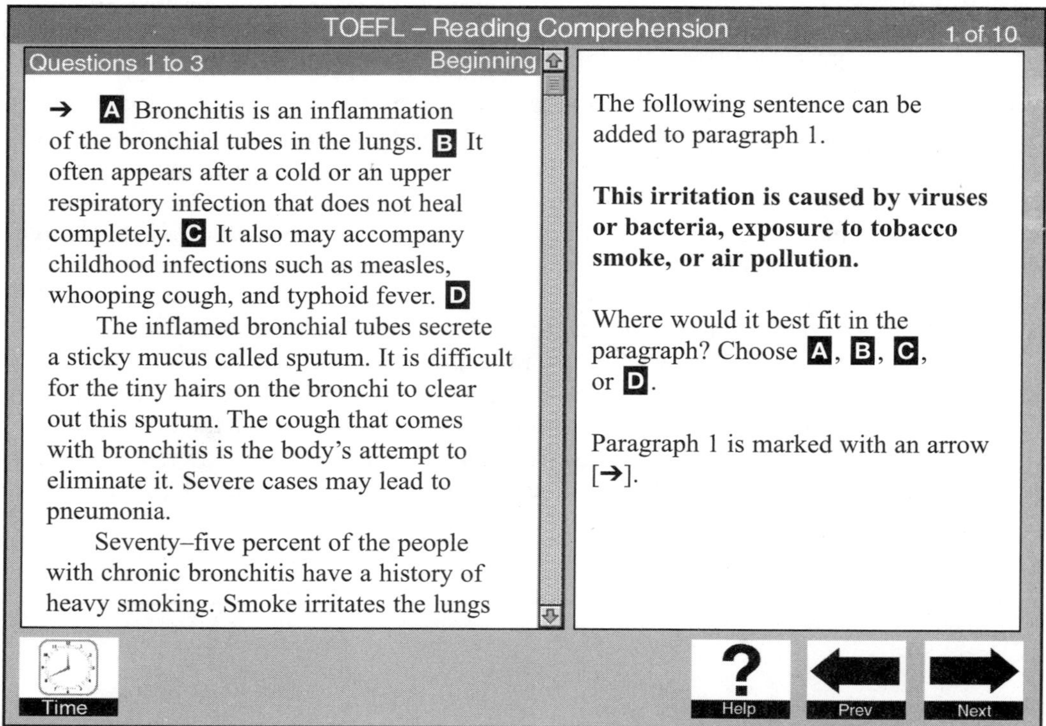

TOEFL – Reading Comprehension 1 of 10

Questions 1 to 3 Beginning

➔ A Bronchitis is an inflammation of the bronchial tubes in the lungs. B It often appears after a cold or an upper respiratory infection that does not heal completely. C It also may accompany childhood infections such as measles, whooping cough, and typhoid fever. D

The inflamed bronchial tubes secrete a sticky mucus called sputum. It is difficult for the tiny hairs on the bronchi to clear out this sputum. The cough that comes with bronchitis is the body's attempt to eliminate it. Severe cases may lead to pneumonia.

Seventy–five percent of the people with chronic bronchitis have a history of heavy smoking. Smoke irritates the lungs

The following sentence can be added to paragraph 1.

This irritation is caused by viruses or bacteria, exposure to tobacco smoke, or air pollution.

Where would it best fit in the paragraph? Choose A, B, C, or D.

Paragraph 1 is marked with an arrow [➔].

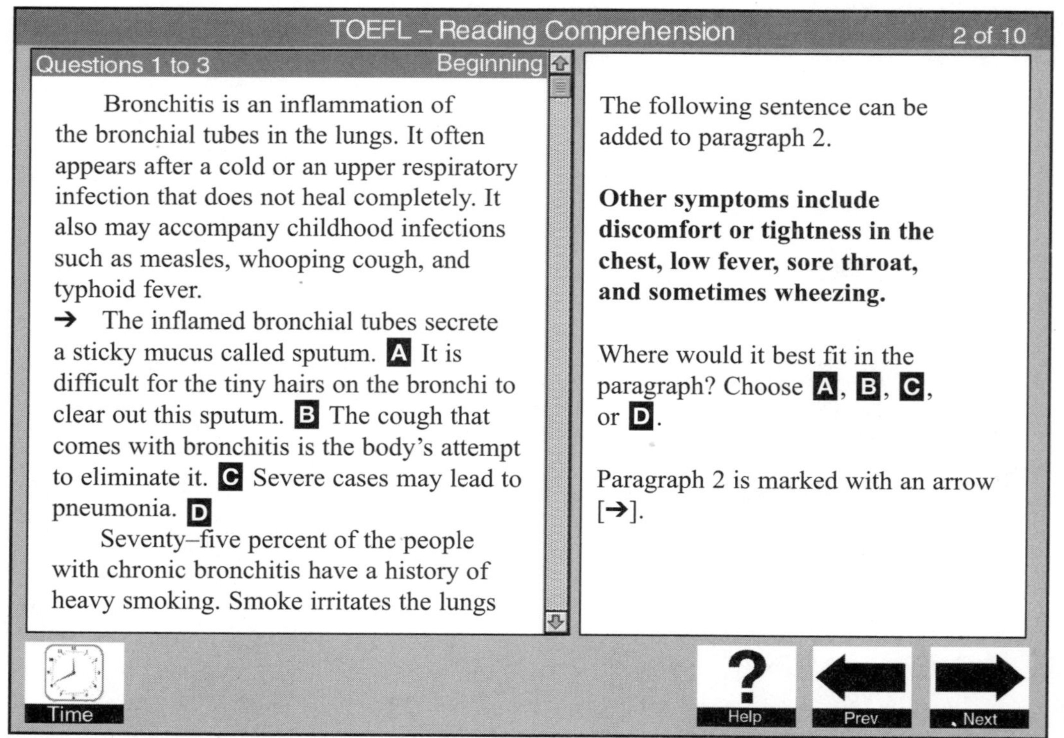

TOEFL – Reading Comprehension 2 of 10

Questions 1 to 3 Beginning

Bronchitis is an inflammation of the bronchial tubes in the lungs. It often appears after a cold or an upper respiratory infection that does not heal completely. It also may accompany childhood infections such as measles, whooping cough, and typhoid fever.

➔ The inflamed bronchial tubes secrete a sticky mucus called sputum. A It is difficult for the tiny hairs on the bronchi to clear out this sputum. B The cough that comes with bronchitis is the body's attempt to eliminate it. C Severe cases may lead to pneumonia. D

Seventy–five percent of the people with chronic bronchitis have a history of heavy smoking. Smoke irritates the lungs

The following sentence can be added to paragraph 2.

Other symptoms include discomfort or tightness in the chest, low fever, sore throat, and sometimes wheezing.

Where would it best fit in the paragraph? Choose A, B, C, or D.

Paragraph 2 is marked with an arrow [➔].

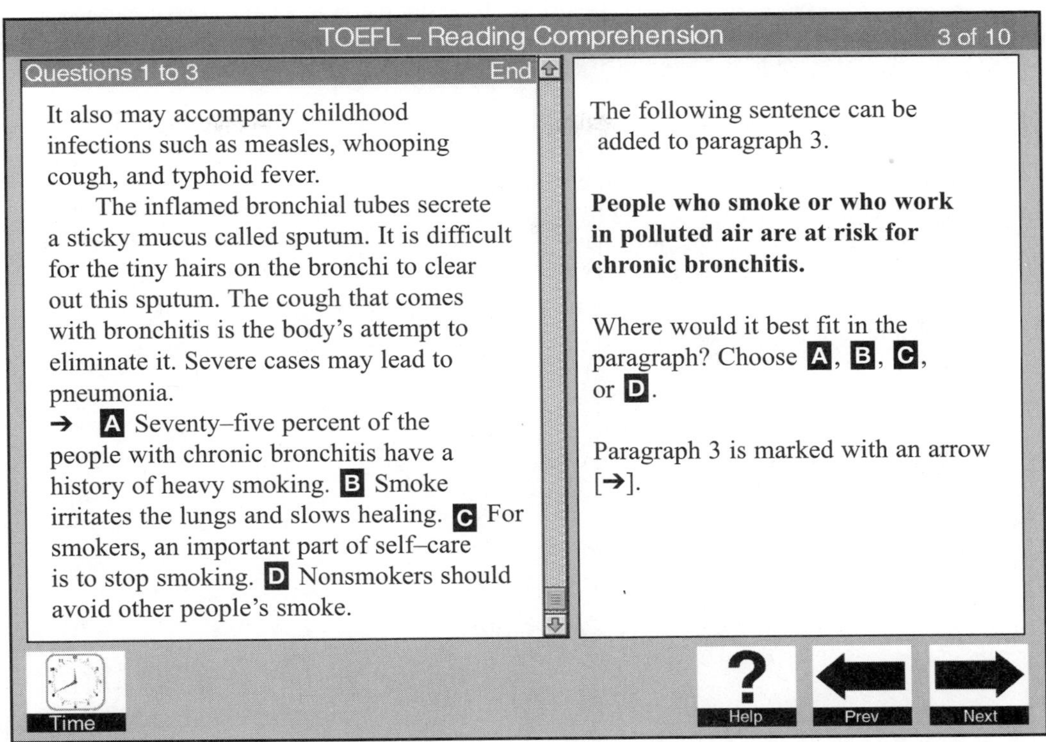
TOEFL – Reading Comprehension 3 of 10

Questions 1 to 3 End

It also may accompany childhood infections such as measles, whooping cough, and typhoid fever.

The inflamed bronchial tubes secrete a sticky mucus called sputum. It is difficult for the tiny hairs on the bronchi to clear out this sputum. The cough that comes with bronchitis is the body's attempt to eliminate it. Severe cases may lead to pneumonia.

➔ **A** Seventy–five percent of the people with chronic bronchitis have a history of heavy smoking. **B** Smoke irritates the lungs and slows healing. **C** For smokers, an important part of self–care is to stop smoking. **D** Nonsmokers should avoid other people's smoke.

The following sentence can be added to paragraph 3.

People who smoke or who work in polluted air are at risk for chronic bronchitis.

Where would it best fit in the paragraph? Choose **A**, **B**, **C**, or **D**.

Paragraph 3 is marked with an arrow [➔].

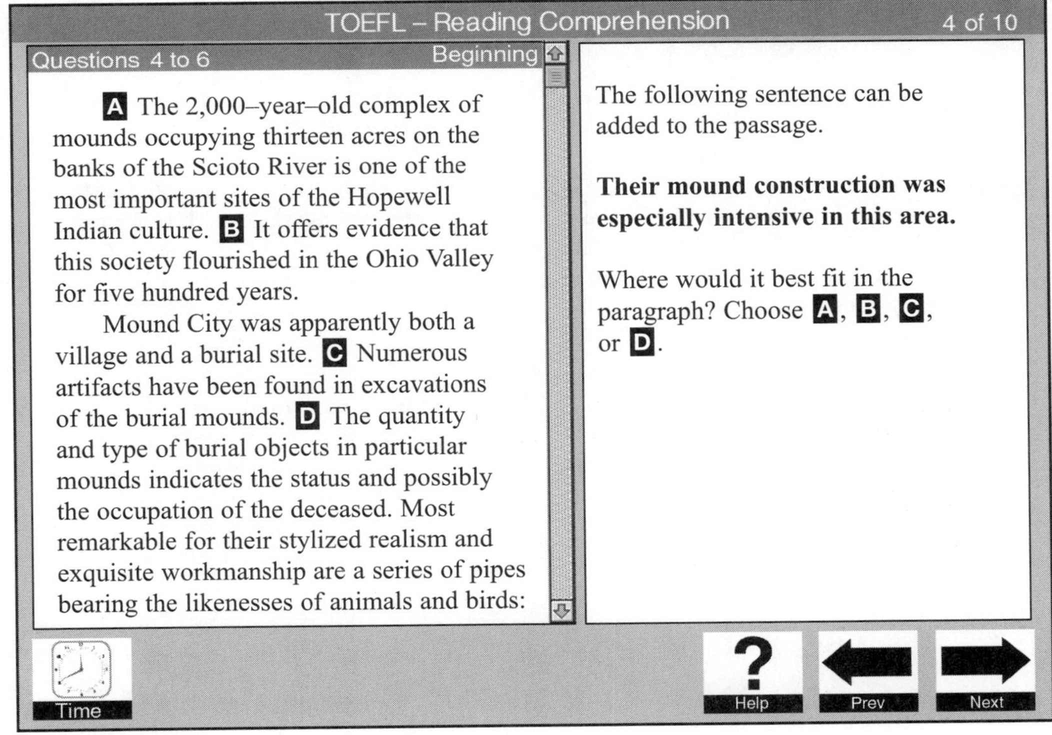
TOEFL – Reading Comprehension 4 of 10

Questions 4 to 6 Beginning

A The 2,000–year–old complex of mounds occupying thirteen acres on the banks of the Scioto River is one of the most important sites of the Hopewell Indian culture. **B** It offers evidence that this society flourished in the Ohio Valley for five hundred years.

Mound City was apparently both a village and a burial site. **C** Numerous artifacts have been found in excavations of the burial mounds. **D** The quantity and type of burial objects in particular mounds indicates the status and possibly the occupation of the deceased. Most remarkable for their stylized realism and exquisite workmanship are a series of pipes bearing the likenesses of animals and birds:

The following sentence can be added to the passage.

Their mound construction was especially intensive in this area.

Where would it best fit in the paragraph? Choose **A**, **B**, **C**, or **D**.

READING

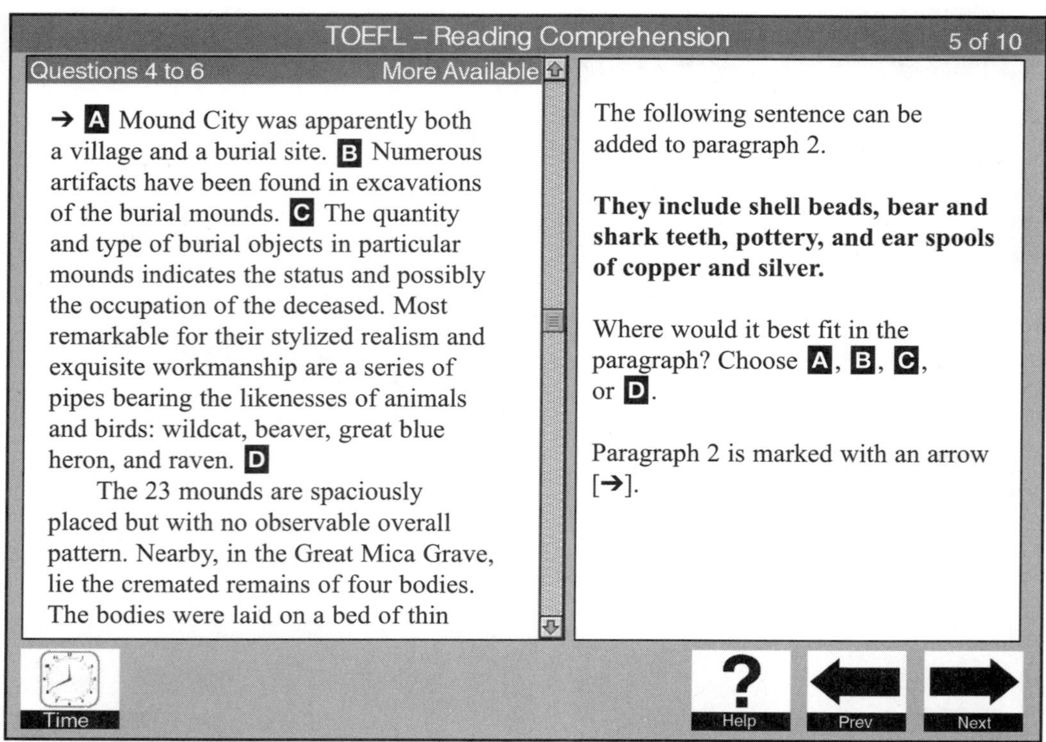
TOEFL – Reading Comprehension 5 of 10

Questions 4 to 6 More Available

➔ A Mound City was apparently both a village and a burial site. B Numerous artifacts have been found in excavations of the burial mounds. C The quantity and type of burial objects in particular mounds indicates the status and possibly the occupation of the deceased. Most remarkable for their stylized realism and exquisite workmanship are a series of pipes bearing the likenesses of animals and birds: wildcat, beaver, great blue heron, and raven. D

The 23 mounds are spaciously placed but with no observable overall pattern. Nearby, in the Great Mica Grave, lie the cremated remains of four bodies. The bodies were laid on a bed of thin

The following sentence can be added to paragraph 2.

They include shell beads, bear and shark teeth, pottery, and ear spools of copper and silver.

Where would it best fit in the paragraph? Choose A, B, C, or D.

Paragraph 2 is marked with an arrow [➔].

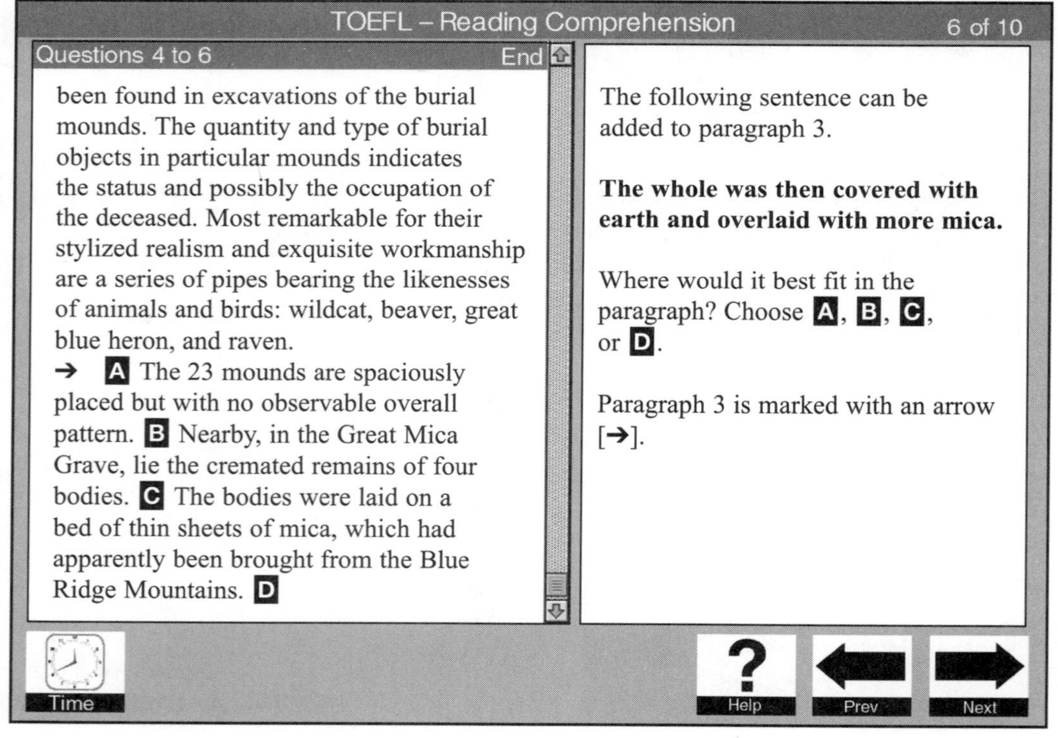
TOEFL – Reading Comprehension 6 of 10

Questions 4 to 6 End

been found in excavations of the burial mounds. The quantity and type of burial objects in particular mounds indicates the status and possibly the occupation of the deceased. Most remarkable for their stylized realism and exquisite workmanship are a series of pipes bearing the likenesses of animals and birds: wildcat, beaver, great blue heron, and raven.

➔ A The 23 mounds are spaciously placed but with no observable overall pattern. B Nearby, in the Great Mica Grave, lie the cremated remains of four bodies. C The bodies were laid on a bed of thin sheets of mica, which had apparently been brought from the Blue Ridge Mountains. D

The following sentence can be added to paragraph 3.

The whole was then covered with earth and overlaid with more mica.

Where would it best fit in the paragraph? Choose A, B, C, or D.

Paragraph 3 is marked with an arrow [➔].

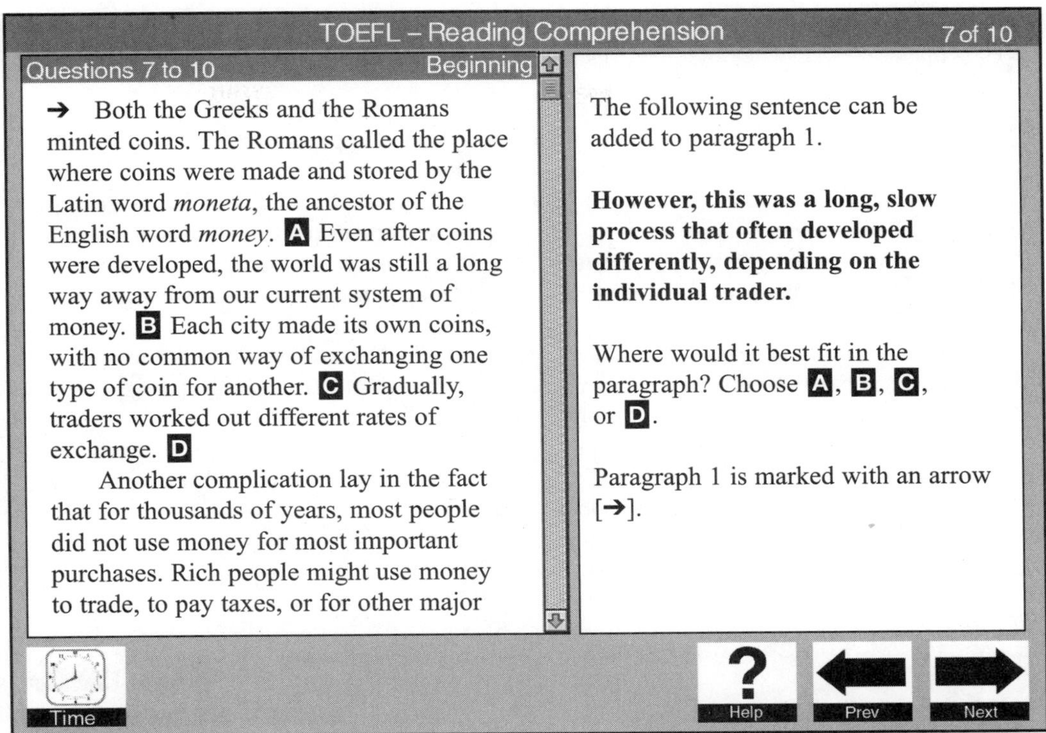
TOEFL – Reading Comprehension
7 of 10
Questions 7 to 10
Beginning
➔ Both the Greeks and the Romans minted coins. The Romans called the place where coins were made and stored by the Latin word moneta, the ancestor of the English word money. A Even after coins were developed, the world was still a long way away from our current system of money. B Each city made its own coins, with no common way of exchanging one type of coin for another. C Gradually, traders worked out different rates of exchange. D
Another complication lay in the fact that for thousands of years, most people did not use money for most important purchases. Rich people might use money to trade, to pay taxes, or for other major
The following sentence can be added to paragraph 1.
However, this was a long, slow process that often developed differently, depending on the individual trader.
Where would it best fit in the paragraph? Choose A, B, C, or D.
Paragraph 1 is marked with an arrow [➔].
Time
Help
Prev
Next

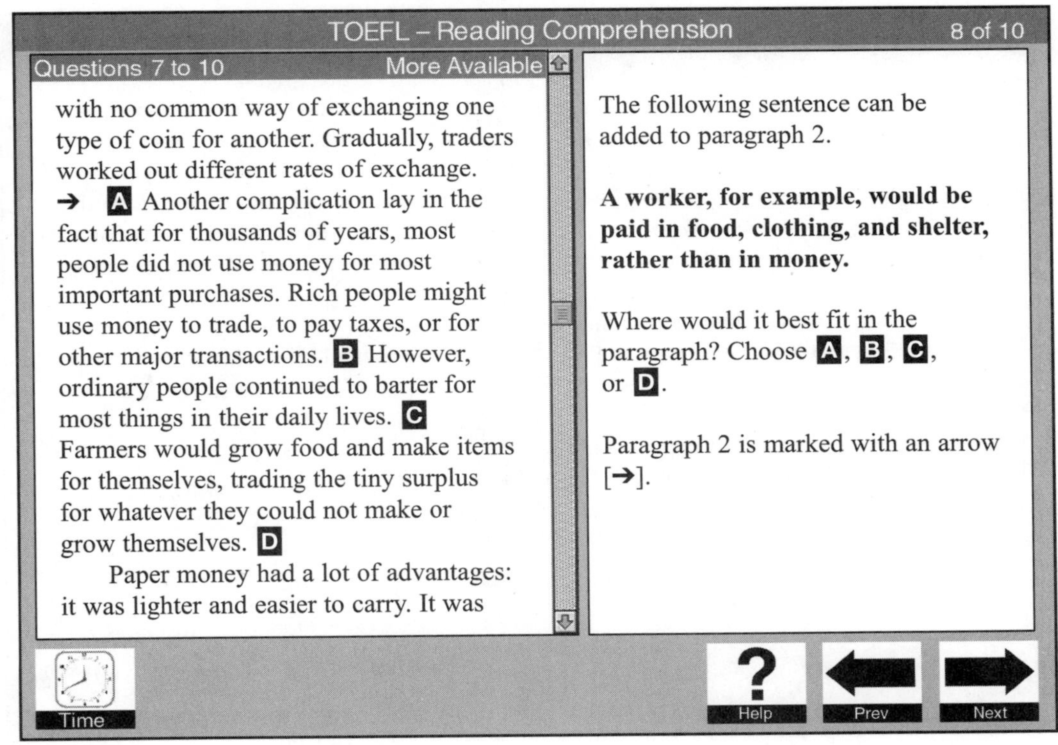
TOEFL – Reading Comprehension
8 of 10
Questions 7 to 10
More Available
with no common way of exchanging one type of coin for another. Gradually, traders worked out different rates of exchange.
➔ A Another complication lay in the fact that for thousands of years, most people did not use money for most important purchases. Rich people might use money to trade, to pay taxes, or for other major transactions. B However, ordinary people continued to barter for most things in their daily lives. C Farmers would grow food and make items for themselves, trading the tiny surplus for whatever they could not make or grow themselves. D
Paper money had a lot of advantages: it was lighter and easier to carry. It was
The following sentence can be added to paragraph 2.
A worker, for example, would be paid in food, clothing, and shelter, rather than in money.
Where would it best fit in the paragraph? Choose A, B, C, or D.
Paragraph 2 is marked with an arrow [➔].
Time
Help
Prev
Next

READING

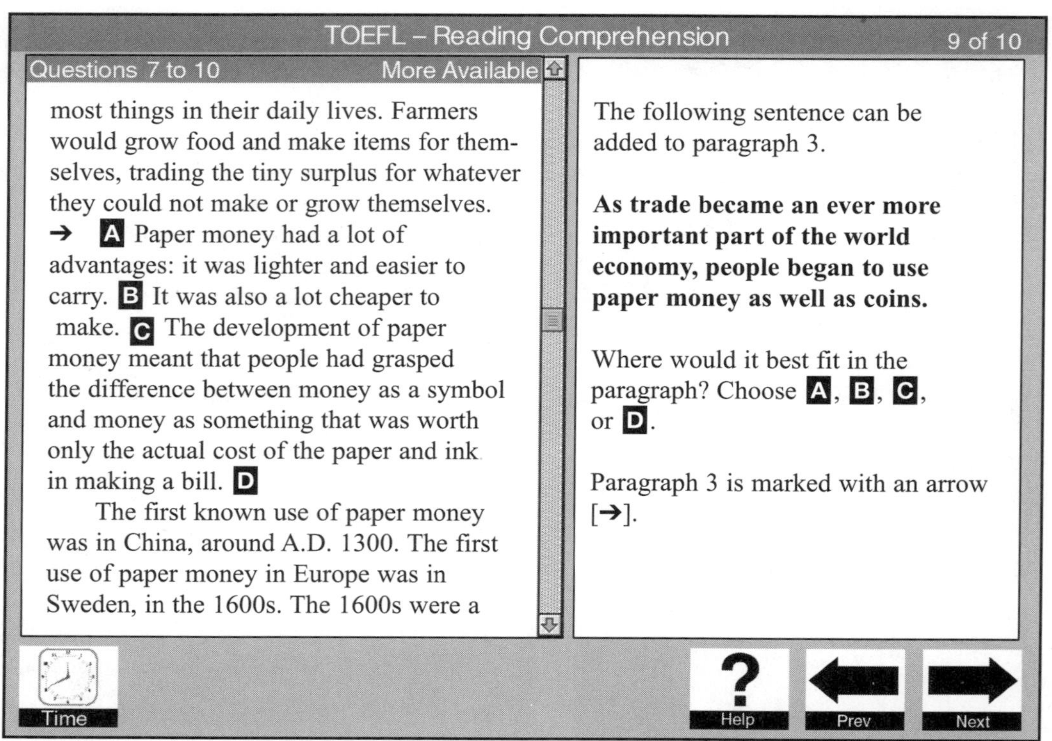

TOEFL – Reading Comprehension 9 of 10

Questions 7 to 10 More Available

most things in their daily lives. Farmers would grow food and make items for themselves, trading the tiny surplus for whatever they could not make or grow themselves.

➔ A Paper money had a lot of advantages: it was lighter and easier to carry. B It was also a lot cheaper to make. C The development of paper money meant that people had grasped the difference between money as a symbol and money as something that was worth only the actual cost of the paper and ink in making a bill. D

The first known use of paper money was in China, around A.D. 1300. The first use of paper money in Europe was in Sweden, in the 1600s. The 1600s were a

The following sentence can be added to paragraph 3.

As trade became an ever more important part of the world economy, people began to use paper money as well as coins.

Where would it best fit in the paragraph? Choose A, B, C, or D.

Paragraph 3 is marked with an arrow [➔].

Time Help Prev Next

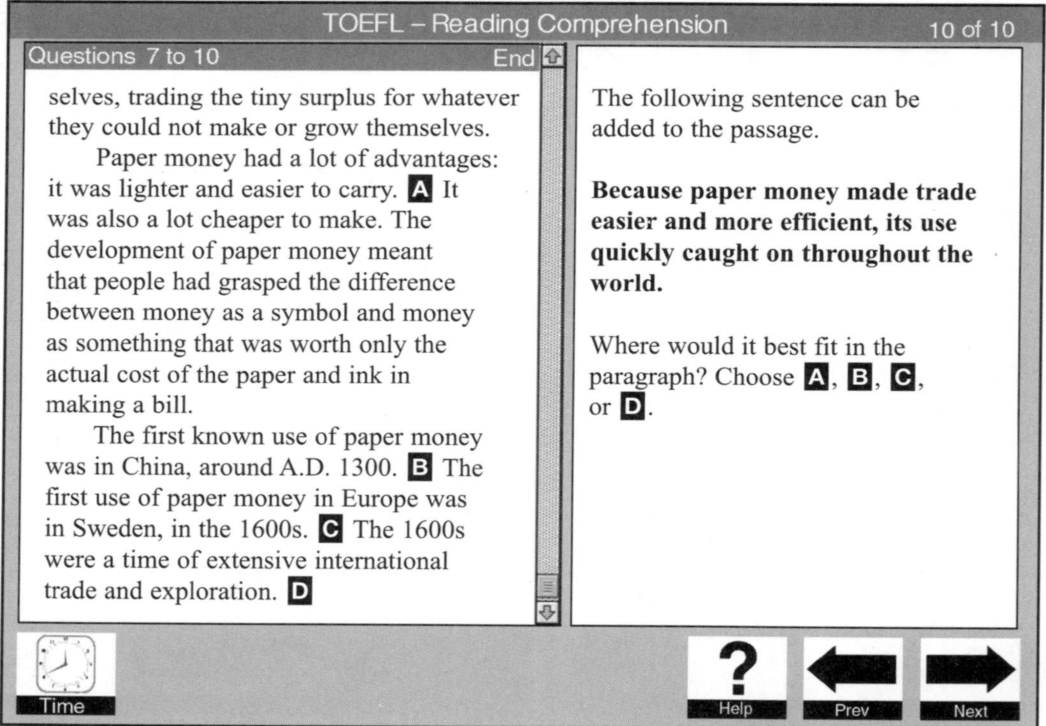

TOEFL – Reading Comprehension 10 of 10

Questions 7 to 10 End

selves, trading the tiny surplus for whatever they could not make or grow themselves.

Paper money had a lot of advantages: it was lighter and easier to carry. A It was also a lot cheaper to make. The development of paper money meant that people had grasped the difference between money as a symbol and money as something that was worth only the actual cost of the paper and ink in making a bill.

The first known use of paper money was in China, around A.D. 1300. B The first use of paper money in Europe was in Sweden, in the 1600s. C The 1600s were a time of extensive international trade and exploration. D

The following sentence can be added to the passage.

Because paper money made trade easier and more efficient, its use quickly caught on throughout the world.

Where would it best fit in the paragraph? Choose A, B, C, or D.

Time Help Prev Next

Answers to Reading Quiz 9 are on page 661.

 ASSESSING PROGRESS – 3.1 through 3.7

QUIZ 10 (Time – 22 minutes)

Read the following passages and choose the one best answer to each question. Answer all questions on the basis of what is stated or implied in that passage.

QUESTIONS 1–10

No actual black hole has yet been located or studied, but the concept has provided endless imaginative fodder for science fiction writers and endless theoretical fodder for physicists and astrophysicists.

Black holes are one of the more exotic theoretical manifestations of general relativity. The standard model for the formation of a black hole involves the collapse of a large star. For extremely massive stars that are four to five times the mass of our sun, the exclusion principle—the resistance between the molecular particles within the star as they are compressed—will not be strong enough to offset the gravity generated by the star's own mass. The star's increasing density will overwhelm the exclusion principle. What follows is runaway gravitational collapse. With no internal force to stop it, the star will simply continue to collapse in on itself, until it reaches a point of infinite density and zero volume, a phenomenon known as a *singularity*.

The star now disappears from the perceivable universe, like a cartoon character who jumps into a hole and pulls the hole in after him. What this process leaves behind is a different kind of hole—a profound disturbance in spacetime, a region where gravity is so intense that nothing, not even light, can escape from it. Any object falling within the boundary of a black hole will be sucked in and will disappear from our universe forever.

What would happen to an object, such as an astronaut, as it vanished into the black hole? Physicists have been amusing themselves with this question for years. Most believe that the astronaut would be destroyed by the intense gravitational forces within the black hole, or would explode in a flash of gamma rays as he or she approached the singularity at the hole's core. Theoretically, an astronaut who managed to survive the passage would experience some very strange things, including acute time distortion, which would enable him or her to know, in a few brief seconds, the entire future of the universe in all its detail.

1. The word "fodder" in line 2 is closest in meaning to

   (A) material
   (B) stories
   (C) support
   (D) problems

2. With what topic is paragraph 2 mainly concerned?

   (A) The theory of relativity
   (B) How to build a model of a black hole
   (C) The cause of a black hole
   (D) Rapid gravitational collapse

3. The opposing force between the molecular particles inside a star is called

   (A) general relativity
   (B) the exclusion principle
   (C) infinite density
   (D) a singularity

4. The word "offset" in line 8 could best be replaced by

   (A) carry
   (B) arrange
   (C) overflow
   (D) counteract

READING

5. It can be concluded from paragraph 3 that light

(A) destroys a black hole
(B) can barely reveal a black hole
(C) does not exist near a black hole
(D) originates in spacetime

6. The word "Most" in line 19 refers to

(A) astronauts
(B) physicists
(C) objects
(D) black holes

7. Which of the following is NOT mentioned as the possible fate of an astronaut who falls into a black hole?

(A) Experience of amusement
(B) Death by gamma rays
(C) Knowledge of the universe
(D) Destruction by gravity

8. Where in the passage does the author describe a vanishing star as a graphic image?

(A) Paragraph 1
(B) Paragraph 2
(C) Paragraph 3
(D) Paragraph 4

9. It can be inferred from the passage that black holes are

(A) soon to be located and studied
(B) a scientific impossibility
(C) the key to the entire future of the universe
(D) a source of inspiration and entertainment

10. The following sentence can be added to the passage.

Nothing in the history of modern astronomy has excited as much speculation and controversy as the object, or event, known as a *black hole*.

Where would it best fit in the passage? Choose **A**, **B**, **C**, or **D**.

A No actual black hole has yet been located or studied, but the concept has provided endless imaginative fodder for science fiction writers and endless theoretical fodder for physicists and astrophysicists.

Black holes are one of the more exotic theoretical manifestations of general relativity. The standard model for the formation of a black hole involves the collapse of a large star. **B** For extremely massive stars that are four to five times the mass of our sun, the exclusion principle—the resistance between the molecular particles within the star as they are compressed—will not be strong enough to offset the gravity generated by the star's own mass. **C** The star's increasing density will overwhelm the exclusion principle. What follow is runaway gravitational collapse. **D** With no internal force to stop it, the star will simply continue to collapse in on itself, until it reaches a point of infinite density and zero volume, a phenomenon known as a *singularity*.

QUESTIONS 11–20

The People of the Longhouse lived in stockaded villages in elevated areas which were easy to defend and were located near a water supply. Twenty–foot long palisades surrounded and protected a group of longhouses. The palisades acted as a defensive wall and also helped keep forest animals from foraging within the village.

Longhouses were the typical dwelling unit within the stockade. A number of families were housed within each longhouse. The longhouse varied in size from twenty feet by sixteen feet, to huge multiple family dwellings sixty feet by eighteen feet. In some instances, longhouses have been known to be more than three hundred feet long in the more populous villages. The longhouse was more than just a shelter; it was the basic unit upon which the entire society was constructed.

In building the longhouse, a row of forked poles was placed in the ground, between four and five feet apart. Cross poles were lashed to the forked uprights to form an arched roof. Slender poles or rafters were then secured to the roof frame, and traverse poles were added to further strengthen the overhead structure. Large pieces of bark were then tied to the frame. The bark was obtained in the spring, by stripping the trees when the sap began to flow. An outer set of poles kept the bark in place on the sides and roof. Smoke holes were built into the roof at about twenty–foot intervals. These were usually covered with a piece of bark. The hearth beneath the smoke hole was shared by two families.

Doors were built at each end of the longhouse. Animal hide or hinged bark was used, and this covering could be lifted up. Along the inside wall, bunks were constructed which served as beds at night and benches in the day. Corn, dried fish, and other foods hung from overhead. The dwelling was compartmentalized to accommodate each family. At the front of the longhouse, over the door, images of clan symbols represented the families living in that longhouse.

11. The passage supports all of the following statements EXCEPT

(A) people ate and slept in longhouses
(B) each longhouse was a separate village
(C) the longhouse was like an apartment building
(D) the longhouse had a cultural function

12. The word "palisades" in lines 2 and 3 is closest in meaning to

(A) roads
(B) fences
(C) bridges
(D) ponds

13. It can be inferred from paragraph 1 that

(A) the villages were sometimes attacked
(B) the People of the Longhouse had a military government
(C) the People of the Longhouse were hunters
(D) animals were kept inside the longhouses

14. Which of the following is NOT mentioned as part of a longhouse?

(A) Bark walls
(B) Arched roof
(C) Hearth
(D) Small windows

15. The word "These" in line 17 refers to

(A) poles
(B) sides and roof
(C) smoke holes
(D) intervals

READING

16. The doors of a longhouse were made of

(A) forked poles
(B) hidden animals
(C) bark or animal skin
(D) wood or bark

17. The word "compartmentalized" in line 23 is closest in meaning to

(A) partitioned
(B) enlarged
(C) opened
(D) decorated

18. It can be inferred from lines 24–25 that

(A) the people knew how to read
(B) some of the families were artists
(C) the door had a religious purpose
(D) each family belonged to a clan

19. Where in the passage does the author give the dimensions of a longhouse?

(A) Lines 2–3
(B) Lines 6–7
(C) Lines 13–15
(D) Lines 20–22

20. The following sentence can be added to paragraph 3 of the passage.

Elm, ash, cedar, fir, spruce, or basswood were the usual sources of bark.

Where would it best fit in the paragraph? Choose **A**, **B**, **C**, or **D**.

In building the longhouse, a row of forked poles was placed in the ground, between four and five feet apart. **A** Cross poles were lashed to the forked uprights to form an arched roof. Slender poles or rafters were then secured to the roof frame, and traverse poles were added to further strengthen the overhead structure. **B** Large pieces of bark were then tied to the frame. The bark was obtained in the spring, by stripping the trees when the sap began to flow. **C** An outer set of poles kept the bark in place on the sides and roof. Smoke holes were built into the roof at about twenty–foot intervals. **D** These were usually covered with a piece of bark. The hearth beneath the smoke hole was shared by two families.

Answers to Reading Quiz 10 are on page 662.

READING COMPREHENSION REVIEW TEST

(Time – 60 minutes)

In the Reading Comprehension section of the TOEFL, you will read several passages. Each one is followed by a number of questions about it. For questions 1–50, you are to choose the one best answer, (A), (B), (C), or (D), to each question.

Answer all questions about the information in a passage on the basis of what is stated or implied in that passage.

Read the following passage:

> The coffees of Central America profit from the area's steady climate and wealth of mountains. The mountains of the Pacific Cordillera, which stretch in a virtually unbroken line from Guatemala to the middle of Panama, provide the best combination of climate, altitude, and soil.
>
> Guatemala was a relative latecomer to the commercial coffee business, exporting beans only since 1875. This mountainous country is ideally suited for coffee production, and its exports now surpass those of much larger countries. European merchants still take about 50 percent of the Guatemalan beans, with most of the best beans today being exported to England.

Example I

It can be inferred from the passage that coffee grows well

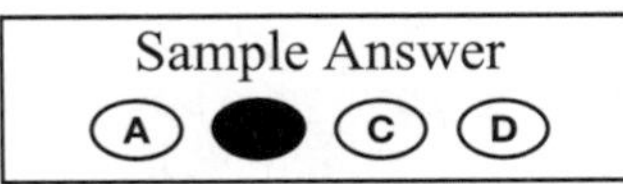

(A) in the northern hemisphere
(B) in mountainous regions
(C) in small countries
(D) near the Pacific Ocean

The passage implies that the mountainous regions of Central America are ideally suited for coffee production. The other answer choices cannot be inferred from the information given. Therefore, you should choose (B).

Example II

The word "surpass" in line 7 is closest in meaning to

Sample Answer
(A) (B) ● (D)

(A) include
(B) surround
(C) exceed
(D) limit

The word *surpass* in this passage means *exceed*. Therefore, you should choose (C).

Now begin work on the questions.

QUESTIONS 1–9

After the United States purchased Louisiana from France and made it their newest territory in 1803, President Thomas Jefferson called for an expedition to investigate the land the United States had bought for $15 million. Jefferson's secretary, Meriwether Lewis, a woodsman and hunter from childhood, persuaded the president to let him lead this expedition. Lewis recruited Army officer William Clark to be his co–commander. The Lewis and Clark expedition led the two young explorers to discover a new natural wealth of variety and abundance about which they would return to tell the world.

When Lewis and Clark departed from St. Louis in 1804, they had twenty–nine in their party, including a few Frenchmen and several men from Kentucky who were well–known frontiersmen. Along the way they picked up an interpreter named Toussant Charbonneau and his Native American wife, Sacajewea, the Shoshoni "Bird Woman" who aided them as guide and peacemaker and later became an American legend.

The expedition followed the Missouri River to its source, made a long portage overland through the Rocky Mountains, and descended the Columbia River to the Pacific Ocean. On the journey, they encountered peaceful Otos, whom they befriended, and hostile Teton Sioux, who demanded tribute from all traders. They also met Shoshoni, who welcomed their little sister Sacajewea, who had been abducted as a child by the Mandans. They discovered a paradise full of giant buffalo herds and elk and antelope so innocent of human contact that they tamely approached the men. The explorers also found a hell blighted by mosquitoes and winters harsher than anyone could reasonably hope to survive. They became desperately lost, then found their way again. Lewis and Clark kept detailed journals of the expedition, cataloging a dazzling array of new plants and animals, and even unearthing the bones of a forty–five–foot dinosaur.

When the party returned to St. Louis in 1806 after traveling almost 8,000 miles, they were eagerly greeted and grandly entertained. Their glowing descriptions of this vast new West provided a boon to the westward migration now becoming a permanent part of American life. The journals written by Lewis and Clark are still widely read today.

1. The purpose of the Lewis and Clark expedition was

   (A) to establish trade with the Otos and Teton Sioux
   (B) to explore territory purchased by the United States
   (C) to purchase land from France
   (D) to find the source of the Missouri River

2. The word "recruited" in line 5 could best be replaced by

   (A) reserved
   (B) substituted
   (C) imparted
   (D) hired

3. It can be inferred that Sacajawea

   (A) married a Shoshoni interpreter
   (B) abducted a child
   (C) demanded tribute from the traders
   (D) is a well–known American heroine

4. The word "they" in line 19 refers to

   (A) elk and antelope
   (B) buffalo herds
   (C) the members of the expedition
   (D) Shoshoni and Mandans

Go on to the next page

5. The word "blighted" in line 20 is closest in meaning to

   (A) increased
   (B) ruined
   (C) swollen
   (D) driven

6. Lewis and Clark encountered all of the following EXCEPT

   (A) dinosaur herds
   (B) buffaloes
   (C) mountains
   (D) friendly people

7. The word "boon" in line 26 is closest in meaning to

   (A) power
   (B) hurdle
   (C) benefit
   (D) conclusion

8. Where in the passage does the author mention hardships faced by the expedition?

   (A) Lines 5–7
   (B) Lines 10–12
   (C) Lines 13–15
   (D) Lines 19–21

9. It can be inferred from the passage that the Lewis and Clark expedition

   (A) experienced more hardships than successes
   (B) encouraged Americans to move to the West
   (C) probably cost the United States more than $15 million
   (D) caused the deaths of some of the explorers

QUESTIONS 10–19

In most discussions of cultural diversity, attention has focused on visible, explicit aspects of culture, such as language, dress, food, religion, music, and social rituals. Although they are important, these visible expressions of culture, which are taught deliberately and learned consciously, are only the tip of the iceberg of culture. Much of culture is taught and learned implicitly, or outside awareness. Thus, neither cultural insiders nor cultural outsiders are aware that certain "invisible" aspects of their culture exist.

Invisible elements of culture are important to us. For example, how long we can be late before being impolite, what topics we should avoid in a conversation, how we show interest or attention through listening behavior, what we consider beautiful or ugly—these are all aspects of culture that we learn and use without being aware of it. When we meet other people whose invisible cultural assumptions differ from those we have learned implicitly, we usually do not recognize their behavior as cultural in origin.

Differences in invisible culture can cause problems in cross–cultural relations. Conflicts may arise when we are unable to recognize others' behavioral differences as cultural rather than personal. We tend to misinterpret other people's behavior, blame them, or judge their intentions or competence without realizing that we are experiencing cultural rather than individual differences.

Formal organizations and institutions—such as schools, hospitals, workplaces, governments, and the legal system—are collection sites for invisible cultural differences. If the differences were more visible, we might have less misunderstanding. For example, if we met a man in a courthouse who was wearing exotic clothes, speaking a language other than ours, and carrying food that looked strange, we would not assume that we understood his thoughts and feelings or that he understood ours. Yet when such a man is dressed similarly to us, speaks our language, and does not differ from us in other obvious ways, we may fail to recognize the invisible cultural differences between us. As a result, mutual misunderstanding may arise.

10. What is the main purpose of the passage?

- (A) To explain the importance of invisible aspects of culture
- (B) To describe cultural diversity
- (C) To point out that much of culture is learned consciously
- (D) To explain why cross–cultural conflict occurs

11. The word "deliberately" in line 4 is closest in meaning to

- (A) slowly
- (B) accurately
- (C) intentionally
- (D) randomly

12. The phrase "the tip of the iceberg" in line 4 means that

- (A) other cultures seem cold to us
- (B) visible aspects of culture are learned in formal institutions
- (C) we usually focus on the highest forms of culture
- (D) most aspects of culture can not be seen

Go on to the next page

13. Which of the following was NOT mentioned as an example of invisible culture?

Ⓐ What topics to avoid in conversation
Ⓑ What food to eat in a courthouse
Ⓒ How late is considered impolite
Ⓓ How people express interest in what others are saying

14. The word "those" in line 12 refers to

Ⓐ people from a different culture
Ⓑ invisible cultural assumptions
Ⓒ people who speak a different language
Ⓓ topics that should be avoided in conversation

15. It can be inferred from paragraph 3 that conflict results when

Ⓐ people think cultural differences are personal
Ⓑ people compete with those from other cultures
Ⓒ one culture is more invisible than another culture
Ⓓ some people recognize more cultural differences than others

16. The author implies that institutions such as schools and workplaces

Ⓐ are aware of cultural differences
Ⓑ teach their employees about cultural differences
Ⓒ reinforce invisible cultural differences
Ⓓ share a common culture

17. The word "exotic" in line 22 could best be replaced by

Ⓐ improper
Ⓑ foreign
Ⓒ outdoor
Ⓓ formal

18. Which of the following would most likely result in misunderstanding?

Ⓐ Learning about our own culture in school
Ⓑ Unusual food being cooked by foreign visitors
Ⓒ Strange behavior from someone speaking a foreign language
Ⓓ Strange behavior from someone speaking our language

19. The following sentence can be added to paragraph 2 of the passage.

Rather, we see them as rude or uncooperative, and we may apply labels to them, such as "passive aggressive."

Where would it best fit in the paragraph? Choose **A**, **B**, **C**, or **D**.

A Invisible elements of culture are important to us. **B** For example, how long we can be late before being impolite, what topics we should avoid in a conversation, how we show interest or attention through listening behavior, what we consider beautiful or ugly—these are all aspects of culture that we learn and use without being aware of it. **C** When we meet other people whose invisible cultural assumptions differ from those we have learned implicitly, we usually do not recognize their behavior as cultural in origin. **D**

QUESTIONS 20–29

The ideas of John Dewey, philosopher and educator, have influenced American thought for over one hundred years. Dewey was born in Vermont in 1859, and throughout his life he kept the respect for experience, individuality, and fair play that shaped the character of the nineteenth–century Vermonter. He viewed his own life as a continuously reconstructive process—with experience and knowledge building on each other.

By the 1930s, Dewey had simplified his theory of experience to its essence. As the intellectual leader of the progressive schools, he asserted that there was danger in rejecting the old unless the new was rooted in a correct idea of experience. He held that experience is an interaction between what a person already knows and the situation at hand. Previous knowledge interacting with the present environment influences future experience.

Dewey believed that experience could not be equated with education because all experiences are not necessarily educative. Experience is educative only when it contributes to the growth of the individual, but it can be miseducative if it distorts the growth of further experience. It is the quality of experience that matters. Thus, productive experience is both the means and the goal of education. Furthermore, since education is a social process, truly progressive education involves the participation of the learner in directing the learning experience.

During his long life, Dewey lectured and published prolifically. These writings were influential both during his lifetime and after his death at the age of ninety–two. He viewed his whole life as an experiment which would produce knowledge that would lead to further experimentation. The range and diversity of Dewey's writings and his influence on society place him among America's great thinkers.

20. The passage mainly discusses

Ⓐ John Dewey's professional growth
Ⓑ the educational methods of John Dewey
Ⓒ the progressive movement in education
Ⓓ John Dewey's theory of experience

21. The author implies that Dewey's Vermont background

Ⓐ provided him with an excellent education
Ⓑ limited the types of experiences he had as a child
Ⓒ inspired him to become a philosopher
Ⓓ contributed to his philosophy of experience

22. The word "reconstructive" in line 5 is closest in meaning to

Ⓐ hardening
Ⓑ unifying
Ⓒ creative
Ⓓ communicative

23. The word "its" in line 7 refers to

Ⓐ progressive education
Ⓑ theory of experience
Ⓒ the 1930s
Ⓓ the old

24. According to John Dewey, the interplay between a person's previous knowledge and the present situation is

(A) dangerous
(B) a rejection of the old
(C) education
(D) a correct idea of experience

25. The word "distorts" in line 15 is closest in meaning to

(A) balances
(B) deforms
(C) mislays
(D) stimulates

26. All of the following were part of Dewey's theory of experience and education EXCEPT

(A) present experience affects future experience
(B) knowledge and experience interact
(C) experience is always educative
(D) experience should develop the individual

27. According to Dewey, progressive education should include

(A) the active participation of the student
(B) both positive and negative experiences
(C) complete rejection of traditional methods
(D) directing new social processes

28. The word "prolifically" in line 20 is closest in meaning to

(A) carefully
(B) progressively
(C) abundantly
(D) intellectually

29. The following sentence can be added to paragraph 4 of the passage.

He wrote several works on education, philosophy, logic, ethics, aesthetics, legal and political theory, and the social sciences.

Where would it best fit in the paragraph? Choose **A**, **B**, **C**, or **D**.

During his long life, Dewey lectured and published prolifically. **A** These writings were influential both during his lifetime and after his death at the age of ninety–two. **B** He viewed his whole life as an experiment which would produce knowledge that would lead to further experimentation. **C** The range and diversity of Dewey's writings and his influence on society place him among America's great thinkers. **D**

QUESTIONS 30–40

If hurricanes are the largest storms on earth, tornadoes are the most violent. Nothing produces more destructive power in a restricted area than a tornado as it passes by, sweeping the ground clear of all movable objects. A tornado's devastating blasts of wind put all human life in jeopardy, sending debris flying and lifting buildings from their foundations. It is small wonder the sight of these intense storms strikes terror.

In recent years, the origin of tornado formation has been the subject of increasingly fruitful research. Nevertheless, some mystery still surrounds tornadoes, and their formation cannot be predicted with absolute accuracy, even when conditions for their occurrence seem just right. Tornadoes are usually associated with thunderstorm conditions. They require a moist airstream that is warm for the season and usually comes from a southerly direction. Tornadoes favor the warmest part of the day, when solar heating and thunderstorm development are at their maximum.

The funnel–shaped cloud of the tornado reaches down to the ground from a parent cloud that is part of an active thunderstorm. Several funnels may develop in a mature tornado system, with small vortices continually forming and dissipating while whirling around the central core of the main tornado. A tornado funnel can assume various forms, from a thin, writhing, rope–like column of grayish white to a thick, amorphous mass of menacing black. In the Northern Hemisphere, tornadoes almost always spin counterclockwise.

87 percent of all tornadoes move from southwest to northeast. Rarely do tornadoes move toward the west. Tornadoes move forward at an average speed of 35 miles per hour, but great variations have been recorded. During part of its course, the great Tri–State Tornado of March 18, 1925, moved at the astonishing rate of 73 miles per hour.

The great Tri–State Tornado killed 695 people in Missouri, Illinois, and Indiana, making it one of the most deadly tornadoes ever recorded. On that same day, seven other tornadoes struck areas in Kentucky, Tennessee, and Alabama, raising the total to 792 deaths; it was clearly the most tragic tornado day in U.S. history.

30. The passage mainly discusses tornadoes in terms of their

(A) characteristics and effects
(B) causes
(C) mysterious origins
(D) direction and speed

31. The word "jeopardy" in line 4 could best be replaced by

(A) ruin
(B) transition
(C) repose
(D) danger

32. It can be concluded from lines 6–9 that

(A) prediction of tornadoes will become more accurate in the future
(B) scientists have studied the effect of tornadoes on fruit trees
(C) if the right conditions exist, a tornado will form
(D) many questions about tornado formation remain unanswered

Go on to the next page

33. According to the passage, tornado formation is related to

(A) dry air from the south
(B) thunderstorms
(C) cold air currents
(D) the season of the year

34. The word "their" in line 12 refers to

(A) tornadoes
(B) the warmest part of the day and a moist airstream
(C) solar heating and thunderstorm development
(D) thunderstorm conditions

35. The word "whirling" in line 15 is closest in meaning to

(A) rotating
(B) binding
(C) leaning
(D) roaring

36. According to the passage, the funnel–shaped cloud of a tornado

(A) is usually rope–like and black
(B) can take different colors or forms
(C) signals the end of a thunderstorm
(D) can be seen only during the afternoon

37. According to the passage, most tornadoes move

(A) in a clockwise direction
(B) faster than 35 miles per hour
(C) forward and backward
(D) toward the northeast

38. Where in the passage does the author describe the appearance of a tornado?

(A) Paragraph 1
(B) Paragraph 2
(C) Paragraph 3
(D) Paragraph 4

39. From the passage, which of the following can be inferred about tornadoes?

(A) They are becoming increasingly unpredictable.
(B) They are among the most powerful forces of nature.
(C) They usually accompany other natural disasters.
(D) They cause more deaths in urban rather than rural areas.

READING

40. The following sentence can be added to paragraph 4 of the passage.

Some tornadoes, however, have been reported to change directions abruptly, follow zigzag paths, or perform complete circles.

Where would it best fit in the paragraph? Choose **A**, **B**, **C**, or **D**.

A 87 percent of all tornadoes move from southwest to northeast. Rarely do tornadoes move toward the west. **B** Tornadoes move forward at an average speed of 35 miles per hour, but great variations have been recorded. **C** During part of its course, the great Tri–State Tornado of March 18, 1925, moved at the astonishing rate of 73 miles per hour. **D**

Go on to the next page

QUESTIONS 41–50

Advertising helps people recognize a particular brand, persuades them to try it, and tries to keep them loyal to it. Brand loyalty is perhaps the most important goal of consumer advertising. Whether they produce cars, canned foods or cosmetics, manufacturers want their customers to make repeated purchases. The quality of the product will encourage this, of course, but so, too, will effective advertising.

Advertising relies on the techniques of market research to identify potential users of a product. Are they homemakers or professional people? Are they young or old? Are they city dwellers or country dwellers? Such questions have a bearing on where and when ads should be placed. By studying readership breakdowns for newspapers and magazines as well as television ratings and other statistics, an advertising agency can decide on the best way of reaching potential buyers. Detailed research and marketing expertise are essential today when advertising budgets can run into thousands of millions of dollars.

Advertising is a fast–paced, high–pressure industry. There is a constant need for creative ideas that will establish a personality for a product in the public's mind. Current developments in advertising increase the need for talented workers.

In the past, the majority of advertising was aimed at the traditional white family—breadwinner father, non–working mother, and two children. Research now reveals that only about 6 percent of American households fit this stereotype. Instead, society is fragmented into many groups, with working mothers, single people and older people on the rise. To be most successful, advertising must identify a particular segment and aim its message toward that group.

Advertising is also making use of new technologies. Computer graphics are used to grab the attention of consumers and to help them see products in a new light. The use of computer graphics in a commercial for canned goods, for instance, gave a new image to the tin can.

41. What does the passage mainly discuss?

(A) How to develop a successful advertising plan
(B) New techniques and technologies of market research
(C) The central role of advertising in selling products
(D) The history of advertising in the United States

42. The word "this" in line 5 refers to

(A) the quality of the product
(B) effective advertising
(C) repeatedly buying the same brand
(D) the most important goal

43. It can be inferred from lines 6–11 that advertisers must

(A) encourage people to try new products
(B) aim their message at homemakers and professional people
(C) place several ads in newspapers and magazines
(D) know about the people who will buy the product

Go on to the next page

44. According to paragraph 2, market research includes

 (A) studying television ratings
 (B) hiring researchers with backgrounds in many fields
 (C) searching for talented workers
 (D) determining the price of a product

45. The author implies that the advertising industry requires

 (A) millions of dollars
 (B) a college–educated work force
 (C) government regulation
 (D) innovative thinking

46. According to the passage, most advertising used to be directed at

 (A) working mothers with children
 (B) two–parent families with children
 (C) unmarried people
 (D) older adults

47. The word "fragmented" in line 20 is closest in meaning to

 (A) collated
 (B) divided
 (C) moved
 (D) forced

48. The phrase "in a new light" in line 24 is closest in meaning to

 (A) differently
 (B) with the use of color enhancement
 (C) more distinctly
 (D) in a more energy–efficient way

49. Where in the passage does the author give an example of a new development in advertising?

 (A) Lines 3–5
 (B) Lines 9–11
 (C) Lines 14–15
 (D) Lines 23–24

50. The following sentence can be added to the passage.

Advertising is an essential part of the marketing process that can be tremendously influential in selling products.

Where would it best fit in the passage? Choose **A**, **B**, **C**, or **D**.

A Advertising helps people recognize a particular brand, persuades them to try it, and tries to keep them loyal to it. Brand loyalty is perhaps the most important goal of consumer advertising. Whether they produce cars, canned foods or cosmetics, manufacturers want their customers to make repeated purchases. **B** The quality of the product will encourage this, of course, but so, too, will effective advertising.

Advertising relies on the techniques of market research to identify potential users of a product. **C** Are they homemakers or professional people? Are they young or old? Are they city dwellers or country dwellers? Such questions have a bearing on where and when ads should be placed. By studying readership breakdowns for newspapers and magazines as well as television ratings and other statistics, an advertising agency can decide on the best way of reaching potential buyers. Detailed research and marketing expertise are essential today when advertising budgets can run into thousands of millions of dollars. **D**

STOP

Answers to the Reading Comprehension Review Test are on page 662.

SECTION 4 – WRITING

The Writing section of the TOEFL measures your ability to write an essay in English. This includes the ability to generate and organize ideas, to support these ideas with examples or evidence, and to compose in standard written English a response to an essay question. The essay questions are about topics that are appropriate for international students and require no specialized knowledge of any subject matter.

You have thirty minutes to plan, write, and revise your essay on both the paper–based test and the computer–based test.

On the paper test, the essay component is called *The Test of Written English*. On the computer–based test, the essay component is in Section 4.

Your essay will be evaluated according to the same procedures on both the paper test and the computer test. It will be read by two qualified essay readers who will rate it on a scale of 1 to 6, with 6 being the highest score possible.

The essay readers will evaluate how well your essay

- answers the question
- shows organization and development
- supports a thesis or main idea
- uses English sentences and words

Neither essay reader will know the score assigned by the other reader. Your essay will receive the average of the two scores unless there is a difference of more than one point. If this happens, a third reader will score your essay. Thus, your essay will receive a final rating of 6.0, 5.5, 5.0, 4.5, 4.0, 3.5, 3.0, 2.5, 2.0, 1.5, or 1. A score of 0 will be given if no essay is written, if the topic is simply copied, or if the essay is written in a language other than English.

THE TEST OF WRITTEN ENGLISH

The Test of Written English (TWE) is given with the paper–based TOEFL at the August, October, December, February, and May administrations. You cannot register to take the TWE only. You must take both the TOEFL and the TWE on the same day.

On the TWE, your essay rating is not incorporated into the total TOEFL score. Instead, a separate TWE score is reported on your TOEFL score report.

The TWE essay question comes at the beginning of the test, before the Listening Comprehension section of the TOEFL.

You will be allowed to make notes or plan your essay in the TWE test booklet. You will write your essay on the essay answer sheet given to you. Only what you write on the answer sheet will be scored by the essay readers.

Sample TWE Essay Question

> Some people prefer occupations in which they work primarily with machines. Others prefer occupations in which they work mainly with people. Which type of occupation do you prefer?
>
> Use specific reasons and examples to support your opinion.

THE COMPUTER–BASED TEST

On the computer test, your essay rating is incorporated into your score for Structure/Writing and counts as one–half of the Structure/Writing score. Your essay rating also appears separately on your score report under the heading "essay rating."

The essay question comes at the end of the test, after the Reading section.

Before the computer gives you the essay topic, you must choose whether to type your essay on the computer or to handwrite it.

- If you choose to type your essay, you will first look at a tutorial on how to type the essay on the computer.
- If you choose to handwrite your essay, the computer will allow you to go directly to the essay question. You can do this by clicking on **Handwrite Essay Now**. If you handwrite your essay, the test supervisor will give you a paper answer sheet to write on.

The test supervisor will give you paper for making notes and planning your essay. However, only the response you type in the essay box on the computer or handwrite on the answer sheet will be scored by the essay readers.

The computer screen will look like this:

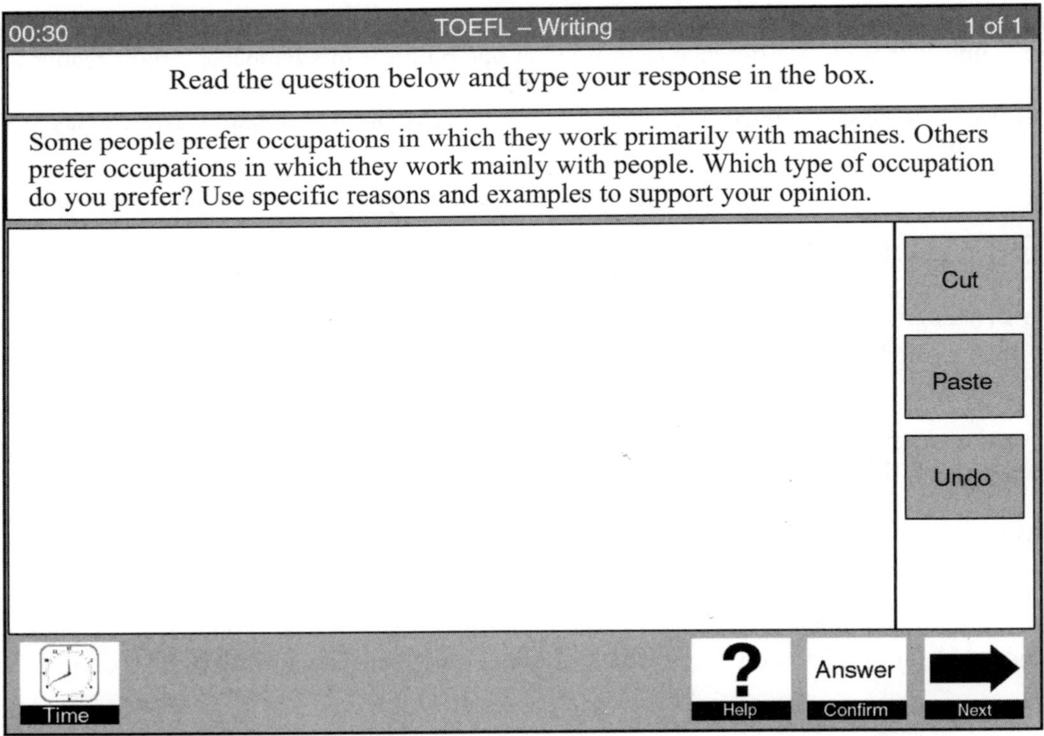

You can end the Writing section at any time by clicking on **Next** and then on **Confirm Answer**. At the end of 30 minutes, the computer will automatically end the Writing section.

QUESTION TYPES

There are four general types of essay questions on both the paper test and the computer test. Here is an example of each type.

Question Type 1 – Agree or Disagree with a Statement

Do you agree or disagree with the following statement?

You should not believe everything you read in the newspaper.

Use specific reasons and examples to support your opinion.

Question Type 2 – Choose and Defend a Point of View

Some people believe that in high school science classes, girls should be in classes with only girls, and boys should be in classes with only boys. Others believe that all high school students should be in science classes that are coeducational, with students of both genders learning together. Which view do you agree with? Use specific reasons and examples to support your opinion.

Question Type 3 – Explain Reasons, Causes, Results, or Qualities

What is the most important product or resource in your country? Why is it important? Use specific reasons and details to explain your answer.

Question Type 4 – Compare and Contrast Two Topics

Compare and contrast two cities or regions in your country. Use specific details and examples to support your answer.

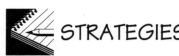

STRATEGIES FOR WRITING THE ESSAY

Prepare before the Test

- If you are taking the computer–based test, decide whether you are going to type or handwrite the essay.
- If you plan to type your essay on the computer, practice by using the Writing section tutorial on the *TOEFL Sampler* CD–ROM.
- Plan to handwrite your essay if you are not comfortable with typing, writing on a keyboard, or using a keyboard with English characters.
- Be familiar with the question types and writing topics typically assigned on the computer–based TOEFL and the Test of Written English. Study the list of TOEFL writing topics on pages 514 to 516. For a longer list of topics, see the TOEFL web site at http://www.toefl.org.

Budget Your Time during the Test

- Use your 30 minutes wisely. Spend your time approximately like this:
  - Prewriting – 5 minutes
  - Writing – 20 minutes
  - Checking – 5 minutes
- During the prewriting phase, read the question carefully and make sure you understand everything it asks you to do. Organize your thoughts by making an outline.
- During the writing phase, support all of your points with evidence: details, examples, facts, reasons, and personal experiences. Write only about the given topic. Use sentence structures and vocabulary that you are familiar with.
- Allow yourself five minutes at the end to check your work. Make sure all of your points are clearly stated and well supported. Check for errors in sentence structure and word choice. If you handwrite your essay, the readers will not mind if errors are crossed out neatly and corrections are written above them.

Know the Scoring Criteria

- Do not be concerned about whether the essay readers agree with your opinion. Be concerned about whether your essay:
  - addresses the writing task
  - shows organization and development
  - supports a thesis or main idea
  - clearly communicates your ideas
  - has good sentence structure
  - uses appropriate vocabulary

OVERVIEW OF THIS SECTION

4.1 Prewriting and Organizing Ideas

FOCUS

Read the following essay question.

> What are some important qualities of a good grandparent? Use specific details and examples to explain why these qualities are important.

How would you plan a response to this question? Check the steps you would take.

__ Just begin writing the essay.
__ Make a list of qualities of grandparents you know.
__ Think about what the question wants you to do.
__ Choose three qualities.
__ Describe your own grandmother.
__ State your opinion about grandparents.

The first thing you would probably do is think about what the question is asking. In the above question, key phrases are *important qualities*, *good grandparent*, *specific details and examples*, and *explain why*. These phrases tell you that the question requires you to do three things:

1. Identify important qualities of a good grandparent.
2. Explain why these qualities are important.
3. Give specific details and examples.

Your next step might be to make a list of qualities. You might add examples from your own life to illustrate these qualities (for example, your own grandparents). You might choose two or three of the most important qualities to explain in your essay.

Another thing you would probably do is decide what the main idea of your essay will be. Your main point should restate in your own words some of the key ideas from the question and communicate your opinion about the topic. For example, a main idea for this essay might be:

> So many qualities make a good grandparent, but the most important are patience, love, and a strong sense of family.

The steps described above are part of the ***prewriting*** phase of writing an essay. Prewriting is an important part of the writing process because very few people can just begin writing and still be able to produce a thoughtful and well–organized essay.

DO YOU KNOW...?

1. An ***essay*** is a written work that is composed of three or more paragraphs. The purpose of an essay is to communicate to a reader an opinion about a topic and to provide information that supports or defends this opinion.

   The essay you write in response to a TOEFL question will do one or more of the following:

   - state one side of an argument and defend it
   - explain or describe something
   - show the similarities or differences between two things

   An essay has three parts:

   1. ***Introduction.*** The introductory paragraph tells your reader what the essay is about. It restates the question in your own words and states your main idea. The main idea of your essay is called the ***thesis statement***. The thesis is often stated in the last sentence of the introductory paragraph.

   2. ***Body.*** The body paragraphs each contain a supporting point to develop your thesis. The body paragraphs are sometimes called ***developmental paragraphs***. They contain specific details, examples, and reasons. On the TOEFL, your essay will probably contain two or three body paragraphs.

   3. ***Conclusion.*** The concluding paragraph summarizes your position and completes the essay.

2. Your essay will be evaluated on how effectively it

   - addresses the writing task (answers the question)
   - shows organization and development
   - supports a thesis or main idea

   Consider the above criteria as you plan your essay during the prewriting phase.

3. ***Prewriting*** is the thinking and planning you do *before* you begin writing your essay. Prewriting consists of:

   - reading and thinking about the question
   - deciding what your thesis or main idea is going to be
   - brainstorming, making notes, and writing an outline

   Brainstorming is quickly generating ideas—examples, details, reasons—in the form of a list or diagram. Brainstorming is thinking on paper. It is coming up with as many ideas as possible in a short amount of time.

   Outlining is organizing your ideas into a logical structure for your essay. Before you write your outline, decide what your thesis is going to be. Then, choose ideas from your brainstorming that will support this main idea. Choose two or three of your best examples or reasons and discard the rest. Decide the most effective order for arranging these ideas, and write your outline. The outline is the plan for writing your essay.

   Note: Spend at least five minutes, but no more than seven minutes, on prewriting.

Look at this example:

> Do you agree or disagree with the following statement?
>
> *The teacher is responsible for motivating students to learn.*
>
> Use specific reasons and examples to support your opinion.

Brainstorming:

Disagree—Student responsible, not teacher
- –learning before & after school, w/o teacher
- –self–discipline
- –If S not self–motivated, T can't help much
- –parents should motivate
- –people naturally want to learn
- –my fifth grade teacher
- –work/all life
- –learning – no teacher

Thesis:

Although many people believe it is the teacher's responsibility to motivate students to learn, students will not learn much unless they are motivated within themselves.

Outline:

1. Natural love of learning
2. Learning during whole life
3. Developing self–discipline

Look at another example:

> Some people like to spend their leisure time doing activities with a lot of people. Others prefer to spend their leisure in quiet ways by themselves or with one other person. Which do you prefer? Use specific reasons and examples to support your answer.

Brainstorming:

Activities with people
reason — job is desk job, alone (computer)
active things/play tennis & basketball
good for exercise, health
socializing with friends
college basketball team
enjoy – hiking, rafting/teamwork important
safety
develop important skills

Thesis:

Since I work mainly by myself in my job as a computer specialist, I prefer leisure activities that provide enjoyment, exercise, and an opportunity to interact with other people.

Outline:

1. Enjoyment and exercise: tennis, hiking
2. Interaction and teamwork: basketball, rafting

PRACTICE

Timed Exercises – 5 minutes each

For each essay question in Exercises 4.1.A through 4.1.E, take five minutes to brainstorm and outline a response that will

- answer the question
- show organization
- support a thesis

In these exercises, you do not have to write the essay. Concentrate only on producing a good thesis and outline in five minutes.

Exercise 4.1.A

Do you agree or disagree with the following statement?

Children should not have to work or help with household tasks. Their only responsibility should be to study.

Use specific reasons and examples to support your opinion.

Exercise 4.1.B

Some people argue for a broad university education in which students learn about many different subjects. Others argue for a specialized university education in which students learn only about a specific field of study. Which position do you agree with? Use specific reasons and examples to support your opinion.

Exercise 4.1.C

If you could change one thing about yourself, what would you change? Use specific reasons and details to support your answer.

Exercise 4.1.D

Society benefits from the work of its members. Compare the contributions of farmers to society with the contributions of business men and women. Which type of contribution do you think is valued more by your society? Give specific reasons and examples to support your answer.

Exercise 4.1.E

What are some important qualities of a good teacher? Use specific details and examples to explain why these qualities are important.

4.1 EXTENSION

1. With your classmates and teacher, discuss which is better: organizing your ideas from least to most important, or from most to least important. What other ways can ideas be organized?

2. Choose one of the outlines you wrote for Exercises 4.1.A through 4.1.E and exchange papers with a classmate. Evaluate how successfully your classmate's outline (1) answers the question, (2) shows organization, and (3) supports a thesis. With your classmate, discuss both of your outlines. Make necessary changes to improve your outline.

3. Write an essay, using your outline from #2 above. Allow yourself 25 minutes to write the essay.

4.2 Supporting the Main Idea

FOCUS

Read the following essay question and two essay outlines.

> Do you agree or disagree with the following statement?
>
> *A student must like a teacher in order to learn from the teacher.*
>
> Use specific reasons and examples to support your opinion.

Outline 1

A student must like a teacher in order to learn from the teacher.
1. Good teachers
2. Learning is more fun
3. Learning is easier
4. Some teachers nicer than others
5. Subject interesting

Outline 2

Disagree—Students do not have to like a teacher to learn from that teacher.
More important:
1. Knows subject, good questions
   Mr. Powell – arrogant but knowledgeable
2. Discipline
   Algebra teacher – strict, but discipline, practice
   Swimming coach

Contrast:

3. H.S. history – nice guy, didn't learn anything

Which outline will probably produce a better essay? Why?

Outline 1 has several ideas, but do these ideas support the writer's opinion, *A student must like a teacher in order to learn from the teacher*?

Outline 2 also has several ideas and examples. Do these ideas support the writer's opinion, *Students do not have to like a teacher to learn from that teacher*?

A very important part of the essay question is *Use specific reasons and examples to support your opinion*. The readers who rate your essay are not interested in what your opinion is, but they are interested in how you support your opinion with specific reasons and examples. Because Outline 2 includes these, it will probably produce a better essay.

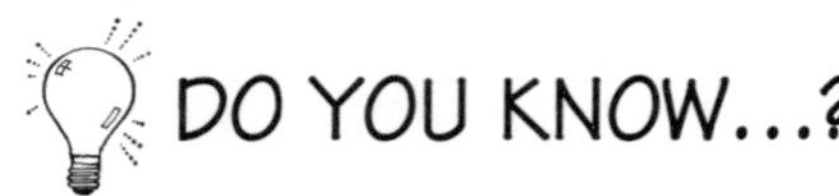

DO YOU KNOW...?

1. The readers who score your essay will look at

   - how the ideas in your essay are organized
   - how well your thesis is developed and supported

   The readers will check to see if your essay is organized with an introduction, body, and conclusion (See 4.1). The introduction contains the ***thesis***, or main idea, which communicates your opinion. The body paragraphs contain supporting ideas.

   Supporting ideas are the points you make to develop your thesis. Each body paragraph should contain one supporting idea which is developed with details. ***Details*** are specific facts, examples, reasons, descriptions, or personal experiences.

   All supporting ideas and details in the body paragraphs must support your thesis.

2. Most of the TOEFL essay questions remind you to support your thesis.

> Use specific reasons and examples to support your opinion.
> Use specific examples and details to support your answer.
> Use specific details to explain why _____.

PRACTICE

Exercise 4.2.A

Read the following essay question and essay. Underline the thesis and supporting ideas. Circle details in the body paragraphs.

> How does advertising influence people's behavior? Use specific details and examples to explain your answer.

People are influenced by the world around them. People see a lot of advertising in newspapers and magazines, on signs, and on television. Today people even see ads in the movie theater! All of this advertising influences how people spend their money, how they look at themselves, and how they communicate with other people.

Advertising influences how people spend their money. People sometimes buy things they can't afford or don't need. I read a story of a family that bought a computer for their children, but they were living in a tent. They didn't even have electricity for the computer. People spend too much because they have to be better than everyone else. In my country, weddings are a big industry, and families spend too much money because of advertising. This is a negative influence of advertising.

Advertising affects how people view themselves. Sometimes it makes people feel bad if they can't buy something. For example, a lot of sports and movie stars advertise shoes, clothes, and so on. Children see this on television and pressure their parents to buy it. There are a lot of crimes because teenagers kill to get designer jackets. Advertising makes them feel like they are nobody without designer clothes. Also, teenagers start to smoke because this looks cool. Moreover, some girls want to be thin like girls in the ads.

Finally, advertising changes people's communication. I hear a lot of little kids saying the phrases they hear on television. They also sing the songs from the commercials. Also, advertising influences spelling. I have seen "night" spelled like "nite." Therefore, advertising affects the ways that people speak and write English.

Advertising has a lot of good points. It is a way to sell things in a capitalist country. However, there are also a lot of bad influences on people's behavior because of advertising.

Could you identify the thesis, supporting ideas, and supporting details?

How well does the essay

- answer the question?
- show organization and development?
- support a thesis?

Analyze and evaluate the essay with your teacher and classmates.

WRITING

Directions for Exercises 4.2.B through 4.2.F: For each essay question, write a thesis statement and two to four supporting statements. Make a list of details that will develop each supporting point.

Exercise 4.2.B

Food is an important part of culture. What have you learned about a country from its food? Use specific examples and details to support your response.

Exercise 4.2.C

Do you agree or disagree with the following statement?

Youth is wasted on the young.

Use specific reasons and examples to support your opinion.

Exercise 4.2.D

Some people think that teachers and education professionals should make all of the important decisions about what is taught in schools. Others think that business and industry professionals should make all of the major decisions. Which view do you agree with? Use specific reasons and examples to support your opinion.

Exercise 4.2.E

Compare and contrast the experiences of children today with the experiences of children thirty or forty years ago. Use specific details and examples to support your answer.

Exercise 4.2.F

Choose one of the following occupations and explain why it is important to society.

artist   banker   engineer   police officer

Use specific reasons and details to explain your answer.

4.2 EXTENSION

Choose one of the essay questions from Exercises 4.2.B through 4.2.F and write an essay. Allow yourself 30 minutes to plan and write the essay. Exchange papers with a classmate. Read your classmate's essay and identify its thesis. Make an outline of your classmate's essay, showing supporting points and details. With your classmate, discuss and evaluate how well both essays (1) answer the question, (2) show organization and development, and (3) support the thesis.

4.3 Writing the Introduction

FOCUS

Read the following essay question and introductory paragraph.

> Some people think that government should spend as much money as possible on developing space technology for the exploration of the moon and other planets. Others think that this money should be spent on solving the problems of society on Earth. Which view do you agree with? Use specific reasons and examples to support your answer.

Society is often divided on major issues involving government spending. While some people believe that as much money as possible should be spent on space exploration, others think we have an obligation to try to solve social problems on Earth. Both views are compelling; however, I believe there are stronger reasons for seeking knowledge beyond our world. If we invest in developing technology for the exploration of space, we may discover knowledge that will benefit society on Earth.

Think about each sentence in the paragraph. What does each sentence do?

The first sentence introduces the general topic of how government should spend money.

> Society is often divided on major issues involving government spending.

The next sentence focuses on the two ways of spending money mentioned in the question.

> While some people believe that as much money as possible should be spent on space exploration, others think we have an obligation to try to solve social problems on Earth.

The next sentence focuses even more on the question and takes a side.

> Both views are compelling; however, I believe there are stronger reasons for seeking knowledge beyond our world.

The last sentence states the writer's opinion.

> If we invest in developing technology for the exploration of space, we may discover knowledge that will benefit society on Earth.

The last sentence is the thesis statement, the idea that must be supported in the rest of the essay.

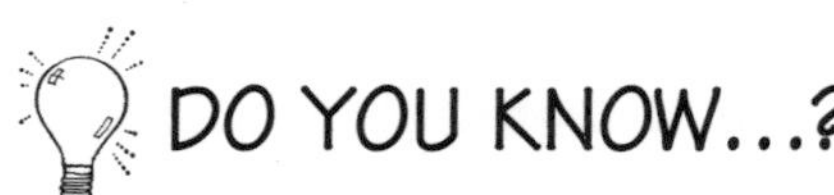

DO YOU KNOW...?

1. The ***introduction*** is the first paragraph of an essay. The purpose of the introduction is to let the readers know what to expect in the body of the essay.

   The introduction contains a ***thesis statement***. The thesis, sometimes called the ***controlling idea***, is the main idea of the essay. The thesis statement is the most important sentence of your essay because it expresses your opinion about the topic. The thesis is usually stated in the last sentence of the introductory paragraph.

   The thesis statement may preview the points you will make in the body of your essay, in the order in which they will be discussed. Previewing your supporting points will help the readers know how your essay will be organized.

2. On the essay test, a good introduction contains three or four sentences.

GENERAL PLAN FOR AN INTRODUCTION	
First sentence	Introduces the general topic of the essay
Second sentence	Narrows the topic to focus on the question
Third sentence	Restates the question in your own words
Fourth sentence	States your thesis or main idea

The above plan will work for any of the four types of essay questions you might see on the TOEFL or TWE.

Look at the following examples of introductory paragraphs.

Question Type 1 – Agree or Disagree with a Statement

In question type 1, your agreement or disagreement with the given statement is the thesis you must support.

> Do you agree or disagree with the following statement?
>
> *You should not believe everything you read in the newspaper.*
>
> Use specific reasons and examples to support your opinion.

Newspapers are an important source of information, and for some people this is their main source of news every day. However, some people think that you should not believe everything you read in a newspaper. There are many reasons why this statement is true. A lot of newspapers have propaganda, focus on scandal, or are not as up to date as the news on television.

Question Type 2 – Choose and Defend a Point of View

In question type 2, your choice of which position you agree with is the thesis you must support.

> Some people believe that in high school science classes, girls should be in classes with only girls, and boys should be in classes with only boys. Others believe that all high school students should be in science classes that are coeducational, with students of both genders learning together. Which view do you agree with? Use specific reasons and examples to support your opinion.

The issue of coeducational science classes is controversial. Some people think that girls should be in science classes with only girls. On the other hand, some people believe that girls and boys should study science in the same class. I believe that girls should have the opportunity to learn science in the best way possible. If girls learn better in an all–girl class, they should be allowed to do so.

Question Type 3 – Explain Reasons, Causes, Results, or Qualities

> What is the most important product or resource in your country? Why is it important? Use specific reasons and details to explain your answer.

Many countries are famous for a certain product or resource. The most important product in my country is information technology. The several related industries involved in the production of information technology have transformed my country by modernizing it and making it an economic power.

Question Type 4 – Compare and Contrast Two Topics

> Compare and contrast two cities or regions in your country. Use specific details and examples to support your answer.

Rural areas are different from urban areas in most countries. In Indonesia there are a lot of differences between the capital city and the small villages. In this essay, I will discuss the similarities and differences between Jakarta, the capital city, and the village of Padua in West–Borneo, where most of my relatives live.

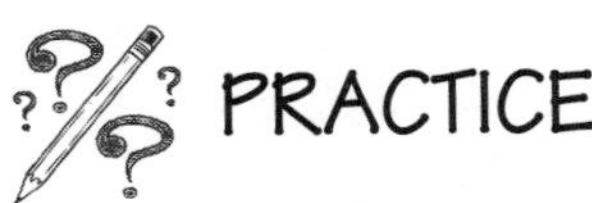

PRACTICE

Timed Exercises – 10 minutes each

For each essay question in Exercises 4.3.A through 4.3.F, write a thesis statement, outline, and introductory paragraph. For the introduction, use the general plan for an introduction on page 494 as a guide.

Spend your time like this:

- 5 minutes on prewriting (thinking, brainstorming, outlining)
- 5 minutes on writing the introduction

Exercise 4.3.A

Some people want to have a job where they can make or do things with their hands. Other people prefer having a job where they can work with their heads and think about things. Which type of job do you prefer? Use specific reasons and examples to support your opinion.

Exercise 4.3.B

Compare the qualities of a good parent with the qualities of a good teacher. Use specific details and examples to support your response.

Exercise 4.3.C

What is the most important change your country has undergone in the past twenty years? What are the results of this change? Use specific details and examples to support your answer.

Exercise 4.3.D

Do you agree or disagree with this statement?

Employers should be required to provide smoking areas for their employees who smoke tobacco.

Use specific reasons and examples to support your opinion.

Exercise 4.3.E

You want to persuade someone to travel to your country. What reasons would you give? Support your answer with specific details.

Exercise 4.3.F

A company has announced that it wishes to build a large shopping mall near your community. Discuss the advantages and disadvantages of this new influence on your community. Do you support or oppose the shopping mall? Use specific reasons and examples to support your opinion.

4.3 EXTENSION

Choose one of the introductory paragraphs you wrote for Exercises 4.3.A through 4.3.F. Exchange papers (introduction only, not the outline) with a classmate. Read your classmate's introduction and identify the thesis statement. Do you think your classmate's essay will successfully answer the question? What do you expect to happen in the body paragraphs of the essay? With your classmate, discuss both of your introductory paragraphs.

4.4 Writing the Body and Conclusion

FOCUS

Read the following essay question and paragraph from the body of the essay.

> Some people learn by reading about things. Others learn by doing things. Which of these methods of learning is better for you? Use specific examples to support your choice.

I learned how to ride a bicycle and drive a car by experience. I rode a bicycle when I was six years old. Because I could not read about it, I had to get on the bicycle and use my feet and hands. I could also learn from my mistake when I fell off my bicycle. Similarly, I learned to drive a car by doing it. Although I had to study a driving manual and take a test on a computer, I could not learn driving well until I practiced driving in a car.

From reading the above paragraph, can you tell which method of learning the writer prefers? How do you know this?

What is the main point of the paragraph? How is this point supported?

The first sentence of the paragraph is important.

I learned how to ride a bicycle and drive a car by experience.

The first sentence gives the topic and main point of the paragraph. This topic—*learning how to ride a bicycle and drive a car by experience*—is developed with several details.

six years old
use my feet and hands
fell off my bicycle
practiced driving in a car

The writer also contrasts learning by doing with learning by reading.

Because I could not read about it
Although I had to study a driving manual

The writer's thesis—a preference for learning by doing things—is supported with specific examples—riding a bicycle and driving a car—which are developed with details in this paragraph from the body of the essay.

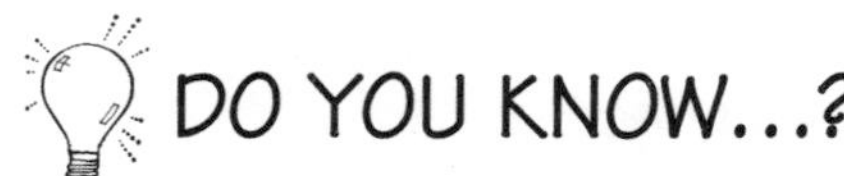

DO YOU KNOW...?

1. The readers who score your essay will look at

- how the ideas in your essay are organized
- how your thesis is developed and supported
- how you use English to express your ideas

2. The ***body*** of the essay consists of the middle paragraphs, which are sometimes called ***developmental paragraphs***. These paragraphs develop the idea expressed in the thesis statement.

   Each body paragraph should have a ***topic sentence*** which expresses the main point of that paragraph. The topic sentence of each body paragraph is developed with specific examples, details, facts, reasons, or personal experiences.

   The topic sentence of each body paragraph should be a point that supports the thesis of the essay. When all of the points in the body support the thesis, the essay has ***unity***.

   The body paragraphs follow the introduction and are arranged in the most effective order for impressing the reader and supporting the thesis. Sometimes the order of the body paragraphs is previewed in the thesis statement. Sometimes the order is arranged from the least important to the most important supporting point, or vice versa.

3. The ***conclusion*** is the last paragraph of an essay. The concluding paragraph should leave your readers with a feeling of completion. The conclusion can do one or more of the following:

- restate the thesis in different words (***paraphrase***)
- summarize the supporting points
- state an opinion
- make a recommendation
- give a solution
- draw a conclusion
- make a prediction

Read the following concluding paragraph from an essay. What does the writer do in the conclusion?

> In summary, a new theater would enrich our school in ways that a new computer lab would not. A theater would enable us to expand our music and drama programs, explore our rich cultural heritage, and strengthen our bonds with the community. For these reasons, I recommend that our prize money be used to build a new theater. Investing in the performing arts is a celebration of our humanity.

The above paragraph states an opinion, which may also restate the thesis.

> In summary, a new theater would enrich our school in ways that a new computer lab would not.

It summarizes the important points.

> A theater would enable us to expand our music and drama programs, explore our rich cultural heritage, and strengthen our bonds with the community.

It also makes a recommendation.

For these reasons, I recommend that our prize money be used to build a new theater.

Finally, the last sentence completes the essay.

Investing in the performing arts is a celebration of our humanity.

Note: On the TOEFL, spend approximately 20 minutes on writing the introduction, body, and conclusion of your essay.

4. An essay has ***coherence*** when all of the ideas within paragraphs, as well as between paragraphs, are connected to each other logically. If your essay is coherent, it is well–organized and easy for your readers to understand.

   Transitions are words and phrases that can help you express relationships between ideas within and between paragraphs. Using transitions gives your essay organization and coherence.

   To show contrast between ideas:

although	in contrast	on the contrary	rather
but	instead	on the one hand…	while
however	nevertheless	…on the other hand	yet

   To introduce examples or reasons:

because	for instance	to illustrate
for example	such as	one example/reason is

   To add examples or reasons:

also	furthermore	next
another example/reason is	in addition	not only…but also
first, second, third…	moreover	similarly

   To emphasize or show importance:

the best example	clearly	in fact	the most important reason
certainly	indeed	most importantly	surely

   To make a conclusion:

at last	finally	in short	therefore
consequently	in conclusion	in summary	thus

PRACTICE

Exercise 4.4.A

Read the following essay. Underline the thesis statement and the topic sentence of each body paragraph. Circle supporting details and transitions.

There are a lot of different ways for people to learn new things. People can learn by reading, or they can learn by doing things. For some people, learning is better either one way or the other. I prefer to learn by doing things because when I do something myself it becomes more real than when I read about it.

I learned how to ride a bicycle and drive a car by experience. I rode a bicycle when I was six years old. Because I could not read about it, I had to get on the bicycle and use my feet and hands. I could also learn from my mistake when I fell off my bicycle. Similarly, I learned to drive a car by doing it. Although I had to study a driving manual and take a test on a computer, I could not learn driving well until I practiced driving in a car.

Another example is mathematics. When I was a child, my teacher made the students measure our classroom. We measured the length and width of the room. This is how we could calculate the area of our classroom. I can never forget this because mathematics became real for me.

Finally, I learned how to use a computer by doing it. I tried to read the computer manual, but this was difficult for me because the book was very complex. I learned more when I sat at the keyboard and tried using several keys. Of course, my teacher explained some things about the computer. However, I could learn best when I experienced it.

It is true that I have to learn some things by reading, such as history and literature. Reading gives me important knowledge. However, for most skills that I need for my life, such as driving and using a computer, I prefer to learn through action. These skills must be experienced for me to really learn them.

Could you identify the thesis, topic sentences, supporting details, and transitions?

What does the writer do in the concluding paragraph?

Analyze and evaluate the essay with your teacher and classmates.

Exercise 4.4.B

Timed exercise – 15 minutes

Choose one of the introductory paragraphs you wrote for Exercises 4.3.A through 4.3.F in the previous unit. Allow yourself 15 minutes to complete the essay with body paragraphs and a conclusion.

4.4 EXTENSION

Form "essay reader" groups of three people to evaluate the essays written for Exercise 4.4.B. You will read the essays of two other people. In turn, your essay will be read by two people. For each essay you read, identify: (1) thesis statement, (2) supporting points, (3) supporting details, and (4) transitions. What does the writer do in the conclusion? Does the essay answer the question? Within your group, discuss all three essays.

4.5 Checking Paragraph and Sentence Structure

FOCUS

Read the following essay question and paragraphs from two different responses.

> Choose one of the following occupations and explain why it is important to society.
>
> athlete journalist politician
>
> Use specific reasons and details to explain your answer.

Paragraph 1

Most importantly, journalists leave behind a record that tells the story of our times. News stories focus on facts such as what, where, when, and why events happen. Because journalists attempt to tell the truth about events in the present, we can later look back at their stories and better understand history. When we want to research the details of the Persian Gulf War or the fall of the Soviet Union, where do we look? Usually we read the news magazines of that time. These are the gifts that journalists left us.

Paragraph 2

The athletes they are good for entertainment. People like to watch athletes play. Especially for children athlete provide a good model. For example, basketball and soccer player. It is something to hope. Also, athletes they show how important is exercise. Because people can see to keep fit. Athletes good for the country. One reason is patriotism. My country likes athletes go to the Olympics. For example, track and field, swimming, and basketball.

Which paragraph is better?

Both paragraphs give specific reasons and details. However, Paragraph 1 is stronger because it is clearer about the point it is developing, *Most importantly, journalists leave behind a record that tells the story of our times*. Paragraph 1 also shows variety in sentence structure.

In Paragraph 2, what point is being developed? Is there a topic sentence? Paragraph 2 also has problems with sentence structure. What is wrong with the following sentences?

For example, basketball and soccer player.
Also, athletes they show how important is exercise.
Because people can see to keep fit.

Remember, you do not have to worry about whether your readers will agree with your opinion. However, you *do* have to be concerned with writing paragraphs and sentences that clearly communicate your opinion by using English appropriately.

WRITING

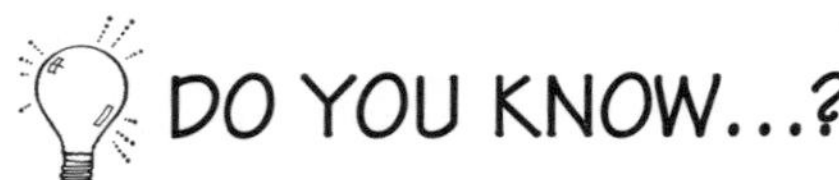

1. The readers who score your essay will look at

   - how the ideas in your essay are organized
   - how you use English to express your ideas
   - the variety and structure of your sentences

   Note: Allow around five minutes at the end of the 30–minute test to check paragraph structure, sentence structure, and word choice, and to make any changes that would clarify your meaning. If you handwrite your essay, cross out errors and write corrections neatly above them.

2. Each paragraph in the body of the essay should develop one point. Usually, this point is stated in the topic sentence of that paragraph. The topic sentence is often the first sentence of the paragraph. All other sentences in the paragraph should provide details, examples, or personal experiences to develop the topic sentence.

   Generally, the body paragraphs in TOEFL essays contain four to seven sentences. However, there is no strict rule for how long each paragraph should be. The essay readers are more interested in what you write than in how much you write.

   Indent the first line of each paragraph. On the computer test, you must use the **Space Bar** to indent the beginning of a paragraph because the **Tab** key will not work.

3. Your essay will be easier and more interesting to read if you

   - use a variety of short and long sentences
   - avoid common sentence errors

   Use conjunctions or subordinating words to join short sentences into longer sentences.

   Example: Athletes provide entertainment. People like to watch athletes play.
   Better: Athletes provide entertainment, and people like to watch them play.
   Because athletes provide entertainment, people like to watch them play.

   Example: The factory is built in my community. It will cause noise.
   Traffic will increase. I oppose building the factory.
   Better: If the factory is built in my community, noise and traffic will increase; therefore, I oppose building the factory.

   Remember, a sentence must have at least one subject and one verb. A sentence can be composed of one or more clauses, which must be joined appropriately with conjunctions or subordinating words (See 2.8, 2.11, 2.20).

   Avoid the following sentence problems:

   Incomplete Sentences (Fragments):

   Example: Because Earth is our home.
   Better: Earth is our home.
   Because Earth is our home, we need to protect our natural resources.

Example: For example, television and computers.
Better: For example, television and computers have impacted family life.

Run–on Sentences:

Example: Children should grow up in the countryside they can know nature.
Better: Children should grow up in the countryside, where they can know nature.
Children should grow up in the countryside because they can know nature.

Example: Some people like living in a rural area, I prefer the urban lifestyle.
Better: Some people like living in a rural area, but I prefer the urban lifestyle.
Some people like living in a rural area; however, I prefer the urban lifestyle.
While some people like living in a rural area, I prefer the urban lifestyle.

Incorrect Duplicate Subject:

Example: Private companies they should spend more money to clean up pollution.
Better: Private companies should spend more money to clean up pollution.

Incorrect Change in Verb Tense:

Example: People are living longer today because they had better health care.
Better: People are living longer today because they have better health care.

Remember, if you handwrite your essay, cross out errors and make corrections neatly. If you type your essay, use the appropriate computer keys to delete errors and insert corrections.

PRACTICE

Exercise 4.5.A

Read the following paragraphs. Check paragraph and sentence structure. Make any changes that will improve the paragraphs. Rewrite the improved paragraphs.

1. My decision not to get married two years ago. I could finish my university studies. My father he wanted me to get married. My parents they allow me to make the decision. If I had married, I have to stay in my husband's home. Because in my culture a married woman she has a duty to her husband. It's our tradition. I chose finish my degree. I will be a graduate student in Toronto. I will pursue my master's degree in business economics.

2. Another good reason to build a school in my neighborhood, is encourage more families to move here, more homes will be built more variety of people. It will encourage more family businesses people will drive more safely the children are walking to school Also a playground sounds of children playing I like this. A school is good for a neighborhood a sense of community, education is a good thing should be close where people live.

4.5 EXTENSION

Choose one of the essays you have written so far for the Practice and Extension exercises in this section. Exchange papers with a classmate. On your classmate's essay, suggest changes in paragraph and sentence structure that will improve the essay. When you get your own essay back, read and think about your classmate's suggestions. What additional improvements can you make?

4.6 Checking Word Choice

FOCUS

Read the following essay question and paragraph from the essay.

> Do you agree or disagree with the following statement?
>
> *You will not learn much about life if you are always comfortable.*
>
> Use specific reasons and examples to support your opinion.

Children must learn about life in a comfortable location. If a child is not safety, the child can't learn nothing. I wanna have children sometimes. My duty is for keep my children safety and protection from bad experience. I'm gonna give my child food, clothes, and other stuffs. Because my child is comfortable, they will learn alot of things about life. On the contrary, I disagree with the statement.

The writer makes several errors in word choice. Can you identify them? Underline words that are inappropriate or confusing.

Look at these words and phrases in the paragraph.

can't learn nothing
wanna
sometimes
for keep my children safety
gonna
stuffs
On the contrary

Why are the above words and phrases inappropriate? What words and phrases would be better? What other words in the paragraph should be changed to improve the paragraph?

The readers who score your essay will look at your word choice. An essay receiving a score of 4 *may contain some errors that occasionally obscure meaning.* An essay receiving a score of 3 *may reveal a noticeably inappropriate choice of words or word forms.*

A few errors are allowed in an essay with a score of 4 or above. However, an inappropriate choice of words or word forms is considered a weakness. Too many errors in word choice can mean the difference between an upper–half score (4 or above) and a lower–half score (3 or below).

WRITING

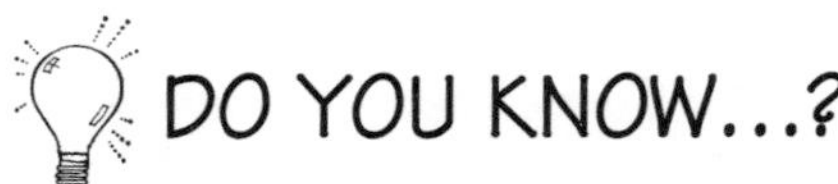

DO YOU KNOW...?

1. The readers who score your essay will look at

   - how you use English to express your ideas
   - the appropriateness of your word choice

   The essay readers are mainly concerned with being able to understand your ideas and how they are supported. Inappropriate word choice or incorrect forms may obscure your meaning, making it difficult to understand.

   It is best to use vocabulary you are familiar with, but avoid slang and other words that would be considered too informal for an academic essay or for writing you do for professional reasons.

   Use words that are as specific as possible to communicate your meaning.

   Example: A parent must get a child food, clothes, and other things.
   Better: A parent must provide a child with food, clothes, and other necessities.

   Example: Practicing sports is a really good thing.
   Better: Practicing sports benefits us in several important ways.

   Note: Allow around five minutes at the end of the 30–minute test to check word choice, sentence structure, and paragraph structure, and to make any changes that would clarify your meaning.

2. Some words that are useful for writing academic essays are:

although	contribute	examine	issue	probably
benefit	controversy	explanation	necessary	provide
cause	dilemma	influence	neither	solution
consequence	essential	instead	prefer	view

   Work to build your written vocabulary. Read as much as you can on a variety of topics, and use the practice exercises in other sections of this book to learn new words in context.

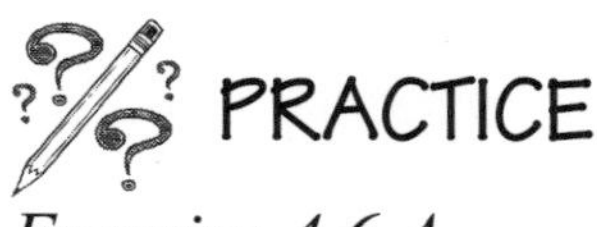

PRACTICE

Exercise 4.6.A

Read the following paragraphs. Check word choice and word form. Rewrite the paragraphs, making changes to clarify meaning and to make details more specific.

1. There are many advantages of having friends who are different me. Such as my friend who is from Turkey learns me a lot about his culture. His family is so big and my family is not big. As a result, I like to go to his house to visiting his family. I enjoy the good food. I enjoy the talking because it is really cool and interesting. Other friend is an artist. My friend makes pictures and does other arts. It is really cool. In conclusion, my artist friend is not alike me, so I learn good things about art from him.

2. I prefer students should have several short vacations throughout the year instead to one long vacation. Students work hardly and need a brake often. On the one hand, students in my country have several short holidays show the seasons. On the contrary, American students have one long vacation in summer. I read a paper say that American students forget what they learned because the long vacation forgetful. I belief several short vacations is good than one long vacation.

4.6 EXTENSION

1. Review the sample paragraphs and essays in units 4.2 through 4.5. Notice the writers' choice of vocabulary. Are there any words and phrases you think are particularly strong or weak? Are there any places where the meaning is confusing? What improvements would you make?

2. Review the paragraphs and essays you have written so far for the Practice and Extension exercises in this section. Are there any words and phrases that make your meaning confusing? What improvements can you make to clarify meaning and make details more specific?

4.7 Analyzing and Scoring Essays

FOCUS

Read the following essay question and essay.

> Some people prefer occupations in which they work primarily with machines. Others prefer occupations in which they work mainly with people. Which type of occupation do you prefer? Use specific reasons and examples to support your opinion.

There are mainly two types of occupations. Some occupations require to work primarily with machines. Other jobs need to work with other people. My job is working with machines, especial a computer. Therefore, I prefer this kind of technical occupation.

Computers are important in the society. I have my job in the medical university. I prefer computers because they are logical, and they can help organization of medical records. In addition, computers have improved business, research, education, and many other fields of study. Many occupations require specialization in computers. People must have technical training to use computers. Therefore, I can improve my education and learn computer skills in my job.

On the other hand, some occupations work mainly with people. It is also neccesary in my job. I work in our team with two other people. Therefore, we must help each one.

In conclusion, I prefer to work with machines. Machines need people to operate, and machines improve human life. However, many occupations need specialization, such as computer programmer, but also they need communication to other people. So, I believe to work with both machines and people are important in the society.

When you ***analyze*** something, you examine its parts. Analyze the above essay and rate the strength of each of its parts by checking the appropriate space between VERY WEAK and VERY STRONG.

Organization	VERY WEAK	__ __ __ __ __ __	VERY STRONG
Thesis statement	VERY WEAK	__ __ __ __ __ __	VERY STRONG
Supporting details	VERY WEAK	__ __ __ __ __ __	VERY STRONG
Sentence structure	VERY WEAK	__ __ __ __ __ __	VERY STRONG
Vocabulary	VERY WEAK	__ __ __ __ __ __	VERY STRONG

With your classmates and teacher, discuss how you scored the parts of the essay. How would you rate the essay overall?

If this essay were rated by TOEFL essay readers, it would probably receive a score of 4. The essay addresses the question, is adequately organized and developed, and uses some details to support the thesis. However, it contains some errors that obscure meaning, such as *Therefore, we must help each one.*

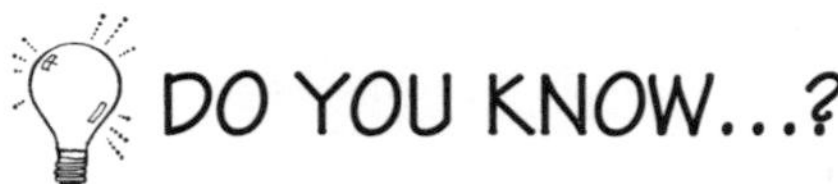

DO YOU KNOW...?

Your TOEFL or TWE essay will be read by two qualified essay readers who will rate it on a scale of 1 to 6, according to the following scale:

6 An essay at this level

- effectively addresses the writing task
- is well organized and well developed
- uses clearly appropriate details to support a thesis or illustrate ideas
- displays consistent facility in the use of language
- demonstrates syntactic variety and appropriate word choice

5 An essay at this level

- may address some parts of the task more effectively than others
- is generally well organized and developed
- uses details to support a thesis or illustrate an idea
- displays facility in the use of language
- demonstrates some syntactic variety and range of vocabulary

4 An essay at this level

- addresses the writing topic adequately but may slight parts of the task
- is adequately organized and developed
- uses some details to support a thesis or illustrate an idea
- demonstrates adequate but possibly inconsistent facility with syntax and usage
- may contain some errors that occasionally obscure meaning

3 An essay at this level may reveal one or more of the following weaknesses:

- inadequate organization or development
- inappropriate or insufficient details to support or illustrate generalizations
- a noticeably inappropriate choice of words or word forms
- an accumulation of errors in sentence structure and/or usage

2 An essay at this level is seriously flawed by one or more of the following weaknesses:

- serious disorganization or underdevelopment
- little or no detail, or irrelevant specifics
- serious and frequent errors in sentence structure or usage
- serious problems with focus

1 An essay at this level

- may be incoherent
- may be undeveloped
- may contain severe and persistent writing errors

0 An essay will be rated 0 if it

- contains no response
- merely copies the topic
- is off–topic, is written in a foreign language, or consists only of keystroke characters

With your classmates and teacher, discuss the above scoring criteria. Discuss the meanings of any unfamiliar words.

PRACTICE

Exercise 4.7.A

Read the following essay question and five essays. Score each essay on a scale of 1 to 6, according to the TOEFL scoring criteria on page 509. With your classmates and teacher, discuss why you scored each essay as you did. Then read the explanations on page 512.

> It has recently been announced that a new hospital may be built in your city. Some people think that your neighborhood would be a good place to locate the hospital. Compare the advantages and disadvantages of locating the hospital in your neighborhood. Use specific details in your discussion.

1. Score _____

A new hospital may be built in my city, and many people think my neighborhood is the best place to locate the hospital. There are some advantages and disadvantages of locating the hospital here. I will compare the two sides and attempt to find a conclusion.

First, a new hospital would benefit my neighborhood because there would be many new jobs for people. For example, a hospital needs not only doctors and nurses but also workers in the cafeteria, laundry, offices, janitor, and so on. Another advantage is that hospitals need a quiet area, and it is peaceful here. It could stay quiet if a hospital is built. The most important reason is that a new hospital would be more convenient for people who live in the west side of the city. People would not have to drive as far if an emergency would come. This is an important advantage for my neighborhood.

However, there are also some disadvantages of this plan. First, many trees must be cut to build a hospital. Second, the hospital would bring more traffic to this area. A hospital needs a large parking lot and a special emergency road for the ambalances. Next, a hospital must use a lot of water. These problems will affect the environment. Furthermore, if the hospital is built here, more development will follow, and this will change the character of the neighborhood from residential to commercial.

Despite the disadvantages, the city is growing very fast, and we need another hospital to serve people in the western part. My neighborhood is an ideal location. Therefore, I recommend that the hospital be built here. The hospital will benefit the people who live here, and the neighborhood will benefit the hospital.

2. Score _____

The main idea is advantage and disadvantage of the hospital in my neighborhood. I believe advantage is more important.

Advantage is for the sick people. They need the hospital for doctors, medicines. In addition, hospital is clean place for the operation and for baby born. Also advantage is for the doctors get a job. My father he is doctor. He rides train to different city for hospital. We need better hospital closely to here. Also sick people they need bigger hospital.

Disadvantage is expensive to built. We need a lot of money. But its very important have hospital closely the sick people are living. Its for AIDS and other disease. We need hospital, so should built hospital in my neighborhood. For help the sick people and advantage for doctors working. We had better to built hospital now.

3. Score _____

My city must decide where to build our new hospital. Some people think that my neighborhood is a good place to locate the hospital. However, there are also many disadvantages which overcome the advantages.

My neighborhood has many tall apartment buildings. The population is a large number. To locate the hospital in my neighborhood will benefit many people who are living in a crowded place. It is good for people to have an available hospital if they are sick or have an injury.

On the contrary, a disadvantage is to locate the hospital there will be very noisy. At present the city has a lot of noise of sirens, but a hospital will increase it because of the emergency vehicles. Another disadvantage is the streets have too many traffic, and it will be difficult to drive to the hospital quickly.

The hospital should be near the university where the medical students are studying. However, this is in a different place in the suburb. It is not in my neighborhood in the city. I recommend the new hospital should be built in the suburb because it has more medical students, better roads, and not many traffic compare with inside the city.

4. Score _____

Every city must have hospitals to assist those who have accidents, diseases, and need tests and treatment. Our city has one old hospital, which is too small for the city's population. Therefore, we must plan to build a new hospital, which will be larger than the old one.

Although there are disadvantages of locating the hospital, such as expensive, more crowded and noisy, there are many advantages also. We must compare which is the best for our city.

A new hospital has many advantages. The hospital provides a service to patients who need a doctor and treatment. The hospital provides researches about illness, such as cancer and dibetes. The hospital provides a job for many nurses and technicals.

The new hospital should built in a location which is convenent for most the people who use it. We must seek a best place, which will advantage most. A new hospital is very expensive; however, we must have a large hospital, which will provide a service for our citizens.

We must examine the advantages and the disadvantages; therefore, we can make a correct decision where locating the hospital.

5. Score _____

I think that the hospital must be built my neighborhood. It's a lot of advantages for my neighborhood.

I plan go to medical school for become doctor. I can work in the hospital, it's near my home, transportation. This can be easy for me. Doctors like a new hospital is modern, clean. My neighborhood is new part in city, good to build a hospital. It's advantage.

I become a doctor I will work very hard to cure people. I like to help the people who are ill. For example, children. We must get a good hospital, clean, modern. It's to cure the children who are very poor and ill. Many this kinds of problems in my city.

Explanation of Essay Scores

1. This essay is strong. It effectively addresses the task of discussing the advantages and disadvantages of building the hospital in one's neighborhood. It is well organized, with transitions providing coherence. The thesis is well developed and supported with appropriate details. The writer uses a variety of sentence structures and appropriate word choice. Score: 6.

2. This essay shows some competence in writing. It shows some organization, but lacks development. For example, there are insufficient details developing the disadvantages. Also, there are several inappropriate word forms, such as *closely*, *to built*, and *its*, as well as an accumulation of errors in sentence structure. Score: 3.

3. This essay is generally well organized and developed. The thesis is supported with some details; however, it lacks the amount of detail, sentence variety, and level of vocabulary expected in a score 6 essay. The essay shows facility in the use of English, although it has a few errors in sentence structure and word choice. Score: 5.

4. This essay shows minimal competence in writing. It addresses the task of discussing the advantages of building a hospital; however, it slights the tasks of discussing the disadvantages and of addressing the specific neighborhood. It also contains some errors that obscure meaning, such as *We must seek a best place, which will advantage most*. Score: 4.

5. This essay suggests incompetence in writing. It is underdeveloped and lacks focus. There is little detail and few specifics. There are frequent errors in sentence structure. Score: 2.

4.7 EXTENSION

1. Read and think about the essay questions in the list of Writing Topics on pages 514 to 516. With your classmates and teacher, discuss the following: (1) what the question requires you to do (the writing task), (2) what a good thesis statement would be, and (3) what details would support this thesis.

2. Write an essay under actual TOEFL conditions. The teacher randomly assigns one of the essay topics from the list on pages 514 to 516. Allow 30 minutes to plan, write, and revise your essay. Handwrite or type your essay on a computer, as you would under actual test conditions. Do not write your name on your essay.

3. Anonymously read, analyze, and score the essays of two classmates written for #2 above. It is important that the names of the writer and readers be unknown. For each of the two essays you read, identify the thesis statement and supporting points. Use the TOEFL scoring criteria on page 509 to give each essay a rating of 6, 5, 4, 3, 2, or 1. When you get your own essay back, compare its two scores. Are they the same or different? Do you agree or disagree with your classmates' analysis and rating of your essay? Think about what you would need to do to improve your essay and get a higher score.

WRITING TOPICS

Topics in the following list (or similar to those on the list) may appear in your actual test. You should become familiar with this list before you take the computer–based TOEFL or the Test of Written English. (For a more complete list of writing topics, see the TOEFL website at http://www.toefl.org.)

1. Do you agree or disagree with the following statement?
   Parents are the best teachers.
   Use specific reasons and examples to support your answer.

2. Some people believe that a college or university education should be available to all students. Others believe that higher education should be available only to good students. Discuss these views. Which view do you agree with? Explain why.

3. Modern life is causing many traditions and beliefs to become less important. Choose <u>one</u> tradition or belief and explain why you think it should be continued and maintained. Use specific reasons and examples to support your answer.

4. It has been said, "Not everything that is learned is contained in books." Compare and contrast knowledge gained from experience with knowledge gained from books. In your opinion, which source is more important? Why?

5. Some people say that the best preparation for life is learning to work with others and be cooperative. Others take the opposite view and say that learning to be competitive is the best preparation. Discuss these positions, using specific examples of both. Tell which one you agree with and explain why.

6. Do you agree or disagree with the following statement?
   Playing games teaches us about life.
   Use specific reasons and examples to support your answer.

7. Films can tell us a lot about the country in which they were made. What have you learned about a country from watching its movies? Use specific examples and details to support your response.

8. When choosing a place to live, what do you consider most important: location, size, style, number of rooms, types of rooms, or other features? Use reasons and specific examples to support your answer.

9. Students at universities often have a choice of places to live. They may choose to live in university dormitories, or they may choose to live in apartments in the community. Compare the advantages of living in university housing with the advantages of living in an apartment in the community. Which would you prefer? Give reasons for your preference.

10. What do you consider to be the most important room in a house? Why is this room more important to you than any other room? Use specific reasons and examples to support your opinion.

11. Some people prefer to live in a small town. Others prefer to live in a big city. Which place would you prefer to live in? Use specific reasons and details to support your answer.

12. Inventions such as eyeglasses and the sewing machine have had important effects on our lives. Choose another invention that you think is important. Give specific reasons for your choice.

13. Some people think that the family is the most important influence on young adults. Other people think that friends are the most important influence on young adults. Which view do you agree with? Use examples to support your position.

14. Do you agree or disagree with the following statement?
    A person's childhood years (the time from birth to 12 years of age) are the most important years of a person's life.
    Use specific reasons and examples to support your answer.

15. Read and think about the following statement:
People behave differently when they wear different clothes.
Do you agree that different clothes influence the way people behave? Use specific examples to support your answer.

16. A university plans to develop a new research center in your country. Some people want a center for business research. Other people want a center for research in agriculture (farming). Which of these two kinds of research centers do you recommend for your country? Give reasons for your recommendation.

17. Do you agree or disagree with the following statement?
There is nothing that young people can teach older people.
Use specific reasons and examples to support your position.

18. What is the most important animal in your country? Why is this animal important? Use reasons and specific details to explain your answer.

19. Your country is going to build a new national university. What academic area should be the main focus of this university? Use specific reasons and examples to support your answer.

20. Many parts of the world are losing important natural resources, such as forests, animals, or clean water. Choose one resource that is disappearing and explain why it needs to be saved. Use specific reasons and examples to support your opinion.

21. In general, people are living longer now. How will this change affect society? Use specific details and examples to develop your essay.

22. Do you agree or disagree with the following statement?
Television has destroyed communication among friends and family.
Use specific reasons and examples to support your opinion.

23. When famous people such as actors, athletes, and rock stars give their opinions, many people listen. Do you think we should pay attention to these opinions? Give specific reasons and examples to support your answer.

24. What are some important qualities of a good supervisor (boss)? Use specific details and examples to explain why these qualities are important.

25. People listen to music for different reasons and at different times. Why is music important to many people? Give specific reasons and examples to support your choice.

26. It is generally agreed that society benefits from the work of its members. Compare the contributions of artists to society with the contributions of scientists. Which type of contribution do you think is valued more by your society? Give specific reasons to support your answer.

27. Do you agree or disagree with the following statement?
When people succeed, it is because of hard work; luck has nothing to do with success.
Use specific reasons and examples to support your answer.

28. Do you agree or disagree with the following statement?
It is more important for students to study history and literature than it is for them to study science and mathematics.
Use specific reasons and examples to support your opinion.

29. When people move to another country, some of them decide to follow the customs of the new country. Others prefer to keep their own customs. Compare these two choices. Which one do you prefer? Support your answer with specific details.

30. Every generation of people is different in important ways. How is your generation different from your parents' generation? Use specific reasons and examples to explain your answer.

31. If you were asked to send one thing representing your country to an international exhibition, what would you choose? Why? Use specific reasons and details to explain your choice.

32. You want to persuade someone to study your native language. What reasons would you give? Support your answer with specific details.

33. Do you agree or disagree with the following statement?
It is better to be a member of a group than to be the leader of a group.
Use specific reasons and examples to support your answer.

34. If you could know something about the future, what would you choose to know about and why? Give reasons and details to support your choice.

35. You have been asked to suggest improvements to a park that you have visited. This might be a city park, a regional park, or a national park. What improvements would you make? Why? Use specific reasons and examples to support your recommendation.

36. Some people say that advertising encourages us to buy things we really do not need. Others say that advertisements tell us about new products that may improve our lives. Which view do you agree with? Use specific reasons and examples to support your answer.

37. Some people think that governments should spend as much money as possible on developing or buying computer technology. Other people disagree and think that this money should be spent on more basic needs. Which one of these opinions do you agree with? Use specific reasons and details to support your answer.

38. A gift (such as a soccer ball, a camera, or an animal) can contribute to a child's development. What gift would you give to help a child develop? Why? Use reasons and specific examples to support your choice.

39. Read and think about the following statement:
Only people who earn a lot of money are successful.
Do you agree or disagree with this definition of success? Use specific reasons and examples to support your opinion.

40. Your community has enough money to hire one new employee. Which one of the following (three choices will be presented in the actual test) should your community hire?

    a community health worker
    an emergency medical technician
    a judge
    a landscaper
    a police officer
    a teacher

    Use specific reasons and details to develop your essay.

PRACTICE TESTS

Tests 1 through 4 are similar in form and content to the actual TOEFL examination. All of the tests include listening, structure, reading, and writing.

Test 1 and **Test 3** are like the computer–based test. The four sections of these tests are:

Section 1 – Listening
Section 2 – Structure
Section 3 – Reading
Section 4 – Writing

Test 2 and **Test 4** are like the paper–based test. The four sections of these tests are:

Test of Written English
Section 1 – Listening Comprehension
Section 2 – Structure and Written Expression
Section 3 – Reading Comprehension

A reproducible answer sheet is provided for each test. Although the actual computer–based TOEFL has no answer sheet, you may find it convenient to use one when you take the practice tests in this book.

Try to take these practice tests under conditions that are as close as possible to the actual test conditions. Work in a quiet room where you will not be disturbed. Each test will take approximately 2½ hours to complete.

Use a clock or watch to time yourself on each section. Times are given for each test section.

Note that the section times for Tests 1 and 3 differ from those for Tests 2 and 4. This is because the computer test differs slightly in format from the paper test. However, the content of both the computer test and the paper test is similar, so completing all four practice tests will help you prepare for either test.

After you finish each test, check your answers in the Answer Key starting on page 664. For items you answer incorrectly, the Answer Key will tell you which units in this book will help you review the appropriate skills.

Section 1

1. (A) (B) (C) (D)
2. (A) (B) (C) (D)
3. (A) (B) (C) (D)
4. (A) (B) (C) (D)
5. (A) (B) (C) (D)
6. (A) (B) (C) (D)
7. (A) (B) (C) (D)
8. (A) (B) (C) (D)
9. (A) (B) (C) (D)
10. (A) (B) (C) (D)
11. (A) (B) (C) (D)
12. (A) (B) (C) (D)
13. (A) (B) (C) (D)
14. (A) (B) (C) (D)
15. (A) (B) (C) (D)
16. (A) (B) (C) (D)
17. [A] [B] [C] [D]
18. (A) (B) (C) (D)
19.

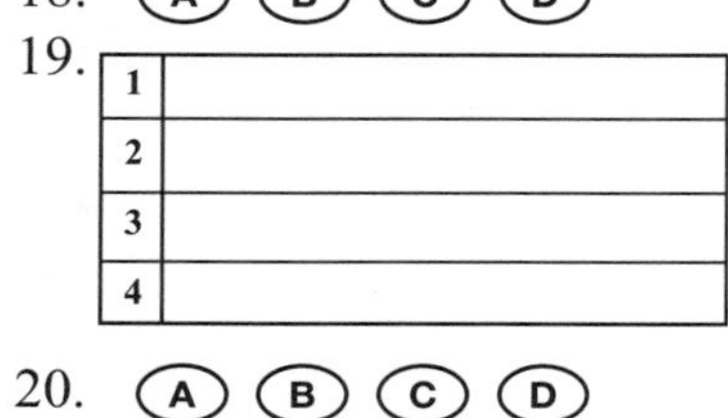

1	
2	
3	
4	

20. (A) (B) (C) (D)
21. (A) (B) (C) (D)
22. (A) (B) (C) (D)
23. (A) (B) (C) (D)
24. (A) (B) (C) (D)
25. (A) (B) (C) (D)
26. (A) (B) (C) (D)
27.

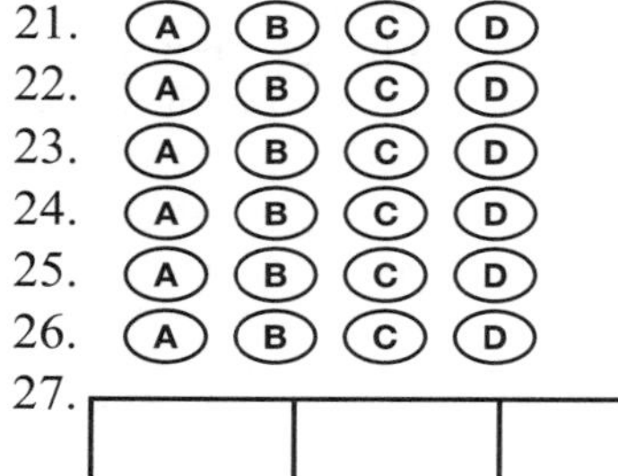

Calcium	Anit–viral properties	No Cholesterol

28. (A) (B) (C) (D)
29. (A) (B) (C) (D)
30. [A] [B] [C] [D]
31.

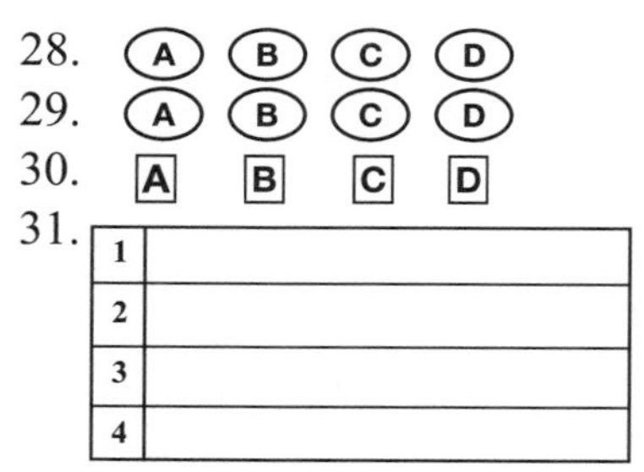

1	
2	
3	
4	

32. (A) (B) (C) (D)
33. (A) (B) (C) (D)
34. [A] [B] [C] [D]
35. [A] [B] [C] [D]
36. (A) (B) (C) (D)
37.

1	
2	
3	

38. (A) (B) (C) (D)
39. (A) (B) (C) (D)
40. (A) (B) (C) (D)
41. (A) (B) (C) (D)
42. [A] [B] [C] [D]
43. (A) (B) (C) (D)
44. (A) (B) (C) (D)
45. (A) (B) (C) (D)

Section 2

1. (A) (B) (C) (D)
2. (A) (B) (C) (D)
3. (A) (B) (C) (D)
4. (A) (B) (C) (D)
5. (A) (B) (C) (D)
6. (A) (B) (C) (D)
7. (A) (B) (C) (D)
8. (A) (B) (C) (D)
9. (A) (B) (C) (D)
10. (A) (B) (C) (D)
11. (A) (B) (C) (D)
12. (A) (B) (C) (D)
13. (A) (B) (C) (D)
14. (A) (B) (C) (D)
15. (A) (B) (C) (D)
16. (A) (B) (C) (D)
17. (A) (B) (C) (D)
18. (A) (B) (C) (D)
19. (A) (B) (C) (D)
20. (A) (B) (C) (D)
21. (A) (B) (C) (D)
22. (A) (B) (C) (D)
23. (A) (B) (C) (D)
24. (A) (B) (C) (D)
25. (A) (B) (C) (D)

Section 3

1. (A) (B) (C) (D)
2. (A) (B) (C) (D)
3. (A) (B) (C) (D)
4. (A) (B) (C) (D)
5. (A) (B) (C) (D)
6. (A) (B) (C) (D)
7. (A) (B) (C) (D)
8. (A) (B) (C) (D)
9. (A) (B) (C) (D)
10. (A) (B) (C) (D)
11. (A) (B) (C) (D)
12. (A) (B) (C) (D)
13. (A) (B) (C) (D)
14. (A) (B) (C) (D)
15. (A) (B) (C) (D)
16. (A) (B) (C) (D)
17. (A) (B) (C) (D)
18. (A) (B) (C) (D)
19. (A) (B) (C) (D)
20. (A) (B) (C) (D)
21. (A) (B) (C) (D)
22. (A) (B) (C) (D)
23. (A) (B) (C) (D)
24. (A) (B) (C) (D)
25. (A) (B) (C) (D)
26. (A) (B) (C) (D)
27. (A) (B) (C) (D)
28. (A) (B) (C) (D)
29. (A) (B) (C) (D)
30. (A) (B) (C) (D)
31. (A) (B) (C) (D)
32. (A) (B) (C) (D)
33. (A) (B) (C) (D)
34. (A) (B) (C) (D)
35. (A) (B) (C) (D)
36. (A) (B) (C) (D)
37. (A) (B) (C) (D)
38. (A) (B) (C) (D)
39. (A) (B) (C) (D)
40. (A) (B) (C) (D)
41. (A) (B) (C) (D)
42. (A) (B) (C) (D)
43. (A) (B) (C) (D)
44. (A) (B) (C) (D)
45. (A) (B) (C) (D)
46. (A) (B) (C) (D)
47. (A) (B) (C) (D)
48. (A) (B) (C) (D)
49. (A) (B) (C) (D)
50. (A) (B) (C) (D)

TEST 1

SECTION 1

LISTENING

Time – approximately 35 minutes

(including the reading of the directions for each part)

 *(Start Tape)*

In the Listening section of the test, you will have an opportunity to demonstrate your ability to understand conversations and talks in English. Answer all the questions on the basis of what is stated or implied by the speakers you hear. Do not take notes or write during the test.

PART A

Directions: In Part A you will hear short conversations between two people. After each conversation, you will hear a question about the conversation. The conversations and questions will not be repeated. After you hear a question, read the four possible answers and choose the best answer.

Here is an example.

On the recording, you hear:

Sample Answer

Ⓐ Ⓑ ● Ⓓ

In your book, you read:

Ⓐ She doesn't want to buy a printer.
Ⓑ She would rather buy something else.
Ⓒ She doesn't want to pay a lot for a printer.
Ⓓ She wants to shop at a better place.

You learn from the conversation that the woman hopes to find a printer at a better price. The best answer to the question, *What does the woman mean?* is Ⓒ, *She doesn't want to pay a lot for a printer.* Therefore, the correct choice is Ⓒ.

1. (A) The man should help Bill with his VCR.
   (B) Bill should read the instructions for programming his VCR.
   (C) Bill should try to take his VCR apart.
   (D) They should use the VCR to record a program.

2. (A) Take botany and zoology this winter.
   (B) Call Dr. Hernandez.
   (C) Register for zoology.
   (D) Change his major to science.

3. (A) She can go with him after work.
   (B) She left work early.
   (C) She avoided having to work this weekend.
   (D) She would rather work than go with the man.

4. (A) He doesn't want to pay a lot for new covers.
   (B) He wrote a check at an upholstery shop.
   (C) He would like to buy an expensive sofa.
   (D) He used to work at an upholstery shop.

5. (A) She is never surprised.
   (B) She is surprised by the news.
   (C) She is less surprised than the man.
   (D) Nothing is surprising.

6. (A) She has been waiting for the man.
   (B) She will start a new job the next day.
   (C) She does not know if she got the job.
   (D) She did not get the job.

7. (A) It takes him several years to build a house.
   (B) His house is at least sixty feet long.
   (C) He has built houses for over six years.
   (D) He built a house sixty–seven years ago.

8. (A) He has difficulty solving the problems.
   (B) He can't understand the teacher.
   (C) He can't draw the diagrams.
   (D) He wishes he hadn't taken the class.

9. (A) He took top honors in bowling.
   (B) He will present awards at the dinner.
   (C) He is a surgeon at the university hospital.
   (D) He teaches in the surgery unit.

10. (A) Pamela wants to go to the play.
    (B) Pamela may decide not to go to the play.
    (C) Pamela will want to sit in the back row.
    (D) Pamela wants to do something else.

11. (A) He can't help her.
    (B) He thinks the woman is bored with walking.
    (C) The woman can find her tour group on the boardwalk.
    (D) She should stop to eat lunch on the boardwalk.

12. (A) She doesn't want to miss her piano lesson.
    (B) She doesn't have anything to do that evening.
    (C) She will miss the recital to meet Tom.
    (D) She is looking forward to hearing Tom play the piano.

13. (A) The man can buy coffee in the lobby.
    (B) The coffee in the lounge is free.
    (C) The coffee and tea is of excellent quality.
    (D) No coffee is available.

14. (A) She must try to manage her problems.
    (B) She should help him with his problems.
    (C) He will try to help her.
    (D) He does not believe she has any problems.

15. (A) The man should get advice from a computer store.
    (B) The man should buy a painting of a deck.
    (C) The man should go to the hardware store to cash a check.
    (D) The man should seek the advice of an expert.

This is the end of Part A.

PART B

Directions: In this part of the test, you will hear several conversations and talks. Each conversation or talk is followed by several questions. The conversations, talks, and questions will not be repeated.

For most of the questions, you will read four possible answers and choose the best answer. Some questions will have special directions.

Here is an example.

On the recording, you hear:

Now listen to a sample question.

Sample Answer

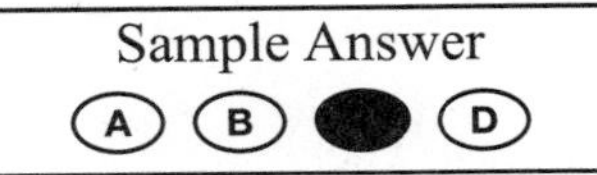

In your book, you read:

(A) It helped scientists see the atmosphere more clearly.
(B) It made it easier for scientists to send messages.
(C) It made data collection from weather stations faster.
(D) It helped airplanes fly higher.

The best answer to the question, *How did the telegraph improve the science of meteorology?* is (C), *It made data collection from weather stations faster.* Therefore, the correct choice is (C).

Now listen to another sample question.

In your book, you read:

Sample Answer
■ B ■ D

Choose 2 answers.

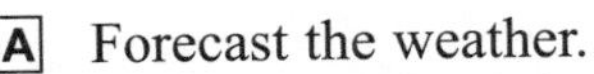

[A] Forecast the weather.
[B] Study trends in rocket science.
[C] Solve air pollution problems.
[D] Study costs of building satellites.

The best two answers to the question, *What do meteorologists do today?* are [A], *Forecast the weather*, and [C], *Solve air pollution problems.* Therefore, the correct choices are [A] and [C].

Remember, you should not take notes during the test.

TEST 1

1 1 1 1 1 1 1 1 1

16. (A) He is transferring to a school in Oklahoma.
(B) He must leave school for a family emergency.
(C) He wants to discuss his term paper.
(D) He needs to have surgery.

17. Choose 2 answers.

[A] Taking the final exam later.
[B] Writing an extra term paper.
[C] Filling out a form.
[D] Taking a six–week make–up course.

18. (A) Road construction.
(B) A change in their route.
(C) Travel by ferry.
(D) What they did last weekend.

19. (A) Drive through Springdale.
(B) Drive east to Ransom.
(C) Drive north on Route 150.
(D) Take the ferry.

1	
2	
3	
4	

20. (A) She wants to go where the scenery is more beautiful.
(B) They might not be able to wake up early enough.
(C) They might be delayed by road construction.
(D) They might not arrive in Ransom in time to catch the ferry.

21. (A) Religious rituals of American Indians.
(B) The role of the shaman in Indian spiritual life.
(C) The role of animals in American Indian culture.
(D) The history of art, mythology, and religion.

22. (A) By reading stories about tribal mythology.
(B) By carving figures of animals into poles.
(C) Through formal religious education.
(D) Through rituals using costumes and masks.

23. (A) They told the history of the tribe.
(B) They showed off the wealth of the tribe.
(C) They inspired song, dance, and ritual.
(D) They provided jobs for tribal shamans.

24. (A) Why orange juice is the most popular breakfast drink.
(B) Disease–fighting breakfast foods.
(C) Causes of heart disease, cancer and stroke.
(D) Painkillers, laxatives, and antacids.

25. (A) It is inexpensive and easy to prepare.
(B) It is better than taking medicine.
(C) It is low in fat and high in nutrients.
(D) It was recommended by Hippocrates.

26. (A) They are likely to be overweight.
(B) They will not get the calcium they need.
(C) They may get cancer or heart disease.
(D) They take too much medicine.

27. (A) Egg substitutes
(B) Orange juice
(C) Milk

Calcium	Anit–viral properties	No Cholesterol

28. (A) Sociology.
(B) Marine Biology.
(C) Geology.
(D) Hotel Management.

29. (A) With a series of earthquakes and avalanches.
(B) Without any prior warning.
(C) With an ash cloud that drifted around the world.
(D) With a massive landslide.

30. Choose 2 answers.

A Water blew out of the lakes.
B Ash and steam erupted.
C Tourists watched in amusement.
D Lava flowed from the crater.

31. (A) The top of the mountain exploded.
(B) Earthquakes caused a huge landslide.
(C) The ash cloud drifted around the world.
(D) The north side of the mountain swelled.

1	
2	
3	
4	

32. (A) It is a rather harmless volcano.
(B) It will remain inactive for a million years.
(C) It is highly likely to erupt again.
(D) Geologists can prevent future eruptions.

33. (A) To train new college administrators.
(B) To recommend that organizations hire more specialists.
(C) To assist college students in career planning.
(D) To inform college counselors of new developments in their field.

34. Choose 2 answers.

A Accountants.
B Managers.
C Writers.
D Teachers.

35. Choose 2 answers.

A Ability to make judgments.
B Concern with technique, tools, and media.
C Ability to coordinate the work of other people.
D Training in a technical or professional field.

36. (A) Specialists have nicer personalities than generalists.
(B) The speaker is a generalist.
(C) Good leaders are usually specialists.
(D) Both specialists and generalists can find jobs.

37. (A) Added lean–to plan
(B) One–room plan
(C) Two–room plan

1	
2	
3	

38.

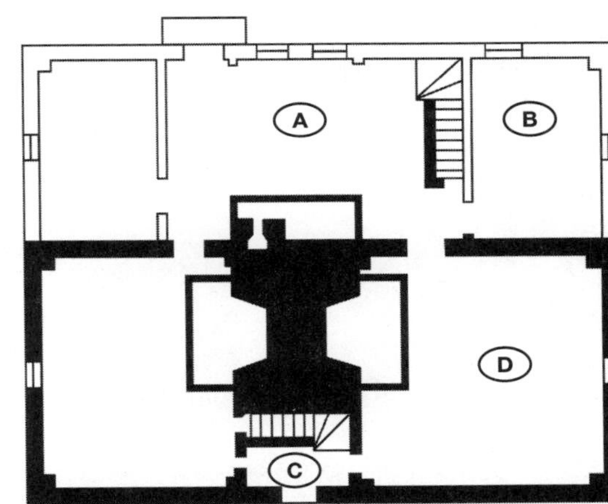

39.

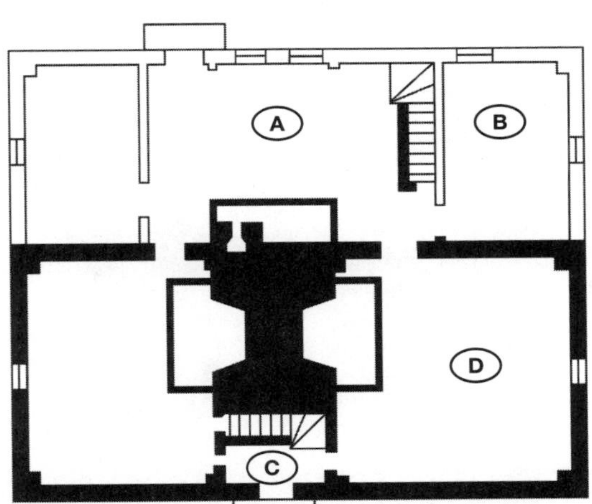

TEST 1

40. (A) The evolution of house styles is impossible to determine.
(B) There is no connection between plan type and the age of the house.
(C) The earliest plan type continued to be built.
(D) Not many colonial houses still exist.

41. (A) A feeling that the heart has jumped.
(B) Severe pain.
(C) Addiction to cigarettes.
(D) Going from a flat road to climbing a hill.

42. Choose 2 answers.

[A] Too much sleep.
[B] Too much coffee.
[C] Anxiety.
[D] Heart attack.

43. (A) The heart stops beating.
(B) The blood pressure drops suddenly.
(C) The body is shocked by a change in temperature.
(D) The pulse rate must be changed quickly.

44. (A) They are a cause of sudden death.
(B) They should be ignored.
(C) They are a message from the body.
(D) They can be cured with medication.

45. (A) Harmony in the Environment.
(B) Symptoms and Causes of Heart Palpitations.
(C) The Effects of Caffeine and Nicotine on the Heart.
(D) How to Avoid Palpitations.

(Stop Tape)

This is the end of Section 1.

STOP

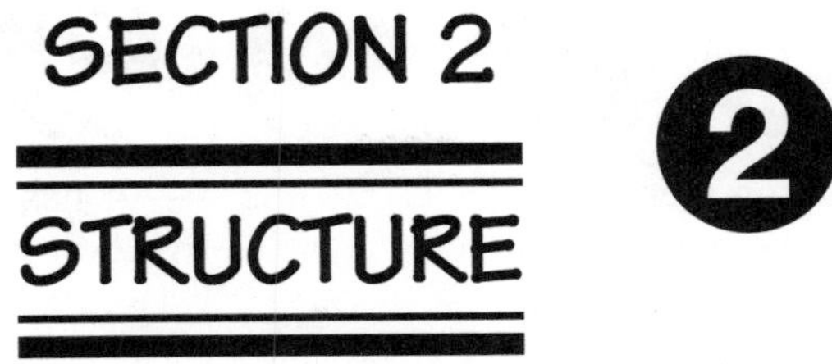

Time – 15 minutes

(including the reading of the directions)

Now set your clock for 15 minutes.

The Structure section of the test measures your ability to recognize language that is appropriate for standard written English. There are two types of questions in this section.

In the first type of question, there are incomplete sentences. Beneath each sentence, there are four words or phrases. Choose the one word or phrase that best completes the sentence.

Example I

Sample Answer
● (B) (C) (D)

Although Chicago is not ——— New York, it has many attractions for visitors.

(A) as large as
(B) larger
(C) larger city
(D) the larger city is

The sentence should read, *Although Chicago is not as large as New York, it has many attractions for visitors*. Therefore, you should choose (A).

The second type of question has four underlined words or phrases. Choose the one underlined word or phrase that must be changed for the sentence to be correct.

Example II

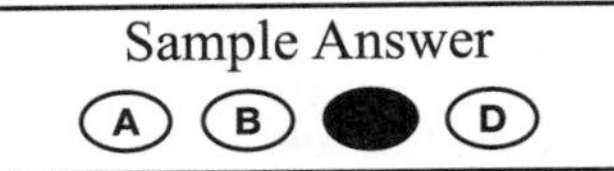

Guglielmo Marconi, the son of (A) a wealthy Italian landowner, made (B) the first successfully (C) transmission using (D) radio waves.

The sentence should read, *Guglielmo Marconi, the son of a wealthy Italian landowner, made the first successful transmission using radio waves*. Therefore, you should choose (C).

Now begin work on the questions.

2 2 2 2 2 2 2 2 2

1. Most of the nation's fighting men were traditionally ------- from the working classes.

   (A) drew
   (B) drawing
   (C) be drawn
   (D) drawn

2. ------- has a powerful influence on the psychological health of a nation.

   (A) Why full employment
   (B) That full employment
   (C) Full employment
   (D) Full employment that

3. Each year, one million teenagers start smoking, and every day about three thousand become
   A B
   addicted to the tobacco.
   C D

4. Fiorello La Guardia made a speech to the United Nations Relief Administration, which he was
   A B
   the director, stating that Europe did not experience prosperity after World War Two.
   C D

5. Victims of carpal tunnel syndrome include electricians drilling holes for wiring, airline workers
   A B
   to type at chest–high terminals, and checkout clerks lifting and twisting groceries to register prices
   C D
   on the scanner.

6. The term *robot*, ------- actually a Czech word meaning *labor*, was first applied to machines in the 1920s.

   (A) which
   (B) which is
   (C) is
   (D) that is

7. -------, the elements in the fuel do not remain the same.

   (A) A nuclear reaction occurs
   (B) When a nuclear reaction occurs
   (C) If a nuclear reaction had occurred
   (D) A nuclear reaction is occurring

8. The purpose of polarizing sunglasses is ------- polarized light and reduce glare.

   (A) to block
   (B) blocking
   (C) which blocks
   (D) block

9. Motorists heading north into Oregon from California should know ------- for the first hundred miles.

   (A) is accessing few major roads
   (B) access towns by the major roads
   (C) that few major roads access towns
   (D) few major roads to access towns

10. Eugene O'Neill, -------, received the Nobel prize in 1936.

   (A) a great American playwright who
   (B) to write great plays
   (C) a great American playwright
   (D) wrote great American plays

11. In 1956 Ella Fitzgerald made the first of several "Songbook" recording that made her an international star.
A B C D

12. When the British partitioned the Bengal area into two administrative units for the purpose of greater
A B
efficient, they overlooked the language and religious groupings within the area.
C D

13. Orville and Wilbur Wright, building on the developments at aviation pioneers of several nations,
A B C
made the first successful flight in 1903.
D

14. Making paper involves reduce a plant to its fibers and then aligning them and coating the fibers with
A B C D
materials such as glues, pigments, and mineral fillers.

15. On April 14, 1865, an actor named John Wilkes Booth, angered by the South's defeat in the Civil War,
A B C
shot and had killed President Abraham Lincoln.
D

16. Economic theory states that in a market economy consumers and technology both helps determine
A B C
what is produced.
D

17. In the mountains of South America -------, the lake with the highest elevation on Earth.

(A) Lake Titicaca lies where
(B) where Lake Titicaca lies
(C) lies Lake Titicaca
(D) Lake Titicaca it lies

18. A zoom lens produces an inverted real image on ------- or the light–sensitive tube of a television camera.

(A) either the film in a camera
(B) which the film in a camera
(C) that is the camera's film
(D) filming with a camera

19. Methods of preserving food in ------- were invented in the early 1800s.

(A) containers sealing
(B) sealing in containers
(C) containers were sealed
(D) sealed containers

20. According to Euclid, if a line were drawn between any two points, -------.

(A) can infinitely extend
(B) it could extend infinitely
(C) it can extend infinitely
(D) infinitely it extends

21. The world's deepest ocean trench, the Mariana Trench in the Pacific Ocean, is almost twice as deep -------.

(A) and Mount Logan's height
(B) that Mount Logan is higher
(C) is higher than Mount Logan
(D) as Mount Logan is high

22. It is true that even the plants of the Kalahari Desert seem have adjusted to the presence of humans.
    A B C D

23. Confucius—a statesman, scholar, and educator of great skill and reputation—is generally held to be China's greatest and most influence philosopher.
    A B C D

24. Although it would take a laboratory analysis to determine the exact proportions of sand, silt, clay, and organic matter in your garden soil, you can get a good idea of what it is by feeling the soil's texture.
    A B C D

25. Alike Seattle, the city of Tacoma is just a few miles away from some of the best places the Northwest has to offer.
    A B C D

This is the end of Section 2.

Time — 60 minutes (including the reading of the directions) Now set your clock for 60 minutes.

In the Reading section of the test, you will read several passages. Each one is followed by a number of questions about it. For questions 1–50, you are to choose the one best answer, (A), (B), (C), or (D), to each question.

Answer all questions about the information in a passage on the basis of what is stated or implied in that passage.

Read the following passage:

The coffees of Central America profit from the area's steady climate and wealth of mountains. The mountains of the Pacific Cordillera, which stretch in a virtually unbroken line from Guatemala to the middle of Panama, provide the best combination of climate, altitude, and soil.

Guatemala was a relative latecomer to the commercial coffee business, exporting beans only since 1875. This mountainous country is ideally suited for coffee production, and its exports now surpass those of much larger countries. European merchants still take about 50 percent of the Guatemalan beans, with most of the best beans today being exported to England.

Example I It can be inferred from the passage that coffee grows well

(A) in the northern hemisphere
(B) in mountainous regions
(C) in small countries
(D) near the Pacific Ocean

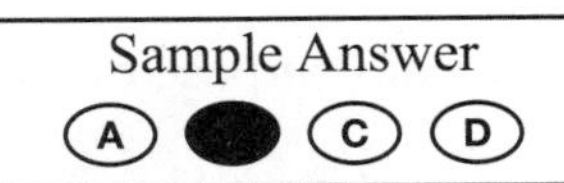

The passage implies that the mountainous regions of Central America are ideally suited for coffee production. The other answer choices cannot be inferred from the information given. Therefore, you should choose (B).

Example II The word "surpass" in line 7 is closest in meaning to

(A) include
(B) surround
(C) exceed
(D) limit

Sample Answer
(A) (B) ● (D)

The word *surpass* in this passage means *exceed*. Therefore, you should choose (C).

Now begin work on the questions.

QUESTIONS 1–8

The Americans with Disabilities Act (ADA) was signed into law in 1990. This law extends civil rights protection to persons with disabilities in private sector employment, all public services, and in public accommodations, transportation, and telecommunications. A person with a disability is defined as someone with a mental or physical impairment that substantially limits him or her in a major life activity, such as walking, talking, working, or self–care. A person with a disability may also be someone with a past record of such an impairment, for example, someone who no longer has heart disease but is discriminated against because of that history.

The ADA states that employers with fifteen or more employees may not refuse to hire or promote a person because of a disability if that person is qualified to perform the job. Also, the employer must make reasonable accommodations that will allow a person with a disability to perform essential functions of the job.

All new vehicles purchased by public transit authorities must be accessible to people with disabilities. All rail stations must be made accessible, and at least one car per train in existing rail systems must be made accessible.

It is illegal for public accommodations to exclude or refuse persons with disabilities. Public accommodations are businesses and services such as restaurants, hotels, grocery stores, and parks. All new buildings must be made accessible, and existing facilities must remove barriers if the removal can be accomplished without much difficulty or expense.

The ADA also stipulates that companies offering telephone service to the general public must offer relay services to individuals who use telecommunications devices for the deaf, twenty–four hours a day, seven days a week.

1. What is the main purpose of the passage?

   (A) To describe discrimination against persons with disabilities
   (B) To explain the provisions of the Americans with Disabilities Act
   (C) To make suggestions for hiring persons with disabilities
   (D) To discuss telecommunications devices for the deaf

2. According to the passage, all of the following are affected by the Americans with Disabilities Act EXCEPT

   (A) someone who has difficulty walking
   (B) a public transit authority
   (C) an employer with fewer than fifteen employees
   (D) a person with a past record of an impairment

3. The word "impairment" in lines 5 and 7 is closest in meaning to

   (A) disability
   (B) violation
   (C) aptitude
   (D) danger

4. The author mentions grocery stores as an example of

   (A) public transit
   (B) barriers
   (C) private sector employment
   (D) public accommodations

5. The word "facilities" in line 19 refers to

(A) barriers
(B) buildings
(C) rail stations
(D) disabilities

6. The author implies all of the following EXCEPT

(A) the ADA requires people with disabilities to pay for special accommodations
(B) the ADA is designed to protect the civil rights of many people
(C) public transportation must accommodate the needs of people with disabilities
(D) the ADA protects the rights of people with mental impairments

7. The word "stipulates" in line 21 is closest in meaning to

(A) supposes
(B) admits
(C) states
(D) requests

8. It can be inferred from the passage that

(A) restaurants can refuse service to people with disabilities
(B) every car of a train must be accessible to persons with disabilities
(C) the ADA is not well–liked by employers
(D) large companies may not discriminate against workers with disabilities

QUESTIONS 9–18

The first American Roosevelt, Claes Martenszen van Rosenvelt, arrived from Holland in the 1640s, when New York was a tiny settlement of 800 people living in eighty houses on Manhattan Island. By the middle of the eighteenth century, when New York had become a bustling port of 25,000, there were fifty Roosevelt families, and Claes's descendants were already showing a talent for associating themselves with the forces of boom and expansion in American economic life.

In the third generation of American Roosevelts, two of the brothers, Johannes and Jacobus, took the family into real estate with the purchase of the Beekman Swamp, a venture that was to have a lasting effect on the city and on their own fortunes. The pre–Revolutionary Roosevelts were prosperous burghers but not of the highest gentry, and in civic affairs they sided with the popular faction against the aristocrats.

The first Roosevelt to achieve gentility and distinction was Isaac, a trader in sugar and rum who ended his business career as president of New York's first bank. For his services to the American Revolution, he was called "Isaac the Patriot." Isaac's cousin James, after service with the Revolutionary army, founded Roosevelt & Son, a New York hardware business that swiftly expanded into building supplies. When James's grandson, Cornelius Van Schaack Roosevelt, was head of the firm, it imported most of the plate glass that was used in the new homes being built in the prospering nation. Cornelius's chief distinction was his wealth; he was listed among the five richest men in New York.

Having played their part in the transformation of New York from a small Dutch outpost into a cosmopolitan city, the Roosevelts had a firm sense of their roots. They remained faithful believers in the Protestant ethic, which sanctified both a ruthless competitive individualism as well as the love and charity that were the basis of the family's strong sense of social obligation. Standards of honor, conduct, and manners were further bred into the Roosevelt sons at Groton and Harvard. They went on to become bankers, sportsmen, and financiers. Two twentieth–century Roosevelts—Theodore and Franklin Delano—became president of the United States.

9. What does the passage mainly discuss?

- (A) The life of Claes Martenszen van Rosenvelt
- (B) The contributions of the Roosevelt family to the American Revolution
- (C) The importance of the Protestant ethic to the Roosevelts
- (D) The history of a prominent American family

10. The word "boom" in line 6 is closest in meaning to

- (A) destruction
- (B) rapid growth
- (C) wealth
- (D) loud noise

11. It can be concluded from lines 7–9 that

- (A) investment in land contributed to the family's wealth
- (B) the American Roosevelts were more successful than their Dutch ancestors
- (C) Johannes and Jacobus had a third brother
- (D) the purchase of the Beekman Swamp was a risky venture

12. According to the passage, who was the first Roosevelt to enter the upper class?

Ⓐ Claes
Ⓑ James
Ⓒ Isaac
Ⓓ Franklin

13. The Roosevelts were involved in all of the following occupations EXCEPT

Ⓐ banking
Ⓑ real estate
Ⓒ teaching
Ⓓ importing

14. The word "outpost" in line 21 is closest in meaning to

Ⓐ port
Ⓑ frontier settlement
Ⓒ sugar plantation
Ⓓ island

15. The word "sanctified" in line 22 is closest in meaning to

Ⓐ influenced
Ⓑ discouraged
Ⓒ cautiously believed
Ⓓ morally approved

16. The word "They" in line 25 refers to

Ⓐ Theodore and Franklin Delano Roosevelt
Ⓑ standards of honor, conduct, and manners
Ⓒ the Roosevelt sons
Ⓓ Groton and Harvard

17. It can be inferred from the passage that the Roosevelt family

Ⓐ has remained in New York since the seventeenth century
Ⓑ will produce another president of the United States
Ⓒ changed its political party more than once
Ⓓ has made significant contributions to American society

TEST 1

18. The following sentence can be added to paragraph 4 of the passage.

By the beginning of the twentieth century, the Roosevelt family was one of the oldest and most distinguished in the United States.

Where would it best fit in the paragraph? Choose **A**, **B**, **C**, or **D**.

A Having played their part in the transformation of New York from a small Dutch outpost into a cosmopolitan city, the Roosevelts had a firm sense of their roots. They remained faithful believers in the Protestant ethic, which sanctified both a ruthless competitive individualism as well as the love and charity that were the basis of the family's strong sense of social obligation. **B** Standards of honor, conduct, and manners were further bred into the Roosevelt sons at Groton and Harvard. **C** They went on to become bankers, sportsmen, and financiers. Two twentieth–century Roosevelts—Theodore and Franklin Delano—became president of the United States. **D**

QUESTIONS 19–29

Jupiter is the largest of the planets. Its equatorial diameter is 88,000 miles, which is eleven times the diameter of the earth. A Jupiter day is only ten earth hours long. For a planet this size, this rotational speed is amazing, and it moves a point on Jupiter's equator at a speed of 22,000 miles an hour, as compared with 1,000 miles an hour for a point on the Earth's equator. Jupiter is at an average distance of 480 million miles from the sun and takes almost twelve of our years to make one complete circuit of the sun.

The only directly observable chemical constituents of Jupiter's atmosphere are methane and ammonia. The temperature at the tops of Jupiter's clouds may be about minus 260 degrees F. The clouds are probably ammonia ice crystals, becoming ammonia droplets lower down. Perhaps Jupiter has no surface—no real interface between the gaseous atmosphere and the body of Jupiter. Jupiter's cloudy atmosphere is a fairly good reflector of sunlight and makes it appear far brighter than any of the stars.

Fourteen of Jupiter's seventeen or more satellites have been found through earth–based observations. Four of the moons are large and bright, rivaling our own moon and the planet Mercury in diameter, and may be seen through a field glass. They move rapidly around Jupiter, and their change of position from night to night is extremely interesting to watch. The other satellites are much smaller, and in all but one instance, they are much farther from Jupiter and cannot be seen except through powerful telescopes. Jupiter's mass is more than twice the mass of all the other planets put together, and accounts for Jupiter's tremendous gravitational field and so, probably, for its numerous satellites and its dense atmosphere.

Photographs of Jupiter were taken by the Voyager and Galileo spacecrafts. Thousands of high resolution multi–color pictures show rapid variations of features both large and small. The Great Red Spot exhibits internal counter–clockwise rotation. The moons Amalthea, Io, Europa, Ganymede, and Callisto were photographed, some in great detail. Each is individual and unique, with no similarities to other known planets or satellites. Io has active volcanoes that probably have ejected material into a doughnut–shaped ring enveloping its orbit about Jupiter. This is not to be confused with the thin, flat, disk–like ring closer to Jupiter's surface. Now that such a ring has been seen by Voyager, older uncertain observations from Earth can be reinterpreted as early sightings of this structure.

19. What does the passage mainly discuss?

    (A) Characteristics of Jupiter and its moons
    (B) Observations of Jupiter by Voyager and Galileo
    (C) Jupiter's many satellites
    (D) Jupiter's position in the solar system

20. According to the passage, Jupiter's rotational speed

    (A) has only recently been calculated
    (B) is a result of Jupiter's great mass
    (C) is faster than Earth's
    (D) has rapidly increased

21. From paragraph 2, which of the following can be inferred about Jupiter's atmosphere?

    (A) It is similar to the atmosphere of Earth.
    (B) It causes ice crystals to form on Jupiter's surface.
    (C) Its chemical composition changes during Jupiter's long circuit of the sun.
    (D) It is very cold.

22. The word "interface" in line 10 is closest in meaning to

    (A) exchange
    (B) interlude
    (C) compromise
    (D) boundary

23. The word "rivaling" in line 14 could best be replaced by

    (A) equaling
    (B) following
    (C) not matching
    (D) fighting

24. According to the passage, why does Jupiter have so many satellites?

    (A) Jupiter's cloudy atmosphere reflects sunlight.
    (B) Jupiter has a large mass and strong gravitational field.
    (C) Volcanoes ejected material into Jupiter's atmosphere.
    (D) Jupiter's day is only ten hours long.

25. The word "Each" in line 26 refers to

    (A) Voyager and Galileo
    (B) the Great Red Spots
    (C) Jupiter's satellites
    (D) planets

26. The author mentions all of the following about Jupiter's satellites EXCEPT

    (A) several can be seen from Earth
    (B) detailed photographs have been taken of them
    (C) one of them has active volcanoes
    (D) one of them has an atmosphere of methane and ammonia

27. Where in the passage does the author compare Jupiter with another planet?

    (A) Lines 2–5
    (B) Lines 10–12
    (C) Lines 17–18
    (D) Lines 24–27

28. It can be concluded from lines 27–31 that

    (A) there are several doughnut–shaped rings around Jupiter
    (B) past observations from Earth may have detected a disk–like ring near Jupiter
    (C) Io's volcanoes are more active than Jupiter's
    (D) scientists are still confused about the structure of a ring near Io

TEST 1

29. The following sentence can be added to paragraph 4 of the passage.

Much turbulence is seen in adjacent material passing north or south of it.

Where would it best fit in the paragraph? Choose **A**, **B**, **C**, or **D**.

Photographs of Jupiter were taken by the Voyager and Galileo spacecrafts. Thousands of high resolution multi–color pictures show rapid variations of features both large and small. The Great Red Spot exhibits internal counter–clockwise rotation. **A** The moons Amalthea, Io, Europa, Ganymede, and Callisto were photographed, some in great detail. **B** Each is individual and unique, with no similarities to other known planets or satellites. **C** Io has active volcanoes that probably have ejected material into a doughnut–shaped ring enveloping its orbit about Jupiter. This is not to be confused with the thin, flat, disk–like ring closer to Jupiter's surface. **D** Now that such a ring has been seen by Voyager, older uncertain observations from Earth can be reinterpreted as early sightings of this structure.

QUESTIONS 30–40

Real estate sales agents work on behalf of property owners and earn a commission, or percentage, of the sale or rental of property. Agents are employed by real estate agencies that sell or rent property as well as manage, appraise, or develop real estate. Some agencies combine their real estate business with an insurance agency or law practice. Most real estate agents sell private homes. Some specialize in commercial property such as factories, apartment buildings, stores and office buildings. Others specialize in undeveloped land sites for commercial or residential use or go into agricultural real estate.

Real estate agents work from a file of listings of property that is for sale or rent. A listing is an agreement, usually in the form of a contract, between the owners of the property and the agent. The owners agree to pay the agent a percentage of the selling price. Real estate agents obtain new listings for their agency by locating property owners interested in selling. For example, they may call home owners who are trying to sell their houses privately through newspaper want ads. Real estate agents visit newly listed properties so that they can familiarize themselves with the features of the property before bringing prospective buyers to see it.

In any sale, the agents have to negotiate with both the seller and the buyer. Many sellers begin by asking more for their property than buyers are willing to pay for it. Agents must be able to convince sellers to set a realistic price. Most of the agents' efforts focus on the buyer, however. Agents try to learn what will motivate the buyer to make a purchase. Agents must be able to convince them that the property suits their needs and is a good buy. Buyers generally offer less for a property than the seller asks. Agents help to negotiate the final price. They usually help buyers arrange bank loans and are generally present at closings, when final contracts of sale are signed.

Real estate agents spend a great deal of time on the telephone, locating property that is for sale and negotiating with clients and property owners. They also spend time in the field checking out new properties and showing real estate to prospective buyers. Most agents work nights and weekends in order to arrange meetings that are convenient to buyers and sellers. Real estate agents can be fairly independent in their work and can feel the satisfaction of finding the right property for the right buyer.

30. The phrase "specialize in" in lines 5 and 7 is closest in meaning to

(A) write about
(B) approve of
(C) concentrate on
(D) refer to

31. A listing is a contract between property owners and real estate agents in which the owners

(A) try to sell their houses privately
(B) agree to pay the agent a percentage of the selling price
(C) obtain new listings for their property
(D) arrange to meet with the agent at a convenient time

TEST 1

32. The word "prospective" in lines 16 and 27 is closest in meaning to

(A) potential
(B) progressive
(C) former
(D) wealthy

33. The word "them" in line 21 refers to

(A) sellers
(B) agents
(C) buyers
(D) owners

34. It can be inferred that negotiating the final price of a property involves

(A) calling an insurance agency
(B) having the seller and the buyer agree on what is realistic
(C) finding a similar property that has a realistic price
(D) motivating the buyer to visit the property

35. In paragraph 3, the author implies that

(A) agents must understand the desires and needs of the buyer
(B) agents are sometimes immoral in their practices
(C) buyers usually pay the price asked by the seller
(D) agents spend more time with sellers than with buyers

36. According to the passage, real estate agents

(A) begin by asking more for a property than buyers are willing to pay
(B) have a college education
(C) own a lot of commercial property
(D) are usually present when final sales contracts are signed

37. The phrase "checking out" in line 27 means

(A) selling
(B) listing
(C) investigating
(D) improving

38. It can be inferred from the passage that

(A) real estate agents are generally wealthy
(B) real estate sales is a growing profession
(C) most real estate agents are also lawyers
(D) real estate agents need strong social skills

39. Where in the passage does the author discuss different types of real estate?

(A) Paragraph 1
(B) Paragraph 2
(C) Paragraph 3
(D) Paragraph 4

40. The following sentence can be added to paragraph 4 of the passage.

However, usually they can set their own hours.

Where would it best fit in the paragraph? Choose **A**, **B**, **C**, or **D**.

A Real estate agents spend a great deal of time on the telephone, locating property that is for sale and negotiating with clients and property owners. They also spend time in the field checking out new properties and showing real estate to prospective buyers. **B** Most agents work nights and weekends in order to arrange meetings that are convenient to buyers and sellers. **C** Real estate agents can be fairly independent in their work and can feel the satisfaction of finding the right property for the right buyer. **D**

Go on to the next page

QUESTIONS 41–50

The human body seems to have been designed for producing language. The mouth is relatively small and can be opened and closed rapidly, and the flexible tongue can be used to shape a wide variety of sounds. The teeth are upright, not slanting outwards like those of apes, and they are roughly even in height. Such characteristics are not needed for eating but are extremely helpful in pronouncing sounds such as *f*, *v* and *th*. The lips have much more intricate muscles than those of other primates, and their flexibility helps with sounds like *p*, *b* and *w*.

Many scholars have studied how the development of language is related to the evolutionary development of the human species. One evolutionary step may have resulted in the development of a vocal tract capable of producing the wide variety of sounds utilized by human language. The assumption of a upright posture moved the head forward and the larynx, or "voice box," lower. This created a longer cavity above the vocal chords, which acted as a resonator for any sounds produced by the larynx.

Another evolutionary step may have been development of a mechanism for perceiving and distinguishing sounds. However, the ability to hear speech sounds is not a necessary condition for the acquisition and use of language. Humans who are born deaf learn the sign languages that are used around them. Still, all languages, including sign language, require the organizing and combining of sounds or signs in specific constructions.

The human brain has specialized functions in each of its two hemispheres. Those functions which are analytic, such as tool–using and language, are largely confined to the left hemisphere of the brain. It may be that there is an evolutionary connection between the tool–using and language–using abilities of humans, and that both are related to the development of the brain.

41. This passage supports all of the following statements EXCEPT

    (A) humans are capable of producing a wide range of sounds
    (B) the development of language is related to human physical development
    (C) humans evolved much later than other primates did
    (D) the human mouth is well–adapted for producing speech

42. The word "intricate" in line 6 is closest in meaning to

    (A) divided
    (B) complex
    (C) powerful
    (D) miniature

43. The word "their" in line 6 refers to

    (A) lips
    (B) other primates
    (C) characteristics
    (D) sounds

44. According to the passage, what happened when humans assumed an upright posture?

    (A) The larynx moved forward.
    (B) Humans developed a mechanism for distinguishing different sounds.
    (C) The human larynx became more similar to that of other apes.
    (D) The cavity above the vocal cords lengthened.

45. The word "resonator" in line 13 is closest in meaning to

(A) regulator
(B) filter
(C) recorder
(D) amplifier

46. Which of the following is NOT mentioned in relation to the development of speech?

(A) Tongue
(B) Larynx
(C) Lungs
(D) Brain

47. In paragraph 3, the author suggests that

(A) deaf children learn sign language by being exposed to it
(B) children must have good hearing to learn sign language
(C) spoken language has more specific constructions than sign language does
(D) the human ear developed at the same time as the voice box

48. In paragraph 4, the author implies that

(A) humans developed language before tool–using
(B) specialization of the human brain is necessary for language
(C) the right hemisphere of the brain is less complex than the left hemisphere
(D) most people use only the left hemisphere of their brain

49. Where in the passage does the author give examples of human functions that are analytic?

(A) Lines 5–7
(B) Lines 8–9
(C) Lines 12–13
(D) Lines 20–22

50. The following sentence can be added to paragraph 3 of the passage.

This suggests that a major step in the development of language relates to evolutionary changes in the brain.

Where would it best fit in the paragraph? Choose **A**, **B**, **C**, or **D**.

A Another evolutionary step may have been development of a mechanism for perceiving and distinguishing sounds. However, the ability to hear speech sounds is not a necessary condition for the acquisition and use of language. **B** Humans who are born deaf learn the sign languages that are used around them. **C** Still, all languages, including sign language, require the organizing and combining of sounds or signs in specific constructions. **D**

This is the end of Section 3.

SECTION 4

WRITING

Time – 30 minutes

In the Writing section of the TOEFL, you will have an opportunity to demonstrate your ability to write in English.

Read the following directions before going on to the next page.

- Read the essay question carefully.
- Think before you write. Making notes may help you to organize your essay.
- It is important to write only on the topic you are given.
- Check your work. Allow a few minutes before the time is up to read over your essay and make changes.
- You must stop writing at the end of 30 minutes. If you continue to write, it will be considered cheating.

Set your clock or watch for 30 minutes.

Now turn the page and begin.

Writing Topic

Directions: Read the topic below and then make any notes that will help you plan your response. Begin typing your response, or write your answer on a separate sheet of paper.

Do you agree or disagree with the following statement?

Subjects such as art, music, and drama should be part of every child's basic education.

Use specific reasons and examples to support your opinion.

This is the end of Test 1.

Answers to Practice Test 1 are on pages 664 to 666.
TOEFL score conversion tables are on page 15.

Section 1

1. Ⓐ Ⓑ Ⓒ Ⓓ
2. Ⓐ Ⓑ Ⓒ Ⓓ
3. Ⓐ Ⓑ Ⓒ Ⓓ
4. Ⓐ Ⓑ Ⓒ Ⓓ
5. Ⓐ Ⓑ Ⓒ Ⓓ
6. Ⓐ Ⓑ Ⓒ Ⓓ
7. Ⓐ Ⓑ Ⓒ Ⓓ
8. Ⓐ Ⓑ Ⓒ Ⓓ
9. Ⓐ Ⓑ Ⓒ Ⓓ
10. Ⓐ Ⓑ Ⓒ Ⓓ
11. Ⓐ Ⓑ Ⓒ Ⓓ
12. Ⓐ Ⓑ Ⓒ Ⓓ
13. Ⓐ Ⓑ Ⓒ Ⓓ
14. Ⓐ Ⓑ Ⓒ Ⓓ
15. Ⓐ Ⓑ Ⓒ Ⓓ
16. Ⓐ Ⓑ Ⓒ Ⓓ
17. Ⓐ Ⓑ Ⓒ Ⓓ
18. Ⓐ Ⓑ Ⓒ Ⓓ
19. Ⓐ Ⓑ Ⓒ Ⓓ
20. Ⓐ Ⓑ Ⓒ Ⓓ
21. Ⓐ Ⓑ Ⓒ Ⓓ
22. Ⓐ Ⓑ Ⓒ Ⓓ
23. Ⓐ Ⓑ Ⓒ Ⓓ
24. Ⓐ Ⓑ Ⓒ Ⓓ
25. Ⓐ Ⓑ Ⓒ Ⓓ
26. Ⓐ Ⓑ Ⓒ Ⓓ
27. Ⓐ Ⓑ Ⓒ Ⓓ
28. Ⓐ Ⓑ Ⓒ Ⓓ
29. Ⓐ Ⓑ Ⓒ Ⓓ
30. Ⓐ Ⓑ Ⓒ Ⓓ
31. Ⓐ Ⓑ Ⓒ Ⓓ
32. Ⓐ Ⓑ Ⓒ Ⓓ
33. Ⓐ Ⓑ Ⓒ Ⓓ
34. Ⓐ Ⓑ Ⓒ Ⓓ
35. Ⓐ Ⓑ Ⓒ Ⓓ
36. Ⓐ Ⓑ Ⓒ Ⓓ
37. Ⓐ Ⓑ Ⓒ Ⓓ
38. Ⓐ Ⓑ Ⓒ Ⓓ
39. Ⓐ Ⓑ Ⓒ Ⓓ
40. Ⓐ Ⓑ Ⓒ Ⓓ
41. Ⓐ Ⓑ Ⓒ Ⓓ
42. Ⓐ Ⓑ Ⓒ Ⓓ
43. Ⓐ Ⓑ Ⓒ Ⓓ
44. Ⓐ Ⓑ Ⓒ Ⓓ
45. Ⓐ Ⓑ Ⓒ Ⓓ
46. Ⓐ Ⓑ Ⓒ Ⓓ
47. Ⓐ Ⓑ Ⓒ Ⓓ
48. Ⓐ Ⓑ Ⓒ Ⓓ
49. Ⓐ Ⓑ Ⓒ Ⓓ
50. Ⓐ Ⓑ Ⓒ Ⓓ

Section 2

1. Ⓐ Ⓑ Ⓒ Ⓓ
2. Ⓐ Ⓑ Ⓒ Ⓓ
3. Ⓐ Ⓑ Ⓒ Ⓓ
4. Ⓐ Ⓑ Ⓒ Ⓓ
5. Ⓐ Ⓑ Ⓒ Ⓓ
6. Ⓐ Ⓑ Ⓒ Ⓓ
7. Ⓐ Ⓑ Ⓒ Ⓓ
8. Ⓐ Ⓑ Ⓒ Ⓓ
9. Ⓐ Ⓑ Ⓒ Ⓓ
10. Ⓐ Ⓑ Ⓒ Ⓓ
11. Ⓐ Ⓑ Ⓒ Ⓓ
12. Ⓐ Ⓑ Ⓒ Ⓓ
13. Ⓐ Ⓑ Ⓒ Ⓓ
14. Ⓐ Ⓑ Ⓒ Ⓓ
15. Ⓐ Ⓑ Ⓒ Ⓓ
16. Ⓐ Ⓑ Ⓒ Ⓓ
17. Ⓐ Ⓑ Ⓒ Ⓓ
18. Ⓐ Ⓑ Ⓒ Ⓓ
19. Ⓐ Ⓑ Ⓒ Ⓓ
20. Ⓐ Ⓑ Ⓒ Ⓓ
21. Ⓐ Ⓑ Ⓒ Ⓓ
22. Ⓐ Ⓑ Ⓒ Ⓓ
23. Ⓐ Ⓑ Ⓒ Ⓓ
24. Ⓐ Ⓑ Ⓒ Ⓓ
25. Ⓐ Ⓑ Ⓒ Ⓓ
26. Ⓐ Ⓑ Ⓒ Ⓓ
27. Ⓐ Ⓑ Ⓒ Ⓓ
28. Ⓐ Ⓑ Ⓒ Ⓓ
29. Ⓐ Ⓑ Ⓒ Ⓓ
30. Ⓐ Ⓑ Ⓒ Ⓓ
31. Ⓐ Ⓑ Ⓒ Ⓓ
32. Ⓐ Ⓑ Ⓒ Ⓓ
33. Ⓐ Ⓑ Ⓒ Ⓓ
34. Ⓐ Ⓑ Ⓒ Ⓓ
35. Ⓐ Ⓑ Ⓒ Ⓓ
36. Ⓐ Ⓑ Ⓒ Ⓓ
37. Ⓐ Ⓑ Ⓒ Ⓓ
38. Ⓐ Ⓑ Ⓒ Ⓓ
39. Ⓐ Ⓑ Ⓒ Ⓓ
40. Ⓐ Ⓑ Ⓒ Ⓓ

Section 3

1. Ⓐ Ⓑ Ⓒ Ⓓ
2. Ⓐ Ⓑ Ⓒ Ⓓ
3. Ⓐ Ⓑ Ⓒ Ⓓ
4. Ⓐ Ⓑ Ⓒ Ⓓ
5. Ⓐ Ⓑ Ⓒ Ⓓ
6. Ⓐ Ⓑ Ⓒ Ⓓ
7. Ⓐ Ⓑ Ⓒ Ⓓ
8. Ⓐ Ⓑ Ⓒ Ⓓ
9. Ⓐ Ⓑ Ⓒ Ⓓ
10. Ⓐ Ⓑ Ⓒ Ⓓ
11. Ⓐ Ⓑ Ⓒ Ⓓ
12. Ⓐ Ⓑ Ⓒ Ⓓ
13. Ⓐ Ⓑ Ⓒ Ⓓ
14. Ⓐ Ⓑ Ⓒ Ⓓ
15. Ⓐ Ⓑ Ⓒ Ⓓ
16. Ⓐ Ⓑ Ⓒ Ⓓ
17. Ⓐ Ⓑ Ⓒ Ⓓ
18. Ⓐ Ⓑ Ⓒ Ⓓ
19. Ⓐ Ⓑ Ⓒ Ⓓ
20. Ⓐ Ⓑ Ⓒ Ⓓ
21. Ⓐ Ⓑ Ⓒ Ⓓ
22. Ⓐ Ⓑ Ⓒ Ⓓ
23. Ⓐ Ⓑ Ⓒ Ⓓ
24. Ⓐ Ⓑ Ⓒ Ⓓ
25. Ⓐ Ⓑ Ⓒ Ⓓ
26. Ⓐ Ⓑ Ⓒ Ⓓ
27. Ⓐ Ⓑ Ⓒ Ⓓ
28. Ⓐ Ⓑ Ⓒ Ⓓ
29. Ⓐ Ⓑ Ⓒ Ⓓ
30. Ⓐ Ⓑ Ⓒ Ⓓ
31. Ⓐ Ⓑ Ⓒ Ⓓ
32. Ⓐ Ⓑ Ⓒ Ⓓ
33. Ⓐ Ⓑ Ⓒ Ⓓ
34. Ⓐ Ⓑ Ⓒ Ⓓ
35. Ⓐ Ⓑ Ⓒ Ⓓ
36. Ⓐ Ⓑ Ⓒ Ⓓ
37. Ⓐ Ⓑ Ⓒ Ⓓ
38. Ⓐ Ⓑ Ⓒ Ⓓ
39. Ⓐ Ⓑ Ⓒ Ⓓ
40. Ⓐ Ⓑ Ⓒ Ⓓ
41. Ⓐ Ⓑ Ⓒ Ⓓ
42. Ⓐ Ⓑ Ⓒ Ⓓ
43. Ⓐ Ⓑ Ⓒ Ⓓ
44. Ⓐ Ⓑ Ⓒ Ⓓ
45. Ⓐ Ⓑ Ⓒ Ⓓ
46. Ⓐ Ⓑ Ⓒ Ⓓ
47. Ⓐ Ⓑ Ⓒ Ⓓ
48. Ⓐ Ⓑ Ⓒ Ⓓ
49. Ⓐ Ⓑ Ⓒ Ⓓ
50. Ⓐ Ⓑ Ⓒ Ⓓ

TEST 2

TEST OF WRITTEN ENGLISH

Time — 30 minutes

In the Test of Written English (TWE), you will have an opportunity to demonstrate your ability to write in English.

Read the following directions before going on to the next page.

- Read the essay topic carefully.
- Think before you write. Making notes may help you to organize your essay.
- Write only on the topic you are given. Write clearly and precisely. How well you write is more important than how much you write, but to cover the topic adequately, you may want to write more than one paragraph.
- Check your work. Allow a few minutes before the time is up to read over your essay and make any changes.
- At the end of 30 minutes, stop writing and put your pencil down. If you continue to write, it will be considered cheating.

Set your clock or watch for 30 minutes.

Now turn the page and begin.

Writing Topic

Directions: Read the topic below and then make any notes that will help you plan your response. Begin writing your essay on a separate sheet of paper.

Developments such as the personal computer have had a major effect on life in the past twenty years. Choose another development and explain why you think it will be influential in the next twenty years.

Use specific reasons and examples to support your opinion.

SECTION 1

LISTENING COMPREHENSION

Time — approximately 35 minutes

(including the reading of the directions for each part)

(Start Tape)

In the Listening Comprehension section of the test, you will have an opportunity to demonstrate your ability to understand conversations and talks in English. There are three parts to this section, with special directions for each part. Answer all the questions on the basis of what is stated or implied by the speakers you hear. Do not take notes or write in your book at any time.

PART A

Directions: In Part A you will hear short conversations between two people. After each conversation, you will hear a question about the conversation. The conversations and questions will not be repeated. After you hear a question, read the four possible answers in your book and choose the best answer. Then, on your answer sheet, find the number of the question and fill in the space that corresponds to the letter of the answer you have chosen.

Here is an example.

Sample Answer

On the recording, you hear:

In your book, you read:

(A) She doesn't want to buy a printer.
(B) She would rather buy something else.
(C) She doesn't want to pay a lot for a printer.
(D) She wants to shop at a better place.

You learn from the conversation that the woman hopes to find a printer at a better price. The best answer to the question, *What does the woman mean?* is (C), *She doesn't want to pay a lot for a printer.* Therefore, the correct choice is (C).

TEST 2

1. (A) She met her friend by chance at the bookstore.
   (B) She went to the bookstore with her friend.
   (C) She saw her friend across from the bookstore.
   (D) She arranged to meet her friend in the bookstore.

2. (A) The woman's assistant is not very capable.
   (B) The woman's assistant has recently started working there.
   (C) The woman's assistant has not done any work so far.
   (D) The woman doesn't have an assistant.

3. (A) The woman didn't like coffee.
   (B) The woman couldn't come to get the coffee table.
   (C) The woman ordered a new table yesterday.
   (D) The woman had not ordered a new table.

4. (A) He has not paid for the stereo yet.
   (B) He bought a stereo last week.
   (C) He bought a stereo two weeks ago.
   (D) He is still waiting for his first paycheck.

5. (A) Dentist.
   (B) Photographer.
   (C) Optometrist.
   (D) Artist.

6. (A) The man should buy new shoes.
   (B) She can help him repair his boots.
   (C) The man can go to the shoe repair shop.
   (D) She wants to go shopping.

7. (A) The woman might find a seat upstairs.
   (B) The woman can sit next to him.
   (C) There are no seats left in the balcony.
   (D) The woman should turn left in the balcony.

8. (A) The man's job is too difficult.
   (B) The man should try to work harder.
   (C) The man should go to bed earlier.
   (D) The man should worry less about his job.

9. (A) He would rather go bowling.
   (B) They should investigate the dance.
   (C) They should check out of the hotel.
   (D) He will ask for the check.

10. (A) Guard her money.
    (B) Read the signs on the train walls.
    (C) Look for a new wallet.
    (D) Not take the train.

11. (A) He must do eight more pages.
    (B) He must finish his paper before morning.
    (C) He cannot come back the next morning.
    (D) He must stop to eat dinner.

12. (A) Amy was running in the park yesterday.
    (B) He was looking for Amy in the park.
    (C) Amy seemed as if she were tired or ill.
    (D) He saw Amy in a parking lot downtown.

13. (A) Buy something to eat on the train.
    (B) Take the five o'clock train.
    (C) Wait to catch a later train.
    (D) Take the train to the airport.

14. (A) What they will do that afternoon.
    (B) Working on an assignment together.
    (C) How they will spend the weekend.
    (D) Returning books to the library.

15. (A) The movie was a waste of time and money.
    (B) He didn't have time to go to the movie.
    (C) The movie was inexpensive.
    (D) He didn't understand what the movie was about.

16. (A) She would rather listen to lectures than do homework.
    (B) She keeps losing her lecture notes.
    (C) She understands most of the assignments in this class.
    (D) She has difficulty doing work at the level of this class.

17. (A) She was not accepted by the business college.
    (B) She earns grades that are above average.
    (C) She does not have a high grade point average.
    (D) She will earn high grades at the business college.

18. (A) The man was in class on Monday, but the woman was not.
    (B) The woman went back to Ohio on Monday.
    (C) Both the woman and the man are from Ohio.
    (D) Both the woman and the man missed class on Monday.

19. (A) Ahmed attended the concert with the speakers.
    (B) Ahmed had not planned to attend the concert.
    (C) Ahmed probably did not attend the concert.
    (D) The concert was probably canceled.

20. (A) She will pay more money than she can afford.
    (B) She will buy the ceramic mugs.
    (C) She will buy the plastic mugs.
    (D) She will spend only fifteen dollars.

21. (A) She prefers to stay home and exercise.
    (B) She likes basketball more than the man does.
    (C) She prefers going to a movie instead of the basketball game.
    (D) She doesn't want to go to a movie.

22. (A) He wouldn't mind spending money that evening.
    (B) He would enjoy going along on a walk.
    (C) He knows a nice store by the lake.
    (D) He would rather drive to the lake.

23. (A) He wants to take a nap.
    (B) He asks the woman to help him carry something.
    (C) He asks the woman to come with him.
    (D) He asks the woman to be patient.

24. (A) She missed taking the exam.
    (B) She studied the wrong material for the exam.
    (C) She thinks she failed the exam.
    (D) She forgot to bring a blue book to the exam.

25. (A) The man is taking a biology class.
    (B) The man is writing a paper about a famous senator.
    (C) The man is reading about the life of a well–known politician.
    (D) The man is reading a book about sanitation.

26. (A) She doesn't like tea.
    (B) She would probably like more tea.
    (C) She likes sugar in her tea.
    (D) She has already gone home.

27. (A) In a library.
    (B) In a book store.
    (C) In a supermarket.
    (D) In a museum.

28. (A) He fell during the soccer game.
    (B) He is not a diligent student.
    (C) He likes accounting more than psychology.
    (D) Matthew wishes he had more time for his studies.

29. (A) They should look at the scenery.
    (B) They should find a nice place to hike.
    (C) They should take care of each other.
    (D) They should look for information about the trail.

30. (A) Step out with the woman.
    (B) Hold the woman's sandwich.
    (C) Watch for a taxi.
    (D) Guard the woman's briefcase.

This is the end of Part A.

        1

PART B

Directions: In this part of the test, you will hear longer conversations. After each conversation, you will hear several questions. The conversations and questions will not be repeated.

After you hear a question, read the four possible answers in your book and choose the best answer. Then, on the answer sheet, find the number of the question and fill in the space that corresponds to the letter of the answer you have chosen.

Remember, you should not take notes or write in your book.

31. (A) Taking pain medication.
    (B) Cleaning teeth.
    (C) Extracting wisdom teeth.
    (D) Recovering from an injury.

32. (A) A lot of pain.
    (B) Putting the patient to sleep.
    (C) Staying in the hospital.
    (D) Making two or three appointments with the nurse.

33. (A) The patient will not be able to find a pharmacy by himself.
    (B) The patient can not recover alone.
    (C) The buses will not be running that week.
    (D) The patient will be drowsy from the anesthesia.

34. (A) He looks forward to feeling relief afterward.
    (B) He is very fearful of pain.
    (C) He is concerned about his roommate's driving him home.
    (D) He doesn't trust the doctor.

35. (A) Hiking.
    (B) Riding the bus.
    (C) Going to college.
    (D) Moving to town.

36. (A) She must stay with her cousin because she can't find an apartment.
    (B) She has been hiking.
    (C) She didn't have much time to pack.
    (D) She can register by telephone.

37. (A) He is majoring in business.
    (B) He is an expert in organizational psychology.
    (C) He teaches a psychology class.
    (D) He rides the bus every day.

38. (A) They both like to travel light.
    (B) They both are looking for an apartment.
    (C) They both think Dr. Robinson is fabulous.
    (D) They both will be taking a psychology course.

This is the end of Part B.

        1

PART C

Directions: In this part of the test, you will hear several talks. After each talk, you will hear some questions. The talks and questions will not be repeated.

After you hear a question, read the four possible answers in your book and choose the best answer. Then, on your answer sheet, find the number of the question and fill in the space that corresponds to the letter of the answer you have chosen.

Here is an example.

On the recording, you hear:

Sample Answer

A B D

Now listen to a sample question.

In your book, you read:

(A) It helped scientists see the atmosphere more clearly.
(B) It made it easier for scientists to send messages.
(C) It made data collection from weather stations faster.
(D) It helped airplanes fly higher.

The best answer to the question, *How did the telegraph improve the science of meteorology?* is (C), *It made data collection from weather stations faster*. Therefore, the correct choice is (C).

Now listen to another sample question.

Sample Answer

A B C

In your book, you read:

(A) Study trends in the earth's climate.
(B) Forecast the weather.
(C) Solve air pollution problems.
(D) Study costs of building satellites.

The best answer to the question, *What is not mentioned as something meteorologists do today?* is (D), *Study costs of building satellites*. Therefore, the correct choice is (D).

Remember, you should <u>not</u> take notes or write in your book.

39. (A) Boaters.
    (B) Weather forecasters.
    (C) Journalism students.
    (D) Radio operators.

40. (A) Television reports.
    (B) Cloud formations.
    (C) People on other boats.
    (D) Nothing.

41. (A) They have accidents when they try to outrun other boats.
    (B) They fall overboard when they stand up in their boat.
    (C) They sit or lie on the bottom of their boat.
    (D) They fall asleep and water enters their boat.

42. (A) Wild animal trainer.
    (B) Botanist.
    (C) Geology professor.
    (D) Forest ranger.

43. (A) It may result in a fine.
    (B) It may cause the death of the babies.
    (C) It is forbidden in the national forest.
    (D) It is not the best way to draw the birds.

44. (A) It might encourage animals to bite or attack people.
    (B) Wild animals usually don't like human food.
    (C) Feeding wild animals is expensive.
    (D) Wild animals would rather find their own food.

45. (A) The dog will have an enjoyable experience.
    (B) The wild animal can always escape.
    (C) The dog might become a wild animal.
    (D) The dog might be killed by a wild animal.

46. (A) Supply and demand in market economics.
    (B) How to be a better consumer.
    (C) The duties of every voter.
    (D) High prices in the supermarket.

47. (A) Consumers prefer goods that are well–made.
    (B) Consumers are like voters who vote by spending money.
    (C) Consumers buy fewer things when prices are low.
    (D) Consumers will supply only high–priced goods.

48. (A) Suppliers.
    (B) Government.
    (C) Consumers.
    (D) Economists.

49. (A) The price will only increase, never decrease.
    (B) The price is determined by an economist.
    (C) If the price is too low, people will not want to buy it.
    (D) The price influences how much people will want to buy.

50. (A) Real examples of how supply and demand influence prices.
    (B) Why consumers complain about cheap goods.
    (C) The required courses for economics majors.
    (D) How the factory system evolved in the real world.

TEST 2

(Stop Tape)

This is the end of Section 1.

SECTION 2

STRUCTURE AND WRITTEN EXPRESSION

2

Time – 25 minutes

(including the reading of the directions)

Now set your clock for 25 minutes.

The Structure and Written Expression section is designed to measure your ability to recognize language that is appropriate for standard written English. There are two types of questions in this section, with special directions for each type.

STRUCTURE

Directions: Questions 1–15 are incomplete sentences. Beneath each sentence you will see four words or phrases, marked (A), (B), (C), and (D). Choose the one word or phrase that best completes the sentence. Then, on your answer sheet, find the number of the question and fill in the space that corresponds to the letter of the answer you have chosen.

Example

Although Chicago is not ——— New York, it has many attractions for visitors.

(A) as large as
(B) larger
(C) larger city
(D) the larger city is

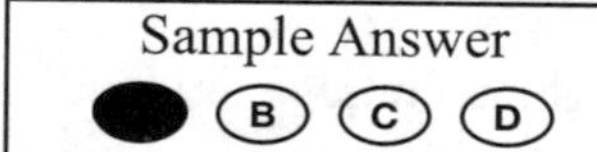

The sentence should read, *Although Chicago is not as large as New York, it has many attractions for visitors*. Therefore, you should choose (A).

Now begin work on the questions.

1. A hare ------- a rabbit in that it has longer ears and hind legs.

   (A) different
   (B) different than
   (C) is different
   (D) differs from

2. John F. Kennedy was elected thirty–fifth president of the United States in 1960, ------- forty–three.

   (A) he was
   (B) at the age of
   (C) the age
   (D) his age of

3. The electron beam of a black–and–white television set is always ------- by the luminance and synchronization signals.

   (A) control
   (B) to control
   (C) controlling
   (D) controlled

4. ------- the rising population of the industrial nations has not suffered from a major epidemic since the last century.

   (A) A miracle that
   (B) It is a miracle that
   (C) That a miracle has been
   (D) Because the miracle

5. A pump increases pressure by pushing the molecules in the fluid ------- the pump closer together.

   (A) that enters
   (B) is entering
   (C) which it enters
   (D) enter

6. ------- two substances do not mix, the one with the lesser density will always float on top of the other.

   (A) Provided that
   (B) The
   (C) It is provided
   (D) To provide

7. Optical instruments such as cameras, microscopes, and ——— all produce images with lenses.

   (A) projecting
   (B) projection
   (C) to project
   (D) projectors

8. A hurricane's life span may be ------- thirty days.

   (A) longer
   (B) as long as
   (C) the longest is
   (D) the longer

9. Not only -------, it also performs an essential function in the reproduction of the plant.

   (A) the flower looks beautiful
   (B) the flower is looking beautiful
   (C) does the flower look beautiful
   (D) the beautiful flower

10. The many temples of the Mayan ceremonial centers ------- limestone covered with white plaster.

   (A) have been built
   (B) built of
   (C) were built of
   (D) to build

11. Although many people do not consider it harmful, alcohol is the ------- in the United States.

    (A) drug commonly abused most
    (B) most commonly abused drug
    (C) most abused commonly drug
    (D) commonly most abused drug

12. Charles Lindbergh's feat put him in a position from which ------- the development of commercial aviation.

    (A) he could encourage
    (B) he encourages
    (C) encouraged
    (D) encouragement

13. Despite recent developments in the genetics of cystic fibrosis, there is still ------- cure for this deadly disease.

    (A) neither
    (B) nor
    (C) not
    (D) no

14. -------, all set in the Chihuahuan Desert, offer scenery ranging from underground caves to high mountain peaks.

    (A) The national parks of the Southwest are
    (B) The national parks of the Southwest
    (C) Not only are the national parks of the Southwest
    (D) In the national parks of the Southwest

15. The traditional Hawaiian value of *ohana* is a cooperative system of social relationships found in -------.

    (A) extended family
    (B) a extended family
    (C) the family extended
    (D) an extended family

Go on to the next page

WRITTEN EXPRESSION

Directions: In questions 16–40 each sentence has four underlined words or phrases. The four underlined parts of the sentence are marked (A), (B), (C), and (D). Identify the one underlined word or phrase that must be changed in order for the sentence to be correct. Then, on your answer sheet, find the number of the question and fill in the space that corresponds to the letter of the answer you have chosen.

Example

Sample Answer
(A) (B) ● (D)

Guglielmo Marconi, the son of (A) a wealthy Italian landowner, made (B) the first successfully (C) transmission using (D) radio waves.

The sentence should read, *Guglielmo Marconi, the son of a wealthy Italian landowner, made the first successful transmission using radio waves*. Therefore, you should choose (C).

Now begin work on the questions.

TEST 2

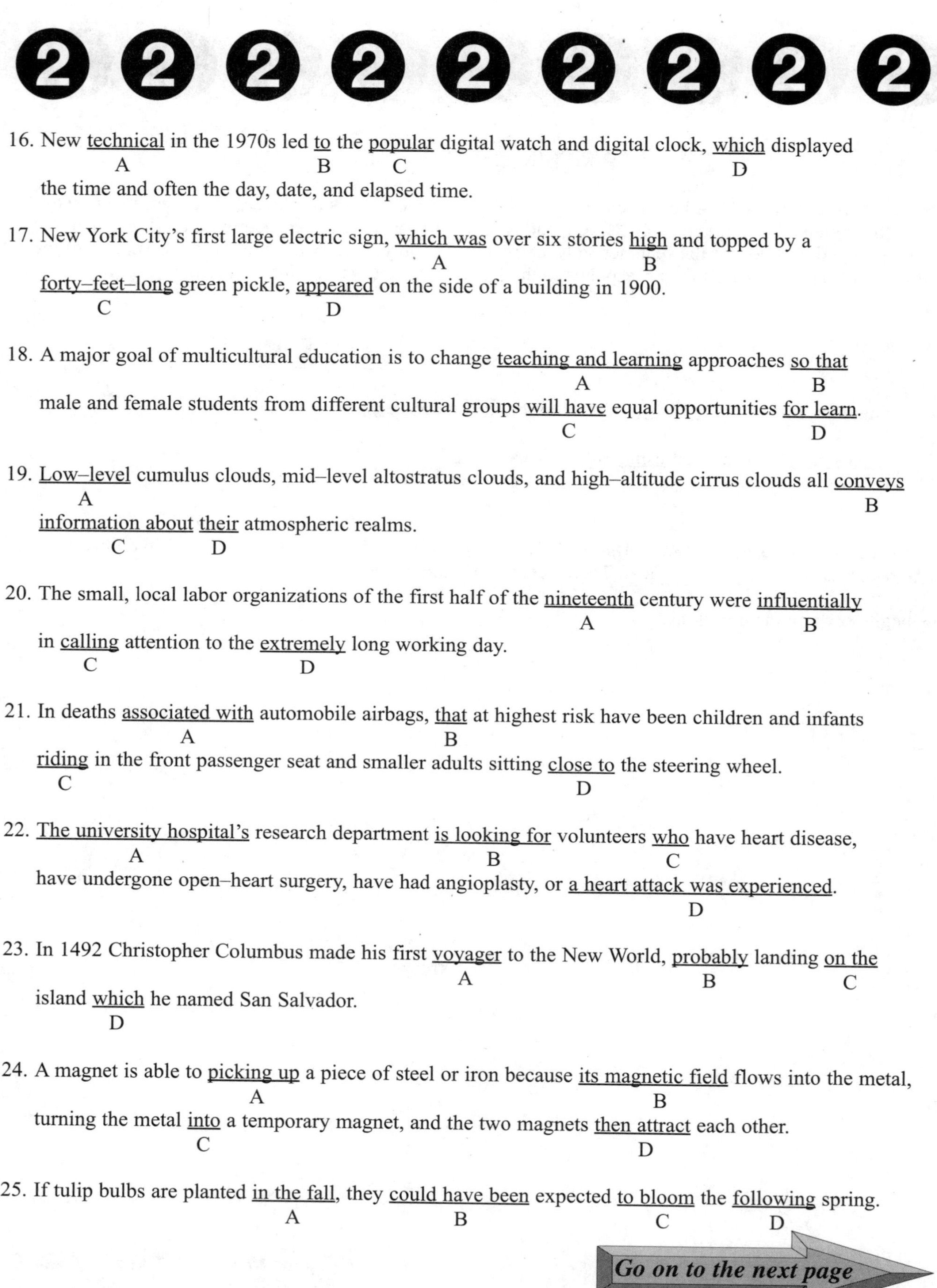

2 2 2 2 2 2 2 2 2

16. New technical in the 1970s led to the popular digital watch and digital clock, which displayed
A B C D
the time and often the day, date, and elapsed time.

17. New York City's first large electric sign, which was over six stories high and topped by a
A B
forty–feet–long green pickle, appeared on the side of a building in 1900.
C D

18. A major goal of multicultural education is to change teaching and learning approaches so that
A B
male and female students from different cultural groups will have equal opportunities for learn.
C D

19. Low–level cumulus clouds, mid–level altostratus clouds, and high–altitude cirrus clouds all conveys
A B
information about their atmospheric realms.
C D

20. The small, local labor organizations of the first half of the nineteenth century were influentially
A B
in calling attention to the extremely long working day.
C D

21. In deaths associated with automobile airbags, that at highest risk have been children and infants
A B
riding in the front passenger seat and smaller adults sitting close to the steering wheel.
C D

22. The university hospital's research department is looking for volunteers who have heart disease,
A B C
have undergone open–heart surgery, have had angioplasty, or a heart attack was experienced.
D

23. In 1492 Christopher Columbus made his first voyager to the New World, probably landing on the
A B C
island which he named San Salvador.
D

24. A magnet is able to picking up a piece of steel or iron because its magnetic field flows into the metal,
A B
turning the metal into a temporary magnet, and the two magnets then attract each other.
C D

25. If tulip bulbs are planted in the fall, they could have been expected to bloom the following spring.
A B C D

Go on to the next page

26. To many early Americans, chicken on the table represented fancy civilized food and suggested that
A B C
a farmer and his wife has found prosperity.
D

27. A heat exchanger is a device in which heat taken from a hot liquid or gas in order to warm a cool one.
A B C D

28. On July 4, 1997, the Pathfinder spacecraft landed on Mars and released a robot that exploration
A B C
the planet's landscape and beamed images back to Earth.
D

29. There was a tremendous appetite for new films for the early moving picture machines called
A B
nickelodeons, and film–makers sought rewarded careers in this new medium.
C D

30. The massive architecture of the ancient Egyptians was advanced than that of the Sumerians and even
A B C
surpassed that of later societies.
D

31. On the one hand, the turkey vulture disgusts people because of its eating habits; on the contrary, it
A B C
fills a useful role by consuming the flesh of dead animals.
D

32. Unlike a stock market, a money market—a network of brokers, buyers, and selling—is not located in
A B C D
a specific place.

33. The earliest works of Finnish architect Alvar Aalto in the early 1930s led the way to a more subtle,
A B C
romanticism, organic type of design.
D

34. The major advantage of a large corporation was that it can raise large sums of money to engage in
A B C
efficient large–scale production.
D

35. The development new building materials and mass–production techniques brought significant changes
A B
to architecture in the first quarter of the twentieth century.
C D

TEST 2

2 2 2 2 2 2 2 2 2

36. It is extremely important and essential to keep accurate financial records that are clear, simple,
A B C
and practical.
D

37. If one plans to hike in the backcountry, you should prepare for the possibility of encountering a bear.
A B C D

38. All fruit contains fiber: an orange provides seven grams, a apple five, and a banana four, but half of a
A B C
grapefruit provides six grams.
D

39. The jumping mouse, especially when startled from its hiding place, may take a few long jumps, but
A B C
generally soon stop and remain motionless.
D

40. Heat rays are harmless, but nuclear radiation can have a highly damaging effect into living cells.
A B C D

This is the end of Section 2.

SECTION 3

READING COMPREHENSION

Time – 55 minutes
(including the reading of the directions)
Now set your clock for 55 minutes.

In the Reading Comprehension section of the test, you will read several passages. Each one is followed by a number of questions about it. For questions 1–50, you are to choose the one best answer, (A), (B), (C), or (D), to each question.

Answer all questions about the information in a passage on the basis of what is stated or implied in that passage.

Read the following passage:

The coffees of Central America profit from the area's steady climate and wealth of mountains. The mountains of the Pacific Cordillera, which stretch in a virtually unbroken line from Guatemala to the middle of Panama, provide the best combination of climate, altitude, and soil.

Guatemala was a relative latecomer to the commercial coffee business, exporting beans only since 1875. This mountainous country is ideally suited for coffee production, and its exports now surpass those of much larger countries. European merchants still take about 50 percent of the Guatemalan beans, with most of the best beans today being exported to England.

Example I It can be inferred from the passage that coffee grows well

(A) in the northern hemisphere
(B) in mountainous regions
(C) in small countries
(D) near the Pacific Ocean

Sample Answer
(A) ● (C) (D)

The passage implies that the mountainous regions of Central America are ideally suited for coffee production. The other answer choices cannot be inferred from the information given. Therefore, you should choose (B).

Example II The word "surpass" in line 7 is closest in meaning to

(A) include
(B) surround
(C) exceed
(D) limit

Sample Answer
(A) (B) ● (D)

The word *surpass* in this passage means *exceed*. Therefore, you should choose (C).

Now begin work on the questions.

Go on to the next page

QUESTIONS 1–11

On March 25, 1911, one of the five hundred employees of the Triangle Shirtwaist factory in New York noticed that a rag bin near her eighth–floor work station was on fire. Workers immediately tried to extinguish the flames. Their efforts proved futile, as piles of fabric ignited all over the eighth floor. The manager of the factory ordered his employees to unroll the fire extinguisher hose, but they found it rotted and useless.

The shirt factory occupied the top three floors of the ten–story Asch Building. The seventy employees who worked on the tenth floor escaped the fire by way of the staircases or climbed onto the roof, where students from New York University, located across the street, stretched ladders over to the Asch Building.

The 260 workers on the ninth floor had the worst luck of all. Although the eighth floor workers tried to warn them by telephone, the call did not reach them, and by the time they learned about the fire, their routes of escape were mostly blocked. Some managed to climb down the cables of the freight elevator. Others crammed into the narrow stairway. Still others climbed onto the single, inadequately constructed fire escape. But that spindly structure could not support the weight of hundreds of people, and it separated from the wall, falling to the ground and carrying many people with it.

To combat the disaster, the New York Fire Department sent thirty–five pieces of equipment, including a hook and ladder. The young women trapped on the ninth–floor window ledge watched in horror as the ladder, fully raised, stopped far below them, reaching only as far as the sixth floor.

Within minutes, the factory—a fire trap typical of the period's working conditions—was consumed by flame, killing 146 workers, mostly immigrant women. City officials set up a temporary morgue on 26th Street, and over the next few days streams of survivors filed through the building to identify the dead.

The Triangle Shirtwaist fire brought a public outcry for laws to regulate the safety of working conditions. The New York Factory Investigating Commission was formed to examine the working conditions in factories throughout the state. Their report introduced many new regulations. The fire had occurred during an era of progressive reform that was beginning to sweep the nation, as people decided that government had a responsibility to ensure that private industry protected the welfare of working people.

1. What does the passage mainly discuss?

(A) The causes of a fire in a shirt factory
(B) Working conditions in New York City
(C) Escaping from a fire in a shirt factory
(D) The events surrounding a tragic fire

2. The word "ignited" in line 4 could best be replaced by

(A) became wet
(B) caught fire
(C) exploded
(D) spread

3. According to the passage, the fire began

(A) on the ninth floor
(B) when a worker dropped a cigarette
(C) when some rags started burning
(D) when a pile of fabric rotted

4. Why does the author mention the fire extinguisher hose in lines 4–5?

   (A) To emphasize the unsafe working conditions
   (B) To show the manager's competence
   (C) To illustrate the factory's modern technology
   (D) To explain how the fire was eventually put out

5. How did many workers on the top floor manage to escape?

   (A) On the fire escape
   (B) On the elevator
   (C) On ladders
   (D) On ropes

6. The phrase "Still others" in line 14 refers to

   (A) the eighth floor workers
   (B) the ninth floor workers
   (C) the routes of escape
   (D) the people in the freight elevator

7. The word "spindly" in line 15 is closest in meaning to

   (A) frail
   (B) wooden
   (C) ugly
   (D) ancient

8. It can be inferred from paragraph 4 that

   (A) New York had a well–equipped fire department
   (B) fire fighters were able to rescue the women on the ninth floor
   (C) the women on the window ledge probably died
   (D) the women probably took the stairs down to the sixth floor

9. According to the passage, most of the workers who died in the fire

   (A) were university students
   (B) had only worked there a short time
   (C) worked on the tenth floor
   (D) were immigrant women

10. The phrase "beginning to sweep the nation" in line 29 means

    (A) changing politics
    (B) becoming more popular
    (C) investigating the government
    (D) starting a controversy

11. Which of the following could NOT be inferred from the passage?

    (A) The Triangle Shirtwaist fire influenced public opinion.
    (B) The Triangle Shirtwaist factory was rebuilt.
    (C) After the fire, new regulations improved working conditions in factories.
    (D) Disasters can lead to a demand for reform.

QUESTIONS 12–20

In the history of technology, computers and calculators were innovative developments. They are essentially different from all other machines because they have a memory. This memory stores instructions and information. In a calculator, the instructions are the various functions of arithmetic, which are permanently remembered by the machine and cannot be altered or added to. The information consists of the numbers keyed in.

An electronic pocket calculator can perform almost instant arithmetic. A calculator requires an input unit to feed in numbers, a processing unit to make the calculation, a memory unit, and an output unit to display the result. The calculator is powered by a small battery or by a panel of solar cells. Inside is a microchip that contains the memory and processing units and also controls the input unit, which is the keyboard, and the output unit, which is the display.

The input unit has keys for numbers and operations. Beneath the keys is a printed circuit board containing a set of contacts for each key. Pressing a key closes the contacts and sends a signal along a pair of lines in the circuit board to the processing unit, in which the binary code for that key is stored in the memory. The processing unit also sends the code to the display. Each key is connected by a different pair of lines to the processing unit, which repeatedly checks the lines to find out when a pair is linked by a key.

The memory unit stores the arithmetic instructions for the processing unit and holds the temporary results that occur during calculation. Storage cells in the memory unit hold the binary codes for the keys that have been pressed. The number codes, together with the operation code for the plus key, are held in temporary cells until the processing unit requires them.

When the equals key is pressed, it sends a signal to the processing unit. This takes the operation code—for example, addition—and the two numbers being held in the memory unit and performs the operation on the two numbers. A full adder does the addition, and the result goes to the decoder in the calculator's microchip. This code is then sent to the liquid crystal display unit, which shows the result, or output, of the calculation.

12. What is the main purpose of the passage?

(A) To summarize the history of technology
(B) To discuss innovative developments in technology
(C) To explain how a calculator works
(D) To compare computers and calculators with other machines

13. The word "innovative" in line 1 could best be replaced by

(A) revolutionary
(B) complicated
(C) important
(D) recent

14. What can be inferred about machines that are not calculators or computers?

    (A) They are older than computers.
    (B) They can not store information in a memory.
    (C) They have simple memory and processing units.
    (D) They are less expensive than computers.

15. In what part of the calculator are the processing and memory units?

    (A) The battery
    (B) The solar cells
    (C) The output unit
    (D) The microchip

16. The word "contacts" in line 14 is closest in meaning to

    (A) locations
    (B) connections
    (C) commands
    (D) codes

17. According to the passage, one function of the memory unit is

    (A) to send codes to the display unit
    (B) to control the keyboard
    (C) to store temporary results during calculation
    (D) to alter basic arithmetic instructions

18. The word "This" in line 25 refers to

    (A) the equals key
    (B) the plus key
    (C) the memory unit
    (D) the processing unit

19. Which of the following could NOT be said about calculators?

    (A) Calculators require a lot of instructions to operate quickly.
    (B) Calculators and computers are similar.
    (C) The calculator's "thinking" takes place in the processing and memory units.
    (D) Pressing a key activates a calculator.

20. Where in the passage does the author list all of the parts of a calculator?

    (A) Paragraph 2
    (B) Paragraph 3
    (C) Paragraph 4
    (D) Paragraph 5

QUESTIONS 21–31

Zora Neale Hurston was born in 1901 in Eatonville, Florida, the seventh child of tenant farmers. When Hurston was nine, her mother's death and her father's speedy remarriage ended her childhood and left her in charge of her own life. Her passion for education took her to Howard University in Washington, D. C., in 1918. While at Howard, Hurston began to write and to make contact with some of the leading figures of the Harlem Renaissance, a flowering of black literature and art in the New York of the 1920s. She eventually moved to New York, where she worked as secretary to the popular romantic writer Fannie Hurst and continued her studies at Barnard College.

A student of anthropology, Hurston devoted the five years following her graduation to the collection of rural black folklore in Haiti, the West Indies, and the American South. Her ear for the rhythms of speech and her daring in seeking initiation into many voodoo cults resulted in ethnographic studies such as *Mules and Men*, which conveyed the color and vigor of rural black culture.

Hurston married twice but found the demands of marriage incompatible with her career. She continued her fieldwork in the Caribbean but eventually followed her most cherished calling, that of fiction writer. *Their Eyes Were Watching God* (1937), a novel about a black woman finding happiness in simple farm life, is now her most famous book, although for thirty years after publication, it was largely unknown, unread, and dismissed by the male literary establishment. In this novel, Hurston gives us a heroic female character, Janie Crawford, who portrays autonomy, self–realization, and independence, while also being a romantic figure subordinate to a man. This novel reveals an African–American woman writer struggling with the problem of the hero as woman and the difficulties of giving a woman character such courage and power in 1937.

From the beginning of her career, Hurston was criticized for not writing fiction in the protest tradition. Her conservative views on race relations put her out of touch with the temper of the times. She argued that integration would undermine the values and vitality of African American culture. Hurston died in poverty and obscurity in 1960, and it was only afterward that later generations of black and white Americans were to rediscover and revere her celebrations of black culture and the black imagination.

21. What does the passage mainly discuss?

    (A) The novels of Zora Neale Hurston
    (B) The biography of an American writer
    (C) African American literature of the 1930s
    (D) Studies of rural black culture

22. What was the Harlem Renaissance?

    (A) A fashionable neighborhood in New York in the 1920s
    (B) A book of folklore by Zora Neale Hurston
    (C) A period of great accomplishments in art and literature
    (D) A famous garden in New York where artists and writers met

23. According to the passage, Hurston's early career focused on

    (A) writing romantic fiction
    (B) writing protest fiction
    (C) making speeches about her initiation into voodoo cults
    (D) studying black culture in the Caribbean and the American South

24. In lines 16–19, the author implies that

    (A) *Their Eyes Were Watching God* was a popular book in 1937
    (B) Hurston was not famous until she published her first novel
    (C) women writers faced discrimination during the mid–twentieth century
    (D) *Their Eyes Were Watching God* is an ethnographic study

25. The word "autonomy" in line 20 is closest in meaning to

    (A) freedom
    (B) selfishness
    (C) intelligence
    (D) physical strength

26. The word "writer" in line 22 refers to

    (A) Fannie Hurst
    (B) Zora Neale Hurston
    (C) Janie Crawford
    (D) a character in the novel

27. The phrase "out of touch" in line 25 means that

    (A) Hurston did not have much contact with other writers
    (B) Hurston ignored the topic of race relations
    (C) Hurston's opinions differed from those of most other people
    (D) Hurston's conservatism made many people angry

28. It can be concluded from lines 24–27 that

    (A) critics did not write about Hurston's protest writings
    (B) late in her career, Hurston began to value racial integration
    (C) Hurston believed black culture would be weakened by racial integration
    (D) Hurston believed integration would add vitality to black culture

29. The word "revere" in line 29 is closest in meaning to

    (A) reread
    (B) analyze
    (C) reconsider
    (D) honor

30. The author's attitude toward Hurston's writings could best be described as

    (A) respectful
    (B) romantic
    (C) critical
    (D) inconsistent

31. It can be inferred from the passage that

    (A) Hurston was well–known throughout her life
    (B) Hurston was an independent thinker throughout her life
    (C) Hurston's books are required reading in American high schools
    (D) Hurston's writings have largely been forgotten

TEST 2

QUESTIONS 32–42

The ancient Mayans played a game in which a ball was thrown through a basket with a vertical–facing hoop attached to a wall. This Mayan game is the only known precedent for the game later invented by Dr. James A. Naismith, an instructor at the YMCA's International Training School in Springfield, Massachusetts.

In the winter of 1891, Naismith was approached by the head of the YMCA's physical training staff, who had concluded that the drop in attendance at his clubs was the result of the dearth of competitive sports in winter. Naismith probably knew nothing about the Mayans, and he was less concerned with history than with the fact that the game he was to create had to be played indoors. All games used a ball, so he decided this one must also. Since it was to be played indoors, the players should not be allowed to run with the ball, as they did in football, or kick it, or knock other players down. Naismith subsequently invented an indoor sport using a round ball and two peach baskets, thus giving birth to the "all–American" game of basketball.

Naismith settled on a rounded goal, rather than uprights as in football, to keep players from charging at it. He placed the goal above their heads to keep defenses from clustering around it. He found some peach baskets, fastened them to the wall, threw in a soccer ball, and came up with half a dozen simple rules.

Because it was simple and easy to learn, basketball caught on quickly. Beginning with seven players per team, which grew to nine, and finally settled at five, the game was being administered by the Amateur Athletic Union. An exhibition game was played at the 1904 Olympics, and after several pioneering seasons played by Yale and Penn, the National Collegiate Athletic Association established its rules officially in 1908. Soon basketball was attracting crowds in high schools and colleges around the country.

By the 1930s, professional basketball was under way, and leagues began showcasing the sport's better players. Players sometimes created new maneuvers. Stanford University's Hank Lusetti invented the jump shot, and scores soared into the sixties and seventies. In later years, Wilt Chamberlain showed that the game could be played "above the rim," ushering in the age of the slam dunk later perfected by Kareem Abdul–Jabbar.

Today, basketball fans love fast–paced, quick–scoring games, but more importantly, they want basketball "stars."

32. Which of the following best describes the organization of the passage?

(A) A description
(B) An illustration
(C) A process
(D) A history

33. The word "precedent" in line 3 is closest in meaning to

(A) early example
(B) comparison
(C) descendant
(D) leader

34. The word "dearth" in line 7 could best be replaced by

    (A) boredom
    (B) elimination
    (C) scarcity
    (D) expense

35. According to the passage, why was basketball invented?

    (A) The National Collegiate Athletic Association established rules for a new game.
    (B) A YMCA leader needed a sport to attract people during winter.
    (C) James Naismith conducted research on the game played by the Mayans.
    (D) It was created for the 1904 Olympics.

36. What was one of Naismith's main considerations when he created the new game?

    (A) The game had to have seven players.
    (B) The game had to be fast–paced.
    (C) The players loved quick, high–scoring games.
    (D) The game had to be played indoors.

37. The phrase "this one" in line 10 refers to

    (A) the ball
    (B) the game
    (C) a basketball player
    (D) James Naismith

38. Why did Naismith place the goal high on the wall?

    (A) To protect players from injury
    (B) To encourage "above the rim" plays
    (C) To prevent players from blocking it
    (D) To give the players more exercise

39. The word "showcasing" in line 25 is closest in meaning to

    (A) displaying
    (B) training
    (C) hiring
    (D) encouraging

40. Which of the following could NOT be said about basketball?

    (A) Basketball has remained unchanged since its invention.
    (B) The popularity of basketball spread quickly after its invention.
    (C) Basketball is an "all–American" sport.
    (D) Basketball "stars" contribute to the game's popularity.

41. Where in the passage does the author compare basketball with another game?

    (A) Lines 5–7
    (B) Lines 10–11
    (C) Lines 16–17
    (D) Lines 18–20

42. What does the paragraph following the passage probably discuss?

    (A) The future of professional basketball
    (B) Games that are similar to basketball
    (C) New maneuvers and rules in basketball
    (D) Famous current basketball players

QUESTIONS 43–50

Birds have evolved many physical attributes that contribute to their flying ability. Wings are important, but adjustable tails, large hearts and light bones play critical roles.

To fly, birds, like airplanes, move air across their wings. Wings are designed so that air above the wing is forced to move faster than air below the wing. This creates higher pressure under the wings, called *lift*, which pushes the bird up. Different wing types evolved for different ways of flying. Prolonged flight requires long wings and an ability to soar. Other birds need superior maneuverability. Finches and sparrows have short, broad wings. Faster birds, like hawks, have built–in spoilers that reduce turbulence while flying. This allows a steeper angle of attack without stalling.

Tails have evolved for specialized use. The tail acts like a rudder helping birds steer. Birds brake by spreading out their tails as they land. This adaptation allows them to make sudden, controlled stops—an essential skill, since most birds need to land on individual branches or on prey.

Flight takes muscle strength. If body builders had wings, they still could not flap hard enough to leave the ground. Birds have large, specialized hearts that beat much faster than the human heart and provide the necessary oxygen to the muscles. The breast muscle accounts for 15 percent of the bird's body weight. On pigeons, it accounts for a third of their total body weight.

Birds carry no excess baggage; they have hollow feathers and hollow bones with struts inside to maintain strength, like cross beams in a bridge. Birds fly to find prey, escape predators, and attract mates—in other words, to survive.

43. What is the main idea of the passage?

    (A) Wings are the most important physical attribute of birds.
    (B) Different wing styles evolved for different types of flight.
    (C) Birds have many specialized features that aid in their survival.
    (D) Birds fly for many reasons.

44. According to the passage, what causes birds to rise when they start flying?

    (A) Long wings with hollow feathers
    (B) Higher air pressure below than above the wings
    (C) Spreading out their tails
    (D) Superior muscle strength

45. The word "prolonged" in line 6 could best be replaced by

    (A) high–altitude
    (B) specialized
    (C) predatory
    (D) sustained

46. The phrase "finches and sparrows" in line 7 refers to

    (A) wings
    (B) maneuvers
    (C) ways of flying
    (D) birds

Go on to the next page

47. According to the passage, what benefit comes from having built–in spoilers?

    (A) An ability to fly faster
    (B) A steeper angle of diving for prey
    (C) Prolonged flight
    (D) Superior maneuverability when climbing

48. It can be concluded from paragraph 3 that

    (A) accurate aim when landing is fundamental
    (B) the tail feathers must be very long
    (C) it is easier for a bird to stop suddenly than gradually
    (D) birds steer by spreading out their tails

49. What does the author imply about body builders having wings?

    (A) If they flapped their wings, they could fly a little.
    (B) If they had wings, their muscles would be strong enough for flight.
    (C) If they had wings, their hearts would still not be large enough for flight.
    (D) Their wings would total 15 percent of their body weight.

50. The word "struts" in line 20 is closest in meaning to

    (A) minerals
    (B) holes
    (C) muscles
    (D) supports

This is the end of Section 3.

This is the end of Test 2.

Answers to Practice Test 2 are on pages 668 to 670.
TOEFL score conversion tables are on page 15.

Section 1

1. A B C D
2. A B C D
3. A B C D
4. A B C D
5. A B C D
6. A B C D
7. A B C D
8. A B C D
9. A B C D
10. A B C D
11. A B C D
12. A B C D
13. A B C D
14. A B C D
15. A B C D
16. A B C D
17. A B C D
18. A B C D
19. A B C D
20. A B C D
21.

Current Term	Spring Term	Summer Term

22. A B C D
23. A B C D
24. A B C D
25. A B C D
26. A B C D
27. A B C D
28. A B C D
29.

1	
2	
3	
4	

30. A B C D
31. A B C D
32. A B C D
33. A B C D
34. A B C D
35. A B C D
36. A B C D
37. A B C D
38. A B C D
39.

1	
2	
3	
4	

40. A B C D
41. A B C D
42. A B C D
43. A B C D
44. A B C D
45.

Cure for scurvy	Naval stores	Root beer

Section 2

1. A B C D
2. A B C D
3. A B C D
4. A B C D
5. A B C D
6. A B C D
7. A B C D
8. A B C D
9. A B C D
10. A B C D
11. A B C D
12. A B C D
13. A B C D
14. A B C D
15. A B C D
16. A B C D
17. A B C D
18. A B C D
19. A B C D
20. A B C D
21. A B C D
22. A B C D
23. A B C D
24. A B C D
25. A B C D

Section 3

1. A B C D
2. A B C D
3. A B C D
4. A B C D
5. A B C D
6. A B C D
7. A B C D
8. A B C D
9. A B C D
10. A B C D
11. A B C D
12. A B C D
13. A B C D
14. A B C D
15. A B C D
16. A B C D
17. A B C D
18. A B C D
19. A B C D
20. A B C D
21. A B C D
22. A B C D
23. A B C D
24. A B C D
25. A B C D
26. A B C D
27. A B C D
28. A B C D
29. A B C D
30. A B C D
31. A B C D
32. A B C D
33. A B C D
34. A B C D
35. A B C D
36. A B C D
37. A B C D
38. A B C D
39. A B C D
40. A B C D
41. A B C D
42. A B C D
43. A B C D
44. A B C D
45. A B C D
46. A B C D
47. A B C D
48. A B C D
49. A B C D
50. A B C D

TEST 3

Time – approximately 35 minutes
(including the reading of the directions for each part)

 *(Start Tape)*

In the Listening section of the test, you will have an opportunity to demonstrate your ability to understand conversations and talks in English. Answer all the questions on the basis of what is stated or implied by the speakers you hear. Do not take notes or write during the test.

PART A

Directions: In Part A you will hear short conversations between two people. After each conversation, you will hear a question about the conversation. The conversations and questions will not be repeated. After you hear a question, read the four possible answers and choose the best answer.

Here is an example.

On the recording, you hear:

Sample Answer
(A) (B) ● (D)

In your book, you read:

(A) She doesn't want to buy a printer.
(B) She would rather buy something else.
(C) She doesn't want to pay a lot for a printer.
(D) She wants to shop at a better place.

You learn from the conversation that the woman hopes to find a printer at a better price. The best answer to the question, *What does the woman mean?* is (C), *She doesn't want to pay a lot for a printer*. Therefore, the correct choice is (C).

1. (A) Buy something to eat or drink.
   (B) Study in the student union building.
   (C) Walk the woman to the cafeteria.
   (D) Get a drink at the fountain.

2. (A) She didn't hear what the man said.
   (B) No explanation is required.
   (C) Money disappears without any reason.
   (D) She doesn't have to tell him why she spends money.

3. (A) The woman said something rude to Lucas.
   (B) The woman told Lucas how rude he was.
   (C) The woman did not speak to Lucas.
   (D) The woman is never angry with Lucas.

4. (A) Charlie stopped going to school.
   (B) Charlie failed all this courses last year.
   (C) Charlie visited her last year.
   (D) She visited Charlie last year.

5. (A) He could not find his way to the lecture hall.
   (B) He lost his notes from the lecture.
   (C) He could not hear the lecture.
   (D) He did not understand most of the lecture.

6. (A) She will miss Robert.
   (B) She didn't want to see Robert.
   (C) She saw Robert just before she left.
   (D) She arrived just after Robert left.

7. (A) She does not understand what the man told her.
   (B) She does not want to speak to the man.
   (C) She does not know Vincent.
   (D) She does not want to give Vincent a ride.

8. (A) Pedro will explain how to make pizza.
   (B) She is going to a show at the student center with Pedro.
   (C) Pedro is having an exhibition of his latest works of art.
   (D) Pedro works for peace.

9. (A) The woman was being rude to him.
   (B) The woman was a dental student.
   (C) The woman did not have any sisters.
   (D) The woman worked at the dental clinic.

10. (A) More than one person will pay for Mark's dinner.
    (B) They will take Mark to an inexpensive place for dinner.
    (C) They will order chips for dinner.
    (D) The man will pay for dinner with a credit card.

11. (A) It was bought at a computer shop.
    (B) It was taken to a repair shop by Jenny.
    (C) It was stolen by Jenny.
    (D) It was repaired by the woman.

12. (A) The man should stay home and finish his assignment.
    (B) The man doesn't need to worry about his report.
    (C) The man wrote a really fine report.
    (D) The man can probably turn his report in late.

13. (A) They are just like the man's binoculars.
    (B) They are less complex than the man's binoculars.
    (C) They don't work as well as the man's binoculars.
    (D) They are heavier than the man's binoculars.

14. (A) Give her something.
    (B) Clean his own garage.
    (C) Leave her to work alone.
    (D) Throw everything away.

15. (A) Get on Flight One–twenty–eight.
    (B) Go to the train station.
    (C) Make a telephone call.
    (D) Leave the airport in fifteen minutes.

This is the end of Part A.

Go on to the next page

        1

PART B

Directions: In this part of the test, you will hear several conversations and talks. Each conversation or talk is followed by several questions. The conversations, talks, and questions will not be repeated.

For most of the questions, you will read four possible answers and choose the best answer. Some questions will have special directions.

Here is an example.

On the recording, you hear:

Now listen to a sample question.

Sample Answer
(A) (B) ● (D)

In your book, you read:

(A) It helped scientists see the atmosphere more clearly.
(B) It made it easier for scientists to send messages.
(C) It made data collection from weather stations faster.
(D) It helped airplanes fly higher.

The best answer to the question, *How did the telegraph improve the science of meteorology?* is (C), *It made data collection from weather stations faster*. Therefore, the correct choice is (C).

Now listen to another sample question.

Sample Answer
■ [B] ■ [D]

In your book, you read:

Choose 2 answers.

[A] Forecast the weather.
[B] Study trends in rocket science.
[C] Solve air pollution problems.
[D] Study costs of building satellites.

The best two answers to the question, *What do meteorologists do today?* are [A], *Forecast the weather*, and [C], *Solve air pollution problems*. Therefore, the correct choices are [A] and [C].

Remember, you should <u>not</u> take notes during the test.

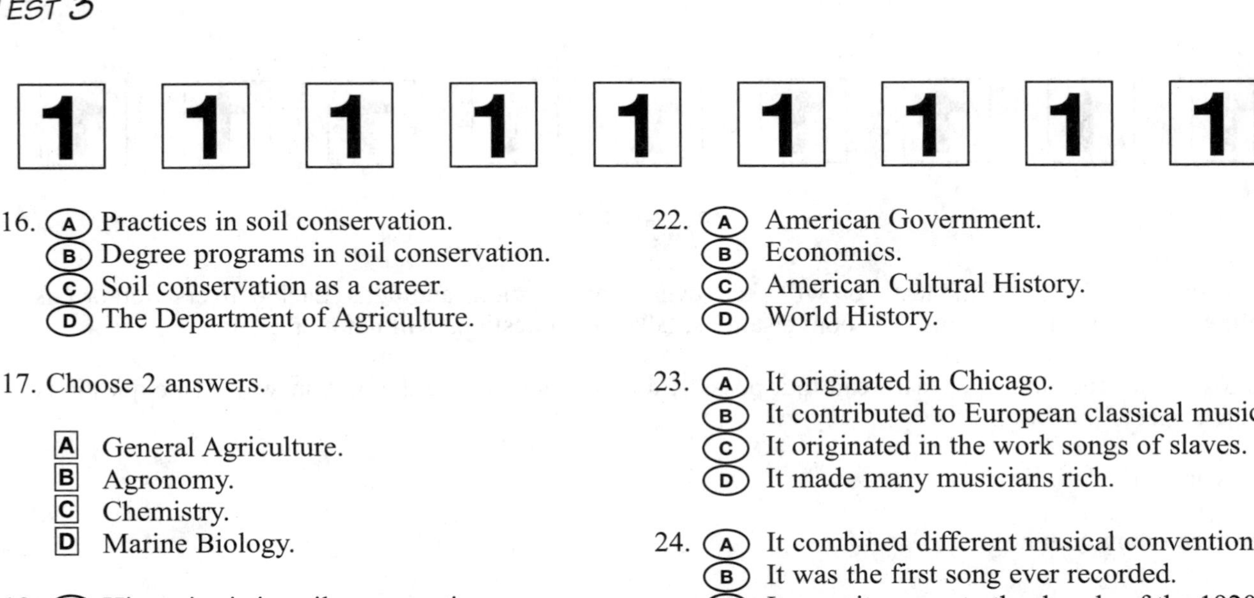

16. (A) Practices in soil conservation.
(B) Degree programs in soil conservation.
(C) Soil conservation as a career.
(D) The Department of Agriculture.

17. Choose 2 answers.

[A] General Agriculture.
[B] Agronomy.
[C] Chemistry.
[D] Marine Biology.

18. (A) His major is in soil conservation.
(B) His major is in wildlife biology.
(C) He wants to develop a program to combat erosion.
(D) He wants to work outdoors.

19. (A) He does not want to take any more math classes.
(B) He wants to take more than three courses in spring.
(C) He wants a third course that will fit his schedule.
(D) He would rather take Speech than English composition.

20. (A) Take Math in spring and Speech in summer.
(B) Drop his one o'clock Business Math course.
(C) Take Economics and Speech in spring semester.
(D) Take more than three courses in spring semester.

21. (A) Speech (B) Biology (C) English

Current Term	Spring Term	Summer Term

22. (A) American Government.
(B) Economics.
(C) American Cultural History.
(D) World History.

23. (A) It originated in Chicago.
(B) It contributed to European classical music.
(C) It originated in the work songs of slaves.
(D) It made many musicians rich.

24. (A) It combined different musical conventions.
(B) It was the first song ever recorded.
(C) It gave its name to the decade of the 1920s.
(D) It was never accepted by white musicians.

25. (A) Jazz blends folk music, blues, popular music, and classical music.
(B) The term "jazz" covers many different kinds of music.
(C) Jazz has been called "America's classical music."
(D) Jazz became less popular after World War One.

26. (A) Protest against the Tea Act by American colonists.
(B) The East India Company.
(C) Intolerable acts in Massachusetts.
(D) The role of the British Parliament in revolutions.

27. (A) It caused a decline in the quality of tea.
(B) It made tea less profitable for the colonists.
(C) It gave a private company a monopoly.
(D) It punished the colony of Massachusetts.

28. (A) A town meeting in Boston.
(B) An outrageous act of Parliament.
(C) A monopoly that controlled the tea trade.
(D) The destruction of tea in Boston Harbor.

Go on to the next page

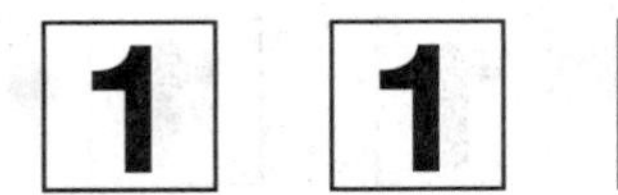

29. (A) Protesters called for a boycott of tea.
(B) Parliament passed the Intolerable Acts.
(C) The Boston Tea Party took place.
(D) Parliament passed the Tea Act.

1	
2	
3	
4	

30. (A) The British Parliament.
(B) Technology in colonial America.
(C) The American Revolution.
(D) The cultivation of tea.

31. (A) Travelers.
(B) Gardeners.
(C) Physicists.
(D) Electricians.

32. (A) They are dominant.
(B) They are lovely and colorful.
(C) They are drab and ugly.
(D) They are moist.

33. (A) Storing the food supply for the plant.
(B) Producing colorful flowers in the winter.
(C) Traveling around the world.
(D) Providing jobs in Japan, Turkey, and Russia.

34. Choose 2 answers.

[A] They are relatively inexpensive.
[B] They produce beautiful flowers.
[C] Some can stay in the ground during winter.
[D] They require a lot of care and attention.

35. (A) How to find interesting rock formations.
(B) The mineral content of rocks.
(C) Different ways to explore the plateau of Utah.
(D) Different shapes of rocks.

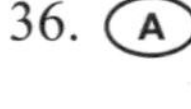

36. (A)  (C) 

(B)  (D) 

37. (A) Erosion causes the edge of its cap to weaken and fall.
(B) Erosion creates interesting and weird forms.
(C) Spires rise and split the mesa into several smaller pieces.
(D) Earthquakes cause the mesa to crack and fall.

38. (A)  (C) 

(B)  (D) 

TEST 3

Go on to the next page

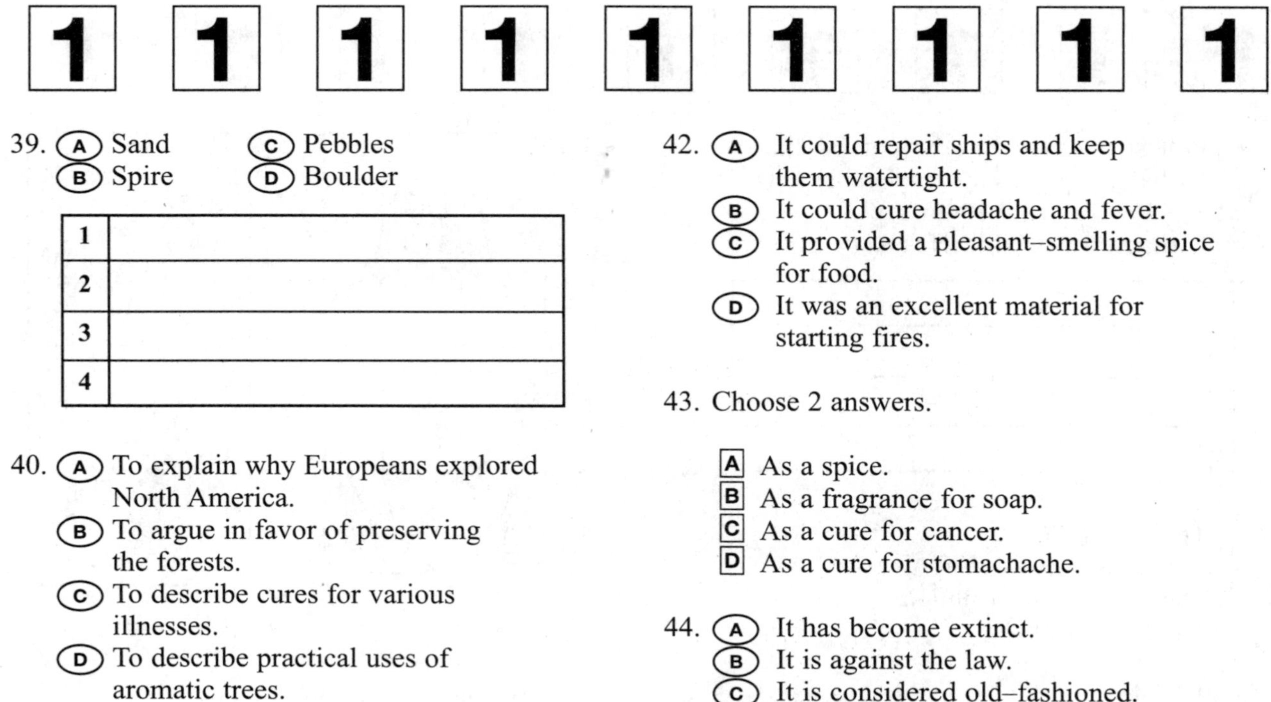

1 1 1 1 1 1 1 1 1

39. (A) Sand (B) Spire (C) Pebbles (D) Boulder

1	
2	
3	
4	

40. (A) To explain why Europeans explored North America.
(B) To argue in favor of preserving the forests.
(C) To describe cures for various illnesses.
(D) To describe practical uses of aromatic trees.

41. (A) The gentle sea breezes.
(B) The beautiful blossoms on the trees.
(C) The smell of the trees.
(D) The density of the forests.

42. (A) It could repair ships and keep them watertight.
(B) It could cure headache and fever.
(C) It provided a pleasant–smelling spice for food.
(D) It was an excellent material for starting fires.

43. Choose 2 answers.

[A] As a spice.
[B] As a fragrance for soap.
[C] As a cure for cancer.
[D] As a cure for stomachache.

44. (A) It has become extinct.
(B) It is against the law.
(C) It is considered old–fashioned.
(D) It has gone up in price.

45. (A) Pine (B) Sassafras (C) Arborvitae

Cure for scurvy	Naval stores	Root beer

(Stop Tape)

This is the end of Section 1.

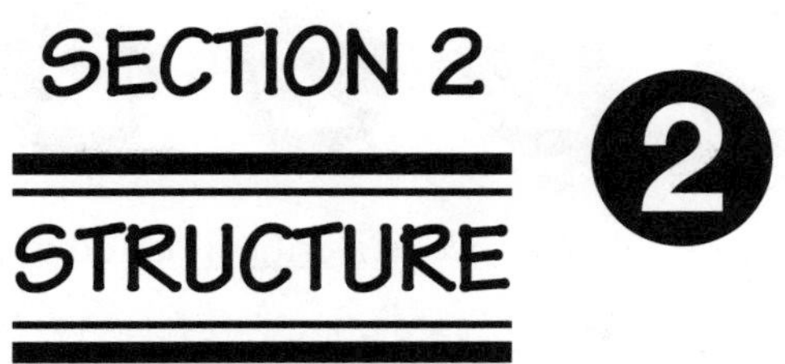

Time – 15 minutes

(including the reading of the directions)

Now set your clock for 15 minutes.

The Structure section of the test measures your ability to recognize language that is appropriate for standard written English. There are two types of questions in this section.

In the first type of question, there are incomplete sentences. Beneath each sentence, there are four words or phrases. Choose the one word or phrase that best completes the sentence.

Example I

Sample Answer

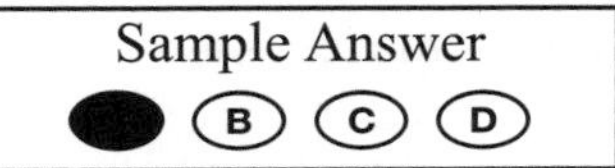

Although Chicago is not ------- New York, it has many attractions for visitors.

(A) as large as
(B) larger
(C) larger city
(D) the larger city is

The sentence should read, *Although Chicago is not as large as New York, it has many attractions for visitors*. Therefore, you should choose (A).

The second type of question has four underlined words or phrases. Choose the one underlined word or phrase that must be changed for the sentence to be correct.

Example II

Sample Answer

Guglielmo Marconi, <u>the son of</u> (A) a wealthy Italian landowner, <u>made</u> (B) the first <u>successfully</u> (C) transmission <u>using</u> (D) radio waves.

The sentence should read, *Guglielmo Marconi, the son of a wealthy Italian landowner, made the first successful transmission using radio waves*. Therefore, you should choose (C).

Now begin work on the questions.

TEST 3

2 2 2 2 2 2 2 2 2

1. Erik Erikson's writings suggest adolescence is a critical (A) period in psychological development because it (B) is no longer characterized (C) by the playful (D) of childhood.

2. Edith Wharton, which (A) many (B) people associate with (C) novels about (D) the upper classes in New York City, also wrote poetry and travel books.

3. All bears (A) are dangerous when accompanying (B) by cubs, surprised by the sudden appearance (C) of humans, or interrupted while feeding (D).

4. The principle of flotation, which explains how things float, was one of the many achievements of Archimedes, -------.

   (A) he was a great Sicilian scientist
   (B) the great Sicilian scientist
   (C) where he was a great scientist
   (D) by the great Sicilian scientist

5. ------- study of a nation's culture would be complete without examination of the informal uses of language.

   (A) Not
   (B) None
   (C) No
   (D) Nothing

6. ------- near the Pacific coast, with warmer temperatures in the south, cooler in the north.

   (A) Moist conditions prevail
   (B) Moist conditions prevailing
   (C) The prevailing moist conditions
   (D) Prevailed moist conditions

7. In the (A) hot climate of India, innumerable (B) caves serving (C) generations of religious men as (D) shrines and retreats.

8. Posters should be attractive and (A) eye–catching and can be put up (B) on bulletin boards and other (C) appropriate places in workplace (D).

9. Erich von Stroheim, whose (A) long acting (B) career spanned many movies and type of (C) roles, played a key role in *Grand Illusion*, a classic study of why men submit (D) to war.

Go on to the next page

10. <u>Besides</u> (A) providing important nutrients and minerals, green vegetables are also <u>high in fiber</u> (B), which has been <u>find</u> (C) to help <u>prevent</u> (D) colon cancer.

11. Psychologists who study human relationships have discovered that friendships appear to be central in early adulthood ------- middle age and beyond.

(A) as soon as
(B) as well as
(C) while
(D) in which

12. ------- discovered has often been a source of disagreement among historians.

(A) Fermentation was how they
(B) How was fermentation
(C) How fermentation that was
(D) How fermentation was

13. An artist ------- will do his best to express innocence and inexperience in the child's face.

(A) portraying a child
(B) which portrays a child
(C) he portrays a child
(D) portrayed a child

14. Many historians believe it was never ------- to practice genocide against the Native Americans.

(A) the government's official policy
(B) official the government's policy
(C) the government's policy official was
(D) been the government's official policy

15. The incidence of asthma <u>is raising</u> (A), but a new class of drugs <u>is fighting back</u> (B) with new approaches that <u>are letting</u> (C) patients <u>breathe</u> (D) more easily.

16. The mechanical parking meter and <u>other</u> (A) similar machines <u>involving</u> (B) lever action <u>has their</u> (C) origin in a <u>fascinating</u> (D) device invented by the Greek scientist Hero.

17. The index <u>of the</u> (A) *New York Times* <u>is valuable</u> (B) not only for finding articles but also <u>location of accounts</u> (C) of similar events <u>contained in other</u> (D) newspapers.

18. Bicycle messengers <u>have existed</u> (A) for a hundred years <u>in</u> (B) San Francisco and New York, and <u>its</u> (C) number in New York reached a peak of around <u>five thousand</u> (D) in the 1990s.

19. Capitalism is <u>traditionally</u> (A) defined <u>as an</u> (B) economic system <u>in which</u> (C) <u>mostly</u> (D) property is privately owned.

TEST 3

20. The success of a picture that shows mainly plants or non–living things ------- how the artist decides to present the subject.

(A) to depend
(B) depends on
(C) are depending on
(D) have depended

21. Under no circumstances ------- in areas where poisonous snakes are known to live.

(A) one should not climb rocks
(B) one should be climbing rocks
(C) should one climb rocks
(D) should be climbing rocks

22. ------- considered a ruthless predator, the grizzly eats mainly grass, berries, and roots.

(A) It is
(B) It can be
(C) Though
(D) For which

23. The older you are, the great (A) your risk for (B) coronary heart disease—the risk begins to rise (C) in men over forty and women over fifty (D).

24. Protein helps for form (A) muscles, blood, skin, hair and nails (B), and it can be (C) a source of (D) heat and energy.

25. In New England before the (A) 1820s, baseball was being (B) played on (C) village greens, with the players dividing to (D) two teams.

This is the end of Section 2.

Time – 60 minutes

(including the reading of the directions)

Now set your clock for 60 minutes.

In the Reading section of the test, you will read several passages. Each one is followed by a number of questions about it. For questions 1–50, you are to choose the <u>one</u> best answer, (A), (B), (C), or (D), to each question.

Answer all questions about the information in a passage on the basis of what is <u>stated</u> or <u>implied</u> in that passage.

Read the following passage:

The coffees of Central America profit from the area's steady climate and wealth of mountains. The mountains of the Pacific Cordillera, which stretch in a virtually unbroken line from Guatemala to the middle of Panama, provide the best combination of climate, altitude, and soil.

Guatemala was a relative latecomer to the commercial coffee business, exporting beans only since 1875. This mountainous country is ideally suited for coffee production, and its exports now surpass those of much larger countries. European merchants still take about 50 percent of the Guatemalan beans, with most of the best beans today being exported to England.

Example I It can be inferred from the passage that coffee grows well

(A) in the northern hemisphere
(B) in mountainous regions
(C) in small countries
(D) near the Pacific Ocean

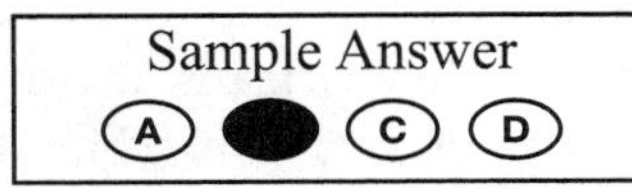

The passage implies that the mountainous regions of Central America are ideally suited for coffee production. The other answer choices cannot be inferred from the information given. Therefore, you should choose (B).

Example II The word "surpass" in line 7 is closest in meaning to

(A) include
(B) surround
(C) exceed
(D) limit

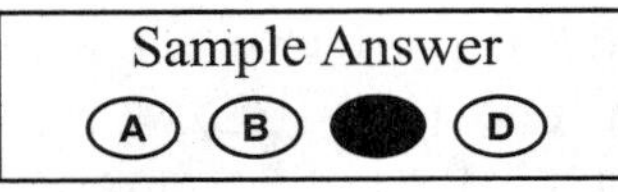

The word *surpass* in this passage means *exceed*. Therefore, you should choose (C).

Now begin work on the questions.

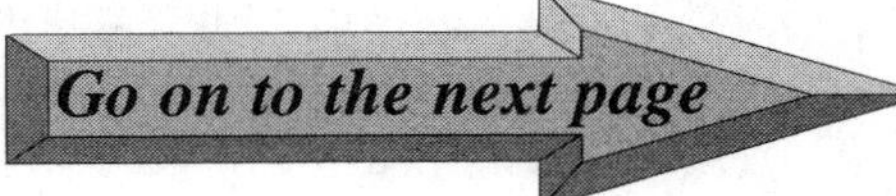

QUESTIONS 1–11

Tides are a natural phenomenon involving the alternating rise and fall in the large fluid bodies of the earth caused by the gravitational attraction of the sun and moon. The combination of these two variable forces produces the complex recurrent cycle of the tides. Tides may occur in both oceans and seas, to a limited extent in large lakes, the atmosphere, and, to a very minute degree, in the earth itself. The period between succeeding tides varies as the result of many factors.

The tide–generating force represents the difference between the centrifugal force produced by the revolution of the earth around the center–of–gravity of the earth–moon system and the gravitational attraction of the moon acting upon the earth's waters. Although the moon is only 238,852 miles from the earth, compared with the sun's much greater distance of 92,956,000 miles, the moon's closer distance outranks its much smaller mass, and thus the moon's tide–raising force is more than twice that of the sun.

The effect of the tide–generating forces of the moon and sun acting along the earth's surface tends to cause a maximum accumulation of the waters of the oceans at two opposite positions on the earth's surface and to withdraw compensating amounts of water from all points 90 degrees away from these tidal bulges. As the earth rotates, a sequence of two high tides, separated by two low tides, is produced each day.

Twice in each lunar month, when the sun, moon, and earth are directly aligned, with the moon between the earth and the sun (at new moon) or on the opposite side of the earth from the sun (at full moon), the sun and the moon exert their gravitational force in an additive fashion. Higher high tides and lower low tides are produced. These are called *spring* tides. At two positions 90 degrees in between, the gravitational forces of the moon and sun tend to counteract each other. These are called *neap* tides.

The actual range of tide in the waters of the open ocean may amount to only one or two feet. However, along the narrow channel of the Bay of Fundy in Nova Scotia, the difference between high and low tides may reach more than 43 feet under spring tide conditions. At New Orleans, the periodic rise and fall of the tide varies with the state of the Mississippi River, being about ten inches at low stage and zero at high. In every case, actual high or low tide can vary considerably from the average, due to weather conditions such as strong winds, abrupt barometric pressure changes, or prolonged periods of extreme high or low pressure.

1. The passage supports all of the following statements EXCEPT

   (A) high tides occur everywhere on Earth at the same time
   (B) tides are largely the result of the moon's gravity
   (C) tides occur in all of Earth's large bodies of water
   (D) the distance between high and low tides varies throughout the year

2. The phrase "these two variable forces" in line 3 refers to

   (A) high and low tides
   (B) the alternating rise and fall
   (C) the gravity of the moon and sun
   (D) oceans and seas

Go on to the next page

3. The word "recurrent" in line 3 is closest in meaning to

(A) simultaneous
(B) repeated
(C) interrupted
(D) resistant

4. According to the passage, tides occur

(A) in the earth's gravity
(B) in the earth's atmosphere
(C) in large rivers
(D) on the moon

5. The word "outranks" in line 11 is closest in meaning to

(A) multiplies
(B) reflects
(C) overcomes
(D) neutralizes

6. According to the passage, the moon

(A) has more mass than the sun
(B) is full at least twice a month
(C) is farther from the earth than the sun
(D) affects tides more than the sun

7. The word "bulges" in line 16 is closest in meaning to

(A) basins
(B) ridges
(C) swellings
(D) pools

8. At full moon, the position of the earth is

(A) between the moon and the sun
(B) on the opposite side of the moon from the sun
(C) on the opposite side of the sun from the moon
(D) determined by the sun

9. What is the main purpose of paragraph 5?

(A) To discuss the range of tide in the open ocean
(B) To show examples of actual high and low tides
(C) To explain the effect of weather on tides
(D) To explain tide–generating forces

10. It can be concluded from lines 28–31 that

(A) high and low tides remain stable throughout the year
(B) high tides can cause extreme weather conditions
(C) changes in atmospheric pressure influence tides
(D) low pressure causes lower tides

11. The following sentence can be added to paragraph 4 of the passage.

As a result, the range between high and low tides is reduced.

Where would it best fit in the paragraph? Choose **A**, **B**, **C**, or **D**.

Twice in each lunar month, when the sun, moon, and earth are directly aligned, with the moon between the earth and the sun (at new moon) or on the opposite side of the earth from the sun (at full moon), the sun and the moon exert their gravitational force in an additive fashion. **A** Higher high tides and lower low tides are produced. **B** These are called *spring* tides. **C** At two positions 90 degrees in between, the gravitational forces of the moon and sun tend to counteract each other. **D** These are called *neap* tides.

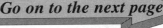

TEST 3

QUESTIONS 12–20

The invention of the Vitascope, a process for the screen projection of movies, represented the realization of an ancient dream. For centuries, people had been seeking a way to simulate objects and creatures in motion. In the seventeenth and eighteenth centuries, there were all sorts of optical entertainments, ranging from primitive shadow shows to elaborate panoramas and magic lantern shows. Then, in 1824, an English scientist, Peter Roget, discovered a principle that was to lead to a new wave of optical devices and eventually to moving pictures. The retina of our eye, Roget revealed, retains the impression of an object for a split second after that object has actually disappeared.

Throughout Europe, imaginative men were fascinated by this principle of persistence of vision. On discs and drums and cylinders they drew pictures of objects in various stages of motion. When these devices were spun, the drawings—viewed through apertures of one sort or another—appeared to be in continuous motion. Such primitive forms of animation could be viewed by only one person at a time, however, and the number of pictures that could be shown on a single disc was obviously quite limited.

The Vitascope debuted triumphantly on April 23, 1896, at Koster and Bial's Music Hall in New York. The first picture shown was the Leigh Sisters in their umbrella dance. The second picture showed the breaking of waves on the seashore. The *Dramatic Mirror* reported that some of the people in the front rows looked about to see where they could run, in case the waves came too close. The Vitascope was a big success, and inventor Thomas Edison was congratulated for his splendid contribution to the people's pleasure.

Edison had lent his name to the Vitascope venture, but in truth, the success of the Vitascope depended heavily on the work of another American inventor, Thomas Armat. Although all devices for the screen projection of movies were based on breakthroughs made some years earlier in Edison's laboratories, Edison himself had little interest in motion pictures and no faith at all in their future. He was far more interested in his phonograph than in photography, and he turned to the latter only when it seemed possible that pictures and sound might be produced on a single wax cylinder.

12. This passage mainly discusses the Vitascope in relation to

(A) the development of motion pictures
(B) a triumph of Thomas Edison
(C) a successful venture
(D) the scientific principles it utilized

13. The author mentions magic lantern shows as an example of

(A) the screen projection of movies
(B) a primitive shadow show
(C) an optical principle
(D) an early optical entertainment

14. The word "retains" in line 7 is closest in meaning to

(A) reverses
(B) holds
(C) impedes
(D) forgets

15. It can be inferred that Peter Roget's principle of persistence of vision

(A) preceded the magic lantern show
(B) was refuted by later discoveries
(C) was probably known by Thomas Armat
(D) caused moving objects to disappear

16. According to the passage, one limitation of early forms of animation was

(A) they were expensive to operate
(B) they required more than a single disc
(C) only one person could watch them
(D) their spinning made people feel ill

17. The author implies that Thomas Edison

(A) received credit that belonged to Thomas Armat
(B) was present when the Vitascope was introduced
(C) produced the first sound picture on a wax cylinder
(D) was interested in making motion pictures

18. The word "breakthroughs" in line 24 is closest in meaning to

(A) models
(B) cylinders
(C) advances
(D) mistakes

19. The word "latter" in line 27 refers to

(A) the future of motion pictures
(B) phonograph
(C) sound
(D) photography

20. The following sentence can be added to paragraph 3 of the passage.

Wave after wave came tumbling in, and as they struck, broke into tiny floods.

Where would it best fit in the paragraph? Choose **A**, **B**, **C**, or **D**.

The Vitascope debuted triumphantly on April 23, 1896, at Koster and Bial's Music Hall in New York. The first picture shown was the Leigh Sisters in their umbrella dance. **A** The second picture showed the breaking of waves on the seashore. **B** The *Dramatic Mirror* reported that some of the people in the front rows looked about to see where they could run, in case the waves came too close. **C** The Vitascope was a big success, and inventor Thomas Edison was congratulated for his splendid contribution to the people's pleasure. **D**

TEST 3

QUESTIONS 21–30

Two–lane highways, like the railways before them, seemed capable of making or breaking a community in the 1920s. The automobile was every American's idea of freedom, and the construction of hard–surface roads was one of the largest items of government expenditure, often at great cost to everything else, including education.

American car registrations rose from one million in 1913 to ten million in 1923. Automobile sales in the state of Michigan outnumbered those in Great Britain and Ireland combined. By 1927, Americans were driving some twenty–six million automobiles, one car for every five people in the country.

The 1920 U.S. Census revealed that for the first time in history more people lived in cities than on farms, and they were leaving the farm and reaching the city by automobile. The growth of roads and the automobile industry made cars the lifeblood of the petroleum industry and a major customer of the steel factories. Cars also caused expansions in outdoor recreation and tourism and related industries—service stations, roadside restaurants, and motels. After World War Two, the automobile industry reached new heights, and new roads led out of the city to the suburbs, where two–car families transported children to shopping malls and segregated schools.

In 1956 Congress passed the Interstate Highway Act, the peak of a half–century of frenzied road building at government expense and the largest public works program in history. The result was the Interstate Highway System, a network of federally subsidized highways connecting major urban centers. Two–hour commutes, traffic jams, polluted cities, and Disneyland became standard features of American life. Like almost everything else in the 1950s, the construction of interstate highways was justified as a national defense measure.

The predominance of private transportation was guaranteed by the federal government. Between 1945 and 1980, 75 percent of federal funds for transportation were spent on highways, while a scant one percent went to buses, trains, or subways. Even before the Interstate Highway system was built, the American bias was clear—which is why the United States has the world's best road system and nearly its worst public transit system.

21. What does the passage mainly discuss?

(A) The construction of roads in the 1920s
(B) The automobile as a ticket to freedom
(C) Expansion of the automobile industry
(D) The importance of roads in American life

22. The word "those" in line 6 refers to

(A) car sales
(B) car registrations
(C) car owners
(D) automobiles

23. It can be inferred from paragraph 2 that

(A) car registration became required in the early 1920s
(B) more cars were sold in Michigan than in any other state
(C) America's passion for cars grew in the 1920s
(D) most people in Ireland could not afford to buy cars

24. The word "frenzied" in line 18 is closest in meaning to

(A) intense
(B) systematic
(C) violent
(D) disorganized

25. According to the passage, which of the following was NOT true?

(A) There was one car for every five Americans in 1927.
(B) The automobile industry grew rapidly after World War Two.
(C) The government said interstate highways were good for national defense.
(D) More Americans lived in rural than in urban areas in 1920.

26. According to the passage, the growth in the number of automobiles influenced all of the following EXCEPT

(A) tourism
(B) the petroleum industry
(C) subway fares
(D) suburban shopping malls

27. The word "scant" in line 26 is closest in meaning to

(A) usually adequate
(B) barely sufficient
(C) more realistic
(D) necessary

28. It can be inferred from the passage that

(A) the federal government usually subsidizes major industries
(B) the government considers roads more expensive than education
(C) the United States needs a better public transit system
(D) Americans value private automobiles over public transportation

29. Where in the passage does the author show the impact of the automobile on the economy?

(A) Paragraph 2
(B) Paragraph 3
(C) Paragraph 4
(D) Paragraph 5

TEST 3

30. The following sentence can be added to paragraph 4 of the passage.

The interstate highways stretched American mobility to new distances.

Where would it best fit in the paragraph? Choose **A**, **B**, **C**, or **D**.

A In 1956 Congress passed the Interstate Highway Act, the peak of a half–century of frenzied road building at government expense and the largest public works program in history. **B** The result was the Interstate Highway System, a network of federally subsidized highways connecting major urban centers. **C** Two–hour commutes, traffic jams, polluted cities, and Disneyland became standard features of American life. Like almost everything else in the 1950s, the construction of interstate highways was justified as a national defense measure. **D**

QUESTIONS 31–39

Adults of different ages encounter different sets of life changes as they move through the normal role acquisitions and losses of adulthood. But at every age, high levels of life change, particularly those involving emotional losses, are linked to higher rates of physical illness and emotional disturbances such as depression. However, there are personal and social resources that may buffer the individual from the potential impact of stress. Such resources may be collectively called *resistance resources*. Central among these is the availability of social support.

Social support can be defined as the receipt of affirmation and aid from others. In many early studies, it was measured only by such objective criteria as marital status and frequency of reported contact with friends and relatives. Recent studies suggest that subjective perception of the adequacy of social support is more strongly related to well–being than are most objective measures. It is not the objective amount of contact with others that is important, but how that contact is interpreted. The tendency to perceive support as being "out there" is related to the security of our attachment to another. The more secure the attachment, the greater our sense of social support is likely to be.

It is clear that adults with adequate social support have a lower risk of disease, death, and depression than do adults with weaker social networks. The beneficial effect of social support is even clearer when an individual is under high stress. That is, the negative effect of stress on health and happiness is smaller for individuals with adequate social support than for those whose social support is weak. For example, one study showed that the link between severe life changes and depression in women was significantly weaker when the woman had a close, intimate relationship. The women who had no confidant were four times as likely to become severely depressed following a major life change than were those whose husband or boyfriend was an intimate confidant.

31. What does the passage mainly discuss?

(A) Studies of social contact and physical strength
(B) The effect of social support on health and happiness
(C) Resistance resources of the human body
(D) Role acquisitions and losses of adulthood

32. Which of the following sentences should NOT be included in a summary of the passage?

(A) Affirmation from friends can lessen the damage caused by stress.
(B) Recovery from depression is linked to an increase in the sense of security.
(C) Social support is a valuable kind of resistance resource.
(D) Major life changes can cause emotional as well as physical illness.

33. The word "buffer" in line 5 is closest in meaning to

(A) protect
(B) transform
(C) return
(D) discourage

34. It can be concluded from lines 10–13 that

(A) there have been several recent studies of social support
(B) objective measures of social support are more reliable than subjective ones
(C) frequency of social contact is a strong indicator of social support
(D) perceived quality of relationships is more important than quantity

35. The phrase "out there" in line 14 is closest in meaning to

(A) far away
(B) available
(C) within oneself
(D) insufficient

36. Which of the following would most likely be experienced by a person with a strong social network?

(A) Less stress on the job
(B) Lower risk of depression
(C) Higher rate of physical illness
(D) More casual relationships

37. The word "those" in line 20 refers to

(A) health and happiness
(B) life changes
(C) individuals
(D) networks

38. Where in the passage does the author discuss a specific study?

(A) Lines 1–4
(B) Lines 8–10
(C) Lines 16–18
(D) Lines 20–24

39. The following sentence can be added to paragraph 3 of the passage.

Similar links between social contact and physical hardiness have been found in studies done in Sweden and Japan.

Where would it best fit in the paragraph? Choose **A**, **B**, **C**, or **D**.

It is clear that adults with adequate social support have a lower risk of disease, death, and depression than do adults with weaker social networks. **A** The beneficial effect of social support is even clearer when an individual is under high stress. **B** That is, the negative effect of stress on health and happiness is smaller for individuals with adequate social support than for those whose social support is weak. For example, one study showed that the link between severe life changes and depression in women was significantly weaker when the woman had a close, intimate relationship. **C** The women who had no confidant were four times as likely to become severely depressed following a major life change than were those whose husband or boyfriend was an intimate confidant. **D**

TEST 3

QUESTIONS 40–50

The election of Andrew Jackson to the presidency in 1828 marked the political ascendancy of the "common man" in American politics. Whereas all previous presidents had been Easterners from well–to–do families, Jackson was a self–made man of modest wealth from the West. Born in 1767, Jackson fought in the American Revolution, in which many of his relatives died. Afterwards, he studied law and moved to the western district of North Carolina. When that territory became the state of Tennessee, Jackson was elected the state's first congressman. His name became a household word during the War of 1812, when, as a U. S. Army major general, he led troops against the Creek Indians in the Mississippi Territory and later defeated the British at New Orleans.

After his presidential inauguration, Jackson rode on horseback to the White House to attend a private party. Crowds of well–wishers suddenly appeared at the reception and nearly destroyed the White House as they tried to glimpse the new president. The common man had made a dramatic entrance onto the national political scene.

Jackson's two terms moved American society toward truer democracy. Many states abandoned property requirements for voting. Elected officials began to act more truly as representatives of the people than as their leaders. As president of the common man, Jackson waged a war against the Bank of the United States, vetoing the bill that rechartered the institution, declaring it a dangerous monopoly that profited the wealthy few.

Although he had built his reputation as an Indian fighter during the War of 1812, Jackson was not an Indian hater. He adopted what was at the time considered an enlightened solution to the Indian problem—removal. Many tribes submitted peacefully to being moved to the West. Others were marched by force to the Indian Territory, under brutal conditions, along what the Cherokees called the Trail of Tears.

One of Andrew Jackson's most enduring legacies was the Democratic Party, which under him became a highly organized political party. In opposition to the Democrats were the Whigs, a party that attracted supporters of the Bank of the United States and opposed the tyranny of the man it called "King Andrew." A less specific but more basic legacy is the populist philosophy of politics that still bears the name "Jacksonian Democracy."

40. The author's perspective toward Andrew Jackson could best be described as

(A) historical
(B) personal
(C) critical
(D) emotional

41. The phrase "became a household word" in line 7 means that

(A) a house style was called Jackson
(B) Jackson acquired fame
(C) Jackson was a popular boy's name
(D) people criticized Jackson

42. The author suggests that Jackson's election and inauguration

(A) brought a new style to the presidency
(B) destroyed the White House
(C) made a lot of the common people angry
(D) put a military man in the White House for the first time

43. The word "institution" in line 18 refers to

(A) the presidency of the United States
(B) American society
(C) democracy
(D) the Bank of the United States

44. According to the passage, why did Jackson oppose the Bank of the United States?

(A) It started a war.
(B) It opposed giving common people the right to vote.
(C) He thought it benefited only rich people.
(D) It opposed electing him "King Andrew."

45. According to the passage, Jackson's policy toward American Indians was

(A) forceful and cruel
(B) developed during the War of 1812
(C) considered progressive at the time
(D) considered his greatest achievement

46. The word "brutal" in line 24 is closest in meaning to

(A) harsh
(B) abrupt
(C) humane
(D) tearful

47. The word "legacy" in lines 25 and 29 is closest in meaning to

(A) trend
(B) philosophy
(C) contribution
(D) legend

48. Which of the following is NOT attributed to Andrew Jackson?

(A) The rise of the "common man"
(B) The Whig Party
(C) The Democratic Party
(D) Jacksonian Democracy

49. Which of the following could NOT be inferred about Andrew Jackson?

(A) He supported democratic reforms.
(B) He was president during a violent war.
(C) He inspired populist politics.
(D) He served his country throughout his life.

50. The following sentence can be added to the passage.

More and more people took advantage of their right to vote.

Where would it best fit in the passage? Choose **A**, **B**, **C**, or **D**.

After his presidential inauguration, Jackson rode on horseback to the White House to attend a private party. Crowds of well–wishers suddenly appeared at the reception and nearly destroyed the White House as they tried to glimpse the new president. **A** The common man had made a dramatic entrance onto the national political scene. **B**

Jackson's two terms moved American society toward truer democracy. Many states abandoned property requirements for voting. **C** Elected officials began to act more truly as representatives of the people than as their leaders. As president of the common man, Jackson waged a war against the Bank of the United States, vetoing the bill that rechartered the institution, declaring it a dangerous monopoly that profited the wealthy few. **D**

This is the end of Section 3.

SECTION 4

WRITING

Time – 30 minutes

In the Writing section of the TOEFL, you will have an opportunity to demonstrate your ability to write in English.

Read the following directions before going on to the next page.

- Read the essay question carefully.
- Think before you write. Making notes may help you to organize your essay.
- It is important to write only on the topic you are given.
- Check your work. Allow a few minutes before the time is up to read over your essay and make changes.
- You must stop writing at the end of 30 minutes. If you continue to write, it will be considered cheating.

Set your clock or watch for 30 minutes.

Now turn the page and begin.

Writing Topic

Directions: Read the topic below and then make any notes that will help you plan your response. Begin typing your response, or write your answer on a separate sheet of paper.

Some students like to work in groups with other students when doing assignments and projects. Others prefer to work independently. Which do you prefer?

Use specific reasons and examples to support your opinion.

This is the end of Test 3. 

Answers to Practice Test 1 are on pages 671 to 673.
TOEFL score conversion tables are on page 15.

TESTS

Section 1

1. A B C D
2. A B C D
3. A B C D
4. A B C D
5. A B C D
6. A B C D
7. A B C D
8. A B C D
9. A B C D
10. A B C D
11. A B C D
12. A B C D
13. A B C D
14. A B C D
15. A B C D
16. A B C D
17. A B C D
18. A B C D
19. A B C D
20. A B C D
21. A B C D
22. A B C D
23. A B C D
24. A B C D
25. A B C D
26. A B C D
27. A B C D
28. A B C D
29. A B C D
30. A B C D
31. A B C D
32. A B C D
33. A B C D
34. A B C D
35. A B C D
36. A B C D
37. A B C D
38. A B C D
39. A B C D
40. A B C D
41. A B C D
42. A B C D
43. A B C D
44. A B C D
45. A B C D
46. A B C D
47. A B C D
48. A B C D
49. A B C D
50. A B C D

Section 2

1. A B C D
2. A B C D
3. A B C D
4. A B C D
5. A B C D
6. A B C D
7. A B C D
8. A B C D
9. A B C D
10. A B C D
11. A B C D
12. A B C D
13. A B C D
14. A B C D
15. A B C D
16. A B C D
17. A B C D
18. A B C D
19. A B C D
20. A B C D
21. A B C D
22. A B C D
23. A B C D
24. A B C D
25. A B C D
26. A B C D
27. A B C D
28. A B C D
29. A B C D
30. A B C D
31. A B C D
32. A B C D
33. A B C D
34. A B C D
35. A B C D
36. A B C D
37. A B C D
38. A B C D
39. A B C D
40. A B C D

Section 3

1. A B C D
2. A B C D
3. A B C D
4. A B C D
5. A B C D
6. A B C D
7. A B C D
8. A B C D
9. A B C D
10. A B C D
11. A B C D
12. A B C D
13. A B C D
14. A B C D
15. A B C D
16. A B C D
17. A B C D
18. A B C D
19. A B C D
20. A B C D
21. A B C D
22. A B C D
23. A B C D
24. A B C D
25. A B C D
26. A B C D
27. A B C D
28. A B C D
29. A B C D
30. A B C D
31. A B C D
32. A B C D
33. A B C D
34. A B C D
35. A B C D
36. A B C D
37. A B C D
38. A B C D
39. A B C D
40. A B C D
41. A B C D
42. A B C D
43. A B C D
44. A B C D
45. A B C D
46. A B C D
47. A B C D
48. A B C D
49. A B C D
50. A B C D

TEST 4

TEST OF WRITTEN ENGLISH

Time — 30 minutes

In the Test of Written English (TWE), you will have an opportunity to demonstrate your ability to write in English.

Read the following directions before going on to the next page.

- Read the essay topic carefully.
- Think before you write. Making notes may help you to organize your essay.
- Write only on the topic you are given. Write clearly and precisely. How well you write is more important than how much you write, but to cover the topic adequately, you may want to write more than one paragraph.
- Check your work. Allow a few minutes before the time is up to read over your essay and make any changes.
- At the end of 30 minutes, stop writing and put your pencil down. If you continue to write, it will be considered cheating.

Set your clock or watch for 30 minutes.

Now turn the page and begin.

Writing Topic

Directions: Read the topic below and then make any notes that will help you plan your response. Begin writing your essay on a separate sheet of paper.

Do you agree or disagree with the following statement?

Progress makes us lazy.

Use specific reasons and examples to support your opinion.

SECTION 1

LISTENING 1

Time – approximately 35 minutes
(including the reading of the directions for each part)

 *(Start Tape)*

In the Listening Comprehension section of the test, you will have an opportunity to demonstrate your ability to understand conversations and talks in English. There are three parts to this section, with special directions for each part. Answer all the questions on the basis of what is stated or implied by the speakers you hear. Do not take notes or write in your book at any time.

PART A

Directions: In Part A you will hear short conversations between two people. After each conversation, you will hear a question about the conversation. The conversations and questions will not be repeated. After you hear a question, read the four possible answers in your book and choose the best answer. Then, on your answer sheet, find the number of the question and fill in the space that corresponds to the letter of the answer you have chosen.

Here is an example.

Sample Answer
(A) (B) ● (D)

On the recording, you hear:

In your book, you read:

(A) She doesn't want to buy a printer.
(B) She would rather buy something else.
(C) She doesn't want to pay a lot for a printer.
(D) She wants to shop at a better place.

You learn from the conversation that the woman hopes to find a printer at a better price. The best answer to the question, *What does the woman mean?* is (C), *She doesn't want to pay a lot for a printer*. Therefore, the correct choice is (C).

TEST 4

1. (A) He will cut the bread for the woman.
   (B) He doesn't have a better knife.
   (C) He is too full to eat another slice of bread.
   (D) The drawer is so full that he can't find a knife.

2. (A) He finds business boring.
   (B) He is slow at learning business.
   (C) Business is never slow.
   (D) Business was better before.

3. (A) Andrew has lived in town for a year.
   (B) Andrew and the speakers moved to town at the same time.
   (C) Andrew has lived in town longer than the speakers have.
   (D) Andrew moved to town a year after the speakers did.

4. (A) She likes to write letters.
   (B) She is looking for a new job.
   (C) She works in a bank.
   (D) She is a graphic artist.

5. (A) They will see an apartment they like.
   (B) They will move before spring.
   (C) They will look at several apartments.
   (D) They agree about what to do.

6. (A) She probably never wears sweatshirts.
   (B) She doesn't like to wear rings.
   (C) She might prefer to buy her own clothes.
   (D) She might not want a pair of earrings.

7. (A) Leave at ten o'clock.
   (B) Leave earlier than she had planned.
   (C) Take the train to avoid the traffic.
   (D) Not leave her tent at home.

8. (A) She is no longer involved with the student assembly.
   (B) The student assembly was active for a few months.
   (C) She quit the student assembly a few months ago.
   (D) She was never in the student assembly.

9. (A) She was trying to find a place to go rafting.
   (B) She was looking for someone to go rafting with.
   (C) She will cancel the rafting trip.
   (D) She wanted to go rafting.

10. (A) The man drank the juice.
    (B) The woman just sat on the counter.
    (C) The man broke the bottle.
    (D) The man crashed a few minutes ago.

11. (A) In a pet shop.
    (B) In a garden.
    (C) In a kitchen.
    (D) In an orchard.

12. (A) She doesn't know where to catch the bus.
    (B) She is going to take a bus to downtown.
    (C) She would rather walk than take the bus.
    (D) She is offering to help the man.

13. (A) His brother has changed his major to botany.
    (B) His brother is looking for a new job.
    (C) His brother makes promises he can not keep.
    (D) His brother has vowed to improve himself.

14. (A) The book is easy to understand.
    (B) The book has a lot of information.
    (C) The explanations in the book are clear.
    (D) The book is a little outdated.

15. (A) Her supervisor likes to have a good time.
    (B) Her supervisor jokes about her too much.
    (C) Her supervisor doesn't work very hard.
    (D) Her supervisor doesn't appreciate her work.

16. (A) The swimming pool looks nice.
    (B) The water is too cold to swim in.
    (C) The water in the lake is not clean.
    (D) He wants to swim somewhere else.

17. (A) Buy a salad.
    (B) Not buy anything at the deli.
    (C) Make a salad.
    (D) Not go to the potluck.

18. (A) The woman should make a decision about what to do.
    (B) The woman should already know what he wants to do.
    (C) The woman should ask someone else.
    (D) The woman should not ask questions.

19. (A) Ask the woman where to get the bus to Worthington Heights.
    (B) Wait for the next bus to Worthington Heights.
    (C) Walk to a bus stop around the corner.
    (D) Apologize for taking the wrong bus.

20. (A) She didn't see the sign for the class.
    (B) She didn't want to take Business Law.
    (C) She regrets not taking Business Law.
    (D) She is sorry she didn't see Professor Lux.

21. (A) In a bank.
    (B) At Tony's office.
    (C) At an apartment building.
    (D) In a restaurant.

22. (A) He is grateful for the help he receives.
    (B) He is sorry because he can not help the woman.
    (C) He thinks the woman is not helpful.
    (D) He wants to check out of town.

23. (A) His job makes him sleepy.
    (B) He is enthusiastic about the new job.
    (C) He has to consider the job offer carefully.
    (D) He expects to have a hectic day tomorrow.

24. (A) There is no possibility for him to date Linda.
    (B) He had to stand in line a long time to see Linda.
    (C) Linda's friends would probably like to meet him.
    (D) He is confused about the date.

25. (A) He finished the page layout.
    (B) Maureen finished the page layout.
    (C) Maureen got tired.
    (D) He lay down after finishing the page.

26. (A) Yoko did not have a sister.
    (B) Yoko's sister would not visit her.
    (C) Yoko would visit her sister.
    (D) Yoko and her sister would go away for the weekend.

27. (A) It was stuffy in the meeting room.
    (B) Ms. Phillips was angry with the men.
    (C) Ms. Phillips seemed very interested.
    (D) Ms. Phillips screamed during the meeting.

28. (A) Help the man with his printer.
    (B) Take a book home.
    (C) Print something at work.
    (D) Take control of the printer.

29. (A) She has a paper due tomorrow.
    (B) She is not in the speakers' presence.
    (C) She will type the man's paper.
    (D) She will probably not see the man today.

30. (A) He is usually a competent boss.
    (B) He is unkind when there is a problem.
    (C) He took them to the wrong room.
    (D) He made a bad decision.

This is the end of Part A.

PART B

Directions: In this part of the test, you will hear longer conversations. After each conversation, you will hear several questions. The conversations and questions will not be repeated.

After you hear a question, read the four possible answers in your book and choose the best answer. Then, on your answer sheet, find the number of the question and fill in the space that corresponds to the letter of the answer you have chosen.

Remember, you should not take notes or write in your book.

31. (A) An exam.
(B) A storm.
(C) An illness.
(D) A movie.

32. (A) She is cold and wet.
(B) She will miss class that day.
(C) She will not be able to turn in her assignment on time.
(D) She feels sleepy because the man is talking too much.

33. (A) Stop worrying about her grade.
(B) Talk to her instructor.
(C) Buy another cup of coffee.
(D) Listen to the rain.

34. (A) Strength.
(B) Crashing.
(C) A rare event.
(D) Electricity.

35. (A) In a video game room.
(B) In a bathroom.
(C) In a dry cleaning shop.
(D) In a self–service laundry.

36. (A) She gives him change for a dollar.
(B) She puts detergent in the machine.
(C) She tells him where he can buy detergent.
(D) She shows him how to use the dryers.

37. (A) How much it costs to use the machine.
(B) Where to do washing on campus.
(C) When to add detergent.
(D) Where to get quarters.

This is the end of Part B.

        1

PART C

Directions: In this part of the test, you will hear several talks. After each talk, you will hear some questions. The talks and questions will not be repeated.

After you hear a question, read the four possible answers in your book and choose the best answer. Then, on your answer sheet, find the number of the question and fill in the space that corresponds to the letter of the answer you have chosen.

Here is an example.

On the recording, you hear:

Now listen to a sample question.

In your book, you read:

(A) It helped scientists see the atmosphere more clearly.
(B) It made it easier for scientists to send messages.
(C) It made data collection from weather stations faster.
(D) It helped airplanes fly higher.

The best answer to the question, *How did the telegraph improve the science of meteorology?* is (C), *It made data collection from weather stations faster*. Therefore, the correct choice is (C).

Now listen to another sample question.

In your book, you read:

(A) Study trends in the earth's climate.
(B) Forecast the weather.
(C) Solve air pollution problems.
(D) Study costs of building satellites.

Sample Answer
(A) (B) (C)

The best answer to the question, *What is not mentioned as something meteorologists do today?* is (D), *Study costs of building satellites*. Therefore, the correct choice is (D).

Remember, you should not take notes or write in your book.

38. (A) Individual counseling.
    (B) Advice on class selection.
    (C) Financial assistance.
    (D) Help with career planning.

39. (A) In the Admissions Office.
    (B) On the job board.
    (C) In the workshop on stress management.
    (D) From other resources in the community.

40. (A) Evenings and weekends.
    (B) Afternoons.
    (C) At the beginning of the quarter.
    (D) By appointment.

41. (A) Speak to another group of students.
    (B) Help the students select classes.
    (C) Provide job search information.
    (D) Answer the students' questions.

42. (A) Her psychology professor observed her.
    (B) She watched complex societies in Samoa.
    (C) She observed her two younger sisters.
    (D) She joined an anthropology club at college.

43. (A) She became interested in anthropology on a trip to Samoa.
    (B) She was fascinated by an anthropology professor.
    (C) She was from a family of anthropologists.
    (D) Her father made her study anthropology.

44. (A) Intellectual courage and pioneers in technology.
    (B) Samoan political institutions.
    (C) Child rearing, cultural change, and race relations.
    (D) The psychology of American children.

45. (A) She made major contributions to the field of anthropology.
    (B) She was a pioneer of the drug culture.
    (C) She was conservative in her approach to her work.
    (D) She did most of her fieldwork in Philadelphia.

46. (A) To give advice about finding an apartment.
    (B) To provide tips for lowering energy costs.
    (C) To make suggestions for decorating a room.
    (D) To sell thermostats and refrigerators.

47. (A) Light bulbs.
    (B) Dishwashers.
    (C) Heating systems.
    (D) Air conditioners.

48. (A) The sun will make walls appear lighter.
    (B) The sun will fade draperies and blinds.
    (C) During the winter, the sun doesn't shine.
    (D) Using the sun's energy can lower costs.

49. (A) Showers use half as much hot water as baths.
    (B) The speaker prefers taking showers.
    (C) This is an advertisement for showers.
    (D) Showers use less hot water than dishwashers.

50. (A) Buy enough light bulbs for a whole year.
    (B) Replace light bulbs every month.
    (C) Use a large bulb instead of many small ones.
    (D) Turn on the lights when you leave a room.

(Stop Tape)

This is the end of Section 1.

SECTION 2

STRUCTURE AND WRITTEN EXPRESSION

Time – 25 minutes

(including the reading of the directions)

Now set your clock for 25 minutes.

The Structure and Written Expression section is designed to measure your ability to recognize language that is appropriate for standard written English. There are two types of questions in this section, with special directions for each type.

STRUCTURE

Directions: Questions 1–15 are incomplete sentences. Beneath each sentence you will see four words or phrases, marked (A), (B), (C), and (D). Choose the one word or phrase that best completes the sentence. Then, on your answer sheet, find the number of the question and fill in the space that corresponds to the letter of the answer you have chosen.

Example

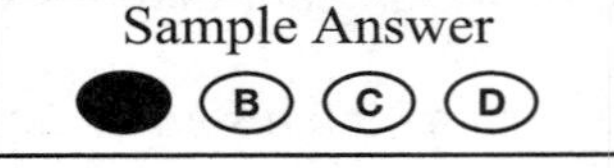

Although Chicago is not ------- New York, it has many attractions for visitors.

(A) as large as
(B) larger
(C) larger city
(D) the larger city is

The sentence should read, *Although Chicago is not as large as New York, it has many attractions for visitors*. Therefore, you should choose (A).

Now begin work on the questions.

1. By displaying its multi–colored tail feathers, ------- female of its species.

   (A) how the peacock attracts
   (B) the peacock attracts the
   (C) attracting the peacock
   (D) being attracted by the

2. Seismology, ------- science of earth quakes, has contributed to our understanding of how the Earth is continuously changing.

   (A) it is the
   (B) which the
   (C) the
   (D) is the

3. The scent glands of the skunk help ------- this unusual animal from its enemies.

   (A) protecting
   (B) being protected
   (C) protect
   (D) protection

4. Critics of the American educational system claim that schools ------- character traits and basic values necessary for leadership.

   (A) apparently fail to teach
   (B) they fail apparently to teach
   (C) to fail apparently to teach
   (D) apparently failing to teach

5. The hummingbird is among ------- in the world.

   (A) a tiny and more colorful bird
   (B) as tiny as the most colorful bird
   (C) tiniest and colorful most the birds
   (D) the tiniest and most colorful birds

6. Snow blindness is impaired vision caused by sunlight ------- from snow surfaces.

   (A) that was reflecting
   (B) the reflection
   (C) reflected
   (D) is reflected

7. ------- a lever is just as important as the amount of effort you apply to it.

   (A) Where you move
   (B) Which you move
   (C) Having been moved
   (D) For moving

8. Writing home in 1711, the governor of Quebec stated that war with the Iroquois ------- at all costs.

   (A) should avoid
   (B) should have avoided
   (C) should be avoiding
   (D) should be avoided

9. Even though a computer is capable of storing ------- in memory devices, one of its main tasks is to print words and results on paper.

   (A) a lot of informations
   (B) masses of information
   (C) an information
   (D) many information

10. Because ------- long tail, the cat possesses an excellent sense of balance.

   (A) with a
   (B) having a
   (C) its
   (D) of its

11. The electrical field produced by a single wire is not very strong, so to increase it, ------- into a coil.

   (A) the wire is wound
   (B) the wire wound
   (C) to wind the wire
   (D) by winding the wire

Go on to the next page

12. Biologist Wynne Edwards believed that animals often did things to help the group -------.

    (A) they lived
    (B) that they lived
    (C) which they lived
    (D) in which they lived

13. In 1870, -------, John D. Rockefeller and others created the Standard Oil Company.

    (A) that oil prices fluctuated
    (B) despite fluctuating oil prices
    (C) but the oil prices fluctuated
    (D) oil prices were fluctuating

14. Although the weather there is not ------- to have a year–round tourist season, British Columbia is popular as a summer destination.

    (A) warm enough
    (B) warmly enough
    (C) enough warm
    (D) as warm enough as

15. A robot's movements can be directed with much precision, enabling it to repeat actions exactly and ------- boring or dangerous tasks.

    (A) for relieving humans
    (B) to relieve humans of
    (C) which relieves humans of
    (D) therefore, it has relieved humans of

Go on to the next page

WRITTEN EXPRESSION

Directions: In questions 16–40 each sentence has four underlined words or phrases. The four underlined parts of the sentence are marked (A), (B), (C), and (D). Identify the one underlined word or phrase that must be changed in order for the sentence to be correct. Then, on your answer sheet, find the number of the question and fill in the space that corresponds to the letter of the answer you have chosen.

Example

Sample Answer

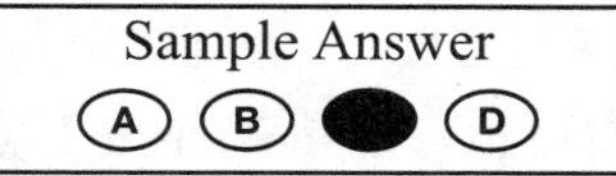

Guglielmo Marconi, the son of (A) a wealthy Italian landowner, made (B) the first successfully (C) transmission using (D) radio waves.

The sentence should read, *Guglielmo Marconi, the son of a wealthy Italian landowner, made the first successful transmission using radio waves*. Therefore, you should choose (C).

Now begin work on the questions.

TEST 4

2 2 2 2 2 2 2 2 2

16. The mallard duck, widespread throughout the Northern Hemisphere, it is recognizable because of its
A B C D
brilliant green head and white collar.

17. In the United States, the number of deads due to heart attack and related conditions fell by 25 percent
A B C
between 1985 and 1990.
D

18. The synthetic functions of the human brain, such as imagining, visualizing, and dreaming, is largely
A B C
associated with the right half of the brain.
D

19. Less women than men are attracted to careers in the physical sciences, even though there are now more
A B C
women in the sciences than ever before.
D

20. While some pirate ships deprived early American colonists of many needed supplies, others smuggled
A B C
in goods, subverted British taxes, and help in the Revolutionary War.
D

21. Flannery O'Connor, which wrote novels and stories about the American South, was best known for
A B C
her portrayals of social and religious fanaticism.
D

22. Plato believed that if we rely on our senses, we would not be able to acquire true knowledge of
A B C
the universe.
D

23. Good research involves much more merely gathering information; it is essentially a thinking activity.
A B C D

24. The main boyhood interesting of psychologist Jean Piaget was observation of animals in their
A B C D
natural habitat.

25. There are a number of reason why population is concentrated in temperate regions, but the wide
A B
variety and availability of animal and vegetable life may be the most important.
C D

Go on to the next page

2 2 2 2 2 2 2 2 2

26. After the development of the steam engine by James Watt in the late 1700s, the Industrial Revolution
A B C
progressed forward rapidly.
D

27. Economist Adam Smith published his book *The Wealth of Nations* in 1776, a year also notably for the
A B C D
Declaration of Independence.

28. Birds whose coloring blends in with the leaves do not seen as easily as those with brighter feathers.
A B C D

29. An American expects his or her conversation partner to respond a statement immediately, but
A B C
in some other cultures, people leave silence between each statement.
D

30. A cartel is an association of producers in a given industry whose purpose is restrict competition.
A B C D

31. In the early grades, the academic performance of girls are equal to that of boys in math and almost
A B C D
equal to boys in science.

32. Thunderstorms occur most frequently during the warm months of the year, except along the Pacific
A B
Coast, where they formation in connection with winter storms.
C D

33. A recent survey showed that teachers considered giving children computers more important than
A B
to reduce class size, improving teachers' salaries, and expanding hours of instruction.
C D

34. In Western societies, an individual's status social is typically defined in terms of education, income,
A B C D
or occupation.

35. All parts of a plant contribute to the human food supply, but perhaps no is as important as the seed,
A B C
from which all our cereals are derived.
D

36. Gospel music has its origin in the ornate vocal style of African American spirituals and of the
A B C D
impassioned speaking of Baptist preachers.

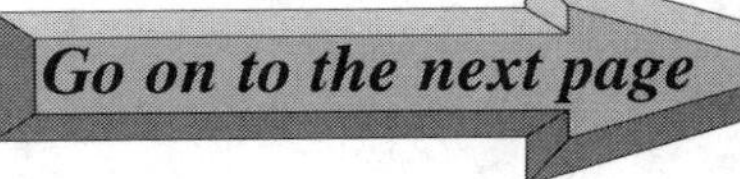

2 2 2 2 2 2 2 2 2

37. A microchip, or integrate circuit, is an electric component containing many tiny circuits that can
A B C
process or store electric signals.
D

38. It was while the Civil War that Abraham Lincoln issued the Emancipation Proclamation, a document
A B
that changed the course of the war.
C D

39. Marriage is associated not only with an increase in life satisfaction and also with a shift toward
A B C
more traditional gender roles.
D

40. Rarely the Park Service allows dogs to visit the national parks, except those kept on a leash at all times.
A B C D

This is the end of Section 2.

SECTION 3

READING COMPREHENSION

Time – 55 minutes

(including the reading of the directions)

Now set your clock for 55 minutes.

In the Reading Comprehension section of the test, you will read several passages. Each one is followed by a number of questions about it. For questions 1–50, you are to choose the one best answer, (A), (B), (C), or (D), to each question.

Answer all questions about the information in a passage on the basis of what is stated or implied in that passage.

Read the following passage:

The coffees of Central America profit from the area's steady climate and wealth of mountains. The mountains of the Pacific Cordillera, which stretch in a virtually unbroken line from Guatemala to the middle of Panama, provide the best combination of climate, altitude, and soil.

Guatemala was a relative latecomer to the commercial coffee business, exporting beans only since 1875. This mountainous country is ideally suited for coffee production, and its exports now surpass those of much larger countries. European merchants still take about 50 percent of the Guatemalan beans, with most of the best beans today being exported to England.

Example I It can be inferred from the passage that coffee grows well

(A) in the northern hemisphere
(B) in mountainous regions
(C) in small countries
(D) near the Pacific Ocean

Sample Answer
(A) ● (C) (D)

The passage implies that the mountainous regions of Central America are ideally suited for coffee production. The other answer choices cannot be inferred from the information given. Therefore, you should choose (B).

Example II The word "surpass" in line 7 is closest in meaning to

(A) include
(B) surround
(C) exceed
(D) limit

Sample Answer
(A) (B) ● (D)

The word *surpass* in this passage means *exceed*. Therefore, you should choose (C).

Now begin work on the questions.

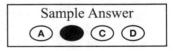

QUESTIONS 1–10

If we believe that clothing has to do with covering the body, and costume with the choice of a particular form of garment for a particular use, then we can say that clothing depends primarily on such physical conditions as climate, health, and textile manufacture, whereas costume reflects social factors such as religious beliefs, aesthetics, personal status, and the wish to be distinguished from or to emulate our fellows.

The ancient Greeks and the Chinese believed that we first covered our bodies for some physical reason such as protecting ourselves from the elements. Ethnologists and psychologists have invoked psychological reasons: modesty in the case of the ancients, and taboo, magical influence and the desire to please for the moderns.

In early history, costume must have fulfilled a function beyond that of simple utility, perhaps through some magical significance, investing primitive man with the attributes of other creatures. Ornaments identified the wearer with animals, gods, heroes or other men. This identification remains symbolic in more sophisticated societies. We should bear in mind that the theater has its distant origins in sacred performances, and in all periods children at play have worn disguises, so as to adapt gradually to adult life.

Costume helped inspire fear or impose authority. For a chieftain, costume embodied attributes expressing his power, while a warrior's costume enhanced his physical superiority and suggested he was superhuman. In more recent times, professional or administrative costume has been devised to distinguish the wearer and to express personal or delegated authority; this purpose is seen clearly in the judge's robes and the police officer's uniform. Costume denotes power, and since power is usually equated with wealth, costume came to be an expression of social caste and material prosperity. Military uniform denotes rank and is intended to intimidate, to protect the body and to express membership in a group. At the bottom of the scale, there are such compulsory costumes as the convict's uniform. Finally, costume can possess a religious significance that combines various elements: an actual or symbolic identification with a god, the desire to express this in earthly life, and the desire to enhance the wearer's position of respect.

1. The passage mainly discusses costume in terms of its

   (A) physical protection
   (B) religious significance
   (C) social function
   (D) beauty and attractiveness

2. What is the purpose of paragraph 1?

   (A) To describe the uses of costume
   (B) To contrast costume with clothing
   (C) To trace the origins of costume
   (D) To point out that clothing developed before costume

3. Psychological reasons for wearing garments include

   (A) protection from cold
   (B) availability of materials
   (C) prevention of illness
   (D) wishing to give pleasure

Go on to the next page

4. The word "investing" in line 11 could best be replaced by

   (A) endowing
   (B) creating
   (C) wrapping
   (D) frightening

5. The word "Ornaments" in line 12 is closest in meaning to

   (A) garments
   (B) representations
   (C) details
   (D) decorations

6. It can be inferred from paragraph 3 that

   (A) the function of costume has become very sophisticated
   (B) children like to identify with other creatures by wearing costumes
   (C) primitive people wore clothes only for sacred performances
   (D) costume no longer fulfills a function beyond simple utility

7. Why does the author mention the police officer's uniform in line 21?

   (A) To illustrate the aesthetic function of costume
   (B) To identify the wearer with a hero
   (C) To suggest that police are superhuman
   (D) To show how costume signifies authority

8. The word "denotes" in lines 21 and 23 is closest in meaning to

   (A) disguises
   (B) describes
   (C) indicates
   (D) denigrates

9. The word "scale" in line 24 refers to

   (A) symbolic identification
   (B) military rank
   (C) social position
   (D) the balance

10. Which of the following would most likely NOT be reflected in a person's costume, as it is defined in the passage?

   (A) Having a heart condition
   (B) Playing in a baseball game
   (C) Working in a hospital
   (D) Participating in a religious ceremony

TEST 4

QUESTIONS 11–18

Psychologists who study information processing have identified and described several memory structures that clarify how our memory works. They include the sensory register, short–term memory, and long–term memory. Each structure varies as to how much information it can hold and for how long.

A description of how humans process information typically begins with environmental stimuli. Our sense receptors are constantly stimulated by visual, auditory, tactile, olfactory, and gustatory stimuli. These experiences are initially recorded in the *sensory register*, so named because information is thought to be encoded there in the same form in which it was perceived. The purpose of the sensory register is to hold information one to three seconds. Information not recognized or otherwise selected by us disappears from the system. The sensory register can hold about twelve items of information at a time. Typists make extensive use of the sensory register in order to remember words just long enough to get them typed. If no further processing takes place, a typist's ability to recall that information later is minimal. Similarly, most of us have had the experience of reading an entire page of text, only to discover when we got to the bottom of the page we couldn't say anything about it except that we had indeed "read" every word.

Once information has been recognized as meaningful, it is sent to *short–term memory*. In this case, short–term is approximately 20 seconds. While this may seem surprising, it can easily be demonstrated. If you were asked to dial an unfamiliar phone number, received a busy signal, and were then distracted by something or someone else for 15 to 20 seconds, chances are you would have forgotten the number at that point. Short–term memory is often referred to as "working" memory.

Most cognitive psychologists believe that the storage capacity of *long–term memory* is unlimited and contains a permanent record of everything an individual has learned and experienced. Information is encoded there to enhance its meaningfulness and organization so that it can be easily retrieved when necessary.

11. What is the purpose of the passage?

    (A) To describe the sensory register
    (B) To compare short–term and long–term memory
    (C) To explain why we sometimes forget information
    (D) To explain how our memory processes information

12. The word "They" in line 2 refers to

    (A) psychologists
    (B) information
    (C) memory structures
    (D) environmental stimuli

13. The word "stimuli" in lines 6 and 7 is closest in meaning to

    (A) objects we consider attractive
    (B) things that help us to later recall what happened
    (C) objects or events that activate our memory
    (D) situations in which we experience emotion

Go on to the next page

14. According to the passage, typists are unable to recall information they type if

    (A) they do not recognize it as meaningful enough to remember
    (B) they are distracted by something or someone
    (C) they have too much work to be able to process it all
    (D) they are tired

15. According to the passage, which type of information is sent to short–term memory?

    (A) Information we need for three seconds or less
    (B) Information that is relevant to us
    (C) Information that surprises us
    (D) Environmental stimuli we do not perceive

16. It can be inferred that short–term memory is called "working" memory because

    (A) we use it extensively when we are working
    (B) it is very difficult to use effectively
    (C) it holds information we are working on at a given moment
    (D) we must work hard to retrieve information from it

17. The word "capacity" in line 24 is closest in meaning to

    (A) quality
    (B) location
    (C) time
    (D) size

18. Which of the following would we most easily retrieve from long–term memory?

    (A) The birth date of our child
    (B) A wrong telephone number we dialed
    (C) The face of a stranger on the street
    (D) Voices from the television in the background

TEST 4

QUESTIONS 19–30

Adolphus Busch came to prominence during the Gilded Age, a time when barons of industry left an indelible mark on the United States. And in the brewing industry, Adolphus Busch was the undisputed baron. Adolphus Busch was born in Germany and emigrated to the U.S. at the age of eighteen. He worked first as a clerk on the Mississippi river front and then decided to sell brewery supplies. One of his customers was Eberhard Anheuser, owner of a struggling brewery. Busch married Anheuser's daughter Lilly in 1861, and three years later he was operating his father–in–law's brewery. Within five years, he more than doubled the brewery's output, from 6,000 to 16,000 barrels. Deciding that brewing was his calling, he became a full business partner in 1869.

Busch decided business would be even better if the market could be expanded. Production was limited by the amount of available storage space. In the days before refrigeration, brewers relied on caves to store their beer. Anheuser's caves were completely full. Expanding the market would also mean shipping beer to other locations, which took time and resulted in spoilage for the highly perishable product. That is why brewing had always been a local business. Busch saw the problems of finite cave space and long–distance shipping simply as obstacles to be overcome.

So, with little more than conviction to sustain him, he set out to overcome these hurdles. He traveled to Europe to learn about the latest advances in brewing. While there, he heard about pasteurization, a process that kept beverages from spoiling. At the 1876 World's Fair in Philadelphia, he got his first glimpse of the newly invented refrigerated railcar. He ordered five. And so, through persistence and experimentation, Busch found a way around spoilage and storage constraints, revolutionizing an entire industry. He was the first to introduce pasteurization and to use artificial refrigeration, ultimately shipping his beer all over the country in a fleet of 850 refrigerated railcars.

Busch was a flamboyant promoter, recognizing early on that making the world's best beers did no good unless people knew about them. His marketing acumen became legendary in the brewing industry. He was a dapper man who wore a white carnation and, in place of calling cards, gave his business associates pocket knives featuring his portrait.

By the time he died in 1913 at the age of seventy–four, Busch had amassed tremendous wealth and attained great position. Few people at that time could dispute the accomplishments of this self–made man.

19. It can be inferred from lines 1–3 that the Gilded Age

(A) caused war among prominent barons
(B) was a time of industrial activity
(C) was marked by economic hardship and ruin
(D) occurred in the early twentieth century

20. While operating his father–in–law's brewery, Adolphus Busch

(A) increased its production of beer
(B) sold brewery supplies
(C) struggled with his customers
(D) emigrated from Germany

Go on to the next page

21. Busch realized that expanding the market for beer would involve

    (A) completely filling the brewery's caves with beer
    (B) increasing the amount of local business
    (C) shipping the beer to nearby cities
    (D) both increasing output and shipping long distances

22. The phrase "the highly perishable product" in line 14 refers to

    (A) the market
    (B) business
    (C) beer
    (D) cave space

23. The word "conviction" in line 17 is closest in meaning to

    (A) success
    (B) intellect
    (C) faith
    (D) despair

24. The phrase "these hurdles" in lines 17–18 refers to

    (A) caves and beer
    (B) shipping and storage
    (C) production and experimentation
    (D) new developments in brewing

25. According to the passage, Busch solved the problem of spoilage by

    (A) using pasteurization and refrigeration
    (B) inventing a refrigerated railcar
    (C) increasing the amount of cave space
    (D) marketing his beer all over the country

26. With what topic is paragraph 3 mainly concerned?

    (A) The latest advances in brewing
    (B) Busch's travels in Europe
    (C) Spoilage and storage problems
    (D) Busch's innovations

27. The word "acumen" in line 26 is closest in meaning to

    (A) department
    (B) skill
    (C) equipment
    (D) predictions

28. It can be concluded from paragraph 4 that

    (A) people didn't recognize the quality of the beer they drank
    (B) people probably thought Busch was dishonest
    (C) Busch thought selling beer was not always good for society
    (D) Busch understood the importance of advertising

29. The word "amassed" in line 29 is closest in meaning to

    (A) controlled
    (B) overcome
    (C) accumulated
    (D) invested

30. The author's attitude toward Adolphus Busch could best be described as

    (A) complimentary
    (B) sarcastic
    (C) persuasive
    (D) neutral

QUESTIONS 31–41

The initial contact between American Indians and European settlers usually involved trade, whereby Indians acquired tools and firearms and the Europeans obtained furs. These initial events usually pitted Indian tribes against each other as they competed for the European trade and for the lands containing fur–producing animals. When the furs had been depleted, the Europeans began a campaign to obtain the lands the Indians occupied. The Indians often formed confederations and alliances to fight back the Europeans; however, the Indians' involvement in the white people's wars usually disrupted these confederations. Indians resisted the attempts by the whites to displace them. They fought defensive wars such as the Black Hawk War in 1832. Indian uprisings also occurred, like the Sioux uprising in the 1860s.

Despite the resistance of the Indians, the Europeans were destined to win the conflict. After Indian resistance was crushed, whites legitimized the taking of Indian lands by proposing treaties, frequently offering gifts to Indian chiefs to get them to sign the treaties. Once an Indian group had signed a treaty, the whites proceeded to remove them from their land. Often the Indians were forced west of the Mississippi into Indian Territory——land the whites considered uninhabitable. If only a few Indians remained after the conquest, they were often absorbed by local tribes or forced onto reservations.

No aspect of American history is more poignant than the accounts of the forced removal of Indians across the continent. As white settlers migrated farther west, Indians were forced to sign new treaties giving up the lands earlier treaties had promised them. Some Indian tribes, realizing the futility of resistance, accepted their fate and moved westward without force. The Winnebagos, who offered little resistance, were shifted from place to place between 1829 and 1866. About half of them perished during their perpetual sojourn. Other tribes, however, bitterly resisted. The Seminoles signed a treaty in 1832 but violently resisted removal. Hostilities broke out in 1835 and continued for seven years. The United States government lost nearly 1,500 men and spent over $50 million in its attempts to crush Seminole resistance. Most of the Seminoles were eventually forced to Indian Territory. However, several hundred remained in the Florida Everglades, where their descendants live today.

31. What does the passage mainly discuss?

    (A) Trade between American Indians and European settlers
    (B) The diverse cultures of American Indian tribes
    (C) Conflict between American Indians and Europeans over land
    (D) Violation of treaties by white settlers

32. What does the author mean by the phrase "pitted Indian tribes against each other" in line 3?

    (A) Trade with Europeans took place in public market pits.
    (B) Contact with Europeans caused opposition among Indian tribes.
    (C) Athletic events were popular with the Indian tribes.
    (D) Indians used European–made firearms in their shooting competitions.

33. The word "legitimized" in line 12 is closest in meaning to

    (A) encouraged
    (B) coordinated
    (C) wrote to support
    (D) justified

34. It can be concluded from lines 11–14 that

    (A) Europeans had greater military, political, and economic power than Indians
    (B) Europeans showed great speaking skill in their treaty proposals
    (C) Indian chiefs were easily bribed by economic offerings
    (D) both Indians and Europeans wanted to end the conflict by signing treaties

35. The author makes the point that Indian Territory was

    (A) considered undesirable by European settlers
    (B) in the western part of Mississippi
    (C) where a few Indians remained
    (D) where several battles between Indians and whites took place

36. According to the passage, which of the following did NOT happen?

    (A) Indian tribes formed alliances with other tribes.
    (B) Treaties allowed Indians to live where they wanted.
    (C) Indians were forced to live on reservations.
    (D) Indians rebelled against European settlers.

37. In lines 19–21, the author implies that

    (A) many accounts of Indian removal are not true
    (B) Indian treaties and removal were minor events in American history
    (C) Indian removal was a shameful tragedy of American history
    (D) new treaties promised Indians more land than had the earlier treaties

38. The word "futility" in line 22 could best be replaced by

    (A) expense
    (B) importance
    (C) advantage
    (D) uselessness

39. The word "perpetual" in line 25 is closest in meaning to

    (A) long–lasting
    (B) seasonal
    (C) victorious
    (D) gradual

40. According to the passage, which tribe did NOT fight against removal?

    (A) Sioux
    (B) Black Hawk
    (C) Winnebago
    (D) Seminole

41. Where in the passage does the author mention the costs associated with removal?

    (A) Lines 9–10
    (B) Lines 12–14
    (C) Lines 19–20
    (D) Lines 27–28

QUESTIONS 42–50

All North American canids have a doglike appearance characterized by a lithe body, long muzzle, erect ears, slender legs, and bushy tail. Most are social animals: wolves travel in packs with a clearly established hierarchy of dominance, coyotes hunt in smaller groups or pairs, and only foxes are solitary. As a result of years of persecution, most canids have decreased greatly. The coyote, however, has thrived alongside man, increasing in both numbers and range.

Its common name comes from *coyotl*, the term used by Mexico's Nahuatl Indians, and its scientific name, *canis latrans*, means "barking dog." The coyote's vocalizations are varied, but the most distinctive are given at dusk, dawn, or during the night and consist of a series of barks followed by a prolonged howl and ending with short, sharp yaps. This call keeps the band alert to the locations of its members. One voice usually prompts others to join in, resulting in the familiar chorus heard at night throughout the West.

The best runner among the canids, the coyote is able to leap fourteen feet and cruise normally at 25–30 miles per hour. It is a strong swimmer and does not hesitate to enter water after prey. In feeding, the coyote is an opportunist, eating rabbits, mice, ground squirrels, birds, toads, snakes, insects, many kinds of fruit, and carrion. To catch larger prey, such as deer or antelope, the coyote may team up with one or two others, running in relays to tire prey or waiting in ambush while others chase prey toward it. Often a badger serves as involuntary supplier of smaller prey: while it digs for rodents at one end of their burrow, the coyote waits for any that may emerge from an escape hole at the other end.

Predators of the coyote once included the grizzly and black bears, mountain lions, and wolves, but with their declining populations these are no longer a threat. Man is the major enemy, especially since coyote pelts have become increasingly valuable, but the coyote population continues to increase, despite efforts at trapping and poisoning.

42. The passage supports all of the following statements EXCEPT

(A) the coyote is a threat to humans
(B) the coyote is an efficient and athletic predator
(C) the coyote is a social animal
(D) the coyote lives successfully near human populations

43. The author mentions wolves and foxes as examples of

(A) prey
(B) canids
(C) rodents
(D) coyotes

44. The word "band" in line 11 is closest in meaning to

(A) leader
(B) choir
(C) group
(D) orchestra

45. The word "opportunist" in line 15 means one who

(A) is very narrow in his interests
(B) likes to team up with others
(C) always has good luck
(D) takes advantage of circumstances

Go on to the next page

46. The word "any" in line 20 refers to

    (A) coyotes
    (B) badgers
    (C) rodents
    (D) burrows

47. Which animal sometimes unknowingly helps the coyote catch food?

    (A) Wolf
    (B) Black bear
    (C) Deer
    (D) Badger

48. The author makes the point that the chief predator of the coyote is

    (A) the human being
    (B) the wolf
    (C) the mountain lion
    (D) the grizzly bear

49. It can be inferred from the passage that

    (A) the coyote is an endangered species
    (B) the coyote is an intelligent and adaptable creature
    (C) people will continue to fear the coyote
    (D) efforts to trap and poison the coyote will increase

50. Where in the passage does the author describe coyote communication?

    (A) Paragraph 1
    (B) Paragraph 2
    (C) Paragraph 3
    (D) Paragraph 4

This is the end of Section 3.

This is the end of Test 4.

TEST 4

Answers to Practice Test 1 are on pages 675 to 677.
TOEFL score conversion tables are on page 15.

ANSWER KEY

QUICK DIAGNOSTIC TEST (p. 17)

Section 1 – Listening

1.	C	1.5
2.	A	1.1, 1.3
3.	D	1.4, 1.5
4.	D	1.2, 1.8, 1.9
5.	B	1.6
6.	D	1.3, 1.8
7.	C	1.1
8.	A	1.2
9.	C	1.1, 1.3, 1.4, 1.7
10.	C	1.14
11.	B–C–A	1.12, 1.13
12.	A	1.15
13.	B	1.10
14.	B, C	1.11
15.	D	1.11
16.	D	1.14
17.	B	1.10
18.	A	1.14
19.	C–A–B	1.12
20.	C	1.15

Section 2 – Structure

1.	C	2.8, 2.1, 2.5	(A) 2.9; (B) 2.9; (D) 2.5, 2.8
2.	A	2.13, 2.8	(B) 2.13; (C) 2.21; (D) 2.5, 2.8
3.	D	2.6, 2.11	(A) 2.6; (B) 2.5, 2.8 (C) 2.9
4.	B	2.2, 2.4	(A) 2.4; (C) 2.16; (D) 2.1, 2.8
5.	A	2.1, 2.17	(B) 2.16; (C) 2.9; (D) 2.16, 2.17
6.	B	2.3	Correction: *much of*. (A) 2.18; (C) 2.7, 2.25; (D) 2.21
7.	C	2.22	Correction: *unlike*. (A) 2.20; (B) 2.25; (D) 2.1, 2.22
8.	D	2.14	Correction: *is short*. (A) 2.21; (B) 2.10; (C) 2.3
9.	C	2.18	Correction: *only*. (A) 2.4; (B) 2.3, 2.4; (D) 2.4, 2.21
10.	D	2.22, 2.25	Correction: *development*. (A) 2.5; (B) 2.21; (C) 2.15
11.	B	2.10, 2.21	Correction: *process in which*. (A) 2.1; (C) 2.21; (D) 2.17
12.	C	2.19	Correction: *as to*. (A) 2.21, 2.17; (B) 2.5; (D) 2.4, 2.19
13.	D	2.7	Correction: *to activate*. (A) 2.3; (B) 2.6, 2.10; (C) 2.22
14.	B	2.15	Correction: *its*. (A) 2.11, 2.23; (C) 2.11; (D) 2.19
15.	B	2.6, 2.12	Correction: *is thrown*. (A) 2.12; (C) 2.21; (D) 2.10

Section 3 – Reading

1.	B	3.1
2.	C	3.3
3.	A	3.5, 3.6
4.	B	3.4
5.	D	3.4
6.	C	3.2
7.	D	3.5
8.	A	3.1, 3.6
9.	D	3.2
10.	C	3.3
11.	B	3.4
12.	B	3.5
13.	A	3.2
14.	D	3.6
15.	C	3.7

SECTION 1 – LISTENING

EXERCISE 1.1.A (p. 38)

1. C A synonym for *arid* is *dry*.
2. D *Refugees* are people who flee their homes to find safety in another place.
3. D A *glimpse* is a quick look.
4. A A synonym for *whirling* is *spinning*.
5. A If something is *bothersome*, it is annoying or irritating.
6. B A synonym for *jeopardy* is *danger*.

EXERCISE 1.1.B (p. 38)

1. A If something is *run–down*, it is worn out or in bad condition.
2. C The man was *lost* during the speech, which means he was confused.
3. C In this context, *pouring* refers to something outside the window; *pouring* means *raining heavily*.
4. B In this context, *hot* means *angry*; Jim and Mr. Kendrick argued angrily.
5. D In this context, *dreams of* means *would like to have*.
6. B In this context, *complimentary* means *praising*.

EXERCISE 1.1.C (p. 39)

1. C A synonym for *fortunate* is *lucky*.
2. A A synonym for *timid* is *shy*.
3. A A synonym for *horrible* is *terrible*.
4. B *Founded* means *established*; the school was established in 1789, which makes it more than two centuries old.
5. D *Inspect* means *examine carefully*.
6. C In this context, *strike* means *beat* or *hit*.

EXERCISE 1.2.A (p. 44)

1. C *Rub (someone) the wrong way* = annoy or irritate.
2. B *On cloud nine* = extremely happy or overjoyed.
3. C *Over and over* = repeatedly.
4. A *Tell apart* = distinguish between.
5. B *See eye to eye* = agree.
6. D *Keep (one's) fingers crossed* = wish or hope for the best. In this context, the man is wishing her good luck on the test.
7. C *Beat around the bush* = avoid the point.
8. C *Close call* = narrow escape.

EXERCISE 1.2.B (p. 45)

1. B *Take turns* = alternate.
2. B *Out of sorts* = irritable or in a bad mood. *Get on (someone's) case* = criticize.
3. C *Lend a hand* = help or assist. *Lumber* is wood for building.
4. B *Hit the nail on the head* = do something exactly right.
5. D *Lose touch* = fail to keep in contact or communication.
6. C *Take it easy* = avoid hard work or worry.
7. A *Night owl* = person who stays up late. *Early bird* = person who gets up early.
8. D *Kill time* = waste time.

EXERCISE 1.2.C (p. 45)

1. A *See through* = detect dishonesty or artificiality.
2. B *Put up with* = tolerate. *Go crazy* = become anxious or impatient.
3. B *Get rid of* = throw away.
4. D *Get out of* = avoid work, trouble, or problems.
5. C *Pass away* = die.
6. C *Take advantage of* = use an opportunity.
7. A *Fed up with* = disgusted by.
8. D *Bring (someone) up* = take care of, raise, or educate a child.
9. D *Show up* = appear.
10. A *Pick on* = bother or tease.

EXERCISE 1.2.D (p. 46)

1. C *Jump at* = accept eagerly.
2. D *Take after (someone)* = resemble.
3. A *Find out* = discover.
4. C *Put off* = delay.
5. B *Run out of* = have no more remaining.
6. B *Steer clear* = stay away from; go around to avoid.
7. B *Look forward to* = anticipate with pleasure.
8. D *Take out* = take someone on a date; *cheer up* = make happy.
9. C *Cut it out* = stop doing something.
10. D *Check out* = investigate.

EXERCISE 1.2.E (p. 47)

1. B *Out of the question* = not to be considered.
2. C *That goes without saying* = It is too obvious to mention.
3. A *No kidding!* is an expression of surprise or pleasure.
4. C *Not on your life* = certainly not; not for any reason.
5. D *You must be kidding* = It's impossible; It's not true; I don't believe you.

QUIZ 1 (p. 49)

1. A *Run out of* = have no more remaining. (1.2)
2. B A synonym for *comprehend* is *understand*. (1.1)
3. D *Take your time* = go slowly; act in an unhurried way. (1.2)
4. C A synonym for *kind* is *considerate*. (1.1)
5. A *Get along with* = exist satisfactorily with; not fight with. (1.2)
6. D The man agrees to watch the woman's purse. In this context, *watch* means *take care of*, and a *purse* is a handbag. (1.1)
7. B *Be hard on* = criticize or treat harshly. (1.2)
8. C *Pull (one's) leg* = tease or joke. (1.2)
9. D *Keep in touch* = communicate. (1.2)
10. A In this context, *coarse* means *vulgar*. (1.1)
11. B *Over (one's) head* = too difficult or strange to understand. (1.2)
12. A *I'll say!* is an expression of agreement. (1.2)
13. C *Get over* = recover from. (1.2)
14. A A synonym for *mandatory* is *required*. (1.1)
15. C *Put up with* = tolerate. The woman doesn't understand how the man could tolerate his brother; this implies the brother is difficult to live with. (1.2)

EXERCISE 1.3.A (p. 54)

1. B The man's condition is "If you'll walk with me." The result is "I can show you my favorite coffee shop."
2. A The causative "lets us design our own assignments" means the students design their assignments; in other words, they direct their own learning.
3. C "I wish my brother would call me more often" means her brother does *not* call her often.

4. B The causative "is having us present our papers in class" means the students will present their papers in class.
5. B "I'd rather stay home and work on my thesis" means he prefers to work on his thesis.
6. D The condition "If I didn't have to work" is unreal; the past tense verb means he *does* have to work, and therefore he cannot help her.

EXERCISE 1.3.B (p. 54)

1. D "I'd rather not bother Dr. Chung" means she prefers not to bother him by asking for an interview when she knows how busy he is.
2. B The condition "If only I'd known" is unreal; the past tense verb means she did not know that Ken's mother had died (passed away). The result "I would have gone with you" means she did *not* go to the funeral. She regrets not going.
3. C The causative "let me have his motorcycle" means she borrowed the motorcycle; this implies that she rode it to the party.
4. A "I wish my professor would hand the papers back" means the professor has not yet handed the papers back; therefore, the man does not know the grade on his paper.
5. A The condition is "If you took a walk with me." The result is "that would refresh your mind." This means a walk would help the man.
6. B The condition "if I knew what it was" is unreal; it means she does *not* know what a ratchet wrench is.

EXERCISE 1.4.A (p. 59)

1. B "There's nowhere like a parking lot to practice driving" means a parking lot is the best place to practice driving.
2. C "He had no choice but to drop out" means he had to leave school.
3. D "Not everyone has responded to the invitation" means they have not yet heard from everyone who was invited; therefore, they do not know how many people are coming.
4. A "Neither Brad nor Satoru can dance" means Brad can't dance and Satoru can't dance (is not a good dancer).
5. A "Rarely do I hear from Martin anymore" means she has heard very little from Martin lately; she has not talked to him in a long time.
6. A "It's not impossible to do well" is a double negative. It means it *is* possible to do well.
7. B "Hardly noticed" is "almost negative." It means *almost was not aware*.
8. B "I've never seen him so excited" means he is more excited than he has ever been before.
9. D "Neither do I" means she agrees with the man's negative statement; she does *not* like having an eight o'clock class either.
10. C "It's not unheard of" is a double negative. It means it *is* heard of; they might get a room without a reservation.

EXERCISE 1.5.A (p. 64)

1. C The man has a class at seven, but the woman's condition for accepting a ride is "If you can pick me up around six," which means she must leave earlier.
2. D Mr. Turner got his teaching job at least two years *before* he moved in next door. This means he moved in next door *after* he started teaching.
3. C The woman says the man's backpack is "a little wider," which means her backpack is *narrower* than the man's.
4. A The man has known the woman's cousin "as long as I've known you," which means he has known the two women the same length of time.
5. D Noah has "only a few credits left to go" (before he can graduate), which means he has almost enough credits to graduate.
6. A The man says he thought they had been married "longer than that" (*fifth anniversary* = married five years), which means he had believed they were married more than five years ago.
7. A *The more, the merrier* = a larger number of people results in a more enjoyable party.
8. B "Almost doubled since I was a freshman" means the tuition is nearly twice as much as it was when he was a freshman.

EXERCISE 1.6.A (p. 68)

1. B The emphasis on "will be able to come" means the woman had assumed the family *would not* be able to come.
2. B The man's rising intonation makes "Bruce is a ballet dancer" a question, which shows his surprise at learning Bruce is a dancer.
3. D The man's rising intonation means he is pleased by being invited to the speedway.
4. A The emphasis on "is running again" means the man had assumed the woman's car *was not* running because something was wrong with it.
5. C The woman's falling intonation means she does *not* think babysitting this weekend is great because she will be busy writing a term paper.
6. C The woman's tone shows she does *not* think the man is helpful.
7. A The woman's rising intonation makes "Levar is a lawyer" a question, which shows her surprise at learning Levar is a lawyer.
8. C The emphasis on "do eat meat" means the man had assumed the woman *did not* eat meat; *vegetarians* do not eat meat.

QUIZ 2 (p. 70)

1. C The condition "If only they would let me know" is unreal; the past tense causative "would let me know" means the woman does *not* know. (1.3, 2.12)
2. D The emphasis on "did remember" means the woman had assumed the man *would not* remember his mother's birthday. (1.6)
3. C *The week before last* = two weeks ago. (1.5)
4. B The conditional "I would if I didn't have to see my adviser" is unreal; the past tense verb means she *does* have to see her adviser; therefore, she cannot have coffee with the man. (1.3, 2.12)
5. D The causative "let us off early" means the man was allowed to leave work early. (1.3)
6. C Last year the speech was "much briefer and to the point," which means this year the speech was longer and less to the point (less focused). (1.5)

7. C "I thought I might see you" means the woman *did not* see the man on the trip. "Not everyone likes putting his life in danger" means some people *do not* like dangerous activities; the man implies he is one who does not like dangerous activities. (1.4)
8. B The man's tone shows he does *not* think she is a lot of fun. (1.6)
9. D "Hardly enough" is "almost negative." It means there was *almost* not enough room; the apartment was too small. (1.4)
10. D "Nowhere does it say" means there is no place in the directions which says what to do with the bolt; the directions are not complete. (1.4)
11. C Astrid is "much taller," which means the T–shirt that fits the woman will be too short for Astrid. (1.5)
12. A The emphasis on "did decide" means the woman had assumed the man *would not* decide to get the convertible. (1.6)
13. A The causative "have my secretary make the arrangements" means the secretary will arrange the details of the speaker's trip. (1.3)
14. C "Seldom hear from anyone" and "never write either" mean the man rarely corresponds with anyone. (1.4)
15. C The condition "if she didn't" is unreal; the past tense verb means Professor Tran *did* like the speech. (1.3, 2.12)

EXERCISE 1.7.A (p. 75)

1. B The woman wonders if Nathalie can take two classes and work full–time, implying Nathalie may be too busy during the summer.
2. B The woman says it took at least two weeks to get her grade, implying the man may also have to wait two weeks.
3. A The man says she had better get used to the class because it is required, implying the woman had better change her attitude.
4. A The radio announcer advises taking Broadway; the woman responds, "If she said to take Broadway, let's take the expressway." The woman suggests doing the opposite of what the radio announcer says, implying she does not believe the radio announcer.
5. B The man needs to hire someone; the woman asks a negative question to remind him how helpful Kimi was, implying Kimi should be hired.
6. A The woman proposes a thriller and a historical drama; the man says he never liked movies about history, implying they should watch the thriller.
7. C The man describes his problem with his roommate; the woman tells him that Yong is looking for someone to share his house, implying the man should become Yong's housemate.
8. D The man asks a negative question, implying the dog will be bothered by all the noise and therefore the woman should not bring the dog to the party.
9. C The man says Brian has two jobs but "needs to work less and focus more on his studies," implying Brian should give up one of his jobs.
10. A The woman has a problem with her car; the man says his best friend is a mechanic, implying his friend may be able to help with her car.

EXERCISE 1.7.B (p. 75)

1. A The woman says she doesn't need the book yet; the man reminds her the report is due next week, implying she should begin working on it.
2. C The man asks the other man about his rock climbing, implying both men are interested in rock climbing.
3. D The woman says she is "a little queasy" (ill) after eating "the last one" (hot dog), implying she does not want another hot dog.
4. A The woman asks a negative question, implying Jerry *should* give as much attention to his studies as he gives to basketball, or spend more time on his studies than he currently does, because his school work is being hurt by the amount of time he spends on sports.
5. C "I'll bet she still hasn't had her brakes fixed" implies Chris should have had her brakes fixed instead of spending five hundred dollars on a bird.
6. B The man can't find his sunglasses; the woman asks if he has looked in the car, implying he might have left his sunglasses in the car.
7. D "I think I'll be repeating this course next year" implies he thinks he failed the exam and will have to take the course again next year.
8. C The man suggests they go look at cars; the woman says, "I have too many other bills at the moment," implying she cannot afford to buy a car now.
9. D "Maybe she'd like to hear from you more often" implies the man should call or write his mother.
10. A The woman says she is going to the ocean for five days; the man reminds her that she has a term paper due next week, implying she may have difficulty getting her paper done.

EXERCISE 1.8.A (p. 78)

1. C The man has to be at work in a half–hour; he will probably turn down the invitation to go out for pizza.
2. A Keys: *grace, balance, strong, performing.*
3. A The man needs a motel; the woman suggests looking in Fairville, which is only thirteen miles away; the man will probably drive to Fairville.
4. D Key: *I'd like to tell you about our special.* A telephone solicitor sells things over the telephone.
5. C "If only I could" means the woman cannot go to the barbecue; everyone at the restaurant "is expected to work an extra shift" implies the woman will probably work an extra shift in the restaurant this weekend.
6. D Keys: *scored more points, player of the year.*
7. B The woman is taking classes in management, marketing, and business economics, which are courses a business major would take.
8. B Keys: *seemed down, won't get back home to see his friends.*
9. C Keys: *go the slow way, gaze at the prairies.*
10. C The man has an upcoming project deadline; his boss does not want to hire more help; the man says he had better postpone his vacation; he will probably work longer hours to finish the project.

EXERCISE 1.8.B (p. 79)

1. A The man missed biology class and needs to borrow the notes; the woman asks, "Weren't you there either?" implying she also missed class.
2. C Professor Garcia assigns a lot of work; the woman says the man will learn much in the class; you can infer Professor Garcia expects his students to work hard.
3. A The man is tired of the food in the cafeteria; he will probably try the food in the deli.

4. D Gloria and Judy are "so much alike" and "both the image of their father"; you can infer they have the same father and are therefore sisters.
5. D The man thinks Shelly would look better in the blue scarf; Shelly is the woman's best friend; the woman will probably buy the blue scarf for Shelly's birthday.
6. A Keys: *get the job*, *checking his references*.
7. C The man is worried about chemistry and got a "D" on the first test; the deadline for dropping classes is next week; the man will probably drop the chemistry class.
8. D Key: *their honeymoon*.
9. B The woman suggests a pizza parlor and two sushi bars; the man has had "enough pizza already this week"; he will probably choose one of the sushi bars.
10. A The man wants postcards; the drugstore sells postcards; he will probably go to the drugstore.

EXERCISE 1.9.A (p. 82)

1. A Keys: *napkins*, *spilled my drink*.
2. D Keys: *brakes were almost out of fluid*, *shocks needed replacing*.
3. C Keys: *biographies*, *nonfiction*.
4. B Keys: *theater*, *overacting*.
5. B Keys: *reviewing chapter five*, *might be a question*.
6. C Keys: *put out your cigarette*, *gas pump*.
7. D Keys: *needles*, *longleaf*, *wood*.
8. A Keys: *x–rays*, *clean your teeth*.

QUIZ 3 (p. 84)

1. A Traffic is heavy; the man says, "It's usually moving a little faster on the Clairmont bridge," implying they should take the Clairmont bridge. (1.7)
2. D Keys: *bouquet of white roses*, *arrangements of white tulips and carnations*. (1.9)
3. A The woman tells the man there are maps of the bus routes at the transfer station, implying he should check the maps there. (1.7)
4. D Keys: *new lab assistant*, *still too early to tell*. (1.8)
5. C The woman tells the man there is a smoking lounge in the basement, implying he should go there to smoke. (1.7)
6. D Keys: *what to order*, *seafood special*. (1.9)
7. C . Keys: *his brothers*, *his two elder sisters*, *three younger sisters*. (1.8)
8. B Keys: *doctor*, *surgery*, *chasing squirrels*. (1.8, 1.9)
9. B "Less afraid of the water than he should be" implies Arnold should be more afraid of the dangers of water; therefore, he should be more aware of water safety. (1.5, 1.7)
10. C "What? Oh, no!" and "There goes my weekend" imply the woman has forgotten to write the bibliography and is therefore not finished with her paper. (1.7)
11. C The woman suggests, "Why not try Ralph's Thriftway?" The man will probably do this.
12. B "Must have already left when I called her" implies the woman could not ask Tracy for a ride to work and therefore did not ride with Tracy. (1.5, 1.8)
13. C Keys: *add the milk*, *butter and flour*, *combined*. (1.9)
14. D The woman wants to take her parents somewhere nice; the man asks if she has tried the new Cajun restaurant, implying she should take her parents there. (1.7)
15. C The man thinks Mr. Nolan's explanations were never clear; he thinks Imelda had Mr. Park's class; the woman is having lunch with Imelda; she will probably ask Imelda's opinion of Mr. Park's class. (1.8)

QUIZ 4 (p. 86)

1. D Keys: *withdrawal slip*, *cash this check*, *account number*. (1.8, 1.9)
2. B *See right through him* = detect that he is dishonest. (1.2)
3. A The man needs a book; the woman tells him where the library catalog is, implying he should use the catalog to find the information he needs. (1.7)
4. A "I have no choice" means the woman is obligated to help Sue move. (1.4)
5. A Keys: *awful music*, *Kasper thinks he knows a lot about music*. The man implies Kasper does *not* know a lot about music; you can infer the speakers do not share Kasper's opinion of music. (1.7, 1.8)
6. C The man is on his way to the barber shop; you can infer he is going to get a haircut. (1.8, 1.9)
7. A The condition "If he were" is unreal; the past tense verb means Jason is *not* angry. (1.3, 2.12)
8. C *Two–faced* = deceitful, disloyal, not sincere. (1.2, 1.7)
9. C In this context, *common* means *coarse* or *ill–bred*. (1.1)
10. B Keys: *leaves and plants*, *use them in his class*. (1.8)
11. C "You could say that again!" is an expression of agreement. (1.2)
12. D The woman wants to know when the man will return her cassette; the man was hoping she had forgotten about it, implying he hoped to keep the cassette. (1.7)
13. B The man must choose someone to work with him on the project; the woman mentions Julie, implying the man should choose Julie. (1.7)
14. B "I haven't seen Tina at all this year" implies Tina must have moved away from next door. (1.4, 1.7)
15. A It is snowing hard; the woman says, "I wouldn't want to drive right now," implying the man should not drive because the snow is too heavy. (1.7)
16. A The emphasis on "will be in town" means the woman is surprised because she had assumed the man would *not* be in town (would be *out of town*). (1.6)
17. D *Put it off* = delay. (1.2)
18. A A synonym for *compulsory* is *required*. (1.1)
19. C The man's coach wants him to lose more weight because he is too heavy. The incorrect answer choices have words that sound similar to *weight* or *coach*. (1.1)
20. A Keys: *intensive care*, *nurse's station*. (1.9)
21. C The woman says the radio is "already quite loud," implying the man should not turn up the volume. (1.7)
22. D "Nothing in the kitchen" means the speakers do not have food at home. "Why don't we try that new place" implies they want to go out to buy some food. (1.4, 1.7)
23. A *Out of the question* = not to be considered; the woman has other bills, which means she cannot afford to have her roof fixed now. (1.2)
24. A Gina had already eaten by the time the woman arrived; you can infer the speaker did not eat lunch with Gina. (1.5, 1.8)

25. D *Call off* = cancel. (1.2)
26. D The condition "if you call and remind me" means the woman will take in the man's mail while he is away, but he must remind her. (1.3, 1.7)
27. D A synonym for *thoughtful* is *kind.* (1.1)
28. A *Take after* = resemble. (1.2)
29. C In this context, *strike* means *stop work.* (1.1)
30. D "Hardly ate" is "almost negative." It means he *almost* did not eat, or he ate only a small amount. (1.4)

Exercise 1.10.A (p. 100)

1. A The man says he doesn't understand his professor or why she said he didn't follow the instructions of the assignment.
2. C The man explains what is wrong with the soup.
3. B The lecture discusses mostly festivals, ceremonies, and religious beliefs of the people.
4. D The first sentence states the topic: "There are several ways to start a business." The rest of the talk gives examples of how to start a business.
5. C The talk discusses the results of a survey of how young Americans feel about socializing with people of different racial and ethnic heritages.
6. A The speaker calls Regionalism a "hype" and a "fraud" that was created "out of thin air," which implies the movement had no substance and therefore was not honest. The speaker also says that Regionalism appealed to values like nativism and racism, which the speaker implies are not admirable.

Exercise 1.11.A (p. 103)

1. D She asks him to buy two dozen fresh clams.
2. A She suggests that he go to Charley's, which has a seafood counter.
3. C They are discussing a survey assignment for an oral report.
4. A The woman wants to interview three people in a family who are of different ages.
5. D The man has not yet decided what to do for the assignment.
6. B The professor says he has a story that he needs translated into English.
7. A Her native language is Norwegian, but she speaks English and has studied Swedish and French.
8. C She asks if next week would be OK, and the professor says that "would be just fine."

Exercise 1.11.B (p. 103)

1. B The professor says osteoarthritis is diagnosed when X–rays show characteristic bone spurs.
2. A The professor says swelling of the membrane lining a joint is common.
3. A The professor says emotional stress often worsens the condition.
4. D One treatment for osteoarthritis is anti–swelling drugs.
5. C Sousa was a bandleader and composer.
6. D The instructor mentions Sousa's marches several times throughout the talk.
7. B Sousa's music is described as having "an upbeat and contagious humanity."
8. A The instructor says, "Now let's hear one of my favorite versions of *The Stars and Stripes Forever.*"

Exercise 1.11.C (p. 104)

1. B The man says, "The hunting season began in the fall and continued until midwinter."
2. C, D The bear and moose were among the animals sought.
3. A The women's job was "to take charge of the camps" on hunting parties.
4. B, D The man says, "women managed all of the agricultural operations" and "a woman headed each clan."
5. A, D Architecture and industrial design are among the fields that require an understanding of perspective.
6. D Perspective is shown when objects in the distance appear smaller than objects close by.
7. B The vanishing point is where two parallel lines—such as the rails in the drawing—appear to meet at a point.
8. C The instructor discusses the eye level (horizontal line) and vanishing point, saying, "I strongly suggest that you sketch them temporarily in every drawing."

Exercise 1.11.D (p. 105)

1. B The speaker defines *volcano* and then discusses three different types of volcanoes.
2. A, B A volcano erupts when hot liquefied rock (magma) pours out of the earth as lava. The lava may be liquid, or it may explode as a solid or liquid particles accompanied by superheated gases.
3. A A shield volcano is gently sloping and resembles a shield.
4. C The magma is blown high into the air and falls as volcanic bombs.
5. C A caldera is a basin–like depression that forms when a volcano's top blows off or when the center of a volcano collapses.
6. A One famous caldera covers much of Yellowstone National Park, and the geysers lie within this caldera.

Quiz 5 (p. 107)

1. A The man asks the woman what she thinks of a history lecture, and the woman says she doesn't understand some of the terms used by the lecturer. (1.10)
2. C *Primo* means *first.* Primogeniture is a system in which the firstborn son inherits his father's property. (1.11)
3. D Most of the discussion deals with the size (mass) and color (magnitude) of stars. (1.10)
4. C The professor says that if the earth were the size of a marble, the sun would be the size of a basketball. The question reverses the order of *earth* and *sun.* (1.11)
5. B, D The various colors of stars are caused by a combination of factors, especially a star's temperature, which is determined by the star's age and mass. (1.11)
6. B An alternate leaf arrangement is when each leaf is attached at a different level on the stem. (1.11)
7. D A basal leaf arrangement is when the leaves are at the base of the stem. (1.11)

8. A The instructor describes the basal leaves of the amaryllis family. (1.11)
9. B The instructor says, "I'd like you to come up and examine these samples of various sunflowers and daisies." (1.11)
10. C, D The instructor says, "Its leaves are long and velvety, with scalloped edges in an opposite arrangement." (1.11)
11. B Most of the lecture discusses Central Park, which is an example of a forested park in New York City. (1.10)
12. D The urban forest includes all the trees in city parks, the trees planted along city streets and highways, and the trees in people's yards. (1.11)
13. B, C Their inspiration came from the gardens of European estates and the romantic landscape paintings of the period. (1.11)
14. C The area had been used as a common pasture for grazing animals. (1.11)
15. A The speaker uses Central Park to illustrate how extending an urban forest can benefit human populations. The speaker calls Central Park "a man–made oasis," "the city's lung," and "one of the best examples of what we can do with the open spaces of our cities." (1.10)

EXERCISE 1.12.A (p. 110)

1. B–C–A Cash a check—in the student union; make a photocopy—near the bookstore; buy coffee—near the computer lab.
2. C The woman says, "You won't get it in the cafeteria, believe me." This implies the coffee in the cafeteria is not good.
3. C–B–A Shrimp—dark zone; bats—twilight zone; early humans—entrance zone.
4. B, C The dark zone has few if any air currents, and the animals there are usually blind because they have adapted to the world of darkness.
5. A Most of the talk gives examples of Native American religious traditions.
6. A–C–B Rain dance—Hopi; war dance—Apache; vision quest—Plains tribes.
7. D The professor says, "Ray's films are known for their compassion, honesty, and quiet dignity."
8. C–A–B Growing up—second film; failure and loss—third film; struggle against hardship—first film.

EXERCISE 1.13.A (p. 113)

1. B The instructor says, "If you are unsure of drawing directly in pen and ink, start off with a light pencil sketch."
2. B–D–A–C 1. Study the subject. 2. Draw the shape of the chair. 3. Draw the outline of the violin. 4. Add the details.
3. D The discussion is about an upcoming speech assignment and focuses on the steps in preparing the speech.
4. A–C–D–B 1. Realize the importance of the speech. 2. Choose your subject. 3. Decide on your purpose. 4. Organize and develop your ideas.
5. B The instructor says, "Why don't you all just take the next few minutes to start brainstorming? Jot down ideas that come to mind."

EXERCISE 1.13.B (p. 114)

1. C The talk describes *photosynthesis*, the process in which trees convert fuel into energy and manufacture foodstuffs to sustain themselves.
2. A All tree leaves carry out photosynthesis.
3. B–A–C 1. A leaf takes in water and carbon dioxide. 2. Solar energy is used to combine carbon dioxide and water. 3. Carbohydrates move throughout the tree.
4. C–D–B–A 1. Hearings are held to hear opinions on the bill. 2. The bill is approved by the Senate. 3. The bill is passed by the House of Representatives. 4. The bill is signed by the president.
5. D A veto occurs when the president refuses to sign a bill and sends it back to the house that originally introduced it.
6. C The topic of the lecture is how a bill becomes a law, which is a likely topic in an American Government course.

QUIZ 6 (p. 115)

1. B The man asks, "Would you mind getting an extra copy of any handouts Professor Young gives out?" (1.14)
2. A The woman says, "I can make a copy of my own notes, too. Do you want me to drop them by after class?" (1.11)
3. C–B–D–A 1. Go over the freeway. 2. Turn right on Lake Boulevard. 3. Go past the mall. 4. Turn right on Harrison. (1.13)
4. B The professor mainly describes the biology of marshes, giving several examples of plants and animals that live there. (1.10)
5. C The professor says, "Marshes are usually absent of trees and shrubs. Vegetation is usually soft–stemmed or herbaceous, consisting of such plants as grasses or sedges." (1.11)
6. B–C–A–D Snapping turtle—reptile; dragonfly—aquatic insect; leopard frog—amphibian; great blue heron-–wading bird. (1.12)
7. C–B–A 1. Plants and animals die in the marsh. 2. Bacteria and fungi break down the biomass. 3. Decaying vegetation turns the water dark brown. (1.13)
8. B, C Defending the colony and gathering pollen are among the many tasks performed by the worker bee. (1.11)
9. D–A–B–C 1. The egg is put into the worker cell. 2. The egg hatches into a larva. 3. The larva enters the pupa state. 4. The adult worker emerges. (1.13)
10. C The professor says, "When the adult worker emerges from the pupa, she usually does not leave the hive until about eight days later. Then, accompanied by other young workers, she takes her first flight in the warmth of the afternoon." (1.11)
11. C–A–B Flying (wings)—thorax; stinging—abdomen; working on the hive (mandibles)—head. (1.12)
12. D The lecture describes the four stages in the development of social reasoning in children. (1.10)

13. A — A four–year–old child is at the Egocentric Level and does not reflect on the thoughts of others. (1.11)
14. D — *Multiple* means *many*. A child at the Multiple Role Taking stage can understand what is expected in many different social situations. (1.11)
15. C–B–D–A — 1. Children have an egocentric perspective. 2. Children can understand two perspectives, but not at the same time. 3. Children can take a third–person perspective. 4. Children develop an analytical and societal perspective. (1.13)

EXERCISE 1.14.A (p. 118)

1. C — The instructor says, "I strongly recommend this video as an excellent way to review the concepts of cell division before our midterm quiz."
2. B — The videotape is on reserve in the library. The instructor says, "Because it's on reserve, it can't be checked out."
3. D — Most of the discussion deals with factors contributing to inflation and the effect inflation had on consumers and companies.
4. C — The professor says economists agree that an increase in the cost of one essential item contributes to inflation, adding, "For example, when oil prices rose sharply in the mid–1970s, inflation went up sharply."
5. A — The professor says, "When oil prices rose sharply in the mid–1970s, inflation went up sharply."
6. B — The professor says, "Because they were hurt by this sudden increase in prices, many companies went out of business or cut back on their growth."

EXERCISE 1.14.B (p. 119)

1. D — The first man says, "I thought it was phony," "That would be impossible," and "It's full of impossibilities."
2. B, C — The woman says, "I liked the way Nathaniel was so bold and also selfless" and "It's a classical story. Nathaniel was a classical hero."
3. C — The second man says, "The English soldier was a greater hero. He sacrificed his life. He did it to save the woman he loved."
4. A — One man thinks a hero must be alive the end of a movie. The other man thinks a character who sacrifices his life is a hero.
5. B — The instructor says, "Because of its potential for cutting costs, the distribution step in the marketing process is receiving more attention."
6. D — The instructor uses the example of fabric softener to illustrate warehousing and transporting in the distribution process.
7. A — The instructor says, "Probably the most crucial area for controlling costs is inventory."
8. A, B — The instructor says, "Computerized information systems give precise and up–to–date accounts of inventory on hand" and "the field of distribution offers good entry–level jobs for persons with training in computer programming."

EXERCISE 1.15.A (p. 122)

1. C — The man says he is curious about the chicken, implying that he will eat chicken.
2. D — The woman says she may go check out the salad bar, implying that she will eat salad.
3. B — The student says, "I have to go to California over the break and won't be back until January 15." This means he will miss more than a week of the next term.
4. A — The professor says, "To get the full benefit of the experience, you need to be there from the start." This implies the student should not miss class time.
5. A — The student asks if the course will be offered again in the spring. This implies that he will take the class in the spring.
6. C — The woman says, "The program you saw was part of the same series as the one I want to tell you about." It can be inferred that the people are discussing a television program.
7. D — The man talks about someone in the documentary who said there was a huge population explosion that turned America into a nation of cities in the nineteenth century. This means the population grew rapidly.
8. A, D — The woman mentions the five separate municipalities of New York, which were officially united as a single city. She also says that each borough maintains traces of its original independence; the man adds that Brooklyn is different from the rest of New York. This implies Brooklyn is a division (borough) of New York.

EXERCISE 1.15.B (p. 123)

1. B — The professor is talking mainly about software design, which would be most appropriate in a Computer Programming course.
2. C — The professor says, "…systems are praised more for the simplicity of their concepts." She adds that if a system is going to be easy to use, the design must be simple and conceptually unified.
3. A — The professor compares software design to architecture and calls the lead software designer "the architect of the system."
4. B — Throughout the talk, the professor stresses that simplicity is very important in software design.
5. D — The professor is discussing the pair of type preferences called *extraversion* and *introversion*.
6. B, D — Extraverted people turn outward and take an active approach to life. Of the answer choices, extraverts would most likely prefer social work and politics because of the social, active nature of these fields.
7. A — Introverted people look inward, take a reflective approach to life, and learn in private, individual ways.
8. C — The professor says, "People often mistakenly treat type preference as a character trait, something that can be worked on and changed. But type preferences are not traits." This implies type preferences cannot be changed.

Quiz 7 (p. 125)

1. B — Raymond says the student employment office sent him, and Ms. Kinney interviews him for a job. (1.14)
2. D — The job requires someone to pick up and deliver parcels all over campus. (1.14)
3. C — Ms. Kinney says they need someone right away, and Raymond says he can start that afternoon. (1.15)
4. C — She took her dog, Tippy, to the veterinarian; the dog has an infection. (1.14)
5. B — The dog has a fever and is being treated. The doctor wants to observe Tippy's response to the fluids and antibiotics he is being given. (1.14)
6. A — The man tries to reassure the woman by saying, "Dogs get infections all the time. Tippy will be all right, I'm sure." (1.11)
7. D — The woman says, "Dr. Adams said I can call tomorrow and see how he's doing." (1.15)
8. C, D — The speaker says the bean germinates (grows from seed) very quickly. The speaker also mentions well–preserved examples of beans that were found in ancient cave sites. (1.14)
9. B — The speaker says, "The Greek philosopher Pythagoras refused to eat beans because he believed they contained blood and were therefore not fit food for a vegetarian." (1.14)
10. A, D — The speaker says that beans have been credited with magic powers and have taught children about the wonders of nature. The speaker also gives examples of bean festivals and rituals. (1.15)
11. C — The talk is given in a cooking class, and the speaker concludes by saying, "…let's take a look at some delicious main dishes that I promise will become traditions in your family." (1.15)
12. B, C — The speaker is discussing the adventures of Brer Rabbit and his rascally friends. He says, "Harris was fascinated by the trickster Brer Rabbit and especially by the masterful storytelling of the old men…." (1.14)
13. B — Brer Rabbit is a "trickster" who has "rascally friends." A *trickster* plays tricks on others; *rascally* means *mischievous*. (1.15)
14. A — The speaker says, "Their enduring appeal…rests in how they offer wise and witty commentary on universal features of the human character…." This, along with the fact that Brer Rabbit is a trickster, implies that the stories examine human nature in an amusing way. (1.15)
15. D — The Brer Rabbit stories come from African–American folklore. The lecture focuses on their literary quality, especially their meaning and their narrative form. (1.15)

Quiz 8 (p. 127)

1. A — The woman is returning a sweater she bought in a department store. (1.10)
2. D — The man says, "Let me know if you see anything you like, and we can make an exchange." (1.11)
3. A — The woman says, "I think he'd rather have a pullover than a cardigan." This implies she wants to look at the pullover sweaters. (1.15)
4. C — The students are discussing the house finch, sparrow, and starling, which are all birds. Keys: *song*; *feathers*. (1.10, 1.15)
5. B–A–C — House finch—red; sparrow—brown; starling—black. (1.11)
6. A, B — The woman says, "I didn't even know they lived in the city." This implies that she previously knew starlings lived outside the city, and now she learns they also live in the city, where the speakers are. The woman says, "I can remember hearing my cousin complain about how the starlings always ate all the fruit in their orchard." This implies that starlings are a nuisance to fruit growers. (1.15)
7. B, D — The student says that tea appealed to Europeans because "…it was a product of the mysterious East" and because "…it brought health and well–being…." (1.14)
8. D — The student says, "Tea was regarded by both monk and emperor as a divine healing herb…" (1.11)
9. A — The student says, "…boiling the wrong leaf could cause trouble" and that the history of poisons is linked to herbals. (1.11)
10. B — The student says, "One of the giants of the herbal world—tea—has been praised for over a millennium" and discusses how tea has been regarded in history. (1.10)
11. C — The talk begins by introducing the topic of skin cancer and then focuses on the most dangerous form of skin cancer, melanoma. (1.10)
12. A — The speaker says the main cause of skin cancer is sun exposure and "The most effective preventative measure is sun avoidance." (1.15)
13. B — The speaker explains that melanoma may begin in or near a mole and "Any sudden growth of a mole should be of concern." (1.14)
14. A — *Asymmetry* is when something does not look the same on both sides. (1.11)
15. D — The speaker says the diameter warning sign is when the size of a mole is greater than six millimeters. (1.11)
16. B, C — The speaker says the foremost factors to be considered are "…talent, training, and personal characteristics." (1.11)
17. B — The speaker says, "Film directors…should be good at leading people…." (1.11)
18. B — The speaker says, "A career in the arts requires a personal sense of commitment—a *calling*—because art *does* have a history of insecure employment." *Insecure* means *uncertain*. (1.14)
19. C–B–A — Photography—take pictures for family wedding; acting—appear in local productions; graphic design—do paste–up for school newspaper. (1.12)
20. B, D — The speaker says that many artists find it difficult to live on the money they make from their art and so must add to their income by teaching or doing other work. (1.15)
21. D — The lecture discusses three different approaches epidemiologists use to gather information about disease. (1.10)
22. B, D — Epidemiologists study several factors, including where people live (environment) and what work they do (occupation). (1.11)

23. A One of the main goals of epidemiology is determining why one group of people is more likely to get a disease than another group of people. (1.14)
24. B–C–A Descriptive: look at trends of diseases over time; observational: observe what people do; experimental: compare treatment and no–treatment groups. (1.12)
25. C The speaker is the director of The Health Research Institute, which "is mostly involved in experimental or intervention studies." (1.11)
26. A The poll focused on "an age group that will have to cope with the anxieties and uncertainties spawned by a rapidly changing society." (1.11)
27. C The poll asked people "about the status of race relations today and how people will get along in the future." (1.10, 1.14)
28. B "Demographers predict that America will be so diverse by 2050 that there will be no majority group." (1.11)
29. B Young Americans are generally optimistic: "Seven out of ten whites say they expect race relations to be better in the next generation." "Asian Americans were the most optimistic, with almost eight of ten predicting improved relations." However, there are some differences between groups: "white Americans have a much rosier perception than black Americans." (1.15)
30. A, D "Black and Native American youth feel most strongly that their race has more to do with their own sense of identity than other things such as income or education." (1.11)

LISTENING COMPREHENSION REVIEW TEST (p. 130)

1. C *Fell through* = failed to happen; he could not get a ride. (1.2)
2. D "Didn't you go…either" means the man did not go to the meeting; the woman did not go because she was studying for an exam. (1.8)
3. A The man's falling intonation means he is disappointed to learn that the meeting was postponed until next week, when he is supposed to be on vacation. He will probably have to change his vacation plans to attend the meeting. (1.6, 1.8)
4. D The man says Dr. Jarrett "makes you write a lot of papers." The woman says, "I'd rather write papers than take exams," which means she would prefer Dr. Jarrett's class. (1.3, 1.8)
5. C "That clock is an hour fast" means the man has another hour to finish typing his paper. (1.5)
6. A The man says he spends "more (time) than I like" fixing gadgets, which means he would like to spend *less* time, implying he doesn't always enjoy fixing gadgets. (1.5)
7. A The man is eating dinner after ten o'clock. He says, "I had to catch a train to my evening class directly after work," implying he did not have time to eat dinner before his class. (1.3, 1.5, 1.7)
8. A *Coming down with the flu* = becoming ill. (1.2)
9. D "Seldom talks" is "almost negative." It means she does *not* often talk to her mother. (1.4)
10. A The man doesn't know the boat trip was canceled; the woman's negative question, "Don't you read your e–mail?," implies he *should* read his e–mail because the cancellation was announced by e–mail. (1.7)
11. B The conditional "I would if I didn't have a physics exam" is unreal; the past tense means he *does have* a physics exam and *will not* join her for dinner. (1.3, 2.12)
12. A *Butt in* = interrupt. (1.2)
13. C Dawn can't find her book bag; the man asks if she has looked in the lounge, implying Dawn might have left her book bag there. (1.7)
14. C "I'd rather just watch" means she prefers to watch other people play. (1.3)
15. C *Close call* = narrow escape. (1.2)
16. D "Is that so? I finished it in no time" means it took the woman very little time to read the book, and she is surprised it took the man so long. (1.4)
17. C "It might get a little stuffy in here" followed by the negative question "don't you think?" implies the room might become uncomfortable if the window is closed. (1.1, 1.7)
18. C A *genius* is someone who is very intelligent. (1.1)
19. B *Fed up* = disgusted. (1.2)
20. B *Get it over with* = complete an unpleasant task. The negative question "Why don't you…" implies the man should finish the assignment. (1.2, 1.7)
21. B The man says, "I'm glad there was nothing on the labor movement. That's the only chapter I didn't study." (1.14)
22. D The woman has a botany test this afternoon at three o'clock. (1.11, 1.15)
23. C The man says, "I was going to tell her I wouldn't be in class today." (1.14)
24. A The secretary says, "Dr. Owada isn't on campus today because she had a conference to go to." (1.11)
25. D The student will probably miss the two o'clock class, even though he would like to hear the speaker; the student says, "it's too bad I'll miss that." (1.15)
26. C Ben says he is confused about his job; he thinks his boss doesn't like him; he doesn't understand why his boss is always watching him. (1.14)
27. B Sandy says that Ben works fast; she advises him to ask Mr. Jackson for more work instead of taking a break when he finishes something. This implies that Ben needs to show Mr. Jackson he is a fast worker because Mr. Jackson may not be aware of it. (1.15)
28. D Sandy advises Ben to let his boss know he can do more work; Ben says, "I'll think about what you said." He wants to solve the problem, so he will probably take her advice and ask his boss for more work. (1.15)
29. A The lecture mainly discusses evidence that the world's climate has shifted abruptly during the past several hundred thousand years. (1.10)
30. D The ice cores were drilled in Greenland. (1.11)
31. B, D During the latest ice age, the temperatures fluctuated wildly, rising and falling several times, "only to slide back into a deep chill lasting thousands of years." (1.11)
32. B The professor says, "The transition about 10,000 years ago from the latest ice age to the present warm period might have taken less than a human lifetime." (1.11)

33. D–C–A–B 1. There is more moisture in the air. 2. More snow falls each winter. 3. Snow builds up as glacial ice. 4. The sun's heat is reflected. (1.13)
34. B Most of the lecture describes the four social classes that make up American society. (A), (C), and (D) are details or supporting ideas, not the main idea of the lecture. (1.10)
35. D The professor says, "If a large group of families are similar to each other in education, income, and values, we call them a *social class*." (1.11)
36. C The professor says, "The lower–middle class is the model for the popular stereotype of America's "common man." (1.11)
37. A The professor describes the lowest class as having many disadvantages, such as the lowest paid jobs and irregular work. (1.11)
38. D–C–A–B Upper—refined living; upper–middle—professional work; lower–middle—manual work; lower—irregular work. (1.12)
39. C The professor says, "...labels may lead us to assume falsely that a community can be neatly divided." This implies labels can be misleading. (1.11, 1.15)
40. B The hydrologic cycle is "the pattern of water movement as it circulates through the natural system." (1.11)
41. A Climatologists study the water in the atmospheric phase of the cycle. Keys: *evaporation*; *atmospheric circulation*; *precipitation of atmospheric water*. (1.11)
42. C Hydrologists study the water in the land phase of the cycle. Keys: *how water moves over and through the land*; *stored on or within the earth*. (1.11)
43. A, C The water that falls to earth "penetrates the surface materials, or runs off over the surface to be stored in rivers, lakes, or oceans." (1.11)
44. A The professor says, "Trees and plants draw up water and return it to the atmosphere by evapotranspiration." From this, you can infer that the loss of trees would affect the cycle because the return of water to the atmosphere would be changed. (B), (C), and (D) are not supported by anything the professor says. (1.15)
45. D Groundwater returns to the surface "either as streamflow or as springs." (1.11)
46. B Most of the talk discusses some effects of inflation, especially how rising prices affect working people. (1.10)
47. B The instructor uses a loaf of bread as an example of how a change in price contributes to inflation. (1.14)
48. D When the price of bread rises from $1.00 to $1.25, but wages stay at ten dollars, a person now has to work one–eighth of an hour, instead of one–tenth, to buy the same loaf of bread. (1.11)
49. A When there is inflation, the same money buys fewer things; therefore, people have less money left over, which means their standard of living goes down. (1.14)
50. C–A–B Moderate inflation—mild; galloping inflation—rapid; hyperinflation—severe. (1.12)

SECTION 2 – STRUCTURE

EXERCISE 2.1.A (p. 147)

1. C The sentence needs a noun structure as the true subject. *There* is the "false" subject. (A) and (D) are clauses (2.8). (B) is a prepositional phrase (2.21).
2. A The sentence needs a noun structure as the subject. (B) and (D) have the subordinators *why* and *because*, which introduce subordinate clauses and would make this sentence incomplete (2.8). (C) is a plural noun, which does not agree with the verb *prides* (2.14).
3. D The sentence needs a noun structure as the subject. Here, the subject is a pronoun that comes after an introductory clause. (A) makes an infinitive, *to make* (2.7), but then the sentence would have no main clause (2.8). (B) is an adverb. (C) has question word order (2.13).
4. C The sentence needs a noun structure as the direct object of the verb. (A) lacks an article (2.4). (B) is a clause (2.8). (D) has the incorrect article (2.4).
5. C The sentence needs a noun structure as the true subject. *It* is the "false" subject. (A) and (B) have the subordinators *when* and *because*, which introduce subordinate clauses (2.8, 2.11). (D) is a clause (2.8).
6. B The sentence needs a noun structure as the direct object of the verb. (A) is a clause (2.8). (C) is a prepositional phrase (2.21). (D) has the possessive adjective *its* (2.15), which does not make sense with *of Spanish America*.
7. A The sentence needs a noun structure as the subject, which comes after an introductory phrase. (B) and (C) have the subordinators *as* and *so that*, which introduce subordinate clauses and would make this sentence incomplete (2.8). (D) has the conjunction, *and*, which connects two main clauses (2.20).
8. D The sentence needs a noun structure that will identify the direct object *candidate*. (A) is a prepositional phrase (2.21). (B) has a verb. (C) has the subordinator *whom*, which introduces noun clauses (2.9), but the structure following it here is not a clause.
9. B *He* is a duplicate subject. *James Fenimore Cooper* is the subject. Correction: omit *he*.
10. A *That* is a subordinator, which introduces subordinate clauses and would make this sentence incomplete (2.8). Correction: omit *that*.

EXERCISE 2.2.A (p. 151)

1. A The sentence needs a noun structure to rename *papyrus*. (B) is a clause (2.8). (C) has the subordinator *as if*, which introduces adverb clauses (2.11). (D) is a prepositional phrase (2.21).
2. C The sentence needs a noun structure to rename the subject, *Edgar Allan Poe*. (A) and (B) are clauses (2.8). (D) ends with the preposition *of*, but the preposition has no object (2.21).
3. C The sentence needs a noun structure as the subject. *The Mongols* is an appositive that renames the subject. (A) has the subordinator *whose*, which introduces adjective clauses (2.10). (B) and (D) are clauses (2.8).

4. C The sentence needs a noun structure to rename the subject, *Barbara Tuchman*. (A) is a clause (2.8). (B) has the subordinator *who*, which introduces adjective clauses (2.10), but the comma before *won* makes this impossible. (D) has a verb.
5. A The sentence needs a noun structure as the object of *containing*. *A narcotic* is an appositive that renames this noun. (B) has the article *the*, which is unnecessary in a generalization about an uncountable noun (2.4). (C) and (D) have verbs.
6. D The sentence needs a noun structure to rename the subject, *African–American dance*. (A) makes an infinitive, *to blend* (2.7), but *of*–phrases do not usually follow infinitives. (B) has a verb, which makes a clause (2.8) instead of an appositive. (C) has the subordinator *which*, which introduces adjective clauses (2.10).
7. D The sentence needs a noun structure as the subject. *All with true horns* is an appositive that renames the subject. (A) and (C) are clauses (2.8). (B) is a prepositional phrase (2.21).
8. D The sentence needs a noun structure to rename the subject, *ichthyology*. (A) is a clause (2.8). (B) is a verb. (C) has the subordinator *which*, which introduces adjective clauses (2.10), but the structure between the commas is not a clause.
9. B The sentence needs a noun structure to rename *Henri Giffard*. (A) is a clause (2.8). (C) is a prepositional phrase (2.21). (D) has the subordinator *whose*, which introduces adjective clauses (2.10).
10. C The sentence needs a noun structure to rename *marten*. (A) has the subordinator *whom*, which introduces adjective clauses (2.10). (B) would make the structure between the commas a main clause (2.8). (D) would make the structure between the commas a prepositional phrase; *as* is a preposition (2.21, 2.23).

EXERCISE 2.3.A (p. 157)

1. B *Less* is not used with countable nouns such as *boys*. Correction: *fewer*.
2. A Adjectives do not have plural forms. Correction: *four–year–old*.
3. A *Much* is not used with countable nouns such as *storms*. Correction: *many*.
4. C The sentence discusses the first of several "Simple" stories. Correction: *stories*, which agrees with the verb *were collected* (2.14).
5. B Uncountable nouns do not usually have plural forms. Correction: *damage*.
6. B Adjectives do not have plural forms. Correction: *million*.
7. D *Scenery* is an uncountable noun. (A) and (C) incorrectly pluralize an uncountable noun. (B) has an incorrect plural of an adjective; adjectives do not have plural forms.
8. C (A) lacks either an article or a number before *thousand*. (B) has an unnecessary word, *of*. (D) has the singular *farmer*, where its plural is necessary.

EXERCISE 2.3.B (p. 158)

1. A *Another* (*an* + *other*) is used only with singular nouns (2.23). Correction: *kind*.
2. A The sentence discusses one (*the largest*) of several carnivores. Correction: *carnivores*.
3. B *Advice* is an uncountable noun, which has no plural form. Correction: *advice*.
4. C *Fewer* is not used with uncountable nouns such as *traffic*. Correction: *less*.
5. A Only one term, *generativity*, is being discussed. Correction: *term*.
6. B *Thousand* is an adjective, but adjectives do not have plural forms. Nouns must be pluralized when there are two or more. Correction: *thousand years ago*.
7. A *Each* is used with singular nouns; it cannot be used with uncountable nouns such as *furniture*. However, furniture can be expressed as a singular by adding a countable noun + *of* phrase. Correction: *item of furniture*.
8. C *Number of* is used with plural countable nouns. Correction: *Japanese Americans*.
9. D *Increase* is uncountable in this context, and *few* is not used with uncountable nouns. Correction: *little increase*.
10. C The singular article *a* (2.4), before the adjectives modifying *supplies*, tells you the noun must be singular. Correction: *supply*.

EXERCISE 2.4.A (p. 164)

1. D *Incoming signal* is a countable noun. Because it is singular here, it should have an article. Correction: *an incoming signal* or *the incoming signal*.
2. C *Expanding economy* is a countable noun. Because it is singular here, it should have an article. Correction: *the expanding economy*.
3. A *Greatest floods* is a superlative that needs the definite article. Correction: *the greatest floods*.
4. C *The* is unnecessary because the sentence is making a generalization about the uncountable noun *nationalism*. Correction: omit *the* before *nationalism*.
5. C *Among most* is incorrect because superlatives need the definite article. Correction: *among the most*.
6. D The definite article *the* before *cheese* is unnecessary because there is an article before *kind of*. In this context, *cheese* is uncountable. Correction: omit *the* before *cheese*.
7. D *A largest* is a superlative that needs the definite article. Correction: *the largest*.
8. D When *such* refers to the class or type of something, it is placed before the entire noun phrase, as it is here before *an adhesive stamp*. (A) has incorrect word order. In (B) *a* is incorrect because *adhesive* begins with a vowel sound. (C) has no article, but one is needed with singular countable nouns such as *stamp*.
9. A No article is used with uncountable nouns, such as *importance*, when they are indefinite or not known to the reader. (B) has the definite article, which is not appropriate because *international importance* is indefinite and uncountable. (C) has an incorrect word form, *international* (2.22), which is an adjective, but the object of a preposition must be a noun (2.21). (D) has *an*, which cannot be used with uncountable nouns such as *importance*.
10. B *Uniformly* is pronounced with a consonant sound and therefore takes *a*. (A) has *an*, which is not used before words that are pronounced with a consonant sound. (C) has incorrect word order (2.16). (D) lacks an article where one is needed.

QUIZ 1 (p. 167)

1. D *Equipment* is an uncountable noun and has no plural form (2.3). Correction: *equipment.*
2. C *It* is a duplicate subject. *The desert pocket mouse* is the subject (2.1). Correction: omit *it.*
3. A *Color images* is made specific and known by the phrase *we see.* Therefore, it should have the definite article (2.4). Correction: *Many of the color images.*
4. C Adjectives do not have plural forms (2.3). Correction: *eighteen–minute.*
5. C The sentence needs a noun structure as the subject, which comes after an introductory clause (2.1). (A) has the subordinator *that,* which introduces noun clauses and would make this sentence incomplete (2.9). (B) has the subordinator *because,* which introduces adverb clauses (2.11). (D) is an incorrect pronoun; *he* refers to a person, but *sunlight* is not a person (2.15).
6. D The sentence needs a noun structure to rename *Telstar* (2.2). (A), (B), and (C) each have a verb, which makes them clauses (2.8).
7. D The sentence needs a noun structure to rename the subject, *Malcolm X* (2.2). (A) is a verb. (B) and (C) are clauses (2.8).
8. C *Human beings* is a plural countable noun that is indefinite; therefore, no article is needed (2.4). Correction: *of human beings.*
9. C *Many* is not used with uncountable nouns such as *information* (2.3). Correction: *much.*
10. B *A* is not used before words that begin with a vowel sound (2.4). Correction: *an individual.*
11. B *A number of* means *several* and is used with plural countable nouns (2.3). Correction: *reasons.*
12. D Adjectives do not have plural forms (2.3). Correction: *fifty–foot–long.*
13. B The sentence needs a noun structure as the subject (2.1). (A) and (D) each have a verb and are not noun structures. (C) is a prepositional phrase (2.21).
14. B The sentence needs a plural noun as the object of the preposition *of* (2.1, 2.21). (A) is a singular noun (2.3) that does not agree with *a set of,* which is a group and needs to be followed by a plural noun. (C) has incorrect word order (2.16). (D) has an incorrect word form, *unfavorably* (2.22).
15. A The sentence needs a noun structure to rename the subject, *Scott Joplin* (2.2). (B) is a verb phrase (2.5). (C) is an infinitive (2.7), which is a noun structure but does not make sense in this context because *Scott Joplin* is a person. (D) has the subordinator *who,* which introduces adjective clauses (2.10).

EXERCISE 2.5.A (p. 174)

1. A The sentence needs a verb. (B) is a verb form that cannot be used without the auxiliary *be.* (C) is an infinitive, which does not function as a verb (2.7). (D) is in passive voice, which is incorrect here because the subject, *millions,* is not the passive receiver of the verb's action (2.6).
2. D The sentence needs a verb. (A) is a verb form that cannot be used without the auxiliary *be.* (B) does not agree with the subject in number (2.14). (C) lacks the auxiliary *be.*
3. D The sentence needs a verb that can be used with the auxiliary *have.* (A) is a form that is not used with *have.* (B) is a preposition + gerund (2.7). (C) is an infinitive, which does not function as a verb (2.7).
4. C The sentence needs a verb + object structure. (A) is a noun phrase (2.1). (B) has an incorrect verb for this context. (D) does not have a noun object; *aggressively* is an adverb.
5. D The sentence needs a verb + object structure to come before *for breaking free.* The adverb *eloquently* comes before the verb it modifies, *stated.* (A) has incorrect word order. (B) is in passive voice, which is incorrect here because *propaganda* is not the passive receiver of the verb's action (2.6). (C) has an incorrect word form, *eloquent,* which is an adjective (2.22).
6. B The sentence needs a verb. (A) is a verb form that cannot be used without the auxiliary *be.* (C) is a verb form that cannot be used without the auxiliary *have.* (D) is an infinitive, which does not function as a verb (2.7).
7. D The sentence needs a verb. This is a generalization; therefore, simple present tense is appropriate. (A) has the incorrect tense of both the modal and the verb. (B) is in passive voice, which is incorrect here because the subject, *consumers,* is not the passive receiver of the verb's action (2.6). (C) has a verb form that cannot be used without the auxiliary *be.*
8. C The sentence needs a verb. (A) is a verb form that cannot be used without the auxiliary *be.* (B) is present tense, but the time markers indicate past time. (D) is present perfect tense, but the time marker *by the end of the 1800s* indicates past perfect is needed.
9. C The first clause needs a verb that will agree in tense meaning with the verb in the second clause, *have adopted.* (A) does not agree in tense with *have adopted.* (B) is a verb form that cannot be used without the auxiliary *be.* (D) is an infinitive, which does not function as a verb (2.7).
10. B The sentence needs a verb + object structure; *and vegetables* is the second part of the compound direct object. (A) does not agree in tense meaning with *in 1993.* (C) has incorrect word order. (D) has a duplicate subject, *forty* (2.1).

EXERCISE 2.5.B (p. 175)

1. A *Belief* is a noun, but a verb is needed. Correction: *believe.*
2. C *Become* does not agree in tense meaning with *in 1867.* Correction: *became.*
3. B *There were* does not agree in tense meaning with the verb in the first clause, *is.* Correction: *there are.*
4. D *Is* does not agree in tense meaning with *until recently,* nor is it used with *been.* Correction: *has.*
5. C *To be* is an infinitive (2.7) where a verb is needed. Correction: *are.*
6. D *Could* is a past tense modal, but the first clause has a present tense modal + verb phrase, *can communicate.* The tense meanings of the two clauses should agree. Correction: *can.*
7. A *Break out* does not agree in tense meaning with *in 1946.* Correction: *broke out.*
8. B *Define* is the incorrect verb form to use with *had.* Correction: *defined.*
9. B *Extend* does not agree in tense meaning with *from 180 million to 135 million years ago.* Correction: *extended.*
10. C *Stressing* does not agree in tense meaning with the verb in the main clause, *gave.* Also, it is a verb form that cannot be used without the auxiliary *be.* Correction: *stressed.*

EXERCISE 2.6.A (p. 181)

1. B The sentence needs a passive voice verb. (A) and (C) are active voice. (D) is an infinitive, which does not function as a verb (2.7).
2. D The sentence needs a passive voice verb. (A) is a preposition (2.21). (B) lacks the auxiliary *be*. (C) has *by*, which does not make sense in this context because *drill holes* cannot *use* construction augers, nor can construction augers *be used by drill holes*. Instead, *drill* is part of an infinitive (2.7).
3. C The sentence needs a passive voice verb. (A) and (D) are active voice. (B) is an incorrect verb form because *can* is never used with past tense verbs such as *accommodated*.
4. C The sentence needs the past participle of the verb after *was*. (A) is the base form of the verb. (B) is the present participle. (D) has an extra, incorrect auxiliary.
5. A The sentence needs a passive voice verb after *may*. (B) lacks the auxiliary *be*. (C) has the incorrect form of *be*; following modals, the base form of *be* is needed. (D) is an infinitive, which does not function as a verb (2.7).
6. A The sentence needs a passive voice verb. (B) is active voice. (C) lacks the auxiliary *be*. (D) has the incorrect form of the auxiliary *be*.
7. B The sentence needs a passive voice verb. (A) is active voice. (C) has the incorrect form of the auxiliary *be*. (D) is an incorrect form because *to* is not used with modals in passive voice verbs.
8. C The sentence needs a passive voice verb. (A) lacks the auxiliary *be*. (B) has incorrect word order. (D) is an incorrect form because *to* is not used with modals in passive voice verbs.

EXERCISE 2.6.B (p. 182)

1. D *Be exported* has the incorrect form of *be*. Correction: *are*.
2. D *Had used* lacks the auxiliary *be*. Correction: *had been used*.
3. B *Attain* is the incorrect form of the verb. Correction: *attained*.
4. B *Was been* has the incorrect form of the first auxiliary. This is a passive voice verb in past perfect tense. Correction: *had been*.
5. C *Be explained* is in passive voice but should be in active voice. In this context, the *migration and feeding habits* of the eel perform the action—they *will explain why its numbers are decreasing*. Correction: *explain*.
6. B *Known* lacks the auxiliary *be*. Correction: *is known*.
7. A *Been* is the incorrect form of *be*. Following modals, such as *had to*, the base form of *be* is needed. Correction: *be*.
8. B *Find* is the incorrect form of the verb. This is an adjective phrase that has been reduced from an adjective clause (2.10). The passive voice is needed. Correction: *found*.

QUIZ 2 (p. 184)

1. C The sentence needs a verb (2.5). (A) is an infinitive, which does not function as a verb (2.7). (B) is a gerund, which does not function as a verb (2.7). (D) has incorrect word order; the direct object *the nest* should come after the verb (2.5).
2. D The sentence needs a verb (2.5). (A) does not agree in tense meaning with *during the nineteenth century* (2.5). (B) lacks a verb. (C) is in passive voice, where active voice is needed (2.6).
3. D The sentence needs a verb (2.5). (A) is a verb form that cannot be used without the auxiliary *be* (2.5). (B) does not agree in tense meaning with the verb in the first clause, *are foraging*, which is in present time because it is a statement of fact (2.5). (C) is an infinitive, which does not function as a verb (2.7).
4. D The subordinate clause needs a passive voice verb (2.5, 2.6, 2.8). (A) is an infinitive, which does not function as a verb (2.7). (B) does not agree in tense meaning with the verb in the main clause, *is* (2.5). (C) is active voice.
5. A The sentence needs a verb (2.5). (B) is a verb form that cannot be used without the auxiliary *be* (2.5). (C) is in passive voice, which is incorrect here because the subject, *surgery*, is not the passive receiver of the verb's action (2.6). (D) is an infinitive, which does not function as a verb (2.7).
6. A The sentence needs a verb (2.5). (B) is a verb form that cannot be used without the auxiliary *be* (2.5). (C) is an infinitive, which does not function as a verb (2.7). (D) is in passive voice, which is incorrect here because the subject, *trial*, is not the passive receiver of the verb's action (2.6).
7. D The sentence needs a passive voice verb (2.6). (A) and (B) are active voice. (C) has the incorrect form of the auxiliary *be* (2.6).
8. A *Had* does not agree in tense meaning with the other verbs in the sentence (2.5). This is a general statement of fact; simple present tense is appropriate. Correction: *has*.
9. B *Characterize* is an incorrect form of the verb; with passive voice verbs, the past participle is needed (2.6). Correction: *characterized*.
10. D *Entertaining* is an incorrect form of the verb; with passive infinitives, the past participle is needed (2.6). Correction: *entertained*.
11. B *Should fertilized* is a passive voice verb that lacks the auxiliary *be* (2.6). Correction: *should be fertilized*.
12. C *Assistant* is a noun, where a verb is needed in a series of verb phrases (2.5, 2.22, 2.25). Correction: *assisted*.
13. C *Do not* has the incorrect auxiliary; with passive voice verbs, *be* is needed (2.6). Correction: *are not*.
14. B *Been doing* has the incorrect form of the auxiliary; following modals, the base form of the auxiliary is needed (2.5). Correction: *be doing*.
15. B *Ever been* lacks the auxiliary *have*, which is needed with the perfect tenses (2.5). Correction: *had ever been*.

EXERCISE 2.7.A (p. 191)

1. A *Tend establish* is a verb + infinitive structure that lacks *to*. Correction: *tend to establish*.
2. D *To reduce* is an incorrect form where a gerund is needed. *To reduce* is not an infinitive here. *Linked to* is a verb + preposition structure. After a preposition, a gerund is needed. Correction: *to reducing*.
3. D *Shaping* is a gerund where an infinitive is needed. After *helps*, *to* may be omitted. Correction: *shape* or *to shape*.
4. D *Change* is a verb where a gerund is needed in a list of gerunds (2.25). Correction: *changing*.

5. B *Enable* is an incorrect form where an infinitive is needed. Correction: *to enable*.
6. D The sentence needs either an infinitive or a gerund following *began*; *testing* is a gerund. (A), (B), and (C) are all verbs (2.5).
7. A The sentence needs an infinitive following *exist*. (B) is in passive voice, which is incorrect here because *machines* is not the passive receiver of the infinitive's action (2.6). (C) introduces an adjective clause (2.10). (D) is a passive voice verb (2.6).
8. C The sentence needs a gerund following the preposition *without*. (A) is a verb phrase (2.5). (B) is an infinitive. (D) is a verb form that is used after a modal (2.5).
9. B The sentence needs an infinitive as an adjective to modify the noun *subject*. (A) is a passive voice verb form that is used after a modal (2.6). (C) is an incorrect structure: preposition + verb. (D) is a gerund.
10. A The sentence needs an adjective to modify the noun *trouble*. Usually, only infinitives, not gerunds, can function as adjectives. However, here the preposition *with* is implied (but omitted) between *trouble* and the gerund: *trouble with sleeping*. (B) has an incorrect preposition. (C) and (D) are verbs.

EXERCISE 2.7.B (p. 192)

1. C *To separated* is an incorrectly formed infinitive. Correction: *to separate*.
2. A *The keeping* has an article where none is needed. Gerunds are uncountable nouns that do not take articles (2.4). Correction: *keeping*.
3. C *Producing* is a gerund where an infinitive is needed. *Unusual*, like *usual*, is an adjective that should be followed by an infinitive. Correction: *to produce*.
4. D *For drive* is an incorrect structure: preposition + verb. Following a preposition, a gerund is needed. Correction: *for driving*.
5. D *Read* is a verb where an infinitive is needed after the indirect object *a player*. Correction: *to read*.
6. D *To glide* is an infinitive where a gerund is needed following a preposition. Correction: *gliding*.
7. D *Analyzing* is a gerund where an infinitive is needed following *help*. After *help*, *to* may be omitted. Correction: *analyze* or *to analyze*.
8. A *Investment* is a noun (2.22) where an infinitive is needed. Correction: *to invest*.

EXERCISE 2.8.A (p. 198)

1. D The sentence needs a verb. (A) has a duplicate subject, *it* (2.1). (B) is a verb form that cannot be used without the auxiliary *be* (2.5). (C) is a preposition + gerund (2.7).
2. C The sentence needs a subject + auxiliary *be*; the verb, *marked*, is in the passive voice (2.6). (A) is a prepositional phrase + verb. (B) has question word order (2.13). (D) is a clause; it has incorrect word order for this context.
3. A The sentence needs a subject + verb. (B) is a verb or a gerund (2.5, 2.7). (C) is a subordinator that introduces adjective clauses (2.10). (D) is a preposition (2.21).
4. D The subordinate clause needs a subject + verb. (A) is an infinitive phrase (2.7). (B) lacks a verb. (C) has question word order (2.13).
5. D The main clause needs a subject + verb. (A) is a verb or a gerund (2.5, 2.7). (B) is an infinitive (2.7). (C) has the conjunction *and*, which is used to join two main clauses (2.20). In this sentence, the first clause is subordinate; it is indicated by the subordinator *after*.
6. B The main clause needs a subject + verb. (A) and (C) lack a verb. (D) has the subordinator *why*, which introduces noun clauses (2.9).
7. C The sentence needs a subject + verb following the appositive. (A) and (B) lack a verb. (D) has question word order (2.13).
8. D The main clause needs a subject + verb. (A) and (C) lack a verb. (B) is a subject + verb, which is incorrect here because the verb *was* must be followed by either a noun complement or a single–word adjective; *founded in 1837* is an adjective phrase (2.10).
9. A *Do not*, the verb of the main clause, lacks a main verb; *do* is an auxiliary verb, and *not* is an adverb. Correction: *do not have*.
10. B *Arm around* is incorrect because it lacks a verb, but here is where the verb of the subordinate clause should be. The subject of this clause is *the various sections of its arm*. Correction: add an appropriate verb between *arm* and *around*, such as *are* or *move*.

QUIZ 3 (p. 200)

1. B The sentence needs an infinitive as an adjective to modify the noun *engine* (2.7). (A) is a verb phrase (2.5). (C) and (D) are preposition + gerund structures (2.7).
2. B The subordinate clause needs a subject + verb (2.8). (A) has incorrect word order; *the only* cannot come before an infinitive such as *to attack* (2.7). (C) is an infinitive phrase (2.7). (D) has incorrect word order.
3. C The clause needs a subject + verb; this clause is the second main clause of a compound sentence (2.8). (A) lacks a verb. (B) has the subordinator *why*, which introduces noun clauses (2.9). (D) lacks a subject.
4. C The sentence needs a verb (2.8). *Is to promote* is a verb + infinitive as subject complement (2.7). (A) is a verb, but it does not agree with the subject, *function* (2.14). (B) and (D) are infinitives, which do not function as verbs (2.7).
5. D The sentence needs a gerund or infinitive as the subject (2.7). *Refining* is a gerund. (A) and (B) are verbs (2.5). (C) is an incorrectly formed infinitive (2.7).
6. D The sentence needs a subject + verb (2.8). (A) is an article (2.4); it has neither a subject nor a verb. (B) has the subordinator *how*, which introduces noun clauses (2.9). (C) lacks a subject.
7. A The sentence needs an infinitive as the direct object of the verb *lets* (2.7). (B) is a gerund (2.7). (C) has *to*, but after *let*, *to* is omitted from an infinitive (2.7). (D) is a verb (2.5).
8. A The main clause needs a subject + auxiliary *be*; the verb, *protected*, is in the passive voice (2.6, 2.8). (B) has question word order (2.13). (C) lacks a verb. (D) has the incorrect auxiliary; passive voice verbs need *be* (2.6).
9. B *Return* is a verb where a gerund is needed following the preposition *before* (2.7). Correction: *returning*.

10. C *Exert* is a verb where an infinitive or gerund is needed as the direct object after *continue* (2.7). Correction: *to exert* or *exerting*.
11. C *Use its* is a verb phrase where a gerund is needed in a series of gerunds that are objects of the preposition by (2.7, 2.25). Correction: *using its*.
12. A *More people in* lacks a verb, but the subordinate clause beginning with *that* needs a verb (2.8). Correction: *more people lived in*.
13. B *Is control* is a verb + infinitive structure that lacks *to* (2.7). Correction: *is to control*.
14. D *Preventing* is a gerund where an infinitive is needed (2.7). After *help*, *to* may be omitted. To be parallel with *conserve*, omit *to* before *prevent* (2.25). Correction: *prevent*.
15. D *For extract* is an incorrect structure: preposition + verb. Here, an infinitive (2.7) would be parallel in structure (2.25) to the infinitive *to process*. Correction: *to extract*.

QUIZ 4 (p. 202)

1. B *Distinguished* is an incorrectly formed infinitive (2.7). An infinitive is formed with *to* + the base form of a verb. Correction: *distinguish*.
2. C *Many* is not used with uncountable nouns such as *cash* (2.3). Correction: *much*.
3. A *Name always* lacks a verb before where one is needed. The sentence has a compound verb joined by *and* (2.8). The two verbs are in the passive voice (2.6). Correction: *name is always*.
4. B *In slide* lacks an article (2.4). *Slide* is a singular countable noun that is made specific by its use in the sentence; therefore, the definite article is needed. Correction: *in the slide*.
5. B The main clause needs a subject + verb (2.8). (A) lacks a verb. (C) has the subordinator *that*, which introduces noun clauses (2.9). (D) lacks a verb.
6. C The sentence needs an infinitive as the subject complement after *is* (2.7). (A) and (B) are verbs. (D) is a noun (2.22).
7. B The sentence needs a noun structure as the direct object of the gerund *using* (2.1, 2.7). (A) lacks the definite article, which is needed because *the inclined plane* is an invention (2.4). (C) is a clause (2.8). (D) is a prepositional phrase (2.21).
8. C The main clause needs a verb (2.8). (A) has an incorrectly formed verb, *had decide* (2.5). (B) is an infinitive, which does not function as a verb (2.7). (D) has *deciding*, which is an incorrect participle in this context. (2.5).
9. A The sentence needs a verb (2.8). (B) has an incorrect form of the verb following the modal (2.5). (C) has an incorrect infinitive following the modal (2.7). (D) does not agree in tense meaning with *thousands of years ago* (2.5).
10. A The sentence needs a noun structure as the true subject; *It* is the "false" subject (2.1). (B) has the subordinator *because*, which introduces adverb clauses (2.11). (C) is a prepositional phrase (2.21). (D) is a clause (2.8).
11. C The main clause needs a subject + verb (2.8). (A) is a subordinating word (2.8). (B) lacks a verb; *would* is a modal auxiliary that is used with other verbs (2.5). (D) lacks a subject.
12. D The sentence needs a noun structure as the subject (2.1). (A) is a verb phrase (2.5). (B) is a prepositional phrase (2.21). (C) has the subordinator *that*, which introduces adjective clauses (2.10).
13. D The first main clause needs a verb that will agree in tense meaning with the verb in the second clause, *are devoted* (2.5). (A) and (B) are infinitives, which do not function as verbs (2.7). (C) does not agree in tense meaning with the verb in the second clause (2.5).
14. B The subordinate clause needs a verb (2.8). (A) and (D) have passive voice verbs, which are incorrect here because the subject, *most Americans*, is not the passive receiver of the verb's action (2.6). (C) has an incorrect form of the verb; following modals such as *used to*, the base form of the verb is needed (2.5).
15. D The sentence needs a noun structure to rename *1954* (2.2). (A) is a clause (2.8). (B) has an incorrect article; the year is specific, so the definite article is appropriate (2.4). (C) has an unnecessary preposition (2.21).
16. B *For to identify* is incorrect because an infinitive is needed as an adjective to modify the noun *term*, but an infinitive cannot be the object of a preposition (2.7). Correction: *to identify*.
17. C *It* is a duplicate subject; *an ice core* is the subject (2.1). Correction: omit *it*.
18. D *Broken* is an incorrect verb form; it is the past participle (2.5). Correction: *broke*, which agrees in tense meaning with *in 1928*.
19. B The singular *tournament* is incorrect because the sentence discusses the first of several *tournaments* (2.3). Correction: *tournaments*.
20. D *Call* is in active voice where passive voice is needed (2.6). A device cannot call, but it can be called something by people. This is an adjective phrase that has been reduced from an adjective clause (2.10). Correction: *called*.
21. D *Saving* is a verb form that cannot be used without the auxiliary *be* (2.5). Simple present tense is appropriate for statements of fact. Correction: *save*.
22. C *Excluding* does not agree in tense or form with the second verb in this clause, *reformed* (2.5). This is a compound verb joined by *but*. Correction: *excluded*.
23. D *Leading* is an incorrect verb form following the modal *can* (2.5) Correction: *lead*.
24. C *A wild birds* has a singular article before a plural noun (2.3, 2.4). Correction: *wild birds*.
25. B Uncountable nouns do not have plural forms (2.3) Correction: *research*.

EXERCISE 2.9.A (p. 209)

1. D The sentence needs a noun structure as the direct object of *includes*. The correct answer is a noun clause. (A) lacks a subordinator. (B) has incorrect word order. (C) has an unnecessary preposition and an incorrect subordinator.
2. A The sentence needs a noun structure as the direct object of *will tell*. The answer is a noun clause that has been reduced to an infinitive phrase. (B) lacks *to* in the infinitive (2.7). (C) has incorrect word order. (D) lacks a verb or infinitive.
3. A The sentence needs a noun clause in a series of noun clauses as the compound subject. (B) and (C) lack a subordinator. (D) has incorrect word order and verb tense.
4. B The sentence needs a noun structure as the direct object of *signals*. The correct answer is the beginning of a noun clause. (A) and (D) lack a subordinator and a verb. (C) has incorrect word order.

5. A The sentence needs a noun structure as the direct object of *finding out* (2.7). The correct answer is a noun clause. (B) and (D) have incorrect word order. (C) lacks a subordinator.
6. B The sentence needs a noun structure as the direct object of *know*. The correct answer is a noun clause. (A) has incorrect word order. (C) has an incorrect subordinator. (D) lacks a subordinator.
7. C The sentence needs a noun structure as the direct object of *to know*. The answer is a noun clause that has been reduced to an infinitive phrase. (A) lacks a subordinator. (B) and (D) have incorrect word order.
8. C The sentence needs a subordinator to introduce its noun clause subject. (A) is not a subordinator. (B) and (D) are subordinators that introduce adverb clauses (2.11).
9. D The sentence needs a noun structure as the object of the preposition *on*. The correct answer is the beginning of a noun clause. (A) has an incorrect subordinator. (B) and (C) lack a subject.
10. C The sentence needs a noun structure as the true subject. *It* is the "false" subject (2.1). The correct answer is the beginning of a noun clause. (A) is a noun + infinitive (2.7). (B) is a prepositional phrase (2.21). (D) has an extra, incorrect verb; the verb of the noun clause is *is*, following *seasonal variation*.

EXERCISE 2.10.A (p. 216)

1. B *Which* lacks a preposition where one is needed before a relative pronoun. Correction: *in which* or *where*.
2. A *Scientist he invents* is incorrect because *scientist* is modified by an adjective clause, which must begin with a relative pronoun. Correction: *scientist who invents*.
3. A The sentence needs an adjective structure to modify *Hammurabi*. The correct answer is the beginning of an adjective clause. (B) and (D) lack a relative pronoun. (C) is an incorrect relative pronoun.
4. B The sentence needs a preposition + relative pronoun to introduce an adjective clause. (A) has an incorrect preposition; *to* is usually used with *introduced*. (C) lacks a preposition. (D) is an incorrect relative pronoun.
5. B The sentence needs an adjective structure to modify *credit line*. The correct answer is a passive voice adjective phrase. (A) has incorrect word order. (C) is active voice. (D) is a verb phrase (2.5).
6. C The sentence needs an adjective structure to modify *blasts*. The correct answer is the beginning of an adjective clause. (A) and (D) lack a relative pronoun. (B) has incorrect word order.
7. C The sentence needs an appositive to explain *buildings* (2.2). The correct answer is the beginning of a noun + adjective phrase that has been reduced from the noun + adjective clause *all of which were restored*. (A) is active voice. (B) is a clause that lacks a relative pronoun. (D) is a noun (2.22).
8. D The sentence needs an adjective structure to modify *art movement*. The correct answer is an adjective clause. (A) lacks a relative pronoun. (B) lacks a relative pronoun and has a duplicate subject (2.1). (C) is a verb phrase (2.5).
9. B The sentence needs an adjective structure to modify *penal colony*. The correct answer is a passive voice adjective phrase. (A) is a main clause (2.8). (C) has incorrect word order. (D) is active voice.
10. B The sentence needs an adjective structure to modify *leaves*. The correct answer is the beginning of an adjective clause. (A) has an incorrect relative pronoun; *that* cannot be used when commas surround the adjective clause. (C) and (D) lack a relative pronoun.

EXERCISE 2.10.B (p. 217)

1. B The sentence needs an adjective structure to modify *device*. The correct answer is the beginning of a passive voice adjective phrase. (A) is active voice. (C) lacks a relative pronoun. (D) has an incorrect relative pronoun.
2. B The sentence needs a relative pronoun to introduce the adjective clause that modifies *Tarascans*. (A) is not a relative pronoun. (C) is incorrect because *that* cannot be used when commas surround the adjective clause. (D) is incorrect because *which* does not refer to people.
3. A The sentence needs an adjective structure to modify *device*. The correct answer is the beginning of an adjective clause. (B) has a duplicate subject (2.1). (C) and (D) lack a relative pronoun.
4. D The sentence needs an adjective structure to modify *dams*. The correct answer is the beginning of a passive voice adjective phrase. (A) is an infinitive (2.7). (B) is a main clause (2.8). (C) lacks a relative pronoun.
5. C The sentence needs an adjective structure to modify *Edouard Daladier*. The correct answer is the beginning of an adjective clause. (A) is a passive verb phrase (2.6). (B) lacks a relative pronoun. (D) is incorrect because *that* cannot be used when commas surround the adjective clause.
6. D The sentence needs an adjective structure to modify *lithographers and publishers*. The correct answer is the beginning of an adjective clause. (A), (B), and (C) all lack a relative pronoun.
7. A The sentence needs an adjective structure to modify *Festival*. The correct answer is the beginning of a passive voice adjective phrase. (B) is active voice. (C) is a main clause (2.8). (D) is the beginning of an adjective clause, which is incorrect here because an adjective clause does not come before the noun it modifies.
8. B The sentence needs an adjective structure to modify *principles of Dada*. The correct answer is the beginning of a passive voice adjective phrase. (A) and (D) are verb phrases (2.5). (C) is a main clause (2.8).

QUIZ 5 (p. 219)

1. D The sentence needs a noun structure as the direct object of *learn*. The correct answer is a noun clause that has been reduced to an infinitive phrase (2.9). (A) is a gerund phrase, which cannot be an object following *learn* (2.7). (B) has an incorrect subordinator. (C) is a main clause (2.8).
2. B The sentence needs an adjective structure to modify *Babism*. The correct answer is the beginning of an active voice adjective phrase (2.10). (A) is passive voice (2.6). (C) has a duplicate subject (2.1). (D) is a noun (2.22).
3. B The sentence needs an adjective structure to modify *intrusions*. The correct answer is an adjective clause (2.10). (A) is a verb phrase (2.5). (C) has an incorrect subordinator. (D) lacks a subordinator.

4. A The sentence needs a noun structure as the direct object of *may not realize*. The correct answer is the beginning of a noun clause with *that* omitted (2.9). (B) has a duplicate subject (2.1). (C) is a prepositional phrase (2.21). (D) is a main clause (2.8).
5. B The sentence needs an adjective structure to modify *soldiers*. The correct answer is a passive voice adjective phrase (2.10). (A) is active voice (2.6). (C) is a main clause (2.8). (D) is an infinitive phrase (2.7).
6. B *Why* is the incorrect subordinator for this context (2.10). Correction: *where*.
7. B *In where* is incorrect because *where* never follows a preposition at the beginning of an adjective clause (2.10). Correction: *where* or *when*.
8. A *Base* is the incorrect form of the verb. In passive voice adjective phrases, the *–ed* form is used (2.10). Correction: *based*.
9. B The sentence needs a noun structure as the subject. The correct answer is a noun clause (2.9). (A) has the subordinator *Because*, which introduces adverb clauses (2.11). (C) has a duplicate subject (2.1). (D) is a main clause (2.8).
10. C The sentence needs an adjective structure to modify *marketplace*. The correct answer is the beginning of an adjective clause (2.10). (A) is a preposition (2.21). (B) and (D) are subordinators that introduce adverb clauses (2.11).
11. C The sentence needs an adjective structure to modify *Igor Stravinsky*. The correct answer is the beginning of a passive voice adjective phrase (2.10). (A) is a passive verb phrase (2.6). (B) is the beginning of a main clause (2.8). (D) is active voice (2.6, 2.10).
12. B The sentence needs a subordinator to introduce its noun clause subject (2.9). (A) is an article (2.4). (C) introduces an adverb clause (2.11). (D) is an adjective expressing quantity (2.3).
13. C The sentence needs a verb + a noun structure as its direct object (2.8, 2.9). (A) is a preposition (2.21). (B) lacks a verb. (D) has a duplicate subject (2.1).
14. D The sentence needs an adjective structure to modify *nomads*. The correct answer is an active voice adjective phrase (2.10). (A), (B), and (C) are all verb phrases (2.5).
15. D The sentence needs a relative pronoun to introduce an adjective clause (2.10). (A) is a preposition (2.21). (B) and (C) have incorrect prepositions.

EXERCISE 2.11.A (p. 225)

1. C The sentence needs a subordinator to introduce an adverb clause of time. (A) is a conjunction that joins main clauses (2.8). (B) introduces adverb clauses of manner. (D) introduces noun clauses (2.9).
2. A The sentence needs an adverb structure to modify the main clause. The correct answer is the beginning of an active voice adverb phrase. (B) is a verb phrase (2.5). (C) is a passive verb phrase (2.6). (D) is an infinitive (2.7).
3. D The sentence needs an adverb structure to modify the main clause. The correct answer is the beginning of an adverb clause. (A) is a preposition (2.21). (B) and (C) lack a subordinator.
4. D The sentence needs an adverb structure to modify the main clause. The correct answer is an adverb clause. (A) is a main clause (2.8). (B) lacks a subject. (C) lacks a subordinator.
5. A The sentence needs an adverb structure to modify the main clause. The correct answer is an active voice adverb phrase. (B) is an infinitive phrase (2.7). (C) is a main clause (2.8). (D) is a main clause with inconsistent use of active and passive voices (2.6).
6. C The sentence needs an adverb structure to modify the main clause. The correct answer is the beginning of an active voice adverb phrase. (A) and (D) are both the beginning of a main clause (2.8). (B) is an infinitive (2.7).
7. B The sentence needs an adverb structure to modify the main clause. The correct answer is the beginning of a passive voice adverb phrase. (A) is an infinitive (2.7). (C) is the beginning of a main clause (2.8). (D) is a noun (2.22).
8. A The sentence needs an adverb structure to modify the main clause. The correct answer is the beginning of an adverb clause. (B) is a preposition (2.21). (C) lacks a subject and verb. (D) does not make sense in this context.
9. D The sentence needs an adverb structure to modify the main clause. The correct answer is the beginning of an active voice adverb phrase. (A) is a main clause (2.8). (B) and (C) are passive voice (2.6).
10. B The sentence needs an adverb structure to modify the main clause. The correct answer is the beginning of an active voice adverb phrase. (A) and (D) are passive voice (2.6). (C) is a verb phrase (2.5).

EXERCISE 2.12.A (p. 231)

1. A The main clause needs a verb that agrees in tense with the verb in the *if*–clause, *is*. (B) is an adverb. (C) is an infinitive (2.7). (D) has incorrect tense.
2. B The sentence needs a subordinator in the condition clause. (A) is an article (2.4). (C) introduces noun clauses (2.9). (D) does not make sense in this context.
3. A The sentence needs a condition clause. (B) has the conjunction *or*, which joins two main clauses (2.8). (C) and (D) lack a subordinator.
4. C The adjective clause modifying *prophecy* needs a verb (2.10). (A) is an infinitive (2.7). (B) does not agree in tense meaning with the other verb in the *if*–clause, *communicate*. (D) is a noun.
5. D The condition clause needs a passive voice verb (2.6). (A) lacks the auxiliary *be*. (B) has the incorrect form of the auxiliary *be*. (C) has incorrect tense.
6. A *Plant* is the incorrect verb form to use with the auxiliary *have* (2.5). Correction: *planted*.
7. C *Was* does not agree in tense meaning with the verb in the condition clause, *will rise*. Correction: *is*.
8. B *Are living* does not agree in tense meaning with the verb in the main clause, *would pass*. Correction: *were living*.
9. D *Has made* does not agree in tense meaning with the verbs in the other clauses, *passed* and *allowed*. Correction: *made*.
10. C *Been* is the incorrect form of the auxiliary *be*. Correction: *be*.

EXERCISE 2.13.A (p. 236)

1. A The sentence needs an inverted subject and verb after *not only*. (B) and (C) do not have an inverted subject and verb. (D) lacks a subject.
2. C The sentence needs an inverted subject and verb after the prepositional phrase of location. (A), (B), and (D) do not have an inverted subject and verb.

3. D The sentence needs an inverted subject and verb after *so*. (A) lacks a verb. (B) does not have an inverted subject and verb. (C) has the incorrect verb.
4. A The sentence needs an inverted subject and verb after *under no circumstances*. (B) has incorrect word order; the direct object does not come before the verb. (C) does not have an inverted subject and verb. (D) has an incorrect subject.
5. D The sentence needs an inverted subject and verb after the prepositional phrase of position in a group. (A) lacks a verb. (B) and (C) do not have an inverted subject and verb.
6. C The sentence needs an inverted subject and verb after the prepositional phrase of location. (A) and (D) do not have an inverted subject and verb. (B) lacks a verb.
7. A The sentence needs an inverted subject and verb after *nowhere*. (B) lacks a subject. (C) and (D) do not have an inverted subject and verb.
8. B The sentence needs an inverted subject and verb after *seldom*. (A) lacks a verb. (C) does not have an inverted subject and verb. (D) is a gerund (2.7).
9. B *The mountain bluebird lives* should have inverted word order because it follows a prepositional phrase of location. Correction: *lives the mountain bluebird*.
10. B *Lincoln issued* should have inverted word order because the subordinate clause begins with the negative expression *only*. Correction: *did Lincoln issue*.

QUIZ 6 (p. 238)

1. C The sentence needs a condition clause (2.12). (A) lacks a subordinator. (B) has the conjunction *and*, which joins two main clauses (2.8). (D) does not agree in tense meaning with the verb in the main clause, *can have*.
2. D The sentence needs an inverted subject and verb after *not often* (2.13). (A) and (B) lack a verb. (C) does not have an inverted subject and verb.
3. B The sentence needs a subordinator to introduce a cause–result adverb clause (2.11). (A) is a preposition (2.21). (C) introduces noun clauses (2.9). (D) is a conjunction that joins main clauses (2.20).
4. D The sentence needs an adverb structure to modify the main clause. The correct answer is the beginning of an adverb clause (2.11). (A) and (B) lack a subordinator. (C) lacks a subject.
5. B *They do* does not agree in tense with the past meaning of the sentence (2.5, 2.12). Correction: *they did*.
6. B *Damascus lies* should have inverted word order because it follows a prepositional phrase of location (2.13). Correction: *lies Damascus*.
7. D The sentence needs a main clause after *and* (2.8). The correct answer has an inverted subject and verb after *neither* (2.13). (A), (B), and (C) do not have an inverted subject and verb. Also, (A) lacks a direct object, and (B) means Toledo lacks two of something, but the statement is incomplete.
8. B The sentence needs an adverb structure to modify the main clause. The correct answer is an active voice adverb phrase (2.11). (A) has the subordinator *that*, which introduces noun clauses (2.9). (C) is a main clause (2.8). (D) is a verb phrase (2.5).
9. A The *if*–clause needs a verb that agrees in tense meaning with the verb in the main clause, *slow down* (2.12). (B) and (D) have incorrect tense. (C) is an infinitive, which does not function as a verb (2.7).
10. D The sentence needs a main clause, which is joined to the second main clause by *but* (2.8). The correct answer is a main clause with an inverted subject and verb after *not only* (2.13). (A) and (B) have the subordinators *if* and *because*, which introduce adverb clauses (2.11). (C) does not make sense in this context.
11. A The sentence needs an adverb structure to modify the main clause. The correct answer is an active voice adverb phrase (2.11). (B) and (D) are verb phrases (2.5, 2.6). (C) is a main clause (2.8).
12. B *Were* is the incorrect auxiliary to use with *not continue* (2.5). This verb must agree in tense meaning with the verb in the main clause, *would be worn away* (2.12). Correction: *did*.
13. C *Although changes* has an incorrect duplicate subordinator, *although* (2.11). The clause beginning with *even if* is subordinate and must be joined to a main clause (2.8). Correction: omit *although*.
14. C The sentence needs an inverted subject and verb after the prepositional phrase of location (2.13). (A) lacks a verb. (B) does not have an inverted subject and verb. (D) is a prepositional phrase (2.21).
15. A The sentence needs an adverb structure to modify the main clause. The correct answer is the beginning of an active voice adverb phrase (2.11). (B) is a main clause (2.8). (C) and (D) are verbs (2.5), which would need to be joined to the main clause with a conjunction such as *and*.

EXERCISE 2.14.A (p. 245)

1. A *Contributes* is a singular verb, but a plural verb is needed with the compound subject. Correction: *contribute*.
2. D *Draws* is a singular verb, but a plural verb is needed with the plural subject, *expressions*. Correction: *draw*.
3. A *Deal with* is a plural verb, but a singular verb is needed with *macroeconomics*, which appears plural but is really singular. Correction: *deals with*.
4. A *Cause* is a plural verb, but a singular verb is needed with the gerund subject *adding extra passengers*. Correction: *causes*.
5. C *Shows* is a singular verb, but a plural verb is needed with *records*, the noun referred to by *that*. Correction: *show*.
6. C *Is* is a singular verb, but a plural verb is needed with the plural subject, *a number of*. Correction: *are*.
7. A *Are called* is a plural verb, but a singular verb is needed with *an association of*, an expression of a group. Correction: *is called*.
8. B The sentence needs a singular verb to agree with its singular subject, *The Book of Changes*. (A) and (C) are plural verbs. (D) is a verb form that cannot be used without the auxiliary *be* (2.5).
9. C The sentence needs a singular verb to agree with its singular pronoun subject, *everyone*. (A) has the relative pronoun *who*, which introduces adjective clauses (2.10). (B) and (D) are plural verbs.
10. D The sentence needs a singular verb to agree with its singular subject, *the physical environment*. (A) is a main clause (2.8). (B) is an infinitive, which does not function as a verb (2.7). (C) is a plural verb.

EXERCISE 2.14.B (p. 246)

1. C *Have* is a plural auxiliary verb, but a singular verb is needed with the uncountable noun subject, *information* (2.3). Correction: *has*.
2. A *Are* is a plural verb, but a singular verb is needed with the subject *the best known*, which is singular because it is the only one of something. Correction: *is*.
3. D *Are excellent* has a plural verb, but a singular verb is needed here. With subjects joined by *either...or*, the verb agrees with the subject it is closer to, which in this case is the gerund *cycling*. Correction: *is excellent*.
4. C *Have been* is a plural auxiliary verb, but a singular verb is needed with the singular subject, *the number of*. Correction: *has been*.
5. C *Help* is a plural verb, but a singular verb is needed with the noun referred to by *that*, which is the gerund *testing*. Correction: *helps*.
6. B *Consumes* is incorrect because the base form of the verb is needed in *that*–clauses following verbs of importance, such as *recommend*. Correction: *consume*.
7. B *Have become* is a plural verb, but a singular verb is needed with the singular subject, *trial*. Correction: *has become*.
8. B *Act* is a plural verb, but a singular verb is needed with the singular subject, *half*. Correction: *acts*.
9. A *Were* is a plural verb, but a singular verb is needed with the "false" subject *there* when the true subject is an uncountable noun such as *experimentation*. Correction: *was*.
10. C *Qualify* is a plural verb, but a singular verb is needed with the singular subject, *a college graduate*. Correction: *qualifies*.

EXERCISE 2.15.A (p. 251)

1. D *Their* is a possessive form where the subject form is needed. Correction: *they*.
2. D *That* does not agree in number with its noun referent, *figures*. Correction: *those*.
3. B *Whom* refers only to people and never to things such as *telescope*. Correction: *which*.
4. D *Your* does not agree in person with *one*; however, both pronouns refer to the same noun and must agree. Correction: *one's* or *his or her*.
5. A *Who is formed* is incorrect because *who* refers only to people and never to things such as *storm*. Correction: *which is formed* or *that is formed*.
6. D *Their* does not agree in number with its noun referent, *child*. Correction: *his, her*, or *his or her*.
7. C *Them* does not agree in number with its noun referent, *a galaxy*, or with the reflexive pronoun *itself*. Correction: *it*.
8. D *His roles* does not agree in gender with its noun referents, *Mary Pickford* and *actress*. Correction: *her roles*.
9. C *Whom* is the object form of the relative pronoun where the subject form is needed (2.10). Correction: *who* or *that*.
10. C *Those* does not agree in number with its noun referent, *coat*. Correction: *that*.

EXERCISE 2.15.B (p. 252)

1. D *It* is a subject pronoun, but a relative pronoun is needed to introduce the adjective clause that modifies *that of the Turks* (2.10). Correction: *which*.
2. C *You should* has a pronoun that does not agree in person with *one*; however, both pronouns refer to the same noun and must agree. Correction: *one should* or *he or she should*.
3. D *Their* does not agree in number with its referent, *state's*. Correction: *its*.
4. B *They* is the subject form where a possessive form is needed. Correction: *their*.
5. D *That* does not agree in number with its noun referents in the compound subject *population, industrial capacity, and financial resources*. Correction: *those*.
6. A *Whose* is the possessive form of the relative pronoun where the object form is needed. Correction: *whom*.
7. D *It* does not agree in number with its noun referent, *people*. Correction: *they*.
8. B *These* does not agree in number with its noun referent, *ledge*. Correction: *that*.

QUIZ 7 (p. 254)

1. C *There is* has a singular verb, but a plural verb is needed with the "false" subject *there* when the true subject is plural, as *similarities* is here (2.14). Correction: *there are*.
2. C *His* is a possessive form where the object form is needed (2.15). Correction: *him*.
3. A *Is* is a singular verb, but a plural verb is needed with the plural subject, *periods* (2.14). Correction: *are*.
4. D *It is* has a pronoun that does not agree in number with its noun referent, *personality differences* (2.15). Also, *is* is a singular verb where a plural verb is needed (2.14). Correction: *they are*.
5. B *Obtains* is incorrect because the base form of the verb is needed in *that*–clauses following expressions of importance, such as *it is important* (2.14). Correction: *obtain*.
6. D *His* does not agree in gender with its referent, *National Geographic Society's*, which is neuter gender (2.15). Correction: *its*.
7. D *Which* refers only to animals and things, and never to people (2.10, 2.15). Correction: *who*.
8. A The main clause needs a subject and a verb that agree in number (2.8, 2.14). *Retail sales* is a noun that appears plural but really is singular. (B) has a plural verb. (C) has question word order (2.13). (D) has an incorrect form of the verb (2.5).
9. C The main clause needs a singular verb to agree with its singular subject, *a demonstration* (2.14). (A) is a preposition (2.21). (B) and (D) are plural verbs.
10. C *They* does not agree in person with *one*; however, both pronouns refer to the same noun and must agree (2.15). Correction: *one* or *he or she*.
11. A *Are* is a plural verb, but a singular verb is needed with *a pair of*, an expression of a group (2.14). Correction: *is*.
12. D *Those* does not agree in number with its noun referent, *system* (2.15). Correction: *that*.
13. B *Causes* is a singular verb, but a plural verb is needed with the plural subject, *role changes* (2.14). Correction: *cause*.

14. A *Are* is a plural verb, but a singular verb is needed with the gerund subject *enforcing minimum wages* (2.14). Correction: *is*.
15. C *Whom* is the object form of the relative pronoun where the possessive form is needed (2.10, 2.15). Correction: *whose*.

QUIZ 8 (p. 256)

1. B *For* is incorrect before the infinitive *to include* because an infinitive cannot be the object of a preposition (2.7). Correction: omit *for*.
2. B *They* does not agree in number with its noun referent, *Halley's Comet* (2.15). Correction: *it*.
3. C *Available* is incorrect because it lacks a verb, but here is where the verb of the second main clause should be (2.5, 2.8). Correction: *is available*.
4. D The sentence needs a noun structure to rename *the 1930s* (2.2). (A) is a main clause (2.8). (B) is part of a main clause (2.8). (C) is an infinitive (2.7).
5. B The sentence needs a main clause after *and* (2.8). The correct answer has an inverted subject and verb after *so* (2.13). (A) does not have an inverted subject and verb. (C) lacks *so* and has the incorrect verb. (D) has the incorrect form of the verb (2.5).
6. C The sentence needs an adverb structure to modify the main clause. The correct answer is the beginning of an active voice adverb phrase (2.11). (A) is a verb phrase (2.5). (B) has incorrect word order. (D) is a main clause (2.8).
7. A The sentence needs a noun structure as the object of the preposition *by* (2.1). The correct answer is a noun clause (2.9). (B) is in passive voice, where active voice is needed (2.6). (C) has question word order (2.13). (D) is a main clause (2.8).
8. B The passive voice sentence needs the past participle of the verb after *is* (2.6). (A) is a noun phrase (2.1, 2.22). (C) is in active voice (2.6). (D) has an incorrect word form; *regular* is an adjective, but an adverb is needed (2.22).
9. B *Considers* is incorrect because the base form of the verb is needed in *that*–clauses following expressions of importance, such as *it is necessary* (2.14). Correction: *consider*.
10. C *Its* is a possessive form where the subject form is needed (2.15). Correction: *it*.
11. C *A water* is incorrect because uncountable nouns such as *water* do not take the singular article *a* (2.3, 2.4). Correction: *water*.
12. C *Report* is an infinitive functioning as an adjective complement, but it lacks *to* (2.7). Correction: *to report*.
13. A The sentence needs a preposition + relative pronoun to introduce the adjective clause that modifies *disorders* (2.10). (B) lacks a preposition (2.10). (C) has *that*, which never follows a preposition at the beginning of an adjective clause (2.10). (D) introduces noun clauses (2.9).
14. A The sentence needs a noun structure as the true subject, which is a compound subject joined by *rather than*. *It* is the "false" subject (2.1). (B) has the subordinator *because*, which introduces subordinate clauses and would make this sentence incomplete (2.8). (C) is a prepositional phrase (2.21). (D) has a verb.
15. D The main clause needs a verb that agrees in meaning with the verb in the *if*–clause, *were* (2.12). (A) and (C) have incorrect tense (2.12). (B) is a main clause (2.8).
16. B The sentence needs an adjective structure to modify *reactions*. The answer is the beginning of a passive voice adjective phrase (2.10). (A) is an infinitive (2.7). (C) lacks the auxiliary *are*, which must follow *that* to be a correct adjective clause in this context (2.10). (D) has incorrect word order and incorrect *–ing* form.
17. A The sentence needs a structure that can introduce a clause. The correct answer is a main clause followed by *that*, which introduces a noun clause (2.9). (B) is an infinitive phrase (2.7). (C) is the beginning of an adverb phrase (2.11), which would make this sentence incomplete. (D) is the beginning of a noun clause (2.9), which would make this sentence incomplete because it would have no subject.
18. D The sentence needs an inverted subject and verb after the prepositional phrase of location (2.13). (A) is a prepositional phrase (2.21). (B) does not have an inverted subject and verb. (C) is an infinitive (2.7).
19. C *Building* is the incorrect verb form to use with *had* (2.5). Correction: *built* or *been building*.
20. C *Occupy* is a plural verb, but a singular verb is needed with the uncountable noun subject *instruction* (2.14). Correction: *occupies*.
21. C *They will* has a verb that does not agree in tense meaning with the verb in the *if*–clause, *were* (2.12). Correction: *they would*.
22. D *Fewer* is not used with uncountable nouns such as *equipment* (2.3). Correction: *less*.
23. D *Which its* is the beginning of an adjective clause, but it lacks a verb where one should be (2.8, 2.10). Correction: *which are its*.
24. A The singular *metal* is incorrect because silver is one of many metals (2.3). Correction: *metals*.
25. C *Do* is a plural verb, but a singular verb is needed with the singular subject *expression* (2.14). Correction: *does*.

EXERCISE 2.16.A (p. 262)

1. B The sentence needs a noun structure as the object of the preposition *of*; *grotesque* is an adjective that modifies this noun. The correct answer has adverb + adjective + noun word order. (A), (C), and (D) all have incorrect word order or word forms.
2. A The sentence needs an adjective to modify *hole* that can be used before an infinitive. The correct answer is an adjective + *enough* structure. (B) has an incorrect adverb. (C) has incorrect word order. (D) is an incorrectly formed comparative (2.19).
3. D The sentence needs a structure to define or describe *aerosol*. The correct answer is an adverb + adjective + noun structure. (A) has *of very fine*, which is incorrect because an adjective cannot be the object of a preposition (2.21). (B) and (C) have incorrect word order.
4. C The sentence needs a structure to define or describe *sizes*. The correct answer is an adjective + *enough* + infinitive structure. (A) has an incorrect gerund (2.7). (B) and (D) have incorrect word order.
5. B *Side opposite* has incorrect word order. Correction: *opposite side*.

6. C *Walls very thick* has incorrect word order. Correction: *very thick walls*.
7. D *Enough heavy* has incorrect word order. Correction: *heavy enough*.
8. C *Songs unrelated* has incorrect word order. Correction: *unrelated songs*.
9. D *Governor territorial* has incorrect word order. Correction: *territorial governor*.
10. C *So weak* has an incorrect word choice. *So* can be used before adjectives or adverbs in cause–result adverb clauses (2.11); *so* is not used before infinitives (2.7). Correction: *too weak*.

EXERCISE 2.17.A (p. 266)

1. D *Surprise* is a verb or noun, but a passive participial adjective is needed. Correction: *surprised*.
2. B *Praising* is an active participial adjective, which is incorrect because *architectural projects* cannot praise. A passive adjective is needed. Correction: *praised*.
3. C *Gift ones* has an incorrect word form, *gift*. A passive participial adjective is needed to modify *ones*. Correction: *gifted ones*.
4. B *Pollution* is a noun, but a passive participial adjective is needed in a series of adjectives modifying *world* (2.25). Correction: *polluted*.
5. C *Specialize role* has an incorrect word form, *specialize*, which is a verb (2.22). A passive participial adjective is needed to modify *role*. Correction: *specialized role*.
6. A The sentence needs a noun phrase in a list of noun phrases (2.1, 2.25). The correct answer is a passive participial adjective + noun. (B) and (C) have incorrect word order. (D) is a verb phrase (2.5).
7. A The sentence needs a subject in the noun clause (2.9). The correct answer is an active participial adjective + noun. (B) has a passive adjective, but *material* performs the action of living. (C) is a clause (2.8). (D) is a noun + infinitive, which implies a future rather than present meaning.
8. C The sentence needs a noun structure as the object of the preposition *for*; *the first continuous–stitch* also modifies this noun. The correct answer is an active participial adjective + noun. (A) is a clause. (B) has *sew*, which is a verb, not an adjective. (D) has incorrect word order.
9. A The sentence needs a noun structure as the direct object of *reflects*. The correct answer is an active participial adjective + noun. (B) has a passive adjective, but *view* performs the action of prevailing. (C) and (D) are main clauses (2.8).
10. D The sentence needs an adjective to modify *painter*. The correct answer is a passive participial adjective. (A) is a noun + infinitive. (B) is an infinitive phrase (2.7). (C) is an active adjective, but *painter* receives the action of teaching; the painter *was taught* by himself.

EXERCISE 2.18.A (p. 271)

1. A The sentence needs a subject and auxiliary verb to come before *known*. (B) has *not only*, which is usually used with *but also* (2.20). (C) is a main clause (2.8). (D) has an infinitive instead of a verb (2.7).
2. A The sentence needs a noun structure as the object of the preposition *of* (2.1, 2.21). (B) has the pronoun *none*, which cannot modify a noun. (C) has *not only*, which is usually used with *but also* (2.20). (D) is an adverb + adjective.
3. C The sentence needs an adjective to modify *types*. (A) is an adverb. (B) is a conjunction. (D) is a pronoun.
4. B The sentence needs a noun structure as the subject (2.1). The correct answer is a pronoun. (A) is an adjective. (C) is a conjunction. (D) is an adverb.
5. C The sentence needs an adjective + noun structure to come after *not*. (A) is a verb phrase (2.5). (B) and (D) have the negative modifiers *neither* and *no*, which cannot follow *not*.
6. A The sentence needs a noun structure as the direct object of *had*. The correct answer has adverb + adjective + noun word order (2.16). (B) and (C) have incorrect word order (2.16). (D) has the adverb *not*, which cannot modify a noun.
7. B The first main clause needs a noun structure as the subject. (A) has *not only*, which is usually used with *but also* (2.20). (C) has the adverb *not*, which cannot modify a noun such as *gear wheels*. (D) has *not*, which has incorrect word order before *are engaged*.
8. D The sentence needs an adjective to modify *sixty–four*. (A) incorrectly uses *only* as a noun. (B) has an unnecessary article. (C) is a conjunction that is usually used with *but also* (2.20).
9. A *Not person* has the adverb *not*, which cannot modify a noun. An adjective is needed. Correction: *no person*.
10. B *None* is a pronoun where an adjective is needed to modify *accident*. Correction: *no*.

EXERCISE 2.19.A (p. 277)

1. B The sentence needs an equative expression. *In the same way as* means *just as*. (A) is a preposition (2.21). (C) is a subordinator that introduces adverb clauses (2.11). (D) is an infinitive (2.7).
2. A The sentence needs a comparative expression to use with *than*. (B) has *lesser*, which is never used with *than*. (C) and (D) are not comparative degree.
3. A The sentence needs an expression that compares two things and can be used with *not*. The correct answer is an equative that is made negative by *not*. (B), (C), and (D) are all incorrectly formed structures.
4. C The sentence needs the second part of a complex equative expression. (A) has *than*, which is used in the comparative degree. (B) is a noun clause (2.9). (D) is a simple equative, which does not make sense following *as beautiful*.
5. B The sentence needs the first part of a double comparative. (A) lacks *the*. (C) is the beginning of a condition clause (2.12). (D) is superlative degree.
6. D The sentence needs a comparative expression to use with *than*. (A) is superlative degree. (B) and (C) lack comparative words.
7. C The sentence needs the first part of a complex equative expression. (A) is a base–form adjective and lacks equative words. (B) is comparative degree. (D) lacks *as* before the adjective.
8. C The sentence needs an expression that compares two things. (A) lacks *than*. (B) is an incorrectly formed equative. (D) is superlative degree.

EXERCISE 2.19.B (p. 277)

1. A *And dry* has the base form of the adjective where the superlative form is needed in a series of superlatives. Correction: *and driest*.
2. C *As if they can* is incorrect because *as if* introduces adverb clauses of manner (2.11). An equative expression is needed with *just as well*. Correction: *as they can*.
3. A *The formalest* is an incorrectly formed superlative. Correction: *the most formal*.
4. B *Least bulky* is a superlative where a comparative is needed. Correction: *less bulky*.
5. B *Far as* is an incorrectly formed equative. Correction: *as far as*.
6. D *Hot* is the base form of the adjective where the comparative form is needed in a double comparative. Correction: *hotter*.
7. C *More greater* is an incorrectly formed comparative. Correction: *greater*.
8. A *The most* does not need *the* because it follows a possessive, *Thomas Edison's*. Correction: *most*.

QUIZ 9 (p. 279)

1. C The sentence needs an equative expression (2.19). (A) incorrectly combines equative and comparative words. (B) has incorrect word order. (D) is a clause.
2. C The sentence needs a structure to define or describe *fatherhood*. The correct answer has adverb + adjective word order (2.16). (A) and (B) have incorrect word forms (2.22). (D) has incorrect word order and word forms.
3. A The sentence needs a noun structure as the direct object of *had*. The correct answer has *only* modifying *a small number* (2.18). (B) and (C) have incorrect word order (2.16, 2.18). (D) is the beginning of a clause (2.8).
4. B *As fixed that* is an incorrectly formed equative (2.19). Correction: *as fixed as that*.
5. A *Person average* has incorrect word order (2.16). Correction: *average person*.
6. D *Most wasteful* is an incorrectly formed superlative (2.4, 2.19). Correction: *the most wasteful*.
7. C *Be* is an incorrect word choice. An equative expression is needed with *just as* (2.19). Correction: *as*.
8. D The sentence needs a noun structure as the object of the preposition *of*. The correct answer has adverb + adjective + noun word order (2.16, 2.17). (A), (B), and (C) all have incorrect word order or word forms.
9. C The sentence needs a comparative expression to use with *more* (2.19). (A) is equative degree (2.19). (B) is a prepositional phrase (2.21). (D) has *others*, which is incorrect before *war* (2.23).
10. B The sentence needs an adjective to modify *fingers* that can be used before an infinitive. The correct answer is an adjective + *enough* structure (2.16). (A) has an unnecessary word, *for*. (C) has incorrect word order. (D) is a comparative expression (2.19), which is incorrect before *to turn*.
11. D The sentence needs the second part of a double comparative (2.19). (A) is superlative degree (2.19). (B) has an unnecessary *–ing* form. (C) is a clause (2.8).
12. A The sentence needs a superlative expression to follow *one of* (2.19). (B) lacks *the* (2.4, 2.19). (C) has an extra word, *one*. (D) is comparative degree (2.19).
13. B The sentence needs an adjective to modify *experience* (2.18). (A) is incorrect without *not*. (C) is an adverb. (D) is a pronoun.
14. C *Appealed* is a passive participial adjective, but an active adjective is needed because *their art* performs the action of appealing (2.17). Correction: *appealing*.
15. C *Much influence* is the base form of the adjective where the comparative form is needed with *than* (2.19). Correction: *more influence* or *much more influence*.

EXERCISE 2.20.A (p. 285)

1. B The sentence needs a noun structure as the direct object of *produces*. The correct answer is a compound object joined by *both...and*. (A) has an unnecessary preposition. (C) lacks a conjunction. (D) is an equative expression (2.19).
2. D The sentence needs a conjunction to join two clauses. The correct answer is a subordinating conjunction. (A) has an incorrect meaning for this context. (B) is an article (2.4). (C) introduces noun clauses (2.9).
3. A The sentence needs a conjunction to join two verb phrases (2.5). The correct answer is the second part of *not only...but also*. (B), (C), and (D) have conjunctions that cannot be paired with *not only*.
4. A The sentence needs a conjunction to join two prepositional phrases (2.21). The correct answer has the second part of *not...but*. (B) lacks the preposition *on*, which must be used with *based* (2.21). (C) and (D) lack a conjunction.
5. B The sentence needs a structure to define or describe *two–thirds of Australia*. The correct answer is two adjectives joined by *either...or*. (A) lacks *or*. (C) and (D) incorrectly pair *either* with *nor* and *and*.
6. B *Therefore* expresses result, but this sentence expresses contrast. Correction: *however*.
7. D *As well* is incorrectly formed. Correction: *as well as*.
8. D *Nor* expresses a negative alternative, but the meaning here is not negative. Correction: *or*.
9. C *As well the* is incorrectly formed. Correction: *as well as the*.
10. D *Either* is incorrectly paired with *and*. Correction: *both*.

EXERCISE 2.21.A (p. 292)

1. D The sentence needs a structure to come between *to pass* and *around the earth*. The correct answer is a preposition + conjunction, which makes a compound preposition, *through and around*. (A), (B), and (C) all have *through* but lack a conjunction to join *through* with *around* (2.20).
2. D The sentence needs a structure to show how *men* and *women* are related. The correct answer is an adjective + preposition structure. (A) lacks *from*, which is needed with *different*. (B) is a verb. (C) is an infinitive (2.7).
3. B The sentence needs the first part of the paired expression *from...to*. (A) lacks a preposition. (C) has an incorrect preposition. (D) has *that*, which introduces noun clauses (2.9).

4. D The sentence needs a structure to come between a verb phrase (2.5) and a prepositional phrase. The correct answer is a *by* + *–ing* structure. (A) is a verb phrase (2.5), which is incorrect here without a conjunction (2.20). (B) has an incorrect structure: preposition + verb. (C) is a clause with question word order (2.13).
5. C The sentence needs a verb (2.8). The correct answer is a verb + preposition structure. (A) is a verb form that cannot be used without the auxiliary *be* (2.5). (B) is an infinitive, which does not function as a verb (2.7). (D) lacks *to*, which must follow *respond*.
6. C *For* is an incorrect preposition. Correction: *of*.
7. C *To the right* lacks a preposition where one is needed. Correction: *to the right of*.
8. D *To* is an incorrect preposition. Correction: *in*.
9. B *Of* is an unnecessary preposition. Correction: omit *of*.
10. A *By* is an incorrect preposition. *Dreams* cannot use terms. However, people use terms for different things. Correction: *for*.

EXERCISE 2.21.B (p. 293)

1. D *Communicate us* lacks a preposition where one is needed. Correction: *communicate with us*.
2. A *Of* is an incorrect preposition with *deal*. Correction: *with*.
3. C *For* is an incorrect preposition. *Breakup* is similar in meaning to *divide* and *division*, so it takes the same preposition they take. Correction: *into*.
4. C *Of* is an incorrect preposition. Correction: *by*.
5. B *Of* is an incorrect preposition. Correction: *by*.
6. B *Out hard gum* has an incorrect preposition. Correction: *of hard gum* or *out of hard gum*.
7. B *Played chromosomes* lacks a preposition where one is needed. Correction: *played by chromosomes*.
8. D *The number deaths* lacks a preposition where one is needed. Correction: *the number of deaths*.
9. D *Of* is an incorrect preposition. Correction: *in*.
10. C *Up* is an incorrect preposition. Correction: *from*.

QUIZ 10 (p. 295)

1. A *By* is an incorrect preposition (2.21). Correction: *of*.
2. A *Also* is an incomplete conjunction (2.20). Correction: *but also*.
3. A *Because its* has an incomplete compound preposition (2.21). Correction: *because of its*.
4. C *Or* is incorrectly paired with *both* (2.20). Correction: *and*.
5. C *At* is an incorrect preposition (2.21). Correction: *by*.
6. B *By* is an unnecessary preposition (2.21). Correction: omit *by*.
7. B The sentence needs a conjunction to join two clauses. The correct answer has a subordinating conjunction (2.20). (A), (C), and (D) all lack a conjunction. Also, (D) has *that*, which introduces noun clauses (2.9).
8. D The sentence needs a conjunction to join two noun phrases (2.20). (A), (B), and (C) all lack a conjunction.
9. C The sentence needs a structure to show how *"simple" ideas and "complex" ideas* and *distinguished* are related. The correct answer is the first part of the paired expression *between...and* (2.21). (A) cannot be paired with *and* (2.20). (B) shows a relationship of three or more things, but only two things are related here: *"simple" ideas* and *"complex" ideas* (2.23). (D) must join structures of the same value (2.20).
10. D The sentence needs a structure to define or describe *the first use of the principle of the airfoil*. The correct answer has the first part of *not...but*, which joins two prepositional phrases (2.20, 2.21). (A) lacks *not* (2.20). (B) and (C) incorrectly pair *neither* and *either* with *but* (2.20).
11. A *Of* is an incorrect preposition (2.21). Correction: *from*, which is part of the paired expression *from...to*.
12. B *Contrary* is incorrectly paired with *on the one hand* (2.20). Correction: *other hand*.
13. B *To the disk drive* has an incorrect preposition (2.21). Correction: *in the disk drive*.
14. A *Is divided to* has an incorrect preposition (2.21). Correction: *is divided into*.
15. B *To* is an incorrect preposition with *differ* (2.21). Correction: *from*.

QUIZ 11 (p. 297)

1. B The sentence needs a structure to follow the passive verb *are marked* (2.6). The correct answer is a prepositional phrase with *by* (2.21). (A) lacks *by*. (C) has incorrect word order. (D) has an incorrect preposition.
2. B The sentence needs a structure with the second part of *either...or* (2.20). (A) incorrectly pairs *either* with *and*. (C) has a structure after *or* that is not parallel to the structure after *either* (2.20, 2.25). (D) lacks *or*.
3. C *In the eighteenth* has an incorrect preposition (2.21). Correction: *to the eighteenth*, which has part of the paired expression *from...to*.
4. C *The much* is an incorrect form where the comparative degree is needed in the second part of a double comparative (2.19). Correction: *the more*.
5. C *Resulted* is a passive participial adjective, but an active adjective is needed because *impact* performs the action of resulting (2.17). Correction: *resulting*.
6. B *Little* is the base form of the adjective where the comparative form is needed with *than* (2.19). Correction: *less*.
7. C *With* is an incorrect preposition (2.21). Correction: *for*.
8. B *But* is incorrectly paired with *neither* (2.20). Correction: *nor*.
9. A *None faction* has a pronoun where an adjective is needed to modify *faction* (2.18). Correction: *no faction*.
10. B *Of* is an incorrect preposition after *determined* (2.21). Correction: *by*.
11. C The sentence needs a noun structure as the subject of an adjective clause (2.1, 2.10). The correct answer is an adjective + noun structure (2.16). (A) has incorrect word order (2.16). (B) has *especially*, an incorrect word form (2.16, 2.23). (D) is a main clause (2.8).
12. D The sentence needs a conjunction that can be used with *not only* (2.20). (A) and (C) are incorrect conjunctions. (B) lacks a conjunction.
13. C The sentence needs an expression that compares two things and can be used with *not as*. The correct answer is an equative that is made negative by *not* (2.19). (A) is part of a clause (2.8). (B) is part of a comparative (2.19). (D) has an incorrect adverb form and lacks *that*, which is necessary for making the compared things parallel (2.25).

14. A The sentence needs a structure to show how *that of youth* and *the work of middle age* are related. The correct answer is an adjective + preposition structure (2.21). (B) lacks *from*, which is needed with *different* (2.21). (C) is an adverb (2.22). (D) is a noun (2.22).
15. D The sentence needs a structure to define or describe *silicon*. The correct answer is a superlative expression (2.19). (A) has incorrect word order. (B) is comparative degree. (C) lacks *the*.
16. B *Volume enormous* has incorrect word order (2.16). Correction: *enormous volume*.
17. C *Depends* lacks a preposition where one is needed (2.21). Correction: *depends on*.
18. B *As well* is an incorrectly formed conjunction (2.20). Correction: *as well as*.
19. A *Because* is a subordinator that introduces adverb clauses (2.11), but it is incorrect here because it is followed by a noun instead of a clause. A preposition is needed (2.21). Correction: *because of*, which is a compound preposition.
20. C *Most* is an incorrectly formed superlative (2.4, 2.19). Correction: *the most*.
21. B The sentence needs a structure to describe *Paul Cezanne* that can be followed by the infinitive *to devote*. The correct answer is an adjective + *enough* structure (2.16). (A) has incorrect word order. (C) is a main clause (2.8). (D) is a gerund phrase (2.7).
22. D The sentence needs the first part of a complex equative expression (2.19). (A) and (B) incorrectly combine equative and comparative words. (C) has incorrect word order.
23. C The sentence needs a comparative expression (2.19). The correct answer has a passive participial adjective (2.17). (A) is a gerund phrase (2.7). (B) has an active adjective, which is incorrect because *people* receive the action; they are driven by *ambition* (2.6). (D) is an infinitive phrase (2.7).
24. C The sentence needs an adjective to modify *precipitation*. The correct answer is an adverb + adjective structure (2.16, 2.18). (A) and (B) have incorrect word order and word forms (2.18). (D) has the pronoun *none* where an adjective is needed (2.18).
25. A The sentence needs a structure to describe or define *which products*. The correct answer is a comparative degree adjective (2.19). (B) has an incorrect word form, *popularly*. (C) has a word that does not exist, *leastly*. (D) is equative degree, which does not make sense in this position (2.19).

EXERCISE 2.22.A (p. 303)

1. A *Elegance* is a noun where an adjective is needed. Correction: *elegant*.
2. B *Cooperatively* is an adverb where an adjective is needed. Correction: *cooperative*.
3. A *Original* is an adjective where a verb is needed. Correction: *originated*.
4. D *Systematic* is an adjective where an adverb is needed. Correction: *systematically*.
5. A *Appearance* is a noun where a verb is needed. Correction: *appears*.
6. B *Technically* is an adverb where an adjective is needed. Correction: *technical*.
7. B *Remarkable* is an adjective where an adverb is needed. Correction: *remarkably*.
8. C *Circulation* is a noun where a verb is needed. Correction: *circulates*.
9. A *Independent* is an adjective where a noun is needed. Correction: *independence*.
10. B *Traditional* is an adjective where a noun is needed. Correction: *tradition*.

EXERCISE 2.22.B (p. 304)

1. C *Skillful* is an adjective where an adverb is needed. Correction: *skillfully*.
2. D *Freeze* is a verb where an adjective is needed. Correction: *frozen*.
3. A *Mass–produce* is a verb where an adjective is needed. Correction: *mass–production*, which is a noun form that functions as an adjective in this context.
4. D *Intensely* is an adverb where an adjective is needed. Correction: *intense*.
5. C *Historically* is an adverb where an adjective is needed. Correction: *historical*.
6. D *Built* is a verb where a noun is needed. Correction: *building*.
7. C *Influence* is a noun or verb where an adjective is needed. Correction: *influential*.
8. A *Different* is an adjective where a noun is needed. Correction: *difference*.
9. A *Maneuver* is a verb where an adjective is needed. Correction: *maneuverable*.
10. B *Vertically* is an adverb where an adjective is needed. Correction: *vertical*.

EXERCISE 2.23.A (p. 311)

1. B *Does* is an incorrect word choice. A verb meaning *causes* is needed. Correction: *makes*.
2. D *Hard* is an incorrect word form. An adverb meaning *scarcely* is needed. Correction: *hardly*.
3. A *Advice* is a noun where a verb is needed. Correction: *advise*.
4. A *A most* is an incorrect word choice. An adverb meaning *nearly* is needed to modify *infinite* (2.16). Correction: *an almost*.
5. C *There* is an incorrect word choice. A possessive adjective is needed (2.15). Correction: *their*.
6. B *Too* is an incorrect word choice because it usually implies a negative result. Correction: *very*.
7. C *Strong prove* has an incorrect word form, *prove*, which is a verb. A noun structure is needed as the direct object of *give* (2.1). Correction: *strong proof*.
8. B *Amount* is not used with countable nouns such as *thunderstorms* (2.3). Correction: *number*.
9. C *To lay* is an incorrect word choice. *Lay* must be followed by a direct object. A word meaning *repose* or *recline* is needed. Correction: *to lie*.
10. C *Many* is an incorrect word choice. An adverb is needed to modify *smaller* (2.16). Correction: *much*.

EXERCISE 2.23.B (p. 312)

1. C *Others* is a pronoun where an adjective is needed to modify *sources*. Adjectives do not have plural forms (2.3) Correction: *other*.
2. B *To raise* is an incorrect word choice. *Raise* must be followed by a direct object. Correction: *to rise*.
3. D *While* is an incorrect word choice because it must be followed by a clause (2.11). A preposition is needed here (2.21). Correction: *during*.
4. C *Drives* refers to an action, but this word refers to people. Correction: *drivers*.

5. D *View* is an incorrect word choice. When *view* is a verb, it must be followed by a direct object. A verb that can be followed by *out* is needed. Correction: *look.*
6. A *Alike* is an incorrect word choice because it is an adjective that usually follows the noun it modifies. A preposition is needed here (2.21). Correction: *like.*
7. A *Then* is an incorrect word choice. A comparative word is needed after *denser* (2.19). Correction: *than.*
8. C *Almost* is an incorrect word choice. A noun or pronoun is needed as the subject of a clause (2.1). Correction: *most*, which functions as a pronoun here.
9. D *As* means *in the role of.* A word meaning *similar to* is needed here. Correction: *like.*
10. A *Beside* is a preposition of location. A word meaning *in addition to* is needed here. Correction: *besides.*

EXERCISE 2.24.A (p. 316)

1. D *Ahead* is redundant when it is used with *advance*, which means *move ahead.* Correction: omit *ahead.*
2. D *Earliest* is redundant because it has the same meaning as *first.* Correction: omit *earliest.*
3. A *And required* is redundant because it has the same meaning as *necessary*. Correction: omit *and required.*
4. C *Fatal* is redundant because it has the same meaning as *that took many lives*. Correction: omit *fatal.*
5. B *Whose numbers are increasing* is redundant because it has the same meaning as *growing*. Correction: omit *whose numbers are increasing.*
6. D *Again* is redundant when it is used with *reread*, which means *read again.* Correction: omit *again.*
7. B *Together with* is redundant when it is used with *joined*. Correction: *with.*
8. D *Progressed forward* is redundant because *progressed* means *moved forward.* Correction: *progressed.*
9. B *Unstable enough* is redundant when it is used with *sufficiently*, which means *enough*. Correction: *unstable.*
10. B *Also* is redundant because it has the same meaning as *in addition to*. Correction: omit *also.*

QUIZ 12 (p. 318)

1. A *Consistent* is an adjective where an adverb is needed (2.22). Correction: *consistently.*
2. D *Director* refers to a person, but this word refers to a thing (2.23). Correction: *direction.*
3. B *Alike* is an incorrect word choice because it is an adjective that usually follows the noun it modifies (2.23). A preposition is needed here (2.21). Correction: *like.*
4. C *Pure* is an adjective where a noun is needed as the object of a preposition (2.21, 2.22). Correction: *purity.*
5. C *Artistic* is an adjective where a noun is needed to refer to a person (2.22). Correction: *artist.*
6. B *Forward* is redundant when it is used with *proceed*, which means *go forward* (2.24). Correction: omit *forward.*
7. B *Reference* is a noun where a verb is needed (2.8, 2.22). Correction: *refers.*
8. B *Almost* is an incorrect word choice (2.23). A noun or pronoun is needed as the direct object of *make up* (2.1). Correction: *most*, which functions as a pronoun here.
9. A *Unlikely* is an incorrect word choice because it is an adverb where a preposition is needed (2.21, 2.23). Correction: *unlike.*
10. B *To achieve* is an infinitive where a verb is needed (2.7, 2.8, 2.22). Correction: *achieved.*
11. D *Another* is an incorrect word choice because it can be used only with singular nouns; *models* is plural (2.3, 2.23). Correction: *other.*
12. C *Into* is redundant when it is used with *entered*, which means *came into* (2.24). Correction: omit *into.*
13. C *Occurrence* is a noun where a verb is needed (2.8, 2.22). Correction: *occurs.*
14. C *Cooperate* is a verb where an adjective is needed (2.22). Correction: *cooperative.*
15. A *While* is an incorrect word choice because it must be followed by a clause (2.11, 2.23). A preposition is needed here (2.21). Correction: *during.*

EXERCISE 2.25.A (p. 323)

1. C The sentence needs a noun in a list of nouns joined by *and.* (A) is a verb phrase (2.5). (B) is a main clause (2.8). (D) is an infinitive (2.7).
2. A The sentence needs a prepositional phrase to modify *emergence*; this structure is parallel to *expansion of the Western economies* (2.21). (B) lacks a preposition. (C) is an adverb + adjective. (D) is a main clause (2.8).
3. D The sentence needs a gerund in a list of gerund phrases joined by *and* (2.7). *Using* is parallel to *partitioning*. (A) is a noun + preposition. (B) is an infinitive (2.7). (D) is a noun (2.22).
4. A The sentence needs *but also* + a verb phrase to be parallel to *not only powers the sun* (2.20). (B) lacks *but* and has incorrect word order. (C) has *it*, making the phrase not parallel to the structure following *not only*. (D) does not agree in verb tense (2.5).
5. B The sentence needs a verb in a list of verbs joined by *and...as well as* (2.20). (A) is a gerund (2.7). (C) is an infinitive (2.7). (D) has a duplicate subject, *they* (2.1).
6. A The sentence needs a noun phrase in a list of noun phrases joined by *and.* (B), (C), and (D) are all main clauses (2.8).
7. C The sentence needs a gerund phrase in a comparison of two things (2.7, 2.19). *Learning to ride a unicycle* is parallel to *learning to swim.* (A) is an infinitive (2.7). (B) is an adverb clause (2.11). (D) is the beginning of a noun clause (2.9).
8. D The sentence needs a noun phrase after *not only* that is parallel to the noun phrase after *but also* (2.20). Both noun phrases are superlatives (2.19). (A) is the first half of a double comparative (2.19). (B) is not parallel. (C) is a main clause (2.8).
9. D The sentence needs an adjective structure that is parallel to *high in carbon dioxide*, to which it is joined by *but.* (A) is a gerund phrase (2.7). (B) and (C) are clauses (2.8).
10. D The sentence needs a noun phrase in a list of noun phrases joined by *and...as well as* (2.20). (A) is an infinitive (2.7). (B) is a main clause (2.8). (C) has the subordinator *which*, which introduces adjective clauses (2.10).

EXERCISE 2.25.B (p. 324)

1. D *Self–esteem is raised* is not parallel to the other verb phrases in the list (2.5). Correction: *raises self–esteem.*

2. D *Managing* is not parallel to *handle*. This is a compound infinitive; *to* is omitted from *handle* because it does not have to be repeated after the first infinitive (2.7). Correction: *to manage*.
3. B *For providing* is not parallel to the verb phrase following *but also* (2.5). Correction: *provides*.
4. C *To install* is not parallel to the other nouns in the list (2.22). Correction: *installation*.
5. C *Reducing* is not parallel to the other infinitives in the list. This is a compound infinitive; *to* is omitted from *boost* and *curb* because it does not have to be repeated after the first infinitive (2.7). Correction: *reduce*.
6. B *The steps* is not parallel to *which contracts*. The verb phrases joined by *and, determines which contracts* and *defines what steps*, should be parallel. Correction: *what steps*.
7. D *To repair* is not parallel to the other nouns in the list (2.22). Correction: *repair*.
8. A *For the* makes *the waterwheel* not parallel to the noun it is being compared to, *the windmill*. Correction: *the*.
9. C *Magnetic pole for the south* is not parallel to *the north magnetic pole*. Correction: *the south magnetic pole*.
10. C *To operate* is not parallel to the other gerunds in the list (2.7). Correction: *operating*.

QUIZ 13 (p. 326)

1. C *Did they* follows *nor*, but it is not parallel to the noun phrase following *neither* (2.20, 2.25). Correction: *the*.
2. D *Plan* is a verb where a noun is needed (2.22). Correction: *planning*.
3. C *Painful* is an adjective where a noun is needed in a list of nouns joined by *and* (2.22, 2.25). Correction: *pain*.
4. D *Activities* refers to things, but this word refers to people (2.23). Correction: *activists*.
5. C *Perform* is a verb where a noun is needed (2.22). Correction: *performance*.
6. A *While* is an incorrect word choice because it must be followed by a clause (2.11, 2.23). A preposition is needed here (2.21). Correction: *during*.
7. B *Providing* is not parallel to the other verbs in the list (2.5, 2.25). Correction: *provide* or *to provide*, an infinitive that is often used with *purpose* (2.7).
8. D The sentence needs a noun in a list of nouns joined by *and...as well as* (2.20, 2.25). (A) is a prepositional phrase (2.21). (B) is a singular noun, which is not parallel to the plural nouns in the list. (C) has the redundancy *also that one sees* (2.24).
9. A The sentence needs a noun in a list of nouns (2.22, 2.25). (B) has *also by*, which is redundant (2.24). (C) is a clause (2.8). (D) has *by*, which is redundant (2.24) and *radiating*, which is not parallel to the other nouns in the list (2.25).
10. C *Among* is an incorrect word choice because it shows a relationship of three or more things, but only two things are related here: *the consumer* and *the stock market* (2.23). Correction: *between*.
11. C *Operate* is not parallel to the other nouns in the list (2.22, 2.25). Correction: *operation*.
12. C *To spend* is not parallel to the thing it is being compared to: *having quiet time by yourself*, which is a gerund (2.7, 2.19, 2.25). Correction: *spending*.
13. D *Intellectually* is an adverb where an adjective is needed (2.22). Correction: *intellectual*.
14. C *To stand* is not parallel to the gerund *swimming*, to which it is joined by *and* (2.7, 2.25). Correction: *standing*.
15. B *To climb* is not parallel to *sliding*, to which it is joined by *as well as* (2.20, 2.25). Correction: *climbing*.

QUIZ 14 (p. 328)

1. A *Nearly* is an incorrect word choice because it is an adverb where a preposition is needed (2.21, 2.23). Correction: *near*.
2. D *To control traffic* is not parallel to the other gerunds in the list (2.7, 2.25). Correction: *controlling traffic*.
3. C *Specialization* is a noun where a verb is needed in an adjective clause (2.10, 2.22). Correction: *specialize*.
4. A *Basic* is redundant because it has the same meaning as *essential* (2.24). Correction: omit *basic*.
5. A *Depends* lacks a preposition where one is needed (2.21). Correction: *depends on*.
6. D *It exaggerates* is a clause where a noun is needed in a list of nouns (2.8, 2.22, 2.25). Correction: *exaggeration*.
7. D *As well a* is an incorrectly formed conjunction (2.20). Correction: *as well as a*.
8. A *Most high* is an incorrectly formed superlative (2.19). Correction: *highest*.
9. B *They have* is a redundant subject and verb which makes the structures following *either* and *or* not parallel (2.24, 2.25). Correction: omit *they have*.
10. A The sentence needs an equative expression (2.19). (B) is an infinitive (2.7). (C) lacks *as* before *productive* (2.19). (D) is an incorrectly formed comparative structure (2.19).
11. D The sentence needs an adjective to modify *source* (2.18). (A) is an adverb (2.18). (B) is a conjunction (2.20). (C) is a pronoun (2.18).
12. B The sentence needs a noun structure as the object of the preposition *through* (2.1, 2.21). (A) and (D) are main clauses (2.8). (C) has incorrect word order: noun + adjective (2.16, 2.17).
13. A *Carve heads* has an incorrect word form, *carve*, which is a verb. A passive participial adjective is needed to modify *heads* (2.17). Correction: *carved heads*.
14. C *To stretch* is an infinitive where a verb is needed in an adjective clause (2.10, 2.22). An infinitive does not function as a verb (2.7). Correction: *stretch*.
15. D *Besides*, which means *also*, is an incorrect word choice (2.23). A preposition meaning *next to* is needed here (2.21). Correction: *beside*.
16. C *Of living expenses* has an incorrect preposition (2.21). Correction: *with living expenses*.
17. D *Accepted generally* has incorrect word order (2.16). Correction: *generally accepted*.
18. A The sentence needs a structure with the second part of *not...but* (2.20). The structure after *but* must be parallel to that after *not* (2.25). (B), (C), and (D) have conjunctions that cannot be paired with *not* (2.20).
19. C The sentence needs a structure to define or describe *field of electronics*. The correct answer has adverb + adjective word order (2.16). (A) is an infinitive (2.7). (B) is a gerund (2.7). (D) is a verb phrase (2.5).

20. D The sentence needs a noun phrase after *nor* that is parallel to the noun phrase after *neither* (2.20, 2.25). (A), (B), and (C) are all main clauses (2.8).
21. D *Its height as* is not parallel to the equative expression *as low as*, to which it is joined by *and* (2.19, 2.25). Correction: *as high as*.
22. B *Along* is an incorrect preposition (2.21). Correction: *of*.
23. B *To invade* is an infinitive where a noun is needed as the object of the preposition *against* (2.1, 2.21). Infinitives cannot be the object of a preposition (2.7). Correction: *invasion*.
24. D *Great than* is an incorrectly formed comparative (2.19). Correction: *greater than*.
25. A *Almost* is an incorrect word choice because it is an adverb where an adjective is needed to modify *thunderstorms* (2.23). Correction: *most*.

STRUCTURE REVIEW TEST (p. 331)

1. D The sentence needs a verb (2.5, 2.8). (A) is a main clause (2.8). (B) has a verb form that cannot be used without the auxiliary *be* (2.5). (C) is in passive voice, which is incorrect because the subject, *high mesa*, is not the passive receiver of the verb's action (2.6).
2. C The sentence needs an adjective to modify *form*. The correct answer has adverb + adjective word order (2.16, 2.17). (A) is a verb phrase (2.5). (B) has incorrect word forms (2.22). (D) has incorrect word order and word forms (2.16, 2.17).
3. D The sentence needs the first part of *not...but* (2.20). The structure after *not* must be parallel to that after *but* (2.25). (A) and (B) lack *as*, which is necessary for parallel structure (2.25). (C) is an adjective, not a conjunction (2.18).
4. D The sentence needs a condition clause (2.12). (A), (B), and (C) lack the subordinator *if*.
5. C *Drawn* is a verb form that does not agree in tense meaning with the other verbs in the sentence or with the time marker *in 1485* (2.5). Correction: *drew*.
6. B *Did the* has an incorrect word choice (2.23). *Make*, which means *produce*, is the verb usually used with *decision*. Correction: *made the*.
7. D *Inventor* is a noun where a verb is needed (2.8, 2.22). Correction: *invented*.
8. C *Been brought* has the extra, incorrect auxiliary *been* (2.5, 2.6). *Was* is correctly used with the passive voice verb. Correction: *brought*.
9. C *Of highest peaks* is an incorrectly formed superlative (2.4, 2.19). Correction: *of the highest*.
10. C *Designed* does not agree in tense meaning with the other verb in the main clause, *produces* (2.5). Correction: *designs*.
11. D *Develop* is a verb where an infinitive or gerund is needed after *begin* (2.7). Correction: *to develop* or *developing*.
12. A *Speaking* is an active participial adjective, which is incorrect because *language* cannot speak. Language *is spoken*; therefore, a passive adjective is needed (2.17). Correction: *spoken*.
13. D The sentence needs a noun structure as the subject of the main clause (2.1, 2.8). The correct answer is a subject pronoun (2.15). (A) is a modal auxiliary (2.5). (B) has the subordinator *so that*, which introduces adverb clauses (2.11). (C) is a preposition (2.21).
14. B The sentence needs a noun in a list of nouns joined by *and* (2.25). (A) and (D) are not parallel to the other nouns in the list (2.25). (C) is a clause (2.8).
15. A The sentence needs a noun structure to rename *Adventures of Huckleberry Finn* (2.2). (B) and (C) are main clauses (2.8). (D) is an equative expression (2.19).
16. A *Much* is not used with countable nouns such as *members* (2.3). Correction: *many*.
17. A *Almost* is an incorrect word choice because it is an adverb where an adjective is needed to modify *hurricanes* (2.23). Correction: *most*.
18. C *Note definite* has incorrect word order (2.16). Correction: *definite note*.
19. A *Repeated* is a verb where an adverb is needed (2.22). Correction: *repeatedly*.
20. C *In where* is incorrect because *where* never follows a preposition at the beginning of an adjective clause (2.10). Correction: *in which*.
21. C *Have been* is a plural verb, but a singular verb is needed with *sensuality*, the uncountable noun referred to by *that* (2.14). Correction: *has been*.
22. B *That of* has a demonstrative pronoun that does not agree in number with its noun referent, *petals* (2.15). Correction: *those of*.
23. D The sentence needs a verb (2.5, 2.8). (A) is a verb form that cannot be used without the auxiliary *be* (2.5). (B) is an infinitive, which does not function as a verb (2.7). (C) lacks a verb; when *used to* means *accustomed to*, it needs *be*.
24. C The sentence needs a noun structure as the subject (2.1). (A) is a clause (2.8). (B) has incorrect word order. (D) is not a noun.
25. A The sentence needs an adverb structure to modify the main clause. The correct answer is the beginning of an active voice adverb phrase (2.11). (B) and (C) are each the beginning of a main clause (2.8). (D) is a noun phrase (2.1).
26. C The sentence needs an inverted subject and verb after the prepositional phrase of location (2.13). (A) lacks a verb. (B) does not have an inverted subject and verb. (D) has the subordinator *that*, which introduces noun clauses (2.9).
27. C The sentence needs an adverb structure to modify *damage*. The correct answer is a *by* + *–ing* prepositional phrase (2.7, 2.21). (A) is a noun phrase. (B) is an adverb clause with incorrect word order (2.11). (D) has incorrect word order.
28. D *And* is incorrectly paired with *either* (2.20). Correction: *or*.
29. C *With* is an incorrect preposition (2.21). Correction: *for*.
30. D *To move* is not parallel to the other verbs in the list, *have* and *are* (2.25). Correction: *move*.
31. C *Whom* is the object form of the relative pronoun where the possessive form is needed (2.10, 2.15). Correction: *whose*.
32. C *The giving of love to* is redundant and not parallel to the other infinitives in the list, *to discover and understand* and *to fulfill* (2.7, 2.24, 2.25). Correction: *to love* or *to give love to*.
33. B The subordinate clause needs a verb (2.8). (A) has an incorrect word choice, *rising* (2.23) and does not agree in number with the noun referred to by *that*, *periods* (2.14). (C) is a main clause (2.8). (D) is in passive voice, where active voice is needed (2.6).

34. C The sentence needs a structure that can introduce a clause. The correct answer is a main clause followed by *that*, which introduces a noun clause (2.9). (A) lacks a subject. (B) has the subject *that* where *it* is needed as the "false" subject (2.1). (D) lacks the auxiliary *be*, which is needed with the passive voice verb *believed* (2.6).
35. B The sentence needs an adjective structure to modify *hydrofoils*. The correct answer is the beginning of an active voice adjective phrase (2.10). (A), (C), and (D) are all verb phrases (2.5).
36. A *Should used* lacks the auxiliary *be* (2.6). Correction: should be *used*.
37. B *Depend* lacks a preposition where one is needed (2.21). Correction: *depend on*.
38. C *Nothing* is a pronoun where an adjective is needed to modify *system* (2.18). Correction: *no*.
39. B *Is normally found* is an incorrectly formed comparative expression (2.19). *Than* must be used with *more*. Correction: *than is normally found*.
40. B *Has* is incorrect because the base form of the verb is needed in *that*–clauses following expressions of importance, such as *it is essential* (2.14). Correction: *have*.

SECTION 3 – READING

EXERCISE 3.1.A (p. 348)

1. C Most of the sentences point out the advantages of radio over field telephones.
2. B Most of the sentences discuss the benefits of rangelands: natural resources, mineral and energy resources, areas for scientific study.
3. D The subject of the paragraph is the first National Football League draft.
4. A The first sentence describes the appearance of dust devils. The second and third sentences contrast the origin of devils with that of tornadoes.
5. C The most general idea of the paragraph is that Marian Anderson had a role in breaking barriers of racial prejudice.
6. A Most of the sentences discuss one or both of the two existing health insurance programs: Medicaid and Medicare.

EXERCISE 3.1.B (p. 350)

1. D The first paragraph discusses causes and the second and third paragraphs discuss effects of middle ear infections.
2. B Paragraph 2 lists the signs (symptoms) of ear infections.
3. C All of the paragraphs discuss the contributions of the Bernoulli family to the mathematics of probability.
4. A All of the paragraphs mention the Bernoullis and probability. Paragraphs 2 and 3 give several examples of the Bernoullis' practical applications of probability.
5. D The passage does not mention the popularity of studying mathematics.
6. D The most general idea of the passage is that packaging plays a role in marketing products.
7. A All three paragraphs discuss ways customers are influenced by packaging.
8. C The passage does not specifically mention customers reading labels.

QUIZ 1 (p. 353)

1. B The controlling idea of the paragraph is that the tiger shark uses many different senses to help it find its food. (A) is inaccurate because the first sentence says the tiger shark *relies mostly on other senses*. (C) is a supporting idea. (D) is not mentioned.
2. D All of the sentences discuss the structure and composition of the earth. (A) is too specific. (B) and (C) are not dealt with.
3. C Most of the sentences discuss laments as a traditional communal form of expressing grief. Some key words are: *ritualized, in the company of other women, participation, communal expression*. (A) and (B) are supporting ideas. (D) is not dealt with.
4. B Most of the sentences discuss the nutritional benefits of almonds. (A) and (C) are supporting details. (D) is implied but is not the idea that controls the passage.
5. A Most of the sentences relate almonds to lowering cholesterol or risk of heart attack. (B) is inaccurate; meat eaters are not mentioned. (C) is inaccurate. (D) is not dealt with.

6. D Most of the sentences discuss words and terms relating to Americans' experiences with imported animals. (A) is not known. (B) and (C) are not dealt with.
7. A All of the sentences in paragraph 2 give examples of terms inspired by monkeys and apes. (B) is a background detail. (C) is implied in some of the details but is not a controlling idea. (D) is inaccurate; vulgarity is not mentioned.
8. C The most general idea of the passage is that there is a transition from youth to adulthood. (A) is not dealt with. (B) is inaccurate; an *initial* life structure, but not a *lifetime* structure, is mentioned as part of the Early Adult Transition. (D) is inaccurate; both external and internal values are mentioned, but not a transition between them.
9. B The first sentence is the topic sentence; the rest of the paragraph describes the two tasks. (A), (C), and (D) are all inaccurate; they try to trick you by using words from the passage.
10. A The passage does not mention young adults facing the Early Adult Transition *on their own*. (B), (C), and (D) are all aspects of the Early Adult Transition.

EXERCISE 3.2.A (p. 363)

1. B See lines 2–4.
2. A See lines 5–6 and 9–10.
3. C The passage does not mention whether *it is difficult to get established* as a writer.
4. D The main idea is stated in the first sentence, and the rest of the passage develops this idea with details.
5. B See lines 5–6.
6. A Burning the woods was a practice of Native Americans. See line7.
7. C See lines 4–5.
8. B See lines 10–11.
9. C See lines 13–15.
10. D The passage does not mention *how to avoid* a tornado.

EXERCISE 3.2.B (p. 366)

1. B The passage states that *about 300 genera...exist in the Northern Hemisphere and nearly a quarter of these genera are native to the United States*. You must calculate a quarter (one fourth) of 300; the answer is 75.
2. B See lines 6–7.
3. D See lines 7–8 and 10.
4. D See lines 11–12.
5. A See line 2. *Industry* is the desirable quality and *Inferiority* is the danger. This idea is explained in paragraph 2.
6. C See line 3.
7. A See lines 5–6.
8. D See lines 6–7.
9. B The passage does not give *proof* that Native Americans came from Asia. *Proof* is conclusive evidence, and what archaeologists now have are *estimates*, *beliefs*, and *theories*, not proof.
10. C The Bering Strait theory does not hold that the first immigrants looked like present–day Asian peoples. See lines 12–13 and 17–19.

EXERCISE 3.2.C (p. 368)

1. B The passage does not mention or imply that Reed was *confused about her career*.
2. B See line 5.
3. A See lines 8–9.
4. C See lines 16–17.
5. A The passage traces the history of buying, selling, marketing, and distribution. Each paragraph discusses a different time period.
6. C See lines 1–3.
7. D See lines 12–14.
8. B See lines 17–18.
9. D The passage says *that people reacted strongly against the typewriter* and gives examples of other inventions that *met with similar resistance initially*. See lines 22–24.
10. C The passage does not mention supermarkets and convenience stores.

QUIZ 2 (p. 371)

1. D The main idea of the passage is that people's attitudes toward money have changed as a result of economic changes and the development of consumer credit. (A) is too general. (B) is inaccurate; see lines 16–18. (C) is inaccurate, see lines 9–10. (3.1)
2. C The belief that people who buy as many things as possible are respectable is a more recent attitude; see lines 16–18. (A), (B), and (D) all paraphrase information in lines 2–4. (3.2)
3. B See lines 7–9. (3.2)
4. A See lines 9–10. (3.2)
5. D This is the main point of paragraph 3; it paraphrases lines 16–18. (A) is untrue; see lines 1–2. (B) is inaccurate; see lines 15–16. (C) is inaccurate; *extravagant* is an exaggeration. (3.2)
6. B All of the paragraphs discuss different things that range managers do. (A) and (D) are not dealt with. (C) is a supporting detail. (3.1)
7. A The passage does not mention enforcing laws relating to rangelands. (B), (C), and (D) are all stated or paraphrased in paragraph 1. (3.2)
8. D See lines 9–10. (3.2)
9. C See lines 11–12. (3.2)
10. C See line 16. (A) is not mentioned. (B) is inaccurate; the passage does not imply that range managers *prefer* working outdoors over indoors. (D) is untrue; the passage states that *employers* generally supply transportation; see lines 16–18. (3.2)

EXERCISE 3.3.A (p. 378)

1. B *The kingdom of Axum* is the subject of the first sentence, and *it* is the subject of the next sentence (you can easily see this if you cross out all introductory and modifying phrases). This parallel position helps you see that *it* refers to *the kingdom of Axum*.
2. B *Sun*, *rain*, and *soil* appear before *these natural elements*. This is the only answer choice that you would *battle...to produce nutritious food for your table*.
3. C *Human beings* appears immediately before *their* and is the only answer choice that could have *behavior*, *values*, *interactions*, and the other things listed in lines 2–4.
4. B *Physical objects* appears immediately before *their*.
5. B *"Duke"* refers to *the strong, silent cowboy*, who is later identified as *John Wayne*.
6. D *The 1940s* is the ten years following 1939, the date that appears before *the next decade*. A *decade* is ten years.

EXERCISE 3.3.B (p. 380)

1. B *Discs and (disc) players* appears before *their*, in the same sentence. (A) is inaccurate because it mentions only *discs*.
2. C *Bit of sound* is the direct object of a verb, and so is *each*. This parallel position helps you see that *each* refers to *bit of sound*. A computer *samples 44,000 bits of sound*...and *assigns each (bit of sound)* a numerical value.
3. C *Pennsylvania* is *the region* that is the land between New York and Maryland, the domain of William Penn, and the subject of this passage.
4. C *Nine broad streets* is the subject of the first clause, and *these* is the subject of the second clause in the same sentence. This parallel position helps you see that *these* refers to *nine broad streets*. (D) is tricky because *two rivers* could also be crossed, but rectangular blocks are formed only when streets are crossed by other streets.
5. D *Each house* appears before *its* and is the only answer choice that could *be placed in the middle* of a lot. (C) is tricky because *grass* could be on a lot, but grass would be planted or grown, not *placed*.
6. A The passage states that *Penn insisted on religious toleration and welcomed all...creeds* (beliefs); see lines 3–4. This does not have the same meaning as *Penn wanted Pennsylvania to be settled only by religious people*. Religious toleration includes acceptance of all beliefs, including belief in no religion.
7. A *Saturn's specific gravity* is the subject of one sentence, and *its diameter* and *its rotational speed* are the subjects of the clauses in the next sentence. This parallel position helps you see that *its* refers to *Saturn*.
8. C *Atmosphere* appears before *that*, closer than any of the other answer choices.
9. B *Saturn's theoretical construction* is the subject of the first clause, and *it* is the subject of the other two clauses in the same sentence. This parallel position helps you see that *it* refers to *Saturn's theoretical construction*.
10. C The passage states that the rings are estimated to be *no thicker than ten miles* (lines 11–12), which means *less than ten miles thick* (1.5, 2.18, 2.19).

EXERCISE 3.3.C (p. 382)

1. *The Amazon River*, or *the Amazon*, is the subject of the first two sentences, and *It* is the subject of the next sentence. This parallel position helps you see that *It* refers to *the Amazon River*.
2. *Most of the river's drainage basin* is the subject of one sentence, and *It* is the subject of the next sentence. This parallel position helps you see that *It* refers to *the river's drainage basin*.
3. *Low, muddy islands* appears immediately before *These*. *These* refers to *low, muddy islands*.
4. *The homeowner* is the one who answers the telephone and has *her* dinner interrupted. Common sense tells you that *her* and *she* refer to *the homeowner*.
5. *Consumers* is the subject of one sentence, and *They* is the subject of the next sentence. This parallel position helps you see that *They* refers to *consumers*.
6. *Telemarketing* is the topic of the passage. *This field* refers to *telemarketing*.

QUIZ 3 (p. 386)

1. B Most of the sentences in paragraph 1 discuss effects of the Great Depression. (A) is not dealt with. (C) and (D) are too general. (3.1)
2. D The previous two sentences discuss people who were unemployed and became poor. (A) would not make sense. (B) and (C) are not mentioned as *thrown out of their apartments*. (3.3)
3. C *Big business owners* appears before *their*, closer than (A) or (B). (D) would not make sense. (3.3)
4. C *Some people* is the subject of the previous clause in the same sentence, a parallel position that helps you see that *others* refers to *people*. (A) would not make sense. (B) and (D) are farther from *others*. (3.3)
5. A The correct answer paraphrases lines 13–15. (B) and (C) are beliefs of President Reagan's supporters, not his critics. (D) is not known; the passage does not mention how many people received more wealth. (3.2)
6. B Whether President Reagan's childhood shaped his philosophy is neither mentioned nor implied. (A) is a major point of paragraph 1. (C) paraphrases lines 1–2. (D) is a major point of paragraph 2. (3.1, 3.2)
7. D The general message of the passage is that merchandising is a way for retail stores to persuade shoppers to buy goods. Most of the sentences in the passage define merchandising by giving examples of merchandising techniques. (A) is a background detail. (B) is inaccurate. (C) is too general. (3.1)
8. B See lines 5–6. (3.2)
9. A *At eye level* appears before *there*, in the same sentence. (B), (C), and (D) are farther from *there*. (3.3)
10. C *Items* appears before *those*, in the same sentence. (A), (B), and (D) are farther from *those*. (3.3)
11. A The passage does not mention shopping carts. (B), (C), and (D) are all mentioned. (3.2)
12. D *Shoppers* appears in the previous sentence, and common sense tells you that shoppers would be *likely to pick up and buy additional items*. (A) and (B) are farther away in both structure and meaning. (C) would not make sense. (3.3)
13. C Most of the sentences in the passage discuss the living habits of muskrats. (A) is too general. (B) and (D) are too specific. (3.1)
14. A The passage does not mention *bushy tail*. *Rudderlike tail* (line 4) has a different meaning. (B), (C), and (D) are all mentioned in paragraph 1 or 2. (3.2)
15. C See lines 6–7. (A), (B), and (D) are not mentioned in relation to the construction of the muskrat's mouth. (3.2)
16. A Muskrats and their habits are the topic of the passage, and common sense tells you *muskrats* is a better answer than (B), (C), and (D), which are all parts of the muskrat's body. (3.3)
17. D *Houses and feeding platforms* appears before *they*, in the same sentence. This is the only answer choice that would be *added to* and *house only one individual*. (A) and (B) would not make sense. (C) is farther away from *they*. (3.3)
18. B The correct answer paraphrases lines 14–17. (A) and (C) are not mentioned. (D) is untrue; it is entrances, not houses, that are underwater. (3.2)
19. C Muskrats are the subject of the passage. (A) would not make sense. (B) appears in the previous paragraph. (D) is not mentioned. (3.3)

20. B The correct answer paraphrases lines 19–21. (A) is inaccurate; see lines 13–14. (C) is inaccurate; see lines 15–17. (D) is untrue; overcrowding is a possible *result*, not a *cause*, of flooding; see lines 18–19. (3.2)

EXERCISE 3.4.A (p. 398)

1. C *Demand it* is similar in meaning to *insist on it.*
2. D *Amounts* renames *denominations*, following *or*.
3. A *Rain* is a type of *precipitation.*
4. C *Change* is similar in meaning to *transformation.*
5. B All of the things in the list (lines 2–3) are people. A rogue is a dishonest person.
6. D *Enhanced* is similar in meaning to *fortified.*
7. A *Additional* is similar in meaning to *supplemental.*
8. B *Insufficiencies* is similar in meaning to *deficiencies.*

EXERCISE 3.4.B (p. 400)

1. A *Prediction* is similar in meaning to *forecasting*. The prefixes *pre–* and *fore–* both mean *before*.
2. B A modem is an electronic device that connects a computer to a telephone line.
3. B *Wares* in this context are items for sale.
4. D An *array* is a collection of things that are arranged in some kind of order.
5. C *Excess* is closest in meaning to *dross*, which is waste material, or something to throw away.
6. B *Called on* is similar in meaning to *invoke*. The stem *–vok–* means *call.*
7. C *Covered* is closest in meaning to *decked* in this context.
8. D *Picking* is closest in meaning to *plucking* in this context.
9. A *Symbol* is closest in meaning to *token* in this context.
10. C Paragraph 3 discusses the rose as a sign of secrecy. *Sub rosa* means *secretly.*

EXERCISE 3.4.C (p. 402)

1. B The topic of the passage is the life span of stars. Paragraphs 2 through 4 each discuss a different stage in a star's existence.
2. C *Unchangeable* is a synonym for *immutable.*
3. D Interstellar clouds are clouds between stars. The prefix *inter–* means *between.*
4. A *Unites* is closest in meaning to *coalesces* in context.
5. C A protostar is the earliest form of a star; during this stage, the star is still forming and is not yet a true star.
6. C A process of fusion reaction, in which hydrogen is converted to helium, is identified in the previous sentence (lines 12–13).
7. A *Forced* is closest in meaning to *exerted* in this context.
8. A See lines 16–18. When a protostar *stops contracting*, it becomes a star and enters its main sequence.
9. D *Enlarges* is similar in meaning to *swells* in this context.
10. B A cinder is an object that is partially or completely burned.

EXERCISE 3.4.D (p. 403)

1. *Stands for* is closest in meaning to *signifies*. Both are verbs with the same subject, *the lotus.*
2. *Derive* has the same meaning as *stem* in this context. Both are verbs with the same subject, *the last two meanings.*
3. *Not dirtied* is closest in meaning to *unsullied.*
4. *Sealed* is closest in meaning to *airtight* in this context.
5. *Loaded* is closest in meaning to *laden* in this context.
6. *Intensify* is closest in meaning to *aggravate*. Both are verbs that mean *make worse* in this context.

QUIZ 4 (p. 407)

1. A *Tool–like* is closest in meaning to *instrumental* in this context. Clues: *shaping rocks, sculpted by the water* (lines 3–4).
2. C *Wear away* is similar in meaning to *erode*. Clues: *softer, at a different rate, creating pockets* (lines 8–9); *until a layer of erosion–resistant harder rock under it emerges* (line 17).
3. D *Successive* is closest in meaning to *alternating.* Clues: *above and below, layers of hard and soft rock* (lines 12–13).
4. B *Breaking* is closest in meaning to *faulting* in this context. Clues: *exposed alternating layers, formed by, and uplifting* (lines 12–14).
5. A *Not numerical* is closest in meaning to *nonquantitative*. Clues: *may relate to history, past experience, instinct, judgment, morality; decision making as an art* (lines 4–6).
6. C *Consequences* is similar in meaning to *outcomes.* Clue: *resulting from these choices* (line 9).
7. A *Express clearly* is closest in meaning to *spell out explicitly*. Clues: *clarify, identify* (lines 11–12).
8. D *Limitations* has the same meaning as *constraints* in this context. Clue: *limiting* (line 12).
9. C *Confused by* is closest in meaning to *confounded by.* Clue: *different uncertainties* (line 14).
10. A *Carried out* is similar in meaning to *implemented.* Clue: *the social and political context in which the decision will be* (line 19).

QUIZ 5 (p. 409)

1. D The passage does not support the idea that Americans are having fewer children than in the past. (A) is supported in lines 1–3. (B) is supported in line 10. (C) is supported in lines 7–8 and paragraph 4. (3.1)
2. A *Adult Americans* appears before *those*, in the same sentence. (B) would be redundant before *more than 90 percent have married* (line 3). (C) is inaccurate; men are not specified. (D) would not make sense with *born in the 1920s*. (3.3)
3. C *Never before seen* is closest in meaning to *unprecedented.* Clues: prefix *pre–* means *before; growing share, postponing marriage for so long* (lines 5–6). (3.4)
4. A See lines 5–6. (3.2)
5. B *Unavoidable* is closest in meaning to *inevitable.* Clues: The general message of paragraph 2 is that people are either not marrying or waiting longer to remarry. Also, a key clause is *put these trends together with our increasing life expectancy* (line 9). (3.4)
6. B *Median age* is defined following the verb *is* (line 13). (3.4)

7. D See lines 14–16. In 1890 the median age at which men first married was 26.1, and in the 1950s (which is between 1947 and 1962), it was 22.6. This is a decrease of more than 3 years. (3.2)
8. C See lines 16–17. (3.2)
9. A See line 18. The prefix *inter–* means *between.* (3.4)
10. C *Unmarried couples* appears before *them*, in the same sentence. (A), (B), and (D) are farther from *them.* (3.3)
11. B The main idea of the passage is that the heroic and the comic were combined and that American popular heroes were comic heroes. (A) and (D) are supporting ideas. (C) is inaccurate. (3.1)
12. B *Heroic themes* appears before *those* and is the subject of the same sentence. (A) and (D) appear in paragraph 1. (C) would not make sense. (3.3)
13. A The passage does not mention fluid use of language as a heroic theme. (B), (C), and (D) are all mentioned or paraphrased in paragraph 2. (3.2)
14. A *Opponents* is similar in meaning to *antagonists.* Clues: *combats, against* (lines 9–10). (3.4)
15. D See lines 20–22 and 25–27. The hero–clown is the topic of the passage, and the blending of heroic and comic themes is illustrated in the Davy Crockett legends. (3.2)
16. C See line 15. (3.2)
17. B *Heroic act* is closest in meaning to *exploit* in this context. Clue: *saving the earth* (line 15). (3.4)
18. C *Bravery* is similar in meaning to *prowess.* Clues: *fearlessness, bold* (line 19). (3.4)
19. D This is an important supporting idea in the passage; it paraphrases lines 22–24. (A) is inaccurate; the author does not imply that American writers *strove* to be distinct. (B) is inaccurate; the author implies only that Americans liked laughing at hero–clowns. (C) is inaccurate; nothing is said about Americans liking the comic *more than* the heroic. (3.2)
20. A *Uncertainty* is a synonym for *ambiguity.* Clues: *vagueness, the unexpected, never quite certain whether to laugh or applaud* (lines 23–27). (3.4)

EXERCISE 3.5.A (p. 418)

1. C Key: *temporary workers are hired by shops during busy seasons such as Christmas.*
2. D Keys: *have a large range, living in hollow trees, hiss, snarl, spit.*
3. C Keys: *vague, burden, terrifying, self–defeating illusion.*
4. B All of the sentences discuss how either communications or transportation has affected business.
5. D Key: *All fifty states have forest lands.*
6. A Keys: *shaping tongues and grooves, making wooden pegs, fitting all these neatly together.*

EXERCISE 3.5.B (p. 420)

1. B Key: *He evidently sighted land.*
2. C Keys: *battling local tribes of Inuits, Thorfinn was killed, continued threats.*
3. A Key: *only the first attack of the European invasion.*
4. A The topic of the passage is baseball statistics. *All those basics* (line 4) means basic statistics.
5. B Key: *sophisticated statistics.*
6. D Ty Cobb and Mickey Cochran are mentioned with Joe Dimaggio (lines 13–14), and Joe Dimaggio is called a *star player* (line 18).
7. B The main idea of the passage is that baseball is the greatest statistics game there is.
8. C Mrs. Lincoln died from drinking the milk of cows that had eaten snakeroot; you can conclude that snakeroot is a plant that is poisonous to humans.
9. A Keys: *a reconstruction of the little house, interpreters, happy to answer one's questions, visitor center.*
10. D Keys: *Thomas Lincoln took his family, Abraham Lincoln's boyhood home, the president's mother.*

EXERCISE 3.5.C (p. 423)

1. A Only plants that can withstand having their roots submerged in water grow in swamps, and red maple is a swamp tree.
2. C Key: *tree, shrub, and herbaceous layers.*
3. B Herbaceous plants grow in the layer beneath shrubs, and cardinal flower, jewelweed, and marsh marigold grow beneath shrubs.
4. C Keys: *half the expenditure of time and money* (line 3), *housed quickly* (line 8), *quick–grown American city* (line 22).
5. D The author compares the time and money it took to build this church with what it usually took to construct a building in 1833.
6. B See lines 4–5.
7. A An *upstart* city is one that grows suddenly and quickly. A *flood of people* is a large number of people.
8. B See lines 9–11 and 17–18.
9. D See lines 18–20.
10. C Balloon–frame construction became *conventional* (standard) and was used extensively in both city and suburban development in the twentieth century.

QUIZ 6 (p. 426)

1. D See lines 4–6. (A) is inaccurate; the author does not imply that *people generally view* culture this way. (B) and (C) are not supported by the information in the passage.
2. C Skin and eye color are physical adaptations to climate. (A), (B), and (D) all involve knowledge, concepts, or values that are shared by members of a group.
3. B The author states that the U. S. is complex and that identifying the core culture of a premodern society is easier than identifying that of the U.S. This implies that the culture of a premodern society is simpler. (A) is not true according to the passage. (C) is not true according to the passage (lines 4–5). (D) is irrelevant here.
4. A See lines 14–15 to see who was excluded from the conception of "men" who were created equal; from this, you can conclude that "men" referred to white men who owned property. (B) is irrelevant here. (C) is inaccurate; the idea had a limited meaning originally. (D) is inaccurate; the idea was expressed by the founding fathers in 1776, but this does not imply it became part of the core culture then.
5. A The idea of equality is *still used by victimized groups* in their struggle for equality (lines 17–18). (B) is not supported by the information in the passage. (C) is not true according to the passage. (D) is inaccurate; no cause–result relationship is implied between core values and victimization.

6. B Keys: *The first man's step onto the moon's surface; In the eight years from 1961 to 1969, ...the reality of a lunar landing.* (A) is inaccurate; several people, including President Kennedy, believed it was possible. (C) and (D) are not supported by the information in the passage.
7. B Nothing in the passage suggests when management science was developed in relation to computers. (A) is implied in lines 9–12. (C) is implied in *tie together a project with thousands of disparate components* (line 11). (D) is implied in *overcome unforeseen obstacles* (lines 10–11).
8. C Keys: *NASA administrators, had to choose the best design, commissioned the Apollo module.* (A), (B), and (D) are not supported by the information in the passage.
9. D The main idea of the passage is that management science played an important role in the space program. (A) and (B) are not supported by the information in the passage. (C) is inaccurate; by stressing the essential role of management science, the author is suggesting the opposite.
10. A Key: *strove to find ways to make the operations as productive and economical as possible* (lines 20–21). (B) and (C) are too general; neither mentions management science. (D) is too general; it does not focus on the space program.

EXERCISE 3.6.A (p. 435)

1. D The author is explaining the work, life, and reputation of Mary Cassatt.
2. C You can infer that Whistler and Sargent were American painters. The author compares Cassatt's "American–ness" to that of Whistler and Sargent.
3. A The author gives three reasons why Cassatt should be seen *in the American context.*
4. B The passage is a historical account of Herschel's contribution to the development of the reflecting telescope.
5. A Key: *much like Galileo and Newton.* You can infer that Galileo and Newton were also scientists who either built or wanted to build telescopes.
6. B The discovery of Uranus was one of Herschel's accomplishments.
7. C *Recording their positions* and *his "Book of Sweeps"* refer to a written record kept by Herschel.
8. D The quotation marks (" ") show where the author quotes Herschel.

EXERCISE 3.6.B (p. 437)

1. A The author states that Gifford Pinchot was *foremost* in promoting forestry as a career.
2. C Key: *the first collegiate school of professional forestry.*
3. D Keys: *do research, teach in colleges and universities.*
4. D *A new class of worker* is a group of employees of a new type; because of telecommunications technology, such as computers and modems, these people can work at home rather than at their company's office.
5. B This paragraph discusses the benefits of telecommuting.
6. B This paragraph discusses the disadvantages—drawbacks—of telecommuting.
7. C *Self–discipline* is the ability to motivate and train oneself. *Without supervision* means independently.
8. A A secretary who works at home four days a week is a telecommuter.

EXERCISE 3.6.C (p. 439)

1. Paragraph 3 outlines the primary functions of most small business owners.
2. Paragraph 2 discusses the three most common types of small business structures.
3. *To give an example of a franchise operation. Such as* tells you that gas stations are an example of *franchise operations* (3.2).
4. *In general, companies are considered as small businesses if their yearly sales are below $9 million.*
5. *The owners are also liable for the firm's debts.* This sentence refers to both sole proprietorships and partnerships. *Liable* means responsible; *debts* are money owed.
6. *Some businesses function with only one person.* The author illustrates this with the example of a bicycle shop owner who performs every job in the business.

QUIZ 7 (p. 443)

1. A The passage illustrates the theory of probability with the example of a coin toss. (B) is not supported; the experiment illustrates the theory. (C) and (D) are supporting details. (3.6)
2. D The author tells you that a tossed coin will land *sometimes heads and sometimes tails*; you can infer that the two sides of a coin are called *heads* and *tails*. (A) is not supported; we cannot say what the result of a coin toss *will be* for certain, but we can *guess*. (B) is irrelevant. (C) is not supported; the author says *perhaps you would argue that the coin has an equal chance*; this does not imply the coin *does* have an equal chance. (3.5)
3. D In lines 13–15 the author summarizes the results of Kerrich's ten thousand trials. (3.6)
4. C Keys: *Probability describes the predictable long–run patterns of random outcomes* (lines 2–3); *after many trials, the proportion of heads settled down to a fixed number* (lines 14–15); also, Kerrich's experiment involved ten thousand coin tosses. (A) is inaccurate; Kerrich's experiment led to the probability of a head as 0.507. (B) is irrelevant. (D) is not true according to the passage; see lines 8–10 and 13–14). (3.5)
5. B The author discusses Franklin in a positive way, focusing on his accomplishments in science and politics. (A) is inaccurate; the author does not try to change your opinion. (C) is inaccurate; the author is not neutral. (D) is inaccurate; the author focuses more on facts than feelings. (3.6)
6. A Keys: *said many things we still say today, new American words.* (B) and (D) are not supported by the information in the passage. (C) is inaccurate; new words were created to describe Franklin's inventions, not him. (3.5)
7. C The author tells you that Franklin owned a printing shop (line 6), and the possessive *his* appears before the names of both the newspaper and the almanac. (A), (B), and (D) are not supported by the information in the passage. (3.5)
8. B *His famous "kite–key experiment."* (3.6)
9. D Paragraph 4 discusses Franklin's political life. (3.6)

10. D Key: *in his will, he listed himself first as "Printer."* (A) is not supported by the information in the passage. (B) is inaccurate; Franklin helped Jefferson, but this does not imply Jefferson could not finish by himself. (C) is inaccurate; *whole man* and *man of the world* mean Franklin was well–rounded and widely influential, not wealthy or materialistic. (3.5)

QUIZ 8 (p. 445)

1. B All of the paragraphs discuss a popular American house style called *Queen Anne*. (A) is too general. (C) and (D) are too specific; they are supporting details. (3.1)
2. C *"Queen Anne"* appears before *This*, closer than (A), (B), or (D). (3.3)
3. A The passage does not mention decorative windows as a characteristic. (B), (C), and (D) are all mentioned or paraphrased in paragraph 2. (3.2)
4. C *Ornate* means elaborate and showy. (A), (B), and (D) are not supported by the information in the passage. (3.5)
5. D *Unbalanced* is closest in meaning to *asymmetrical* in this context. Clue: *how drastically different the right and left sides are*. (3.4)
6. C See lines 17–18. (3.2)
7. D *Fans* is closest in meaning to *buffs* in this context. Clues: *favorite symbols, painstakingly and lovingly*. (3.4)
8. B Keys: *favorite symbols of the past, painstakingly and lovingly restored, reproduced by contemporary builders*. (A) is untrue according to the passage. (C) is not supported by the information in the passage. (D) is too general. (3.5)
9. A *The style was loosely based on medieval buildings.* (3.6)
10. A Paragraphs 2–4 discuss either European or American exploration of Colorado. (B) is a background detail. (C) is a supporting detail. (D) is an implied detail; the emphasis is on exploration for potential future exploitation. (3.1)
11. C Anasazi buildings can still be seen; they were built of stone, which has withstood the wear of the centuries since the 1200s. Clues: *Anasazi archaeological site* (lines 19–20), *stone houses and other Anasazi remains* (line 28). (3.4, 3.5)
12. D Gold, pelts, and slaves had commercial value. Keys: *prospecting and trading party* (lines 7–8), *commercial value* (line 11). (A) is inaccurate; Rivera found little of commercial value. (B) is irrelevant. (C) is not supported; the author's attitude is more objective than critical. (3.5, 3.6)
13. C *Southwestern Colorado* is the subject of the passage and *the region* explored by Rivera. (3.3)
14. B Key: *left names on the land*. (A) is inaccurate; *unsuccessful* can have many meanings. (C) is inaccurate; some details are known. (D) is not supported by the information in the passage. (3.5)
15. C See lines 16–17. (3.2)
16. B *Stronghold* is closest in meaning to *fastness* in this context. Clues: *penetrated deeply, mountain*. (3.4)
17. A Keys: *adventurous, a tough bunch, penetrated deeply into the mountain fastness*. (B) is inaccurate; Peg–leg Smith obtained his supplies in the trapping town of Taos. (C) and (D) are not supported by the information in the passage. (3.5)
18. D William Becknell was *the father of the Santa Fe Trail*; this implies he discovered or built the trail. (A), (B), and (C) are not supported by the information in the passage. (3.5)
19. C The passage is an account of a certain period in Colorado's history. (A), (B), and (D) are all inaccurate or relate to details instead of the main purpose. (3.6)
20. B The passage does not mention the discovery of gold and mentions only some *insignificant silver–bearing rocks* (line 9). (A) is the topic of paragraph 1. (C) is stated in lines 5–6. (D) is an important idea implied throughout the passage. (3.2)

EXERCISE 3.7.A (p. 453)

1. A In the added sentence, *Most of them* refers to *kindergartners*, the subject of the previous sentence.
2. B In the added sentence, *However* is a transition that shows contrast between *appear relatively dry* in the previous sentence and *spongy and wet to the touch*.
3. C The added sentence introduces *peat accumulation*, which is expanded on in the following sentence, *Peat deposits 6 to 12 meters deep are not uncommon*.
4. B In the added sentence, *The most obvious benefit* refers to *trees are good for the environment* in the previous sentence.
5. C The added sentence introduces *the demand for air–conditioning*, which the following sentence develops with *This translates into reduced emissions*.
6. C In the added sentence, *It* refers to *Corn*, the subject of the previous sentence.
7. A The purpose of the added sentence is to introduce the topic of paragraph 2. The rest of the sentences give examples.
8. D In the added sentence, *All activities* refers back to *planting and harvesting* in the previous sentence. Also, the added sentence introduces the concept of *unity*, which the following sentence expands on.

QUIZ 9 (p. 458)

1. B In the added sentence, *This irritation* refers to *an inflammation of the bronchial tubes* in the previous sentence (3.3). (A) would not make sense. (C) would interrupt the ideas in consecutive sentences. (D) would be less coherent than the correct answer.
2. C In the added sentence, *Other symptoms* naturally follows *the cough* in the previous sentence. (A) and (B) would interrupt the ideas in consecutive sentences. (D) would be less coherent than the correct answer.
3. A The added sentence introduces the topic of *chronic bronchitis*, which is developed in the rest of the paragraph. (B) would be less coherent than the correct answer. (C) and (D) would interrupt the ideas in consecutive sentences.
4. B In the added sentence, *Their* refers to Hopewell Indians in the previous sentence (3.3). (A) would not make sense. (C) and (D) are too far away from the referent of *Their*.
5. C In the added sentence, *They* refers to *artifacts* in the previous sentence. (A) would not make sense. (B) would be less coherent than the correct answer. (D) would not make sense; the pipes do not *include shell beads, bear and shark teeth*, and so on.

6. D The purpose of the added sentence is to describe part of a process; *then covered with earth and overlaid* is a clue; this sentence logically follows *the bodies were laid* in the previous sentence. (A) and (B) would not make sense. (C) would be less coherent than the correct answer.
7. D In the added sentence, *However* is a transition that shows contrast between *traders worked out different rates of exchange* in the previous sentence and *this was a long, slow process*. (A) would not make sense. (B) and (C) would be less coherent than the correct answer.
8. C In the added sentence, *for example* tells you the purpose of the sentence is to illustrate something; here it illustrates *ordinary people continued to barter*, the idea introduced in the previous sentence. (A) would not make sense. (B) would not make sense because the added sentence would not illustrate the previous sentence. (D) would be less coherent than the correct answer.
9. A The added sentence introduces the topic of *paper money*. (B) would interrupt the ideas in consecutive sentences. (C) and (D) would be less coherent than the correct answer.
10. D The added sentence expresses cause, *Because paper money made trade easier and more efficient*, and result, *its use quickly caught on throughout the world*. The sentence functions best as the conclusion of the passage. (A), (B) and (C) would interrupt the ideas in consecutive sentences.

QUIZ 10 (p. 463)

1. A *Material* is closest to meaning to *fodder* in this context. Black holes give writers and scientists material to work with. (3.4)
2. C The paragraph describes the conditions that lead to the formation of a black hole. (A) is too general. (B) is inaccurate; the paragraph does not instruct in *how to build*. (D) is a supporting detail. (3.1)
3. B See lines 7–8. The dashes are a punctuation clue; the information between the two dashes defines *exclusion principle*. (3.2, 3.4)
4. D *Counteract* is similar in meaning to *offset*. Clues: *will not be strong enough, will overwhelm* (lines 8–9). The prefix *counter–* means *against*. (3.4)
5. C Key: *nothing, not even light, can escape* (line 16). (A), (B), and (D) are not supported by the information in the passage. (3.5)
6. B *Physicists* is the subject of one sentence, and *Most* is the subject of the next sentence. This parallel position helps you see that *Most* refers to *physicists*. (A), (C), and (D) are farther from *Most*. (3.3)
7. A The passage does not mention experience of amusement. (B), (C), and (D) are all mentioned or paraphrased in paragraph 4. (3.2)
8. C *A cartoon character who jumps into a hole* (lines 13–14) is a graphic image. (3.6)
9. D Keys: *provided endless imaginative fodder…endless theoretical fodder* (lines 1–2), *physicists have been amusing themselves* (line 19). (A), (B), and (C) are not supported by the information in the passage. (3.5)
10. A The purpose of the added sentence is to introduce the topic of black holes. The sentence functions best as the opening of the passage. (B), (C), and (D) would interrupt the ideas in consecutive sentences. (3.7)
11. B The stockaded villages contained longhouses (lines 1–5), but nothing in the passage suggests that each longhouse was a separate village. (A) is supported in paragraphs 3–4. (C) is supported in paragraph 2. (D) is supported in lines 9–10 and 24–25. (3.1, 3.2)
12. B *Fences* is closest in meaning to *palisades* in this context. Clues: *twenty–foot long, surrounded and protected, acted as a defensive wall*. (3.4)
13. A Keys: *elevated areas which were easy to defend, palisades surrounded and protected, defensive wall*. (B), (C), and (D) are not supported by the information in paragraph 1. (3.5)
14. D The passage does not mention small windows as part of a longhouse. (A), (B), and (C) are all mentioned in paragraph 3. (3.2)
15. C *Smokes holes* is the subject of one sentence, and *These* is the subject of the next sentence. This parallel position helps you see that *These* refers to *smoke holes*. (A) and (B) are farther from *These*. (D) would not make sense; *intervals* means the spacing between smoke holes. (3.3)
16. C See line 20. *Animal hide* is animal skin. (3.2)
17. A *Partitioned* is closest in meaning to *compartmentalized* in this context; both words have the stem *–part–*. Clue: *accommodate each family*. (3.4)
18. D Key: *images of clan symbols represented the families*. From this, you can infer that each family in the longhouse was a member of a clan. (A) and (B) are not supported by the information in the passage. (C) is inaccurate; the clan symbols were *over* the door, not part of the door. (3.5)
19. B *The longhouse varied in size from twenty feet by sixteen feet, to huge multiple family dwellings sixty feet by eighteen feet.* (3.6)
20. C The purpose of the added sentence is to give examples of the trees from which bark was obtained. (A), (B), and (D) would interrupt the ideas in consecutive sentences. (3.7)

READING COMPREHENSION REVIEW TEST (p. 467)

1. B See lines 2–3. (3.2)
2. D *Hired* is closest in meaning to *recruited* in this context. Clue: *to be his co–commander*. (3.4)
3. D The author states that Sacajawea *later became an American legend* (line 12). From this, you can infer that she is a well–known heroine. (A) is inaccurate; the author implies Charbonneau was not Native American but Sacajawea was (lines 10–11). (B) is inaccurate; Sacajawea *had been abducted* as a child (line 17). (C) is inaccurate; the *Teton Sioux* demanded tribute (line 16). (3.5)
4. A *Elk and antelope* appears before *they*, in the same sentence, and is modified by the phrase *so innocent of human contact that*; common sense tells you this is the most likely answer choice to tamely approach the men. (B) and (D) are farther from *they*. (C) would not make sense. (3.3)
5. B *Ruined* is closest in meaning to *blighted* in this context. Clues: *a hell, by mosquitoes*. (3.4)
6. A Lewis and Clark did not encounter dinosaurs, which are extinct, but they did find dinosaur bones (line 23). (B), (C), and (D) are all mentioned in paragraph 3. (3.2)

7. C *Benefit* is closest in meaning to *boon* in this context. Clues: *Their glowing descriptions...provided a, to the westward migration now becoming a permanent part.* (3.4)
8. D *The explorers also found a hell blighted by mosquitoes and winters harsher than anyone could reasonably hope to survive. They became desperately lost, then found their way again.* (3.6)
9. B Keys: *a new natural wealth of variety and abundance* (lines 6–7); *their glowing descriptions of this vast new West provided a boon to the westward migration* (lines 25–26). (A), (C), and (D) are not supported by the information in the passage. (3.5)
10. A All of the paragraphs develop the idea that the invisible aspects of culture are important. (B) is too general. (C) and (D) are supporting details. (3.1, 3.6)
11. C *Intentionally* is closest in meaning to *deliberately* in this context. Clues: *learned consciously* (line 4). (3.4)
12. D Most aspects of culture can not be seen, just as most of an iceberg can not be seen because it is underwater; only the tip of the iceberg is visible, just as only the explicit aspects of culture are visible. (3.4, 3.5)
13. B The passage does not mention what food to eat in a courthouse. (A), (C), and (D) are all mentioned or paraphrased in lines 8–10. (3.2)
14. B *Invisible cultural assumptions* appears before *those*, in the same sentence. (A), (C), and (D) are farther from *those*. (3.3)
15. A The author states that conflicts may arise when we fail to recognize others' behavioral differences as cultural rather than personal. (B), (C), and (D) are not supported by the information in paragraph 3. (3.5)
16. C Key: *collection sites for invisible cultural differences* (line 20). (A) is untrue according to the passage. (B) is not supported; in fact, the context suggests otherwise. (D) is irrelevant. (3.5)
17. B *Foreign* is closest in meaning to *exotic* in this context. Clue: *Yet when such a man is dressed similarly to us* (lines 24–25). (3.4)
18. D Strange behavior from someone speaking our language is an example of an invisible cultural difference; because that person speaks like us, we might misinterpret their behavior as a personal rather than a cultural difference. (A) involves no cultural difference and thus no misunderstanding. (B) and (C) would probably not be misinterpreted because they involve visible, rather than invisible, cultural differences. (3.5)
19. D In the added sentence, *Rather* is a transition that shows contrast between *we usually do not recognize their behavior as cultural in origin* in the previous sentence and *we see them as rude or uncooperative*. Also, *them* refers to *other people* in the previous sentence. (A), (B), and (C) either would not make sense or would be less coherent than the correct answer. (3.7)
20. D All of the paragraphs develop the topic of Dewey's theory of experience. (A), (B), and (C) are all supporting details. (3.1)
21. D Key: *born in Vermont in 1859; throughout his life he kept the respect for experience...that shaped the character of the nineteenth–century Vermonter* (lines 2–4). (A), (B), and (C) are not supported by the information in the passage. (3.5)
22. C *Creative* is closest in meaning to *reconstructive* in this context. Clue: *experience and knowledge building on each other*. You can also analyze the parts of *reconstructive*: *re–* means again; *con–* means together; *–struct–* means *build*. (3.4)
23. B *Theory of experience* appears before *its*, in the same sentence, closer than (A), (C), or (D). (3.3)
24. D The interplay between one's previous knowledge and one's present situation is Dewey's definition of *experience*; see lines 9–11. (A) and (B) are inaccurate; rejecting the old could be dangerous unless the new were rooted in a correct idea of experience. (C) is inaccurate; Dewey believed that education and experience were not the same thing (line 13). (3.2)
25. B *Deforms* is closest in meaning to *distorts* in this context. Clues: *contributes to the growth of, but, miseducative*. (3.4)
26. C Dewey believed that experience *can be miseducative if it distorts the growth of further experience* (lines 15–16). (A), (B), and (D) are all paraphrased in paragraph 2 or 3. (3.2)
27. A See lines 18–19. (B) is untrue according to lines 14–16. (C) is inaccurate according to lines 8–9. (D) is not dealt with in the passage. (3.2)
28. C *Abundantly* is closest in meaning to *prolifically* in this context. Clues: *long life, lectured and published, range and diversity of Dewey's writings*. (3.4)
29. A The added sentence gives examples that develop *lectured and published prolifically* in the previous sentence; also, *These writings* in the following sentence refers to *several works* in the added sentence. (B), (C), and (D) would be less coherent than the correct answer. (3.7)
30. A Most of the information in the passage discusses the characteristics and effects of tornadoes. (B), (C), and (D) are all supporting ideas. (3.1)
31. D *Danger* is similar in meaning to *jeopardy*. Clues: *devastating blasts, sending debris flying, lifting buildings from their foundations*. (3.4)
32. D Keys: *some mystery still surrounds tornadoes, cannot be predicted*. (A) is not supported by the information in lines 6–9. (B) is irrelevant. (C) is inaccurate according to the information in lines 6–9. (3.5)
33. B See lines 9–10. (3.2)
34. C *Solar heating and thunderstorm development* appears before *their*, in the same sentence. (A), (B), and (D) are all farther from *their*. (3.3)
35. A *Rotating* is closest in meaning to *whirling* in this context. Clues: *vortices, around the central core, spin*. (3.4)
36. B See lines 16–18. (A) is inaccurate; the funnel can be grayish white (line 17). (C) is not supported; the passage does not mention the *end* of a thunderstorm. (D) is inaccurate; tornadoes favor the warmest part of day (line 11), but this does not imply they occur *only* during the afternoon. (3.2)
37. D See line 20. (3.2)
38. C Paragraph 3 discusses the shape and color of tornadoes.
39. B The passage develops the idea that tornadoes are a powerful and destructive force of nature. (A) is inaccurate; see paragraph 2. (C) is inaccurate; tornadoes accompany thunderstorms, which are not generally considered to be disasters. (D) is not supported by the information in the passage. (3.5)

40. B In the added sentence, *however* is a transition that shows contrast between the discussion of a tornado's direction in the two previous sentences and the discussion of tornadoes that change directions. (A) would not make sense. (C) would interrupt the ideas in consecutive sentences. (D) would be less coherent than the correct answer. (3.7)
41. C All of the paragraphs discuss the central role of advertising in selling products. (A) is inaccurate; the passage does not describe a process. (B) and (D) are supporting details. (3.1)
42. C Repeatedly buying the same brand is mentioned in the previous sentence. (A) and (B) would not make sense. (D) is too far from *this*. (3.3)
43. D Key: *identify potential users of a product*. (A) is inaccurate; *new* products are not specified. (B) is inaccurate; homemakers and professional people are not specified. (C) is inaccurate; newspapers and magazines are not the only places for ads. (3.5)
44. A See lines 9–10. (B) and (D) are not dealt with in the passage. (C) is inaccurate; searching for workers is not part of market research according to the passage. (3.2)
45. D Key: *constant need for creative ideas*. (A) is inaccurate; it repeats words from lines 12–13 to confuse you. (B) is inaccurate; *college–educated* workers are not necessarily the same as *talented* workers (line 16). (C) is irrelevant. (3.5)
46. B Traditional families had two parents and two children; see lines 17–18. (3.2)
47. B *Divided* is closest in meaning to *fragmented* in this context. Clue: *into many groups*. (3.4)
48. A *Differently* is closest in meaning to *in a new light* in this context. Clue: *for instance, gave a new image* (line 25). (3.4)
49. D *Computer graphics* is an example of a new technology. (3.6)
50. A The purpose of the added sentence is to introduce the topic of advertising as an essential part of the marketing process. The sentence functions best as the opening of the passage. (B) and (C) would interrupt the ideas in consecutive sentences. (D) would be less coherent than the correct answer. (3.7)

PRACTICE TESTS
TEST 1

SECTION 1 – LISTENING (p. 519)

1. B Bill doesn't know how to program his VCR; the woman asks a negative question, "Why doesn't he just read the instruction manual?" implying Bill should read the instructions. (1.7)
2. C The woman says Dr. Hernandez is great and inspired her to major in science; the man says Dr. Hernandez is teaching zoology in winter; the man will probably register for zoology. (1.8)
3. C *Get out of* = avoid work or trouble. The woman managed to avoid working this weekend. (1.2)
4. A The man asked at an upholstery shop, but new covers would be "really expensive"; he implies he does not want to pay a lot for new covers. (1.1, 1.7)
5. B The negative expression "Nothing could surprise me more" means the news of Gregorio being accepted into medical school surprises her more than any other news she might hear. (1.4)
6. C The condition "if only they would call" is unreal; the past tense verb means they did *not* call; therefore, the woman does not know if she got the job. (1.3, 2.12)
7. C Rick has been building houses *at least* six or seven years, which means more than six years. (1.5)
8. A *Figure out* = find the answer, solve a problem. (1.2)
9. C Keys: *intern in surgery, continue working at the university hospital*. (1.8)
10. B *Back out* = withdraw from a promise or agreement. (1.2, 1.7)
11. C The woman is looking for her tour group; the man says, "There's a bunch of folks over on the boardwalk." A *bunch of folks* is a group of people. (B) and (D) have words that sound similar to *bunch* and *boardwalk*. (1.1)
12. D "I don't want to miss that" implies she is looking forward to hearing Tom play at his piano recital. (1.8)
13. B In this context, *complimentary* means free of charge. (1.1)
14. A *Deal with* = control or manage. (1.2)
15. D The man's house and deck need work; the woman mentions someone at the hardware store who gave her excellent advice, implying the man should also seek the advice of a professional. (1.7)
16. B The student's father had surgery; therefore, the student must leave school for family reasons. (1.14)
17. A, C The student will have to take the final exam within six weeks; there is also a form to fill out. (1.11)
18. B The man says, "I've been rethinking our route." Most of the conversation is about a change in their driving route to avoid delays due to construction. (1.10)
19. C–A–B–D 1. Drive north on Route 150. 2. Drive through Springdale. 3. Drive east to Ransom. 4. Take the ferry. (1.13)
20. D The woman reminds the man that they must be in Ransom by eleven o'clock to make the ferry; she asks, "…are you sure we can go that way and still catch the ferry?" (1.14)

21. C Most of the discussion deals with the importance of animals in American Indian culture. (A) and (B) are too specific. (D) is too general. (1.10)
22. D The shaman helped people gain contact with the spiritual world through rituals using masks, costumes, song, and dance. (1.11)
23. A The professor says that the animal–like figures on totem poles "served as valuable collective memory devices for tribes that lacked a written language. The animals and other mythological creatures told the story of the tribe." (1.14)
24. B Most of the talk discusses breakfast foods that can help prevent disease. (A) and (D) are too specific. (C) is too general. (1.10)
25. C The speaker says, "A bowl of cereal, fresh fruit,– and low–fat milk is the model meal: low in fat, and high in fiber, vitamins and minerals." (1.14)
26. A The speaker says, "Breakfast skippers…are more likely to be overweight, to have high cholesterol levels and to eat too many fatty foods." (1.11)
27. C–B–A Egg substitutes—No cholesterol; Orange juice—Anti–viral properties; Milk—Calcium. (1.12)
28. C The lecture describes a volcanic eruption, which is a *geologic* activity. (1.15)
29. A The eruption cycle had a rather harmless beginning when a strong earthquake occurred and was followed over the next week by more earthquakes that caused several avalanches. (1.11)
30. B, C The professor says, "There were occasional steam and ash eruptions during April and early May—to the delight of the many tourists and hikers who came to watch the show." [A] did not occur until after the great explosion. [D] is not mentioned. (1.11)
31. D–B–A–C 1. The north side of the mountain swelled. 2. Earthquakes caused a huge landslide. 3. The top of the mountain exploded. 4. The ash cloud drifted around the world. (1.13)
32. C The professor says that Mount St. Helens has had a long history of explosive activity and concludes, "…geologists who've studied this mountain believe that future eruptions are near certainty and can not be prevented." (A), (B), and (D) are not supported by anything the professor says. (1.15)
33. C The speaker, a career counselor, describes two kinds of employees and says, "It is your job to find out, during your college years, into which of these two job categories you fit, and to plan your career accordingly." (1.10)
34. A, D The speaker says that careers emphasizing specialization include accounting and teaching. (1.11)
35. A, C The speaker says generalists must be able to make overall judgements and to plan and organize other people's work. [B] and [D] characterize specialists. (1.11)
36. D The speaker says, "Any organization needs both kinds of people, although different organizations need them in different ratios." From this, you can infer that both specialists and generalists can find jobs. (A) and (B) are not supported by anything the speaker says. (C) is inaccurate; the speaker implies generalists, not specialists, make good leaders. (1.15)
37. B–C–A 1. One–room plan. 2. Two–room plan. 3. Added lean–to plan. (1.13)
38. A The kitchen in the added lean–to plan was in the space added to the back of the house, where "the cooking was done in a fireplace added to the back of the central chimney mass." (1.11)
39. C The porch (in all three plan types) was the small room into which the front door opened. The porch had "a steep staircase crowded up against an immense chimney." (1.11)
40. C The speaker says, "These plan types form a logical evolutionary sequence. But a one–room plan might have been built at any time in the seventeenth century." This means the earliest plan type (one–room) continued to be built even after the other two types were introduced. (1.14)
41. A The health educator says, "The symptom is usually reported as a fluttering in the chest, or a feeling that the heart has jumped." (1.11)
42. B, C Anxiety and too much coffee are two causes mentioned by the speaker. (1.11)
43. D When one gets out of bed too quickly, the heartbeat regulator has trouble adjusting to the quick change from a horizontal to a vertical circulatory system, and the pulse rate must be changed. (1.14)
44. C The health educator says, "An irregular heartbeat is a warning to slow down before your motor burns out." (1.11)
45. B The talk discusses causes and symptoms of an irregular heartbeat. (A) is too general. (C) and (D) are too specific. (1.10)

SECTION 2 – STRUCTURE (p. 525)

1. D The sentence needs the past participle of the verb after *were* (2.6). (A) is the past form. (B) is the present participle. (C) has an extra, incorrect auxiliary.
2. C The sentence needs a noun structure as the subject (2.1). (A) and (B) have the subordinators *Why* and *That*, which introduce subordinate clauses and would make the sentence incomplete (2.8, 2.9). (D) has the relative pronoun *that*, which introduces adjective clauses (2.10).
3. D The sentence makes a generalization about the uncountable noun *tobacco*; therefore, no article is needed (2.4). Correction: *tobacco*.
4. B *Which* is incorrect because it lacks a preposition (2.10, 2.21). Correction: *of which*. La Guardia was the director *of* the U. N. Relief Administration.
5. C *To type at* is not parallel to the other present participles in the list (2.10, 2.25). Correction: *typing at*.
6. B The sentence needs an adjective structure to modify *robot*. The correct answer is the beginning of an adjective clause (2.10). (A) lacks a verb. (C) lacks a relative pronoun. (D) has *that*, which cannot begin an adjective clause between commas.
7. B The sentence needs an adverb structure to modify the main clause. The correct answer is an adverb clause (2.11). (A) and (D) lack a subordinator. (C) has a verb that does not agree in tense meaning with the verb in the main clause, *do not remain* (2.12).
8. A The sentence needs an infinitive as the subject complement after *is* (2.7). (B) is a gerund, which would not be parallel to *reduce*, an infinitive joined by *and* (2.25). (C) is the beginning of an adjective clause (2.10). (D) is a verb.

9. C The sentence needs a noun structure as the direct object of *should know*. The correct answer is a noun clause (2.9). (A) and (B) are verb phrases (2.5). (D) has the infinitive *to access* where a verb is needed (2.7).

10. C The sentence needs a noun structure to rename *Eugene O'Neill* (2.2). (A) has the subordinator *who*, which introduces adjective clauses (2.10). (B) is an infinitive (2.7). (D) is a verb phrase (2.5).

11. B *Recording* is singular where a plural is needed after *several* (2.3). Correction: *recordings*.

12. C *Efficient* is an adjective where a noun is needed (2.22). Correction: *efficiency*.

13. B *At aviation pioneers* has an incorrect preposition (2.21). Correction: *of aviation pioneers*.

14. A *Reduce* is a verb where a gerund is needed after *involves* (2.7). Correction: *reducing*.

15. D *Had killed* does not agree in tense meaning with the other verb in the main clause, *shot* (2.5). Correction: *killed*.

16. C *Helps determine* is a singular verb phrase, but a plural verb is needed with the compound subject (2.14). Correction: *help determine*.

17. C The sentence needs an inverted subject and verb after the prepositional phrase of location (2.13). (A) does not have an inverted subject and verb. (B) has the subordinator *where*, which introduces subordinate clauses (2.8, 2.10). (D) has a duplicate subject. (2.1)

18. A The sentence needs a noun structure as the object of the preposition *on*. The correct answer is *either* + noun phrase, which is parallel to *or* + noun phrase (2.1, 2.20, 2.25). (B) has the subordinator *which*, which introduces adjective clauses (2.10). (C) is a main clause (2.8). (D) is a gerund phrase, which would not be parallel to the noun phrase following *or* (2.7, 2.25).

19. D The sentence needs a noun structure as the object of the preposition *in*. The correct answer is a passive participial adjective + noun (2.1, 2.17). (A) has incorrect word order and form (2.16). (B) has an unnecessary preposition. (C) is a clause (2.8).

20. B The sentence needs a main clause to follow a condition clause (2.8, 2.12). (A) lacks a subject. (C) and (D) have verbs that do not agree in tense meaning with the verb in the *if*–clause, *were drawn* (2.12).

21. D The sentence needs the second part of a complex equative expression (2.19). (A) is a conjunction + noun (2.1). (B) is a noun clause (2.9). (C) is comparative degree (2.19).

22. C *Have adjusted* is an incorrectly formed perfect–tense infinitive which is the direct object of the verb *seem* (2.7). Correction: *to have adjusted*.

23. D *Influence* is a verb where an adjective is needed (2.22). Correction: *influential*.

24. C *It is* has a pronoun and verb that do not agree in number with the noun referent *proportions* (2.14, 2.15). Correction: *they are*.

25. A *Alike* is an incorrect word choice because it is an adjective where a preposition is needed (2.23). Correction: *like*.

SECTION 3 – READING (p. 529)

1. B Most of the paragraphs explain the provisions of the ADA. (A) and (C) are not dealt with. (D) is a supporting detail. (3.1, 3.6)

2. C See line 9. (A) and (D) identify people who fit the definition of *a person with a disability* in paragraph 1. (B) is mentioned in paragraph 3. (3.2, 3.5)

3. A *Disability* is closest in meaning to *impairment* in this context. Clue: *substantially limits him or her in a major life activity*. (3.4)

4. D See lines 17–18. Clues: *are, such as*. (3.2, 3.4)

5. B *Buildings* is the subject of the previous clause in the same sentence, a parallel position that helps you see that *facilities* refers to *buildings*. (A) and (D) would not make sense. (C) is dealt with in the previous paragraph. (3.3)

6. A The passage does not state or imply that people with disabilities must pay for special accommodations. (B), (C), and (D) are all stated or implied in paragraph 1 or 3. (3.5)

7. C *States* is closest in meaning to *stipulates* in this context. Clue: *The ADA states* (line 9). (3.4)

8. D Companies with fifteen or more employees may not refuse to hire or promote a person because of a disability and must make reasonable accommodations for persons with disabilities (paragraph 2). (A) is untrue according to lines 16–18. (B) is untrue according to lines 14–15. (C) is not supported by the information in the passage. (3.5)

9. D Each paragraph discusses a period in the history of the Roosevelt family. (A), (B), and (C) are supporting details. (3.1)

10. B *Rapid growth* is closest in meaning to *boom* in this context. Clues: *bustling port, expansion in American economic life*. (3.4)

11. A Buying the Beekman Swamp had *a lasting effect* on the fortunes, or wealth, of the two brothers. (B), (C), and (D) are not supported by the information in the passage. (3.5)

12. C Isaac was the first Roosevelt *to achieve gentility and distinction* (line 12); gentility is associated with the upper class. (3.2)

13. C Teaching is not mentioned as an occupation of any of the Roosevelts. (A), (B), and (D) are all mentioned in the passage. (3.2)

14. B *Frontier settlement* is closest in meaning to *outpost* in this context. Clues: *from a small...into a cosmopolitan city* (lines 20–21); *a tiny settlement of 800 people* (line 2). (3.4)

15. D *Morally approved* is closest in meaning to *sanctified* in this context. Clues: *ethic* (line 22); *standards of honor, conduct, and manners were further bred into* (lines 24–25). (3.4)

16. C *The Roosevelt sons* appears before *They*, in the previous sentence. (A) is farther from *They*. (B) would not make sense; *standards of honor, conduct and manners* are things and cannot become bankers, sportsmen, and financiers. (D) would not make sense; Groton and Harvard are schools. (3.3)

17. D The passage gives several examples of Roosevelts who made significant contributions, including two who served as U. S. president. (A), (B), and (C) are not supported by the information in the passage. (3.5)

18. A In the added sentence, *by the beginning of the twentieth century* serves as a transition to *the transformation of New York from a small Dutch outpost into a cosmopolitan city* in the next sentence. The sentence functions best as the opening of the paragraph. (B) and (C) would interrupt the ideas in consecutive sentences. (D) would be less coherent than the correct answer. (3.7)
19. A Each paragraph discusses the characteristics of either Jupiter or its satellites. (B) and (D) are supporting details. (C) is the topic of paragraph 3. (3.1)
20. C See lines 3–5. (3.2)
21. D Keys: *minus 260 degrees F., ice crystals*. (A) and (C) are not supported by the information in the paragraph. (B) is inaccurate; Jupiter may have no surface (line 10). (3.5)
22. D *Boundary* is closest in meaning to *interface* in this context. Clue: *between the gaseous atmosphere and the body of Jupiter*. (3.4)
23. A *Equaling* is similar in meaning to *rivaling* in this context. Clues: *large and bright, our own moon*. (3.4)
24. B See lines 19–21. (A), (C), and (D) are all true according to the passage but irrelevant to the question of the number of satellites. (3.2)
25. C *The moons Amalthea, Io, Europa, Ganymede, and Callisto* is the subject of one sentence, and *Each* is the subject of the next sentence. This parallel position helps you see that *Each* refers to the moons, or satellites, of Jupiter. (A) and (B) are farther from *Each*. (D) is inaccurate; *planets* and *moons* are different. (3.3)
26. D Jupiter, not its satellites, has an atmosphere of methane and ammonia (lines 7–8). (A), (B), and (C) are all mentioned or paraphrased in paragraph 3 or 4. (3.2)
27. A In lines 2–5 Jupiter is compared with Earth. (3.6)
28. B Observations by the Voyager spacecraft have revealed a disk–like ring close to Jupiter's surface; older observations from Earth may have detected this same ring. (A) is inaccurate; a doughnut–shaped ring surrounds Io's orbit of Jupiter. (C) and (D) are not supported by the information in the passage. (3.5)
29. A In the added sentence, *it* refers to *the Great Red Spot* in the previous sentence. (B) is incorrect because *it* would not agree with any possible referent. (C) would not make sense. (D) would interrupt the ideas in consecutive sentences. (3.7)
30. C *Concentrate on* is closest in meaning to *specialize in* in this context. Lines 5–7 list different types of real estate that different agents concentrate on. (3.4)
31. B See lines 9–11. (3.2)
32. A *Potential* is closest in meaning to *prospective* in this context. Clue: *buyers*. (3.4)
33. C *Buyers* appears before *them*, in the previous sentence. (A) and (D) are farther from *them*. (B) would not make sense. (3.3)
34. B The agent must convince the seller to set a realistic price (line 19) and also convince the buyer that the property is a good buy (lines 21–22). (A) is irrelevant. (C) is not supported by the information in the passage. (D) is irrelevant; you can reasonably assume the buyer has already visited the property. (3.5)
35. A Agents must try to understand what (desires and needs) will motivate the buyer (lines 20–22) (B), (C), and (D) are not supported by the information in paragraph 3. (3.5)
36. D See lines 22–23. (3.2)
37. C *Investigating* is similar in meaning to *checking out* in this context. Clue: *visit newly listed properties so that they can familiarize themselves with the features of the property* (lines 14–15). (3.4)
38. D Keys: *have to negotiate with both the seller and the buyer; convince sellers to set a realistic price; learn what will motivate the buyer; arrange meetings that are convenient to buyers and sellers*. (A) and (B) are not supported by the information in the passage. (C) is inaccurate; *some* agencies combine real estate with a law practice (lines 4–5); this does not imply that most agents are lawyers. (3.5)
39. A See lines 5–8. (3.6)
40. C In the added sentence, *However* is a transition that shows contrast between *work nights and weekends* in the previous sentence and *usually they can set their own hours*. (A) would not make sense. (B) and (D) would be less coherent than the correct answer; little or no contrast is expressed. (3.7)
41. C The passage does not compare human evolution with that of other primates. (A), (B), and (D) are all supported in the passage. (3.1)
42. B *Complex* is closest in meaning to *intricate* in this context. Clues: *more...muscles, flexibility helps with sounds like p, b, and w*. (3.4)
43. A *Lips* is the subject of the first clause in the same sentence, a parallel position that helps you see that *their* refers to *lips*. (B), (C) and (D) would not make sense. (3.3)
44. D See lines 11–13. (3.2)
45. D *Amplifier* is closest in meaning to *resonator* in this context. Clue: *a vocal tract capable of producing the wide variety of sounds* (line 10). (3.4)
46. C The passage does not mention lungs in relation to the development of speech. (A), (B), and (D) are all mentioned in the passage. (3.2)
47. A Key: *Humans who are born deaf learn the sign languages that are used around them*. (B) is untrue according to lines 15–17. (C) and (D) are not supported by the information in the paragraph. (3.5)
48. B The human brain has specialized functions in each hemisphere (half), and language is an analytic function occurring in the left hemisphere. (A), (C), and (D) are not supported by the information in the paragraph. (3.5)
49. D *Such* as tells you that *tool–using* and *language* are examples of analytic functions of the human brain. (3.2, 3.6)
50. D In the added sentence, *This* refers to *all languages... require the organizing and combining of sounds or signs in specific constructions* in the previous sentence. (A) and (C) would be less coherent than the correct answer. (B) would interrupt the ideas in consecutive sentences. (3.7)

TEST 2

SECTION 1 – LISTENING COMPREHENSION (p. 547)

1. A *Come across* = meet by chance. (1.2)
2. B Keys: *new assistant, the work he has done so far.* (1.1, 1.8)
3. D The emphasis on *did order* means the man had assumed the woman *did not* order the new table. (1.6)
4. C *The week before last* = two weeks ago. (1.5)
5. C Keys: *eyes, frames, glasses, contact lenses*. An optometrist tests eyes and prescribes corrective lenses. (1.8, 1.9)
6. C The man needs his boots fixed; the woman asks a negative question, "Isn't there a shoe repair shop…?" implying he can have his boots fixed there. (1.7)
7. A The woman needs a seat; the man says there might be some seats remaining "in the balcony" (upstairs), implying she might be able to find a seat there. (1.1, 1.7)
8. D The man is always tired; the woman says, "Maybe you're worrying too much about your work," implying he should worry less about his work (job). (1.1, 1.5, 1.7)
9. B The man mentions a dance and asks a negative question, "Why don't we check that out instead?" implying they should check out the dance. *Check out* = investigate. (A) is inaccurate. (C) and (D) use *check* incorrectly. (1.2, 1.7)
10. A *Keep an eye on* = watch, guard. (1.2)
11. B The computer lab is closing and will not open until nine o'clock the next morning; the man's paper is due at eight o'clock; he will have a problem finishing his paper before morning without a computer. (1.5, 1.8)
12. C In this context, *run–down* means *tired* or *ill*. (A), (B), and (D) repeat words from the conversation incorrectly. (1.1)
13. A The woman asks if there is a "snack bar" on the train, implying she would like to buy something to eat (a snack) on the train. (1.1, 1.8)
14. B Keys: *our project, meet, go to the library*. (1.9)
15. A "Worth neither the time nor the money" means not worth the time and not worth the money; in other words, the movie was a waste of time and money. (1.4)
16. D *Keep up* = stay at the same level. The woman has a "hard time" keeping up, which means she has difficulty doing the work at the level of the class. (1.1, 1.2)
17. C Laura was accepted by the business college; the man says he thought the college required a high grade point average, implying Laura does *not* have a high grade point average, and he is surprised at her being accepted. (1.7)
18. D "Weren't you in class…either" implies the woman was not in class; the man also was not in class because he was taking his brother to the bus station. You can infer that both the woman and man missed class. (1.8)
19. C The man doesn't see Ahmed and wonders about this; the woman says Ahmed told her he would be at the concert. You can infer that the speakers are at the concert and that Ahmed has not made it to the concert. (1.8)
20. C The ceramic mugs are fifteen dollars each, but the woman can't afford to pay that much; the plastic mugs are cheaper; she will probably buy the plastic mugs. (1.5, 1.8)
21. C "I'd rather go to a movie" means she prefers going to a movie. (1.3)
22. B The man's exclamation shows he is pleased by being invited along on a stroll by the lake. A *stroll* is a walk. (A) and (D) repeat words from the conversation incorrectly. (C) has *store by the lake*, which sounds similar to *stroll by the lake*. (1.1, 1.6)
23. D *Bear with* = have patience. (1.2)
24. C *Blow it* = fail, do poorly. (1.2)
25. C A *biography* is a book about a person's life; *famous* means *well–known*; a *senator* is a politician. (A) and (D) have words that sound similar to *biography* and *senator*. (B) is inaccurate. (1.1)
26. B The man says Brenda's cup seems to be empty, implying she might like more tea. (1.7)
27. C Key: *finding the detergent*. (1.9)
28. B "I wish he felt the same way about psychology and accounting" means Matthew *does not* feel the same about his studies as he does about soccer. This implies Matthew may not be a diligent student. (1.3, 1.7)
29. C *Look out* = be careful. The man advises them to take care of each other. (1.2)
30. D The man agrees to watch the woman's satchel. In this context, *watch* means *guard*, and a *satchel* is a briefcase or bag. (B) and (C) have words that sound similar to *satchel*. (1.1)
31. C The man and the oral surgeon are discussing the extraction of the man's wisdom teeth (*molars*). (1.10)
32. B The oral surgeon says that the man will need to be anesthetized and will need some time to "wake up" in the recovery room; this means he will be put to sleep. (1.11, 1.15)
33. D The man will be sleepy (*drowsy*) from the sleep–inducing drug (*anesthesia*) for several hours after the surgery; therefore, he will not be able to drive himself home. (1.14)
34. A The man says, "It will be a relief to have these wisdom teeth out." (1.11)
35. C They are discussing college and the classes they will be taking. (1.10)
36. C The woman had to pack quickly because she just got the acceptance letter from the college two days ago. (1.14)
37. A The man says he is studying "business—mostly marketing this quarter." This suggests that business is his major field of study. (B) and (C) are inaccurate. (D) is not supported by anything the man says. (1.15)
38. D They both will be taking a psychology course from Dr. Robinson and may be in the same class. (1.11)
39. A The talk is mostly about storms and boat safety; therefore, boaters would be an appropriate audience. (1.15)
40. B The speaker says the first visual sign of a storm will be a high cloud formation with a dirty bottom and a tall, stringy top. (1.11)
41. B The speaker says, "Many people drown in storms because they stand up, swing their arms, and holler for help." (1.14)

42. D The speaker says that if visitors see any injured animals, they should report it "here at the ranger station." The speaker also wishes the visitors "a pleasant experience in the Thompson National Forest." You can infer the speaker is probably a forest ranger. (1.15)
43. B Disturbing a bird's nest will upset the bird and cause it to leave the nest, leaving the eggs uncovered. The speaker says, "Eggs that are left uncovered will cool quickly, killing the embryos." *Embryos* are the unhatched babies. (1.14)
44. A When people feed wild animals, the animals get used to being fed and lose their fear of humans. The animals then might bite or attack people if they can't get human food. (1.14)
45. D The speaker says, "Your dog might end up being the victim of a bear or a mountain lion." (1.11)
46. A The lecture mainly discusses supply and demand in market economics. (B) and (D) are details. (C) is inaccurate. (1.10)
47. B The professor says, "Consumers are like voters. They use their money votes to buy what they want." (1.11)
48. C The professor says, "The consumers with the most dollar votes have the most influence over *what* gets produced and *to whom* goods go." (1.11)
49. D The professor says, "It is generally held that the quantity of a particular good that people will buy depends on its price." This implies the reverse: the price determines the quantity of a good that people will buy. (1.15)
50. A The professor says, "Tomorrow we will look at just how demand and supply work in the real world." You can infer that the professor will discuss real examples of how supply and demand influence prices. (1.15)

SECTION 2 – STRUCTURE AND WRITTEN EXPRESSION (p. 554)

1. D The sentence needs a verb (2.5, 2.8). (A) is an adjective. (B) is an adjective + conjunction. (C) lacks *from*, which is needed with *different* (2.21).
2. B The sentence needs a preposition to introduce the modifying phrase with *forty–three* (2.21). (A) is the beginning of a main clause (2.8). (C) and (D) lack an introductory preposition.
3. D The sentence needs the past participle of the verb after *is* (2.6). (A) is the base form of the verb. (B) is an infinitive, which does not function as a verb (2.7). (C) is the present participle.
4. B The sentence needs a structure to introduce a clause. The correct answer is a main clause + *that*, which introduces a noun clause (2.8, 2.9). (A) lacks a verb and has the subordinator *that*, which would make the sentence incomplete (2.8). (C) and (D) have the subordinators *That* and *Because*, which would make the sentence incomplete (2.8).
5. A The sentence needs an adjective structure to modify *fluid*. The correct answer is the beginning of an adjective clause (2.10). (B) and (D) are verbs. (C) has a duplicate subject, *it* (2.1, 2.10).
6. A The sentence needs a subordinator to introduce an adverb clause of condition (2.11, 2.12). (B) and (C) would make two incorrectly joined main clauses (2.8). (D) is an infinitive (2.7).
7. D The sentence needs a noun in a list of nouns referring to things and joined by *and* (2.25). (A) is a gerund, which would not be parallel to the other nouns in the list (2.7, 2.25). (B) is a noun that refers to an activity, not a thing (2.23). (C) is an infinitive, which would not be parallel to the other nouns in the list (2.7, 2.25).
8. B The sentence needs an adjective structure to modify *thirty days*. The correct answer is an equative degree adjective (2.19). (A) is a comparative expression that cannot be used without *than*. (C) has an unnecessary verb. (D) has an unnecessary article (2.4).
9. C The subordinate clause needs an inverted subject and verb after *Not only* (2.8, 2.13). (A) and (B) do not have an inverted subject and verb. (D) lacks a verb.
10. C The sentence needs a passive voice verb + preposition (2.5, 2.6, 2.21). (A) is active voice and lacks *of*. (B) lacks the auxiliary *be*. (D) is an infinitive, which does not function as a verb (2.7)
11. B The sentence needs a noun structure as the subject complement after *is* (2.1). (A), (C), and (D) all have incorrect word order (2.16).
12. A The adjective clause needs a subject + verb after *from which* (2.8, 2.10). (B) has a verb that does not agree in tense meaning with the verb in the main clause, *put* (2.5). (C) lacks a subject. (D) lacks a verb.
13. D The sentence needs an adjective to modify *cure* (2.18). (A) and (B) are conjunctions. (C) is an adverb.
14. B The sentence needs a noun structure as the subject (2.1). (A) and (C) have verbs. (D) is a prepositional phrase (2.21).
15. D The sentence needs a noun structure as the object of the preposition *in* (2.1, 2.4). (A) lacks an article where one is needed (2.4). (B) has an incorrect article (2.4). (C) has incorrect word order (2.16).
16. A *Technical* is an adjective where a noun is needed (2.22). Correction: *technology*.
17. C *Forty–feet–long* is an adjective, but adjectives do not have plural forms (2.3). Correction: *forty–foot long*.
18. D *For learn* is an incorrectly formed infinitive (2.7). Correction: *to learn*.
19. B *Conveys* is a singular verb, but a plural verb is needed with the compound subject (2.14). Correction: *convey*.
20. B *Influentially* is an adverb where an adjective is needed (2.22). Correction: *influential*.
21. B *That* is a demonstrative pronoun that does not agree in number with its noun referent, *deaths* (2.15). Correction: *those*.
22. D *A heart attack was experienced* is not parallel to the other verb phrases in the list (2.5, 2.25). Correction: *have had a heart attack*.
23. A *Voyager* is an incorrect word choice because it refers to a person, but this word refers to a thing (2.23). Correction: *voyage*.
24. A *Picking up* is the incorrect verb form to use with *able to* (2.5). Correction: *pick up*.
25. B *Could have been* does not agree in tense meaning with the verb in the *if*–clause, *are planted* (2.6, 2.12). Correction: *can be*.

26. D *Has found* does not agree in tense meaning with the verbs in the main clause, *represented* and *suggested* (2.5). Correction: *had found.*
27. C *Heat taken* lacks the auxiliary *be*, which is needed with passive voice verbs (2.6). Correction: *heat is taken.*
28. C *Exploration* is a noun where a verb is needed (2.22). Correction: *explored.*
29. C *Rewarded* is a passive participial adjective, but an active adjective is needed because *careers* performs the action of rewarding (2.17). Correction: *rewarding.*
30. B *Was advanced* has an incorrectly formed comparative expression (2.19). Correction: *was more advanced.*
31. C *On the contrary* is incorrectly paired with *on the one hand* (2.20). Correction: *on the other hand.*
32. B *Selling* is not parallel to the other nouns in a list of nouns referring to people (2.23, 2.25). Correction: *sellers.*
33. D *Romanticism* is a noun where an adjective is needed in a list of adjectives (2.22, 2.25). Correction: *romantic.*
34. B *Was that* has a verb that does not agree in tense meaning with the other verb in the sentence, *can raise* (2.5). Correction: *is that.*
35. A *New building materials* lacks a preposition where one is needed (2.21). Correction: *of new building materials.*
36. B *And essential* is redundant because it has the same meaning as *extremely important* (2.24). Correction: omit *and essential.*
37. B *You should* has a pronoun that does not agree in person with *one* (2.15). Correction: *one should* or *he or she should.*
38. B *A apple five* has an incorrect article (2.4). Correction: *an apple five.*
39. D *Stop and remain* is a plural verb, but a singular verb is needed with the singular subject *mouse* (2.14). Correction: *stops and remains.*
40. D *Into living cells* has an incorrect preposition (2.21). *On* usually comes after *effect*. Correction: *on living cells.*

SECTION 3 – READING COMPREHENSION (p. 561)

1. D Each paragraph discusses the cause, progress, or effects of the fire. (A), (B), and (C) are supporting details. (3.1)
2. B *Caught fire* is similar in meaning to *ignited* in this context. Clues: *on fire, the flames.* (3.4)
3. C See lines 2–4. (3.2)
4. A The rotted, useless hose emphasizes the unsafe working conditions in the factory. (B) is irrelevant. (C) and (D) are inaccurate. (3.6)
5. C See lines 7–9. (3.2)
6. B *The ninth floor workers* is the subject of most of the sentences in the paragraph and the referent of *Still others.* (3.3)
7. A *Frail* is closest in meaning to *spindly* in this context. Clues: *inadequately constructed, could not support the weight.* (3.4)
8. C Keys: *trapped; the ladder...stopped far below them, reaching only as far as the sixth floor.* (A), (B), and (D) are not supported by the information in the passage. (3.5)
9. D See line 22. (3.2)
10. B *Becoming more popular* is similar in meaning to *beginning to sweep the nation.* Clues: *public outcry, people decided.* (3.4)
11. B Nothing in the passage suggests that the Triangle Shirtwaist factory was rebuilt. (A), (C), and (D) are all supported by information in paragraph 6. (3.5)
12. C Most of the paragraphs discuss what a calculator does and how it works. (A) and (B) are too general. (D) is a supporting detail. (3.1, 3.6)
13. A *Revolutionary* is similar in meaning to *innovative* in this context. Clue: *essentially different.* (3.4)
14. B Calculators and computers are different from all other machines because they can store information in a memory (lines 2–3). (A) and (D) are irrelevant. (C) is untrue according to lines 2–3. (3.5)
15. D See lines 10–11. (3.2)
16. B *Connections* is closest in meaning to *contacts* in this context. Clues: *circuit board, closes the...and sends a signal.* (3.4)
17. C See lines 20–21. (3.2)
18. D *The processing unit* appears before *This*, closer than (A), (B), or (C). (3.3)
19. A Nothing in the passage suggests that calculators require a lot of instructions to operate quickly. (B) is supported in paragraph 1. (C) is supported in paragraphs 4–5. (D) is supported in paragraph 3. (3.5)
20. A See lines 8–9. (3.6)
21. B Each paragraph discusses an aspect of the life of writer Zora Neale Hurston. (A) is a supporting detail. (C) and (D) are too general. (3.1)
22. C See lines 6–7. In this context, *flowering* means creativity and accomplishment. (3.2, 3.4)
23. D See lines 9–11. (3.2)
24. C For thirty years, Hurston's novel was *largely unknown, unread, and dismissed by the male literary establishment.* This suggests that women writers faced discrimination. (A) is inaccurate; the book is *now* Hurston's most famous book. (B) is inaccurate; Hurston's book was largely unknown. (D) is untrue; the book is a novel. (3.5)
25. A *Freedom* is closest in meaning to *autonomy* in this context. Clues: the prefix *auto–* means *self*; *independence; while...subordinate to a man.* (3.4)
26. B Zora Neale Hurston was the African American woman writer who struggled with the problem of the hero as woman. (3.3)
27. C Clues: *Hurston was criticized, conservative views, the temper of the times.* (A) is not supported by the information in the passage. (B) and (D) are inaccurate. (3.4, 3.5)
28. C Hurston believed that integration would undermine, or weaken, black culture. (A) is inaccurate; Hurston did not write in the protest style. (B) and (D) are untrue; Hurston did not support integration. (3.5)
29. D *Honor* is closest in meaning to *revere* in this context. Clues: *poverty and obscurity...only afterward that, rediscover, the black imagination.* (3.4)
30. A In paragraphs 2–4, the author shows respect for the value of Hurston's writings. Keys: *conveyed the color and vigor* (line 13); *gives us a heroic female character* (lines 19–20); *celebrations of black culture and the black imagination* (line 29). (3.6)
31. B Keys: *in charge of her own life* (line 3); *found the demands of marriage incompatible with her career* (lines 14–15); *out of touch with the temper of the times* (lines 25–26). (A) and (D) are inaccurate. (C) is not supported by the information in the passage. (3.5)

32. D Most of the paragraphs discuss the history of basketball. (A), (B), and (C) may be included in the passage but do not describe the passage's overall structure. (3.6)
33. A *Early example* is closest in meaning to *precedent* in this context. Clue: the prefix *pre–* means *before*; *for the game later invented.* (3.4)
34. C *Scarcity* is similar in meaning to *dearth*. Clue: *drop in attendance*. (3.4)
35. B See lines 5–9. (A) is inaccurate; the NCAA established rules later. (C) is untrue according to lines 7–8. (D) is inaccurate; basketball was invented in 1891. (3.2)
36. D See lines 8–9. (3.2)
37. B *All games* appears before *this one* and is the subject of the sentence. *This one* refers to *the game* that Naismith was creating. (A), (C), and (D) would not make sense. (3.3)
38. C He placed the goal above the players' heads to keep the defensive players from clustering around and blocking it (lines 15–16). (3.2)
39. A *Displaying* is closest in meaning to *showcasing* in this context. A showcase is a container, usually made of glass, in which items are displayed. The basketball leagues began displaying the players to amuse the fans. (3.4)
40. A Some changes mentioned in the passage include the number of players (lines 18–19), professionalization (line 24), and the creation of new maneuvers (lines 25–29). (B), (C), and (D) are all mentioned or implied in the passage. (3.5)
41. B Lines 10–11 compare basketball with football. (3.6)
42. D Key: *Today; more importantly, they want basketball "stars."* (A), (B) and (C) are not suggested by the information in paragraph 6. (3.5)
43. C All of the paragraphs discuss features of birds that contribute to their flying ability, and thus their survival. (A), (B), and (D) are supporting ideas. (3.1)
44. B See lines 4–5. Higher air pressure below the wings causes "lift." (3.2)
45. D *Sustained* is similar in meaning to *prolonged* in this context. Clue: *ability to soar*. (3.4)
46. D *Other birds* is the subject of one sentence, and *Finches and sparrows* is the subject of the next sentence. This parallel position helps you see that finches and sparrows are types of birds. (3.3)
47. B See lines 8–9. Built–in spoilers reduce turbulence; this allows a steeper angle of diving to catch prey. (3.2)
48. A Keys: *controlled stops—an essential skill; need to land on individual branches or on prey*. (B) is not supported; nothing implies the feathers must be *very long*. (C) is not supported. (D) is inaccurate; birds *brake* this way. (3.5)
49. C Keys: *they still could not flap hard enough to leave the ground; birds have large, specialized hearts that beat much faster than the human heart.* (A) and (B) are untrue according to the passage. (D) is inaccurate; it incorrectly repeats words from line 17. (3.5)
50. D *Supports* is closest in meaning to *struts* in this context. Clues: *to maintain strength, like cross beams in a bridge*. (3.4)

TEST 3

SECTION 1 – LISTENING (p. 573)

1. A The man asks if the cafeteria is still open, implying he would like to buy something to eat or drink. (1.8)
2. B *That goes without saying* = It is too obvious to mention; no explanation is necessary. (1.2)
3. C The conditional "If I hadn't still been so mad, I might have spoken to Lucas" is unreal; the verb tenses mean the woman *was* still mad and *did not* speak to Lucas. (1.3, 2.12)
4. A *Drop out* = quit school. (1.2)
5. D In this context, *lost* means *confused*; the man did not understand the lecture. (A) uses a different meaning of *lost* that is incorrect here. (B) uses *lost* inaccurately. (1.1)
6. D Robert "dropped by" (visited) *before* the woman got home, but she "missed" him, which means she arrived *after* Robert had left. (1.2, 1.5)
7. D The man told Vincent the woman would take him to the airport. "Tell me you didn't!" implies the woman does not want to give Vincent a ride. (1.7, 1.8)
8. C In this context, "showing his new pieces" means "exhibiting his most recent works of art." (A) and (D) have words that sound similar to *pieces*. (1.1)
9. D Keys: *How are things at the dental clinic?, Weren't you the technician who took my x–rays?* (1.8)
10. A *Chip in* = the cost is shared; more than one person pays. (C) uses a meaning of *chip* that is incorrect here. (1.2)
11. B The causative "got Jenny to take my computer to the shop" means that Jenny took the computer to the (repair) shop; the computer was repaired, so the speaker was able to finish her report. (1.3)
12. A The man says he is going out; the woman asks a negative question, "Don't you want to finish your report first?" implying he should stay home and finish the report. (1.7)
13. D The man says his binoculars "may be lighter," which means the woman's binoculars are heavier than his. (1.5)
14. D *Get rid of* = throw away. (1.2)
15. C The man missed his flight and then asks where the nearest telephone is; he will probably make a telephone call. (1.8)
16. C The conversation takes place at a career fair; the main subject is soil conservation as a career. (A), (B), and (D) are details mentioned by the speakers. (1.10)
17. A, B The soil conservationist says, "Most soil conservationists have degrees in agronomy, agricultural education, or general agriculture." (1.11)
18. D He says he would like to have a job where he can work outdoors, and soil conservationists do most of their work "in the field" (outdoors). (1.14)
19. C He is trying to figure out his schedule for spring semester. He has already chosen two classes but can't find another class to fit his schedule. (1.14)
20. A Mrs. Kim says, "Why not take Math in spring? You could take Business Math," and "Speech will be offered again during the summer term. Can you take it then?" (1.11)
21. B–C–A Speech—Summer term; Biology—Current term; English—Spring term. (1.12)

22. C The instructor talks about the origins, characteristics, and influences of jazz—ideas most likely to be discussed in a course in American Cultural History. (1.15)
23. C The instructor says, "African Americans began performing the folk music known as 'the blues,' whose origins lay in the work songs of slavery days." (1.11)
24. A "St. Louis Blues" adapted the African–American folk idiom to European conventions of orchestration and harmony, thus becoming influential among both black and white musicians. (1.14)
25. D (A), (B), and (C) are all mentioned by the speaker. (D) is inaccurate; in fact, jazz gave its name to the decade of the 1920s, the period after World War One. (1.11)
26. A The lecture discusses the Tea Act and the response of the American colonists to it. (1.10)
27. C The Tea Act required that all tea shipped to the colonies be imported by the East India Company, which means it gave a private company a monopoly on tea. (1.14)
28. D The Boston Tea Party was an act of protest that involved throwing tea off ships into the water of Boston Harbor. (1.11)
29. D–A–C–B 1. Parliament passed the Tea Act.
2. Protestors called for a boycott of tea.
3. The Boston Tea Party took place.
4. Parliament passed the Intolerable Acts. (1.13)
30. C The speaker concludes by saying, "Thus, we can see that in a dispute over tea, a revolution began." (1.15)
31. B The talk is about flower bulbs, so the most likely audience would be gardeners. (1.15)
32. C The speaker says bulbs look drab and generally ugly. (A) has *dominant*, which does not relate to the bulb's appearance. (B) is inaccurate; it is the *flowers* that grow from bulbs, *not* the bulbs, that are lovely and colorful. (D) is inaccurate; bulbs can survive for months without moisture. (1.11)
33. A The bulb is a self–contained "storehouse" that helps the plant to survive for months without soil or moisture. (1.11)
34. B, C Bulbs produce beautiful flowers, and some bulbs are hardy—able to stay in the ground all winter. [A] is not mentioned. [D] is inaccurate; bulbs require a *minimum* of care. (1.11)
35. D The professor mainly discusses the shapes of various rock formations. (A) and (B) are details. (C) is not mentioned. (1.10)
36. C A mesa is a flat–topped hill that is wider than it is high; a mesa looks like a table. (1.11)
37. A A mesa reduces (shrinks) in size because its softer base recedes with erosion, weakening the edge of the mesa's cap, which eventually cracks, splits, and falls. (1.14)
38. A A butte is a part (remnant) of an eroded mesa; a butte is at least as high as it is wide. (1.11)
39. B–D–C–A 1. Spire. 2. Boulder. 3. Pebbles. 4. Sand. (1.13)
40. D The talk mainly describes various practical uses of aromatic trees. (A) and (B) are not supported by anything the speaker says. (C) is a detail. (1.10)
41. C The European explorers first noticed the "pungent aroma," or pleasant smell, of the trees. (1.11)
42. A Sailors valued pine sap because it produced "naval stores"—pitch and pine tar that healed wounds in wooden ships and kept the ships watertight and seaworthy. (1.14)
43. A, D Powdered sassafras leaves were used as spice by the Choctaw Indians. Sassafras was "a cure for everything from fever to stomachache." [B] is not mentioned. [C] is inaccurate; in fact, sassafras was found to be a potential "carcinogen," a cancer–causing substance. (1.11)
44. B The U. S. Food and Drug Administration found sassafras oil a potential carcinogen, so sassafras has become a "banned" substance, which means it is against the law to use it as a food or drink. (1.15)
45. C–A–B Pine—Naval stores; Sassafras—Root beer; Arborvitae—Cure for scurvy. (1.12)

SECTION 2 – STRUCTURE (p. 579)

1. D *Playful* is an adjective where a noun is needed (2.22). Correction: *playfulness*.
2. A *Which* refers only to animals or things and never to people (2.10, 2.15). Correction: *whom*.
3. B *Accompanying* is not parallel to the other past participles in the list (2.6, 2.11, 2.25). Correction: *accompanied*.
4. B The sentence needs a noun structure to rename *Archimedes* (2.2). (A) is a clause (2.8). (C) has the subordinator *where*, which introduces subordinate clauses (2.10, 2.11). (D) is a prepositional phrase (2.21).
5. C The sentence needs an adjective to modify *study* (2.18). (A) is an adverb. (B) is a pronoun. (D) is a noun.
6. A The sentence needs a subject + verb (2.8). (B) has a verb form that cannot be used without the auxiliary *be* (2.5). (C) lacks a verb. (D) has incorrect word order.
7. C *Serving* is a verb form that cannot be used without the auxiliary *be* (2.5). Correction: *have been serving, have served,* or *serve*.
8. D *In workplace* lacks an article where one is needed (2.4). Correction: *in the workplace*.
9. C *Type of* is singular where a plural is needed before *roles* (2.3). Correction: *types of*.
10. C *Find* is the incorrect form of the verb; the passive voice is needed (2.6). Correction: *found*.
11. B The sentence needs a conjunction to join two noun phrases (2.20). (A) and (C) introduce adverb clauses (2.11). (D) introduces adjective clauses (2.10).
12. D The sentence needs a noun structure as the subject. The correct answer is the beginning of a noun clause (2.9). (A) and (B) have incorrect word order for this context. (C) has *that*, which would incorrectly introduce an adjective clause (2.10).
13. A The sentence needs an adjective structure to modify *artist*. The correct answer is an active voice adjective phrase (2.10). (B) has *which*, which refers only to things and never to people (2.10). (C) is a main clause (2.8). (D) is a verb phrase (2.5).
14. A The sentence needs a noun structure as the true subject. *It* is the "false" subject (2.1). (B) has incorrect word order (2.16). (C) is a clause (2.8). (D) has a verb form that would not agree with *was* (2.6).

15. A *Is raising* is an incorrect word choice (2.23). *Raise* must be followed by a direct object. Correction: *is rising*.
16. C *Has their* has a singular verb, but a plural verb is needed with the compound subject *parking meter and other similar machines* (2.14). Correction: *have their*.
17. C *Location of accounts* follows *but also*, but it is not parallel to the *for* + gerund phrase following *not only* (2.20, 2.25). Correction: *for locating accounts*.
18. C *Its* does not agree in number with its noun referent, *bicycle messengers* (2.15). Correction: *their*.
19. D *Mostly* is an adverb where an adjective is needed to modify *property* (2.22). Correction: *most*.
20. B The main clause needs a verb. The correct answer is a verb + preposition structure (2.8, 2.21). (A) is an infinitive, which does not function as a verb (2.7). (C) and (D) are plural verbs, but a singular verb is needed with the singular subject *success* (2.14).
21. C The sentence needs an inverted subject and verb after *under no circumstances* (2.13). (A) and (B) do not have an inverted subject and verb. (D) lacks a subject.
22. C The sentence needs a subordinator to introduce an adverb phrase (2.11). (A) and (B) are subject + verb structures (2.8). (D) introduces adjective clauses (2.10).
23. A *Great* is the incorrect form of the adjective in a double comparative (2.19). Correction: *greater*.
24. A *For form* is an incorrect structure, preposition + verb, where an infinitive is needed (2.7). Following *helps*, *to* may be omitted. Correction: *form*.
25. D *To* is an incorrect preposition (2.21). Correction: *into*.

SECTION 3 – READING (p. 583)

1. A A maximum accumulation of water at two opposite positions on earth (high tide) is balanced by withdrawal of water from all points 90 degrees away (low tide); see lines 14–16. (B) is supported in paragraph 2. (C) is supported in paragraph 1. (D) is supported in paragraph 4. (3.1)
2. C *The gravitational attraction* (gravity) *of the sun and moon* appears before *these two variable forces*, closer than (A), (B), or (D). (3.3)
3. B *Repeated* is closest in meaning to *recurrent* in this context. Clues: *rise and fall; cycle;* the prefix *re–* means *again*. (3.4)
4. B See lines 4–5. (3.2)
5. C *Overcomes* is closest in meaning to *outranks* in this context. The moon's mass is smaller but its tide–raising force is greater than that of the sun. (3.4)
6. D See line 12. The moon's tide–raising force is *more than twice that of the sun*. (3.2)
7. C *Swellings* is closest in meaning to *bulges*. Clues: *maximum accumulation of waters, away from these*. (3.4)
8. A See lines 19–20. The moon is *on the opposite side of the earth from the sun* at full moon. This means the earth is between the moon and the sun. (3.2, 3.5)
9. B Paragraph 5 gives some examples of actual high and low tides. (A) and (C) are supporting details. (D) is the topic of paragraph 2. (3.1, 3.6)
10. C Actual high and low tides can vary due to *abrupt barometric pressure changes*. (A) is untrue according to the passage. (B) and (D) are not supported by the information in the passage. (3.5)
11. D In the added sentence, *As a result* is a transition that shows a cause–result relationship between *the gravitational forces of the moon and sun tend to counteract each other* in the previous sentence and *the range between high and low tides is reduced*. (A), (B), and (C) would not make sense. (3.7)
12. A The Vitascope is discussed in the context of the development of motion pictures. (B), (C), and (D) are supporting details. (3.1)
13. D See lines 4–5. (3.2)
14. B *Holds* is closest in meaning to *retains* in this context. Clues: *the impression...for a split second after that object has actually disappeared*; the prefix *re–* means *again*. (3.4)
15. C Inventors who worked on motion pictures probably knew about Roget's principle (lines 9–11), and Thomas Armat worked on motion pictures (lines 22–23). (A) and (B) are not supported by the information in the passage. (D) is inaccurate; see lines 7–8. (3.5)
16. C See lines 12–13. (A) and (D) are not mentioned. (B) is inaccurate. (3.2)
17. A Keys: *Edison was congratulated for his splendid contribution; but in truth, the success of the Vitascope depended on...Thomas Armat* (lines 20–23). (B), (C), and (D) are not supported by the information in the passage. (3.5)
18. C *Advances* is closest in meaning to *breakthroughs* in this context. All devices for the screen projection of motion pictures were based on something made in Edison's laboratories—in this case, developments, or advances. (3.4)
19. D *Photography* appears before *latter*, in the same sentence. (A) and (C) are farther from *latter*. (B) is the former, not the latter, thing mentioned. (3.3)
20. B The added sentence describes the waves, developing the idea introduced in the previous sentence. (A) and (D) would not make sense. (C) would be less coherent than the correct answer; it is more logical to describe the appearance of the waves before the reaction to them. (3.7)
21. D All of the paragraphs develop the idea that automobile roads are important in American life. (A), (B), and (C) are supporting ideas. (3.1)
22. A *Automobile sales* (car sales) appears before *those*, in the same sentence. (B), (C), and (D) are farther from *those*. (3.3)
23. C The increase in car registrations and the number of cars suggests that America's passion for cars grew in the 1920s. (A) and (D) are not supported by the information in the passage. (B) is inaccurate; Michigan car sales are compared to those in other nations, not other states. (3.5)
24. A *Intense* is closest in meaning to *frenzied* in this context. Clues: *one of the largest items of government expenditure* (lines 3–4); *the growth of roads* (line 11). (3.4)
25. D See lines 9–10. (A), (B), and (C) are all paraphrased in paragraphs 2–4. (3.2)
26. C The passage does not mention subway fares in relation to the growth in the number of cars. (A), (B), and (D) are all mentioned in paragraph 3. (3.2)

27. B *Barely sufficient* is closest in meaning to *scant* in this context. Clues: *one percent, worst public transit system*. (3.4)
28. D Keys: *The predominance of private transportation; the American bias; the world's best road system; its worst public transit system*. (A) and (C) are not supported by the information in the passage. (B) is inaccurate; see lines 3–4. (3.5)
29. B Paragraph 3 gives examples to show how the growth of roads and the automobile industry affected other industries. (3.6)
30. C The added sentence functions as a transition between *interstate highways*, which is introduced in the previous sentence, and the ideas of *mobility* and *distances*, which are developed with examples in the following sentence. (A) would not make sense. (B) and (D) would be less coherent than the correct answer. (3.7)
31. B All of the paragraphs discuss social support and its effect on physical and emotional health. (A) is inaccurate; physical strength is not emphasized. (C) and (D) are too general. (3.1)
32. B The passage does not deal with recovery from depression. (A), (C), and (D) are important supporting ideas. (3.2)
33. A *Protect* is closest in meaning to *buffer* in this context. Clue: *from the potential impact*. (3.4)
34. D Subjective perception of the adequacy, or quality, of social support is more important than objective measures such as frequency of social contact. (A) is inaccurate; the passage does not mention how many studies there have been. (B) is untrue according to lines 10–13. (C) is inaccurate; frequency of social contact is important, but not as important as quality of contact. (3.5)
35. B *Available* is closest in meaning to *out there* in this context. Clue: *the security of our attachment*. (3.4)
36. B Key: *adults with adequate social support have a lower risk of...depression than do adults with weaker social networks* (lines 16–17). (A), (C), and (D) are not supported by the information in the passage. (3.5)
37. C *Individuals* appears before *those*, in the same sentence; both are the object of the preposition *for*, a parallel position that helps you see that *those* refers to *individuals*. (A), (B), and (D) are farther from *those*. (3.3)
38. D Lines 20–24 discuss a study of depression in women. (3.6)
39. D The added sentence expands on the idea of a link between social support and health by adding information about other studies. (A), (B), and (C) would interrupt the ideas in consecutive sentences. (3.7)
40. A The author presents Andrew Jackson in a historical perspective, focusing on his life and presidency. (3.6)
41. B Jackson acquired fame because of his leadership during the War of 1812. His name was frequently mentioned in conversation, thus it *became a household word*. (3.4)
42. A Keys: *marked the political ascendancy of the "common man"; whereas all previous presidents* (lines 1–2); *made a dramatic entrance* (line 13). (B) is inaccurate; they *nearly* destroyed the White House. (C) and (D) are not supported by the information in the passage. (3.5)
43. D *The Bank of the United States* appears before *institution*, in the same sentence. (A), (B), and (C) are farther from *institution*. (3.3)
44. C See lines 17–19. Jackson believed the Bank profited only a small number of rich people. (3.2)
45. C See lines 21–22. Jackson's policy of Indian removal was *at the time considered an enlightened solution*. (3.2)
46. A *Harsh* is closest in meaning to *brutal* in this context. Clues: *marched by force, Trail of Tears*. (3.4)
47. C *Contribution* is closest in meaning to *legacy* in this context. Paragraph 5 discusses the enduring contributions that Jackson made to American politics. (3.4)
48. B See lines 26–28. The Whig Party opposed Jackson. (A), (C), and (D) are all contributions of Jackson. (3.2)
49. B Nothing in the passage suggests that Jackson was president during a war; the "war" he waged against the Bank of the United States was political, not violent. (A), (C), and (D) are all supported by the information in the passage. (3.5)
50. C The added sentence expands on the idea of abandoning property requirements for voting that is introduced in the previous sentence. (A), (B), and (D) would be less coherent than the correct answer; there is no logical connection to other ideas. (3.7)

TEST 4

SECTION 1 – LISTENING COMPREHENSION (p. 601)

1. D The conditional "if this drawer weren't so full, I might be able to find one" is unreal; the verb tenses mean the drawer is very full and the man *can't* find a knife. (A), (B), and (C) repeat words from the conversation incorrectly. (1.3, 2.12)
2. D The negative expression "business has never been slower" means business is now the slowest it has ever been; in other words, business was better before. (B) and (C) repeat words from the conversation incorrectly. (1.4, 1.5)
3. C Andrew moved to town "at least a year before" the speakers did, which means Andrew has lived there longer than the two speakers have. (1.5)
4. D Keys: *sketches, lettering, color.* (1.8)
5. D *See eye to eye* = agree. (1.2)
6. D The woman wants to buy Jill some earrings; the man asks a negative question, "Are you sure she wouldn't prefer…?" implying Jill might not want earrings. (1.7)
7. B The man says she "had better leave early anyway," implying she should leave earlier than she had planned. (1.3, 1.7)
8. A The woman was active in the student assembly "only for a few months," a short amount of time, implying she is not active at present. (1.5, 1.7)
9. D *Look forward to* = anticipate with pleasure. (1.2)
10. C Keys: *bottle of juice, hear that crash.* (1.8)
11. B Keys: *roses, taken good care of them, the weather was perfect for roses.* (1.9)
12. D "I can show you where to wait" means she is offering to help him if he walks with her. (1.3)
13. D *Turn over a new leaf* = change for the better. (1.2)
14. B In this context, *comprehensive* means *including a lot.* (1.1)
15. B *Make fun of* = joke about. (1.2)
16. C A synonym for *polluted* is *not clean.* (1.1)
17. A The negative question "Why don't you just get a salad…?" implies the man should buy a salad at the deli. (1.7)
18. B "Need you even ask?" implies the woman does *not* need to ask because she already knows what he wants to do. (1.7)
19. B The man wants to know where he can get a bus to Worthington Heights; the woman says he is in the right place; the man will probably wait for the next bus. (1.8)
20. C The woman says she is "really sorry" she didn't "sign up" for that class (Business Law), which means she regrets not taking the class. In this context, *sign up* means *register*. (1.1, 1.2)
21. C Key: *the check for my rent.* (1.9)
22. C The man's tone shows he does *not* think the woman helped him; he is disappointed because he cannot write a check. (1.6)
23. C *Sleep on it* = consider carefully. (1.2)
24. A *Stand a chance* = have a possibility. (B) and (D) repeat words from the conversation incorrectly. (1.2, 1.4)
25. B The causative "got Maureen to do it" means Maureen did it (finished the page layout). (C) has *tired*, which sounds like *tied–up*. (D) has *lay down*, which sounds like *layout*. (1.3)
26. A The man's rising intonation makes "Yoko has a sister" a question, which shows his surprise at learning Yoko has a sister; he had assumed she did *not* have one. (1.6)
27. B In this context, *steamed* means *angry*; Ms. Phillips was angry because the men were not prepared. (1.1)
28. A The man's printer won't work; the woman asks if he would like her to take a look at it; the woman will probably help the man with his printer. (1.8)
29. B The speakers are discussing Molly; the woman says she has not seen Molly today; you can infer Molly is not present. (1.8)
30. B *Take it out on (someone)* = be unpleasant or unkind to someone when you are upset. (1.2, 1.7)
31. B Keys: *wind, branches snapping, power went out.* (1.10, 1.15)
32. C She says, "I'm upset because I have a paper due this morning, and I couldn't finish it without my computer." (1.14)
33. B The man says, "Why don't you just go talk to him? I'm sure he'll allow it this time." He is advising her to talk to her instructor. (1.11)
34. D Keys: *power went out around eight o'clock; the power is still not on; that means no heat; couldn't finish (my paper) without my computer.* (1.11, 1.15)
35. D Keys: *vending machine for detergent; this is the closest place where I can do my washing; put the detergent in; my clothes.* (1.15)
36. C The woman tells him where the detergent vending machine is. (A) is inaccurate; she tells him where the change machine is. (B) and (D) are inaccurate. (1.11)
37. B (A), (C), and (D) are all mentioned. Neither speaker mentions where to do washing on campus. (1.11)
38. C (A), (B), and (D) are all mentioned. The speaker does not mention financial assistance. (1.11)
39. B The speaker says, "We have a job board, where we post listings of job openings both on and off campus." (1.11)
40. A Many of the special workshops have sessions that meet on evenings or Saturdays. (1.11)
41. D The speaker says, "Now, I'd like to show you our facilities and introduce you to one of our counselors, but before that, are there any questions?" You can infer the speaker will probably answer questions from the audience. (1.15)
42. C Mead was trained in observation from early childhood, when her grandmother taught her to keep a detailed daily record of the infant development of her two younger sisters. (1.11)
43. B Mead was fascinated by the brilliance of Ruth Benedict, an anthropology professor; Mead then decided to do graduate work in anthropology. (1.14)
44. C Child rearing, cultural change, and race relations are among the many subjects Mead wrote about. (1.11)
45. A The speaker says, "No one has denied the extent of her contribution to anthropology…and her willingness to tackle large subjects of major intellectual consequence." Also, the fact that Mead published ten major works shows that she made major contributions to the field of anthropology. (1.15)
46. B The speaker says, "Consider trying to cut energy costs by following these tips." (1.10)
47. C The speaker says, "During the winter, more energy is used for heating than anything else" (1.11)

48. D The speaker advises using the sun's heat by opening draperies and blinds and using the sun's light as a way to get along with as few lights as possible. Both of these practices can lower energy costs. (1.14)
49. A About half as much hot water is used for a shower as for a tub bath. (1.14)
50. C The speaker recommends using one large bulb rather than several smaller ones. (1.11)

SECTION 2 – STRUCTURE AND WRITTEN EXPRESSION (p. 608)

1. B The sentence needs a subject + verb (2.8). (A) is a noun clause (2.9). (C) and (D) are gerund phrases (2.7).
2. C The sentence needs a noun structure to rename the subject, *seismology* (2.2). (A) would make a clause instead of an appositive (2.8). (B) has the subordinator *which*, which introduces adjective clauses (2.10). (D) is a verb.
3. C The sentence needs an infinitive after *help*; *to* may be omitted after *help* (2.7). (A) and (B) are gerunds (2.7). (D) is a noun (2.22).
4. A The subordinate clause needs a verb (2.5, 2.8). (B) has a duplicate subject, *they* (2.1). (C) is an infinitive, which does not function as a verb (2.7). (D) has a verb form that cannot be used without the auxiliary *be* (2.5).
5. D The sentence needs a noun structure as the object of the preposition *among* (2.1, 2.19). (A) has base–form and comparative adjectives where the superlative degree is needed (2.19). (B) has the equative expression *as tiny as*, which cannot follow *among* (2.19, 2.21) (C) has incorrect word order.
6. C The sentence needs an adjective structure to modify *sunlight*. The correct answer is the beginning of a passive voice adjective phrase (2.10). (A) has a verb that does not agree in tense meaning with the verb in the main clause, *is* (2.5). (B) is a noun (2.22). (D) is a passive voice verb phrase (2.6).
7. A The sentence needs a noun structure as the subject. The correct answer is the beginning of a noun clause (2.1, 2.9). (B) has *which*, which introduces adjective clauses (2.10). (C) is in passive voice, which is incorrect here because *a lever* is the direct object (2.5, 2.6). (D) is a *for* + gerund prepositional phrase (2.7, 2.21).
8. D The sentence needs a passive voice verb (2.6). (A) and (B) are active voice. (C) is an active voice modal + verb (2.5).
9. B The sentence needs a noun structure as the direct object of *storing* (2.1, 2.3). (A) has an incorrect plural form for the uncountable noun *information* (2.3). (C) has *an*, which cannot be used with an uncountable noun (2.3, 2.4). (D) has *many*, which cannot be used with an uncountable noun (2.3)
10. D The sentence needs a preposition as part of a compound preposition after *because* (2.21). (A) has an incorrect preposition. (B) and (C) lack prepositions.
11. A The second main clause needs a subject + verb. The correct answer has a passive voice verb (2.6, 2.8). (B) lacks the auxiliary *be* (2.6). (C) is an infinitive, which does not function as a verb (2.7). (D) is a prepositional phrase (2.21).
12. D The sentence needs an adjective structure to modify *group*. The correct answer is an adjective clause (2.10). (A) lacks a subordinator. (B) and (C) lack a necessary preposition; they lived *in* the group (2.21).
13. B The sentence needs a structure to come between commas. The correct answer is a prepositional phrase that functions as an adverb (2.21). (A) is a noun clause (2.9). (C) is a conjunction + main clause (2.8). (D) is a main clause (2.8).
14. A The sentence needs an adjective to modify *weather* that can be used before the infinitive *to have*. The correct answer is an adjective + *enough* structure (2.16). (B) has an incorrect adverb form. (C) has incorrect word order. (D) incorrectly combines *enough* with an equative expression (2.19).
15. B The sentence needs a structure that is parallel to the infinitive phrase *to repeat actions exactly* and is joined by *and* (2.7, 2.25). (A) lacks a preposition where one is needed. (C) is the beginning of an adjective clause (2.10). (D) has a verb that does not agree in tense meaning with the verb in the main clause, *can be directed* (2.5, 2.6).
16. B *It* is a duplicate subject (2.1). *The mallard duck* is the subject. Correction: omit *it*.
17. A *Deads* is an incorrect form; adjectives do not have plural forms. A plural noun is needed (2.3, 2.22). Correction: *deaths*.
18. B *Is* is a singular verb, but a plural verb is needed with the plural subject *functions* (2.14). Correction: *are*.
19. A *Less women* is incorrect because *less* is not used with countable nouns such as *women* (2.3). Correction: *fewer women*.
20. D *Help* does not agree in tense meaning with the other verbs in the sentence, *deprived, smuggled*, and *subverted* (2.5). Correction: *helped*.
21. A *Which* refers only to animals or things and never to people (2.10, 2.15). Correction: *who*.
22. B *Rely on* does not agree in tense meaning with the verb in the main clause, *would not be*; this is a present unreal conditional sentence (2.12). Correction: *relied on*.
23. A *More* is an incorrectly formed comparative expression (2.19). Correction: *more than*.
24. A *Interesting* is an adjective where a noun is needed (2.22). Correction: *interest*.
25. A *Reason* is incorrect because *a number of* means *several* and is used with plural countable nouns (2.3, 2.14). Correction: *reasons*.
26. D *Forward* is redundant when it is used with *progressed*, which means *move forward* (2.24). Correction: omit *forward*.
27. D *Notably* is an adverb where an adjective is needed (2.22). Correction: *notable*.
28. B *Do not* has the incorrect auxiliary (2.6). Correction: *are not*.
29. B *To respond* lacks a preposition where one is needed (2.21). Correction: *to respond to*.
30. D *Restrict* is a verb where an infinitive is needed as the subject complement after *is* (2.7). Correction: *to restrict*.
31. B *Are* is a plural verb, but a singular verb is needed with the singular subject *performance* (2.14). Correction: *is*.
32. D *Formation* is a noun where a verb is needed (2.5, 2.8, 2.22). Correction: *form*.

33. C *To reduce* is not parallel to the other gerunds in the list, *improving* and *expanding* (2.7, 2.25). Correction: *reducing*.
34. A *Status social* has incorrect word order (2.16). Correction: *social status*.
35. B *No* is an adjective where a noun or pronoun is needed (2.18). Correction: *none*.
36. D *Of* is an incorrect preposition (2.21). Correction: *in*.
37. A *Integrate circuit* has an incorrect word form, *integrate*, which is a verb where a passive participial adjective is needed to modify *circuit* (2.17). Correction: *integrated circuit*.
38. A *While* is an incorrect word choice because it must be followed by a clause, but a preposition is needed here before a noun object (2.11, 2.21, 2.23). Correction: *during*.
39. B *And also* is incorrectly paired with *not only* (2.20). Correction: *but also*.
40. A *The Park Service allows* should have an inverted subject and verb after the "almost negative" expression *rarely* (2.13). Correction: *does the Park Service allow*.

SECTION 3 – READING COMPREHENSION (p. 615)

1. C Most of the paragraphs discuss the social functions of costume. (A), (B), and (D) are supporting details. (3.1)
2. B The paragraph lists differences between costume and clothing. (3.1, 3.6)
3. D See lines 8–9. *The desire to please* is given as a psychological reason for covering our bodies. (A), (B), and (C) are physical reasons. (3.2)
4. A *Endowing* is similar in meaning to *investing* in this context. Clue: *with the attributes of other creatures*. Costume gave people, or endowed them with, certain qualities. (3.4)
5. D *Decorations* is closest in meaning to *ornaments* in this context. Clues: *beyond that of simple utility, identified the wearer with*. (3.4)
6. B Key: *in all periods children at play have worn disguises, so as to adapt gradually to adult life*. (A), (C), and (D) are not supported by the information in the paragraph. (3.5)
7. D The police officer's uniform is given as an example of how costume expresses *personal or delegated authority* (lines 19–20). (3.2, 3.6)
8. C *Indicates* is closest in meaning to *denotes* in this context. Clues: *costume...power; military uniform... rank*. (3.4)
9. C *The scale* refers to *social position* in this context. Clues: *an expression of social caste* (line 22); *At the bottom...there are such compulsory costumes as the convict's uniform* (lines 24–25). The convict has a low social position. (3.4)
10. A Having a heart condition is a physical reason. (B), (C), and (D) are all social reasons, expressing membership in a group or profession. (3.5)
11. D Each paragraph explains how a memory structure works in processing information. (A) and (C) are supporting details. (B) is inaccurate. (3.1, 3.6)
12. C *Memory structures* appears before *They*, in the previous sentence. *Memory structures* is the only answer choice that could include the three things listed (lines 2–3). (A) would not make sense. (B) and (D) are farther from *They*. (3.3)
13. C Objects or events that activate our memory are environmental stimuli. Clues: *sense receptors; stimulated; visual, auditory, tactile, olfactory, and gustatory*. (3.4)
14. A See lines 10–14. Information that is not recognized as meaningful receives no further processing and is therefore forgotten. (3.2)
15. B See lines 18–19. (3.2)
16. C Keys: *approximately 20 seconds*; the example of forgetting an unfamiliar phone number. Short–term memory holds information just long enough for the task we are currently working on, such as remembering a phone number long enough to dial it. (A) may be true, but cannot be inferred from paragraph 3. (B) and (D) are not supported by the information in the passage. (3.5)
17. D *Size* is closest in meaning to *capacity* in this context. Clues: *storage, contains*. (3.4)
18. A Because the birth date of our child is important to us, we would be more likely to encode it so that it could be easily retrieved when necessary. (B), (C), and (D) would probably be less meaningful to us. (3.5)
19. B Key: *a time when barons of industry left an indelible mark*. (A), (C), and (D) are not supported by the information in the passage. (3.5)
20. A See lines 7–8. (3.2)
21. D See lines 10–11 and 13–14. Increasing production (output) would involve increasing storage space. (3.2)
22. C Common sense tells you that beer is the product under discussion and thus the most logical referent of *the highly perishable product*. (A), (B), and (D) are not products. (3.4)
23. C *Faith* is closest in meaning to *conviction* in this context. Busch had only his belief, or faith, that he could overcome the problems of storage and shipping. (3.4)
24. B The obstacles of shipping and storage are discussed in the previous paragraph; Busch saw them as *obstacles to be overcome* (lines 15–16). Paragraph 3 discusses Busch's effort to *overcome these hurdles*. Common sense tells you that *these hurdles* are *shipping and storage*. (A), (C), and (D) would not make sense. (3.3)
25. A See lines 22–24. (3.2)
26. D The most general idea in the paragraph is Busch's innovations in the brewing industry. (A), (B), and (C) are supporting details. (3.1)
27. B *Skill* is closest in meaning to *acumen* in this context. Clue: *recognizing early on*. (3.4)
28. D Keys: *flamboyant promoter, unless people knew about them, marketing acumen*. (A), (B), and (C) are not supported by the information in the passage. (3.5)
29. C *Accumulated* is closest in meaning to *amassed* in this context. Clues: *tremendous wealth, self–made man*. (3.4)
30. A The author focuses on Busch's accomplishments in the industry, calling him a *self–made man* (line 31). (3.6)
31. C All of the paragraphs develop the idea of conflict between American Indians and Europeans over land. (A) and (D) are supporting ideas. (B) is not dealt with here. (3.1)

32. B Trade with Europeans caused the Indian tribes to compete with each other for the land containing the fur–producing animals that the Europeans wanted. (3.2, 3.6)
33. D *Justified* is closest in meaning to *legitimized* in this context. The author is saying that the Europeans proposed treaties and offered gifts as a way to make taking the land lawful and acceptable. (3.4)
34. A Keys: *Despite the resistance...the Europeans were destined to win; Indian resistance was crushed; offering gifts*. (B), (C), and (D) are not supported by the information in the passage. (3.5)
35. A Indian Territory was considered *uninhabitable* (line 16), or unable to be lived in. (3.2).
36. B See lines 12–15. Treaties usually meant that Indians had to move away from land that Europeans wanted. (A) and (D) are paraphrased in paragraph 1. (C) is mentioned in lines 17–18. (3.2)
37. C Key: *No aspect of American history is more poignant*. The author implies that the forced removal of the Indians is distressing and tragic. (A) and (D) are not supported by the information in the passage. (B) is untrue according to the author. (3.5)
38. D *Uselessness* is similar in meaning to *futility* in this context. Clue: *accepted their fate*. (3.4)
39. A *Long–lasting* is closest in meaning to *perpetual* in this context. Clue: *between 1829 and 1866*. (3.4)
40. C See lines 22–24. (3.2)
41. D Lines 27–28 discuss the cost to the U. S. government for removal of the Seminoles. (3.6)
42. A Nothing in the passage supports the idea that the coyote is a threat to humans. (B) is supported in paragraph 3. (C) and (D) are supported in paragraphs 1–2. (3.1)
43. B See lines 1–4. The word *Most* in line 2 refers to *canids* in line 1. (3.2, 3.3)
44. C *Group* is closest in meaning to *band* in this context. Clue: *its members*. (3.4)
45. D An *opportunist* is one who seizes any opportunity. The coyote takes advantage of circumstances, eating whatever it can find (lines 15–16). (3.4)
46. C *Rodents* appears before *any*; both are the object of the preposition *for*, a parallel position that helps you see that *any* refers to *rodents*. The badger digs for rodents at one end of the rodents' burrow, and the coyote waits for rodents that may come out the other end of the burrow. (3.3)
47. D See lines 19–21. (3.2)
48. A See lines 23–24. (3.2)
49. B Keys: *has thrived alongside man* (line 5); *is an opportunist* (line 15); *may team up with one or two others* (line 17); *population continues to increase, despite efforts at trapping and poisoning* (line 25). (A) is untrue according to line 25. (C) and (D) are not supported by the information in the passage. (3.5)
50. B Paragraph 2 discusses the coyote's vocalizations. (3.6)

TAPESCRIPT

QUICK DIAGNOSTIC TEST (p. 17)

Section 1 — Listening

In the Listening section of the test, you will have an opportunity to demonstrate your ability to understand conversations and talks in English. Answer all the questions on the basis of what is stated or implied by the speakers you hear. Do not take notes or write during the test.

Part A

Directions: In Part A you will hear short conversations between two people. After each conversation, you will hear a question about the conversation. The conversations and questions will not be repeated. After you hear a question, read the four possible answers and choose the best answer.

Here is an example.

On the recording, you hear:

(Man) Why don't you buy this printer?
(Woman) I'm hoping to find one at a better price.
(Narrator) What does the woman mean?

In your book, you read:

(A) She doesn't want to buy a printer.
(B) She would rather buy something else.
(C) She doesn't want to pay a lot for a printer.
(D) She wants to shop at a better place.

You learn from the conversation that the woman hopes to find a printer at a better price. The best answer to the question, "What does the woman mean?" is (C), "She doesn't want to pay a lot for a printer." Therefore, the correct choice is (C).

1. M: Last year around seventy people came to the management training.
   W: I think we can expect at least that many this year.
   N: What does the woman mean?

2. W: I just finished an excellent novel. I'd be happy to lend it to you.
   M: Thank you, but I'd rather read a biography.
   N: What does the man mean?

3. M: I ran into Dominic today and hardly recognized him. He's a different man.
   W: I know what you mean. I've never seen him happier.
   N: What does the woman say about Dominic?

4. W: Thanks for coming in on your day off.
   M: No problem. I could sure use the money. Where do you want me to work?
   W: We're short–handed out in front. I had to fire one of the waiters, and two busboys called in sick.
   N: What is the woman's job?

5. W: Today in my calculus class Professor Moore used some of her skating routines to explain the theory.
   M: Professor Moore is a figure skater?
   N: What does the man mean?

6. W: A group of us are going hiking on Mount Adams this weekend. How'd you like to join us?
   M: I would if I didn't have my organic chemistry final on Monday morning.
   N: What will the man probably do this weekend?

7. W: Where are you going?
   M: To the gym on the corner. I always lift weights on Saturdays.
   N: What does the man mean?

8. M: My algebra test is tomorrow, and I still can't figure out how to set up story problems.
   W: Let's go over them one more time.
   N: What does the woman suggest they do?

9. W: I'm really looking forward to our field trip in the canyon.
   M: If we're lucky, it won't be so blazing hot this time.
   N: What does the man imply?

Part B

Directions: In this part of the test, you will hear several conversations and talks. Each conversation or talk is followed by several questions. The conversations, talks, and questions will not be repeated.

For most of the questions, you will read four possible answers and choose the best answer. Some questions will have special directions.

Here is an example.

On the recording, you hear:

(Narrator) Listen to part of a talk in a general science class. The instructor is talking about the science of meteorology, the study of the earth's atmosphere.

(Man) Progress in the field began with the development of physics and the invention of basic instruments. In the nineteenth century, the invention of the telegraph was important because it improved rapid data collection from remote weather stations. Today, because of such modern research tools as high–altitude airplanes, weather balloons, rockets, earth satellites, and space probes, meteorologists are able to provide more sophisticated understanding and forecasting of weather, their best known function. They also work at solving air pollution problems and studying trends in the earth's climate.

Now listen to a sample question.

(Narrator) How did the telegraph improve the science of meteorology?

In your book, you read:

(A) It helped scientists see the atmosphere more clearly.
(B) It made it easier for scientists to send messages.
(C) It made data collection from weather stations faster.
(D) It helped airplanes fly higher.

The best answer to the question, "How did the telegraph improve the science of meteorology?" is (C), "It made data collection from weather stations faster." Therefore, the correct choice is (C).

Now listen to another sample question.

(Narrator) According to the instructor, what do meteorologists do today?

In your book, you read:

Choose 2 answers.

[A] Forecast the weather.
[B] Study trends in rocket science.
[C] Solve air pollution problems.
[D] Study costs of building satellites.

The best two answers to the question, "What do meteorologists do today?" are [A], "Forecast the weather" and [C], "Solve air pollution problems." Therefore, the correct choices are [A] and [C].

Remember, you should not take notes during the test.

Questions 10 through 12. Listen to a conversation between two teaching assistants.

M: Hi, Sarah, do you have a minute?
W: Uh, sure, Dave. I have a few minutes, but then I have to run. I've got a class at two o'clock. You know how it is!
M: Well, that's exactly what I'm concerned about. It seems like I have no time to breathe, either. I'm teaching with Professor Chapman—it's a large class—and that means I have almost fifty papers to grade every week. It really takes a lot of time, and I can barely get my own coursework done. I think they're asking us to work too much.
W: That's the most common complaint of first–year teaching assistants. They give us a lot of work the first year.
M: Do you think we should say something to the department head?
W: It's hard on us now, but think of what we're learning. If I were you, I'd try to stick it out this term. Do a good job and impress Professor Chapman. He's fair, and he understands what it's like for us. When they give us our assignments next term, he'll give you more choice in which class you teach.
M: Well, maybe I'd better just bear with it. If I can only get through this term!
W: I've heard it will get better for us next year. They'll assign us only a few students so we'll have more time to work on our thesis projects.
M: I look forward to that.
W: I've got to go now. Hang in there, OK? It does get better.
M: Thanks, Sarah. See you later.

10. Why is the man concerned?
11. According to the woman, in what order are the following given to teaching assistants?
12. What will the man probably do now?

Questions 13 through 16. Listen to a small business owner speak to an introductory business class.

To be successful as a small business owner, you must be a competent and knowledgeable manager. You also need a thorough knowledge of your field. You should have a combination of formal education and practical training suited to the kind of business you want to operate. To run a store, for example, you need experience in retailing and college courses in bookkeeping, accounting and business. You should also be familiar with tax laws and with state and federal laws regulating business.

Small business owners usually consider themselves successful when they can support themselves solely from the operation and profits of their business. Many expand their businesses or branch out into other fields. Many large department stores, supermarket chains, wholesale distributors, and even giant manufacturing corporations started out as small businesses. However, most small businesses remain small.

Small businesses generally face stiff competition from established companies at first. For example, large companies generally have cash reserves on hand that enable them to absorb losses more easily than small firms can. This is why many small businesses fail each year. Others, however, become highly successful. Hard work, good management, and a product or service for which there is a demand are the essentials for making it as a small business.

13. What is the talk mainly about?
14. According to the speaker, what is required to operate a store?
15. When is a small business considered to be successful?
16. According to the speaker, why do many small businesses fail?

Questions 17 through 20. Listen to an introductory lecture given to university students who are majoring in the social sciences.

The term *research* can mean any sort of careful, systematic investigation in some field of study that is undertaken to discover or establish knowledge.

One of the most common forms of research is survey research. It involves asking a large group of people questions about a particular topic or issue. This can be done in a number of ways—face–to–face with individuals, by mail, by telephone, and now on the Internet. Each method has its advantages and disadvantages, but obtaining information from a large group of people lies at the heart of survey research.

Another kind of research is experimental research, one of the most powerful methodologies researchers can use. Experimental research is the most conclusive of scientific methods because it enables researchers to go beyond the description and identification of relationships, to at least a partial determination of what causes them. An experiment usually involves two groups of subjects—an experimental group, which receives a treatment of some sort, and a control group, which receives no treatment. The control group enables the researcher to determine whether the treatment has had an effect.

But sometimes a researcher wants an in–depth look at a particular individual or situation. Instead of asking "*What* do people think about this?" as in survey research, or "*What* would happen if I do this?" as in experimental research, the researcher asks "How do these people act?" or "How are things done?" To answer this type of question, researchers use a number of methodologies that come under the label *qualitative research*. Think of qualitative research as the investigation of the *quality* of relationships, activities, or situations.

Over the next several weeks, we'll take a closer look at several methodologies, and each of you will begin designing a project that will try out a specific research method.

17. What is the purpose of the lecture?
18. According to the speaker, why is experimental research one of the most powerful methodologies?
19. With which characteristic is each type of research associated?
20. What will the next lecture in this course probably be about?

SECTION 1 – LISTENING

1.1 LISTENING FOR KEY WORDS (p. 36)

Focus

M: Have you heard the forecast for this weekend?
W: There's supposed to be a blizzard coming this way.

M: Have you heard the forecast for this weekend?
W: There's supposed to be a blizzard coming this way.
N: What does the woman mean?

Exercise 1.1.A

1. M: The air feels different here in the mountains.
   W: Yes, I can feel how arid it is.
   N: What does the woman mean?

2. W: I really enjoyed meeting your new neighbors.
   M: They're great. Did you know they fled their country as refugees?
   N: What does the man mean?

3. M: Why were you hanging around the front office all morning?
   W: I was hoping to get a glimpse of our new president.
   N: What does the woman mean?

4. M: Look at that strange cloud over there.
   W: We'd better get back inside. A whirling cloud is bad news.
   N: What does the woman mean?

5. M: My family had a lovely trip at the lake last summer.
   W: When I was there in August, the mosquitoes were quite bothersome.
   N: What does the woman say about her trip to the lake?

6. W: I didn't expect to see you home so soon.
   M: Well, Jeff drove like a maniac. My life was in jeopardy all the way home.
   N: What does the man say about Jeff?

Exercise 1.1.B

1. W: I was a little shocked to see where Nadine lives.
   M: Her place was run–down, wasn't it? Did you see the stairway?
   N: What does the man mean?

2. W: How did you like the president's speech about our school's vision?
   M: I'm afraid I was completely lost.
   N: What does the man mean?

3. M: Have you looked out the window recently?
   W: Oh, it's pouring! We'd better wait a while before we walk home.
   N: What do you know from the conversation?

4. W: I was sorry I had to leave early. How did the rest of the meeting go?
   M: You missed the best part. Things got really hot between Jim and Mr. Kendrick.
   N: What does the man mean?

5. M: It's good to hear that your brother finally finished college.
   W: Yes, and now he dreams of having his own company.
   N: What does the woman mean?

6. W: What did your instructor say about your presentation?
   M: She was very complimentary.
   N: What does the man mean?

Exercise 1.1.C

1. W: This term I'll be taking marketing, management, and sociology.
   M: You were fortunate to get into marketing. That class usually fills up.
   N: What does the man mean?

2. M: I'd really like it if Teresa went to the party with me.
   W: Well, why don't you stop being so timid and ask her?
   N: What does the woman mean?

3. M: How was your weekend with your parents?
   W: Nice, except my mother's meals are still horrible.
   N: What does the woman say about her mother?

4. M: There are some beautiful buildings on this campus.
   W: Yes, and many are old. The school was founded in 1789.
   N: What do you know from the conversation?

5. W: I think we should take this apartment.
   M: I'd rather inspect it more before we decide.
   N: What does the man mean?

6. M: I'm having a hard time training my dog.
   W: But it won't help if you strike him like that!
   N: What does the woman mean?

1.2 LISTENING FOR IDIOMS (p. 41)

Focus

W: I just heard the news! Congratulations on getting into medical school!
M: Thank you. It's a real load off my mind.

W: I just heard the news! Congratulations on getting into medical school!
M: Thank you. It's a real load off my mind.
N: What does the man mean?

Exercise 1.2.A

1. W: I think it's wonderful having Dr. Williamson next door.
   M: Really? He always rubs me the wrong way.
   N: What does the man mean?

2. W: How does Ellen like her new kitten?
   M: She's been on cloud nine ever since she got him.
   N: What does the man say about Ellen?

3. M: You've been doing homework for the past four hours.
   W: My instructor said I would have to do the exercises over and over before I got them correct.
   N: What does the woman mean?

4. W: I just found out that Karen has a twin sister.
   M: I've met them both, and you can hardly tell them apart.
   N: What does the man mean?

5. M: Why do you seem so tense lately?
   W: Maybe it's because my boss and I don't see eye to eye about anything.
   N: What does the woman say about her boss?

6. W: I'm taking the TOEFL next week.
   M: I'll keep my fingers crossed for you.
   N: What does the man mean?

7. M: I think we should talk about this. I've been wondering how you felt about our last discussion. What I want to know is, I mean...
   W: Would you please stop beating around the bush?
   N: What does the woman want the man to do?

8. W: Look out for that car!
   M: Wow! Now that was a close call!
   N: What do you know from the conversation?

Exercise 1.2.B

1. M: You drove to Alaska in three days? How did you get there so fast?
   W: We took turns driving.
   N: What does the woman mean?

2. W: You sure are out of sorts.
   M: Sorry. I guess it's because my supervisor has been getting on my case.
   N: What does the man mean?

3. W: Is there anything you want me to do?
   M: How about lending a hand with this lumber?
   N: What does the man want the woman to do?

4. W: Kurt thinks you need to look for a job where you can use both your head and your hands.
   M: As usual, Kurt hit the nail on the head.
   N: What does the man say about Kurt?

5. W: How does Aaron like living in Texas?
   M: Actually, I've lost touch with Aaron.
   N: What does the man mean?

6. M: What a headache! Even if I work the next two weekends, I still won't be able to finish the project on time. And my boss doesn't seem to care!
   W: Then why don't you just take it easy?
   N: What does the woman suggest the man do?

7. W: Christine just started working the night shift at the electronics plant.
   M: She always was more of a night owl than an early bird.
   N: What does the man say about Christine?

8. W: I walk past the coffee house every day, and I always see Leo there, either playing a game or reading the paper.
   M: Leo knows more ways to kill time than anyone.
   N: What does the man say about Leo?

Exercise 1.2.C

1. W: I think Fred has been lying to me again.
   M: Finally, you can see through him!
   N: What does the man mean?

2. M: We haven't had this much rain in a long time.
   W: I won't be able to put up with it much longer without going crazy.
   N: What does the woman mean?

3. W: I think you need a new jacket for your suit.
   M: I'd like to get rid of the whole suit.
   N: What does the man mean?

4. M: Can you come to the lake with me this weekend?
   W: Let me see if I can get out of helping my brother paint his house.
   N: What does the woman want to do?

5. W: I didn't see Rachel in class today.
   M: Didn't you hear? Her father passed away, and she had to go home.
   N: What does the man mean?

6. M: Do you feel like going to the concert this evening?
   W: The movies at the museum are free. We should take advantage of them.
   N: What does the woman suggest?

7. M: I thought you liked owning a wooden boat.
   W: I used to, but now I'm fed up with all the work it requires.
   N: What does the woman mean?

8. W: It was a such pleasure to meet the Martinez children.
   M: Yes, their parents have brought them up very well.
   N: What does the man mean?

9. W: Eric, are you still here? You've been drinking coffee for three hours!
   M: I'm still waiting for my girlfriend to show up.
   N: What does the man mean?

10. M: Shunji is so serious. He never laughs at my jokes.
    W: Maybe he thinks you're picking on him.
    N: What does the woman mean?

Exercise 1.2.D

1. M: Mr. Tung has offered me a job in Hong Kong.
   W: If I were you, I'd jump at the opportunity.
   N: What does the woman think the man should do?

2. W: You sure seem to spend a lot of time on your boat.
   M: I take after my grandfather. He was a captain in the navy.
   N: What does the man mean?

3. M: Sorry, but I haven't seen Stefan for several months. Why do you ask?
   W: I have a letter from his sister. Maybe I can find out where he moved.
   N: What does the woman say about Stefan?

4. W: I guess I'd better make an appointment with a dentist.
   M: You shouldn't put it off any longer.
   N: What does the man mean?

5. M: Can you stop and get us a pizza for dinner?
   W: Why? Did we run out of food at home?
   N: What does the woman want to know?

6. M: Warren offered to sell me all his old term papers.
   W: Well, if I were you, I'd steer clear of Warren.
   N: What does the woman suggest?

7. M: I told my parents I'd fly to Boston to visit them at Christmas.
   W: Oh, I'm sure they're looking forward to that.
   N: What does the woman mean?

8. W: I think Masami has been feeling homesick.
   M: Maybe we should take her out to cheer her up.
   N: What does the man mean?

9. W: Did you notice how Patrick is always correcting what Nina says?
   M: Yes. I wish he would cut it out.
   N: What does the man think Patrick should do?

10. W: Where have you been all afternoon?
    M: I've been checking out motorcycles with Greg.
    N: What does the man mean?

Exercise 1.2.E

1. W: We need a bigger apartment just to store all of our books and tapes!
   M: That's out of the question!
   N: What does the man mean?

2. W: Mr. Shimada is the best teacher at this school. Everyone should be required to take his psychology class.
   M: That goes without saying.
   N: What does the man mean?

3. W: Reema has been accepted into the School of International Studies.
   M: No kidding!
   N: What does the man mean?

4. M: Won't you change your mind and come to the boxing match with us on Saturday?
   W: Not on your life!
   N: What does the woman mean?

5. M: Maria, I want you to have all my laundry ready by the time I get home.
   W: You must be kidding!
   N: What does the woman mean?

QUIZ 1 (p. 49)

Directions: In this quiz you will hear short conversations between two people. After each conversation, you will hear a question about the conversation. The conversations and questions will not be repeated. After you hear a question, read the four possible answers and choose the best answer.

Here is an example.

On the recording, you hear:

(Woman) Did Sarah have a good time on her trip to Mexico?
(Man) Oh, I heard that fell through.
(Narrator) What does the man mean?

In your book, you read:

(A) Sarah fell on her trip to Mexico.
(B) Sarah enjoyed her trip to Mexico.
(C) Sarah had a terrible trip to Mexico.
(D) Sarah did not go to Mexico.

You learn from the conversation that Sarah's trip to Mexico fell through. *Fell through* is an idiom that means failed to happen. The best answer to the question, "What does the man mean?" is (D), "Sarah did not go to Mexico." Therefore, the correct choice is (D).

1. W: This soup is delicious. Did you make it differently this time?
   M: Actually, I ran out of salt, so I used miso.
   N: What does the man mean?

2. W: I found Dr. Salcedo's lecture extremely inspiring.
   M: Oh, really? I didn't comprehend a single word.
   N: What does the man mean?

3. M: I hate to keep you waiting. Why don't you go on ahead?
   W: Take your time. It's still early.
   N: What does the woman mean?

4. W: Look at what your grandmother sent us for our anniversary.
   M: She is so kind. I'm sure she made that herself.
   N: What does the man say about his grandmother?

5. W: Why did you move out of your apartment? I thought you liked being by the park.
   M: I guess I never got along with my roommate.
   N: What does the man mean?

6. W: Would you mind watching my purse for five minutes?
   M: I'd be happy to.
   N: What does the man agree to do?

7. W: Dennis is depressed about not getting the scholarship.
   M: I think he's being too hard on himself.
   N: What does the man say about Dennis?

8. W: Mario said he's got an invitation from the Algerian ambassador.
   M: Oh, really? Well, Mario is pulling your leg.
   N: What does the man say about Mario?

9. M: Well, I guess this is good–bye until September.
W: I'll miss you, Taro. Please keep in touch over the summer.
N: What does the woman mean?

10. M: Allen is fun to hang out with, don't you think?
W: He's a little too coarse for me.
N: What does the woman think of Allen?

11. M: How do you like Dr. Lim's organic chemistry class?
W: I like Dr. Lim, but most of his lectures are over my head.
N: What does the woman mean?

12. W: Isn't it nice how Scott helps Carla take care of her mother?
M: I'll say!
N: What does the man mean?

13. M: If you're tired, I can take you home.
W: Thank you. I feel OK, but I'm still getting over the flu.
N: What does the woman mean?

14. M: Oh, I really don't want to take any more calculus classes.
W: But two years of calculus are mandatory in your program.
N: What does the woman mean?

15. M: Good news! My brother decided to move out at the end of this month.
W: I don't see how you put up with him for this long.
N: What does the woman imply?

1.3 LISTENING FOR CONDITIONALS, CAUSATIVES, AND MODALS (p. 51)

Focus

M: I wonder if Caleb is still annoyed because I dented his car.
W: If he were, he would let you know.
N: What does the woman say about Caleb?

W: How did you like your first day of class?
M: It was interesting. The instructor had us introduce someone we didn't already know.
N: What does the man say about his class?

Exercise 1.3.A

1. W: Hi, Nick! Do you know where I can get a good cup of coffee?
M: If you'll walk with me, I can show you my favorite coffee shop.
N: What does the man want the woman to do?

2. M: So, you have Dr. Levensky for sociology? She sure makes you work, doesn't she?
W: Yes, she does, but I love her style. She lets us design our own assignments.
N: What does the woman say about Dr. Levensky?

3. M: I'm afraid to see my phone bill. My brother and I talked for two hours last night.
W: I wish my brother would call me more often.
N: What does the woman say about her brother?

4. W: Why are you still typing? I thought you'd finished your paper.
M: I just remembered Dr. Grant is having us present our papers in class, and I wanted to make my introduction better.
N: What does the man mean?

5. W: How would you like to go to a potluck at Phil's house on Saturday?
M: I'd rather stay home and work on my thesis.
N: What does the man mean?

6. W: Will you still be able to help me move this weekend?
M: If I didn't have to work, I would. Why don't you ask Troy?
N: What does the man mean?

Exercise 1.3.B

1. M: Maybe you could ask Dr. Chung to let you interview him.
W: I'd rather not bother Dr. Chung. I know how busy he is.
N: What does the woman mean?

2. W: Where were you last weekend? We missed seeing you at the beach.
M: I had to go to a funeral. Ken's mother passed away.
W: Oh, if only I'd known. I would have gone with you.
N: What does the woman mean?

3. M: I'm glad you could make it to the party after all.
W: I was lucky. My brother let me have his motorcycle for the weekend.
N: What does the woman mean?

4. W: How did you do on your term paper?
M: I wish my professor would hand the papers back.
N: What does the man mean?

5. M: I think I reached a dead end on my paper. I just can't seem to be able to finish it.
W: Then why don't you take a break?
M: I can't. I have to keep working.
W: If you took a walk with me, maybe that would refresh your mind.
N: What does the woman mean?

6. M: Would you please hand me the ratchet wrench?
W: I would if I knew what it was.
N: What does the woman mean?

1.4 LISTENING FOR NEGATIVE EXPRESSIONS (p. 56)

Focus

W: Did you hear that Doug and Claudia got married?
M: Nothing could surprise me more!
N: What does the man mean?

Exercise 1.4.A

1. W: Where are you taking me?
M: To the mall. There's nowhere like a parking lot to practice driving.
N: What does the man mean?

2. M: I haven't seen Ernie in a long time, have you?
   W: Didn't you hear? He had no choice but to drop out because he missed so much time from his classes.
   N: What does the woman say about Ernie?

3. M: Are we ready to order the food for the picnic?
   W: Not everyone has responded to the invitation yet.
   N: What does the woman mean?

4. W: I ran into Brad and Satoru at the dance club on Saturday.
   M: You're kidding! Neither Brad nor Satoru can dance!
   N: What does the man say about Brad and Satoru?

5. M: I wonder what Martin and all the others are up to these days.
   W: Rarely do I hear from Martin anymore.
   N: What does the woman mean?

6. W: I'm afraid I won't get a good score on the TOEFL.
   M: Don't worry. It's not impossible to do well the first time.
   N: What does the man mean?

7. W: Professor Snow seemed a little unsteady at the lectern this morning.
   M: I hardly noticed.
   N: What does the man mean?

8. M: Raul told me he's been accepted into the graduate program at Stanford.
   W: I know. I've never seen him so excited.
   N: What does the woman say about Raul?

9. M: I don't like having an eight o'clock lecture class.
   W: Neither do I.
   N: What does the woman mean?

10. W: We'll probably never find a hotel room.
    M: It's not unheard of to get a room without a reservation.
    N: What does the man mean?

1.5 Listening for Time, Quantity, and Comparisons (p. 61)

Focus

W: Congratulations on getting the job!
M: Thanks, Lena.
W: When does it start?
M: The week after next. I'm really looking forward to it.
N: What do you know about the man?

Exercise 1.5.A

1. M: Do you need a ride to campus this evening? I have a class at seven.
   W: If you can pick me up around six. I have to stop at the library before my class.
   N: What does the woman mean?

2. M: How long has Mr. Turner been teaching high school?
   W: He got that job at least two years before he moved in next door.
   N: What do you know about Mr. Turner?

3. M: Say, don't we have the same backpack?
   W: They look similar, but I think yours is a little wider.
   N: What do you know about the woman's backpack?

4. W: I didn't know you worked with my cousin Maria. How long have you known her?
   M: As long as I've known you.
   N: What does the man mean?

5. W: Noah won't be able to graduate this year after all.
   M: Oh, really? That's too bad. He has only a few credits left to go!
   N: What does the man say about Noah?

6. W: Bill and Ayumi just celebrated their fifth anniversary.
   M: Really? I thought they'd been married longer than that.
   N: What had the man believed about Bill and Ayumi?

7. M: How many people is Oskar inviting to his graduation party?
   W: Oh, you know Oskar. The more, the merrier!
   N: What does the woman say about Oskar?

8. W: I can't believe the cost of tuition for next year!
   M: It's almost doubled since I was a freshman.
   N: What does the man mean?

1.6 Understanding Intonation (p. 66)

Focus

M: Mr. Tumpek wants to see you in his office. I think he's giving you the Acme project.
W: That's just what I wanted to hear...
N: What does the woman mean?

W: I'm sorry, but we don't accept this credit card here.
M: Gee, thanks... That helps me a lot.
N: What does the man mean?

Exercise 1.6.A

1. M: My sister says we should expect the whole family at the cabin this weekend.
   W: Oh, so they *will* be able to come!
   N: What had the woman assumed?

2. W: You should have come to the dance recital with me. Bruce was fabulous as the prince!
   M: Bruce is a ballet dancer?
   N: What does the man mean?

3. W: Are you interested in going to the speedway on Saturday? My boss can get us some tickets.
   M: The speedway! What a way to spend a Saturday!
   N: What does the man mean?

4. W: Do you still need a ride to San Francisco?
   M: Then your car *is* running again?
   N: What had the man assumed?

5. M: Your sister called. She wants you to babysit your nephews this weekend.
   W: Oh, great... And I have a term paper to write.
   N: What does the woman mean?

6. M: I won't be able to help you install your computer this weekend after all. Steve and I are going to the football game.
   W: Thanks a lot! You're a big help!
   N: What does the woman mean?

7. M: I'm celebrating with Levar tonight. He won his first big case!
   W: Levar is a lawyer?
   N: What had the woman assumed about Levar?

8. W: I think I'll order the steak and onions.
   M: Then you *do* eat meat?
   N: What does the man mean?

QUIZ 2 (p. 70)

Directions: In this quiz you will hear short conversations between two people. After each conversation, you will hear a question about the conversation. The conversations and questions will not be repeated. After you hear a question, read the four possible answers and choose the best answer.

Here is an example.

On the recording, you hear:

(Man) Why are you working so late? It's almost seven o'clock.
(Woman) My boss is making me give a presentation tomorrow.
(Narrator) What does the woman mean?

In your book, you read:

(A) She must prepare her presentation.
(B) She must help her boss give a presentation.
(C) Her boss is making a presentation tomorrow.
(D) She will miss the presentation tomorrow.

The woman says her boss is *making* her give a presentation, which means that *she*, not her boss, will be giving the presentation. The best answer to the question, "What does the woman mean?" is (A), "She must prepare her presentation." Therefore, the correct choice is (A).

1. M: Did you find out if you got into graduate school?
   W: If only they would let me know. I can't stand the suspense.
   N: What does the woman mean?

2. M: My mother was so happy I remembered her birthday. We talked for over an hour.
   W: Oh, so you *did* remember!
   N: What had the woman assumed?

3. W: I didn't realize your roommate had moved out. When did that happen?
   M: The week before last, at the end of the month.
   N: What do you know about the man's roommate?

4. M: Hi, Carol! Can you join me for coffee after class?
   W: I would if I didn't have to see my adviser at three o'clock.
   N: What does the woman mean?

5. W: I'm glad to see you! I didn't know if you would be able to make it.
   M: My boss let us off early for the weekend.
   N: What does the man mean?

6. W: Wasn't the president's speech better than it was last year?
   M: Last year his speech was much briefer and to the point. I could barely stay awake through it this time.
   N: What does the man say about the president's speech?

7. W: I thought I might see you on the rafting trip.
   M: Not everyone likes putting his life in danger.
   N: What does the man imply?

8. W: I'm sorry, but I have too much homework. I can't go to the game with you.
   M: You're a lot of fun!
   N: What does the man mean?

9. M: I heard there was a good party at Eli's. I was sorry to miss it.
   W: Oh, but there was hardly enough room in Eli's apartment for all those people.
   N: What does the woman mean?

10. W: Why do you look so puzzled?
    M: I can't figure out how to put this chair together.
    W: Didn't it come with directions?
    M: Yes. But nowhere does it say what to do with this bolt.
    N: What does the man mean?

11. W: I think this T–shirt will fit Astrid, don't you?
    M: Well, it fits you just fine, but Astrid is much taller.
    N: What does the man mean?

12. M: My new car arrives at the dealership next week.
    W: Oh, then you *did* decide to get the convertible?
    N: What does the woman mean?

13. M: Are you going to the conference in Atlanta?
    W: Oh! I'm glad you reminded me. I'll have my secretary make the arrangements.
    N: What does the woman mean?

14. W: I got two letters and eight e–mails from old friends this week.
    M: Oh, really? I seldom hear from anyone. But I never write either.
    N: What does the man mean?

15. W: Do you think Professor Tran liked my speech?
    M: Well, if she didn't, she would let you know.
    N: What does the man mean?

1.7 LISTENING FOR IMPLICATIONS BY THE SPEAKERS (p. 72)

Focus

M: Do you mind if I open this window?
W: I just closed it. I thought it felt drafty in here.
N: What does the woman imply?

Exercise 1.7.A

1. M: Nathalie is taking two classes this summer.
   W: Can she do that and work full–time?
   N: What does the woman imply about Nathalie?

2. M: I still haven't received my grade on the final exam. Maybe I should call the department secretary.
   W: Don't worry so much. It took me at least two weeks to get my grade.
   N: What does the woman think the man should do?

3. W: I really hate this class. It's so boring!
   M: Well, you'd better get used to it. It's required for graduation.
   N: What does the man suggest?

4. M: Maybe we should take Broadway this morning. The radio announcer said traffic is heavy on the expressway.
   W: Well, if she said to take Broadway, let's take the expressway!
   N: What does the woman imply about the radio announcer?

5. M: I can't decide which of our research assistants to hire full–time for the summer.
   W: Wasn't Kimi a big help to us on that quarterly report?
   N: What does the woman imply?

6. W: There are two really good movies on TV tonight. One is a historical drama and the other is a thriller.
   M: I've never liked movies about history. I can never follow what's going on.
   N: What does the man imply?

7. M: My roommate and I have lived together for six months, and I still can't get used to his habits. He does his laundry in the middle of the night.
   W: I know someone who needs a housemate. You know Yong, don't you?
   M: Yong? Your lab partner from biology last year?
   W: Yes. He's really nice. He's looking for someone to share his house.
   N: What does the woman think the man should do?

8. W: Do you mind if I bring my dog to your party?
   M: Wouldn't he be bothered by all the noise?
   N: What does the man imply?

9. M: I don't know how Brian manages to take five classes and work at two jobs.
   W: I heard he's not doing very well in his courses. And he still wants to go to medical school.
   M: He needs to work less and focus more on his studies.
   N: What does the man imply about Brian?

10. W: My car has been making funny noises whenever I go uphill.
    M: Really? My best friend is a mechanic.
    N: What does the man imply?

Exercise 1.7.B

1. W: Oh, I don't need that book yet.
   M: But your report is due next week!
   N: What does the man imply the woman should do?

2. W: Todd, meet my brother, Daniel.
   M: Nice to meet you, Daniel. Maria tells me you're a rock climber, too. I heard you also climbed Devil's Tower last year.
   N: What does the man imply?

3. M: I want another hot dog. Would you like me to get you one, too?
   W: I'm a little queasy after the last one.
   N: What does the woman imply?

4. M: Jerry made the most points in the basketball game last night.
   W: Shouldn't Jerry give as much attention to his studies?
   N: What does the woman imply about Jerry?

5. W: Chris just bought a bird, and she paid five hundred dollars for it!
   M: And I'll bet she still hasn't had her brakes fixed.
   N: What does the man imply about Chris?

6. M: I can't seem to find my sunglasses anywhere.
   W: Have you looked in the car?
   N: What does the woman imply?

7. W: How did your geology exam go?
   M: I think I'll be repeating this course next year.
   N: What does the man imply?

8. M: Haven't you been driving this wreck for too long? Let's go look at cars.
   W: I have too many other bills at the moment.
   N: What does the woman imply?

9. W: Your mother called again.
   M: Oh, really? She also sent two letters in the past week.
   W: Maybe she'd like to hear from you more often.
   N: What does the woman imply?

10. W: I'm going to the ocean for five days with Helen and her cousin.
    M: Didn't you say you had a term paper due next week?
    N: What does the man imply?

1.8 MAKING INFERENCES ABOUT PEOPLE (p. 77)

Focus

M: Kelly, would you help me with these blood samples?
W: Sure, but first I need to rush these charts up to Dr. O'Brien on the fifth floor.
N: What can be inferred about Kelly?

W: I've been having trouble with my dishwasher. Water is leaking out on the floor.
M: My friend's did that once. I think I know how to solve the problem.
N: What will the man probably do?

Exercise 1.8.A

1. W: Do you want to join me and Randy for pizza? We're meeting in fifteen minutes.
   M: I have to be at work in a half–hour.
   N: What will the man probably do?

2. W: Yvonne was wonderful, wasn't she? I've never seen such grace and balance.
   M: I never realized just how strong she must be.
   W: Just like everyone in her family. They've been performing all of their lives.
   N: What can be inferred about Yvonne?

3. W: I'm sorry, sir, but all of the motels in town are filled because of the convention. I suggest you try looking in Fairville.
   M: How far is Fairville?
   W: Thirteen miles down the highway.
   N: What will the man probably do?

4. M: Good morning, Mrs. Williams. This is Steve from Central Carpet Cleaning Service. I'd like to tell you about our special for this month.
   W: No, thank you. I'm not interested.
   N: What is the man's job?

5. M: Would you like to go to a barbecue at my parents' beach house this weekend?
   W: Oh, if only I could! But two people at the restaurant are on vacation, and everyone is expected to work an extra shift.
   N: What will the woman probably do this weekend?

6. W: How is your little brother doing?
   M: He's busier than ever. He scored more points than anyone this season, and his team is naming him player of the year.
   W: Oh, you must be so proud of him!
   N: What can be inferred about the man's brother?

7. M: What classes are you taking next semester?
   W: Management, marketing, and business economics.
   M: It sounds like you'll be busy.
   N: What can be inferred about the woman?

8. W: I saw Antoine today and he sure seemed down.
   M: Maybe it's because he has to take classes this summer and won't get back home to see his friends.
   N: What can be inferred about Antoine?

9. M: Did you get your plane tickets yet?
   W: I decided to go the slow way instead. I just want to relax, read my book, and gaze at the prairies.
   N: What is the woman planning to do?

10. M: We're going to have trouble meeting our project deadline.
    W: Can you hire more help?
    M: My boss doesn't think that's a good solution. I'd better postpone my vacation.
    N: What will the man probably do?

Exercise 1.8.B

1. M: Say, Becky, could I borrow your notes from biology?
   W: Weren't you there either?
   M: No, I had to pick up my roommate at the airport.
   W: Oh. Maybe Susan took notes.
   N: What can be inferred from the conversation?

2. M: I can't believe how much work Professor Garcia assigns! I don't see how I can possibly get it all done.
   W: Oh, but he's great, isn't he? You'll learn so much in his class!
   N: What can be inferred about Professor Garcia?

3. M: I'm getting sick of this cafeteria food. It's always the same.
   W: That's why I eat at the deli. The selection there is better.
   M: What deli?
   W: Didn't you know there was a deli upstairs from the bookstore?
   N: What will the man probably do?

4. M: Gloria and Judy are so much alike, aren't they?
   W: They're both the image of their father.
   N: What can be inferred about Gloria and Judy?

5. W: Do you think Shelly would like this scarf?
   M: I think Shelly would look better in this blue one.
   W: Hmm. The blue one is more expensive, but she is my best friend and tomorrow is her birthday.
   N: What will the woman probably do?

6. W: Did Ahmad get the job in the physics lab?
   M: He hasn't heard. They must be checking his references.
   N: What can be inferred about Ahmad?

7. M: Eighteen credits may be too much for me this term. I'm worried about chemistry.
   W: That class is a lot of work.
   M: I just don't have enough time to study, and I got a "D" on the first test.
   W: Oh. Well, you know it's not too late to drop classes. The deadline is next week.
   N: What will the man probably do?

8. W: I ran into Joe and Susan in front of the Greek market today.
   M: Are they back from their honeymoon already?
   N: What can be inferred about Joe and Susan?

9. M: Where is a good place to buy lunch around here?
   W: Let's see. I know of two sushi bars that are both very good. And there's an excellent pizza parlor nearby.
   M: Oh, I've had enough pizza already this week.
   N: What will the man probably do?

10. M: Do you know where I can buy postcards?
    W: I think the drugstore next door sells them.
    N: What will the man probably do?

1.9 MAKING INFERENCES ABOUT CONTEXT (p. 81)

Focus

W: I'd like to get this prescription refilled, please.
M: I'm sorry, but according to the label, this prescription can't be refilled.
N: Where does this conversation take place?

M: Hey now, Dash! Where do you think you're going?
W: Oh, he's splashing water all over the floor! Try to hold him while I rinse him off.
N: What are the speakers doing?

Exercise 1.9.A

1. W: Would you mind getting me some more napkins? I just spilled my drink.
   M: No problem. I'll be right back.
   N: Where does this conversation probably take place?

2. W: Could you identify the problem?
   M: Well, your brakes were almost out of fluid and all of your shocks needed replacing. You're lucky to be alive!
   N: What are the speakers discussing?

3. M: Excuse me. Where can I find the biographies?
   W: They would be in nonfiction. Right over there, to the left of the window.
   N: In what kind of store does this conversation take place?

4. M: Well, that was just awful! I almost walked out of the theater.
   W: It was pretty disappointing, wasn't it? I've never seen such overacting!
   N: What are the speakers discussing?

5. W: Why are you reviewing chapter five? I thought Professor Sanders said chapter six.
   M: But all of the important formulas are in chapter five. There might be a question about one of them.
   N: What are the speakers doing?

6. M: Ma'am, you'll have to put out your cigarette before you can use that gas pump.
   W: Oh, all right.
   N: Where does this conversation take place?

7. W: The needles of both the longleaf and the loblolly are in clusters of three. How can we tell them apart?
   M: Dr. Chow said the longleaf has harder wood.
   N: What are the speakers discussing?

8. W: Mr. Richards, since we didn't take x–rays last time, we'll need to do a full set today before we clean your teeth.
   M: Oh, all right. But I am in a bit of a hurry.
   N: Where does this conversation take place?

QUIZ 3 (p. 84)

Directions: In this quiz you will hear short conversations between two people. After each conversation, you will hear a question about the conversation. The conversations and questions will not be repeated. After you hear a question, read the four possible answers and choose the best answer.

Here is an example.

On the recording, you hear:

(Woman) Did I miss anything important at the department meeting yesterday?
(Man) Didn't you go either? I was hoping you could fill me in.
(Narrator) What can be inferred from the conversation?

In your book, you read:

(A) The man has an important form he must fill out.
(B) The man will inform the woman about the meeting.
(C) Neither speaker attended the meeting.
(D) An important announcement was made at the meeting.

The woman implies that she missed the meeting, and the man responds, "Didn't you go either?" which means he also did not go to the meeting. The best answer to the question, "What can be inferred from the conversation?" is (C), "Neither speaker attended the meeting." Therefore, the correct choice is (C).

1. W: I've never seen the traffic so heavy. It seems to be backed up quite a ways.
   M: It gets worse on the freeway every month.
   W: Something must have happened on the freeway bridge.
   M: It's usually moving a little faster on the Clairmont bridge.
   N: What does the man imply?

2. M: I'd like a bouquet of white roses.
   W: Oh, I'm sorry, but we have only red roses today. But we do have some beautiful arrangements of white tulips and carnations.
   N: Where does this conversation probably take place?

3. M: Excuse me, do you know if there is a bus that goes to Sherwood Park?
   W: There are maps of the bus routes at the transfer station across the street.
   N: What does the woman imply the man should do?

4. W: How is your new lab assistant doing?
   M: Well, it may still be too early to tell. He does try hard, though.
   N: What can be inferred about the man's lab assistant?

5. M: Do you mind if I smoke?
   W: It's not allowed here, but there's a smoking lounge in the basement.
   N: What does the woman imply?

6. M: I've never been here before. Do you have any idea what to order?
   W: No, but the seafood special looks good.
   N: What are the speakers discussing?

7. M: Abdul's sisters are coming to visit. Can they stay with you for a few days? His brothers are staying with me.
   W: Sure. But didn't his sisters visit just last month?
   M: That was his two elder sisters. This time it's three younger sisters.
   W: Oh my!
   N: What can be inferred about Abdul?

8. M: I'm Scott Blanchard, here to pick up Smokey.
   W: Oh, yes. The doctor said Smokey came through the surgery just fine, but I'm afraid he won't be chasing squirrels for a while.
   N: What is the woman's job?

9. W: I was shocked to learn that Arnold took up sailing. He can't swim!
   M: It seems he's less afraid of the water than he should be.
   N: What does the man imply?

10. M: How long is the bibliography on your sociology paper?
    W: What? Oh, no!
    M: Remember? Dr. Patel wants us to write a short review of each of our sources and then make copies for everyone.
    W: There goes my weekend.
    N: What does the woman imply?

11. M: Where is the best place to buy bagels?
    W: Bagels? Otto's Bakery is best, but I think it's closed today. Why not try Ralph's Thriftway on Lake Drive?
    N: What will the man probably do?

12. M: I thought you were going to ask Tracy for a ride to work today.
    W: She must have already left when I called her at seven.
    N: What can be inferred from the conversation?

13. M: When should I add the milk?
    W: After the butter and flour are thoroughly combined. Make sure there are no lumps.
    N: What are the speakers doing?

14. W: My parents are visiting this weekend, and I want to take them somewhere nice.
    M: Have you tried the new Cajun restaurant in Melville?
    N: What does the man suggest?

15. W: I need to take algebra next quarter. Both Mr. Park and Mr. Nolan are teaching it.
    M: I had Mr. Nolan for algebra, but his explanations were never very clear. I think Imelda had Mr. Park.
    W: Oh, I'm having lunch with Imelda today.
    N: What will the woman probably do?

QUIZ 4 (p. 86)

Directions: In this quiz you will hear short conversations between two people. After each conversation, you will hear a question about the conversation. The conversations and questions will not be repeated. After you hear a question, read the four possible answers and choose the best answer.

Here is an example.

On the recording, you hear:

(Woman) It's nice to have Peter working with us now.
(Man) Yes. His talent is essential to the success of our project.
(Narrator) What does the man mean?

In your book, you read:

(A) Peter will manage the project.
(B) The project needs Peter's abilities.
(C) The central problem is finding successful people.
(D) Peter tolerates working with them.

You hear the man use the key words *talent* and *essential*. A synonym for *talent* is *ability*, and something that is *essential* is *needed*. The best answer to the question, "What does the man mean?" is (B), "The project needs Peter's abilities." Therefore, the correct choice is (B).

1. M: Do I need a withdrawal slip to cash this check?
   W: No. Just sign your name and write your account number on the back of the check.
   N: What is the woman's job?

2. W: I thought you and Brent were good friends.
   M: I used to think so, too, but now I can see right through him.
   N: What does the man mean?

3. M: I need to find a book on unemployment.
   W: The library catalog is right over there. Just follow the directions on the screen. If you have any trouble, I'll be happy to help you.
   N: What does the woman imply the man should do?

4. M: If you're too busy, why don't you tell Sue you can't help her move this weekend?
   W: I have no choice. She's done so much for me.
   N: What does the woman mean?

5. W: Did you hear that awful music Kaspar was playing at his party?
   M: Oh, Kaspar thinks he knows a lot about music.
   N: What can be inferred from the conversation?

6. W: Where are you headed?
   M: To the barber shop.
   N: What can be inferred from the conversation?

7. W: Do you think Jason is angry about what I said?
   M: If he were, he'd let us know.
   N: What does the man say about Jason?

8. M: You seem agitated. Is something bothering you?
   W: I thought Lucy was my friend, but today I realized she is really two–faced.
   N: What does the woman imply about Lucy?

9. M: How was dinner with your parents and your new roommate?
   W: My father thinks my roommate is common, but she is really very sweet.
   N: What does the woman mean?

10. W: Mr. Bond just got in his car carrying a lot of leaves and plants.
    M: He's probably going to use them in his class.
    N: What can be inferred about Mr. Bond?

11. M: Henry is the best buddy a guy could ask for.
    W: You could say that again!
    N: What does the woman mean?

12. W: When are you going to return my cassette?
    M: Oh, I was hoping you'd forgotten about that.
    N: What does the man imply?

13. M: I'm having a hard time deciding who should work with me on the project.
    W: Don't you think Julie would be the best researcher?
    N: What does the woman suggest?

14. M: Does Tina still live next door to you?
    W: I haven't seen Tina at all this year.
    N: What does the woman imply?

15. M: It's snowing so hard that I can't see my neighbor's house.
    W: I wouldn't want to drive right now.
    M: Don't worry. I'll be careful.
    N: What does the woman imply?

16. M: Is your offer to take me to lunch on Friday still good?
    W: Oh! Then you *will* be in town!
    N: What had the woman assumed?

17. W: When are you going to do something about your brakes?
    M: I guess I can't put it off any longer.
    N: What does the man mean?

18. M: Can you go to Chicago with us on Friday?
    W: I think I've got a compulsory workshop on Friday.
    N: What does the woman mean?

19. W: Hi, Ed! Why so glum?
    M: My coach wants me to lose more weight before the next game.
    N: What does the man mean?

20. M: Could you please tell me what room David Phillips is in?
    W: Yes. Mr. Phillips is in intensive care on the third floor. I advise you to stop at the nurse's station next to the elevator before going in.
    N: Where does this conversation take place?

21. M: Do you mind if I turn up the volume on the radio?
    W: It's already quite loud.
    N: What does the woman imply?

22. W: I'm starving, and there is nothing in the kitchen.
    M: Why don't we try that new place on the corner?
    N: What do both speakers want to do?

23. M: It looks like your roof needs fixing.
    W: I know, but with all my other bills, it's just out of the question.
    N: What does the woman mean?

24. M: Did you have lunch with Gina today?
    W: She had already eaten by the time I arrived.
    N: What can be inferred from the conversation?

25. M: If you've started packing, you may as well stop.
    W: Why? Has the ski trip been called off?
    N: What does the woman want to know?

26. M: Would you take in my mail while I'm on vacation next week?
    W: If you call and remind me right before you leave.
    N: What does the woman imply?

27. M: In case you get hungry, I packed some snacks.
    W: How thoughtful of you.
    N: What does the woman mean?

28. W: My nephews are the nicest little boys I know.
    M: They must take after their aunt.
    N: What does the man mean?

29. W: Why was there no trash pick–up today?
    M: I guess the city workers are still on strike.
    N: What does the man mean?

30. M: I'm a little worried about Frank.
    W: I know. Did you notice that he hardly ate his cake?
    N: What does the woman mean?

1.10 IDENTIFYING THE TOPIC AND MAIN IDEAS (p. 98)

Focus

Listen to a conversation between a student and his tutor.

M: I'm really confused when the diagrams on the test don't look right. A problem might say the base of a triangle is three and the height is, say eight, but the picture doesn't look right.
W: Do you mean the diagram isn't drawn to scale?
M: Right. And sometimes the caption even says "Not drawn to scale." Why do they do that?
W: To confuse you. But here's a tip that always works for me. If a drawing is not done to scale, then the first thing you should do is make a quick sketch that is to scale. The sketch doesn't have to be elaborate. When you make your own drawing, sometimes the solution is obvious right away.

What is the subject of the conversation?

Exercise 1.10.A

Question 1. Listen to a conversation between two students.

W: Hi, Nestor! How's it going?
M: Well, I don't know. I just got my sociology paper back, and I don't understand my professor. She didn't give it a grade.
W: Did she write any comments on the paper?
M: She said I didn't follow the instructions of the assignment, so she didn't know how to grade it. She wanted us to write about the family in society, and I wrote about my family.
W: You'd better go talk to her. I'm sure she'll allow you to rewrite the paper.
M: I sure hope so because I need a grade for this class.

What is the man's problem?

Question 2. Listen to a conversation in a college cafeteria.

M: Excuse me, I hate to bother you, but there's something wrong with this soup.
W: What's wrong with it?
M: Well, it's cold for one thing. And there are big lumps of flour in it.
W: Oh. Well, I'd better tell the cooks.
M: Can I have a salad instead?
W: Of course, go ahead and help yourself. You won't need to come through the line again.
M: Thank you.

What is the purpose of the conversation?

Question 3. Listen to part of a lecture given by an anthropology instructor.

Most of the winter festivals centered around the agricultural cycle, except for midwinter, which concluded the fall hunting expedition. From the time the maple sap started to flow in the early spring, to the fall harvest, the people had ceremonies to express gratitude for the gifts of the Creator. Such festivals conveyed a feeling of oneness with nature.

For instance, when the corn and other garden crops had ripened, the people called a meeting to give thanks for the corn through a series of dances. People and corn were considered sisters, and the corn was said to whisper to a person in the fields. This illustrates how the animate and inanimate were united as one, according to the beliefs of the people.

What would be the best title for the lecture?

Question 4. Listen to part of a talk given to members of a college business club.

There are several ways to start a business. You may buy an established enterprise or become a partner or shareholder in one. You can purchase a franchise. Or you may wish to begin completely on your own. If you want to find a partner, check the classified sections of newspapers. You can also place your own ad to find partners.

You will need money to invest. After the initial starting costs are met, you still need enough money to cover costs until the business begins to pay for itself. You should have at least part of that sum. You can borrow money from investors, family members, and lending institutions. If you start a corporation, you can sell stock in the company to raise money.

What is the purpose of the talk?

Question 5. Listen to part of a talk in a sociology class.

A survey of young Americans of different racial and ethnic backgrounds suggests parity among the groups in how they feel about socializing with one another. Almost nine out of ten say they don't mind hanging out with people of different racial or ethnic heritage. But only about half say they feel very comfortable with other groups. And when it comes to romantic involvement, less than a third say they would be extremely likely to get romantically involved with someone of a different race or ethnic group.

What is the talk mainly about?

Question 6. Listen to part of a lecture in an art history class.

The creation of the movement known as "Regionalism" was the first full–scale American art–world hype. Its instigator was a journalist from Kansas turned art dealer in New York. Regionalism's appeal to bedrock American values, to nativism and racism, and to the anxiety of the Depression of the 1930s might not have spread past Kansas City if the journalist's article had not been picked up by *Time* magazine. *Time* praised the restoration of American values through art, while at the same time criticizing modernism as an outlandish foreign import.

This was the only time that *Time* magazine ever created an art movement out of thin air. Suddenly, the front page of American visual culture was taken over by a fraud.

What is the speaker's main point?

1.11 COMPREHENDING DETAILS (p. 101)

Focus

Listen to an instructor speak to a world history class.

I'd like to tell you about an interesting program that will be shown on television next Wednesday. It's on channel 10, from eight until nine o'clock. The show will deal with how geography has impacted history. Topics will include how inventions such as the wheel spread quickly through Europe and Asia, and how the domestication of wild grass helped some societies evolve more rapidly than others. I think it will be an especially interesting follow–up to our discussion of the native North Americans in the seventeenth century.

I highly recommend this program. So, remember to check it out next Wednesday evening on channel 10. Be sure to set your VCR.

Now choose the best answer to each of the following questions.

1. When will the program be on television?
2. What topics will the program cover?

Exercise 1.11.A

Questions 1 through 2. Listen to a conversation between two friends.

M: I'm going to the grocery store now. Is there anything you need me to pick up?
W: Yes. A few ingredients for the stew: a lime, some parsley, and two dozen fresh clams. Oh, and some ice cream for dessert.
M: Does the supermarket have clams?
W: Yes, if you go to Charley's, there's a seafood counter in the back.
M: OK. Will two dozen be enough for everyone?
W: Well, only five people called to say they were coming. I also have a lot of shrimp and whitefish.
M: OK, then. I'll see you soon.

1. What does the woman ask the man to buy?
2. What does the woman suggest the man do?

Questions 3 through 5. Listen to a conversation between two students.

M: Have you decided what to do for your oral report?
W: I think I'll interview the people in the family I'm living with.
M: But I thought we had to do a survey of a lot of people.
W: Ms. Weintraub said we could either survey a large group of people or interview a few people in depth. I want to interview three people of different ages. The grandmother has a lot of opinions. I want to compare her ideas and the ideas of the mother and the fourteen–year–old son.
M: That sounds like it might be interesting. I don't know what to do yet. Any ideas?
W: It should be something that's interesting to you.
M: Yeah, I know. But I have too many interests.
W: I'm sure you'll be able to narrow it down.

3. What are the students discussing?
4. What does the woman want to do?
5. What is the man's problem?

Questions 6 through 8. Listen to a conversation between a student and a professor.

W: Professor Grady, did you want to see me?
M: Yes, please come in, Hildegunn. I have a proposition for you. I have a story that I need translated into English. You know Swedish, don't you?
W: My native language is Norwegian, but I studied Swedish and French in school.
M: Oh, that's good. Would you like to take a look at the story? I have it right here.
W: Of course.
M: As you can see, it's not very long, only three pages. Are you interested? The English department will pay you.
W: I would like to help you, Professor Grady, but I have three tests this week. Would next week be OK?
M: Next week would be just fine. I can count on you then?
W: Yes, of course.

6. What does the professor want the student to do?
7. What is the student's native language?
8. According to the student, when will the work be ready?

Exercise 1.11.B

Questions 1 through 4. Listen to part of a lecture given to students in a nursing program. The professor is talking about osteoarthritis, a disease affecting the joints.

Osteoarthritis is the most common form of arthritis—or inflammation of the joints. It affects virtually all older adults to one degree or another. Most have few symptoms, and the disease is diagnosed only when X–rays of the vertebrae show characteristic bone spurs or when the fingers are knobbed by bony growths.

With osteoarthritis, lumps may form in bone tissue. Cartilage that normally cushions the joint becomes soft and breaks down. Small pieces of bone may become loose and get caught inside the joint, causing pain or forming bony spikes or bone spurs that point out into the joint.

Swelling of the membrane lining the joint is common. Its cause is unknown, but may include chemical, mechanical, or inborn factors. Emotional stress often worsens the condition. The condition usually begins with pain after exercise or use of the joints.

Treatment for osteoarthritis includes rest of the joints that are affected, heat, and anti–swelling drugs. Surgery is sometimes necessary and may reduce pain and greatly improve the working of a joint. Replacing the hip and joining together the parts of the joint are some of the kinds of surgery used in treating serious cases of osteoarthritis.

1. How is osteoarthritis usually diagnosed?
2. What often occurs with osteoarthritis?
3. According to the professor, what factor makes osteoarthritis worse?
4. How is osteoarthritis treated?

Questions 5 through 8. Listen to an instructor speak to a music appreciation class about John Philip Sousa.

A great leap forward in American music came in 1880, when the U. S. Marine Band needed a leader and John Philip Sousa was offered the job. Only twenty–six years old, Sousa brought to the band discipline and new musical standards. Under Sousa, the Marine Band played the music of Rossini, Berlioz, Tchaikowsky, and Wagner, as well as some of his own composed marches. His famous *Washington Post March* was written during this period.

Later, Sousa left to form his own private concert band. Thus, a new era was inaugurated—that of the world famous Sousa Band. It played from coast to coast and made repeated European tours, always to enthusiastic audiences.

Sousa was a democratic composer. The appeal of his marches lay in the fact that they were always composed for an occasion, and Sousa's mind was on the occasion and the presence of the people involved in it. His marches have an upbeat and contagious humanity. His most famous march, *The Stars and Stripes Forever*, was a singing march for which he also wrote the words. Sousa's fans at the time wanted to have it declared the national anthem.

Now let's hear one of my favorite versions of *The Stars and Stripes Forever* and try to discover why Sousa was, and still is, considered "the people's musician."

5. How did John Philip Sousa contribute to American music?
6. What type of music was Sousa famous for?
7. How does the instructor characterize Sousa's music?
8. What does the instructor want the students to do next?

Exercise 1.11.C

Questions 1 through 4. Listen to part of a discussion in a Native American studies class.

M: The men of the northwoods tribes were the hunters. The hunting season began in the fall and continued until midwinter. These expeditions frequently took the hunters away from the village for long periods of time. Moose, deer, beaver, bear, and elk were the animals sought. Large deer drives were common, and small animals were taken with snares or the bow and arrow.
W: Did the women ever go hunting with the men?
M: The women often accompanied their husbands on hunting parties. Their job was to take charge of the camps.
W: Do you mean they just cooked for the men? I thought the Native Americans had more of a system of equality.
M: Overall, men and women shared the labor. On hunting expeditions, women basically supported the men, whose job was to procure the game. On the other hand, women controlled other realms of life. For example, women managed all of the agricultural operations. Also, a woman headed each clan, and these women were respected for their role as keepers of the clan.

1. When did the hunting season take place?
2. What animals were hunted by the northwoods tribes?
3. According to the man, how did women participate in hunting?
4. Which tribal activities were controlled by women?

Questions 5 through 8. Listen to part of a talk in a drawing class. The instructor is discussing perspective.

An understanding of perspective is mandatory for all students and professionals who do representational drawing. This includes a variety of fields, such as illustration, interior design, architecture, industrial design, and fine arts.

The fundamental principle of perspective is that objects appear smaller as their distance from the observer increases. For instance, someone across the street appears smaller than the person next to you, someone down the street appears still smaller, and so on. Buildings in a landscape, the cross–ties of railroad tracks, and the cars of a train are just a few examples of things that we know are approximately equal in size yet which appear to diminish with distance.

A related concept is that any two or more lines that are in reality parallel will, if extended indefinitely, appear to come together or meet at a point. This point is called the *vanishing point* of these lines. When you draw a building, the vanishing point creates a feeling that the building recedes in space and seems to grow smaller. Yet in reality the sides of the building are parallel. If lines are drawn along these sides, they converge at a distant point—the vanishing point.

In views of real life, and therefore in realistic pictures, the eye level—the horizontal line—is rarely visible, and vanishing points virtually never are. Yet you must always work with an awareness of them. I strongly suggest that you sketch them temporarily in every drawing, to assist you in conveying perspective.

5. According to the instructor, what fields require an understanding of perspective?
6. Select the drawing that illustrates the concept of perspective.
7. Identify the part of the drawing that represents the vanishing point.
8. What does the instructor advise the students to do?

Exercise 1.11.D

Questions 1 through 6. Listen to part of a talk in a geology class.

A volcano is a vent in the earth which erupts when hot liquified rock, or magma, moves to the earth's surface, pouring out as lava. The lava may flow out as a liquid, or it may explode from the vent as solid or liquid particles accompanied by superheated gases. Ash and cinders form a cone around the vent.

There are several types of volcanoes. The most fluid magmas erupt quietly and flow from the vent to form gently sloping shield volcanoes. The name *shield volcano* comes from their resemblance to the shields of early Germanic warriors. The lava flows from shield volcanoes are usually only one to ten meters thick but may extend for great distances from the vent. The volcanoes of Hawaii and Iceland are typical volcanoes of this type.

Cinder cone volcanoes are formed when magmas with high gas contents and high viscosity are blown high into the air during an eruption. The magma falls as volcanic bombs which accumulate around the vent and form steep–sided cones.

Calderas, large basin–like depressions, are formed when a violent eruption blows the top off of an existing cone or when the center of a volcano collapses. One famous caldera covers much of Yellowstone National Park. Six hundred thousand years ago there was a huge volcanic explosion which devastated the landscape. At the center there remained only a smoldering caldera, a collapsed crater more than forty miles wide. Yellowstone's famous geysers and hot springs lie within this giant basin.

1. What is the talk mainly about?
2. Identify the types of substances that erupt from volcanoes.
3. Select the diagram that represents a shield volcano.
4. How does the speaker describe the magma that erupts from cinder cone volcanoes?
5. Select the diagram that represents a caldera.
6. Which type of volcano is associated with the geysers in Yellowstone National Park?

QUIZ 5 (p. 107)

Directions: In this quiz you will hear several conversations and talks. Each conversation or talk is followed by several questions. The conversations, talks, and questions will not be repeated.

For most of the questions, you will read four possible answers and choose the best answer. Some questions will have special directions.

Here is an example.

On the recording, you hear:

(Narrator) Listen to part of a talk in a biology class. The instructor is talking about North American mammals.

(Woman) The cougar, or mountain lion, has occasionally been known to injure people, but usually it avoids people unless cornered. There have been a few rare reports when a cougar has slaughtered several deer or a flock of domestic sheep in one night. For many years the cougar was persecuted as a threat to livestock, but now it is fully protected where it is rare and classified as a game animal where it is abundant.

Now listen to a sample question.

(Narrator) What does the instructor say about the cougar?

In your book, you read:

(A) It is becoming more abundant.
(B) It normally does not attack people.
(C) It is a serious threat to domestic animals.
(D) It eats mainly deer and sheep.

The best answer to the question, "What does the instructor say about the cougar?" is (B), "It normally does not attack people." Therefore, the correct choice is (B).

Questions 1 through 2. Listen to a conversation between two students.

M: That was a pretty good history lecture, don't you think?

W: Well, to be honest, I didn't understand what Dr. Marquez meant by "partible inheritance," and it seems like that's an important thing to know.

M: Partible inheritance means that a man's property would be divided equally among all his children. After the man died, that is.

W: Oh. Then what's "primogeniture"?

M: That's when all the property goes to the eldest son. Just think about the word "primogeniture." "Primo" means "one" or "first," right?

W: Right. Oh, I get it! "Primogeniture" is when the first son gets everything.
M: That's right.
W: Now it's starting to make sense.

1. What are the students discussing?
2. What does *primogeniture* mean?

Questions 3 through 5. Listen to a discussion in an astronomy class.

W1: A famous solar astronomer often used to say, "The sun is a star!" delighted that one of these miraculous objects had been placed close to the earth for the benefit of people like himself. When we look at the sun, we have an up–close view of one of the estimated *billion billion* stars that inhabit the universe. But what *is* a star?
M: A ball of burning stuff that twinkles in the sky.
W1: You're absolutely right. But it's even more than that. A star is a super hot, massive ball of gas. Words such as "massive" quickly lose their impact when discussed on a cosmological scale, but in relative terms, a star is certainly massive. If the earth were the size of a marble, for example, what would the sun be the size of?
M: An orange?
W1: A basketball is more like it. And our sun is an average smallish star in the white–yellow color range. Who can tell me what gives a star its color?
W2: Is the color because of the material it's made of?
W1: That's only part of it. The various colors, or magnitudes, of the stars are the result of a combination of interrelated factors, but especially a star's temperature. The temperature is in turn determined by the star's mass and age. Generally speaking, hotter stars range toward blue in color, while cooler stars are reddish, with the whitish–yellowish stars like our sun falling in between the two extremes.

3. What is the discussion mainly about?
4. According to the professor, if the sun were the size of a basketball, what would the earth be the size of?
5. What factors influence the color of a star?

Questions 6 through 10. Listen to part of a talk in a botany class. The instructor is talking about the leaf arrangements of plants.

There are several common arrangements of leaves on wild flowering plants. In the usual arrangement, called "alternate," each leaf is attached at a different level on the stem. For example, look at this poppy. See how there is a leaf on the left side of the stem, and above it a leaf on the right, and above that on the left again, and so on up the stem. In contrast, when two leaves are attached at one level but on opposite sides, as on this bee plant, they are said to be "opposite."

Leaves that appear at ground level, at the base of the stem, are called "basal." If there are many, they form a basal rosette. The amaryllis family is a group of herbs growing from bulbs, with narrow basal leaves and a long, leafless flowering stalk. The basal leaves of the amaryllis are grasslike and sharply pointed, with teeth along the edges.

Several families of wildflowers have leaves of different arrangement types. I'd like you to come up and examine these samples of various sunflowers and daisies. These are all members of the sunflower family, which includes species with mostly alternate and opposite leaf arrangements. I think you'll find the chocolate flower especially beautiful. Its leaves are long and velvety, with scalloped edges in an opposite arrangement. This is one of my favorites.

6. Select the drawing that best represents a plant with an alternate leaf arrangement.
7. Select the drawing that best represents a plant with a basal leaf arrangement.
8. What example does the instructor give of a plant family with basal leaves?
9. What does the instructor want the students to do?
10. How does the instructor describe the chocolate flower?

Questions 11 through 15. An expert in urban studies has been invited to speak to an environmental studies class. Listen to part of the lecture.

One of the greatest benefits that trees can provide for human populations is being realized by extending and improving what today's foresters call the "urban forest." This includes all the trees in city parks, the trees planted along city streets and highways, and the trees in people's yards. The extent of this forest is surprising. About one–third of the surface area of the average city is given to streets and buildings. The rest is covered by trees and grass.

The concept of a tree–lined village green has a long history, but one of North America's first public parks that was planned and created as a unified project was Central Park in New York City. Central Park was designed by landscape architects Olmsted and Vaux in the late nineteenth century. Their inspiration came from the gardens of European estates and the romantic landscape paintings of the period.

Central Park was set in a rectangular site that covered over 800 acres in the middle of Manhattan Island. The site had once been forested, but by then the original forest was long gone. The area had been used as a common pasture and eventually had deteriorated into a kind of urban wasteland, dotted with garbage dumps.

The vision of Olmsted and Vaux transformed this wasteland into a semblance of its original appearance, with rolling hills, grassy meadows, and woody thickets. Workers planted thousands of trees. The result was a man–made oasis in the midst of steel and stone. Central Park has been called "the city's lung," and it remains one of the best examples of what we can do with the open spaces of our cities.

11. What is the lecture mainly about?
12. What is the definition of *urban forest*?
13. What inspired the designers of New York City's Central Park?
14. How had the site of Central Park been used before it was made into a park?
15. What is the speaker's main point about Central Park?

1.12 MATCHING WORDS AND CATEGORIES (p. 109)

Focus

Listen to part of a talk in a botany class.

Most North American trees fall into one of two categories—evergreen or deciduous—depending on the type of leaf they bear. The leaves of evergreens—pines, firs, spruces, and redwoods—tend to be narrow and needlelike, whereas most deciduous trees—oaks, maples, and nut trees—have broad, flat leaves that are either simple or compound.

Now, uncover the box.

Match the four words above the box with the correct category. Put one word in each box.

Exercise 1.12.A

Questions 1 through 2. Listen to a conversation between two students.

M: Pardon me, but can you tell me where I can cash a check?
W: Sure. The cashier's office is in the student union. There's a bank in there, too, but I think you have to have an account.
M: I want to open an account. Oh, and do you know where I can make a photocopy?
W: The best machines are in front of the bookstore, in the lobby.
M: Thank you. Oh, and one more thing. Where can I get a decent cup of coffee?
W: You won't get it in the cafeteria, believe me. I always go to the espresso cart outside the computer lab.
M: Thanks for your help.

1. Where can the man do each of the following things?
2. What does the woman imply about the cafeteria?

Questions 3 through 4. Listen to part of a talk in a biology class. The professor is talking about caves.

The interior of a cave is divided into three zones. The entrance zone may serve as a place of shelter for animals or people. Prehistoric humans used entrance zones of caves as shelters and burial grounds. Therefore, such zones are of interest to archaeologists, as they provide clues to the habitat of early human beings.

The next zone is called the twilight zone. The twilight zone is sheltered from direct sunlight and is home to a large, diverse population of animals such as salamanders, bats, and during severe winters, bears.

The third zone, the dark zone, is the true cave environment. Perpetually dark, it has only slight seasonal changes in temperature, few if any air currents, and a constant relative humidity of nearly 100 percent. In the dark zone live animals that have adapted to the world of darkness, including small shrimp, beetles, spiders, and fish. These animals are usually blind, and some lack eyes altogether. Since no green plants grow in caves, these animals depend largely on food that is washed in by streams or mud.

3. Match each cave inhabitant with the appropriate cave zone.
4. What characterizes the dark zone of a cave?

Questions 5 through 6. Listen to part of a talk in a Native American studies class.

Although the original American Indian cultures were highly diverse, they were similar in many of their traditions. Religious beliefs and rituals permeated every aspect of Indian life. Southwest tribes such as the Hopi and the Apaches had a rich and elaborate year–round sequence of ceremonials including songs, dances, and poetry. The Hopi performed dances to bring rain. The Apaches engaged in special dances and ceremonies to gain the support of the spirits before undertaking raids or going into war. The Plains tribes often sought contact with the spirits by going on a vision quest.

5. What is the talk mainly about?
6. Which Native American group practiced each tradition?

Questions 7 through 8. Listen to a humanities professor talk about a filmmaker.

Today I'd like to talk a little about the early work of an Indian filmmaker, Satyajit Ray, who is still regarded by many film critics as one of the world's great directors. Ray's films are known for their compassion, honesty, and quiet dignity.

His Apu Trilogy, three films about Bengali life, were hailed as a national epic in the 1950s. The first film, *Pather Panchali*, is the story of a Bengali family's noble struggle against poverty and the heartbreaks of life. In the second film, called *Aparajito*, the son of the family, Apu, grows to manhood. And in the third film, *The World of Apu*, he marries, fails at his life's ambitions, and then, after losing his wife, wanders across the country for several years before returning to claim his son.

Satyajit Ray's movies have never been very popular in India itself, but those who appreciate his unobtrusive technique and his compassion for his characters view his films as a poetic record of Indian life.

7. According to the professor, what characterizes the films of Satyajit Ray?
8. Which film in the Apu Trilogy deals with each of the following themes?

1.13 SEQUENCING EVENTS IN A PROCESS (p. 112)

Focus

Listen to a conversation between two university students.

W: Excuse me, could you please tell me the way to the swimming pool?
M: Sure. It's in the recreation center. Just turn right on the next street. Then go straight until you come to the science building. To the left of the science building, you'll see another street with a lot of trees along it. Turn there and go—oh a little ways—past the round arts building. The rec center will be right in front of you. A big building with a green roof. You can't miss it.
W: I'm sorry. Did you say turn left at the next street?
M: No, right. The name of the street is State.
W: Thank you.
M: Have a nice swim!

Now, uncover the page and answer the following question.

How will the woman get to the swimming pool? Put the steps in the correct order.

Exercise 1.13.A

Questions 1 through 2. Listen to part of a talk in an art class. The instructor is talking about drawing with pen and ink.

If you are unsure of drawing directly in pen and ink, start off with a light pencil sketch. This will allow you to make sure that your proportions are correct and that you are happy with the composition.

Take a few minutes to study your subject—this chair and violin. Notice how the straight lines of the chair differ from the curves of the violin. Once you are ready to begin drawing, define the shape of the chair with clean straight lines. Then add contrast by drawing the outline of the violin with gently curved lines. You may have to apply more pressure to the nib when drawing curved lines to allow the ink to flow easily.

When you have drawn the outlines of both objects, add in the finer details, such as the seat of the chair and the violin strings. Suggest the texture of the woven seat by using light and dark strokes of the pen.

1. What does the instructor recommend for students who do not want to begin drawing directly in ink?
2. The instructor explains how to draw the subject. Summarize the process by putting the steps in order.

Questions 3 through 5. Listen to a discussion in a speech class.

W1: For your speaking assignment, you will want to follow a logical series of steps in preparing your speech. The first step, of course, is to realize the importance of the speech to you.

M: But isn't that always the same in this class? After all, you give us an assignment and we want to get a good grade for it.

W1: Yes, that's true, but the grade isn't the only thing that's important.

W2: Yeah, Paul, think of us, your listeners! We want you to believe in what you're saying!

W1: Next, of course, you select your subject. Then, decide on your purpose. Do you simply want to inform us about your subject? Or do you want to influence us in some way? Write down a statement of exactly what you wish to accomplish in the speech. This is the first step in organizing your thoughts.

M: Is entertainment a purpose?

W1: It could be, yes. Your purpose could be to make your audience laugh.

W2: I expect you to be really funny, Paul!

W1: After you decide on your purpose and organize your ideas, you are ready to develop your ideas interestingly and soundly. Why don't you all just take the next few minutes to start brainstorming? Jot down ideas that come to mind—things that matter to you, things you feel strongly about.

3. What is the discussion mainly about?
4. According to the instructor, what is the logical order of steps in preparing a speech?
5. What does the instructor want the students to do next?

Exercise 1.13.B

Questions 1 through 3. Listen to part of a talk in a biology class.

A tree can be seen as a complex engine, converting fuel into energy and manufacturing new products from available resources. The complicated but almost instantaneous process that takes place inside a leaf employs energy from the sun to convert water and carbon dioxide into sugars and other organic molecules. This process is called *photosynthesis*. All tree leaves carry out photosynthesis in basically the same way.

The pores on the outer skin of the leaf open and take in molecules of carbon dioxide as needed. Meanwhile, water that was absorbed by the roots and transported upward through the trunk enters the leaf through its stem. Once carbon dioxide and water are present in a leaf that is drenched in sunlight, photosynthesis can begin.

When sunlight shines on a leaf, its energy is absorbed by molecules of chlorophyll, the pigment that gives leaves their green color. This energy is used to combine water and carbon dioxide molecules to make carbohydrates, or sugars, and other energy–rich organic molecules. In the process, oxygen is released to the outside air through the leaf's pores. Microscopic veins in the leaf carry the newly made foodstuffs out through the stem into the twigs and branches, where they begin their journey throughout the tree. This process continues all through the growing season, as long as the leaves remain green.

1. What is the talk mainly about?
2. Where does photosynthesis take place?
3. The speaker explains what happens during photosynthesis. Summarize the process by putting the events in order.

Questions 4 through 6. Listen to part of a lecture about how a bill becomes a law in the United States Senate.

A Senator introduces a bill by sending it to the clerk of the House, who assigns it a number and title. This procedure is called the first reading.

The bill is then sent to the appropriate committee. If the committee opposes the bill, they immediately kill it. Otherwise, they hold hearings to listen to opinions and facts offered by interested people. The committee then votes on the bill, and if the bill is approved, it is sent back to the clerk of the House.

The clerk gives the bill a second reading. Senators may debate the bill and suggest changes to it. The bill is then put to a vote in the Senate, and if it is passed, it goes to the House of Representatives.

Now, the House of Representatives votes on the Senate bill. If they defeat it, the bill dies. If they pass it, the bill is sent to the president. If the president signs it, the bill becomes a law. But the president may refuse to sign it. This is called a *veto*. When the president vetoes a bill, it is sent back to the house where it originated, along with the president's reasons for refusing to approve it.

4. How does a bill originating in the Senate become a law? Summarize the process by putting the steps in order.
5. What is a veto?
6. In what course was this lecture probably given?

QUIZ 6 (p. 115)

Directions: In this quiz you will hear several conversations and talks. Each conversation or talk is followed by several questions. The conversations, talks, and questions will not be repeated.

For most of the questions, you will read four possible answers and choose the best answer. Some questions will have special directions.

Here is an example.

On the recording, you hear:

(Narrator) Listen to part of a talk in an environmental studies class.

(Man) The first two centuries of colonization had almost no effect on the vast virgin forests blanketing North America. But in the first half of the nineteenth century, industry and agriculture expanded, and by 1850, millions of acres of old–growth forest had been cut or burned off. By 1920, the population of the United States and Canada had topped 100 million, and nearly half the primal old–growth forest was gone. The southeastern U. S. had been virtually clear cut. It was only then that government began to realize the extent of the devastation and to pass laws to conserve our forests.

Now listen to a sample question.

(Narrator) The professor briefly explains a sequence of events. Put the events in the correct order.

In your book, you read:

(A) Agriculture and industry expanded.
(B) Conservation laws were passed.
(C) Forests covered North America.
(D) Old–growth forests were half gone.

The correct order of events given by the professor is:

1. Forests covered North America.
2. Agriculture and industry expanded.
3. Old–growth forests were half gone.
4. Conservation laws were passed.

Therefore, the correct answer is C–A–D–B.

Questions 1 through 3. Listen to a telephone conversation between two college students.

M: Hello, Chiyo? This is Len.
W: Hi, Len, how are you?
M: Not well. I have strep throat and can't come to class. Would you mind getting an extra copy of any handouts Professor Young gives out?
W: I'm sorry about your throat. Of course I'll get the handouts. I can make a copy of my own notes, too. Do you want me to drop them by after class?
M: That would be extremely kind of you.
W: Would you give me the directions to your house?
M: OK. As you leave campus, go over the freeway. When you come to Lake Boulevard, turn right. Go past the mall and then turn right on Harrison. My house is on the next block. 507 Harrison.
W: I'm sure I can find it.
M: Thank you very much, Chiyo.
W: No problem. I'll see you after class.

1. Why does the man call the woman?
2. What does the woman offer to do?
3. How will the woman get to the man's house? Put the steps in the correct order.

Questions 4 through 7. Listen to a professor give a talk in an environmental science class.

Wetlands often result from the surface exposure of groundwater—that is, the water that has percolated down through the soil and accumulated on a layer of rock. One type of wetland is a marsh, whose soil is permanently or regularly saturated with water. Marshes are usually absent of trees and shrubs. Vegetation is usually soft–stemmed or herbaceous, consisting of such plants as grasses or sedges.

Animal life is highly diverse and includes an array of aquatic insects, some of which spend only their early stages in the water and then become terrestrial adults, such as dragonflies. Common amphibians include the green and leopard frogs, and reptiles include the painted and spotted turtles, as well as the snapping turtle in deepwater marshes. In the Florida Everglades, alligators are especially common during the dry season. The Everglades also support wading birds such as the great blue heron and egret.

Because marshes are so biologically productive, several tons of dead plant and animal material become available to the food chain each year. Much of this energy–rich biomass is broken down by bacteria and water fungi. The water in marshes may be tea–colored or dark brown because of the presence of organic acids from the decaying vegetation.

4. What is the professor mainly discussing?
5. Which type of vegetation grows in marshes?
6. Based on the professor's description, classify the following animals.
7. The professor briefly explains a biological process that occurs in marshes. Summarize the process by putting the events in order.

Questions 8 through 11. Listen to part of a talk in a biology class. The professor is talking about bees.

The worker bees, underdeveloped females, do all the work that is done in the hive. They secrete the wax, build the comb, gather pollen, feed and rear the brood, and fight all the battles necessary to defend the colony. The worker bees possess the whole ruling power of the colony and regulate its economy.

The worker develops from the egg into a perfect adult bee in twenty–one days. Each egg is laid by the queen bee, who deposits it in the bottom of the worker cell. After three days, the egg hatches into a small white worm called a larva, which, being fed by the adult bees, increases rapidly in size. When the cell is nearly filled by the growing larva, it is closed up by the bees. The larva then enters the pupa state.

When the adult worker emerges from the pupa, she usually does not leave the hive until about eight days later. Then, accompanied by other young workers, she takes her first flight in the warmth of the afternoon.

The body of the worker bee is divided into three segments—head, thorax, and abdomen. On the head are the mandibles, the jawlike organs which enable the bees to perform the necessary hive duties and to mold the wax and build their combs. The honey bee's four wings and six legs are fastened to the thorax. Located in the abdomen are the honey sac and the sting, with its highly developed poison sac. The sting is used by the workers for self–defense and for the protection of their colony. The worker uses her sting only once, for in doing so, she loses her life.

8. What tasks does the worker bee perform?
9. The professor describes the stages of a worker bee's development. Summarize the process by putting the events in order.
10. When does a worker bee begin to fly?
11. What segment of the bee's body contains the feature necessary for each activity?

Questions 12 through 15. Listen to part of a lecture given by a psychology professor.

The work of Robert Selman revealed that during the elementary school years children gradually grasp the fact that a person's actions or words do not always reflect inner feelings. Toward the end of the elementary school years—and increasingly during adolescence—children become capable of taking a more detached and analytical view of their own behavior as well as the behavior of others.

As children begin school, at about age four to six, they do not recognize that other people may interpret the same social event differently than they do. They do not reflect on the thoughts of others. Selman called this the Egocentric Level.

From about age six to ten, children become able to distinguish between their own interpretations of social interactions and those of others in limited ways. However, they are usually not yet able to view the two perspectives at the same time.

Between the ages of ten and twelve, children become capable of taking a third–person view, which permits them to understand the expectations of themselves and of others in a variety of situations. Selman called this the Multiple Role Taking stage.

Finally, from around twelve to fifteen years and older, a societal perspective begins to develop. Children now are able to judge actions by how they might influence *all* individuals, not just themselves or those who are immediately concerned.

12. What is the main idea of the lecture?
13. At what age is a child least able to recognize the thoughts of other people?
14. What characterizes a child at the Multiple Role Taking stage?
15. The professor briefly explains the development of the social perspective of children. Put the stages in the correct order.

1.14 Determining Reasons (p. 117)

Focus

Listen to a telephone conversation between a student and her adviser.

W: Hello, Mr. Hanfman. This is Denise Anderson.
M: Hello, Denise.
W: I'm sorry, but I can't make my advising appointment at ten o'clock. My car broke down and I have to see my mechanic. May I reschedule for tomorrow?
M: Let's see. Can you make it at eight o'clock?
W: Oh, no, I'm sorry. I have algebra at eight.
M: Hmm. Later in the morning then? I'll be in a meeting until around noon. How about twelve–fifteen?
W: Twelve–fifteen? Yes, I can come then.
M: All right then. I'll see you tomorrow.
W: Thank you, Mr. Hanfman.

Now choose the best answer to each of the following questions.

1. Why must the student reschedule her appointment?
2. Why can't the student meet at eight o'clock the next day?

Exercise 1.14.A

Questions 1 through 2. Listen to an instructor talk about a videotape.

There's a video I would have shown in class, but because of our snow days, there unfortunately will not be enough time to do that. So, instead, I've put the video on library reserve for the quarter. Just go to the reserve desk and ask for "DNA Revealed." It contains some spectacular photography of the events surrounding the mitotic cycle. I strongly recommend this video as an excellent way to review the concepts of cell division before our midterm quiz.

Because it's on reserve, it can't be checked out, but there are several viewing rooms in the library. The tape is not long, only around twenty–five minutes. I hope you all get a chance to see it.

1. Why does the instructor recommend the videotape?
2. Why must the videotape be viewed in the library?

Questions 3 through 6. Listen to a discussion in an economics class.

W1: As with most economic issues, economists disagree deeply about exactly what causes inflation. They generally do agree that a sharp increase in the cost of one essential item is likely to be a contributing factor. For example, when oil prices rose sharply in the mid–1970s, inflation went up sharply. Can anyone tell me why?
W2: Was it because people had to pay more for oil, and then prices of other things also went up?
W1: That was pretty much the case. All of a sudden, consumers were hit with higher prices for oil and for many other things. These higher prices were a form of inflation. Just think of it. All the companies that used oil—to heat their buildings or run their machines—suddenly had to raise their prices to cover the increased cost of the oil.
M: So that would mean anything transported by truck would cost more.

W1: Precisely. At the same time, all the consumers who bought oil—mainly in the form of gasoline for their cars—had to spend a much bigger portion of their paychecks on oil.
M: I remember hearing my parents talk about how they had to wait in a long line to buy gas.
W2: I can remember when my grandfather and uncle lost their jobs. Was that because of inflation?
W1: Possibly. Because they were hurt by this sudden increase in prices, many companies went out of business or cut back on their growth. They fired or laid off people, or stopped hiring.

3. What is the discussion mainly about?
4. Why does the professor mention oil prices?
5. According to the professor, why did inflation occur in the mid–1970s?
6. According to the professor, why did companies lay people off?

Exercise 1.14.B

Questions 1 through 4. Listen to a discussion in an English class. The students have just watched a film.

M1: Well, I thought it was phony because no one could survive going over a waterfall like that. And did you see how he shot two guys, with a rifle in each hand? That would be impossible while you're running.
W: But he was a hero! It's a classical story. Nathaniel was a classical hero.
M1: I realize that, but it still bothers me when a story is supposed to be a true but it's full of impossibilities.
W: Was it supposed to be true?
M1: I thought so.
W: Well, I liked the film. I liked the way Nathaniel was so bold and also selfless. Everything he did was for his people, their way of life, not for himself.
M2: I don't think Nathaniel was the hero. The English soldier was a greater hero. He sacrificed his life. He did it to save the woman he loved. That's more heroic.
M1: I don't think a character who dies before the end of the movie can be a hero. A hero has to be the one who survives.
M2: I disagree. The one who survived was a bloodthirsty killer! That makes him the villain, not the hero.
M1: But wasn't it just a basic adventure story?

1. Why does the first man criticize the film?
2. Why does the woman like the film?
3. Why does the second man think the English soldier was a hero?
4. Why do the two men disagree?

Questions 5 through 8. Listen to a talk in a marketing class. The instructor is discussing distribution.

Because of its potential for cutting costs, the distribution step in the marketing process is receiving more attention. Distribution involves warehousing, transporting and keeping inventory of manufactured products. Take an everyday product like fabric softener. After it comes off the assembly line, it's packed in cartons and trucked to warehouses around the country. When orders come in from retailers, the fabric softener is delivered to supermarket shelves. This is distribution.

Probably the most crucial area for controlling costs is inventory. Companies don't want to overproduce and have unsold stock of their product piled up in warehouses. Wholesale companies and large retail chains employ several techniques for inventory control. This is where the computer revolution really had an impact. Computerized information systems give precise and up–to–date accounts of inventory on hand. And the field of distribution offers good entry–level jobs for persons with training in computer programming or data processing.

Overseeing the whole area of distribution is the distribution manager. This job is becoming increasingly important and can lead to an executive position.

5. According to the instructor, why is the distribution step in marketing getting more attention?
6. Why does the instructor mention fabric softener?
7. Why is inventory control so important?
8. Why are computers important in distribution?

1.15 MAKING INFERENCES AND PREDICTIONS (p. 121)

Focus

Listen to part of a lecture in an American history class. The professor is discussing the history of women's rights.

American women had been trained from childhood to assume the role of housekeepers, taught that they were naturally inferior to men, and denied the right to hold property. Women were excluded from responsible professional positions and encouraged to bear a lot of children. After the American Revolution, women faced too many social, psychological, and biological obstacles to be able to assume a full and independent role in society. The appearance of a feminist movement that would demand civil rights for women depended on the disappearance of some of the customs that had kept women in a position of inferiority. The first signs of this process were apparent well before 1815.

Now answer the following questions.

1. What can be inferred from the lecture?
2. What will the professor probably discuss next?

Exercise 1.15.A

Questions 1 through 2. Listen to a conversation in a college cafeteria.

W: What's the lunch special today?
M: Meatloaf with potatoes and gravy and something with chicken and pineapple. The meatloaf is usually pretty good, but I eat that all the time. I'm curious about the chicken.
W: They both sound disgusting to me. I wonder if they have anything without meat. I'm thinking of becoming a vegetarian.
M: Oh, really? Since when?
W: I think since I started eating in this cafeteria. Maybe I'll go check out the salad bar.

1. What will the man probably eat for lunch?
2. What will the woman probably eat for lunch?

Questions 3 through 5. Listen to a conversation between a student and a professor.

M: Professor Jenson, I've registered for your intercultural communications class next quarter. But I just found out I have to go to California over the break and won't be back until January 15.
W: Oh, I see. That means you would miss more than a week of class.
M: I know. Is there any way I can make up the time?
W: We'll cover some very important concepts the first week. And students will be forming learning groups and starting to plan their term projects. The first group paper will be due on January 15.
M: Would I still be able to join a group?
W: To get the full benefit of the experience, you need to be there from the start.
M: I understand. Will this course be offered again in the spring?
W: Yes, it will. In fact, during spring term there will be two sections of the class.

3. Why does the student go to see the professor?
4. What does the professor imply?
5. What will the student probably do?

Questions 6 through 8. Listen to a discussion in a history class.

W: Did anyone happen to catch "The American Metropolis" last night? It was about the growth of cities.
M: I didn't see *that*, but I did see part of a documentary last week that told about a guy—I think he was a visitor from another country—who wrote a book about the growth of industry and so on—the things we've just studied. I remember he said there was a huge population explosion that turned America into a nation of cities, all within a decade. He was talking mostly about Baltimore.
W: Baltimore then or now?
M: In the nineteenth century, right after the Civil War.
W: The program you saw was part of the same series as the one I want to tell you about. Last night the topic was New York City. As early as 1880, the federal government wrote a report on how the five separate municipalities of New York actually constituted one vast metropolitan area. It was a progressive way of thinking at the time. And within twenty years, those five municipalities were officially united as a single city, by a vote of the people. To this day, however, each borough maintains traces of its original independence.
M: I agree with that. I'm from Brooklyn, and it's definitely different from the rest of New York.

6. What are the people discussing?
7. What can be inferred about the United States in the nineteenth century?
8. What can be inferred about New York City?

Exercise 1.15.B

Questions 1 through 4. Listen to a professor talk about software design.

The purpose of a programming system is to make a computer easy to use. Because ease of use is the purpose, the ultimate test of software design is the ratio of function—or usefulness—to complexity. In the past, function, not simplicity, was always the measure of excellence for designers. Now, however, systems are praised more for the simplicity of their concepts.

Simplicity comes from conceptual unity. What is conceptual unity? It's when every part of the system reflects the same philosophy, when every part uses the same language and the same techniques. If a computer system is going to be easy to use, the design must have conceptual unity.

To achieve unity, a design must proceed from one person's mind, or from the minds of a small number of people who share a way of thinking about the project. A large building is most successful when it comes from the vision of one architect. Similarly, a software design is most successful when it is unified under the vision of one lead designer—the architect of the system. When a system is simple, functional, and conceptually unified, it is a well–constructed work of architecture.

1. In what course was this talk probably given?
2. What does the professor imply about the usefulness of a software design?
3. What does the professor imply about architecture?
4. What can be inferred from the talk?

Questions 5 through 8. Listen to part of a talk given by a psychology professor.

The theory of personality types suggests that we can examine several pairs of what are called *type preferences*. One pair of preferences is extraversion–introversion, which shows the broad areas of people's natural interests.

Extraverted people are, by nature, continuously alerted to events outside themselves. Extraverts turn outward to pick up ideas, expectations, values, and interests. Thus, extraverts generally have a variety of interests and take an active approach to life.

In contrast, introverted people naturally look inward for resources. Introverts pursue fewer interests but on a deeper level. Introverts take a reflective approach to life and involve themselves in inner events, ideas, and impressions. Introverted people prefer to learn in private, individual ways.

People often mistakenly treat type preference as a character trait, something that can be worked on and changed. But type preferences are not traits. They are preferred ways of being in the world, different mind–sets, different ways of experiencing life's daily events. Type preferences like extraversion and introversion represent different motivations, interests, and learning styles.

5. What is the talk mainly about?
6. What type of job would an extraverted person probably prefer?
7. What type of assignment would an introverted student probably prefer?
8. What does the professor imply about type preferences?

QUIZ 7 (p. 125)

Directions: In this quiz you will hear several conversations and talks. Each conversation or talk is followed by several questions. The conversations, talks, and questions will not be repeated.

For most of the questions, you will read four possible answers and choose the best answer. Some questions will have special directions.

Here is an example.

On the recording, you hear:

(Narrator) Listen to part of a talk in a biology class. The instructor is talking about the gray wolf.

(Woman) War against the gray wolf started when this region began to be settled significantly. By 1900, hunting had taken a heavy toll on the once plentiful supply of deer and elk. In an effort to maximize hunting harvests, misguided early settlers began a systematic campaign to wipe out the gray wolf, and the number of wolves fell dramatically. This year the government is studying a plan to reintroduce the wolf to our region. Wolf opponents fear that a wolf, if reintroduced, will kill and eat domestic animals. Supporters of the wolf, though, note that when this happens—and it rarely does—ranchers are repaid for their losses.

Now listen to a sample question.

(Narrator) What does the instructor imply about the early settlers in the region?

In your book, you read:

Choose 2 answers.

[A] They supported the reintroduction of the wolf.
[B] Their hunting decreased deer and elk populations.
[C] They were experienced soldiers.
[D] They viewed the wolf as a competitor.

The best two answers to the question, "What does the instructor imply about the early settlers in the region?" are [B], "Their hunting decreased deer and elk populations," and [D], "They viewed the wolf as a competitor." Therefore, the correct choices are [B] and [D].

Now listen to another question.

(Narrator) Why do some people oppose the reintroduction of the wolf?

In your book, you read:

(A) They believe it will threaten livestock.
(B) They believe it will kill people.
(C) They think it will be expensive for the government.
(D) They are afraid the wolves will starve.

The best answer to the question, "Why do some people oppose the reintroduction of the wolf?" is (A), "They believe it will threaten livestock." Therefore, the correct choice is (A).

Questions 1 through 3. Listen to a conversation between a student and a university administrator.

M: Ms. Kinney?
W: Yes?
M: I'm Raymond Lee. The student employment office sent me.
W: Oh, yes, Raymond. Come in. I've been expecting you. Did they tell you anything about the job?
M: Just a little.
W: Do you know your way around campus pretty well?
M: Yes. This is my second year here.
W: Good. We need someone who knows the campus and who can help out with a lot of different tasks, like picking up and delivering parcels, including on the west campus. Do you have a car?
M: Um, no. But I have a bicycle.
W: That's even better. Parking on the west campus is getting tight. Is your bicycle fast?
M: I used to race.
W: That's wonderful! Sometimes we have to do things in a hurry. Can you work every day?
M: Yes. I'd like to.
W: We need someone right away, someone who can work a few hours every day.
M: I can start this afternoon. I'm finished with my classes at one–fifteen.

1. Why does Raymond meet with Ms. Kinney?
2. Why is Raymond's bicycle important?
3. What will probably happen next?

Questions 4 through 7. Listen to a conversation between two friends.

M: You seem distracted. Is something wrong?
W: I'm worried about Tippy. I had to take him to the vet today.
M: Why? What happened?
W: Oh, he just wanted to sleep all the time. That's not so unusual, but I got concerned when he didn't want to go for a walk. He didn't eat his food either, and that is really strange.
M: I'm sorry to hear that. What did the vet say?
W: Well, it's some kind of infection, but Dr. Adams couldn't really say what caused it. She called it a "fever of unknown origin." I can't stop thinking about him. He was dehydrated, so they had to give him fluids. They're also giving him antibiotics. Dr. Adams wants to keep him there for a couple of days.
M: Dogs get infections all the time. Tippy will be all right, I'm sure.
W: I hope you're right. Dr. Adams said I can call tomorrow and see how he's doing.
M: I'm sure it will turn out all right. Will you let me know?
W: OK. I'll call you.

4. Why is the woman worried?
5. Why must Tippy stay with Dr. Adams?
6. How does the man respond?
7. What will the woman probably do?

Questions 8 through 11. Listen to a talk in a cooking class. The speaker is discussing some traditions of the bean.

The humble bean was traditionally credited with magic powers. For one thing, it germinates very quickly and is a favorite of preschool teachers for teaching young children about the wonders of Nature. Also, the bean is one of our most ancient foods. Well–preserved examples have been found in Bronze Age cave sites in Switzerland.

The Greeks and Romans actually considered this vegetable the food of the gods. The Greek philosopher Pythagoras refused to eat beans because he believed they contained blood, and were therefore not fit food for a vegetarian. One story tells how he refused to step on beans even when fleeing his enemy, since he thought they held the souls of the dead.

Beans have been a central item in the diet of many agricultural societies. The Iroquois of North America held an annual bean festival, with ritual dances and ceremonies thanking the gods for their gifts. And the Hopi used beans in rituals connected with spring and puberty. Famous bean festivals were also held in Europe and were related to Christian tradition. On Twelfth Night, a King and Queen of the Bean were chosen and crowned. A great feast took place, and part of the ritual involved eating a beancake that had been baked on the previous evening.

Now that you have an idea of some of the rich traditions surrounding the bean, let's take a look at some delicious main dishes that I promise will become traditions in your family.

8. According to the speaker, why was the bean believed to have magic powers?
9. Why did the philosopher Pythagoras refuse to eat beans?
10. What can be concluded from the talk?
11. What will the speaker probably do next?

Questions 12 through 15. Listen to part of a lecture about the Brer Rabbit stories.

The adventures of Brer Rabbit and his rascally friends—Brer Fox, Brer Wolf, and Brer Bear—were first written down by an American journalist named Joel Chandler Harris. Harris was born in Georgia in 1848, and as a young boy he used to visit the workers' cabins and listen to the stories being told by the old men sitting around the fire. Harris was fascinated by the trickster Brer Rabbit and especially by the masterful storytelling of the old men, which blended African folklore with European narrative forms.

Later, when Harris was writing a daily column for a newspaper in Atlanta, he remembered his boyhood days and wrote one of the stories he had heard about Brer Rabbit. It was an immediate success. From then on, stories about the doings of Brer Rabbit and his friends, narrated by an old character named Uncle Remus, were a regular feature in the newspaper.

The Brer Rabbit stories have been popular ever since, although not without controversy and charges of ethnic stereotyping. Their enduring appeal, however, rests in how they offer wise and witty commentary on universal features of the human character, while being delivered in a satisfying narrative form.

12. Why was the young Harris interested in the Brer Rabbit stories?
13. What can be inferred about Brer Rabbit?
14. Why are the Brer Rabbit stories still popular?
15. In what course was this lecture probably given?

QUIZ 8 (p. 127)

Directions: In this quiz you will hear several conversations and talks. Each conversation or talk is followed by several questions. The conversations, talks, and questions will not be repeated.

For most of the questions, you will read four possible answers and choose the best answer. Some questions will have special directions.

Here is an example.

On the recording, you hear:

(Narrator) Listen to part of a talk in a geology class.

(Woman) Large caves such as Carlsbad Caverns in New Mexico are famous for their many underground chambers and varied and majestic landscapes. Delicate flowerlike and strawlike structures grow from the ceiling, as do massive curtains of stone. Among the most interesting and well–known formations are icicle–like stalactites, which hang from the ceiling, and stalagmites, which are found on the cave floor.
Groundwater seeping into a cave chamber contains carbon dioxide absorbed from the atmosphere or the soil. This carbon dioxide may unite with limestone to form calcium carbonate. Stalagmites are produced when water drops directly to the cave floor. The impact of the water striking the floor causes it to break into droplets or into a film, releasing the excess carbon dioxide, and the crystals begin to grow upward.

Now listen to a sample question.

(Narrator)What is the talk mainly about?

In your book, you read:

(A) Groundwater in caves
(B) The formation of Carlsbad Caverns
(C) Structures that form in caves
(D) Majestic landscapes

The best answer to the question, "What is the talk mainly about?" is (C), "Structures that form in caves." Therefore, the correct choice is (C).

Now listen to another sample question.

(Narrator) What types of formations hang from the ceiling of a cave?

In your book, you read:

Choose 2 answers.

[A] Cave flowers
[B] Curtains of stone
[C] Stalactites
[D] Icebergs

The best two answers to the question, "What types of formations hang from the ceiling of a cave?" are [B], Curtains of stone," and [C], "Stalactites." The correct choices are [B] and [C].

Questions 1 through 3. Listen to a conversation in a department store.

M: May I help you?
W: Yes. I'd like to return this sweater.
M: Is there something wrong with it?
W: No, I bought it as a gift for someone, but then I realized he might not like this style. I think he'd rather have a pullover than a cardigan.
M: OK. Would you like to take a look at our pullovers?
W: Sure.
M: The wools are on these tables, and the cottons are over there on the wall. We have a lot of different styles. Feel free to look around.
W: OK.
M: Let me know if you see anything you like, and we can make an exchange.
W: I will. Thank you.

1. What is the purpose of this conversation?
2. What does the man want the woman to do?
3. What will the woman probably do?

Questions 4 through 6. Listen to a conversation between students on a biology field trip.

W: Look! Isn't that a house finch?
M: No, I think it's just a little brown sparrow.
W: It seems reddish to me. And its song is like a recording we heard of a house finch. Professor Flynn said we'd probably see a lot of red finches today.
M: Well, maybe you're right. We'd better write it down anyway. But I still say it's too brown to be a house finch. I'll put a question mark by it.
W: We've sure seen enough starlings. I didn't even know they lived in the city. I can remember hearing my cousin complain about how the starlings always ate all the fruit in their orchard.
M: They are kind of pretty, though, don't you think? Look at how the black is mixed with a little green, making their feathers look iridescent.

4. What are the students discussing?
5. Match each word with the correct color.
6. What can be inferred about starlings?

Questions 7 through 10. Listen to a student give an oral report in a world history class. The student is talking about tea.

Over the years, hundreds of herbs have proved virtuous for every sort of disease. One of the giants of the herbal world—tea—has been praised for over a millennium.

From the very beginning, tea had the ultimate in herbal virtues: it brought health and well–being, enabling one to stay awake to work. It is no wonder that tea was so well received in early modern Europe. Tea had special appeal in Europe because it was a product of the mysterious East. Europeans readily adopted drinks brought from the Land of Spice.

Buddhist monks brought tea to Japan as early as 794 A.D. Tea was regarded by both monk and emperor as a divine healing herb, and the royal tea garden was managed by the emperor's Bureau of Medicine. The Japanese tea ceremony presents every step in the making of the tea before the eyes of the guests, including the gathering of the water, its boiling, the cleaning of the utensils, and the addition of the tea.

Of course, boiling the wrong leaf could cause trouble. Even in modern times, there are stories of migrants who, coming to a new country, made tea from a plant that looked just like one they had used at home—but with deadly results. The history of poisons as well as the history of cures is intimately tied to herbals. The longtime resistance to commercial preparations of herbal tea may be due to the traditional association of herbal teas with witch's brews and the mysterious cures that wrinkled old wives used to make.

7. According to the student, why was tea so well received in Europe?
8. According to the student, how was tea regarded in Japanese history?
9. What negative aspect of herbs does the student mention?
10. What would be a good title for this report?

Questions 11 through 15. Listen to a talk in a health science class.

Skin cancer is the most prevalent of all cancers. The principal cause of skin cancer is overexposure to sunlight, according to most medical experts. Chronic sun exposure—especially when it causes burning or blistering—results in more skin cancer than does any other risk factor, including exposure to x–rays and a family history of skin cancer. The most effective preventative measure is sun avoidance.

The most dangerous of all skin cancers is malignant melanoma. Melanoma has its beginnings in melanocytes, the skin cells that produce the dark protective pigment called melanin. Melanoma may suddenly appear without warning, but it may also begin in or near a mole or other dark spot in the skin. Thus, it's important that we know the location and appearance of the moles on our bodies so any change will be noticed.

Now I'd like to go over the ABCDs of melanoma—an easy guide to recognizing the warning signs of this disease. *A* is for asymmetry—when one half of a mole doesn't match the other half. *B* is for border irregularity. This is when the edges of a mole are ragged, notched, or blurred. *C* stands for color—when the pigmentation is not uniform—when shades of tan, brown, black, red, white, or blue are present. And finally, *D* for diameter—when the size of a mole is greater than six millimeters, which is about the size of a pencil eraser. Any sudden growth of a mole should be of concern.

11. What is the purpose of the talk?
12. What can be inferred about skin cancer?
13. Why is it important for people to be familiar with the moles on their bodies?
14. Select the drawing that illustrates the melanoma warning sign of asymmetry.
15. Select the drawing that illustrates the melanoma warning sign of diameter.

Questions 16 through 20. A guest artist has been invited to a college campus to give a talk on choosing a career in the arts. Listen to the beginning of the talk.

While the outlook is generally good, there are a number of factors to be considered before undertaking a career in the arts. Foremost among these are talent, training, and personal characteristics. Whether a person's goal is to be an actor or an animator, a saxophonist or a sculptor, talent is an essential consideration. But talent alone will not guarantee a successful career in the arts. Most careers also require training.

All people in the arts need to be self–disciplined, creative, and able to express themselves through their art, whatever it may be. Beyond the need for these general attributes, each career calls for distinct personal characteristics. Film directors, for instance, should be good at leading people; fiction writers should be prepared to spend hours with only their imagination and a word processor.

A career in the arts requires a personal sense of commitment—a *calling*—because art *does* have a history of insecure employment. Those who are interested should talk with arts professionals or work in the arts themselves. Professionals can give good firsthand advice, but experience is the best way to get a feel for the field. This experience does not have to be formal. It can be part–time or volunteer work. Those who think they might want to be graphic designers could work as paste–up artists for a school newspaper. Aspiring actors could appear in local productions, and photographers could start by snapping photos for a family wedding.

Finally, another very important consideration is that many artists find it difficult, or even impossible, to live on the money they make from their art. Many have to supplement their income by teaching, by working behind the scenes, or by doing other work not related to the arts.

16. According to the speaker, what factors are important in choosing a career in the arts?
17. According to the speaker, what personal attribute should a film director have?
18. Why does the speaker warn students that a career in art requires a special calling?
19. How does the speaker suggest one gain experience in the following fields?
20. What does the speaker imply about a career in the arts?

Questions 21 through 25. An administrator in the field of public health has been invited to speak to a statistics class. Listen to part of the lecture.

As an epidemiologist, I look at factors that are involved in the distribution and disease frequency in human populations. What is it about what we do, what we eat, what our environment is, what our occupations are, that leads one group of people to be more or less likely to develop a disease than another group of people? It is these factors that we try to identify.

We go at it from a couple of different angles. One is called *descriptive epidemiology*, or looking at the trends of diseases over time as well as trends of diseases in one population relative to another population.

Another way is through *observational epidemiology*, in which we observe what people do. We take a group of people who have a disease and a group of people who don't have a disease. We look at their patterns of eating or drinking and their medical history. We also take a group of people who have been exposed to something, such as smoking, and a group of people who haven't, and follow them over time to see whether they develop a disease or not. In observational epidemiology, we don't interfere in the process. We just observe it.

A third approach is *experimental epidemiology*, sometimes called an intervention study. The Health Research Institute, of which I am the director, is mostly involved in experimental or intervention studies. We study a group of people who have a particular treatment and a group of people who do not and compare the outcomes.

From these three different approaches—descriptive, observational, and experimental—we can judge whether a particular factor causes or prevents the disease that we are looking at.

21. What is the lecture mainly about?
22. What factors are studied by epidemiologists?
23. Why do epidemiologists often study two groups of people?
24. Which method is used by each type of epidemiology?
25. With which type of epidemiology does the speaker mainly work?

Questions 26 through 30. Listen to a radio news story.

Young Americans will face the challenges of a more diverse nation. A recent poll of people 15 to 25 years old provides a snapshot of the attitudes among an age group that will have to cope with the anxieties and uncertainties spawned by a rapidly changing society. Demographers predict that America will be so diverse by 2050 that there will be no majority group.

The poll showed that white Americans have a much rosier perception than black Americans about the status of race relations today and how people will get along in the future. Seven out of ten whites say they expect race relations to be better in the next generation, while just more than half of the blacks felt that way. Asian Americans were the most optimistic, with almost eight of ten predicting improved relations.

A majority of blacks also feel strongly that race is still a factor in how people are judged, compared to roughly a third of the white and Hispanic respondents. Black and Native American youth feel most strongly that their race has more to do with their own sense of identity than other things such as income or education.

26. Who were questioned in the poll?
27. Why was the poll conducted?
28. What do demographers predict about American society in 2050?
29. What can be concluded about how young Americans perceive race relations?
30. Which groups feel that race is closely linked to self–concept?

LISTENING COMPREHENSION REVIEW TEST (p. 130)

In the Listening section of the test, you will have an opportunity to demonstrate your ability to understand conversations and talks in English. Answer all the questions on the basis of what is stated or implied by the speakers you hear. Do not take notes or write during the test.

Part A

Directions: In Part A you will hear short conversations between two people. After each conversation, you will hear a question about the conversation. The conversations and questions will not be repeated. After you hear a question, read the four possible answers and choose the best answer.

Here is an example.

On the recording, you hear:

(Man) Why don't you buy this printer?
(Woman) I'm hoping to find one at a better price.
(Narrator) What does the woman mean?

In your book, you read:

(A) She doesn't want to buy a printer.
(B) She would rather buy something else.
(C) She doesn't want to pay a lot for a printer.
(D) She wants to shop at a better place.

You learn from the conversation that the woman hopes to find a printer at a better price. The best answer to the question, "What does the woman mean?" is (C), "She doesn't want to pay a lot for a printer." Therefore, the correct choice is (C).

1. W: I thought you were going skiing this weekend.
   M: I was, but my ride fell through.
   N: What does the man mean?

2. M: Didn't you go to the club meeting last week either?
   W: No, I was studying for my geometry exam.
   N: What can be inferred from the conversation?

3. W: Did you hear that Mr. Maddox postponed our meeting until next Wednesday?
   M: Oh, great… And I was supposed to be on vacation next week.
   N: What will the man probably do next week?

4. W: Should I take history with Dr. Marcus or Dr. Jarrett?
   M: Dr. Marcus mostly gives lectures and exams. I had Dr. Jarrett, and he makes you write a lot of papers. But in his class we had some great discussions.
   W: I think I'd rather write papers than take exams.
   N: What is the woman probably going to do?

5. M: Oh, no! It's already nine–thirty and I haven't finished typing my term paper.
   W: Don't panic. That clock is an hour fast.
   N: What does the woman mean?

6. W: You seem to know so much about gadgets. You must spend a lot of time fixing them.
   M: More than I like, actually.
   N: What does the man mean?

7. W: It's after ten o'clock. Why are you eating dinner so late?
   M: I had to catch a train to my evening class directly after work.
   N: What does the man imply?

8. M: Hi, Michelle. How are you doing?
   W: Not too well. I think I'm coming down with the flu.
   N: What does the woman mean?

9. M: Rebecca calls her mother a lot, doesn't she?
   W: As a matter of fact, she seldom talks to her family.
   N: What does the woman say about Rebecca?

10. M: Hi! Are you all ready for the boat trip this weekend?
    W: It was canceled. Didn't you know? At our meeting last week, we decided to go next month instead.
    M: Oh. I wish someone had told me.
    W: Don't you read your e–mail?
    N: What does the woman imply?

11. W: You'll join me for dinner after the ball game, won't you?
    M: I would if I didn't have a physics exam tomorrow morning.
    N: What does the man mean?

12. M: Do you think Melissa likes John?
    W: Hmm. She always does try to butt in when I'm talking to him.
    N: What does the woman say about Melissa?

13. W: Dawn can't seem to find her book bag.
    M: Has she looked in the lounge?
    N: What does the man imply?

14. M: I thought you liked to play golf.
    W: I used to, but now I'd rather just watch.
    N: What does the woman mean?

15. W: How was your hike in the desert?
    M: Great, except I had a close call with a rattlesnake!
    N: What does the man mean?

16. W: What did you think of that book?
    M: It was dense. I barely had enough time to finish it before class.
    W: Is that so? I finished it in no time.
    N: What does the woman mean?

17. W: Do you mind if I close the window?
    M: It might get a little stuffy in here, don't you think?
    N: What does the man imply?

18. W: What do you think of our new co–worker?
    M: Leonard? I think he's some kind of genius.
    N: What does the man think about Leonard?

19. W: Is something bothering you today?
    M: Oh, I'm a little fed up with my roommate.
    N: What does the man mean?

20. M: I really don't want to do this assignment.
    W: Why don't you just get it over with?
    N: What does the woman suggest?

Part B

Directions: In this part of the test, you will hear several conversations and talks. Each conversation or talk is followed by several questions. The conversations, talks, and questions will not be repeated.

For most of the questions, you will read four possible answers and choose the best answer. Some questions will have special directions.

Here is an example.

On the recording, you hear:

(Narrator) Listen to part of a talk in a general science class. The instructor is talking about the science of meteorology, the study of the earth's atmosphere.

(Man) Progress in the field began with the development of physics and the invention of basic instruments. In the nineteenth century, the invention of the telegraph was important because it improved rapid data collection from remote weather stations. Today, because of such modern research tools as high–altitude airplanes, weather balloons, rockets, earth satellites, and space probes, meteorologists are able to provide more sophisticated understanding and forecasting of weather, their best known function. They also work at solving air pollution problems and studying trends in the earth's climate.

Now listen to a sample question.

(Narrator) How did the telegraph improve the science of meteorology?

In your book, you read:

(A) It helped scientists see the atmosphere more clearly.
(B) It made it easier for scientists to send messages.
(C) It made data collection from weather stations faster.
(D) It helped airplanes fly higher.

The best answer to the question, "How did the telegraph improve the science of meteorology?" is (C), "It made data collection from weather stations faster." Therefore, the correct choice is (C).

Now listen to another sample question.

(Narrator) According to the instructor, what do meteorologists do today?

In your book, you read:

Choose 2 answers.

[A] Forecast the weather.
[B] Study trends in rocket science.
[C] Solve air pollution problems.
[D] Study costs of building satellites.

The best two answers to the question, "What do meteorologists do today?" are [A], "Forecast the weather" and [C], "Solve air pollution problems." Therefore, the correct choices are [A] and [C].

Remember, you should <u>not</u> take notes during the test.

Questions 21 through 22. Listen to a conversation between two students.

W: How did your history test go?
M: Not too bad. I was just glad there was nothing on the labor movement. That's the only chapter I didn't study. How about you? Didn't you have a test today, too?
W: Yeah, in botany, this afternoon at three o'clock.
M: At three I'll be in the pool. I'll be thinking of you.
W: Thanks. I'd rather be in the pool myself.

21. Why is the man glad about his history test?
22. What will the woman do this afternoon?

Questions 23 through 25. Listen to a conversation between a student and the physics department secretary.

M: Hello. May I leave a message here for Dr. Owada?
W: Yes. I can give her a message, or if you've written her a note, you can put it in her mailbox over there.
M: I didn't write her a note, but I can. May I sit here and write it?
W: Sure. Oh, I just realized that Dr. Owada isn't on campus today because she had a conference to go to. She'll get the message tomorrow. Would that be all right?
M: I was going to tell her I wouldn't be in class today, but maybe I don't need to now. Is her two o'clock class canceled?
W: No, Professor Strong will be giving the lecture today.
M: Oh, it's too bad I'll miss that. He's a great speaker. Well, thank you for your help.
W: It's OK. Have a nice day.

23. Why does the student want to leave a message for Dr. Owada?
24. What does the secretary say about Dr. Owada?
25. What will the student probably do?

Questions 26 through 28. Listen to a telephone conversation between two co–workers.

W: Hello.
M: Hello, Sandy? This is Ben.
W: Hi, Ben. How are you?
M: Oh, not so good. I'm a little confused about my job.
W: Why? What's the matter?
M: I don't think Mr. Jackson likes me. He always watches me and asks me why I'm not working.
W: Why would he do that?
M: I don't know. When he tells me to do something, I do it as fast as I can. When I finish, I take a break until he gives me something else to do.
W: Maybe Mr. Jackson thinks you take too many breaks.
M: But I do everything he tells me to do.
W: Yes, and that's good. You're a fast worker. But when you finish something, you should ask Mr. Jackson if there's anything else he wants you to do.
M: Do you mean I should ask for more work?
W: If you let him know you can handle more work, he'll see you have initiative.
M: Well...OK then. I guess I'll think about what you said. I'll see you tomorrow. Thanks.
W: Bye–bye.

26. Why does Ben call Sandy?
27. What does Sandy imply about Mr. Jackson?
28. What will Ben probably do?

Questions 29 through 33. Listen to part of a lecture in an earth science class. The professor is discussing the world's climate.

The world's climate is more unstable than previously believed. Ice cores drilled from Greenland reveal the world's climate has been changing, even under the undisturbed conditions of past eons. Researchers have discovered an erratic, "flickering climate" during the past several hundred thousand years, with sudden swings from warm to cold and back again in as little as a few decades.

Based on an analysis of oxygen isotopes in the Greenland ice, European and U.S. researchers have concluded that during the latest ice age, the ancient climate might have fluctuated wildly, with average annual temperatures rising as much as 11 degrees in as little as five years, only to slide back into a deep chill lasting thousands of years. Scientists discovered evidence of several abrupt shifts between 15,000 and 100,000 years ago, when temperatures rose suddenly and snowfall and methane levels in the air doubled.

The transition about 10,000 years ago from the latest ice age to the present warm period might have taken less than a human lifetime, not the centuries of gradual warming most scientists had once assumed.

Analysis of the earth's ice suggests global warming will result in thousands of years of glacial cold. When the climate becomes warmer, there will be more moisture in the air. Therefore, more snow will fall each winter. More snow will build up as glacial ice, which in turn will reflect more of the sun's heat. This will lower global temperature dramatically. Then, if glaciers spread over enough of the earth, this will quickly refrigerate the planet.

29. What would be a good title for this lecture?
30. Where were the ice cores drilled?
31. According to the professor, what happened during the latest ice age?
32. What does the professor say about the transition from the latest ice age?
33. The professor explains what will happen if the earth's climate becomes warmer. Summarize the process by putting the events in order.

Questions 34 through 39. Listen to a lecture given by a sociology professor.

A stratified society is one marked by differences among people that identify them as being "higher" or "lower." The simplest form of inequality is based on age and sex. Old people may have a high or low position; women are often ranked below men. But in every society there is another form of inequality that ranks families rather than individuals. If a large group of families are similar to each other in education, income, and values, we call them a *social class*. Many scholars agree that contemporary American society can be described as having four social classes. These classes can be labeled as follows:

First, the upper class. This is the wealthy families who have a stable pattern of refined living. In the past, the upper class was based on inherited property. Today, the upper class contains many newly successful persons who learn the gracious way of life. Second, the upper–middle class—the successful business and professional families. Their income is mostly from current occupations. They live in large houses in good suburbs or in the best apartment houses, and most are college graduates. Third, the lower–middle class. They are the less successful members of government and business, as well as the more successful manual workers. The lower–middle class is the model for the popular stereotype of America's "common man." And finally, the lower class—people who have the lowest paid jobs, work irregularly, and live in slums.

These class descriptions will help us order our thinking about the complexities of social reality, but the labels may lead us to assume falsely that a community can be neatly divided with each family conveniently labeled.

34. What is the main idea of the lecture?
35. According to the professor, what characterizes the members of a social class?
36. Which social class fits the stereotype of America's "common man"?
37. How does the professor describe the lowest class?
38. Match each social class with the characteristic mentioned by the professor.
39. What does the professor imply about labels for social classes?

Questions 40 through 45. Listen to part of a lecture in an environmental science class. The professor is discussing the *hydrologic cycle*.

Water is essential for life, and in some parts of the world, it is a most precious commodity. Water from earth is continuously absorbed into the atmosphere as vapor, which in turn condenses or freezes and falls as rain, hail, or snow. Vegetation plays an important part in this cycle, which is called the *hydrologic cycle*, the pattern of water movement as it circulates through the natural system.

Our understanding of how the cycle operates has resulted from research in climatology and hydrology. Climatologists study the role of solar energy in evaporation, atmospheric circulation, and the precipitation of atmospheric water. Hydrologists are concerned with how water moves over and through the land and how it is temporarily stored on or within the earth.

Hydrologists study the vast quantities of water that are involved in the land phase of the cycle. Of the precipitation that falls on a land area, small amounts are evaporated while still in the air or are intercepted by vegetation. The remainder reaches the surface of the land. Then it is stored on the surface, penetrates the surface materials, or runs off over the surface to be stored in rivers, lakes, or oceans.

Some of the absorbed moisture is stored temporarily in the upper soil layers and used later by the vegetation. Trees and plants draw up water and return it to the atmosphere by evapotranspiration through and from their leaves. In the ground, if the soil is already saturated, the absorbed water will seep downward through the upper soil layers, possibly reaching the water table, where it passes into groundwater storage. Ultimately, most of the groundwater returns to the surface–water system either as streamflow or as springs.

40. What is the hydrologic cycle?
41. Identify the area in the diagram that is studied by climatologists.
42. Identify the area in the diagram that is studied by hydrologists.
43. According to the professor, what happens to water that falls to earth as precipitation?
44. What can be inferred about the role of trees in the hydrologic cycle?
45. How does groundwater reappear on the earth's surface?

Questions 46 through 50. Listen to a talk given by an economics instructor.

One of the major problems in our economy is inflation, a situation in which prices are going up faster than wages. Thus, a person has to work more hours to pay for the same items.

For example, let's say that this year a loaf of bread costs $1.00 and the average salary in the United States is $10.00 per hour. That means a person could earn enough money to buy a loaf of bread in one–tenth of an hour, or six minutes. Then, halfway through the year, the price of the bread goes up to $1.25, while wages stay the same. That means that a person now has to work one–eighth of an hour—seven and a half minutes—to buy the same loaf of bread.

Now let's say that at the end of the year, wages go up to $11.00 per hour, but the price of bread goes up to $1.50. Now a person has to work more than one–seventh of an hour—over eight minutes—to buy the same loaf of bread. As you can see, if more and more work time is spent earning money to buy loaves of bread, employees will have less money left over to buy other things. Inflation means that the same money buys fewer things, and everybody's standard of living goes down, even if salaries are going up.

Some kinds of inflation are worse than others. Moderate inflation does not distort relative prices or incomes severely. Galloping inflation happens rapidly, say at a rate of 100 percent or more within a year. And then there is hyperinflation—inflation so severe that people try to get rid of their currency before prices rise further and render the money worthless. Times of hyperinflation are usually characterized by social and political turmoil.

46. What is the main purpose of the talk?
47. Why does the instructor mention a loaf of bread?
48. What happens when prices go up but salaries remain the same?
49. Why does an employee's standard of living go down when there is inflation?
50. Match the types of inflation with the correct descriptions.

PRACTICE TESTS

TEST 1 (p. 519)

SECTION 1 — LISTENING

In the Listening section of the test, you will have an opportunity to demonstrate your ability to understand conversations and talks in English. Answer all the questions on the basis of what is stated or implied by the speakers you hear. Do not take notes or write during the test.

Part A

Directions: In Part A you will hear short conversations between two people. After each conversation, you will hear a question about the conversation. The conversations and questions will not be repeated. After you hear a question, read the four possible answers and choose the best answer.

Here is an example.

On the recording, you hear:

(Man) Why don't you buy this printer?
(Woman) I'm hoping to find one at a better price.
(Narrator) What does the woman mean?

In your book, you read:

(A) She doesn't want to buy a printer.
(B) She would rather buy something else.
(C) She doesn't want to pay a lot for a printer.
(D) She wants to shop at a better place.

You learn from the conversation that the woman hopes to find a printer at a better price. The best answer to the question, "What does the woman mean?" is (C), "She doesn't want to pay a lot for a printer." Therefore, the correct choice is (C).

1. M: Bill can't figure out how to program his VCR.
   W: Why doesn't he just read the instruction manual?
   N: What does the woman imply?

2. W: Have you registered for winter quarter yet?
   M: I'm headed there now. But I haven't decided whether I should take botany or zoology.
   W: I had Dr. Hernandez for zoology last year. She's great! She inspired me to major in science.
   M: I'm glad you told me that. She teaches zoology this winter.
   N: What will the man probably do?

3. M: Don't you have to work this weekend?
   W: I got out of it, so I'll be able to go with you after all.
   N: What does the woman mean?

4. W: The cushions on your sofa could use new covers.
   M: I know. I've checked at an upholstery shop, but it's really expensive.
   N: What does the man imply?

5. M: Did you hear the news? Gregorio has been accepted into medical school.
   W: Nothing could surprise me more!
   N: What does the woman mean?

TAPESCRIPT

6. M: Did you find out if you got the job?
   W: No, if only they would call. I've been waiting all day.
   N: What does the woman mean?

7. M: How long has your brother Rick been building houses—six, seven years?
   W: Oh, at least that long.
   N: What does the woman say about Rick?

8. W: How are you doing in your calculus class?
   M: I can't figure out most of the problems.
   N: What does the man mean?

9. W: Hey, would you like to go bowling with us tonight?
   M: Another time. I'm going to Hasan's award dinner. He took top honors as intern in surgery.
   W: Oh, that's great! Will he continue working at the university hospital?
   M: He wants to. He says they have the best surgery unit in the area.
   N: What can be inferred about Hasan?

10. M: Are you and Pamela going to the play?
    W: Well, she said she would go with me, but she may back out.
    N: What does the woman imply?

11. W: Excuse me, I can't find my tour group from the university.
    M: There's a bunch of folks over on the boardwalk.
    N: What does the man mean?

12. M: Tom is giving his piano recital this evening.
    W: Oh, really? I don't want to miss that.
    N: What can be inferred about the woman?

13. M: Is there a coffee shop in the lobby?
    W: No, but there is complimentary coffee and tea in the lounge every morning.
    N: What does the woman mean?

14. W: Why can't you help me?
    M: You've got to deal with your own problems.
    N: What does the man mean?

15. M: My house needs painting, and something has to be done about that deck.
    W: Mrs. Johnson at the hardware store gave me excellent advice about my house.
    N: What does the woman imply?

Part B

Directions: In this part of the test, you will hear several conversations and talks. Each conversation or talk is followed by several questions. The conversations, talks, and questions will not be repeated.

For most of the questions, you will read four possible answers and choose the best answer. Some questions will have special directions.

Here is an example.

On the recording, you hear:

(Narrator) Listen to part of a talk in a general science class. The instructor is talking about the science of meteorology, the study of the earth's atmosphere.

(Man) Progress in the field began with the development of physics and the invention of basic instruments. In the nineteenth century, the invention of the telegraph was important because it improved rapid data collection from remote weather stations. Today, because of such modern research tools as high–altitude airplanes, weather balloons, rockets, earth satellites, and space probes, meteorologists are able to provide more sophisticated understanding and forecasting of weather, their best known function. They also work at solving air pollution problems and studying trends in the earth's climate.

Now listen to a sample question.

(Narrator) How did the telegraph improve the science of meteorology?

In your book, you read:

(A) It helped scientists see the atmosphere more clearly.
(B) It made it easier for scientists to send messages.
(C) It made data collection from weather stations faster.
(D) It helped airplanes fly higher.

The best answer to the question, "How did the telegraph improve the science of meteorology?" is (C), "It made data collection from weather stations faster." Therefore, the correct choice is (C).

Now listen to another sample question.

(Narrator) According to the instructor, what do meteorologists do today?

In your book, you read:

Choose 2 answers.

[A] Forecast the weather.
[B] Study trends in rocket science.
[C] Solve air pollution problems.
[D] Study costs of building satellites.

The best two answers to the question, "What do meteorologists do today?" are [A], "Forecast the weather" and [C], "Solve air pollution problems." Therefore, the correct choices are [A] and [C].

Remember, you should <u>not</u> take notes during the test.

Questions 16 through 17. Listen to a conservation between a student and his professor.

M: Professor Park?
W: Hello, Tony. How can I help you?
M: Professor Park, I have a problem. My father had to have surgery, and I have to go to Oklahoma. I don't know how long I'll be gone. I was wondering if I could take an Incomplete for your class.

W: I'm so sorry to hear about your father. Of course, you can take a grade of Incomplete. It means you would have six weeks to make up the term paper and the final exam. There is also a form that you need to fill out that I have to sign.
M: I've got the form right here.
W: Oh, then why don't we take care of it right now?

16. Why does the student go to see his professor?
17. What is required for an Incomplete?

Questions 18 through 20. Listen to a telephone conversation between two friends.

W: Hello.
M: Hi, Lisa. This is Rob.
W: Hi! Are you ready to go this weekend?
M: Almost. But I've been rethinking our route. I heard there's construction on Highway 28 that's causing long delays. Some work on the bridges or something. So, I think we should take Route 150 north and go through Springdale before we head east to Ransom.
W: Springdale? Isn't that out of the way? We have to be in Ransom by eleven to make the ferry.
M: I know. That's why I suggest we leave a little earlier and go north first. That way we can avoid the road work and have a nice drive at the same time. The scenery is beautiful around Springdale this time of year.
W: Yes, I've heard that. But are you sure we can go that way and still catch the ferry?
M: If we leave here by seven o'clock, we can.
W: Seven! Well, all right. It will be good to get an early start.
M: OK then. I'll pick you up on Saturday at seven.
W: All right. I'm looking forward to it. See you then.

18. What are the people discussing?
19. Rob explains his plan for their trip. Summarize his plan by putting the steps in order.
20. Why is the woman concerned?

Questions 21 through 23. Listen to part of a discussion in an anthropology class.

M1: Most North American Indians were deeply religious and saw people as existing within a spiritual world that included all other living things. Animal spirits often played major roles in their religions. Can anyone think of an example of how the importance of animals was expressed? Yes, Sandra?
W: I've seen some different Indian masks, and a lot of them looked like animals or birds.
M1: That's a good example. The tribes of the northwest Pacific Coast believed in many spirits, such as those of the eagle, beaver, and whale. They sought the protection of these spirits through various ceremonies and rituals. The shaman, who played a key role in many Indian religions, helped them to gain contact with the spiritual world. Masks, costumes, song, and dance figured prominently in these rituals.
M2: What about the animals on totem poles?
M1: Another great example. The fanciful animal–like figures carved into totem poles served as valuable collective memory devices for tribes that lacked a written language. The animals and other mythological creatures told the story of the tribe. Every pole told a story of some kind—a symbolic story that could be read by anyone familiar with the imagery of a particular tribe or clan.

21. What is the discussion mainly about?
22. According to the professor, how did people contact the spiritual world?
23. Why were totem poles important to some tribes?

Questions 24 through 27. Listen to a talk on the radio about health.

When we're sick, some of us may still rush to the drugstore for painkillers, laxatives and antacids. But some of us know we need to look no further than the shelves of our grocery store for an array of disease–fighters. Although I'm not recommending that food replace medicine, there are surprising super foods that can prevent disease.

Breakfast is the easiest meal to eat healthfully. A bowl of cereal, fresh fruit, and low–fat milk is the model meal: low in fat, and high in fiber, vitamins and minerals. Researchers found that people who eat a nutritious breakfast get 30 percent of the recommended daily amounts of thiamin, riboflavin, calcium and vitamin C, as well as 25 percent of iron and vitamin B12. Breakfast skippers, on the other hand, are more likely to be overweight, to have high cholesterol levels, and to eat too many fatty foods.

If you feel your breakfast is incomplete without eggs, I recommend skipping the egg in a shell in favor of egg substitutes, especially for people with coronary artery disease or hypertension. Not only are egg substitutes cholesterol–free, they are also fat–free.

Orange juice is still the breakfast drink of choice for most people. OJ is a good source of vitamins and has anti—viral properties that can help fight infection. And, of course, there is milk, still a breakfast natural, but only if it's skim or one percent. Adults should have two or three glasses of milk every day to ensure they get the calcium they need. Finally, a cup of tea may be one of your best defenses against heart disease, cancer and stroke.

Hippocrates got it right when he advised his patients, "Let food be your medicine."

24. What is the talk mainly about?
25. Why is a breakfast of cereal, fruit, and milk the model meal?
26. What does the speaker say about people who skip breakfast?
27. According to the speaker, what are the benefits of each of the following foods?

Questions 28 through 32. Listen to a professor give a lecture about Mount St. Helens.

Mount St. Helens is in the Cascade Range, a chain of volcanoes, many of which are only sleeping. Mount St. Helens has had a long history of explosive activity. The eruptions of 1980 were not unexpected. Geologists familiar with the mountain had predicted such activity.

The eruption cycle had a rather harmless beginning on March 20, 1980, when a strong earthquake was recorded near the mountain. During the next week, the earthquakes increased rapidly, causing several avalanches. Then, there was a loud boom, and a small crater opened on top of the awakening mountain. There were occasional steam and ash eruptions during April and early May—to the delight of the many tourists and hikers who came to watch the show.

Then scientists noticed vibrations thought to be magma moving deep in the volcano. By early May, the north side of the mountain swelled, and steam and ash eruptions became frequent. The top of the volcano was coming apart.

On the morning of May 18, after a few quiet days, earthquakes triggered a massive landslide, and much of the north face slid down the mountain. This landslide released a tremendous sideways blast. Next, the summit exploded, sending an ash cloud over 60,000 feet into the air, blocking the sunlight.

The blast leveled all trees for 17 miles to the northeast and blew all of the water out of some lakes. The eruption killed the mountain's goats, millions of fish and birds, thousands of deer and elk, and dozens of people. The ash cloud drifted around the world.

Now, Mount St. Helens is sleeping again, but geologists who've studied this mountain believe that future eruptions are near certainty and can not be prevented.

28. In what course was this lecture probably given?
29. According to the professor, how did the cycle of eruptions begin?
30. What occurred during the months before the great explosion of Mount St. Helens?
31. The professor explains what happened during the great eruption. Summarize the process by putting the events in order.
32. What can be concluded about Mount St. Helens?

Questions 33 through 36. Listen to a career counselor speak about two different types of employees.

Are you going to be more effective and happy as a specialist or as a generalist? Do you find real satisfaction in the precision, order, and system of a clearly laid–out job? Or are you one of those people who tend to grow impatient with anything that looks like a "routine" job?

There are a great many careers in which the emphasis is on specialization. You find these careers in engineering and in accounting, in production, in statistical work, and in teaching. But there is an increasing demand for people who are able to take in a great area at a glance. There is, in other words, a demand for people who are capable of seeing the forest rather than the trees, of making overall judgments. And these "generalists" are particularly needed for administrative positions, where it is their job to see that other people do the work, where they have to plan for other people, to organize other people's work, to initiate it and appraise it.

Specialists understand one field; their concern is with technique, tools, media. They are "trained" people, and their educational background is technical or professional. Generalists—and especially administrators—deal with people. Their concern is with leadership, with planning, with direction, and with coordination. They are "educated" people, and the humanities are their strongest foundation.

Any organization needs both kinds of people, although different organizations need them in different ratios. It is your job to find out, during your college years, into which of these two job categories you fit, and to plan your career accordingly.

33. What is the purpose of the talk?
34. According to the speaker, which people are probably specialists?
35. According to the speaker, what characterizes a generalist?
36. What can be inferred from this talk?

Questions 37 through 40. A historian has been invited to speak to an architecture class. She will be discussing styles of housing in colonial New England. Listen to part of the lecture.

There was considerable variety in the plans of seventeenth–century houses. Each house, naturally, was shaped by circumstances of family need, available means, site, and the accidents of time. It is nonetheless possible to define the three most common plan types in New England, and even to suggest how these probably succeeded one another in an evolutionary sequence.

The *one–room plan* was the simplest and the earliest type. The front door opened into a small room, in those days called the porch, with a steep staircase crowded up against an immense chimney. The main room was a combination living–dining–cooking room of ample size. The staircase led to one large sleeping room upstairs.

The *two–room plan* was simply the one–room plan with a parlor added at the other side of the chimney and porch, giving two fireplaces back–to–back.

The *added lean–to plan* was the result of an addition at the back of the house, with roof rafters leaning from one–story eaves at the back against the top of the wall of the main house. The added space was used for a separate kitchen. The cooking was done in a fireplace added to the back of the central chimney mass. On the cold side of the kitchen was a pantry, and on the warm side, facing the southern sun, a downstairs bedroom.

These plan types form a logical evolutionary sequence. But a one–room plan might have been built at any time in the seventeenth century, and it is wisest not to regard plan type strictly as a determiner of the age of a colonial house.

37. In what order did the three plan types probably develop? Put the three types in order.
38. Identify the kitchen in the floor diagram of the added lean–to plan.
39. Identify the room called the porch in the floor diagram of the added lean–to plan.
40. Why does the speaker advise against determining a house's age strictly by plan type?

Questions 41 through 45. Listen to a health educator talk about irregular heartbeats.

An irregular heartbeat can be quite frightening. But fortunately it's rarely serious, because it's one body signal that people seldom ignore.

One type of irregular heartbeat is known as palpitations. Palpitations are painless and represent an extra beat of the heart that can be caused by too much coffee, tobacco, medication, or anxiety. The symptom is usually reported as a fluttering in the chest, or a feeling that the heart has jumped. It may be felt while inhaling slowly. The patient may experience palpitations during times of stress: after several days with less sleep than usual, or before a test or an important meeting.

Sometimes medications such as cold tablets or thyroid medications may be a factor in bringing on the attacks. Another triggering factor is quick change of position, such as getting out of bed too quickly or jumping out of a chair to answer the phone. The body says, "I'm lighthearted" or "I think I'm going to faint." With palpitations, the heartbeat regulator has trouble adjusting to the quick switch from a circulatory system that is horizontal to one that is vertical. The pulse rate must be changed. It's no wonder the heart may skip a few beats—like a car motor missing when it goes from a flat road to climbing a hill.

Palpitations are an example of lack of harmony between the body and its environment. It may mean that your body disapproves of the chemicals you are putting into it. It resents the caffeine and nicotine being forced into the electrical circuits of your heart. It could also be telling you that you are working too hard. An irregular heartbeat is a warning to slow down before your motor burns out.

41. What is a symptom of palpitations?
42. What causes palpitations?
43. Why do people sometimes have palpitations when they get out of bed too quickly?
44. What does the health educator imply about palpitations?
45. What would be the best title for this talk?

TEST 2 (p. 547)

SECTION 1 – LISTENING COMPREHENSION

In the Listening Comprehension section of the test, you will have an opportunity to demonstrate your ability to understand conversations and talks in English. There are three parts to this section, with special directions for each part. Answer all the questions on the basis of what is stated or implied by the speakers you hear. Do not take notes or write in your book at any time.

Part A

Directions: In Part A you will hear short conversations between two people. After each conversation, you will hear a question about the conversation. The conversations and questions will not be repeated. After you hear a question, read the four possible answers in your book and choose the best answer. Then, on your answer sheet, find the number of the question and fill in the space that corresponds to the letter of the answer you have chosen.

Here is an example.

On the recording, you hear:

(Man) Why don't you buy this printer?
(Woman) I'm hoping to find one at a better price.
(Narrator) What does the woman mean?

In your book, you read:

(A) She doesn't want to buy a printer.
(B) She would rather buy something else.
(C) She doesn't want to pay a lot for a printer.
(D) She wants to shop at a better place.

You learn from the conversation that the woman hopes to find a printer at a better price. The best answer to the question, "What does the woman mean?" is (C), "She doesn't want to pay a lot for a printer." Therefore, the correct choice is (C).

1. M: Why are you so happy today?
   W: I was in the bookstore and came across my best friend from grade school.
   N: What does the woman mean?

2. M: How do you like your new assistant?
   W: I'm really pleased with the work he has done so far.
   N: What do you know from the conversation?

3. W: The new coffee table came yesterday.
   M: Oh, so you *did* order it after all!
   N: What had the man assumed?

4. W: When did you get your new stereo?
   M: The week before last, when I got my first paycheck.
   N: What does the man mean?

5. W: Your eyes are fine. If you'd like new frames for your glasses, you could look at our selection.
   M: I was thinking of trying contact lenses.
   N: What is the woman's job?

6. M: Where can I get these boots fixed?
   W: Isn't there a shoe repair shop on this block?
   N: What does the woman imply?

7. W: Excuse me, but is this seat taken?
M: Yes, it is. But I think there are some seats left in the balcony.
N: What does the man suggest?

8. M: I feel tired all the time, but I have trouble sleeping at night.
W: Maybe you're worrying too much about your work.
N: What does the woman imply?

9. W: Do you want to go bowling with us tonight?
M: I heard there's a dance at the Palms Hotel. Why don't we check that out instead?
N: What does the man suggest?

10. W: I'm taking the train downtown to go shopping.
M: Well, you'd better keep an eye on your wallet.
N: What does the man advise the woman to do?

11. W: I'm sorry. The computer lab is closing in ten minutes. We open again at nine a.m.
M: But my paper is due at eight!
N: What is the man's problem?

12. W: I haven't seen much of Amy lately, have you?
M: I met her yesterday in the park, and she looked a lot run–down.
N: What does the man say about Amy?

13. M: Here are your tickets, miss. The train will depart from Gate Five at one o'clock.
W: Thank you. Could you please tell me if there is a snack bar on the train?
N: What will the woman probably do?

14. M: I'm anxious to get started on our project. Can you meet sometime before the weekend?
W: If we meet Friday morning, I'll have time to go to the library that afternoon.
N: What are the speakers discussing?

15. W: What did you think of the movie?
M: It was worth neither the time nor the money.
N: What does the man mean?

16. M: What do you think of Professor Chen's philosophy class?
W: I enjoy his lectures, but I have a hard time keeping up with the rest of his class.
N: What does the woman mean?

17. W: Did you hear that Laura was accepted by the business college?
M: Really? I thought they required a high grade point average.
N: What does the man imply about Laura?

18. W: Weren't you in class Monday either?
M: No, I had to take my brother to the bus station. He went back to Ohio.
N: What can be inferred from the conversation?

19. M: I wonder what happened to Ahmed. I don't see him anywhere.
W: I can't imagine. He told me he would be at the concert tonight.
N: What can be inferred from the conversation?

20. M: The plastic mugs are quite a bit cheaper than the ceramic ones.
W: I know. I prefer ceramic, but I can't afford fifteen dollars each.
N: What will the woman probably do?

21. M: There's a basketball game at the arena tonight.
W: Oh, really? I'd rather go to a movie.
N: What does the woman mean?

22. W: Would you like to join us for a stroll by the lake?
M: What a nice way to spend the evening!
N: What does the man imply?

23. W: Roger, come on! What's taking you so long to get ready?
M: Bear with me. I'm a little tired today.
N: What does the man mean?

24. M: You seem down today. Is something bothering you?
W: I think I blew it on my math exam, and I don't know what to do.
N: What does the woman mean?

25. W: What have you been reading all afternoon?
M: A book for my class. It's a biography of a famous senator.
N: What do you know from the conversation?

26. W: Do you think Brenda would like more tea?
M: Well, it looks like her cup is empty.
N: What does the man imply about Brenda?

27. W: Were you able to find everything that you were looking for?
M: Not really. You've moved things around since the last time I was here, and I had trouble finding the detergent.
N: Where does this conversation probably take place?

28. W: Matthew sure seems excited about being on the soccer team!
M: Yeah, but I wish he felt the same about psychology and accounting.
N: What does the man imply about Matthew?

29. W: My roommate and I are going hiking this weekend.
M: I hope you have a good time. Look out for each other, OK?
N: What does the man mean?

30. W: I need to step out for a few minutes. Would you mind watching my satchel?
M: I'd be happy to.
N: What does the man agree to do?

Part B

Directions: In this part of the test, you will hear longer conversations. After each conversation, you will hear several questions. The conversations and questions will not be repeated.

After you hear a question, read the four possible answers in your book and choose the best answer. Then, on the answer sheet, find the number of the question and fill in the space that corresponds to the letter of the answer you have chosen.

Remember, you should <u>not</u> take notes or write in your book.

Questions 31 through 34. Listen to a conversation between a patient and an oral surgeon.

W: Mr. Novak, I believe it would be best to extract all four of your molars.
M: Oh. Can all four be taken out at the same time?
W: Yes, if that's the way you'd like it.
M: How long will it take?
W: We'll need to anesthetize you, of course. The procedure will take around an hour, but then you'll need some time to wake up in the recovery room. Two or three hours all together.
M: Oh.
W: You'll be sleepy for several hours afterward, and you'll need someone to drive you home.
M: I guess my roommate can do that.
W: Good. Do you have any more questions?
M: Um, will there be any pain?
W: Not much. I'll write a prescription and you can have it filled on the way home after the surgery.
M: That's good to know. It will be a relief to have these wisdom teeth out.
W: That's what people usually say. Now, if you'll just make an appointment with the nurse, we'll be able to take care of those teeth.
M: Thank you, doctor.

31. What is the main subject of this conversation?
32. According to the doctor, what will the surgery involve?
33. Why must someone drive the patient home?
34. How does the man feel about the surgery?

Questions 35 through 38. Listen to a conversation on a bus.

M: That backpack looks heavy. Here, let me help you.
W: Thank you.
M: Have you been hiking?
W: Not exactly. I'm just moving to town. I start college tomorrow.
M: Oh, really? You travel light.
W: My parents are bringing the rest of my things this weekend. I had to pack quickly because I just got the acceptance letter from college two days ago. I registered by telephone, and now, well, here I am. I'm staying with my cousin until I can find an apartment.
M: Which college are you going to?
W: Central City College.
M: No kidding! That's where I go. What are you studying?
W: Math, accounting, and psychology. What about you?
M: Business—mostly marketing this quarter. But I have to take psychology, too, and I'm actually looking forward to that. I heard the instructor is fabulous—Dr. Robinson. He's an expert in organizational psychology.
W: Did you say Dr. Robinson? I think that's who I have for psychology.
M: Maybe you'll be in my class.
W: Wouldn't that be a coincidence! Oh, if this is Broad Street, I get off here.
M: It was nice to meet you. Maybe I'll see you at school.

35. What are the people mainly discussing?
36. Why is the woman traveling with a backpack?
37. What can be inferred about the man?
38. What do these two people have in common?

Part C

Directions: In this part of the test, you will hear several talks. After each talk, you will hear some questions. The talks and questions will not be repeated.

After you hear a question, read the four possible answers in your book and choose the best answer. Then, on your answer sheet, find the number of the question and fill in the space that corresponds to the letter of the answer you have chosen.

Here is an example.

On the recording, you hear:

(Narrator) Listen to a part of a talk in a general science class. The instructor is talking about the science of meteorology, the study of the earth's atmosphere.

(Man) Progress in the field began with the development of physics and the invention of basic instruments. In the nineteenth century, the invention of the telegraph was important because it improved rapid data collection from remote weather stations. Today, because of such modern research tools as high–altitude airplanes, weather balloons, rockets, earth satellites, and space probes, meteorologists are able to provide more sophisticated understanding and forecasting of weather, their best known function. They also work at solving air pollution problems and studying trends in the earth's climate.

Now listen to a sample question.

(Narrator) How did the telegraph improve the science of meteorology?

In your book, you read:

(A) It helped scientists see the atmosphere more clearly.
(B) It made it easier for scientists to send messages.
(C) It made data collection from weather stations faster.
(D) It helped airplanes fly higher.

The best answer to the question, "How did the telegraph improve the science of meteorology?" is (C), "It made data collection from weather stations faster." Therefore, the correct choice is (C).

Now listen to another sample question.

(Narrator) What is *not* mentioned as something meteorologists do today?

In your book, you read:

(A) Study trends in the earth's climate.
(B) Forecast the weather.
(C) Solve air pollution problems.
(D) Study costs of building satellites.

The best answer to the question, "What is *not* mentioned as something meteorologists do today?" is (D), "Study costs of building satellites." Therefore, the correct choice is (D).

Remember, you should not take notes or write in your book.

Questions 39 through 41. Listen to a talk given by the leader of a student club.

Water is a continually changing, dynamic surface. This makes studying the weather much more important on the water than on land. For this reason, a simple 24–hour, pocket–sized weather radio should be standard equipment for your boat.

Storms send advance warnings *if* you know what to look for. Many weather changes can be read in the ever–changing cloud patterns. The first visual signs of a storm will appear in the west, southwest, or northwest. There will be a high cloud formation with a dirty bottom and a tall, stringy top. As beginning boaters, my friends and I admired these beautiful cloud formations from our kayak on the Connecticut River on a day we will not forget. The violence of the hurricane–force winds that hit us in our small kayak will be remembered forever.

If you are in your boat, and a storm is on its way, don't try to outrun it. Head for a protected area. If you get stuck, use a bucket or any kind of drag attached to the anchor line, and sit or lie on the bottom of the boat. Many people drown in storms because they stand up, swing their arms, and holler for help. After the storm passes, the boat is floating peacefully without occupants. They fell overboard and drowned.

39. To what group of people would this talk most likely be given?
40. According to the speaker, what will warn you if a storm is coming?
41. According to the speaker, why do many people drown in storms?

Questions 42 through 45. Listen to a talk given to a tour group.

Do you enjoy watching wild animals? They may actually enjoy watching you, too! If you sit still, like a rock, the birds may fly closer, seeing that you are not a threat. Deer may approach you out of curiosity. There are a lot of wild animal "don'ts" but if you are observing right, you'll have an enjoyable and safe experience, and so will the wildlife.

The first rule is to avoid disturbing the animals. If a bird appears upset by you, you are probably too close to its nest and may be affecting the survival of its eggs or young. Curiosity may draw you to a bird nest, but beware of the consequences to the inhabitants of the nest. Eggs that are left uncovered will cool quickly, killing the embryos.

Second, don't feed the animals! Wild animals who get used to being fed forget how to fend for themselves. Human food is bad for animals. Most importantly, wild animals who lose their fear of humans might bite or attack people if they are teased or denied their favorite human treat. A wild animal who attacks a human usually has to be killed.

My last rule is don't let your dog chase wildlife. This puts great stress on wild animals, and they may use too much energy trying to escape. Besides, your dog might end up being the victim of a bear or a mountain lion.

If you should see an obviously injured animal, report it here at the ranger station. Now, I want to wish you all a pleasant experience in the Thompson National Forest.

42. What is probably the speaker's job?
43. According to the speaker, why should one avoid disturbing a bird's nest?
44. Why is it important *not* to feed wild animals?
45. What might happen if a dog chases wildlife?

Questions 46 through 50. Listen to a professor give an introductory lecture in an economics class.

In this course, we will look at the basic problems every economy must face: *what* goods shall be produced and *for whom* goods shall be produced. We will look at how a modern mixed economy solves the problems of supply and demand by relying on a system of markets and prices.

Basically, the system goes something like this: consumers are like voters. They use their money votes to buy what they want. Your votes compete with my votes over the goods we both want to buy. The consumers with the most dollar votes have the most influence over *what* gets produced and *to whom* goods go. We will examine how this spending of money votes operates in a market system. In other words, we will examine the theory of supply and demand. We will look at how these two central forces—supply and demand—are brought into balance by the price of goods.

Let's consider demand. It is generally held that the quantity of a particular good that people will buy depends on its price. The higher the price, the less of it people will want to buy. The lower the price, the more people will want to buy. Now, about supply: there is one major factor underlying the supply of a good, and that is the cost of producing that good.

I've just given you the briefest summary of market economics. Tomorrow we will look at just how demand and supply work in the real world and how the market price of a good comes at the point where the amount of a good that consumers wish to buy is equal to the amount sellers wish to sell.

46. What is the lecture mainly about?
47. How does the professor describe consumers?
48. According to the professor, who has the most influence over what goods are produced?
49. What does the professor imply about the price of a good?
50. What will the next lecture probably be about?

TEST 3 (p. 573)

SECTION 1 — LISTENING

In the Listening section of the test, you will have an opportunity to demonstrate your ability to understand conversations and talks in English. Answer all the questions on the basis of what is stated or implied by the speakers you hear. Do not take notes or write during the test.

Part A

Directions: In Part A you will hear short conversations between two people. After each conversation, you will hear a question about the conversation. The conversations and questions will not be repeated. After you hear a question, read the four possible answers and choose the best answer.

Here is an example.

On the recording, you hear:

(Man) Why don't you buy this printer?
(Woman) I'm hoping to find one at a better price.
(Narrator) What does the woman mean?

In your book, you read:

(A) She doesn't want to buy a printer.
(B) She would rather buy something else.
(C) She doesn't want to pay a lot for a printer.
(D) She wants to shop at a better place.

You learn from the conversation that the woman hopes to find a printer at a better price. The best answer to the question, "What does the woman mean?" is (C), "She doesn't want to pay a lot for a printer." Therefore, the correct choice is (C).

1. M: Excuse me, can you tell me where the student union is?
   W: Sure, it's that two–story brick building by the fountain.
   M: Do you know if the cafeteria is still open?
   W: I think it stays open until eleven on weeknights.
   M: Thanks!
   N: What will the man probably do?

2. M: If you keep spending money, you won't have any for an emergency.
   W: That goes without saying.
   N: What does the woman mean?

3. M: When you saw Lucas, did you tell him how rude he was?
   W: If I hadn't still been so mad, I might have spoken to Lucas.
   N: What can be inferred from the conversation?

4. M: I haven't seen Charlie all semester, have you?
   W: I heard he dropped out at the end of last year.
   N: What does the woman say about Charlie?

5. W: Did you like Professor Turner's lecture about the Federal Reserve system?
   M: Yes, but I was lost during most of it.
   N: What does the man mean?

6. M: Robert dropped by just before you got home.
   W: Oh. I'm sorry I missed him.
   N: What does the woman mean?

7. M: Vincent needs a ride to the airport, and I said you would take him.
   W: Oh, no. Tell me you didn't!
   N: What can be inferred about the woman?

8. M: Where are you going?
   W: To the student center. Pedro is showing his new pieces in the gallery.
   N: What does the woman say about Pedro?

9. M: Hi! It's nice to see you again. How are things at the dental clinic?
   W: I really wouldn't know.
   M: Weren't you the technician who took my x–rays?
   W: You might be thinking of my sister. She works there.
   N: What had the man assumed?

10. W: Are you planning anything for Mark's birthday?
    M: A group of us are chipping in to take him out to dinner.
    N: What does the man mean?

11. M: So, were you able to get your report done after all?
    W: Only after I got Jenny to take my computer to the shop.
    N: What happened to the woman's computer?

12. M: See you later. I'm going out now.
    W: Really? Don't you want to finish your report first?
    N: What does the woman imply?

13. W: My binoculars are just like yours, aren't they?
    M: They're almost the same. Mine may be lighter, but they don't work as well.
    N: What can be inferred about the woman's binoculars?

14. M: Thanks for coming to help me clean my garage.
    W: Why don't you just get rid of all this stuff?
    N: What does the woman suggest the man should do?

15. W: I'm sorry, sir, but Flight One–twenty–eight departed fifteen minutes ago.
    M: Oh. Well then, could you please tell me where the nearest telephone is?
    N: What will the man probably do?

Part B

Directions: In this part of the test, you will hear several conversations and talks. Each conversation or talk is followed by several questions. The conversations, talks, and questions will not be repeated.

For most of the questions, you will read four possible answers and choose the best answer. Some questions will have special directions.

Here is an example.

On the recording, you hear:

(Narrator) Listen to part of a talk in a general science class. The instructor is talking about the science of meteorology, the study of the earth's atmosphere.

(Man) Progress in the field began with the development of physics and the invention of basic instruments. In the nineteenth century, the invention of the telegraph was important because it improved rapid data collection from remote weather stations. Today, because of such modern research tools as high–altitude airplanes, weather balloons, rockets, earth satellites, and space probes, meteorologists are able to provide more sophisticated understanding and forecasting of weather, their best known function. They also work at solving air pollution problems and studying trends in the earth's climate.

Now listen to a sample question.

(Narrator) How did the telegraph improve the science of meteorology?

In your book, you read:

(A) It helped scientists see the atmosphere more clearly.
(B) It made it easier for scientists to send messages.
(C) It made data collection from weather stations faster.
(D) It helped airplanes fly higher.

The best answer to the question, "How did the telegraph improve the science of meteorology?" is (C), "It made data collection from weather stations faster." Therefore, the correct choice is (C).

Now listen to another sample question.

(Narrator) According to the instructor, what do meteorologists do today?

In your book, you read:

Choose 2 answers.

[A] Forecast the weather.
[B] Study trends in rocket science.
[C] Solve air pollution problems.
[D] Study costs of building satellites.

The best two answers to the question, "What do meteorologists do today?" are [A], "Forecast the weather" and [C], "Solve air pollution problems." Therefore, the correct choices are [A] and [C].

Remember, you should <u>not</u> take notes during the test.

Questions 16 through 18. Listen to a conversation between a soil conservationist and some students at a career fair.

M1: Most of the soil conservationists in this country are employed by the federal Department of Agriculture or Department of the Interior. Smaller numbers are employed by state and local governments, and some teach at colleges and universities.
W: Do colleges have degree programs in soil conservation?
M1: Not very many colleges offer degrees with a major in soil conservation. Most soil conservationists have degrees in agronomy, agricultural education, or general agriculture. A few have degrees in related fields of the natural sciences.
W: My major is wildlife biology. Would I qualify for work in soil conservation?
M1: Yes. A background in biology would be a plus. Your course work should also include at least thirty hours in natural resources, including the study of soils.
M2: I'd like to have a job where I could work outdoors. How much time does a soil conservationist spend outside?
M1: If you want to work outdoors, this might be a field for you to consider. Soil conservationists do most of their work in the field. For example, if a farmer is experiencing an erosion problem, the soil conservationist will visit the farm, find the source of the problem, and develop a program to combat the erosion.

16. What is the main subject of this conversation?
17. What educational background do soil conservationists usually have?
18. Why might the male student be interested in soil conservation as a career?

Questions 19 through 21. Listen to a conversation between a student and his adviser.

M: Mrs. Kim, may I speak with you?
W: Hello, James. Please have a seat. How can I help?
M: I'm trying to figure out my schedule for spring semester. I want Economics and Speech, but I can't find another class to fit my schedule.
W: Have you completed all your science credits?
M: Yes. I have Biology this term.
W: I see. Let's have a look at your record. Hmm. I see you need another math credit. Why not take Math in spring? You could take Business Math. It meets at one o'clock.
M: But then I wouldn't be able to take Speech because it also meets at one o'clock.
W: Speech will be offered again during the summer term. Can you take it then?
M: I was planning to work in my uncle's store this summer.
W: It will be an evening class.
M: Oh, really? Well, maybe I can handle that. I really want Speech, so I'll have to take it in summer. But if I take Math instead of Speech in spring, I still need a third class.
W: Then take English composition. It's a requirement.
M: I was afraid you were going to say that. Well, OK, I'd better take English. Thank you for your help, Mrs. Kim.
W: You're welcome. Good–bye, James.

19. Why does James come to see Mrs. Kim?
20. What does Mrs. Kim advise James to do?
21. In which term will James probably take each class?

Questions 22 through 25. Listen to an instructor give a talk about jazz.

The origins of jazz are as richly textured as the music itself. The term "jazz" really covers many different kinds of music. In the late nineteenth century, African Americans began performing the folk music known as "the blues," whose origins lay in the work songs of slavery days. Within the African—American community, the blues evolved into popular commercial music.

In 1914, a black orchestra leader named W. C. Handy wrote "The St. Louis Blues." Adapting the African–American folk idiom to European conventions of orchestration and harmony, Handy produced a hit song. "The St. Louis Blues" was tremendously influential among black and white musicians, and Handy's style of music became famous under the name of "jazz."

Early jazz musicians were active in many cities and towns throughout the southern United States. It was New Orleans, with its long tradition of African—American music, that was the home of many "fathers" of jazz. After World War One, the musicians of New Orleans joined the general northward migration of African–Americans. The first great national center of jazz was Chicago. From there, the music entered the mainstream and even gave its name to the decade of the 1920s.

Jazz, blending African–American folk roots with elements of popular music and European classical traditions, has been called "America's classical music."

22. For what course would this talk be most appropriate?
23. What does the instructor say about the style of music known as "the blues?"
24. According to the instructor, why is the song "St. Louis Blues" significant?
25. What is *not* mentioned about jazz?

Questions 26 through 30. Listen to a lecture in an American history class.

By the 1760s, the American colonies were moving closer to a break with Great Britain. In 1773, the colonists saw the British Parliament's passage of the Tea Act as yet another affront to their rights. The Tea Act required that all tea shipped to the colonies be imported by the East India Company, and that only officers of the company could then sell tea. This legislated monopoly was a disaster for most colonial tea merchants, who were put out of business.

To the American colonists, the granting of a monopoly to a private business was considered an outrage. They feared this act was the beginning of Parliamentary interference in the affairs of the colonies. In Boston, protesters called on the officers of the East India Company to resign their commissions. They refused. Then, at a town meeting, protest leaders called for a boycott of tea. At this time, several ships loaded with tea sat in Boston Harbor.

On the night of December 16, 1773, the Boston protesters took action. A group of sixty men dressed as Mohawk Indians boarded the ships and threw overboard 342 tea chests, worth 18,000 pounds. This act of protest became known as the Boston Tea Party.

Parliament's response was almost immediate. Four new laws were passed to punish the colony of Massachusetts. These laws were known as the "Intolerable Acts." Although three of the laws were directed at Massachusetts alone, citizens from other colonies joined Massachusetts in outrage. Throughout the colonies, protest leaders called for the formation of a Continental Congress. Thus, we can see that in a dispute over tea, a revolution began.

26. What is the lecture mainly about?
27. Why did the American colonists dislike the 1773 Tea Act?
28. What was the Boston Tea Party?
29. The speaker explains a sequence of events. Put the events in the order in which they happened.
30. What is the most likely topic for the next lecture in this class?

Questions 31 through 34. Listen to a talk given by the leader of a club. The speaker is discussing bulbs.

Although bulbs don't look like much, they travel well. They may look drab and generally ugly, but they are like well–wrapped packages. From those plain brown lumps come lovely and colorful flowers—tulips, daffodils, lilies, and dahlias. The unexciting but functional packaging of bulbs enabled these plants to withstand the rigors of early travel from Japan, Turkey, Russia, and other corners of the globe to Europe and the New World.

When dormant, the bulb holds the life of a whole plant. It is a self–contained storehouse that helps the plant to survive for months without soil or moisture. Nutrients are gathered from the leaves and packed into the bulb as support for the plant when it begins to grow again.

Many different types of bulbs are popular today. The true bulbs are the daffodils and tulips. Rhizomes produce the lovely calla lily, and tuberous roots produce the dahlia and begonia.

Some are hardy—able to stay in the ground all winter. Others are tender and must be dug up and stored when temperatures drop. But, whether true bulb, rhizome, or tuberous root, all produce flowers year after year with a minimum of care.

31. To what group of people would this talk most likely be given?
32. What does the speaker say about the appearance of bulbs?
33. What is the main function of the bulb?
34. According to the speaker, why are bulbs so popular?

Questions 35 through 39. Listen to a talk in a geology class. The professor is talking about what the students will see on an upcoming field trip.

Now that you are acquainted with some of the ways sedimentary rocks are formed, the next step is to look at various shapes and learn how to read their clues. On our field trip, we'll see several of the rock formations called *mesas*. It's the flat–topped cap that gives this landform its name, since the Spanish who explored Utah thought these flat–topped hills that were wider than they were high looked like tables, or mesas.

The sides of a mesa below the cap are often made of shales or softer sandstones. Within time, even the durable cap of a mesa reduces in size, for as its softer base recedes with erosion, the edge of the cap rock is undermined. It eventually cracks, splits, and falls. As a mesa is shrunk in size by seasonal erosion, it may also be cut into smaller landforms by rivers. If these smaller mesa remnants are at least as high as they are wide, they are called *buttes*. Further erosion may narrow a butte to a tower or spire.

The shaft of a spire is usually harder than the base on which it stands and, like a mesa or butte, is capped with a narrow rim of even harder rock. Erosion of the softer rock may reduce the spire to a variety of interesting and weird forms. We'll see some hourglass–shaped rocks, delicate mushroom–shaped rocks, and strangely eroded pillars. Over time, erosion finally topples these rocks to the ground. There they remain as boulders until further erosion demolishes them completely and they disintegrate into pebbles, and finally to the sand we will walk on as we explore the surface of the plateau.

35. What is the talk mainly about?
36. Select the picture that best represents a mesa.
37. Why does a mesa shrink in size?
38. Select the picture that best represents a butte.
39. The professor briefly explains the process of erosion and disintegration of a rock spire. Put the rock's stages in the order in which they appear.

Questions 40 through 45. Listen to part of a talk in a biology class. The professor is discussing the original forests of North America.

The first thing that European explorers noticed about the forests of North America, even before they set foot on the continent, was the pungent aroma carried to their ships by the offshore breezes. Some hopeful sea captains took this aroma as a foretaste of the valuable Oriental spices that had prompted their voyages of exploration. In fact, the agreeable smells came not from spices but from the rich and varied vegetation of the North American forests.

The aromas of the forests came from the blossoms of numerous trees and from the volatile oils in pine sap. Pine trees exude a resinous sap that heals wounds in ships caused by wind, fire, and lightning. To sailors, these fragrances hinted at an abundant supply of what were known as naval stores—the pitch and pine tar that kept wooden ships watertight and seaworthy.

Farther south along the Atlantic coast, the air was perfumed by such species as the sassafras tree. Powdered sassafras leaves were used as spice by the Choctaw Indians. The strong but pleasant smell of its leaves, bark, wood, and roots—once familiar as the dominant flavoring in root beer—had long recommended sassafras as a cure for everything from fever to stomachache. Sassafras was one of the first exports from the English colonies. However, in the 1960s, the U. S. Food and Drug Administration found sassafras oil a potential carcinogen, so even grandma's sassafras tea has become a banned substance.

Another aromatic tree the Europeans found was the arborvitae tree, which, like the limes that were prescribed for scurvy victims, was rich in vitamin C. A decoction made from the bark and leaves of the arborvitae tree was given to the men of Jacques Cartier's expedition up the St. Lawrence River in 1535, saving their lives from the scurvy that ailed them.

40. What is the purpose of the talk?
41. According to the professor, what did European explorers first notice as they sailed toward the shores of North America?
42. Why did sailors value pine sap?
43. How was the sassafras tree used?
44. What can be inferred about sassafras today?
45. Match each tree with one of its past uses.

TEST 4 (p. 601)

(p. 601)

SECTION 1 — LISTENING COMPREHENSION

In the Listening Comprehension section of the test, you will have an opportunity to demonstrate your ability to understand conversations and talks in English. There are three parts to this section, with special directions for each part. Answer all the questions on the basis of what is <u>stated</u> or <u>implied</u> by the speakers you hear. Do <u>not</u> take notes or write in your book at any time.

Part A

Directions: In Part A you will hear short conversations between two people. After each conversation, you will hear a question about the conversation. The conversations and questions will not be repeated. After you hear a question, read the four possible answers in your book and choose the best answer. Then, on your answer sheet, find the number of the question and fill in the space that corresponds to the letter of the answer you have chosen.

Here is an example.

On the recording, you hear:

(Man) Why don't you buy this printer?
(Woman) I'm hoping to find one at a better price.
(Narrator) What does the woman mean?

In your book, you read:

(A) She doesn't want to buy a printer.
(B) She would rather buy something else.
(C) She doesn't want to pay a lot for a printer.
(D) She wants to shop at a better place.

You learn from the conversation that the woman hopes to find a printer at a better price. The best answer to the question, "What does the woman mean?" is (C), "She doesn't want to pay a lot for a printer." Therefore, the correct choice is (C).

1. W: Would you please get me a better knife to slice this bread with?
   M: Well, if this drawer weren't so full, I might be able to find one.
   N: What does the man imply?

2. W: Why do you seem so unhappy?
   M: I'm really just bored. Business has never been slower.
   N: What does the man mean?

3. M: Has Andrew been living in town as long as we have?
   W: He moved here at least a year before we did.
   N: What do you know about Andrew?

4. M: Hi Sylvia! How do you like your new job?
   W: I love it. Last week I did some sketches and lettering. Next week, I'll probably work more with color.
   N: What can be inferred about Sylvia?

5. M: I think we should wait until spring before we look for a new apartment.
   W: I'm so glad we see eye to eye about that.
   N: What does the woman mean?

6. W: While we're in the gift shop, I think I'll look for some earrings for Jill.
   M: Are you sure she wouldn't prefer a sweatshirt?
   N: What does the man imply about Jill?

7. W: I don't have to be there until ten.
   M: But you'd better leave early anyway. The traffic will be really bad.
   N: What does the man suggest the woman do?

8. M: Weren't you active in the student assembly last year?
   W: Only for a few months.
   N: What does the woman imply?

9. M: I heard the rafting trip has been canceled.
   W: Yes, and I was looking forward to it.
   N: What does the woman mean?

10. W: Where's the bottle of juice I just set on the counter?
    M: Oh, didn't you hear that crash a few minutes ago?
    N: What can be inferred from the conversation?

11. W: What beautiful roses! You must have taken good care of them.
    M: Thank you. I did, but also the weather was perfect for roses this year.
    N: Where does this conversation probably take place?

12. M: Hi, Sarah! Say, do you know where I can catch a bus to downtown?
    W: If you'll walk with me, I can show you where to wait.
    N: What does the woman mean?

13. W: Your brother sure has been in a lot of trouble lately.
    M: Yes, but he's promised the family that he's turned over a new leaf.
    N: What does the man mean?

14. W: Why are you always looking at that old economics book?
    M: It may be old, but it's still the most comprehensive text I've ever seen.
    N: What does the man mean?

15. M: Why don't you like your supervisor?
    W: Oh, it always seems like he's making fun of me.
    N: What does the woman mean?

16. W: What a beautiful lake!
    M: It may look nice, but it's too polluted for swimming.
    N: What does the man mean?

17. M: I've been invited to a potluck at Jim's house, but I'm an awful cook.
    W: Why don't you just get a salad from the deli?
    N: What does the woman suggest the man do?

18. W: Do you feel like dancing or going to the ball game?
    M: Need you even ask?
    N: What does the man imply?

19. M: Do you know if this is where I can get the bus for Worthington Heights?
    W: It's the right place, but I'm sorry to say that bus went by just a few minutes ago.
    N: What will the man probably do?

20. M: I thought you'd be in Business Law with Professor Lux this semester.
    W: No, but I'm really sorry I didn't sign up for that class.
    N: What does the woman mean?

21. W: Good morning, Tony. How are you today?
    M: Fine. I'm on my way to work, and I just wanted to drop off the check for my rent.
    N: Where does this conversation probably take place?

22. W: I'm sorry, but we do not accept checks from out of town.
    M: Thanks a lot! That really helps me!
    N: What does the man mean?

23. W: So you were offered a new job? That's great!
    M: Well, I told them I'd give my answer tomorrow. I want to sleep on it.
    N: What does the man mean?

24. W: You know, Erik, I think Linda likes you.
    M: Yeah, but she's got so many other friends I don't stand a chance for a date.
    N: What does the man mean?

25. W: This page layout looks great! When did you have time to finish this?
    M: Oh, I was tied–up, so I got Maureen to do it.
    N: What does the man mean?

26. W: Yoko's sister is visiting her this weekend.
    M: Yoko has a sister?
    N: What had the man assumed?

27. W: How did your committee meeting go?
    M: Not that well. Ms. Phillips was really steamed when she realized Kevin and I weren't prepared.
    N: What does the man mean?

28. M: I don't understand why my printer won't work.
    W: Would you like me to take a look at it?
    N: What will the woman probably do?

29. M: Do you think I could get Molly to type my paper? It's due tomorrow.
    W: I haven't seen her today.
    N: What can be inferred about Molly?

30. W: Mr. Wilson sure is in a bad mood this morning.
    M: Yeah, he takes it out on us whenever anything goes wrong.
    N: What does the man imply about Mr. Wilson?

Part B

Directions: In this part of the test, you will hear longer conversations. After each conversation, you will hear several questions. The conversations and questions will not be repeated.

After you hear a question, read the four possible answers in your book and choose the best answer. Then, on your answer sheet, find the number of the question and fill in the space that corresponds to the letter of the answer you have chosen.

Remember, you should not take notes or write in your book.

Questions 31 through 34. Listen to a conversation between two students in a coffee shop.

W: Hi, Victor! I'm glad you made it. I wasn't sure you could.
M: Neither was I. After last night, I wasn't sure I'd wake up this morning!
W: I couldn't sleep. Wasn't the wind incredible?
M: What a racket! All I could hear were branches snapping and limbs crashing down. My power went out around eight o'clock and didn't come back on until this morning.
W: Oh, really? Where I live, the power is still not on. And that means no heat. I'm upset because I have a paper due this morning, and I couldn't finish it without my computer.
M: Oh, your instructor will understand. I heard the whole town was without power. Probably no one did the paper.
W: Professor Gray said late papers will receive a lower grade, and I can't afford that. I need to pass this class.
M: Why don't you just go talk to him? I'm sure he'll allow it this time. Last night was a rare event. Can you believe how hard it's still raining?
W: All this rain is making me drowsy. I didn't get much sleep because it was freezing in my house. At least it's warm in here. I think I'll get more coffee. Would you like some?
M: Thanks, I'd love some coffee.

31. What are the people mainly discussing?
32. Why is the woman concerned?
33. According to the man, what should the woman do?
34. In this conversation, what does *power* mean?

Questions 35 through 37. Listen to a conversation between two students.

M: Excuse me, but are you planning to use this machine?
W: No, that machine's not taken, as far as I know.
M: Thank you. Could you tell me how much it costs?
W: It's a dollar a load. You need four quarters.
M: Do you know where I can get change for a dollar?
W: There's a change machine over there next to the dryers.
M: Thank you. And where can I get some detergent?
W: I think there's also a vending machine for detergent somewhere. Oh, yeah, it's by those kids who are playing the video game.
M: Thank you.
W: No problem. Is this your first time here?
M: Yes. I just started at the university last week. I live off campus, and this is the closest place where I can do my washing.
W: I see. Well, have fun. I have to finish my reading now.
M: I'm sorry. I hate to interrupt you again, but do I put the detergent in before or after my clothes?
W: You do have a lot to learn!

35. Where does this conversation take place?
36. How does the woman help the man?
37. What is *not* mentioned?

Part C

Directions: In this part of the test, you will hear several talks. After each talk, you will hear some questions. The talks and questions will not be repeated.

After you hear a question, read the four possible answers in your book and choose the best answer. Then, on your answer sheet, find the number of the question and fill in the space that corresponds to the letter of the answer you have chosen.

Here is an example.

On the recording, you hear:

(Narrator) Listen to a part of a talk in a general science class. The instructor is talking about the science of meteorology, the study of the earth's atmosphere.

(Man) Progress in the field began with the development of physics and the invention of basic instruments. In the nineteenth century, the invention of the telegraph was important because it improved rapid data collection from remote weather stations. Today, because of such modern research tools as high–altitude airplanes, weather balloons, rockets, earth satellites, and space probes, meteorologists are able to provide more sophisticated understanding and forecasting of weather, their best known function. They also work at solving air pollution problems and studying trends in the earth's climate.

Now listen to a sample question.

(Narrator) How did the telegraph improve the science of meteorology?

In your book, you read:

(A) It helped scientists see the atmosphere more clearly.
(B) It made it easier for scientists to send messages.
(C) It made data collection from weather stations faster.
(D) It helped airplanes fly higher.

The best answer to the question, "How did the telegraph improve the science of meteorology?" is (C), "It made data collection from weather stations faster." Therefore, the correct choice is (C).

Now listen to another sample question.

(Narrator) What is *not* mentioned as something meteorologists do today?

In your book, you read:

(A) Study trends in the earth's climate.
(B) Forecast the weather.
(C) Solve air pollution problems.
(D) Study costs of building satellites.

The best answer to the question, "What is *not* mentioned as something meteorologists do today?" is (D), "Study costs of building satellites." Therefore, the correct choice is (D).

Remember, you should <u>not</u> take notes or write in your book.

Questions 38 through 41. Listen to an orientation talk given to new college students.

The Counseling and Career Center provides a supportive atmosphere where you can reflect on major decisions or talk about important issues in your life. Some of the issues our counselors can help with include choosing a career, succeeding in college, and just dealing with the pressures that you might face from time to time.

Our services include help with the admissions process, program and class selection, and transferring to other programs. We also have individual counseling, by appointment, as well as group counseling sessions that focus on the issues in your life. All of our counselors are knowledgeable of other programs and resources in the community and can refer you to these other resources.

One of the main things we do is provide occupational and job search information. We have a job board, where we post listings of job openings both on and off campus. We also have special classes and workshops in career and life planning, some of which you can receive college credit for. I'll pass around this quarter's schedule for these special classes. You'll see that in addition to career planning, there are workshops in stress management, study skills, and test taking, all of which are very popular with students. Most of these classes are free of charge, and as you'll see, several have sessions that meet on evenings or Saturdays.

Now, I'd like to show you our facilities and introduce you to one of our counselors, but before that, are there any questions?

38. What service is *not* provided by the Counseling and Career Center?
39. Where can students learn about job openings?
40. When do many of the special workshops meet?
41. What will the speaker probably do next?

Questions 42 through 45. Listen to a lecture about Margaret Mead, an American anthropologist.

Margaret Mead was from an academic family in Philadelphia. She was trained in observation from early childhood, when her grandmother taught her to keep a detailed daily record of the infant development of her two younger sisters.

Mead's father reluctantly allowed her to have a college education. At Barnard College, Mead was fascinated by the brilliance of Ruth Benedict, who was then a professor of anthropology at Columbia University. Although majoring in psychology, Mead decided to do graduate work in anthropology.

In 1923, she set out to pursue her first fieldwork assignment in Samoa. This study resulted in her famous book, *Coming of Age in Samoa*. A woman of tremendous energy and openness to new issues, new technologies for research, and new media for communication, Mead published ten major works between 1928 and 1977, moving from studies of child rearing in the Pacific to the cultural and biological bases of gender, the nature of cultural change, the structure and functioning of complex societies, race relations, and the origins of the drug culture. Throughout her life, Mead remained a pioneer in her willingness to think of new ways anthropology could serve society.

Although Margaret Mead's approach to her fieldwork has been criticized, no one has denied the extent of her contribution to anthropology, her intellectual courage, and her willingness to tackle large subjects of major intellectual consequence.

42. How was Margaret Mead first trained in observation?
43. Why did Mead decide to study anthropology?
44. What subjects did Mead write about?
45. What can be inferred about Margaret Mead?

Questions 46 through 50. Listen to a talk given on the radio.

If you live in a house or apartment where utilities are not included in the rent, you are probably aware of the costs of energy consumption. Consider trying to cut energy costs by following these tips.

During the winter, more energy is used for heating than anything else. Therefore, you should set your thermostat no higher than 68 degrees. When no one is home, or when everyone is sleeping, turn the setting down to 60 degrees or lower. On sunny days, use the sun's heat by opening draperies and blinds.

Hot water uses a lot of energy. Run your dishwasher and clothes washer only when you have a full load. Use warm or cold water for laundry when you can. Take showers instead of tub baths. About half as much hot water is used for a shower. Don't leave the hot water running when rinsing dishes or shaving.

The refrigerator operates 24 hours a day, every day, so it is one of the biggest users of energy in your home. Before opening your refrigerator door, pause and think of everything you will need so you do not have to go back several times. When you do open the door, close it quickly to keep the cool air in.

Get in the habit of turning off lights when you leave a room, even if you will be gone only for a short time. During the day, try to get along with as few lights as possible. Let the daylight do the work. White or light–colored walls make a room seem brighter. Use light bulbs of lower wattage, and whenever possible, use one large bulb rather than several smaller ones.

46. What is the purpose of the talk?
47. According to the speaker, what uses the most energy during the winter?
48. Why does the speaker mention the sun?
49. Why does the speaker recommend taking showers instead of tub baths?
50. What does the speaker recommend about light bulbs?

INDEX

A

B

C

D

E

F

G

H

I

J

K

L

M

Q

R

S

W

Y

Notes

Notes

Notes

NOTES

NOTES